Lecture Notes in Computer Science 12211

More information about this series at http://www.springer.com/series/7409

Xiaowen Fang (Ed.)

HCI in Games

Second International Conference, HCI-Games 2020
Held as Part of the 22nd HCI International Conference, HCII 2020
Copenhagen, Denmark, July 19–24, 2020
Proceedings

 Springer

Editor
Xiaowen Fang
DePaul University
Chicago, IL, USA

ISSN 0302-9743   ISSN 1611-3349   (electronic)
Lecture Notes in Computer Science
ISBN 978-3-030-50163-1   ISBN 978-3-030-50164-8   (eBook)
https://doi.org/10.1007/978-3-030-50164-8

LNCS Sublibrary: SL3 – Information Systems and Applications, incl. Internet/Web, and HCI

This Springer imprint is published by the registered company Springer Nature Switzerland AG
The registered company address is: Gewerbestrasse 11, 6330 Cham, Switzerland

Foreword

The 22nd International Conference on Human-Computer Interaction, HCI International 2020 (HCII 2020), was planned to be held at the AC Bella Sky Hotel and Bella Center, Copenhagen, Denmark, during July 19–24, 2020. Due to the COVID-19 coronavirus pandemic and the resolution of the Danish government not to allow events larger than 500 people to be hosted until September 1, 2020, HCII 2020 had to be held virtually. It incorporated the 21 thematic areas and affiliated conferences listed on the following page.

A total of 6,326 individuals from academia, research institutes, industry, and governmental agencies from 97 countries submitted contributions, and 1,439 papers and 238 posters were included in the conference proceedings. These contributions address the latest research and development efforts and highlight the human aspects of design and use of computing systems. The contributions thoroughly cover the entire field of human-computer interaction, addressing major advances in knowledge and effective use of computers in a variety of application areas. The volumes constituting the full set of the conference proceedings are listed in the following pages.

The HCI International (HCII) conference also offers the option of "late-breaking work" which applies both for papers and posters and the corresponding volume(s) of the proceedings will be published just after the conference. Full papers will be included in the "HCII 2020 - Late Breaking Papers" volume of the proceedings to be published in the Springer LNCS series, while poster extended abstracts will be included as short papers in the "HCII 2020 - Late Breaking Posters" volume to be published in the Springer CCIS series.

I would like to thank the program board chairs and the members of the program boards of all thematic areas and affiliated conferences for their contribution to the highest scientific quality and the overall success of the HCI International 2020 conference.

This conference would not have been possible without the continuous and unwavering support and advice of the founder, Conference General Chair Emeritus and Conference Scientific Advisor Prof. Gavriel Salvendy. For his outstanding efforts, I would like to express my appreciation to the communications chair and editor of HCI International News, Dr. Abbas Moallem.

July 2020   Constantine Stephanidis

HCI International 2020 Thematic Areas and Affiliated Conferences

Thematic areas:

- HCI 2020: Human-Computer Interaction
- HIMI 2020: Human Interface and the Management of Information

Affiliated conferences:

- EPCE: 17th International Conference on Engineering Psychology and Cognitive Ergonomics
- UAHCI: 14th International Conference on Universal Access in Human-Computer Interaction
- VAMR: 12th International Conference on Virtual, Augmented and Mixed Reality
- CCD: 12th International Conference on Cross-Cultural Design
- SCSM: 12th International Conference on Social Computing and Social Media
- AC: 14th International Conference on Augmented Cognition
- DHM: 11th International Conference on Digital Human Modeling and Applications in Health, Safety, Ergonomics and Risk Management
- DUXU: 9th International Conference on Design, User Experience and Usability
- DAPI: 8th International Conference on Distributed, Ambient and Pervasive Interactions
- HCIBGO: 7th International Conference on HCI in Business, Government and Organizations
- LCT: 7th International Conference on Learning and Collaboration Technologies
- ITAP: 6th International Conference on Human Aspects of IT for the Aged Population
- HCI-CPT: Second International Conference on HCI for Cybersecurity, Privacy and Trust
- HCI-Games: Second International Conference on HCI in Games
- MobiTAS: Second International Conference on HCI in Mobility, Transport and Automotive Systems
- AIS: Second International Conference on Adaptive Instructional Systems
- C&C: 8th International Conference on Culture and Computing
- MOBILE: First International Conference on Design, Operation and Evaluation of Mobile Communications
- AI-HCI: First International Conference on Artificial Intelligence in HCI

Conference Proceedings Volumes Full List

38. CCIS 1224, HCI International 2020 Posters - Part I, edited by Constantine Stephanidis and Margherita Antona
39. CCIS 1225, HCI International 2020 Posters - Part II, edited by Constantine Stephanidis and Margherita Antona
40. CCIS 1226, HCI International 2020 Posters - Part III, edited by Constantine Stephanidis and Margherita Antona

http://2020.hci.international/proceedings

Second International Conference on HCI in Games
(HCI-Games 2020)

Program Board Chair: **Xiaowen Fang, DePaul University, USA**

- Amir Zaib Abbasi, Pakistan
- Abdullah Azhari, Saudi Arabia
- Ikram Bououd, France
- Barbara Caci, Italy
- Benjamin Ultan Cowley, Finland
- Khaldoon Dhou, USA
- Kevin Keeker, USA
- Xiaocen Liu, P.R. China
- Haipeng Mi, P.R. China
- Keith Nesbitt, Australia
- Sergio Nesteriuk, Brazil
- Fabrizio Poltronieri, UK
- Daniel Riha, Czech Republic
- Owen Schaffer, USA
- Fan Zhao, USA
- Miaoqi Zhu, USA

The full list with the Program Board Chairs and the members of the Program Boards of all thematic areas and affiliated conferences is available online at:

http://www.hci.international/board-members-2020.php

HCI International 2021

The 23rd International Conference on Human-Computer Interaction, HCI International 2021 (HCII 2021), will be held jointly with the affiliated conferences in Washington DC, USA, at the Washington Hilton Hotel, July 24–29, 2021. It will cover a broad spectrum of themes related to Human-Computer Interaction (HCI), including theoretical issues, methods, tools, processes, and case studies in HCI design, as well as novel interaction techniques, interfaces, and applications. The proceedings will be published by Springer. More information will be available on the conference website: http://2021.hci.international/.

General Chair
Prof. Constantine Stephanidis
University of Crete and ICS-FORTH
Heraklion, Crete, Greece
Email: general_chair@hcii2021.org

http://2021.hci.international/

Contents

User Engagement and Game Impact

Serious Games

Designing Games and Gamified Interactions

Generalised Player Modelling: Why Artificial Intelligence in Games Should Incorporate Meaning, with a Formalism for so Doing

Benjamin Ultan Cowley[1,2]($\boxtimes$) ®

[1] Data Science, Faculty of Educational Sciences,
University of Helsinki, Helsinki, Finland
ben.cowley@helsinki.fi
[2] Cognitive Science, Faculty of Arts, University of Helsinki, Helsinki, Finland
https://blogs.helsinki.fi/bcowley/

Abstract. General game-playing artificial intelligence (AI) has recently seen important advances due to the various techniques known as 'deep learning'. However, in terms of human-computer interaction, the advances conceal a major limitation: these algorithms do not incorporate any sense of what human players find *meaningful* in games.

I argue that adaptive game AI will be enhanced by a generalised player model, because games are inherently human artefacts which require some encoding of the human perspective in order to respond naturally to individual players. The player model provides *constraints* on the adaptive AI, which allow it to encode aspects of what human players find meaningful. I propose that a general player model requires parameters for the subjective experience of play, including: player psychology, game structure, and actions of play. I argue that such a player model would enhance efficiency of per-game solutions, and also support study of game-playing by allowing (within-player) comparison between games, or (within-game) comparison between players (human and AI).

Here we detail requirements for functional adaptive AI, arguing from first-principles drawn from games research literature, and propose a formal specification for a generalised player model based on our 'Behavlets' method for psychologically-derived player modelling.

Keywords: Artificial intelligence · Game AI · General player model · Player personality · Behavlets · Formal models · Category theory

1   Introduction

Computer games have the potential to adapt themselves through changes to their difficulty, appearance, story, or even rules. Computer games thus offer a unique opportunity for play that is completely tailored to the individual player by adaptive artificial intelligence (AI) - instantiated as opponent agent AI or 'game-management' AI. Any non-trivial adaptation requires a player model, to encode relevant aspects of player individuality [36]. The concept of a generalised

© Springer Nature Switzerland AG 2020
X. Fang (Ed.): HCII 2020, LNCS 12211, pp. 3–22, 2020.
https://doi.org/10.1007/978-3-030-50164-8_1

player model extends this, to describe the subjective experience of play in terms of validated constructs, which could include psychology profiles, game design patterns, action patterns, and more. The aim is not to provide a one-size-fits-all model, but to provide a system for expressing the supra-specific elements that apply to all players, especially cognition, emotion, and personality. The specific implementation then depends on the game.

In this paper, I suggest that adaptive game AI will be optimised by a generalised player model. This is because games are inherently human artefacts which, therefore, require some encoding of the human perspective in order to effectively autonomously respond to the individual player. This argument is built on the idea that the player model will impose *constraints* which guide the AI to optimal performance.

In brief, game-playing AI must typically be constrained to function (see Sect. 2.2). For example, in their ground-breaking Go and Atari-playing agents, Silver *et al.*, and Mnih *et al.* [25,29] imposed well-chosen constraints on the problem domain to enable their solutions. Such constraints can be, e.g. dimensionality reduction, or *simulation* of the original system according to some simplification. Here it is proposed that a generalised player model gives a partial solution, built on two requirements: i) to capture information about player psychology (cognition, emotion and personality) and activity; ii) to represent that information in the context of the game. Requirement i) *constrains* the model of player behaviour to well-understood theoretical constructs; ii) presents the model as input to a learning algorithm.

A generalised player model requires a foundation of parameters that describe the subjective experience of play. The foundation will draw on established modelling tools, including at least: a) psychology of behaviour; b) general game design; and c) actions in the context of a given game. This foundation should also be integrated with the computational intelligence that drives the model. The ultimate aim is to *improve efficacy and viability of the artificial intelligence required to power games which adapt to their players*.

A generalised player model can bring added benefits. It can be more efficient than creating a novel model for every game, and can even improve algorithmic performance of a real-time player model [14]. It also allows comparison between games which makes it a useful tool for studying play in general.

In Part A, I discuss why adaptive game AI benefits from a general model of player psychology. First, the concept and meaning of an adaptive game is described, stating the aspects of player psychology to which games can adapt. I then make my case from first principles, drawing on the literature of games studies.

In Part B, I discuss possible but speculative solutions, and develop one as a proposal: a formal category theoretic basis to a 'Behavlets'-driven generalised player model. The Behavlets method is designed to build facets a) to c) above into composite features of game-play defined over entire action sequences [10], and thus model players for, e.g. personality type classification [9]. This paper is built on several prior preprint papers exploring research questions related to Behavlets [11,12].

2 Part A: Adaptivity in Games

2.1 Background

Games can roughly be split into two categories: single player and multiplayer. Adaptive algorithms may be used in a multiplayer game for a range of reasons; in the main, the challenge in these games is due to other human players. In an online multiplayer game, with an interface via network but without camera or microphone, the players do not see each other nor do they have access to traditional social cues for understanding their opponents, e.g. body language. Such a game environment is *stigmergic*, as players do not interact directly but through the shared environment of the game space. They will read the signs left by their opponent, build a 'theory of mind' model around the complete set of actions observed, and classify the other player based on both what they know of the types of player of that game, and natural social recognition skills. This process contributes to the decision making process for how to play the game and is very different from a single player game.

In certain games, the inclusion of good quality, artificially-intelligent non-player characters (NPCs) can be central to gameplay design and is important for the player experience. Games can be created to be adaptive to the player through changes to NPC behaviour, or by altering other parameters of the game that affect the gameplay [36]. In both cases, a player learns to be more effective at playing a game by learning the rules of the game, including how NPCs behave. Unlike real players, NPC behaviour is usually more predictable and typically it is easier to develop strategies to be successful in competitive gameplay. Players expect NPCs to behave consistently. Nevertheless, one of the reasons that people like to play against other real players is that it is often more satisfying. People behave differently from each other, have complex capability profiles, and are motivated by different ways of playing. Players understand that other players are less predictable than NPCs and accept this.

Dynamic Difficulty Adjustment (DDA) is a popular approach to implement adaptive AI, e.g. [6]. It can work, for example, by altering the number of power-ups in a game or by making non-player characters more or less co-operative or competitive. Some of the earliest games to implement DDA systems were *Max Payne* (3D Realms 2001) and *Prey* (3D Realms 2006). However, the AI can do much more than control an opposing force. Forms of adaptive AI demonstrated in commercial games include adjusting player character attributes *MarioKart* (Nintendo 1992), appearance *Fable* (Lionhead Studios 2004), story *Facade* (Mateus and Stern 2005), character learning *Black and White* (Lionhead Studios 2001), and reactive squad tactics *Fear* (Monolith Productions 2005). Related research (from disciplines including game AI, computational intelligence, and machine learning), has been reviewed [35] and categorised into three main areas: Player Experience Modelling (PEM), Procedural Content Generation (PCM), and Massive-Scale Game Data Mining (MDM).

I consider a game AI system holistically (with NPC behaviour as a core aspect), in which the AI has two coordinated systems: α) a user model to capture some aspect of player psychology, which then supplies parameters to β) controller(s) for adjusting some relevant game system(s). The user model α is intended to model relevant data about some area of the player's state, as discussed further in Sect. 2.3. The issue of what the AI can control is somewhat out of scope, and thus is only briefly discussed here. In many ways the ultimate adaptive system would be based around a human or team of humans who dynamically adjust the gameplay experience based on player choice. Consider a Dungeon Master in table top role play games or the alleged human guidance of the Big Blue Chess playing algorithm. In both cases human guidance provides additional nuances, e.g. flexibility or experience, to the dynamic adjustment of a game playing experience. A game AI based on these principles could be more effective in tailoring fun experiences for a greater range of players. This is part of the motivation for the approach underlying our research.

Modus Operandi. Adaptive AI should be built around creating a *more engaging* game for the individual player. Obviously, a separate class of game-playing AI can be created with the sole purpose (utility function) of beating the opposing player, e.g. as Chess or Go playing programs. In this class of AI, player psychology is more or less irrelevant because maximising the utility of winning does not necessarily require opponent modelling.

A standard game is constrained by its ruleset, but an adaptive game has the potential to exceed known constraints, or the known/explored state space. Thus I contend that *unconstrained* adaptive AI can violate certain principles of good game design, such as logical consistency and a coherent Magic Circle [19], by exhibiting emergent behaviour. It follows that adaptive AI must be explicitly constrained to adhere to the prior assumptions of the player, which can be encoded as a player model.

Further, undesirable and unpredictable game play bugs can emerge from adaptive components, which could be difficult to test exhaustively. Thus adaptive AI requires a certain level of *formal understanding* of the game that is being designed, in order to give designers the tools to build meta-constraints in the abstract level of the game's possibility space. The use of formal modelling can also benefit the creation of a generalised player model, as described in Sect. 3 below (and earlier [11]).

Interaction Modes. It is useful to briefly describe the varying forms of player-game interaction, as this can affect how adaptive AI could be deployed. Salen and Zimmerman [27] illustrated four different modes of game interactivity:

1. Cognitive: psychological, emotional and intellectual interaction with the game.
2. Functional: essentially, the interaction with the game interface and the primary means for accessing the game mechanics.
3. Explicit: the interaction with the underlying game mechanics – this is the core of the game, the mechanics and the formal rules.

4. Cultural: occurs outside the bounds of the game in the form of fan sites, creation of and use of cheats, eSports events, etc.

Here we are interested in the first three modes of interactivity and how these relate to game adaptation. This interactivity is illustrated by the relational schema shown in Fig. 1. This is a combination of ideas following on from LeBlanc's Mechanics Dynamics Aesthetics (MDA) method [20] and the USE model of user interaction with an automated system [8].

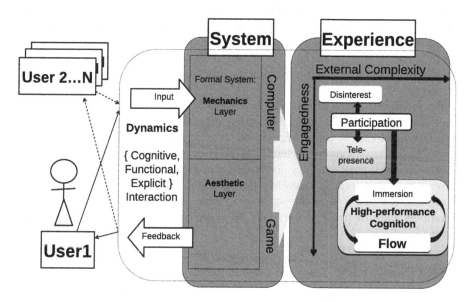

Fig. 1. A model of player interaction with a computer game, for two or more players. Adaptive AI involves leveraging information from the 'User(s)' to dynamically alter the elements of the central 'System' module, thus regulating activity within the right-hand 'Experience' module, which feeds back to the 'User(s)'.

At the highest level the model illustrates how a player's experience of the game arises from a player's participation in a game in several modes of interaction. A player's interaction with the underlying formal game system gives rise to a unique set of game play dynamics and a player receives either negative or positive feedback on performance etc. Thus one description of a game is as cybernetic system [27], i.e. a system with a control loop.

Adaptation as a part of this feedback loop can potentially provide improved control of the game system and thus a more tailored experience for individual players. This then gives rise to a more complex game dynamic and potential emergent game behaviour.

2.2   AI Under Constraint

One key constraint for adaptive AI is that the player's original conception of the game rules and elements, including *a priori* knowledge[1], must not change.

For instance, if the game is a simulation of competition or *agôn* [5] the player's opponents usually appear to have abilities similar to the player—an example would be a fighting game like Street Fighter II (Capcom 1991). Adaptive AI should not suddenly change those abilities in an obvious way in mid-play, to adjust a game mechanic such as difficulty. Early examples of DDA in racing games caused dissonance among players by doing this: a terrible opponent who suddenly becomes lightning fast on the last lap would hurt players' immersion.

In the DDA system for *Max Payne* (3D Realms 2001) was designed with this in mind, trying to make it invisible to players. The aim was to not be obvious when the game is self-adjusting its difficulty level, to maintain the game's immersion.

Yet hiding the rules in this way is a form of "black-box mechanics". Some game designers think this is bad practice, ergo the player should know about the adaptive elements, but I argue that there is always a complexity limit on players' knowledge of game mechanics. Thus they can be made aware of adaptive AI, if and only if they can be sufficiently informed of the logic under which the adaptive system works, so that they have some idea of why the game performs its actions. For instance, if the adaptive system is non-linear and/or composed of complex rules or predicates, it may be excessively difficult to explain to the player.

Logical Consistency. The great thing in game design is to create a game with no *capricious logic*. Capricious logic occurs when the game mechanics are not internally consistent, and this can occur for many reasons. A major cause is the fact that players *observe* a game logic whose rules are often bent or broken for expediency or speed within the game engine.

That players demand a self-consistent logic from their games can be seen in Steinkuehler and Duncan's [30] study of *World of Warcraft* (Vivendi Universal 2004) players. They examined the cultural activities surrounding the game, such as online discussion forums. Here they discovered that players had been analysing game elements in an attempt to uncover hard information that would be useful in 'beating' the game. They claim that these are players of a young age with no scientific training, applying the scientific method to a game world because *they trust that the internal logic of that world will be self-consistent*, so that applying logical analysis will bear fruit. The rule-based structure of games demand logic even if their playfulness should allow logic to be sometimes set aside.

---

[1] *A priori* knowledge includes knowledge of 'realistic' or 'natural' elements. This can help when adapting, as some changes need not be explicitly explained, such as the trivial example of player opponents that increase in toughness as they increase in size. *A priori* can also refer to game design patterns, existing conventions which somewhat binds developers to the forms of previous work in their chosen genre.

Logical self-consistency sufficient to cope with this type of meta-gaming analysis could be considered a benchmark objective for in-game adaptive AI, since it would be proof (through 'natural use') that the autonomic component of the game engine can withstand scrutiny. Pre-facing development of autonomous computer systems by modelling through formal methods should help to ensure their operational stability [32].

Coherent 'Magic Circle'. The second reason adaptive AI must be constrained is that players are temporarily redefining themselves and their world in terms of a new set of rules, defined by the game: a 'game world'. Huizinga [19] describes play as a free and meaningful activity, carried out for its own sake, spatially and temporally segregated from the requirements of practical life, *and bound by a self-contained system of rules that holds absolutely.* If these rules change players will be forced to 'step out' of the game to re-evaluate their perceived definition of the game world. This would destroy the sense of immersion in a game world which is important to the player's enjoyment of the 'fantasy' element of play.

This concept of a game world is known as the Magic Circle [19] to games researchers. The Magic Circle pertains to the attitudinal psychology that is a prerequisite of play, as individuals must take on the role of players in order to play. Huizinga held that the 'cheater' is less deleterious to other players' enjoyment than the 'spoil-sport', because the latter is denying the validity of the Magic Circle while the former is only trying to exploit it [31]. The above example of *World of Warcraft* players applying the scientific method can be thought of in the same way, since they are rejecting the attitude of playfulness in favour of production, sometimes known as 'the grind'.

[23, 24] also identified fantasy as an important part of enjoyment in gaming. Drawing on the psychology of intrinsic motivation, he was among the first to experiment on the relation between fantasy and game-play in educational games. The fact that fantasy is hugely motivating in game play is quite well-established now, and it is more interesting *how* that fantasy is structured. It is necessary to provide some comprehensible metaphor within the fantasy, so that players can easily digest the information content of the fantasy and go directly to dealing with the game mechanic. Thus, here again adaptive AI requires constraint.

Constraint Summary. So there is a potential conflict of interest between adaptive AI which can alter game mechanics, and preservation of logical consistency and the Magic Circle. For instance, one way to introduce novice players to a complicated control scheme is to begin with a restricted subset of the full scheme. But if this is how the player initially understands the game, they will question the introduction of new control dimensions unless they are explained within the narrative - i.e. in the acquisition of new equipment, skills, companions etc. Meeting the player's expectations for the logic and fantasy of their game is the key to creating effective adaptive components. These constraints on adaptive AI mean that great care must be taken when adapting in-game elements in real time - the player must either be forewarned that adaptation may take place (making it part of the game's rule set, which may conflict with realism), or must not be able to notice it at all.

2.3   Aspects of Players to Adapt to

Ability. Ability within a game is influenced by a player's position within the *learning curve* of the game. The learning curve is the sine qua non of game design: as argued by Koster [22], learning is the key ingredient that makes games fun.

Player ability is also influenced by their knowledge of the game's design patterns [3]. A player who is fluent with a particular design pattern, such as the 'Aim and Shoot' pattern, can have a higher skill level when beginning to play than a player who is not so familiar.

Learning and ability are related in information processing terms. In [8] it was pointed out that players process information from the game world, trying to balance the complexity of this environment with internal cognitive complexity. The complexity of the game comes from its control scheme, narrative, objectives, opponents and other such elements; while cognitive complexity refers to the player's ability to take all that in and react, enabled through prior experience of the form or innate ability. So a balance between the two is desired. If the player cannot comprehend everything being thrown at him, he will be overwhelmed and unable to function in an ideal way. If the game does not provide sufficient challenge or interest, the player will be left unengaged and will lose motivation.

Thus, negative imbalance leads to confusion and anxiety, and positive imbalance leads to boredom and apathy [26]. There is an echo of Ashby's Law of Requisite Variety in this formulation, since the variety needed to support learning and thus optimal game play must be present in both sides: player and game. In this sense, an adaptive single-player system would resemble a pair of linked homeostats [16]. On one side, the player learns the game system and/or narrative, attempting to 'beat' it by application of experience-based skill. On the other side, the game maintains its novelty by adapting to the player's current ability level. Therefore if one homeostat is a human player, the first requirement of an automated adaptive AI system is homeostasis of the player's experience. This means being able to keep up with the player's inevitable learning of the game system. Once that requirement is met, then the system can be tweaked to provide different levels of difficulty, types of experience, etc.

Learning. Learning is a key aspect of game play, and the fact of learning implies the necessity of some form of teaching. At the least, one can say that there is a didactic process inherent in the way game content is structured so that the player can learn it without being over- or underwhelmed. In a standard game, designing how this structure is revealed during play is the job of the game developer. In an adaptive game, the adaptive AI is forced to deal with player learning, perhaps by constraint to a given possibility space.

Controlling the pace of learning of players is integral to a game's design, as the quality of the play experience depends heavily upon it. Some games demand mastery with a levelling or 'power-up' structure in a very discrete, 'building block' way. Another class of games have learning built into the basic structure of game play. For instance Tetris or Chess have relatively easy-to-learn mechanics but a great depth of emergent complexity, and the pace of learning follows the player's own ability to uncover this complexity, enabled through practice.

DDA attempts to address these issues, but it must deal with a major hurdle: players vary in how much challenge they want to face, and DDA smoothes out the challenge. In other words, some players want to be challenged beyond their current abilities, and grow in skill to meet the challenge by replaying sections of the game over and over until they conquer the game. At the other end of the scale, some players want simply to wander, enjoy the game world and never be overly challenged, as discussed next.

Personality & Interaction Style. The act of playing requires an attitude to the game being played that constitutes a personality, even in the case of AI agents where 'attitude' would only be attributable on observation by humans. The act of play requires commitment to a course of action that ends with an invested outcome, winning or losing being the most common type of outcome. The *perseverance* of a player, and their particular *style* in undertaking the play actions, contribute to their play personality. Perseverance in play refers to continuing in the face of setbacks, e.g. replaying until the point of mastery of a level, strategy, or skill. Style of play is used to encapsulate the differences between players in their approach to play tasks. As with any form of personality, a play personality is not to be thought of as static but quite contextualised and relative. It thus requires constant monitoring, with a dynamic player model.

Adapting play based on a fixed metric of player performance ignores the opportunity to refine adaptive AI based on types of players. This is a major problem with DDA, because adjusting difficulty adjusts the challenge of the game, and one difference between types (in many of the existing player typologies) [1], the pure *Conqueror* type requires very high challenge, while the pure Wanderer type requires stress-free play, i.e. little or no challenge. These are mutually exclusive and yet core requirements (of each type), so a game that ignores this in favour of adapting only to the player's evinced skill risks alienating both types. The subtle indicators of a player's type are in their *approach* to play, not their skill in playing. Thus adapting play based on an evaluation of the player's type involves shifting the focus of play *overall*, encompassing cohesive changes to difficulty, reward structure, aesthetics and automated assistance.

A player approaches a game from the unique perspective of her own play history and personality, as discussed above; in addition, players vary fundamentally in information processing styles. This has been addressed in the study of temperament theory, which is regarded as biologically based, while personality is culturally based. I, and others, have previously covered this topic in detail [2,10,13]. Thus it is sufficient to reiterate that there is a close link between the interaction styles that characterise people, and the patterns which reoccur throughout game design – and this is no accident because games are human artefacts designed for human minds.

Behavlets. As stated in the Introduction, a general model should provide insight into different facets of player behaviour, for example the cognitive information processing 'style' of a player. It thus requires a foundation of parameters that describe the subjective experience of play. The foundation will draw on established modelling tools, including at least: i) psychology of behaviour; ii) general game design; and iii) actions in the context of a given game.

I previously proposed the *Behavlets* method [10] to build facets i) to iii) above into composite features of game-play defined over entire action sequences. The aim is to create player-modelling features linked to valid psychological theory. The Behavlet process integrates descriptive models for temperament theory, game design patterns, and patterns of player actions. The core concept is to capture behaviours with certain known bias of personality; e.g. aggression, caution; and thus observe the players' self-expression. Behavlets have been used to model players for, e.g. personality type classification [9] and move prediction [14]. Thus I use the Behavlets method to fulfil requirement i (from the Introduction): to capture information about player psychology (cognition, emotion, personality).

How to fulfil requirement ii, and represent the Behavlet model in the context of a game AI? Below I propose an abstract mathematical formalisation, to provide a foundation for more specific solutions in future.

3   Part B: A General Player Model Proposal

This section aims to provide a notation to represent Behavlets as action sequences in a formally defined simulation of a game system, by extending [32]. The motivation is to generate a representation of possible player actions, and the archetypal behaviour traits that can shape those actions, such that the representation can be used as input for a learning system. Ultimately, the goal is to learn from real human behaviour.

3.1   Background

Formalism. To represent Behavlets (or any other psychological model) 'in the game', i.e. in a manner both machine- and human-comprehensible, is (in principle) best done by *simulation*. As stated in the inspirational work of [18], simulation "models' main purposes are to leave out certain aspect of complex systems to facilitate study of those systems".

Note that games can be neatly modelled as a mathematical system because they rely on rule-based interactions defined on a possibility space, and the mechanics of play are essentially functions over that space.

Restricting the games under consideration to those with strictly bounded rules, observe that a state at time t is determined by the game state at time $t-1$. Thus the game can usually be represented by a finite-state Markov process[2].

---

[2] With a non-rational learning human player at the core of gameplay (who may display high *choice variance*, i.e. infer different predicates based on the same observations), game processes are usually strictly non-Markovian; however they can still be given Markovian representations as a simplifying assumption.

A state-based model is often used for game representation, and Markov methods are often used for computational intelligence in games [35].

However, observe that play involves spaces and control systems; these can be either discrete, or approximately continuous with minimum lower bound, sometimes defined by the frame rate of e.g. 60 fps or 16.67 ms per frame.

For purpose of player modelling, the difference between approximate and truly continuous is not as important as the player's *understanding* of the nature of the play space. A general player model must capture the player's understanding, and deal with 'approximately continuous' data.

If the model must capture every frame of the game, it is hardly an efficient simulation. Far more parsimonious to use a modelling framework that can handle continuous entities.

For example, consider Go played with clocks. Players make a single discrete move while their clock elapses continuous time. The elapsed time value can be captured with a simple integer, but the elapsed psychological experience cannot.

Fortunately, the required tools are already in [32]'s category theory framework to model interactive control systems. The framework in [32] models both discrete and continuous control systems, in hybrid form and as abstraction simulations. I will draw on the definition of hybrid control systems (HCS), following [18] and building on [32].

[18] is an excellent complement for the reader; it works lucidly through the foundational technical aspects of applying this formalism to games. It also concludes at about the point where I aim to depart: the composition of micro-games (e.g. Behavlets) to form complete games (e.g. player models). The approach is more applied than [18], but as in that paper the aim here is to produce a simulation model with reduced complexity compared to the original game.

[18] described the *how* of game specification using HCS methods, but he himself questioned *why* one would wish to do it. I am interested in providing this motivating vision.

Prior Work. A general player model has the difficult task to account for the variation between players, variability in their behaviour over time, and the reciprocal relationship of players to the game. For example, such a model should account not only for player learning, but also player emotions' impact on play. There are many relevant fields of study in that problem, and I have previously reviewed literature contributing to generalised player modelling [13]. Below, literature on formal models is briefly reviewed.

Various *descriptive* models of game play have tried to include aspects of player psychology, such as emotions. For example, I proposed the User-System-Experience (USE) model [7,8], to describe the intrinsic motivation of games in terms of the cognitive neuroscience of information processing and learning. However the specification of games themselves was lacking in detail. Järvinen [21, pp. 99–247] built a player experience model on top of a game decomposition theory. The model has two concepts: game experiences are composed of sequences of emotions; and game elements embody conditions that elicit emotions.

[17] define a formalisation of 'synthetic' emotions using Decision Theory, to be used for player modelling or for communication of AI agent states to the player. Methods which codify game mechanics allow a model to capture player-game interactions. [28] attempts this, using the object oriented programming paradigm to define game mechanics as "methods invoked by agents". [4] developed a formal modelling toolset to analyse player behaviour by action sequence mining. The method finds all action sequences and their frequency in a game log, representing common sequences as features, which are selected by ranking according to their mutual information with the class variable.

Formal specification of the play space can support the integration of game and psychological models. [33] defined game theory, which gives useful tools to analyse player behaviour: assuming that players are rational agents with definable utilities for action. Such assumptions do not serve our purpose to learn from real human behaviour. More generally, formal methods such as category theory [34], enable specification and verification of the objects and actions of the play space, and thus support rigorous testing of system coherence. Category theory was applied to game specification in [18], which leveraged [32]'s system of notation for abstractions. In [18]'s abstract specification, a game "consists of objects which change their state during the play, where the evolution of their state is governed by rules and influenced by the players or other objects". [18] defined a game as a *triple* $(S, \mathcal{M}, F)$, where S is a set of game states; $\mathcal{M}$ is a monoid describing the inputs to the system; and F is an action of the monoid on the set, i.e. the rules. [18] also showed how the operation of composition defined in [32] could be used to create novel games; this was a useful abstract discussion.

This approach is flexible, but the complexity of the domain poses a large problem for this method. [18] agrees: "describing a game with this formalism seems to be a cumbersome task". The task is cumbersome because the approach relies too much on one system; any such system will be either unwieldy or insufficiently descriptive. In a multi-step modelling approach, methods for action-tracking [4], design pattern analysis [3], and player psychology profiling [10] can first describe the game; i.e. requirement i) above. These descriptions can then be associated with a coding formalism for rigour, i.e. requirement ii) above.

Next section describes such an approach – note, some background knowledge about HCS literature and algebraic definitions is assumed.

3.2   Formal Model

Here, the full HCS defined by Tabuada et al. [32] is extended. A game is modelled as a HCS; some rectifying operations are also defined, to force the HCS to behave as games do.

Model Foundation

Definition. A game $G = (\mathcal{X}, \mathcal{M}, \Phi)$, consisting of:

- the state space $\mathcal{X} = \{\mathcal{X}_q\}_{q \in Q}$
- a monoid $\mathcal{M} = \coprod_{n \in \mathbb{N}} (U^* \cup \Sigma^*)^n$
- a partial action Φ of $\mathcal{M}$ on $\mathcal{X}$, such that there exist invariants $Inv(q) \subseteq \mathcal{X}_q$

Note. Here, $\mathcal{X}$ is a set of smooth manifolds parametrised by discrete states $q \in Q$; this allows modelling of any simulated spaces with entities, such as a game's 3D environment with typical player-controlled unit(s) and opponent(s).

Note. Monoid $\mathcal{M}$ is defined as the product union of the sets U^*, the set of smooth manifold inputs, and Σ^*, the set of discrete inputs[3]; which allows modelling of combined analogue and digital inputs, such as a joystick and buttons. Individual inputs are denoted by m, a map in $\mathbb{N}_0^+$, defined as a composition of finite $u^{t1...i}$ with finite $\sigma_{1...j}$. In this system, $u^{t'}$ indexes time, with 'embedded' discrete inputs from Σ^*, if modelling game time is required.

Note. The partial action Φ implies a ruleset that can be defined over a subset of the state space; this allows modelling of rules such as power-ups, which alter some core function in a restricted area of state-space, i.e. after a power-up item has been consumed, and perhaps within limited time/space.

This general-form model may be revised to obtain the core framework for specific games. For example perfect-information purely-discrete games, such as Chess and Go, can be obtained when $\mathcal{X}_q$ is a singleton and $U = \emptyset$.

Example. Let us model the game of *Noughts & Crosses* (TicTacToe in American) as a demonstration.

- $X_{\mathsf{xo}} = (pos_\psi)_{\{\psi \in 1...9\}}$, the set of 3×3 board positions, uniquely ordered by the magic square $n = 3^4$.
- $\mathcal{M}_{\mathsf{xo}} = \sigma_{\mathsf{x} \in \psi} \cup \sigma_{\mathsf{o} \in \psi}$, the act of placing an x or an o.
- $\Phi_{\mathsf{xo}} = \phi : \{1, 2, 3\}$, a map to three 'rules',
  1. $\sigma_{\mathsf{x}} \times \sigma_{\mathsf{o}} \longrightarrow {}_4 P_\psi$, paired player turns involve sampling without replacement from the magic square $n = 3$, up to four times,
  2. $\mathsf{x} \cap \mathsf{o} = \emptyset$, choices are disjoint,
  3. $win \iff \sum \Sigma^* = 15$, winning condition such that player wins if and only if 3 choices sum to 15.

---

[3] Although continuous systems are constrained to have finite duration of input times, they may have infinite number of inputs defined as vector field maps from an input manifold. This permits a model consistent with the player's point of view, which is an important part of creating psychologically relevant models.

[4] This is a rare occasion when a magic square becomes a Magic Circle (in the sense of Huizinga, not Yang Hui)!.

Although *Noughts & Crosses* is a trivial child's game, it is a simple matter to adapt this specification to model *Gomoku*, which is also an m, n, k-game. From there, it is straightforward to model Go, at least for $(\mathcal{X}, \mathcal{M})$. To define Φ for the core Go rules, which for brevity are not stated here, would require significant effort but tractable complexity because the rules are all simply derived from the board and input definitions $\mathcal{X}, \mathcal{M}$.

In order to more flexibly create games, it helps to exploit modularity; for this one can use the operation *composition of monoids*. Composition implies that, given two monoids $\mathcal{M}_1$ and $\mathcal{M}_2$, one can form the composition $\mathcal{M}' = \mathcal{M}_1 \otimes \mathcal{M}_2$, which is also a monoid. $\mathcal{M}'$ has all possible evolutions of the composed monoids and no interaction between their parts.

For such a model $(\mathcal{X}, \mathcal{M}, \Phi)$ as described, a common shorthand notation is $\Phi_{\mathcal{X}}$, denoting $\Phi_{\mathcal{X}} : \mathcal{X} \times \mathcal{M}_x \to \mathcal{X}$. With this notation, and composition, one can thus describe a basic game, Φ_0, and compatible game-parts $\Phi_{\mathcal{X}a}$ and $\Phi_{\mathcal{X}b}$, and obtain a complete game by composition, $\Phi_{\mathcal{X}b} \times \Phi_{\mathcal{X}a} \times \Phi_{\mathcal{X}0} \to \Phi_{\mathcal{X}ab}$. The goal is that such game-parts are used to represent Behavlets, as described below, Sect. 3.3.

However as [18] pointed out, with such a framework it is not yet possible to build any reasonably interesting game, in the sense of a system which produces meaningful decisions and outcomes [27]. This is because the composition operator does not impose any interaction on the composed parts, leaving the resultant system causally heterogeneous and un-gamelike. Composition should also impose constraints on the composed monoids, such that the inputs of each are influenced by the other. And, tracking activity patterns allows us to see more clearly how the defined influences work in practice. Thus, two more concepts complete our core toolset: **composition with restriction**, and **orbits**.

Definition. **Composition with restriction**, denoted $\otimes$, from [32], imposes a restriction of $\Phi_{\mathcal{X}}$ to a subset of $\mathcal{X} \otimes \mathcal{M}'_x$, such that the composed monoids are forced to synchronise by the restriction.

Definition. An **orbit** is a set O_x containing all points visited on an evolution starting at x and controlled by some input $m \in \mathcal{M}$. Formally, $O_x = \{x' \in \mathcal{X} : x' = \Phi_{\mathcal{X}}(x, m')$ for some prefix m' of $m\}$. [34] defines an orbit as the behaviour of an imperative program f, i.e. the effect of a series of inputs a on an initial state x, such that $f_{ai}(x_{i-1}) = x_i$.

For our purposes, an orbit of monoid $\Phi_{\mathcal{X}}$ will represent instances when the game-play activity pattern defined by $\Phi_{\mathcal{X}}$ is played. For example, in Noughts & Crosses there are well-known tactics, which when played according to the correct selection criteria will generate a perfect game. These include *Play Center*, *Block*, *Fork* and others defined in [15]. They can be modelled with a triplet, defining: player's move, state of the board, and a test for the type of tactic played.

In the game of Go there are also various well-known patterns of play, such as *atari*, *gote* vs. *sente*, *joseki*, *ko* fighting. These concepts may be captured by orbits, when the analysis of the pattern characteristics is algorithmic and tractable (as in Go, some expert judgement is often involved in assessing patterns).

To make a well-formed map from games to models, an orbit for modelling behaviour is under two constraints. It cannot be a cycle, as cycles are not game-like: consider the *ko* rule in Go. It cannot consist only of a stable state, as this cannot evolve (by definition [34]), and is therefore uninteresting from a player modelling point of view.

Complete Model. Based on this framework, a modelling scheme for game behaviour is proposed, which is descriptive rather than generative; i.e. the aim is to simulate the game components that relate to player actions, rather than deriving a simulation of game play from a model of the engine mechanics.

Definition. A game G' is a composition of HCSs $\Phi_{\mathcal{X}i}$, $1 < i \leq k$, where each $\Phi_{\mathcal{X}i}$ is used to model a distinct game play pattern, and the composition (by the properties of composition of monoids) is also a HCS.

The 'base' monoid $\Phi_{\mathcal{X}0}$ represents the core game framework, with no orbit restrictions. A single game play pattern is represented by a monoid, $\Phi_{\mathcal{X}i}$: $(\mathcal{X}_i, \mathcal{M}_i, \Phi_i)$, instantiated by an orbit $O_{\mathcal{X}i}$, with a starting condition $(q, x_0)_i$, an initial condition from $\mathcal{X}_{qi}$ which corresponds to the opening state of the game pattern. Such monoids are constrained from having initial or terminal objects (as defined by [34]), because they would then be allowed to define only a single function, violating the principle that games should be uncertain.

Modelling of the complete game is achieved by composition with restriction, where three restriction operators are defined.

1. $\mathcal{X}_{qi} \subseteq \mathcal{X}_{qi-1}$, i.e. state space is reduced every time by composition. This models the progression of games, i.e. the fact that a game can generally be modelled as a tree traversal, such that every move will reduce the remaining possible states.
2. $m_i \otimes m_{i-1}$ iff m_{i-1} is a prefix of m_i, such that e.g. in a time-indexed system $m_{t^1} \geq m - 1_{t^1}$, i.e. the start time of the orbit for the next monoid to be composed must be greater than or equal to the prior monoid, such that game progression is modelled.
3. $O_{xi} \neq O_{xi-1}$ where $(q, x_0)_i \cap (q, x_0)_{i-1} \neq \emptyset$ without any other restriction on $x \in O_{\mathcal{X}i}$. I.e. monoids composed such that their orbits have overlapping time sequences, shall not be isomorphic.

Thus, based on this approach, a game G' is a basis monoid $\Phi_{\mathcal{X}0}$: $(\mathcal{X}_0, \mathcal{M}_0, \Phi_0)$, which provides the complete state space and time registration, without inputs. The basis monoid is composed with $1..k-1$ additional game pattern monoids, to describe those activities in the game that reduce the possibility space until game end. Each pattern monoid Φ_i is restricted to join the base monoid in a time-ordered fashion, without overlap of isomorphs, and without expanding the game tree with nodes excluded by previously composed monoids $\Phi_{1..i-1}$.

3.3 Behavlets-Based Formal Model

As mentioned, the intention is to formalise the 'Behavlets' player modelling method. Per the formal model definition, this can be done by using orbits to represent the play patterns arising in-game, as elaborated here.

A Behavlet is essentially a game play pattern associated with a temperament trait. Thus, a well-chosen monoid representation of a pattern, $\Phi_{\mathcal{X}i}$, can also represent a Behavlet, and thereby be associated with a temperament trait. To select the right monoid for the Behavlet is quite straightforward. The instantiation orbit $O_{\mathcal{X}i}$ is equivalent to the Behavlet logic, defined in [10]. Further, the orbit starting condition $(q, x_0)_i$ is equivalent to the Behavlet concept of a *constraint harness*, defined in [10].

An example will illustrate the approach, for which are used already peer-reviewed [10] and empirically tested [14] Behavlets, derived for the game *Pac-Man* (Namco 1980). The formal framework for the Behavlets model of a given game Γ is obtained and used with the following five step process:

1. define basis monoid for Γ
2. define compositional Γ play pattern monoids, each with temperament trait
3. define model *instance* as label for play personality in Γ
4. model reduction by the operation of *simulation*, giving representations of behaviour patterns in Γ-like games which can be compared
5. obtain generalised player model by iterating this process

I will apply this process to the Pac-Man Behavlets using the Pac-Man specification from my previous work (see e.g. appendix D to [9]). This specification was totally state-based, discretising the smooth movement of original Pac-Man. Thus, as with Chess or Go, this Pac-Man does not need U^*, and $\mathcal{X}$ is singleton. For brevity, further simplifications are made which do not relate to the example Behavlet. Only a single level is modelled, to avoid extra complications surrounding *tests* that would be needed to model end-of-level or loss of lives (for a description of test function construction, see e.g. [34, p. 46]). There are no extra state variables to model bonus items, points scored, or Pac-Man's lives (these values are referenced but not defined). There is also no model of the driver of Ghost behaviour, which in the prior specification is simply a probabilistic map to adjacent positions, weighted toward Pac-Man in normal play and away from Pac-Man when a power pill is in effect. These features can be trivially added.

First, the basis monoid for a Pac-Man game $\mathcal{P}$:

Definition. $\Phi_{\mathcal{P}} = (\mathcal{X}_{\mathcal{P}0}, \mathcal{M}_{\mathcal{P}0}, \Phi_{\mathcal{P}0})$,

- $\mathcal{X}_{\mathcal{P}0} = \{mat, xy_p\}$, where $mat = (hpos_x) \cup (vpos_y), \{x, y \in \mathbb{N}, 1\ldots20\}$ the Pac-Man 'map' matrix with values drawn from $\{\emptyset, wall, pill, powerpill\}$; and xy_p is a set of current position values for Pac-Man and the Ghosts $\{xy_p \mid p \in PM, G1..4\}$,
- $\mathcal{M}_{\mathcal{P}0} = m : \{\leftarrow, \uparrow, \downarrow, \rightarrow\} \times \mathcal{X}_{xy_{PM}} \xrightarrow{d=1} \mathcal{X}$, a map from the four directions of movement to the matrix position adjacent to Pac-Man's current position,

- $\Phi_{\mathcal{P}0} = \phi : \{1,2,3\}$, a map to three 'rules',

  1. $m \times pill \longrightarrow \{+5_{points}, \mathcal{X}_{xy_{PM}} = \emptyset\}$, Pac-Man passes through a matrix position with a pill: increase points by +5, position becomes empty,
  2. $m \times powerpill \longrightarrow \{+10points, \mathcal{X}_{xy_{PM}} = \emptyset, \phi = \phi' : \{1,2,3'\}, t : (1..n)\}$, similar effects as $pill$; also transition to the map ϕ', where vulnerability of Pac-Man to the Ghosts is inverted for a limited time n,
  3. $m \times xy_{G1..4} \longrightarrow -1_{life}$, Pac-Man and a Ghost enter the same matrix position: Pac-Man loses a life,
  3'. $m \times xy_{G1..4} \longrightarrow \{+50points \times i, i \in (1..4), xy_{G_i} = xy_{0G_i}\}$, Pac-Man and a Ghost enter the same matrix position: +50 points (multiplied by consecutive Ghost order), Ghost returns to starting position

Second, the Behavlets themselves are modelled. To illustrate, I select a Behavlet listed in [10, p. 293], *A1_Hunt Close To Ghost House*. Behavlet *A1* (for short) tracks how often a player follows the Ghosts right up to their house while attacking them in *powerpill* mode.

Definition. $\Phi_{A1} - (x', m', O_{\mathcal{P}A1})$,

- $x' = \forall 1..4, \mathtt{dist}(xy_{G_i}, xy_{0G_i}) \leq 3$, the manhattan distance of each Ghost to its own starting position is three or less,
- $m' \subseteq \mathcal{M}_{\mathcal{P}0} \forall t_{(1..n)}$, the orbit elapses for all inputs until the end of the *powerpill* timer,
- $O_{\mathcal{P}A1} = \{x' \in \mathcal{X}_{\mathcal{P}0} : x' = \Phi_{\mathcal{P}0}(x, m')\}$, an orbit defined on the Pac-Man basis monoid

Third, the composited game is produced, $\mathcal{P} = \Phi_{A1} \otimes \Phi_{\mathcal{P}} = \Phi_{\mathcal{P}A1}$. Game instances where this Behavlet monoid appears can be labelled as examples of *cautious play*, with a quantification scheme as described above.

Fourth, model reduction by simulation creates a simpler representation without reference to the specifics of the game. Thus one does not need to define, for example, the dimensions of game space states $\mathcal{X}_q$, only to define the *type* of spaces as they appear to the player. In this way, one can make an equivalence between models for Pac-Man, Go, even Noughts & Crosses if wished. Given the game produced by composition with restrictions $\Phi_{\mathcal{P}A1}$, two simulations of the composed parts are defined: β_{A1} and $\beta_{\mathcal{P}}$. The map φ which defines each β is an abstraction of the part of the model *which is not relevant to comparison with another simulated game.* βs are composed by restriction to produce a more general version of the model, $\beta_{\mathcal{P}A1}$.

$$
\begin{array}{ccccc}
\beta_{A1} & \otimes & \beta_{\mathcal{P}} & \longrightarrow & \beta_{\mathcal{P}A1} \\
\varphi \uparrow & & \varphi \uparrow & & \uparrow \\
\Phi_{A1} & \otimes & \Phi_{\mathcal{P}} & \longrightarrow & \Phi_{\mathcal{P}A1}
\end{array}
\qquad (1)
$$

The complete approach to simulation is detailed in [32], and is also discussed in [18]. Here it is enough to note that, given proven models of games such as those described above, the reduction can be pursued and the simulations are then 'safe' to study without reference to the messy details.

Fifth and finally, obtaining the generalised player model from the given framework is perhaps possible for a class of games between which simulation is well-defined. Proving this is clearly a matter for future work.

4   Discussion

It is clear that adaptive AI can be enhanced using in-depth knowledge of the player in real-time. It is our primary argument in this paper that a generalised player model is the most efficient way to capture player individuality which is required for good function of adaptive AI. Properly constraining adaptive AI should therefore be a function of a player modelling approach.

The approach described in Sect. 3 for a generalised player model draws on the Behavlet method to create psychologically-based features of game play, and redefines them as parts of a category theoretic formal model. The value of this approach is that, under a formal framework, Behavlet models of particular games can be further generalised by the operation of simulation.

The primary use case for the described method is to capture player variation. Consider that, if Behavlets are modelled as game parts Φ_{χ}, then by the Behavlets method [10], each $\Phi_{\chi i}$ will have an associated behaviour trait. Thus, a game instance with a specific Φ composition will reflect the 'character' of a particular player's play style. Potentially, characteristics of human play can be learned through enough such instances.

Also consider that the method allows abstraction and specificity: one can build a canonical game model and also simulate game instances quite easily from the same definitions. This allows exploration of the space of possible games.

This is a work at the concept stage, and like any concept there are many details lacking. The state of the method presented is probably sub-optimal, and this may frustrate the more engineering-minded reader; but the aim is initiate a conversation. It is to be hoped that the concept will provide fertile soil to grow more detailed methods.

In future work, we will study a single game under a finite set of adaptive AI conditions. We will use Behavlets [10] to provide the generalised player model, and the formal method (described above) to provide a rigorous framework for comparison. We will iteratively evaluate progressively more complex adaptations of this testbed game. The testbed game, such as a first-person shooter, will be chosen to provide a well-understood experience (in the sense of being well-studied), and also a rich activity (in the sense of allowing players to express varying behaviours). [10] has guidelines on choosing a viable testbed game.

Thus, in the first instance the formally defined player model will be built for the testbed game with no adaptation conditions. The game will then be altered in a simple way, in order to demonstrate abstract game comparison-by-simulation [11], comparing the original and altered versions. Thereafter, adaptive AI will be added to the modelled game, in multiple conditions with increasing complexity. Based on the generalised player model, each adaptation will be designed to respond to some aspect of the player profile, for example a player's tendency towards cautious play, creating multiple versions of the game. These versions will be evaluated by play testing to establish whether the generalised player model does in fact support adaptive AI. To further demonstrate that the system can facilitate adaptive AI, the versions with more complex adaptations will be compared with the simpler versions, using the simulation features of the formal model. The threshold for complexity will be set where it is no longer possible to manually test all possible adaptive outcomes. This will show that issues of logical consistency can be dealt with more readily when the profile of the player is known through a formal generalised player model.

References

1. Bateman, C., Boon, R.: 21st Century Game Design, vol. 1. Charles River Media, London (2005)
2. Bateman, C., Lowenhaupt, R., Nacke, L.: Player typology in theory and practice. In: Digital Games Research Association conference, Utrecht, Netherlands (2011)
3. Björk, S., Holopainen, J.: Patterns in Game Design. Charles River Media, Hingham (2005)
4. Breining, S., Kriegel, H.P., Schubert, M., Zufle, A.: Action sequence mining. In: Croonenborghs, T., Driessens, K., Missura, O. (eds.) Second International Workshop on Machine Learning and Data Mining in Games, at European Conference on Machine Learning, Athens, Greece (2011)
5. Caillois, R.: Man, Play, and Games. Free Press of Glencoe, New York (1961)
6. Chanel, G., Rebetez, C., Bétrancourt, M., Pun, T.: Emotion assessment from physiological signals for adaptation of game difficulty. IEEE Trans. Syst. Man Cybern. Part A Syst. Hum. **41**, 1052–1063 (2011)
7. Cowley, B., Charles, D., Black, M., Hickey, R.: User-system-experience model for user centered design in computer games. In: Wade, V.P., Ashman, H., Smyth, B. (eds.) AH 2006. LNCS, vol. 4018, pp. 419–424. Springer, Heidelberg (2006). https://doi.org/10.1007/11768012_62
8. Cowley, B., Charles, D., Black, M., Hickey, R.: Toward an understanding of flow in video games. Comput. Entertain. **6**(2), 1–27 (2008)
9. Cowley, B., Charles, D., Black, M., Hickey, R.: Real-time rule-based classification of player types in computer games. User Model. User-Adapt. Interact. **23**(5), 489–526 (2012). https://doi.org/10.1007/s11257-012-9126-z
10. Cowley, B., Charles, D.: Behavlets: a method for practical player modelling using psychology-based player traits and domain specific features. User Model. User-Adapt. Interact. **26**(2), 257–306 (2016)
11. Cowley, B.U.: How to advance general game playing artificial intelligence by player modelling. arXiv 1606.00401, June 2016
12. Cowley, B.U., Charles, D.: Adaptive artificial intelligence in games: issues, requirements, and a solution through Behavlets-based general player modelling. arXiv 1607.05028, July 2016
13. Cowley, B.U., Charles, D.: Short literature review for a general player model based on Behavlets. arXiv 1603.06996, 7 March 2016

14. Cowley, B.U., Charles, D.: Utility of a Behavlets approach to a decision theoretic predictive player model. arXiv 1603.08973, March 2016
15. Crowley, K.: Flexible strategy use in young children's tic-tac-toe. Cogn. Sci. **17**(4), 531–561 (1993)
16. Espejo, R., Harnden, R.: The Viable System Model: Interpretations and Applications of Stafford Beer's VSM. Wiley, New York (1989)
17. Gmytrasiewicz, P.J., Lisetti, C.L.: Modeling users' emotions during interactive entertainment sessions (2000)
18. Grünvogel, S.: Formal models and game design. Games Stud. **5**(1), 1–9 (2005)
19. Huizinga, J.: Homo Ludens: A Study of the Play-element of Culture. Routledge, London (1949)
20. Hunicke, R., LeBlanc, M., Zubek, R.: MDA: a formal approach to game design and game research. In: Proceedings of the Challenges in Game AI Workshop. AAAI Press, Stanford University in Palo Alto, CA (2004)
21. Järvinen, A.: Games Without Frontiers: Methods for Game Studies and Design. VDM Verlag, Copenhagen (2009)
22. Koster, R.: A Theory of Fun for Game Design. Paraglyph Press, Scottsdale (2005)
23. Malone, T.W.: What makes things fun to learn? Heuristics for designing instructional computer games. In: SIGSMALL 1980: Proceedings of the 3rd ACM SIGS-MALL Symposium and the First SIGPC Symposium on Small Systems, Palo Alto, California, United States, pp. 162–169. ACM Press (1980)
24. Malone, T.W.: What makes computer games fun? [for education]. BYTE **6**(12), 258–277 (1981)
25. Mnih, V., et al.: Human-level control through deep reinforcement learning. Nature **518**(7540), 529–533 (2015)
26. Rauterberg, M.: About a framework for information and information processing of learning systems. In: Falkenberg, E.D., Hesse, W., Olivé, A. (eds.) Information System Concepts. IAICT, pp. 54–69. Springer, Boston, MA (1995). https://doi.org/10.1007/978-0-387-34870-4_7
27. Salen, K., Zimmerman, E.: Rules of Play: Game Design Fundamentals, vol. 1. MIT, London (2004)
28. Sicart, M.: Defining game mechanics. Games Stud. **8**(2) (2008)
29. Silver, D., et al.: Mastering the game of Go with deep neural networks and tree search. Nature **529**(7587), 484–489 (2016)
30. Steinkuehler, C., Duncan, S.: Scientific habits of mind in virtual worlds. J. Sci. Educ. Technol. **17**(6), 530–543 (2008)
31. Swalwell, M., Wilson, J., Kücklich, J.: Forbidden pleasures - cheating in computer games. In: The Pleasures of Computer Gaming: Essays on Cultural History, Theory and Aesthetics. McFarland & Co., Jefferson, N.C. (2008)
32. Tabuada, P., Pappas, G.J., Lima, P.: Compositional abstractions of hybrid control systems. Discret. Event Dyn. Syst. **14**(2), 203–238 (2004)
33. Von Neuman, J., Morgenstern, O.: Theory of Games and Economic Behavior. Wiley, New York (1944)
34. Walters, R.: Categories and Computer Science. Cambridge University Press, Cambridge (1991)
35. Yannakakis, G.N.: Game AI revisited. In: Proceedings of the 9th Conference on Computing Frontiers, CF 2012, pp. 285–292. ACM, New York (2012)
36. Yannakakis, G.N., Togelius, J.: A panorama of artificial and computational intelligence in games. IEEE Trans. Comput. Intell. AI Games **7**(4), 317–335 (2015). https://doi.org/10.1109/TCIAIG.2014.2339221

Hermeneutic Relations in VR: Immersion, Embodiment, Presence and HCI in VR Gaming

Leighton Evans[1]([✉]) [iD] and Michal Rzeszewski[2] [iD]

[1] Swansea University, Swansea, Wales, UK
l.evans@swansea.ac.uk
[2] Adam Mickiewicz University, Poznan, Poland

Abstract. The emergence of Virtual Reality (VR) as a viable consumer medium for gaming offers an opportunity to reconceptualise understandings of immersion, embodiment and presence in gaming. However, many of the discourses and attempts to conceptualise experience in VR games conflate these terms rather than understanding each as a state of engagement with a VR environment or game. This results in a lack of understanding of the importance of design and intentionality in the VR game with regards to immersion, embodiment and presence. Using a post-phenomenological approach, this paper differentiates immersion, embodiment and presence as three kinds of relation utilising the I – technology – world schema. This approach allows for an understanding of these states of engagement as layered and hierarchical rather than instantly emergent on the part of the technology. The hermeneutic relation between the user and VR game [I → (technology – world)] that indicates presence can be understood as a feeling of place or placehood in VR and is intentionally the state aimed for as optional in VR games. The importance of technological intentionality as a co-constructor of embodiment and presence is exemplified through an analysis of user reviews of VR games either built-for VR or ported to VR. Built-for VR games create the possibility of a sense of place for the games by incorporating the possibility of embodiment and presence into the design of control and movement while ported VR games fail to immerse because of a lack of technological intentionality towards these goals.

Keywords: Virtual Reality · Post-phenomenology · Gaming

1 Introduction

The emergence of virtual reality (VR) as a medium for games since 2012 poses a challenge to researchers and designers with regards to reconceptualising the relationship between system, player and game play – in essence, a reconsideration of the human-computer interface (HCI) of gaming. The challenge has deep roots; the euphoric techno-utopianism of the discourses around 1990s VR was a reflection of the implicit and explicit revolutionary nature of VR as radically immersive and intimate compared to other interfaces. This discourse has been replicated in the publicity and hype surrounding the contemporary re-emergence of VR, particularly in gaming which has quickly become

© Springer Nature Switzerland AG 2020
X. Fang (Ed.): HCII 2020, LNCS 12211, pp. 23–38, 2020.
https://doi.org/10.1007/978-3-030-50164-8_2

the most profitable and visible use of VR. When considering the human-computer inter-action of VR and games, the notion of immersion as an a priori property of VR is problematic. The notion of immersion as a given creates a confusion when considering the relationship between immersion, embodiment and presence in VR, and fails to con-sider the intertwined relationship between these states felt by the gamer and how they are contingent on but also independent from one another. The enrolment of presence and embodiment into the concept of immersion ignores the critical functions and feelings of the experience of these states in VR, and potentially minimises the importance of presence and embodiment as states of experience that differentiate VR as a medium. In particular, the conflation of immersion and embodiment minimises the attention that can be paid to the creation of the sense of place and placehood in VR, and how a feeling of placehood emerges from a design and comportment towards embodiment, and a sense of embodiment is contingent on a feeling of place on the part of the user – a hermeneutic circle that is elided in a conception of embodiment as an extension or division of immer-sion, without which presence in VR cannot be achieved In short, the user and the mood and comportment of the user towards the game environment is ignored in conceptual-ising the user experience in VR. This paper explores how conceptualising immersion, embodiment and presence through a theoretical lens of post-phenomenology can avoid conflation of key experiential aspects of VR gaming and can also explain theoretically.

Gaming and VR

Arguably gaming is the most visible form of VR. The Sony PlayStation 4 is one of the most popular platforms for VR through the PSVR with over 5 million units sold, and the Oculus Rift and HTC Vive are closely associated with games through the use of the Steam VR platform as a game distribution platform. VR should, in theory, aid the sense of presence in games for the player. Pimentel and Teixeira [1] explain that VR requires the same mental shift that happens when you become absorbed in playing a computer game. Tamborini and Skalski [2] argue that VR technology enhances spatial presence in games by the game technology being able to match user expectations of bodily movement and orientation in a manner that playing on a screen cannot. For example, when a player in a VR game environment turns her head, there is an expectation to see the surrounding environment move accordingly. Therefore, VR incorporates bodily movement and orientation into the game environment, arguably improving the sense of 'being there' in the game and from an HCI perspective, one would argue, an enhanced ludic experience.

Empirical research on the effects of VR on user satisfaction in gaming is promising. Shelstad et al. [3] found that VR gaming on the Oculus Rift enhanced perceptions of overall satisfaction, enjoyment, engrossment, creativity, sound, and graphics quality in gamers. Madsen [4] argues that the commercialisation of VR has brought horror video games to the highest level of immersion and presence, generating more arousing mediated experiences in the genre. These findings are supported by Lin et al. [5], who found that in participants who identified themselves as easily scared, playing a horror game (*The Brookhaven Experiment*) on the HTC Vive led to significantly greater enjoyment ratings compared less predisposed participants. These players experienced more immersion, perceived enjoyment and perceived fear in the VR environment. However, there is a danger in reading the results of research as VR being a panacea with regards to enjoyment.

Unpicking why these ratings occur is critical. Depth of presence in a game environment is contingent on how the graphics, sound, narrative, interface and orientation of the user are harnessed in the game for immersion to lead to presence [6]. The success of games in VR in creating this increased sense of presence may not be a function of the use of VR as a medium for the game, but instead is a function of the design and immersive qualities of the game itself and the mood of the user towards orientation. While this furthers a position of questioning why VR games may be more enjoyable, it is only a vantage point for further investigation rather than a satisfactory answer as to why this may occur.

Gaming in VR, at least at the early stages of consumer VR, is marked by a tension between existing and emerging gaming forms. Gaming and the kinds of games popular in VR ask fundamental questions about the kind of investment and development being put into VR in its early consumer iteration. At the early stage of development of consumer VR, games can be divided into two kinds: VR ports, which are games developed for non-VR systems and converted into VR; and built-from-the-ground-up for VR games, games developed for VR specifically. In the former, Bethesda have led the way with conversions of major console and PC titles into VR: *Doom, Skyrim,* and *Fallout IV* have been converted to VR. Other successful ports have included *Superhot, Resident Evil VII* (with the VR version released simultaneously for PSVR) and a slew of games that have had additional VR expansions such as *Star Wars: Battlefield, The Last Guardian, Tekken 7* and *Wipeout Omega.* Popular built-from-the-ground-up games have included *Job Simulator, I Expect you to Die* and *Beat Saber.* The built-from-the-ground-up games are considerably more original than the console ports; for example, *Beat Saber* is a VR rhythm game, where the goal is to slash light sabres to hit objects (the 'beats') in perfect rhythm with the music of the game. *Beat Saber* has an innovative game design with the immersive elements of vision, sound, touch and orientation working together to provide a unique experience. Games such as this can be seen as part of a developing language of VR [7] which can emerge from the experimental tone of such games, and the utilising of the unique features of VR (such as being able to mimic light sabres in the hand in a VR environment through haptic devices), where conventions of gaming are remediated and altered in the VR medium. The ported games take existing games and remediate the perspective from which they are played from on the part of the gamer. This is not to underestimate the vast amount of effort and work that goes into the creation of such games, but the underlying logic and language of the game is created for another medium and transposed to VR.

The schism between ported games and built-for VR games offers an opportunity to explore the differences and co-dependence of immersion, embodiment and presence in VR through the experience of gamers. This paper argues that built-for VR game environments alter the experience of place and space in VR games by using embodiment as the mechanism for the creation of a sense of place in VR. This is achieved through a shift in the relationality of the player to the game and game environment, creating a hermeneutic relationship between gamer, system and game environment. Avoiding the conflation of immersion with embodiment and presence as different kinds of the former necessitates a critical understanding of the relationship between the user and the medium at a phenomenological and post-phenomenological level, that is at the level where the user interacts with and experiences VR rather than at a material, medium or essentialist level. Using Don Ihde's post-phenomenological concept of embodied and hermeneutic relations with technology, the importance of the relationship between place and presence in VR can be understood through the lens of place being embodied in a multi-stable manner in VR games. This approach draws attention to the gamer and their embodied experience as well as considering the role of the system and the game environment as co-creators of a sense of place and embodiment in the user. The experience of place in VR is situated, embodied, specific and fully signifying through embodiment in an experiential locale or world. This approach allows for a critical analysis of the kinds of experience that users have with contemporary VR games as well as analysing how VR developers may develop embodied, place-creating experiences in the future that afford the possibility of a feeling of presence in VR.

To exemplify this conceptual approach, we consider the two typical kinds of VR games available today: VR ports, games converted into VR; and built-for VR games such as *Beat Saber* that utilise immersive elements of vision, sound, touch and orientation to create a game experience. Ported games create worlds that use familiar geographical clues to build a sense of place without a consideration for embodiment that comes would allow for the development of a hermeneutic relation. Priority is given to the architecture of the game rather than the phenomenological experience of the game for the user. From a post-phenomenological perspective, built-for VR games shift the relationality of the player to the game from an embodiment relation (seeing through VR) to a hermeneutic relation (understanding the game as a virtual experience). In ported games, the body or embodiment is not considered in the original design of the experience of place. This lack of embodiment contributes to a lack of virtual place. We consider user experiences of *Job Simulator, Moss* and *Beat Saber* as examples of the development of a hermeneutic relation in VR gaming, compared to the simple embodied but not-place building experience of *Borderlands 2 VR and Doom VR*. The post-phenomenological framework proposed offers both an analytic and developmental framework for VR games as well as proposing a theoretical framework to avoid the conflation of immersion, embodiment and presence in VR. In addition, this framework takes the form of a topology of states of engagement in VR that can inform HCI debate and VR design.

2   Post-phenomenology, Human-Technology Relations and VR

The framework we develop here is derived from post-phenomenological or mediation theory. Classical phenomenology studies our experience of the world; post-phenomenology studies how our experience is mediated by technology [8]. Eschewing Heidegger's concerns with Dasein, the approach retains the rejection of the Cartesian subject by replacing it with the existential, lived body as a fundamental concern [9]. Post-phenomenology specifically updates phenomenology by understanding the world through the 'I – technology – world' schema [10], and thanks to this structuring of technology a mediator of experience, post-phenomenology is also known as mediation theory. Ash et al. [11] argue that an advantage of a post-phenomenological approach is that this approach interrogates how digital interfaces appear as objects, and therefore allow researchers in HCI to think about the ways that interfaces are structured to modulate actions without reducing the modulation effect. The approach therefore gives an account of human experience by expanding what is meant by 'human' and by re-evaluating the role of non-human objects in the construction of experience. Interfaces in this approach refer to how multiple objects work and communicate together to construct experience. Critically, post-phenomenology considers these objects or technologies as cultural instruments which are non-neutral and deeply embedded in daily life processes. Cultural instruments are transmitters of a particular culture or ideology [12].

Critical to the use of post-phenomenology to understanding the differences between immersion, embodiment and presence in VR is that embodiment replaces subjectivity in a post-phenomenological analysis, in effect giving a non-subjective phenomenology [13]. Action, experience and knowledge is always situated as an embodied experience, and because of this self-knowledge is reflexive as a factor in being-in-the-world and activity with other things as an embodied agent in the world. In the context of VR, the kind of engaged attitude or mood that the gamer has through their embodied engagement with the VR game will shape their mode of engagement as immersed, embodied or present (or none of these). The importance of the body and embodiment in post-phenomenological theory can be thought of as the human body being caught in the fabric of the world that enmeshes us, and digital technology is part of that fabric [14]. Stacey O'Neal terms this entanglement as the 'digital attitude' [14] when digital technology is familiar, the body is often engaged in digital experience in a taken for granted manner (such as occurs in VR with body and avatar acceptance). Digital technology is an object in the lifeworld, but it is also part of the fabric of the everyday world and is therefore a co-constructor of our everyday world [15]. In our average everydayness, we incorporate digital media into our own body and life experience in a habitual manner. For the understanding of VR, this approach sets a groundwork for a kind of analysis. VR is part of a wider context in which our bodies and lives are enmeshed with the digital; the body is critical in all our engagements with the digital as we are embodied agents in the world, and the digital and our embodied activity act as a co-creator of our world (even if that world is virtual).

Embodiment is therefore a critical part of the post-phenomenological framework, and as such should lend itself to an analysis of VR that has embodiment as a core component. The use of and digital media creates a technologically-mediated pluraculture [16], and embodiment is an element of that pluraculture as a particular form of the I – technology – world schema. This schema has four relational shifts that affect the way that technology shapes relationships between humans and their world: focal relations; embodiment relations; hermeneutic relations; and alterity relations. This analysis forsakes alterity relations as they refer to the quasi-otherness of relations to particular forms of digital technology which would be incongruous with video games and VR in particular. Focal relations refer to phenomenon of technology in the foreground being focussed upon, while other technology works in the background. This relation is akin to a focus on a particular object, experience or technology while that technology works in the background, away from circumspection on the part of the user. In this analysis, the focal relation is posited as immersion where the attention of the gamer is on the game or experience, not the technology or the inter-connectivity of the technology with other technical devices, or the functioning of hardware or software in the background. This corresponds with Bortulussi and Dixon's definition of immersion [17] as a hybrid, dynamic and interactive phenomenon that involves convergence and divergence to the state of immersion. Such a view emphasises the role of the individual in the construction of immersion, as immersion involves an orientation towards engagement with the media in question. Thon [18] positions this as a kind of attentional focus, a psychological immersive shift of attention that goes hand-in-hand with the construction of situational models of engagement. Ryan [19] furthers this notion of the psychological aspect of immersion by arguing that immersion is a kind of directed, intentional consciousness that relates to another world and reorganises the 'universe of being' around that world.

The embodiment relation is more significant, expressed as:

(I – technology) → world

Arrows and parentheses allow for permutations on the I – technology – world schema, and arrows denote intentionality towards that unit of the schema [8]. Selinger [20] describes embodiment relations as the relation that occurs when we use technology to amplify the body's perceptual abilities (in a sense, a McLuhanist extension of man). In an embodiment relation, the technology is always in a ready-to-hand state, being used to perceive the world through the technology itself. We have embodiment relations with many technologies, from eyeglasses to television. Ihde [21] argues that computers have an embodiment relation to users, as we use computers in our everyday understanding of the world; computers are part of the fabric of the everyday and our interactions with them are with an intentionality towards the world. Embodiment is, therefore, always limited by the scope of the programme being used [22] and our embodiment relations are always inter-relational. The embodiment relation in this analysis or VR and gaming translates as embodiment directly. When using VR, the technology itself is embodied (HMD on the head of the user) and the world is being 'seen' or experienced through that technology, with bodily motion and perceptual attention being mapped by the VR equipment and fed back to the gamer as an experience that has visual fidelity and congruence.

More significant again is the hermeneutic relation. In a hermeneutic relation, we are perceiving the world through the technology itself.

I → (technology – world)

The interpreting or reading of the world is through the technology. Hermeneutic relations involve entering into practices with artefacts to gain knowledge of the world otherwise not available [23]. Wellner [24] argues that hermeneutic relations are our main post-phenomenological vehicle to understanding our special relation to media. Andrew Feenberg [25] describes hermeneutic relations like "a screenplay in which the interpreted message is, in effect, a world". Feenberg's point is that in a hermeneutic relation, technology and the world are not just two parts of a unit – technology-world as a co-entity replaces the world as a focus of our intentionality. This relation is mapped to the feeling of presence in VR. In a hermeneutic relation, the world and technology form a singular unit where intentionality is directed. understanding extended embodiment through technology is a hermeneutic circle. The hermeneutic relation involves a translational mediation of technology and technological codes back to the human, but those codes and the technology are a co-constructor of the world in which the user is an active participant. Therefore, in a hermeneutic relation we feel 'present' in the experiential world that has been co-created by the technology.

The notion of technology as a co-constructor of world leaves some room for a technologically determinist critique of the theory, but the importance of intentionality on the part of the human and the technology itself as a co-constructors is a means to avoid this critique. Verbeek [26] added to the 4 post-phenomenological relations with 'cyborg intentionality' indicating intentionality of the part of technology, as it has been programmed to commit intentional acts, and 'composite intentionality' where intentionality is distributed between human and technology [27]. In this view, "intentionality is not a bridge between subject and object, but a fountain from which the two of them emerge" [28]. Hence, technological intentionality is a co-constructor of the world rather than a determinist shaper of the world, as the intentionality on the part of the user towards the (technology – world) unit is as critical as any intentionality programmed into the technology itself. Wellner [29] proposes a new relation to explain this:

I → (technology → world)

The intentionality of the technological artefact to represent the world in a manner where the world itself becomes a part of the (technology – world) unit does not detract from there needing to be a human being with intentionality directed to that unit in order for the hermeneutic relation to exist and for there to be a hermeneutic effect i.e. the world is read through the technology and is therefore contingent upon the technology to be meaningful as a world. Intentionality plays a critical role in the establishment of presence in VR, as the analysis of ported and built-for VR games will illustrate. The intentional nature of how those games should be played, experienced and embodied defines the gaming experience and possibility of presence as an elevated and deep engagement with the VR game.

Having mapped the three relations onto the three states of engagement with VR:

Immersion - Focal relation
Embodiment - Embodiment relation
Presence - Hermeneutic relation

the relations between each relation need to be understood. The contention of this analysis is that these relations should not be read as discreet, but as O'Neal [30] argues the schema can be laid on one another at the same time. Presence in VR is therefore a combination of the focal + embodiment + hermeneutics relations, where the hermeneutic relation is critical, but cannot be achieved without focal immersion and embodiment. The framework also allows for shifts between these different states of engagement with the VR experience. Ihde's outlines that relations between humans and technology shift thanks to 5 potential variational distinctions [31]: materiality of the technology; bodily technique of use; cultural contents of the practice; embodiment in trained practice; and the appearance of differently structured lifeworlds. The variations between different relations occur due to pivot points. A pivot "stresses the degree to which the material of the artefact and human attentions can create different uses" [32], with the movement between pivots and stabilities creating multistabilities of use. The structure of technologies is multistable with regards to use, cultural embeddedness, politics and ethics, and most critically to a sense of place and placehood that emerges from the use of technology.

3 The Role of Place

Borgmann [33] argues that orientation to place is critical to human 'being', and that disorientation is to be in trouble as a human being. Disorientation in a mediated space is the restless pursuit of the unobtainable, but focal presence in virtual reality emphasises the near. In the post-phenomenological model immersion, embodiment and presence in VR are all based on the focal relation between the user and technologically-mediated experience. Ihde [34] argues that post-phenomenologically, we do not experience space singularly, but always our spatiality is multistable – we self-organise into different spatial arrangements. This is important when thinking about the difference between immersion, embodiment and presence. Presence is, in this analysis, akin to a feeling of place or placehood in VR. Experientially and developmentally, places are critically important to the wellbeing of humans, particularly as spaces to dwell. Dwelling is a feeling of being-at-home in a place in the world, and while dwellings are wildly multistable the possibility of feeling place in VR is critically important.

Another source of confusion comes from psychologists, who call immersion presence and posit that spatial presence is the closest thing to immersion [35]. A spatial presence usually denotes a feeling when media content is perceived as real in the sense that media users experience a sensation of being spatially located in the mediated environment. This kind of sensation is closer to embodiment in this post-phenomenological analysis. For presence, the most ubiquitous component of definitions is 'being there' [36].

In the world of game design, questions of space and place have always been important, even to the point that spatiality have been called a defining element of a computer game [37]. The ability of a given game to evoke a sense of place is a factor that is often used to decide on the quality of the game – a good game is the one with a captivating world[1]. Therefore, from the very beginning creators of virtual game worlds strived to make them more immersive by making them similar to the real world. In 2001 Martin Dodge [38] wrote that "Virtual worlds (...) attempts to simulate characteristics of real-world places in the hope of making the online experience less virtual and more naturalistic, therefore more enjoyable and fulfilling". Further technological advancements made it possible to create increasingly larger and multidimensional worlds that include intricate spatial designs, even mimicking in complexity the existing real spatial arrangements. Some gaming studios even hired architects to help them create believable objects and structures [39]. However, it was understood very early that this similarity could not be provided through a simple mirroring because the resulting representation is always imperfect and cracks in the imperfect mirror are easily spotted and this breaks the immersion. In his widely cited book Bartle [40] noticed this and instead proposed a set of guidelines designed to ensure the creation of a believable world through, among

---

[1] See for example a thread on the NeoGAF forums started the user "Piano" in which forum users discuss this issue: https://www.neogaf.com/threads/games-with-a-strong-sense-of-place-screen shots.1029850/.

other factors, adherence to a principles of a geographical consistency (rivers run from mountains to seas etc.).

This state of affairs was further complicated with the introduction of VR. When finally made available to a wider audience, VR brought something new to the equation - the promise of technologically induced immersion and presence. However, this promise is not easy to fulfil in practice as it requires a different approach at virtual world building and the reliance on geographical consistency is no longer enough. As argued by game designer Jeff Murray "*Just because something is realistic in terms of math or physics does not mean it will feel good in the virtual world. The virtual is different to the real world and it is a place*" [41]. When experiencing VR, however rich the environment it provides, we cannot rely on our knowledge of spatial structure of the world and are instead reliant on the structure provided by the game designers. In the same way that imperfections in virtual representations of the real places make them less believable, the inconsistencies of the spatial arrangement of the body and VR environment prevent the player of building a sense of place and achieving presence. It may be tempting to think that there is just something missing in the technology itself. That adding a full set of sensory inputs to the VR experience - to simulate the sense of smell, touch, kinaesthetic sensations etc., would be more convincing and place-building. However, this relation is hard to prove [42] and recreating full range of human senses is hardly practical. There is even evidence that a more realistic representations may not effective in certain real-life applications [43] and on the other hand a deliberately non-immersive low fidelity virtual environments still can be designed to successfully evoke a sense of place [44].

The phenomenological point of view on place itself can provide a perspective on this problem of creating a sense of presence and place in VR. We may think of place as an event (congruent with the idea of a relation), as a coming-into-presence mediated by various stimuli and as an encounter between location and human modes of existence [45]. This location can be either virtual or real and, in both case, there is a virtuality component in the sense of place - the sustained relation of creating something new, the possibility of experiencing something unexpected. VR worlds that try to be realistic by mimicking the real world loose the 'virtuality' in this process and instead become 'virtuzalizations" [46]. So, in order to create the embodiment and hermeneutic relations a game designer needs to provide the element of surprise and creative experimentation. It is necessary to decouple from the real world into the virtual world that is accepted as a place, and the VR technology can achieve this if designed with this in mind [47]. In our view the certain built-for-VR games represent the effectiveness of this decoupling in creating a sense of place and presence by encompassing a technological intentionality towards these relations.

4 Gaming Experience in Ports and Built-for VR

Reinhard [48] argues that in VR, the materiality of the landscape is always experienced because of the withdrawal of the HMD. Following this post-phenomenological framework, we argue that if a hermeneutic relation is established between the user and the technology to experience the VR world, then the materiality of the landscape in VR is experienced as place thanks to the feeling of presence on the part of the gamer that feels immersed, embodied and present in the environment. However, this is contingent on the technological intentionality coded into the VR experience to create a sense of place on the part of the programmers and designers of the game. The importance of this can be seen in the different reactions' gamers have to built-for VR games and ported VR games. Built-for VR games look to utilise the features of VR to create an immersive experience that can facilitate the feeling of embodiment and presence on the part of the user by including embodied experience and place creation at the core of the gaming experience. Essentially, VR game utilise the immersive elements of sound, touch, vision and orientation [49] in VR systems to create a game experience. Ported games use familiar geographical cues to build a sense of place in VR, and wayfinding and navigation based on traditional gaming. As built-for VR games have embodiment as the mechanism for the creation of a sense of space and place in VR, this shifts the relationality of the player towards an embodied and hermeneutic relation with the game. In ported games, embodiment is not crafted into the design of the game itself but is an addition to the original game that may, or may not, facilitate the development of a hermeneutic relation within this new medium for the game. To assess how this difference may manifest in gaming experience, we briefly consider some of the feedback given to different ported and built-for VR games. Using reviews contributed to the site *Metacritic*, a thematic analysis [50] of reviews indicated that the major issues identified by gamers were movement, control, lack of embodiment and nausea.

Issues with movement were prevalent with the ported game *Borderlands 2 VR*, with the mechanisms for movement in the original game not being replicated in the VR version causing major issues for the flow of the game experience (and hence for the possibility of focal relations or an immersive experience in the first instance):

> Move controller support is awful. Teleport move is very slow to engage and seems to get blocked by invisible walls if you're not standing way out in the open, making it essentially unusable around any kind of background cover or uneven terrain.
>
> BillLikesVR 14/12/2018

The inability to move smoothly and in a realistic fashion without glitches in the game clearly prevents a sense of immersion developing for the gamer. This is supported by other comments:

> the jittery neck movement is downright horrible and breaks the immersion big time. It's also inexplicable, as the game isn't a technical marvel, either. One of the pleasures I get from virtual reality is being able to look around naturally, to get that physical sensation you can't find anywhere in a "flat" game, but that's something Borderlands 2 VR just doesn't deliver.
>
> Mlnsfn 09/03/2019

Again, immersion is prevented but also the sense of not being able to look around the environment 'naturally' indicates that there is not an embodied relation with the game, where the 'world' is seen through the technology as the rendering of the game environment itself makes this impossible. The constraining nature of limited movement is also commented upon elsewhere:

If you want push to move (like you play on a monitor) you can only walk directly in the way you are staring. Which is really stupid. No strafing, no backpedaling, nothing. The direction you move should be tied to the direction you point with your left hand.

Timo98 29/10/2019

The directional movement in the original game is suited to the interface of controller-monitor where the viewpoint of the gamer is distanced from the display. In VR, for directional movement to be intuitive and natural the game needs to be responsive in a different way, but the ported game makes no affordance for this difference in perspective, embodiment and relation. This leads to issues with nausea:

Movement just doesn't feel right: I'm able to play Skyrim VR or Gran Turismo for more than 3 h without a single problem, but I can't play for more than 15 min Borderlands 2 VR because of the dizziness. It's awful, I've bought a really expensive game that I can't play because it's a sickness generator.

Selve 02/01/2019

The uncanniness of the movements and the difficulty of translating console-based movement systems to a VR experience are not exclusive to *Borderlands 2 VR*. *Doom VFR*, another ported version of a very successful first-person shooter, was reported as having similar issues with constraint of movement and nausea-induction:

Built for the PSVR Move controllers, you are unable to turn less than 180°, and strafing left and right are both mapped to right facing buttons.

Spidor 19/05/2019

the gameplay is clunky and is mostly about running around which is not so pleasant in VR

tobivv 27/11/2019

The problems with movement around the environment are complimented with issues with the control interfaces in ported games. Again, porting a control system to VR ignores the differences in embodiment in VR as a medium, and creates awkward and uncanny gaming interfaces which prevent the establishment of a smooth, focal experience that could lead to a sense of embodiment or presence:

[Discussing *Borderlands 2* VR] Wrong pivot point on Move controllers: for some reason, the pivot point has been set in the wrist instead of the hand, so you always feel like you are holding a hand which is holding a weapon, so weird.

Selve 02/01/2019

[Discussing *Doom* VFR] I was excited to have another game that uses the Aim Controller, but the gun doesn't even line up well with what you're seeing. It doesn't give the illusion that you're holding the weapons. The tracking seems messed up as well.

OutlawTX 03/12/2017

These issues on movement and control are fundamental in preventing the focal relation between gamer and VR system developing as the building block towards immersion, embodiment and presence. The possibility of a sense of place is therefore non-existent in ported games which ignore the unique needs and features of VR technologies, interfaces and control systems. Interestingly, reviews of built-for VR games rarely mention controls, movement or nausea because the design of the game has incorporated the idiosyncrasies of these parts of the game experience. Reviews of built-for VR games emphasised a sense of presence:

[Discussing *Job Simulator*] Once it's done, there isn't an awful lot of replay value, but it's great to show people the sense of presence you can get in VR

Crazymurdock 16/11/2016

In particular, reviews of *Beat Saber* emphasised how the game avoided inducing nausea through an intuitive control and movement system that limited the possibility for nausea while not limiting embodied experience:

The game is very fun and one of the best for any VR system. It also is one of the least taxing VR games, I think, in terms of motion sickness. It makes great use of only requiring the player to look forward for the game itself.

Kenmei 10/01/2019

I get motion sick with most Vomit Reality games, but I can play this one for hours without any motion sickness whatsoever.

Inconnux, 17/02/2019

The nature of control in built-for VR was also frequently assessed as a key factor in developing a sense of immersion and embodiment. Control interfaces that take account of the affordances and limitations of VR can increase the feeling of presence and place in a VR game:

[Discussing *Job Simulator*] The implementation of room scale and controller experience is perfect. It's a game that is guaranteed to absolutely stun anyone new to the room scale VR experience.

Scimajor 18/12/2016

This was commented on frequently in gamer reviews of the VR game *Moss:*

Fantastic immersion and a really clever implementation of the VR controls and your interaction with the environment (I'm sure more VR games will use this style in the future).

Rustigsmed 01/01/2019

The game fully immerses you in the world, from the backdrops, to the little characters running around, you really feel like a giant looking into a world of mice and other forest dwellers. All the levels are designed so that you can remain in one position and still easily see all the objectives, interactive objects, enemies and objects. You can even get up and look around to find hidden secrets and still feel part of the world.

LivewireHD 07/01/2019

Immersion through a fidelity between control, visuals and embodied action clearly makes gamers feel part of the 'world', which in the post-phenomenological framework posited here may indicate a sense of presence and placehood through a hermeneutic relation with the technology and world.

5 Conclusions

Gunkel [51] stresses that when thinking of human-technology associations, these are not relations between existing subjects who perceive and act on a pre-existing world of objects but as sites where both the objectivity of the world and subjectivity of those experiencing the world it and existing in it are created [52]. Such an approach to considering human-technology relations recasts HCI as a speculative science of self-reflecting knowing, and the post-phenomenological approach we outline in this paper is intended as a contribution to and advancement of this 'third-wave' approach to HCI. In particular, seemingly inevitable development of more VR gaming in the future challenges researchers and theorists to engage with the conceptual difficulties and possibilities of immersion, embodiment and presence and how these moods or states of being for gamers can be fostered, built and exploited. The opening theoretical gambit proposed in this paper should be seen as a starting point for further research, with close attention paid to gamer accounts of experience through empirical research supported by both qualitative and quantitative methods. The technological intentionality or towards-which of game developers is critical in the possibility of being able to develop different variations on the I-technology-world schemas, and the difference between ported cash-in games capitalising of the emergence of VR and carefully-crafter built-for VR games is a basic illustration of how this intentionality effects in-game experience. The position forwarded in this paper is intended as a potential guide towards understanding these different issues and an analytical framework for identifying contemporary, and future, issues with the development of presence in VR.

References

1. Pimentel, K., Teixeira, K.: Virtual Reality: Through the New Looking Glass. Intel/McGraw-Hill, New York (1995)
2. Tamborini, R., Skalski, P.: The role of presence in the experience of electronic games. In: Bryant, J., Vorderer, P. (eds.) Playing Video Games: Motives, Responses, and Consequences, pp. 225–240. Routledge, New York (2006)
3. Shelstad, W.J., Smith, D.C., Chaparro, B.S.: Gaming on the rift: how virtual reality affects game user satisfaction. In: Proceedings of the Human Factors and Ergonomics Society Annual Meeting, vol. 61, no. 1, pp. 2072–2076 (2017)

4. Madsen, K.E.: The differential effects of agency on fear induction using a horror-themed video game. Comput. Hum. Behav. **56**, 142–146 (2016)
5. Lin, J.T., Wu, D., Tao, C.: So scary, yet so fun: the role of self-efficacy in enjoyment of a virtual reality horror game. New Media Soc. **20**(9), 3223–3242 (2017)
6. Evans, L.: The Re-emergence of Virtual Reality, pp. 63–66. Routledge, London (2018)
7. Evans, L.: The Re-emergence of Virtual Reality, pp. 71–74. Routledge, London (2018)
8. Wellner, G.: From cellphones to machine learning a shift in the role of the user in algorithmic writing. In: Romele, A., Terrone, E. (eds.) Towards a Philosophy of Digital Media, p. 209. Palgrave Macmillan, New York (2018)
9. Ihde, D.: Postphenomenology: Essays in the Postmodern Context, p. 1. Northwestern University Press, Evanston (1993)
10. Verbeek, P.P.: Toward a theory of technological mediation: a program for postphenomenological research. In: Friis Berg, J.K., Robert, P.C. (eds.) Technoscience and Postphenomenology: The Manhattan Papers, pp. 189–204. Lexington Books, London (2016)
11. Ash, J., Anderson, B., Gordon, R., Langley, P.: Unit, vibration, tone: a post-phenomenological method for researching digital interfaces. Cult. Geogr. **25**(1), 165–181 (2018)
12. Ihde, D.: Postphenomenology: Essays in the Postmodern Context, p. 13. Northwestern University Press, Evanston (1993)
13. Ihde, D.: Embodied Technics, p. 41. University of New York Press, New York (2010)
14. Irwin, S.O.: The unbearable lightness (and Heaviness) of being digital. In: Romele, A., Terrone, E. (eds.) Towards a Philosophy of Digital Media, p. 185. Palgrave Macmillan, New York (2018)
15. Irwin, S.O.: The Unbearable Lightness (and Heaviness) of Being Digital. In: Romele, A., Terrone, E. (eds.) Towards a Philosophy of Digital Media, p. 189. Palgrave Macmillan, New York (2018)
16. Ihde, D.: Postphenomenology: Essays in the Postmodern Context. Northwestern University Press, Evanston (1993)
17. Bortolussi, M., Dixon, P.: Psychonarratology: Foundations for the Empirical Study of Literary Response. Cambridge University Press, Cambridge (2003)
18. Thon, J.: Immersion revisited on the value of a contested concept. In: Leino, O., Wirman, H., Fernandez, A. (eds.) Extending Experiences: Structure, pp. 29–43. Analysis and Design of Computer Game Player Experience. Lapland University Press, Rovaniemi (2008)
19. Ryan, M.: Narrative as Virtual Reality 2: Revisiting Immersion and Interactivity in Literature and Electronic Media. John Hopkins University Press, Baltimore (2015)
20. Selinger, E.: Postphenomenology: A critical Companion to Ihde. SUNY Press, Albany (2006)
21. Ihde, D.: Embodied Technics, p. 47. University of New York Press, New York (2010)
22. Ihde, D.: Embodied Technics, p. 51. University of New York Press, New York (2010)
23. Selinger, E.: Postphenomenology: A critical Companion to Ihde, p. 6. SUNY Press, Albany (2006)
24. Wellner, G.: From cellphones to machine learning. a shift in the role of the user in algorithmic writing. In: Romele, A., Terrone, E. (eds.) Towards a Philosophy of Digital Media, p. 211. Palgrave Macmillan, New York (2018)
25. Feenberg, A.: Active and passive bodies: don Ihde's phenomenology of the body. In: Selinger, E. (ed.) Postphenomenology: A Critical Companion to Ihde, p. 194. SUNY Press, Albany (2006)
26. Verbeek, P.P.: Cyborg intentionality: rethinking the phenomenology of human–technology relations. Phenomenol. Cogn. Sci. **7**(3), 387–395 (2008)
27. Wellner, G.: From cellphones to machine learning. a shift in the role of the user in algorithmic writing. In: Romele, A., Terrone, E. (eds.) Towards a Philosophy of Digital Media, p. 214. Palgrave Macmillan, New York (2018)

28. Rosenberger, R., Verbeek, P.P.: Postphenomenological Investigations: Essays on Human-Technology Relations, p. 15. Lexington Books, Lexington (2015)
29. Wellner, G.: From cellphones to machine learning. a shift in the role of the user in algorithmic writing. In: Romele, A., Terrone, E. (eds.) Towards a Philosophy of Digital Media, p. 215. Palgrave Macmillan, New York (2018)
30. Irwin, S.O.: The unbearable lightness (and Heaviness) of being digital. In: Romele, A., Terrone, E. (eds.) Towards a Philosophy of Digital Media, p. 198. Palgrave Macmillan, New York (2018)
31. Ihde, D.: Postphenomenology and Technoscience: The Peking University Lectures, p. 190. SUNY Press, Albany (2009)
32. Whyte, K.: What is multistability? a theory of the keystone concept of postphenomenological research. In: Friis Berg, J.K., Robert, P.C. (eds.) Technoscience and Postphenomenology: The Manhattan Papers, p. 76. Lexington Books, Lanham (2015)
33. Borgmann, A.: Orientation in technological space. First Monday (2010). https://doi.org/10.5210/fm.v15i6.3037
34. Ihde, D.: Phenomenology and places. In: Champion, E. (ed.) The Phenomenology of Real and Virtual Places, p. 52. Routledge, London (2018)
35. Madigan, J.: Getting Gamers: The Psychology of Video Games. Rowan and Littlefield, London (2015)
36. Slater, M.: How colorful was your day? Why questionnaires cannot assess presence in virtual environments. Presence Teleoperators Virtual Environ. 13(4), 484–493 (2004)
37. Aarseth, E.: Allegories of space: the question of spatiality in computer games. In: Eskelinen, M., Koskimaa, R., (eds.) Cybertext Yearbook 2000, pp. 154–171. University of Jyväskylä, Jyväskylä (2001)
38. Dodge, M.: Explorations in alphaworld: the geography of 3D virtual worlds on the internet. In: Unwin, D., Fisher, P. (eds.) Virtual Reality in Geography. Taylor & Francis, London (2001)
39. Dinnen, S.: Architecture in video games: how real-world designers are helping to build virtual worlds (2007). http://www.cityam.com/272826/architecture-video-games-realworld-designers-helping-build
40. Bartle, R.A.: Designing Virtual Worlds. New Riders, San Francisco (2004)
41. Murray, J.W.: Building Virtual Reality with Unity and Steam VR. CRC Press, Boca Raton (2017)
42. Turner, P., Turner, S.: Place, sense of place, and presence, Presence Teleoperators Virtual Environ. 15, 204–217 (2006)
43. Bowman, D.A., McMahan, R.P.: Virtual reality: how much immersion is enough? IEEE Comput. 40(7), 36–43 (2007)
44. Turner, P., Turner, S., Burrows, L.: Creating a sense of place with a deliberately constrained virtual environment. IJCPS 1, 54 (2013)
45. Janz, B.B.: Virtual place and virtualized place. In: Champion, E. (ed.) The Phenomenology of Real and Virtual Places, p. 60. Routledge, London (2018)
46. Janz, B.B.: Virtual place and virtualized place. In: Champion, E. (ed.) The Phenomenology of Real and Virtual Places, p. 61. Routledge, London (2018)
47. Turner, S., Huang, C.-W., Burrows, L., Turner, P.: Make-believing virtual realities. In: Turner, P., Harviainen, J.T. (eds.) Digital Make-Believe, pp. 27–47. Springer, Cham (2016). https://doi.org/10.1007/978-3-319-29553-4_3
48. Reinhard, A.: Landscape archaeology in skyrim VR. In: Champion, E. (ed.) The Phenomenology of Real and Virtual Places, p. 33. Routledge, London (2018)
49. Evans, L.: The Re-emergence of Virtual Reality. Routledge, London (2018)
50. Joffe, H., Thompson, A.R.: Thematic Analysis. In: Harper, D. (ed.) Qualitative Research Methods in Mental Health and Psychotherapy: A Guide for Students and Practitioners, pp. 210–223. Wiley, New York (2011)

51. Gunkel, D.J.: The relational turn: third wave HCI and phenomenology. In: Filimowicz, M., Tzankova, V. (eds.) New Directions in Third Wave Human-Computer Interaction. Springer, New York (2018). https://doi.org/10.1007/978-3-319-73356-2_2
52. Verbeek, P.P.: Moralizing Technology: Understanding and designing the Morality of Things, p. 15. University of Chicago Press, Chicago (2011)

A Tool to Support Players Affective States Assessment Based on Facial Expressions Analysis

Marcos C. Fleury[1], Tiago B. P. e Silva[2], Mauricio M. Sarmet[3],
and Carla D. Castanho[1(✉)]

[1] Department of Computer Science, University of Brasilia, Brasilia, Brazil
`carlacastanho@unb.br`
[2] Federal Institute of Education, Science and Technology of Paraiba,
João Pessoa, Paraiba, Brazil
[3] Department of Design, University of Brasilia, Brasilia, Brazil

Abstract. Digital games are played by a large variety of players with different profiles and backgrounds. Understanding their reactions and experiences while playing is crucial to support game expansion or creation. This paper presents a tool to support affective states assessment based on facial analysis. It allows the configuration of different testing scenarios to gather in-game information as well as webcam feed for the facial expressions analysis and further affective reaction processing. Also, it outputs all the data collected and processed into three different formats: graphs, videos and CSV files. Experimental tests with a 2D puzzle game were made to demonstrate that the tool is able to gather and properly provide information about players' affective experience.

Keywords: Games · Affective states · Facial recognition · Game analytics · Player experience

1 Introduction

Digital games are consumed by players with different backgrounds, and the same games may be experienced differently by people with different profiles [22]. Therefore, it is important to have a way to understand their reactions and preferences in order to make better games [17]. Comprehending their experiences during playing time can be valuable to both game developers or researchers, and several tools and methodologies are used to provide an in-depth representation of the players experience [9].

Among those methodologies, the use of biometrics is constantly growing, especially because of their role in understanding players experience when used in conjunction with other techniques like direct observation, interviews and questionnaires [16]. The latter, like the GEQ (Game Experience Questionnaire) [11], are frequently used to get information either after or between game sessions.

© Springer Nature Switzerland AG 2020
X. Fang (Ed.): HCII 2020, LNCS 12211, pp. 39–57, 2020.
https://doi.org/10.1007/978-3-030-50164-8_3

However, it lacks the possibility of collecting information during gameplay, something that biometric measures can fulfill. Besides, the use of biometrics allows the researcher to collect data that is not necessarily available to the player's conscious processes or that is less susceptible to player's biases, like affective states.

According to [4] an affect is an intense and relatively short emotional state caused by a sudden change in the environment. Affective states are related to bodily responses that can be measured and used by an external observer to infer what was being felt. There is no definitive way of measuring an affective state [18], but there are various possibilities like electroencephalography (EEG), galvanic skin response (GSR), electromyography (EMG), and electrodermal activity (EDA), to name a few [16]. There are several advantages in using psychophysiology data when used together with other methods like play testings or questionnaires. However, there may be some difficulties related to data gathering and analysis [10].

Another way of measuring emotions is by facial expression analysis. Facial expressions are commonly represented using discrete representations of basic emotions with physiologic and expressive symptoms that can be categorized based on studies of researchers like Paul Eckman and his six basic emotions [7]. The work in [19], for example, used a machine learning algorithm to analyze facial expressions, infer their affective states and compare these readings to participant's self reports.

This paper presents a tool to support affective states assessment based on facial analysis. It allows the configuration of different testing scenarios to gather in-game information as well as webcam feed for the facial expressions analysis and further affective reaction processing. The affective state face analyzer employed, developed by Vieira [21], uses a machine learning algorithm to learn how to distinguish between seven different affective states. From each individual video, the tool provides different outputs and can be used with games of different sizes and genres.

Experimental tests were made to check if the tool was able to gather and properly provide information about players' affective experience. The tests were ran with Lumen, a 2D puzzle game [15]. Ten participants were asked to play four phases and answer a questionnaire regarding their gaming profiles and preferences. Each phase of the game was designed to test a specific aspect of the game and a corresponding affective reaction. In other words, the aim was to check if the players were reacting as expected at certain points of the game or to determine if the challenge was well structured for the different player profiles. After data analysis and processing, the use of the proposed tool allowed the researchers to assess the reliability of the stimuli (based on players' expected and observed affective response) and of the settings used on each game phase.

The rest of this paper is organized as follows. Section 2 gives a brief overview of the fundamental concepts of this research, such as affective states and facial expression, while Sect. 3 describes some related works. Section 4 presents the tool proposed in this work, its main features and some implementation details.

In Sect. 5 are presented the experiments that were conducted with the tool and in Sect. 6 the respective results are shown. Finally, Sect. 7 presents the final considerations of this study and some future work.

2 Affective States and Facial Expression

The field of emotion experience research has grown significantly in recent years. However, researchers are still struggling to consolidate their core definitions. Emotion, Affect, feelings, and affective states are examples of concepts used by various researchers in numerous situations [13]. Despite this, it is understood that the study of emotions is fundamental to understand various components of human behavior and how people interact with the world [6]. This work is interested in understand how affective states, "an intense and relatively short emotional state brought about by a sudden change in any circumstances vital for the person or animal" [4], can be measured and used to understand the impact of game characteristics.

These affective states and all of its reactions are felt by individuals and only they can experience the complexity of such states [18]. Considering that is not possible for a person to have a fully consciousness emotional experience, researchers have proposed the measure of bodily reactions as an alternative for an external observer to infer or guess what was being felt. When a person is feeling fear their heart accelerates, their respiration is suspended, the lips shake, the legs feel weak and the skin crawls [8]. Some of these reactions can be seen or measured by external agents or sensors, while others cannot. Although there is no definitive correct way of measuring an affective state [18], there are various possibilities that display good accuracy when confronted with self reports and descriptions.

The usual way of visualizing affective states is by either representing it in a dimensional space or by using discrete terms to characterize them. The dimensional space representation can be defined by three values, these being arousal, valence and tension (or dominance), that when combined would describe the affection that was felt. As for the discrete representation, it consists of linguistically representing a finite amount of basic emotions with physiologic and expressive symptoms that can be observed and distinguished. Facial expressions are commonly represented using the latter based on the work of Paul Eckman and his six basic emotions [7].

An individual's affective state is usually inferred from their facial expression by observing the eyes region, the mouth, the eyebrows and the mouth edges. In order to automatically infer these states, two methods are usually used: facial recognition through machine learning or Electromyography (EMG). The EMG technique consists of using electrodes to measure the activity of the muscles of the face. It has the advantages of instantly picking up minor variations of the muscles. On the other hand, it suffers from a lot of noise from the equipment itself and from the activity of unrelated muscles. As for the facial detection, it first uses algorithms to separate the facial elements that are of importance and then measure their sizes and angles in accordance to databases of facial expressions already categorized by the emotion they represent. Then, it uses learning algorithms to relate these measures to each of the their emotions. Although being very influenced by the learning algorithms and by the databases used, this method has the advantage of being less intrusive then the EMG since no equipment needs to be physically touching the subject.

It is also possible to have the affective states inferred from facial expressions by non automatic methods. One possibility is recording the face of a person and then have judges watch the video and, based on professional experience or study, infer what the person might have felt at each moment. Another possibility is having the subjects themselves describe what was felt either as it happens or post-factum. One weakness of such methods is their dependence on subjective knowledge and understanding by either the judges or the subject, also, it is harder to recreate and evaluate the experiment using the same data.

3   Related Work

Although a work that tried to achieve the same goal of developing a tool to analyze an user's game experience through both their face and game variables has not been found, some studies have been conducted on correlated areas. A study [19] conducted in Sydney's University of Technology used a machine learning algorithm to analyze facial expressions, infer their affective states and compare these readings to participant's self reports. They observed that the facial expressions readings presented plenty of data and that this data significantly related to the self reports. They also observed that different genres incite different expressions.

Other authors, such as [23], proposed a model based on heartbeat and brainwaves measures for emotion assessment. The authors argue that those measures are more precise than facial and vocal expressions because of cultural variations. After collecting the cited biometric measures, Yoshida et al. used the data to verify the accuracy of subjective self-evaluation based on the Emotional Intelligence Quotient (EQ).

A study [10] from the Breda University of Applied Sciences used four different measures (skin conductivity, facial muscular activity, heart rate and blood pressure) to aid on the development of a casual mobile game. They concluded that there are several advantages in using psychophysiology data during development stages when used together with other methods like play testing or questionnaires. Through this combination they could more effectively understand which challenges were pleasurable for the players, what visuals could bring confusion, which speeds where ideal in specific game-play situations and other findings. However, they also encountered some difficulties related to the analysis of the amount of data collected and the obstructiveness of some of the sensors used.

Inventado et al. [12], from Osaka University, developed a tool to aid the recording, annotation and revision of emotion-related data. This tool used a computer's web-cam to record a user's facial expression while also recording the computer's desktop image. Then, the tool presented both videos alongside with an emotion annotation tool in which the user labeled what they experienced at each moment of the recorded session. Finally, the annotations were used to understand brainwave readings that were recorded during the sessions. It was concluded that the tool was effective in giving context to the annotation process, making it easier, and also in making non observational reading, such as the brainwaves, understandable.

Based on the Circumplex Model of Affect, Tangnimitchok et al. [20] developed a system for emotion assessment based on facial expressions and pupil diameter. Using pictures from the International Affective Picture System (IAPS) as stimulus, Arousal and Affect measures were collected and a model of emotional states was developed. Tangnimitchok et al. suggested that the use of physiological data can be an non-intrusive alternative to infer the emotions of interface users.

Another study from [5] proposed a model of difficulty adjustment based on facial expression measures of affect. As a result, they were able to predict the perceived difficulty of the game used based on facial expression measures, with an accuracy rate of 77%. An experimental design was used to compare groups that played a game with and without the difficulty adjustment algorithm. In this study, the measures of facial expressions were used to measure the degree of difficulty experienced by the participant, since negative affective states may be associated with greater difficulty in the game.

4   The Tool

The main goal of the tool presented in this work is to facilitate the understanding of a developer, designer or researcher about what is being experienced by those who play a game. To accomplish that, three guidelines directed the development of the tool: it should be general, non intrusive, and also computationally light. In the following section these will be detailed.

4.1   Preliminary Guidelines

The idea of the tool being general is that it should not be designed for restrict research uses, that is, not for a specific game or genre. This was decided for a few different reasons. First of all, games can be developed in many different ways. Currently, there are various free engines, like Unity [1] or Unreal Engine 4 [2], which were developed by well established companies and can be used to develop entire games. At the same time, many developers still prefer to develop their own engines. In addition, some games can be fully developed by just one or two people or by teams made up of hundreds of professionals. Considering all that, a tool to help understand players reactions, or affective state, must be general enough to be used in at least most of these cases.

One of the goals of this research is to gather information of game sessions in the least intrusive and artificial way possible. Thus, the use of large accessories to gather psychophysiology data from users was discarded. Some sensors can limit the user's movement, cause discomfort or increase the feeling of self-awareness during gaming sessions, which can alter the results of players' reactions. Therefore, in this work, a non-invasive way of collecting player information was considered. The player's reactions will be obtained from recordings of images of his/her face during a game session, which will be submitted to an affective state face analyzer. This resulted in a smaller pool of information regarding psychophysiological reactions, but it also meant less interference on the player and a simpler setup for test sessions. Using only facial expression data simplifies the equipment needed to a single notebook with a webcam.

Game questionnaires like the GEQ [11] are an effective and often tested way to get information of game sessions either after or in intervals while the game is played. However, the process of asking players to answer questionnaires, rate and analyze them is demanding and time-consuming. Considering this, the tool was designed to acquire information whilst the game is running. This means that the same machine has to run the game and the tool at the same time. The tool receives information from the game, records the game screen and the webcam feed to obtain the image sequences of the player's face. Currently, games can take a lot of resources from the machines they are running on, they can have complex logic or graphics that require a lot of computing power to be playable. For this reason, another main guideline for the software developed was that it should be as light as possible.

4.2   Overview

To simplify, from now on, we will mention anyone who uses the tool as the researcher, although this person may be a scientist, a programmer, a designer, or anyone interested in identifying the affective states of a player during a game session.

Figure 1 shows an overview of how the tool works. The researcher uses the tool to setup test scenarios and decides what are the variables that the tool will send their preset values to the game during the test. After the setup is done, the researcher can run the game for each test subject while the tool records the videogame screen, the webcam feed (with the player's face) and receives outputs from the game. Finally, after as many test sessions as desired, the tool can export graphs of the affective states and specified internal variables, videos of the sessions with the identified affective states and also a CSV file with all the collected data which can be used to perform additional or specialized analyzes.

The tool runs any executable file and can be used with a game as it is. However, it also allows the researcher to configure some variables of the game, and in this case, some modifications are necessary to be made in its source code. In order to make this process as simple as possible, the tool uses a single method of sending information to the game and a single method of receiving information back. To be able to modify the selected variables in the game the tool sends ordered values as command-line variables that can then be read by the game, which then sets them to the specified values or uses them as configuration variables. This strategy reduces the amount of work necessary to adapt each game to be compatible with the tool and make it as general as possible. The researcher only needs to decide what are the game variables of interest to the tests, the position in the code where each variable is updated, and right after that write a command to print a single string containing the triplet (date/time, name, value).

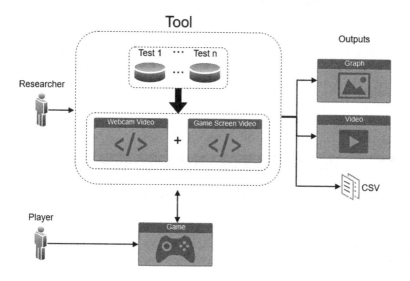

Fig. 1. Tool overview

When creating test sessions, the tool allows for three different kinds of tests. The first one, called "*Empty*" is used when there is no configuration being done from the tool in the game, so all that is needed to run the test is the location of the execution file. The second kind of possible test, is called "*Lightweight*". Here, at the start of each new test session, the researcher specifies the variables whose values will be send from the tool to the game. In this case only the name of the variables and location of the execution file are needed when creating the test. This type of test can be used, for example, when the researcher is performing preliminary tests and is still trying to find reference values to the variables to be changed in the game. Last, is the "*Scenarios*" test (Fig. 2), which is used to set up both the variable names and their values for each defined scenario. This setting is used when the purpose is to test different setups for each sessions and compare them, for example. Also, in this option the researcher may choose which scenario he/she wants to run or let the tool do it randomly.

The tool does not do any kind of processing during the game sessions, it only records the values of the in-game variables received from the game and the two video feeds, the webcam (player's face recording) and the game screen video. The test sessions are processed, that is, the facial expressions are analysed when

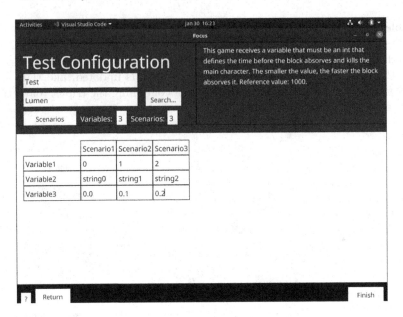

Fig. 2. Tool's test configuration screenshot.

the tool user chooses to do so by pressing a button. This is to avoid interfering with the game that is running. Also, every session needs to be processed only once, since all data is then stored in each respective test file.

For each session, the output options of the tool are graphs, a video and a CSV file. Each graph can present the results from one to eight different variables in the session timeline. Figure 3 gives an example of a graph generated by the tool, where the first four variables (in blue) are the affective states of *Neutral*, *Happiness*, *Sadness* and *Anger*, and the other four are in-game variables.

The video output is generated by the synchronized merging of the webcam video with the game screen video in addition to the affective states that are being identified at each moment. This combination of outputs is exemplified in Fig. 4. Finally, the CSV file gathers all the information for each variable in each session and can be used as input to other software for further analysis of the collected data.

4.3 Implementation Details

For the development of the tool, Rust programming language [14] was chosen. Rust offers fast execution speed while being safe when it comes to possible failures, something highly desirable since a software crash can mean the loss of entire test sessions recordings. In addition, the use of Rust addresses the need for a lightweight software.

Concerning the facial expressions analyses we used the analyzer created by Vieira [21]. It was developed using the OpenCV library [3] for Python and a

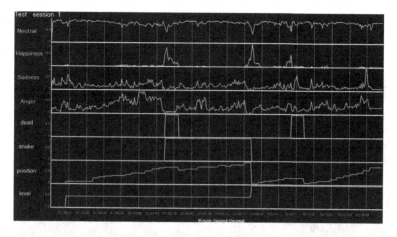

Fig. 3. Graph output example which shows the players affective states and the in-game variables through the test timeline. (Color figure online)

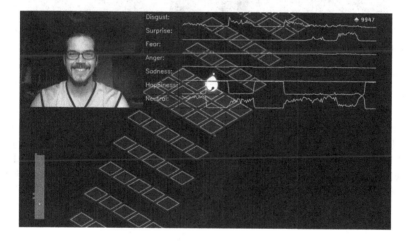

Fig. 4. Video output example.

machine learning algorithm to learn how to distinguish between seven different affective states (Happiness, Sadness, Anger, Fear, Surprise, Disgust and Neutral) from a facial expression database. The assessment is based on each individual frame of the videos recorded by a webcam.

5 Experiments

We performed some experimental tests with our tool and a 2D puzzle game called *Lumen*. The goal was to verify the affective states of the players at each phase of the game, as they were designed with some particularities. The results also helped to determine whether the game level design was appropriate for different player profiles. The Lumen game and details about the tests settings are described below.

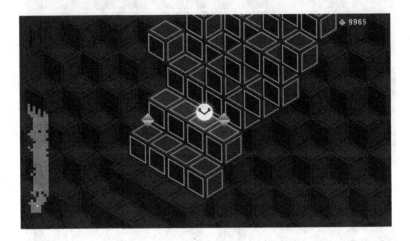

Fig. 5. A screenshot of the Lumen game.

5.1   The Lumen Game

Lumen (Fig. 5) is a 2D puzzle game inspired by the game Catherine by Atlus. It consists of a main character who has the ability to enter into cubes and move them. The game map has a ladder shape formed by these cubes which should be moved by the player in order to create a way to climb until the top of the level. Meanwhile, several obstacles appear in order to eliminate the main character or hinder the ascent. The main challenge is to figure out how to organize the blocks in a way that allows the character to continue climbing.

5.2   The Tests Settings

All tests were conducted in the same experimental setting, and only the researcher was present besides the participant. The researcher provided the participants with information about the basic playing instructions and asked for the participant's consent. Only then the experimental session could begin.

In total, ten test sessions were conducted (three women and seven men). Six of the participants categorized themselves as experienced and four as casual players. Five of them played 10 or more hours per week and only one person did not report playing at least weekly. Considering the most played games, only three people mentioned games that they classified as puzzle games as their most played ones, and no one had ever played the Lumen game itself.

Each test session was designed to be uninterrupted and consisted of two game levels and four parts distributed among the levels. These parts do not have a clear separation between them. Each one was created for a particular evaluation

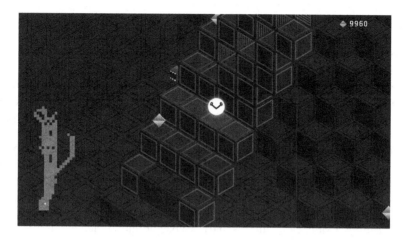

Fig. 6. Screenshot of the hidden snake element in the game Lumen.

purpose, which are detailed below. Between levels, the player receives a kind of reward for overcoming the first challenges and, therefore, having a sense of accomplishment.

The test was configured for the game to send four distinct values to the tool: *"dead"*, which is true when the main character is dead and false when it is alive back again; *"position"*, which is an integer value of the number of blocks climbed minus the number of blocks dropped down from; *"snake"*, which value becomes true when a specific block containing a snake is activated for the first time; and *"level"*, which value is either 1 or 2 depending on what level the player is currently in.

Each of the four parts that comprise a test session is described below.

1) Adaptation Evaluation: in this part, there is no challenge for the player, only the basic movements and commands are necessary to get used to the way the character moves and behaves in the game. The player uses the arrow keys to move and the shift key to enter the blocks and move them. The goal of this part is to analyze how much time the player takes to understand the game core mechanics. The data used in this evaluation are the current position of the character, represented by *"position"*, and its respective time.

2) Surprise/Happiness Evaluation: in this part, a special game element, represented by a snake, will suddenly appear to the player. A colorful snake is hidden behind one of the blocks (Fig. 6) and the moment the character moves in front of this block, the snake attacks. If the player can move the character away fast enough, the snake will miss it, otherwise, if the snake hits the character, it will be eliminated and will return to the last checkpoint. This game element was designed to be a threat but also something visually appealing and fun, causing a positive reaction in the players when they first see the snake. In this part,

the data used for the evaluation are the value *"snake"* that becomes true when the snake block is first activated and also the player's affective responses, specially Happiness and Surprise, obtained from the facial expressions.

3) Challenge Evaluation: this part presents a complex task that requires more attention and gameplay mechanics understanding to be solved. The challenge is to enter and move four blocks in order to create a stair for the character, however, the player must figure out that a block may be moved to places without a block immediately below it. The goal of this test is to identify if the challenge causes frustration and, if so, how long it takes for the player to feel it. Also, it is intended to capture possible reactions if the challenge is overcame. The data used is this evaluation are the character's position and the player's affective responses, with emphasis on Disgust, Anger, Happiness and Neutral.

4) Fine Tuning Evaluation: in this part a specific game element is presented to the player. It is a block which kills the character if it stays in front of it for a certain amount of time. This time is set in the game according to a value passed from the tool through a command line variable. The test is done with three different time settings for this special block, which are 500, 1000 and 1500 milliseconds, and respectively named as *Fast*, *Moderate* and *Slow* scenarios. The goal is to find out the most suitable scenario so that the challenge is not frustrating nor tedious. The data used in this test evaluation are the amount of time set for each session, the number of deaths of the character, obtained from the variable *"dead"*, and the player's affective responses, with emphasis on Neutral and Disgust.

After each test session the participants answered a questionnaire with the purpose of gathering information about their gaming profile as well as their familiarity with games having similar gameplay mechanics to the Lumen Game. This questionnaire asked, among other questions related to demographics, the amount of hours per week they usually spend playing video games and also the titles of their favorite games. This information was useful to better contextualize each of the evaluations described above.

6   Results

After the ten test sessions were carried out, then they were all processed by the tool. This processing basically consists in identifying the affective states from the user's face recorded videos, synchronize these information with the in-game data collected during the game session, and produce the outputs, which are two graphs and one video for each session, and one CSV file containing the data of the entire test (ten sessions). The reason for two output graphs is that all the affective states and in-game variables do not fit in only one graph. So, for visualization purposes each graph shows four affective states on the top (in blue), followed by the in-game variables which are repeated in both graphs.

Below we describe the conclusions and findings for each evaluation test based on the analysis of the data generated by the tool.

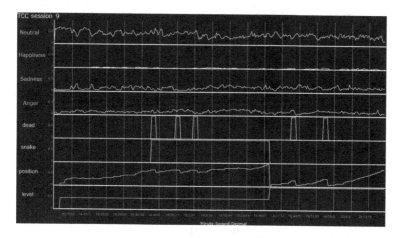

Fig. 7. Output graph 1 of participant No. 8.

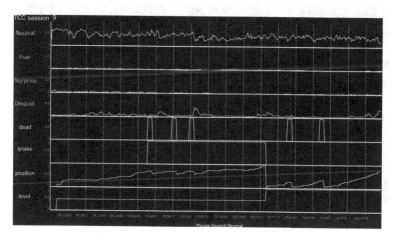

Fig. 8. Output graph 2 of participant No. 8.

1) Adaptation Evaluation: Table 1 shows the time (in seconds) that each participant took to advance in the initial part of the game. From the responses to the questionnaires, it was observed that those who reported themselves as experienced players had a shorter time to adapt to the game. On the other hand, from the affective states detected by the tool, it was not possible to identify frustration (disgust or anger) in the players who took more than two minutes to complete the adaptation part. For those who took less than a minute at this stage, it was possible to notice surprise, disgust or anger. For example, Figs. 7 and 8 show, respectively, anger and disgust for Participant No. 8. These affective states may be due to some kind of discomfort with the game controls, when compared to the games these hardcore players are used to. Nevertheless, it was observed that all the participants acquired at least a

Table 1. Adaptation test duration for each test session

Session	Duration (in seconds)
1	26.99982542
2	67.00045514
3	151.0000676
4	73.99987981
5	38.00001031
6	112.0000641
7	98.99958061
8	56.00049853
9	128.9995475
10	106.0002487

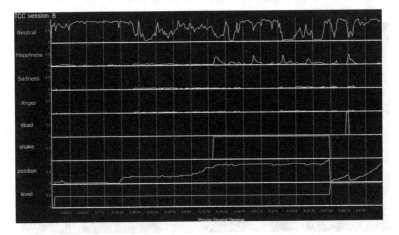

Fig. 9. Output graph 1 of participant No. 7.

basic understanding of the game controls in a short period of time (up to two and a half minutes) without further instructions. Thus, we conclude that the tutorial, or initial, phase was suitable and effective for both experienced and casual players.

2) Surprise/Happiness Evaluation: the results of this test may suggest a possible design problem in the game, since a mixture of different reactions were identified in the snake's first appearance. While it was a new element that was supposed to cause both surprise and joy, the player experienced the death of the character when the snake appeared for the first time. This caused a common reaction of sadness or anger as it resulted in the character going down a few blocks. Nevertheless, in four participants, the affective state of happiness was observed at different levels. Figures 9 and 10 show the output graphs of the participant No. 7. In Fig. 9, for example, we can see happiness being

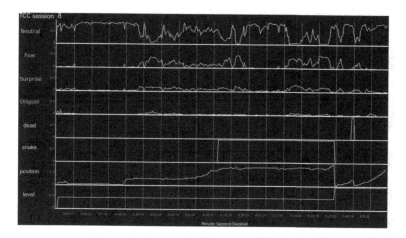

Fig. 10. Output graph 2 of participant No. 7.

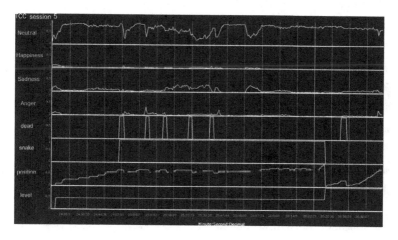

Fig. 11. Output graph 1 of participant No. 4.

identified at the same moment the snake appears. On the other hand, probably due to the character's deaths, anger was noted in participant No. 4 (Figs. 11 and 12) and disgust in participant No. 3 (Figs. 13 and 14). Thus, the results showed that the snake element produced the desired effect in almost half of the participants, while also causing an unexpected and negative reaction in some.

3) Challenge Evaluation: Table 2 shows the time (in seconds) that each participant took to go through the challenge. There is a significant difference between the time spent by the five fastest players and the five slowest players. From the players' profile, four of the five fastest considered themselves to be experienced players, while only two of the slowest did so. All players were able to pass the challenge, meaning either a good understanding of the core

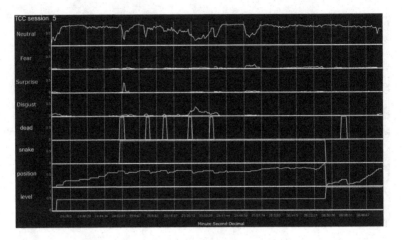

Fig. 12. Output graph 2 of participant No. 4.

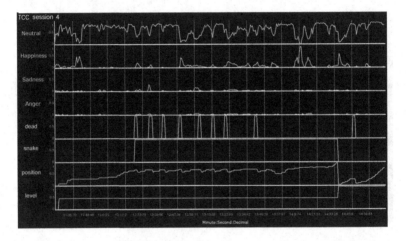

Fig. 13. Output graph 1 of participant No. 3.

mechanics and physics of the game or possibly indicating that the challenge was too easy. Concerning the affective states, in general, it was not observed a common standard reaction of happiness of the players when they managed to overcome the obstacle. Thus, the video output was used to analyze each session to identify possible reactions during the Challenge. It was possible to see peaks of happiness throughout it, which may mean that the reaction does not necessarily occur the moment the player progresses through the challenge, but when the solution is clear and a sense of accomplishment is felt.

4) Fine Tuning Evaluation: for each session, one of three values (500, 1000 and 1500 ms) were randomly chosen by the tool and assigned to the special block. Although, in the tests, all the players had their characters killed at least once,

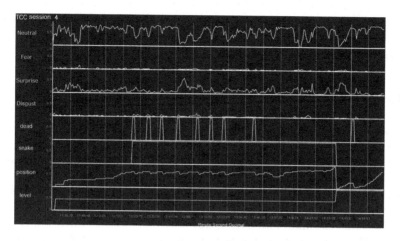

Fig. 14. Output graph 2 of participant No. 3.

Table 2. Challenge test duration for each test session

Session	Duration (in seconds)
1	28.00019802
2	24.00079454
3	26.00040845
4	125.0665281
5	29.99982022
6	187.9813782
7	180.7350982
8	20.99966244
9	204.7591664
10	140.7246334

we could notice from the video recordings that some players were just curious about it and stayed in front of the special block just to see what would happen. Only two of the participants had their characters killed more than once for staying too much time in front of the special block. In this case, one participant is an experienced player in the *Moderate* scenario (1000 ms) and the other is a casual player in the *Fast* scenario (500 ms). Due to the randomness of the values defined for the special block, only two participants went through the *Fast* scenario, that is, an experienced player and a casual player. From the results of this evaluation it was observed that the *Slow* scenario (1500 ms) was not challenging enough for none of the four participants that played it. Regarding the *Moderate* scenario, we can consider that it showed a small level of difficulty, because one of the four players who passed through it experienced some kind of challenge. Last, the *Fast* scenario did not have enough participants for a more concrete conclusion. Nevertheless, it is worth mentioning that one of the two participants in the *Fast* scenario had the character killed.

7 Conclusion

The goal of this research was to develop a tool that could simplify the way that both researchers can test the reaction that players have to the games they are interested in. The tool was meant to be simple to use, to be compatible to different genres and kinds of games while presenting relevant information to help on the detection of problems or possible enhancements in a game. To accomplish that the use of facial expression was considered an non intrusive and effective way of gathering the information regarding players' reactions. As for the outputs, the possibility of various options such as graphs, videos and CSV file, provide flexibility to the user of the tool.

A limitation of the tool is on the operational system end, since it was developed for Linux and it is the only platform in which the tool currently runs. In addition, having used Python for facial expression analysis and face recording, the software has lower than expected execution speed, both during the game session and the video processing.

The preliminary tests conducted with the tool aimed to demonstrate some of its features, possibilities of use and the combinations of output data for inferences. We intend to carry out new tests with the Lumen game with a larger number of participants so that quantitative results can be obtained in the analyzes. Future works also involve carrying out tests with games of different genres. Finally, improvements on the tool graphical user interface are part of the next steps.

References

1. Unity. https://unity.com/. Accessed 15 Jan 2020
2. Unreal engine. https://www.unrealengine.com/en-US/. Accessed 15 Jan 2020
3. Opencv (2018). https://opencv.org/about.html. Accessed 15 Jan 2020
4. Aboulafia, A., Bannon, L.J.: Understanding affect in design: an outline conceptual framework. Theor. Issues Ergon. Sci. **5**(1), 4–15 (2004). https://doi.org/10.1080/1463922031000086708
5. Blom, P.M., Bakkes, S., Spronck, P.: Modeling and adjusting in-game difficulty based on facial expression analysis. Entertain. Comput. **31**, 100307 (2019)
6. Cacioppo, J.T., Gardner, W.L.: Emotion. Annu. Rev. Psychol. **50**, 191–214 (1999)
7. Dalgleish, T., Power, M.: Handbook of Cognition and Emotion. Wiley Interscience, New York (2005)
8. Damásio, A.R.: O Erro de Descartes: Emoção. Razão e o Cérebro Humano, Companhia das Letras, November 2012
9. El-nasr, M.S., Drachen, A., Canossa, A.: Game Analytics. Springer, London (2013). https://doi.org/10.1007/978-1-4471-4769-5

10. Gualeni, S., Janssen, D., Calvi, L.: How psychophysiology can aid the design process of casual games: a tale of stress, facial muscles, and paper beasts. In: Proceedings of the International Conference on the Foundations of Digital Games, FDG 2012, pp. 149–155. ACM, New York (2012). https://doi.org/10.1145/2282338.2282369
11. IJsselsteijn, W., de Kort, Y., Poels, K.: The Game Experience Questionnaire. Technische Universiteit Eindhoven (2013)
12. Inventado, P.S., Legaspi, R., Numao, M., Suarez, M.: Observatory: a tool for recording, annotating and reviewing emotion-related data. In: 2011 Third International Conference on Knowledge and Systems Engineering, pp. 261–265, October 2011. https://doi.org/10.1109/KSE.2011.48
13. Keltner, D.: Toward a consensual taxonomy of emotions. Cogn. Emot. **33**(1), 14–19 (2019)
14. Klabnik, S., Nichols, C.: The Rust Programming Language, 2nd edn. No Starch Press, San Francisco (2018)
15. Moraes, M., et al.: Lumen: puzzle tridimensional de raciocínio lógico. Workshop G2 : Games na Graduação. In: XV Brazilian Symposium on Computer Games and Digital Entertainment (2016)
16. Nacke, L.E.: Introduction to biometric measures for games user research. In: Drachen, A., Mirza-Babaei, P., Nacke, L.E. (eds.) Games User Research, pp. 281–299. Oxford University Press, Oxford (2018)
17. Schell, J.: The Art of Game Design: A Book of Lenses. Morgan Kaufmann Publishers Inc., San Francisco (2008)
18. Scherer, K.R.: What are emotions? and how can they be measured? Soc. Sci. Inf. **44**(4), 695–729 (2005). https://doi.org/10.1177/0539018405058216
19. Tan, C.T., Bakkes, S., Pisan, Y.: Inferring player experiences using facial expressions analysis. In: Proceedings of the 2014 Conference on Interactive Entertainment, IE 2014, pp. 7:1–7:8. ACM, New York (2014). https://doi.org/10.1145/2677758.2677765
20. Tangnimitchok, S., O-larnnithipong, N., Ratchatanantakit, N., Barreto, A.: Affective monitor: a process of data collection and data preprocessing for building a model to classify the affective state of a computer user. In: Kurosu, M. (ed.) HCII 2019. LNCS, vol. 11567, pp. 179–190. Springer, Cham (2019). https://doi.org/10.1007/978-3-030-22643-5_14
21. Vieira, L.C.: Assessment of fun from the analysis of facial images. Ph.D. thesis, Universidade de São Paulo (2017)
22. Williams, D., Yee, N., Caplan, S.E.: Who plays, how much, and why? Debunking the stereotypical gamer profile. J. Comput. Med. Commun. **13**(4), 993–1018 (2008)
23. Yoshida, R., Sugaya, M.: Influence of EQ on the difference of biometric emotion and self-evaluated emotion. In: Kurosu, M. (ed.) HCII 2019. LNCS, vol. 11567, pp. 191–200. Springer, Cham (2019). https://doi.org/10.1007/978-3-030-22643-5_15

Can We Predict the Best Gamification Elements for a User Based on Their Personal Attributes?

Wad Ghaban[(⊠)] and Robert Hendley

School of Computer Science, University of Birmingham, Birmingham B15 2TT, UK
{whg360,R.j.Hendley}@cs.bham.ac.uk

Abstract. Different studies have reported on the various effects of gamification on learners in the online learning course. Thus, it may be valuable to build a learner model that can be used to adapt gamification elements to learners' attributes (e.g. personality). To do this, it is important to understand the relationship between gamification and the learner's personality. A few empirical studies have tried to understand this relationship, but they were based on self-report questionnaires obtained from learners at the end of the study. Using this approach may bias the results because they ignore the learners who dropped out in the middle of the experiment. In the work presented here, we report on a series of studies, each using different gamification elements and each using dropping out as a proxy for motivation. Furthermore, we measured the learners' knowledge gain and satisfaction. The results show that gamification affects learners with different personality dimensions in different ways. Some personality dimensions gain significant benefits from some forms of gamification, while other personality dimensions do not. This variation in the results shows that it can be useful to use personality (ideally with other factors) as a basis for adapting gamification elements. The results can also be used to build a prediction model to match the most beneficial gamification elements to different personality dimensions.

Keywords: Gamification · Motivation · Online learning · Personality · Dropout · Survival

1 Introduction

Previous research has shown that gamification, which is the use of game elements in non-game contexts, can enhance the motivation and engagement of some learners in an online learning environment [18]. However, some learners become annoyed with gamification elements and others are distracted by them [4]. Considering these variations, we suggest building a model that could be used to adapt gamification elements based on the learners' personality profile [20]. The objective is to be able to utilise the gamification elements that would be most beneficial to a specific learner and avoid the negative effects from others.

To build this model, we needed to understand the relationship between gamification elements and the learners' dimensions. A few studies have attempted to address this relationship; however, their results may not be reliable because these studies were

© Springer Nature Switzerland AG 2020
X. Fang (Ed.): HCII 2020, LNCS 12211, pp. 58–75, 2020.
https://doi.org/10.1007/978-3-030-50164-8_4

based on self-report questionnaires that were completed after a gamified course was finished. Moreover, they either forced the completion of the course, which misses the main aim of gamification, or the analysis excluded the learners who dropped out part way through the experiment [8,29]. Thus, in our research, we aim to utilise a more objective approach to measure the effect of different combinations of gamification elements on learners' with different personality profiles.

Within this paper, we aimed to answer the following main research question:

Do learners with different personality dimensions respond differently to different gamification elements?

To answer this question, we conducted three different studies with different gamification elements, but we used the same overall method. In these three studies, we used different measurements. Learners' dropout rate is measured and used as a proxy for learners' motivation. We hypothesised that learners who are more motivated by gamification elements will use the gamified version longer. We also measured the learners' knowledge gain and satisfaction at the end of the experiment.

In these studies, we hypothesised that personality dimensions will respond differently toward different gamification elements.

Our results supported our hypotheses for the variations in the effects of gamification elements. Some learners (e.g. highly extroverted ones) obtain significant benefits (at least, in terms of time spent on the course), whereas others (e.g. highly conscientious ones) obtain little benefit from gamification. The results from the three studies must be combined to build a model that can predict the best gamification elements to provide for each personality dimension.

In this paper, we discuss the method that was used to understand the relationship between gamification and personality type. This method requires a special kind of analysis (survival analysis), which will be discussed in the following sections.

2   Background

Online learning is growing rapidly due to its potential benefits, such as flexibility in terms of time and location. Learners can subscribe to any course from any place at any time without incurring the cost of travel time and accommodation [2]. However, one major drawback of online courses is the lack of engagement and motivation that comes from real world classes. Many learners drop out from online courses after just a few weeks after enrolling [30]. Therefore, studies have evaluated techniques that can be used to enhance learner motivation and engagement. Changing the learning content into a video game is one strategy that has been implemented to motivate learners [16]. However, using video games and other kinds of games, such as serious games and game-based learning, may distract learners causing them to engage more with playing the game rather than learning the curriculum. Furthermore, different research studies have argued that the main purpose of a game is to entertain learners, whilst the main purpose of online courses is to teach learners [14].

Moreover, changing the learning content to make it more game-like requires extra time and cost for teachers and developers. Consequently, different research studies have suggested using gamification as a technique to enhance the motivation and the engagement of online learners [7,13,34].

2.1 Gamification

The term 'gamification' is defined in different ways based on the area of concern. For example, in the field of marketing, gamification is defined as the integration of game elements into a state or community to change the users' behaviour and engage them [5]. However, all gamification definitions can be integrated into a single definition: the use of game elements (e.g. points and badges) in a non-game context (e.g. learning or business).

Studies have identified the positive impact of gamification on enhancing online learners' motivation [12,14]. These studies have shown that if gamification elements are designed well, they will enhance the learners' motivation, engagement and satisfaction [24]. Gamification elements provide instant and quick feedback that will motivate and engage learners to do more. Furthermore, in the gamified system, some learners may feel that they are in a game so they are less likely to fear failure [15]. Even in the worst case, learners might not feel depressed or anxious, and they will have sufficient feedback about their progress [14,21].

Some studies have identified the relationship between self-determination theory and gamification. For example, Wilson et al. [42] mapped gamification to learners' intrinsic motivation, finding that gamification can satisfy the three elements of intrinsic motivation. For example, presenting points and badges allows learners to receive quick feedback about their progress, giving them the feeling that they can do the task. However, Martí-Parreño et al. [31] believed that gamification can only be linked to extrinsic motivation. The authors [31] use examples of gamified sports applications to justify their claims. They argue that users will not participate in any exercises if they do not have the ability and tendency to complete it [31]. Wilson et al. [42] noted that gamification elements can be considered either intrinsic or extrinsic motivators based on the learners' interest and on their need for the content.

From another point of view, Hamzah et al. [24] pointed out that gamification elements can be annoying and boring, especially if they are not integrated well. Some learning gamified applications add different elements without any relationship between the elements and the learners' behaviour during the learning process [35].

Martí-Parreño et al. argued that learners' perceptions of gamification elements differ [31]. For example, some learners are properly motivated by gamification elements, while others may be distracted. These learners spend their time collecting points and competing with their friends in the leaderboard, while other learners dislike gamification elements because they find them tedious [29].

To overcome the variations in the users' perceptions of gamification, we argue that a learner model should be developed that can be used to adapt the gamification elements to the learners' different attributes. For example, the learners' mood and affective state may be used as a basis for this adaptation. However, these attributes are dynamic and difficult to detect. In contrast, personality is usually argued to be a stable attribute, and reliable psychological instruments can be used to assess it [3]. Thus, we will focus on personality in the rest of this paper.

2.2 Personality

Personality is a set of characteristics that determine how individuals interact with the outside world [25]. Different models have been developed to describe personality. In this research study, we used the Big Five model (sometimes referred to as the Five-Factor model), which has been widely used in similar research. The Big Five model is used to describe and classify personality into the following five categories or dimensions: conscientiousness (individuals who are careful, hardworking, responsible and organised), extroversion (individuals who are social, active and energetic), agreeableness (individuals who are helpful, friendly and kind), neurotic tendencies (individuals who are anxious, depressed, angry and insecure) and openness to experience (individuals who are imaginative, curious and open-minded) [25]. Table 1 summarises the five dimensions of the Big Five model [23].

Different tools have been developed to measure the Big Five model, such as the Neo-Five Factor Inventory (NEO-FFI) and the Big Five Inventory (BFI). These tools provide reliable measurements on the five personality dimensions. However, the length of these tools (usually more than 100 questions) make it difficult to apply them. Consequently, different shorter versions of these tools have been developed that vary in length. For example, some tools used a smaller version of the NEO-FFI that consists of 10 questions. However, these smaller versions mostly suffer from several reliability issues [36]. Therefore, we used a more accurate and reliable personality test that is neither too long nor too short. We utilised a special version of the BFI that is designed for children that consists of 46 questions. This tool is free and available in different languages [10].

Table 1. A summary of the big five personality traits (adapted from [41])

Personality	Characteristics
Conscientiousness	Leadership skills, the capability to make long-term plans and often an organised support network
Extroversion	Has good social skills and numerous friendships, often participating in team sports and having club memberships
Agreeableness	Forgiving attitude and a belief in cooperation
Neuroticism	Low self-esteem and irrational and perfectionistic beliefs
Openness to experiences	Interested in different hobbies and knowledgeable about foreign cuisine

2.3 Adaptivity in Gamification

Adapting the gamification elements based on the learners' personality dimensions requires one to investigate how different personality dimensions are influenced by the gamification elements. Theoretical works have suggested different gamification elements for different personality dimensions based on the attributes associated with each type of personality [34,36]. For example, highly conscientious learners are described as hard-workers, and they may only need gamification elements to provide them with instant and quick feedback, which will motivate them. Highly extroverted learners enjoy gamification elements, especially the social elements. They like to interact and compete with others.

In terms of practical and empirical research, a few studies have addressed the relationship between gamification elements and personality dimensions. For example, Codish and Ravid [8] focused on one dimension of personality (extroversion). Another study [9] included all the Big Five personality dimensions. These two studies, along with other similar work [29,38], examined the effects of the gamification elements on learners with different types of personality dimensions; the results showed that learners with different personality dimensions prefer different gamification elements. Table 2 summarises the findings from the related research studies that have examined the effect of gamification on different personality dimensions.

The methods used in the previous related research studies were based on self-report questionnaires that asked learners about their preferred elements. However, using this type of approach may provide unreliable results [20]. These studies only analysed the results from learners who completed the study, which may cause bias in the results; this conflicts with the main aim of gamification. Further, these studies did not include data on the learners who dropped out in the middle of the experiment. It is important to identify the reasons why the learners dropped out. For example, is the dropout rate the result of the gamification elements? Thus, the current study takes a more objective approach, which will be explained in the next section.

3   Method

This research aims to build a learner model that can be used to adapt gamification to individual learner's personality dimensions. To accomplish this, three stages must be completed. First, we need to understand the relationship between gamification and personality dimensions. Second, we use the obtained understanding to build the adaptive model. Finally, the proposed adaptive model must be evaluated to examine if it is beneficial for learners (Fig. 1). In this paper, we focus on the first stage.

To build a strong understanding of the relationship between gamification and personality dimensions, we conducted three different studies at different times with different participants. In each study, we used different gamification elements and we measured the learners' motivation, knowledge gain and satisfaction.

3.1 Setup

We built an online learning website for a course that teaches learners how to use Microsoft Excel. The course consists of 15 lessons, beginning with simple topics, such

Table 2. A summary of related research studies that present how different personality dimensions benefit from gamification elements

Personality	Points	Badges	Leaderboard	Social elements	Avatars	No gamification elements
High conscientious	[33,38]					[9,37]
Low conscientious	[20,22]	[20,22]	[20,22]	[22]		
High extrovert	[20,22,33,38]	[8,20,22,37]	[20,22,28,29,33,37,38]	[22,37,38]		
Low extroversion		[9]	[8,29]			
High agreeableness	[20,33,38]	[9,20]	[20,28,33,38]	[38]		
Low agreeableness						[20,22]
High neuroticism	[20,29,37]	[20]	[20]			[22]
Low neuroticism	[22]	[22]	[22,28]	[22]	[33]	
High openness	[20,22,33,38]	[20,22]	[20,22]	[22]	[37]	
Low openness	[20,22]	[20,22]	[20,22,28,33]	[22]	[8,33]	

Fig. 1. The process required to build model

as 'What is Excel?' and 'How can tables can be created in Excel?' The course then moves onto more advanced topics, such as mathematical and logical operations. Each lesson was followed by a short test to provide learners with feedback and to inform them about their progress.

Two versions of the course were designed. One version had integrated gamification elements and the other version did not. We used a variety of gamification elements in the design of each study. For example, in the first study, we used the most common gamification elements, points, badges and a leaderboard, as argued by [29]. Points could be obtained each time a learner gave a correct answer on the lesson test. By collecting five points, a learner earned a badge. The number of collected badges could change the learner's position on the leaderboard.

In the second study, we aimed to increase the cost of the gamification elements. Thus, we added some social gamification elements that allowed the learners to interact with others, and to chat.

Finally, in the third study, we used another gamification element: avatars. However, it is important to identify the way that an avatar is presented to the learner. For example, a learner can build his/her own avatar to present himself/herself while experiencing the system. Thus, avatars will be presented differently to the learners based on their choices [39].

To prevent this, in this study, we decided to use the avatar as a form of guidance for the learners. The avatar is presented in the same way for all learners every few minutes carrying a regular motivational phrases, such as 'You are doing great. Carry on!', are also presented. Thus, in the third study, we used points, badges, a leaderboard, an avatar and motivational phrases.

3.2 Participants

We asked 600 high school learners from Saudi Arabia (almost 200 learners in each of the three studies) ranging in age from 16 to18 years to participate in our studies.

Before conducting the studies, we obtained approval from the schools, the learners' parents and the learners, and we specified that all collected data would be anonymous and securely stored. The learners were made aware that they were free to drop out of the studies at any time.

3.3 Procedure

After establishing these agreements, we conducted our studies with a between-subjects design. At the schools, we asked the learners to register on our website by completing three forms: 1) one that obtained their demographic information (e.g. age, gender), 2) a pre-test consisting of eight questions related to the course to measure the learners' prior knowledge level and 3) a BFI to measure the learners' personality dimensions.

Unlike other studies that classified personality dimensions into high and low, we classified each dimension of a learner's personality into three classes: high, average or low. We believe that classifying personality dimensions into two classes at the mid-point is not sensible, as argued by [27].

These three classes were determined (for each personality dimension) by taking the mean (μ) and standard deviation (σ). Then, we classified the learners who scored lower than $\mu - \sigma$ as low. Learners between $\mu - \sigma$ and $\mu + \sigma$ as average and learners above $\mu + \sigma$ as high, for that personality dimension.

Afterwards, we divided the learners equally into two groups, balanced according to their age, gender, personality profile and prior knowledge level. One group used the gamified version of the website, and the other group used an identical version of the website without any gamification elements.

The learners were free to dropout at any time, and we used this variable as a proxy for motivation and engagement. We hypothesised that the learners who were more motivated would use the system for a longer period of time [22].

When all the learners in both versions either had completed the course or stopped using it, we asked them to complete a post-test that had the same structure as the pre-test. We calculated learners' knowledge gain using the following formula:

Learners' knowledge gain = Learners' post-test − Learners' pre-test

We also asked the learners to complete an e-learner satisfaction tool [40]. Figure 2 shows the flow of the studies.

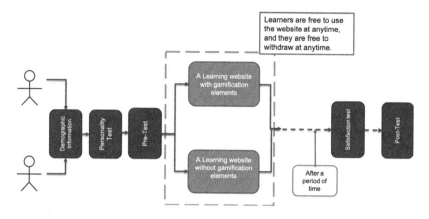

Fig. 2. The flow of our studies.

4   Results

In this paper, we provide an overview of three experimental studies that aimed to understand the influence of different combination of gamification on online learners' personality dimensions. We measured the influence of gamification elements by using three different measurements, such as: learners' motivation, knowledge gain and satisfaction.

As the space allotted in this paper does not permit us to report all the results, we will summarise the most interesting findings in below:

4.1   Motivation

Unlike other related research studies that used self-report questionnaires to measure the effect of gamification on motivation, we used a more objective approach by measuring the dropout rate and using it as a proxy for motivation. Because we used a different approach, we needed to apply a special analysis known as survival analysis.

One way to perform a survival analysis is to use the Kaplan-Meier estimator, which visualises the dropout rate of the two groups [11]. Figures 3 and 4 show an example of Kaplan-Meier estimator after it is applied on the high and low extrovert learners in the second experiment, respectively.

The Kaplan-Meier estimator can provide an understanding of which version is better, but it does not present the degree of difference between the dropout rate for the two groups. Furthermore, as Mills (2010) [32] pointed out, the Kaplan-Meier estimator may provide unreliable results if it is applied with continuous data. Thus, we used a different kind of survival analysis, the Cox Proportional Hazards Model, which evaluates the effect of specific factors in a particular event (e.g. death, dropout). This factor is called the hazard rate (HR). The model analyses the relationship between the hazard function and the predictors by assuming a nonlinear relationship between them [11]. We used the Cox model to examine whether there were any significant differences between the dropout rate of the two groups. Thus, we identified the extent of the dropout rate difference between the two groups. Table 3 shows the results obtained using the Cox model.

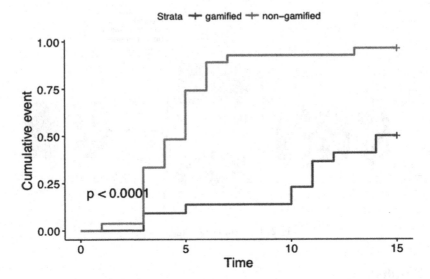

Fig. 3. The Kaplan-Meier estimator for the highly extrovert learners in the second experiment.

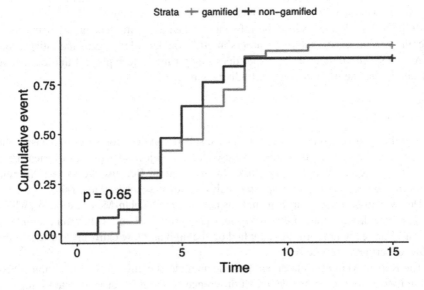

Fig. 4. The Kaplan-Meier estimator for the low extrovert learners in the second experiment.

The results show that most of the learners were more motivated in the gamified version. This can be clearly seen from the sign of the *coef*. The positive value shows that the dropout rate is higher in the second version (the non-gamified version). While, the value of the HR shows the difference in the dropout rate between the two groups.

From the table, it can be noticed that the dropout rate varies between the different personality dimensions. Some personality dimensions, such as highly extroverted learners, gain a significant benefit from the points, badges and leaderboard. This benefit is increased when the social elements are added. While other personality dimensions, such as highly conscientiousness learners, gained a slight benefit from the gamification elements. The dropout rate was almost the same between the two versions in the three studies. However, we did notice that highly neurotic learners were demotivated by some of the gamification elements, such as the avatars.

4.2 Satisfaction

Following the results from the effect of gamification elements on learners' motivation, we compared the satisfaction of the learners in the two versions. Our results support what is suggested from [6] as there is a good correlation between learners' motivation and satisfaction. Most of the learners were motivated because of the gamification elements, and they were also more satisfied. Table 4 shows an example of the learners' satisfaction results from the second study.

4.3 Knowledge Gain

As we are measuring the effect of gamification on the learning environment, it is obvious that we should measure learners' knowledge gain. In the studies, we aimed to measure learners' short-term gain by asking them to fill in a post-test directly after finishing the study. In addition, we aimed at measuring learners' long-term knowledge gain by asking them to fill in another post-test four weeks after finishing the study. However, for different reasons related to the schools and the participants, we were unable to measure learners' long-term knowledge gain.

Regarding learners' short-term knowledge gain, the results were different from those obtained for learners' motivation and satisfaction. Some of the learners were

Table 3. The results from Cox model in the three studies

Independent variables	Experiment (1)			Experiment (2)			Experiment (3)		
	P-value	Coef	HR	P-value	Coef	HR	P-value	Coef	HR
Overall learners	<0.00001	0.66	1.9	<0.00001	0.63	1.8	0.4	−0.13	0.87
High conscientious	0.05	0.48	1.6	0.06	0.2	1.8	0.6	−0.23	0.79
Low conscientious	0.01	0.84	2.3	0.04	0.6	1.9	0.1	0.62	1.8
High extraversion	0.01	1.0	2.7	<0.00001	1.9	7.0	0.9	−0.03	0.96
Low extraversion	0.3	−0.4	0.6	0.6	0.15	1.1	0.02	−1.04	0.35
High agreeableness	0.001	1.4	4.2	0.1	0.89	2.4	0.4	−0.73	0.48
Low agreeableness	0.5	0.25	1.3	0.1	0.43	1.5	0.9	0.03	0.96
High neuroticism	0.01	0.92	2.5	0.7	0.1	1.1	0.04	−0.67	0.5
Low neuroticism	0.3	0.43	1.5	<0.00001	1.4	4.2	0.2	−0.58	0.56
High openness	0.01	1.2	3.5	0.02	0.6	1.9	0.5	0.27	1.31
Low openness	0.02	0.99	2.7	<0.00001	1.4	4.2	0.06	−0.97	0.37

highly motivated by the gamified version. However, their knowledge gain in the gamified version was worse than in the non-gamified version. For example, highly extroverted learners enjoyed and were motivated by the gamification elements, especially the social elements. However, we found that their knowledge gain in the gamified version was lower. This was not expected, as we had hypothesised that improving learners' motivation would improve their knowledge gain. However, this was not the case. Instead, gamification might be a distraction for learners from concentrating on the course. Table 5 shows an example of the learners' knowledge gain in the gamified and non-gamified versions in the second experiment.

Overall, our results showed a variation in the responses of different personality dimensions towards gamification.

The results from our three studies indicate that gamification had a positive effect on most of the learners. However, this positive result varied across different types of personality dimensions. Some learners, such as the highly conscientious ones, only experienced a slight positive effect from the use of points, badges and the leaderboard. In contrast, low conscientious learners benefitted the most from these gamification elements.

5   Discussion

In this paper, we discuss a series of studies that were conducted to understand the effect of different gamification elements on learners' personality dimensions. We asked about 600 learners to participate in our studies (almost 200 learners in each of the three studies). After registration, we divided the learners into two groups, in which they were balanced in terms of their age, gender, prior knowledge level and personality profile. Then, we asked the learners to use the online learning website at any time and any place they wished; they were also free to drop out at any time. After, we compared the dropout rate in both groups, and we used that data as a proxy for motivation. Furthermore, we measured the learners' knowledge gain and satisfaction.

The results from the studies showed a variation in the response of different personality dimensions towards gamification. Furthermore, the learners' motivation, knowledge gain and satisfaction were different under the same gamification element. For example, highly extroverted learners were found to be very motivated by and satisfied with the gamification elements, especially the social elements. However, their knowledge gain was lower in the gamified version. Thus, we tried to trace the behaviour of the highly extroverted learners when they were interacting with the gamification elements. We found that these learners were using the social gamification elements, and they were talking about topics that were not related to the course. Moreover, some highly extroverted learners used the social elements to compete with their friends by asking them about the number of collected points and badges. Consequently, we can suggest that the presence of the social gamification elements may distract highly extroverted learners from concentrating on the course content. Thus, we can conclude that social elements are very important to highly extroverted learners, since they are motivated by and satisfied with these elements. However, the presence of these elements must be controlled. In the case of the existing social elements, learners should be supervised by the administrator or the teacher. Thus, for example, if the social elements start to distract highly

Table 4. An example of the summary of the results of the satisfaction for the personality dimensions in the second experiment

Personality	Total number of learners	Satisfaction in the gamified version			Satisfaction gain in the non-gamified			Benefit from gamification
		N	μ	Sd	N	μ	Sd	
Overall learners	194	97	6.62	0.311	97	6.17	0.3	0.45
High conscientious	37	23	6.6	0.8	14	6.4	0.78	0.2
Low conscientious	33	18	6.4	0.78	15	6.07	0.73	0.33
High extrovert	47	23	6.64	0.58	24	6.1	0.49	0.54
Low extroversion	40	24	6.54	0.58	16	6.1	0.76	0.44
High agreeableness	54	26	6.64	1.3	28	6.4	1.1	0.24
Low agreeableness	50	28	6.32	0.8	22	6.28	0.87	0.04
High neuroticism	48	26	5.7	0.83	22	6.3	0.87	−0.6
Low neuroticism	40	26	6.3	0.78	14	6.3	0.75	0
High openness	40	21	6.5	0.78	19	6.3	0.83	0.2
Low openness	37	23	6.27	0.88	14	6.3	0.8	−0.03

extroverted learners, the teacher must redirect the topics to be related to the course. Another suggestion is to make the social elements be a reward for highly extroverted learners. Thus, learners can begin the course with a basic level with no social elements and then work harder to move onto the next level that has the social elements.

Another issue in our studies is the presence of the avatar. We chose to present the same avatar to all learners in the same way. The same avatar will be presented to the learners every couple of minutes, along with some motivational phrases. Choosing to present the avatar in this way may be the reason why some of the learners were demotivated. Most learners prefer to choose their own avatar to best represent themselves, their personality, their hobbies and their preferences, as argued by [39]. However, we designed our study using the same avatar for all learners in the same way to avoid introducing any new effect that may bias the results.

The use of the between-subjects design is another issue related to the design of our studies. Designing an experiment in this way is effective and prevents the impact of any learning effect, as argued by [1]. However, this type of study design requires a large number of participants. Furthermore, there is a significant chance of having noise in the results. Thus, when building our model based on the obtained results, there is a risk that it would be based on noisy data.

The previous results indicate that it is worthwhile to adapt gamification elements, and personality can be a good predictor for learners' behaviour in a gamified system. However, the issues presented above make the process of building an adaptive model based on our results more challenging. For that reason, we suggest building the adaptive model based on the obtained results from our studies and the related studies in the literature [8,9,29,38]. We will also include suggestions from theory that explain the

Table 5. An example of the summary of the results of the knowledge gain for the personality dimensions in the second experiment.

Personality	Total number of learners	Knowledge gain in the gamified version			Knowledge gain in the non-gasified			Benefit from gamification
		N	μ	Sd	N	μ	Sd	
Overall learners	194	97	1.39	2.14	97	1.97	1.91	−0.58
High conscientious	37	23	2.12	1.5	14	2.6	1.7	−0.48
Low conscientious	33	18	2.51	0.45	15	2.16	1.86	0.35
High extrovert	47	23	1	2.1	24	2.04	1.45	−1.04
Low extroversion	40	24	2.04	1.9	16	1.73	1.65	0.31
High agreeableness	54	26	1.81	2.1	28	2.4	1.61	−0.59
Low agreeableness	50	28	2.01	2.39	22	2.23	1.14	−0.22
High neuroticism	48	26	1.42	1.8	22	1.78	2.01	−0.36
Low neuroticism	40	26	1.61	1.9	14	2.5	1.28	−0.89
High openness	40	21	1	2.4	19	2.37	1.5	−1.37
Low openness	37	23	1.27	1.53	14	1.64	10.94	−0.37

best gamification elements based on the characteristics of each personality dimension. Using this approach, we can have a set of predictions on how to match a combination of multiple gamification elements to the learners' personality profile.

For example, as suggested from our results, learners who are highly conscientious did not gain any significant benefit from the gamification elements. These learners are usually described as being hardworking, and they always do their job. They do not need any techniques to motivate them. Thus, we suggested avoiding using any gamification elements for these learners.

In our studies, the highly neurotic learners did not benefit from the gamification elements. Integrating avatars and motivational phrases was found to have a negative effect. Moreover, highly neurotic learners are usually described as being emotionally unstable, and they are usually more anxious and sadder than other personality dimensions [26]. Thus, it may be risky to integrate gamification elements into an online learning venue for these learners because they may find them tedious and childish. We suggest avoiding any gamification elements for this kind of personality dimension when building our model.

In contrast, the highly extroverted learners were shown to gain the most significant benefit from the different gamification elements. From our studies, these learners were motivated by points, badges, leaderboard and the social elements. This result confirmed what was suggested by [38]. Furthermore, highly extroverted learners are usually active and full of energy [26]. They also prefer to talk and interact with others. Thus, in building our model, we suggest providing different gamification elements. At the same time, the presence of these elements must be controlled. The suggested adaptive model must track the learners' behaviour; if there is any risk that the gamification elements might distract learners, the system must dynamically update the presence of the gamification elements, either by blocking the existing gamification elements or adding a new gamification element.

After predicting how to match a combination of the gamification elements to the learners' personality dimensions, we will build the model based on these predictions. Then, the proposed adaptive model will be evaluated to assess its effectiveness. One way to evaluate the model is by using the match/mismatch approach [19]. To accomplish that, we divided the participants into two groups: one group was asked to use an adaptive version of the learning website that matched their personality dimensions. The other group was asked to use the same online learning system but with gamification elements that did not match their personality. The main objective was to examine if there was a variation in the response of the learners in the matched and the mismatched groups.

The proposed adaptive model can be considered to be an effective technique to improve learners' motivation, knowledge gain and satisfaction. However, the model must be evaluated with other groups of learners, as we believe that the effectiveness of the obtained model might be restricted to the target learners who are aged 16–18 years old. Further, the model may not consider learners with special needs; for example, learners with colour-blindness or dyslexia. In addition, most of the studies that focused on the effect of gamification, including ours, ran on a short-term basis only. However, we believe that the effect of gamification may be reduced over time. Thus, learners may become bored after a period of time from using the adaptive gamified system. In that case, we suggest that it may be better to make the system half-adapted. Thus, the adaptive model provides the initiative's adaptive gamification elements. Then, the learners have the freedom to change the gamification elements if they get bored. This also allows us to understand how users' preferences change and which attributes, other than personality, can affect learners' behaviour. This understanding can be used for optimising the adaptive gamified system to improve users' experience.

6   Conclusion

Recently, gamification has been used to improve users' motivation and engagement [7]. However, some studies have shown that gamification has a varied effect on users. For example, some users are motivated by these elements for a short period of time, but they then become bored and demotivated [17]. Other users enjoy these elements, but become overwhelmed by them [23]. For example, some users may distract themselves by collecting points and badges rather than concentrating on the task. Furthermore, [29] pointed out that some users may dislike the presence of the gamification elements because they find them to be tedious, while other users describe these gamification elements as a waste of time. For this variation in the response of users, we suggest building a model that can be used to match learners with different personality dimensions with the most beneficial combination of multiple gamification elements. However, accomplishing that required going through several stages. First, it is important to understand the relationship between the gamification elements and the personality dimensions. Then, this understanding can be used to build and evaluate the proposed model.

In this paper, we focused on the first stage that aimed to understand the influence of the gamification elements on personality dimensions. While a few studies [8,9,29,38] have tried to understand the relationship between gamification elements and personality dimensions, they were based on self-report questionnaires obtained from learners who completed the study. However, using that approach may bias the results because the participants are forced to complete the entire study. Furthermore, these studies ignored the users who dropped out in the middle of the study without examining the reason for dropping out, which could be due to the gamification elements.

To address these limitations, we decided to examine the relationship between the gamification elements and the personality dimensions. We applied a more objective approach by using different measurements to understand the influence of the gamification elements on different personality dimensions. We used the dropout rate as a proxy for motivation. We also measured the learners' knowledge gain and satisfaction.

We conducted a series of studies with 600 learners. In each of these studies, we assigned learners (balanced by age, gender, prior knowledge level and personality type) into two groups: one group used a website integrated with gamification elements and the other group used a website that was not integrated with gamification elements. We used different gamification elements in each study. In the first study, we used points, badges and a leaderboard. In the second study, we added social gamification elements, such as chat. In the third study, we used points, badges, the leaderboard, avatars and motivational phrases. The learners were free to dropout at any time, and we used their dropout rate as a proxy for motivation. After ensuring that all the learners had either dropped out or completed the course, we measured the learners' knowledge gain and satisfaction.

The results from the three studies did not show a significant negative effect from gamification (except for the effect of the avatars on the highly neurotic learners). However, we did observe positive effects, which varied among the different personality dimensions. Some personality dimensions, such as the highly extroverted learners, benefitted significantly from the gamification elements, such as the social elements. Others, such as the highly conscientious learners, experienced less extensive benefits from gamification. The motivation of the highly conscientious learners was almost the same in the gamified and non-gamified versions. Furthermore, the highly neurotic learners did not obtain any significant benefit from the gamification elements, such as points, badges or the leaderboard. These learners had a negative effect from some of the gamification elements, such as avatars.

This variation in the effects of gamification shows that a learner's personality can be considered to be a good predictor of their behaviour in gamified online courses. However, we need to consider other factors, such as learners' friendships, moods and physical contexts, which may influence their behaviours. For example, happy conscientious learners may prefer to use gamification elements, but when these learners are angry or sad, they may dislike using those elements.

Furthermore, we could not apply all the gamification elements in the design of our studies. Our studies used a between-subjects design, which is considered to be an effective way to design this type of study. However, the results from this kind of study may provide noisy data. Consequently, in the next stage of this process, we combined the results obtained from our studies with suggestions from theoretical work and data from related empirical studies to generate a prediction. The prediction was used to build an adaptive model. This model matched each combination of multiple gamification elements to the learners' personality profile. The chosen gamification elements must be those that are most beneficial to the learners. Thus, the chosen gamification elements must improve the learners' motivation, knowledge gain and satisfaction. It is also important to note that the proposed adaptive model must be built dynamically because it must track the users' behaviour. Then, the model must be able to update the presence of the gamification elements based on the learners' behaviour (either by blocking the existing gamification elements or integrating new ones). The proposed adaptive model must be then evaluated to assess its effectiveness, and to ensure that it can provide learners with the best experience when using a gamified system. In addition, the model must be evaluated with other group of learners, such as younger or older learners. Further, it may better to assess the effective of the adaptive gamification elements on learners in the long-term. This understanding can help to improve users' experience.

References

1. Alshammari, M.: Adaptation based on learning style and knowledge level in e-learning systems. Ph.D. thesis, University of Birmingham (2016)
2. Anderson, T., Elloumi, F.: The Theory and Practice of Online Learning, 2nd edn. Athabasca University, Athabasca (2008). Accessed 3 Mar 2009
3. Bennet, N.L., Fox, R.D.: Learning styles in continuing medical education. J. Contin. Educ. Health Prof. **4**(4), 89–92 (1984)
4. Blohm, I., Leimeister, J.: Gamification: design of it-based enhancing services for motivational support and behavioral change. Bus. Inf. Syst. Eng. **5**(4), 275–278 (2013)
5. Bunchball, I.: Gamification 101: An introduction to the use of game dynamics to influence behavior. White paper 9 (2010)
6. Chen, P.S., Chih, J.T.: The relations between learner motivation and satisfaction with management training: an empirical study in Taiwan. Int. J. Manage. **28**(1), 77 (2011)
7. Cheong, C., Cheong, F., Filippou, J.: Quick quiz: a gamified approach for enhancing learning. In: PACIS, p. 206 (2013)
8. Codish, D., Ravid, G.: Personality based gamification-educational gamification for extroverts and introverts. In: Proceedings of the 9th CHAIS Conference for the Study of Innovation and Learning Technologies: Learning in the Technological Era, vol. 1, pp. 36–44 (2014)
9. Codish, D., Ravid, G.: Personality based gamification: How different personalities perceive gamification (2014)
10. Costa Jr., P.T.: Revised NEO Personality Inventory and NEO Five-Factor Inventory. Research Psychologists Press, London (1992). Professional manual
11. Cox, D.R.: Analysis of Survival Data. Routledge, London (2018)
12. Da Rocha Seixas, L., Gomes, A.S., de Melo Filho, I.J.: Effectiveness of gamification in the engagement of students. Comput. Hum. Behav. **58**, 48–63 (2016)
13. Dichev, C., Dicheva, D., Angelova, G., Agre, G.: From gamification to gameful design and gameful experience in learning. Cybern. Inf. Technol. **14**(4), 80–100 (2014)
14. Dicheva, D., Dichev, C., Agre, G., Angelova, G., et al.: Gamification in education: a systematic mapping study. Educ. Technol. Soc. **18**(3), 75–88 (2015)
15. Domínguez, A., Saenz-De-Navarrete, J., De-Marcos, L., Fernández-Sanz, L., Pagés, C., Martínez-Herráiz, J.J.: Gamifying learning experiences: practical implications and outcomes. Comput. Educ. **63**, 380–392 (2013)

16. Duncan, S.C.: Minecraft, beyond construction and survival. Well Played J. Video Games Value Mean. **1**(1), 1–22 (2011)
17. Fernandes, F.T., Junior, P.T.A.: Gamification aspects in the context of electronic government and education: a case study. In: Nah, F.F.-H.F.-H., Tan, C.-H. (eds.) HCIBGO 2016. LNCS, vol. 9752, pp. 140–150. Springer, Cham (2016). https://doi.org/10.1007/978-3-319-39399-5_14
18. Fitz-Walter, Z., Tjondronegoro, D., Wyeth, P.: Orientation passport: using gamification to engage university students. In: Proceedings of the 23rd Australian Computer-Human Interaction Conference, pp. 122–125. ACM (2011)
19. Ford, N., Chen, S.Y.: Matching/mismatching revisited: an empirical study of learning and teaching styles. Br. J. Educ. Technol. **32**(1), 5–22 (2001)
20. Ghaban, W., Hendley, R.: Investigating the interaction between personalities and the benefit of gamification. In: Proceedings of the 32nd International BCS Human Computer Interaction Conference, p. 41. BCS Learning & Development Ltd. (2018)
21. Ghaban, W., Hendley, R.: How different personalities benefit from gamification. Interact. Comput. **31**(2), 138–153 (2019). https://doi.org/10.1093/iwc/iwz009
22. Ghaban., W., Hendley., R.: Understanding the effect of gamification on learners with different personalities. In: Proceedings of the 11th International Conference on Computer Supported Education - Volume 2: CSEDU, pp. 392–400. INSTICC, SciTePress (2019). https://doi.org/10.5220/0007730703920400
23. Ghaban., W., Hendley., R., Fleck., R.: Investigating how social elements affect learners with different personalities. In: Proceedings of the 11th International Conference on Computer Supported Education - Volume 2: CSEDU, pp. 416–423. INSTICC, SciTePress (2019). https://doi.org/10.5220/0007732404160423
24. Hamzah, W.A.F.W., Ali, N.H., Saman, M.Y.M., Yusoff, M.H., Yacob, A.: Enhancement of the arcs model for gamification of learning. In: 2014 3rd International Conference on User Science and Engineering (i-USEr), pp. 287–291. IEEE (2014)
25. Hofstee, W.K.: Who should own the definition of personality? Eur. J. Pers. **8**(3), 149–162 (1994)
26. Hotard, S.R., McFatter, R.M., McWhirter, R.M., Stegall, M.E.: Interactive effects of extraversion, neuroticism, and social relationships on subjective well-being. J. Pers. Soc. Psychol. **57**(2), 321 (1989)
27. Hurtz, G.M., Donovan, J.J.: Personality and job performance: the big five revisited. J. Appl. Psychol. **85**(6), 869 (2000)
28. Jia, Y., Liu, Y., Yu, X., Voida, S.: Designing leaderboards for gamification: perceived differences based on user ranking, application domain, and personality traits. In: Proceedings of the 2017 CHI Conference on Human Factors in Computing Systems, pp. 1949–1960. ACM (2017)
29. Jia, Y., Xu, B., Karanam, Y., Voida, S.: Personality-targeted gamification: a survey study on personality traits and motivational affordances. In: Proceedings of the 2016 CHI Conference on Human Factors in Computing Systems, pp. 2001–2013. ACM (2016)
30. Kim, K.J., Frick, T.W.: Changes in student motivation during online learning. J. Educ. Comput. Res. **44**(1), 1–23 (2011)
31. Martí-Parreño, J., Seguí-Mas, D., Seguí-Mas, E.: Teachers' attitude towards and actual use of gamification. Procedia Soc. Behav. Sci. **228**, 682–688 (2016)
32. Mills, M.: Introducing Survival and Event History Analysis. Sage, London (2010)
33. Orji, R., Nacke, L.E., Di Marco, C.: Towards personality-driven persuasive health games and gamified systems. In: Proceedings of the 2017 CHI Conference on Human Factors in Computing Systems, pp. 1015–1027. ACM (2017)
34. Stannett, M., Sedeeq, A., Romano, D.M.: Generic and adaptive gamification: A panoramic review (2016)

35. Stott, A., Neustaedter, C.: Analysis of gamification in education. Surrey, BC, Canada **8**, 36 (2013)
36. Tondello, G.F., Mora, A., Nacke, L.E.: Elements of gameful design emerging from user preferences. In: Proceedings of the Annual Symposium on Computer-Human Interaction in Play, pp. 129–142. ACM (2017)
37. Tondello, G.F., Orji, R., Nacke, L.E.: Recommender systems for personalized gamification. In: Adjunct Publication of the 25th Conference on User Modeling, Adaptation and Person-alization, pp. 425–430. ACM (2017)
38. Tondello, G.F., Wehbe, R.R., Diamond, L., Busch, M., Marczewski, A., Nacke, L.E.: The gamification user types Hexad scale. In: Proceedings of the 2016 Annual Symposium on Computer-Human Interaction in Play, pp. 229–243. ACM (2016)
39. Vasalou, A., Joinson, A.N.: Me, myself and I: the role of interactional context on self-presentation through avatars. Comput. Hum. Behav. **25**(2), 510–520 (2009)
40. Wang, Y.S.: Assessment of learner satisfaction with asynchronous electronic learning systems. Inf. Manag. **41**(1), 75–86 (2003)
41. Wiggins, J.S.: The Five-Factor Model of Personality: Theoretical Perspectives. Guilford Press, New York (1996)
42. Wilson, D., Calongne, C., Henderson, B.: Gamification challenges and a case study in online learning. Internet Learn. J. **4**(2), 84–102 (2015)

Pixel Perfect: Fashion Styling in Virtual Character Design Process

Nandhini Giri[✉] and Erik Stolterman

Indiana University, Bloomington, IN 47405, USA
Nandhini.giri@gmail.com

Abstract. The main objective of this paper is to understand the process of designing 3D virtual characters in the gaming and animation industry in terms of clothing, hair styling and body proportions modeling. It focuses on the design practices and the creative decisions made by Computer Graphics (CG) professionals to bring virtual characters to life through fashion styling and character performance. A descriptive understanding of industry design practices can help build theories about the motivation and other human factors that goes into character design from the designers' perspective.

Keywords: Character design process · Fashion styling · Character performance

1 Introduction

This paper explores the process of designing virtual characters in the gaming and animation industry. It focuses on the design practices and the creative decisions made by Computer Graphics (CG) professionals to bring virtual characters to life through fashion and character performance. Fashion Styling is a creative process that facilitates designers to bring together mental imagery, innovative design, aesthetics and culture to shape fashion images and visuals. With ever increasing computing power and better designer tools for graphics modeling, texturing and animating, the creativity and diversity in the field of CG fashion styling, define the future of the fashion industry.

Though fashion seems to be the vehicle behind gamers narrating their stories in online worlds (Klastrup and Tosca 2009), there is very less research done in this area. Seo and Kim (2015) categorize game characters into five categories based on their fashion styles. Playstyles (Bowman et al. 2012) and game play enjoyment (Oliver and Raney 2011) have a direct connection in player-avatar interactions. Digital animation is an embodied performance (Silvio 2010) that requires more research on theory-practice relationships. American Manga and cosplay culture are evolving into our lifestyle (Napier 2007).

There is a whole body of scholarly work in fan culture, media spectatorship and para social relationship with media characters that try to explain these phenomena. However, a better understanding of industry design practices can help build theories about the motivation and human factors that help create these characters from the designers' perspective.

© Springer Nature Switzerland AG 2020
X. Fang (Ed.): HCII 2020, LNCS 12211, pp. 76–87, 2020.
https://doi.org/10.1007/978-3-030-50164-8_5

The main objective of this paper is to understand the process of designing 3D virtual characters in the gaming and animation industry in terms of clothing, hair styling and body proportions modeling. It focuses on the design practices and the creative decisions made by Computer Graphics (CG) professionals to bring virtual characters to life through fashion styling and character performance. A descriptive understanding of industry design practices can help build theories about the motivation and other human factors that goes into character design from the designers' perspective.

2 Related Research

2.1 Fashion in Gaming

Fashion and computer graphics character development are two topics that have received very less attention in the research field. Klastrup and Tosca (2009), talk about "the neglected area of clothing and fashion in computer games, particularly MMORPGs", which they claim as an important aspect of game aesthetics and player performance (pg. 3). By combining cultural studies of fashion and the functional importance of clothing in the game world 'World of Warcraft' (WoW), they argue that fashion in an online game world like WoW is a vehicle for personal storytelling and individualization. The qualitative study revealed that "Fashion is a way for people to notice each other in WoW, to express oneself and to make sure that they are not lost in the immensity of the unchanging world".

Another study conducted by Seo and Kim (2015) proposes the fashion typology suitable for game by analyzing the fashion styles of game characters. Five styles were identified with the focus on clothing, hairstyle and accessories – "Creative style, attractive style, grotesque style, usual style and suit style emerged as the main style classifications" (pg. 1). The analysis bridged the difference of opinions between gamers and developers related to fashion style and helped enhance the competitiveness of game design. These qualitative studies explore gamers preferences of designing their digital identities in online game worlds, and the way CG fashion styling, influences people's fashion sense of everyday lifestyle clothing, hair styling and accessories preferences. The studies combine design theories, cultural studies of fashion and the social behavior/psychology of humans in virtual and real world.

2.2 Game Design and Clothing

Books on Game Design briefly mention clothing, but do not elaborate on its significance in the process of designing virtual characters or their influence on the gamers. Rollings and Adams briefly mention "cosmetic things such as clothing color" as one of the "intangible" attributes that goes into defining an avatar in an MMORPG (Rollings and Adams 2003, p. 522). In Edward Castronova's Synthetic worlds, he points out that "shiny clothes" is one of the elements through which status can be expressed, concluding that "the status distinctions found in synthetics worlds engage emotions that correspond to the ones we have on Earth" (Castronova 2005, p. 113).

Fron et al. (2007) examine the functions of dress-up from a gender perspective, both in general as cultural practice, and more specifically, as it takes place in various forms in digital games and worlds. The authors make a distinction between two forms of dress-up: dressing up dolls and dressing-up as somebody, for instance when you play a character in a MMORPG. The later form of "dress-up" can take place in many ways, including what they describe as the very typical MMORPG "instrumental" activity of "donning armor, which for many players are typically "dressing up by numbers" (p. 6). They point out that some players prefer to combine the "statistical and aesthetic" features of armor.

2.3 Technical Perspective

Clothing and fashion have received some attention from the technical and programming perspective of computer graphics field. While research work focuses more on how to portray and represent clothing to be more realistic, there is not much attention paid to the function of clothing. However, authors do recognize clothing as "a key storytelling tool used to convey an intended impression to the audience" (Bridson et al. 2005, p. 1). On another note, research work also points out that the traditional practices of the garment industry can be improved by using virtual garment simulation. "The garment industry is still attached to the traditional way of designing garments, which is based on designing patterns (shapes of fabric) which are then seamed together on a mannequin" (Volino et al. 2005, pg. 597). The authors point out that this approach is still quite inefficient because of the lack of integration between the 2D pattern design process and the 3D simulation. Interactivity between design and simulation is the key idea for solving this bottleneck. While current systems require the re-assembly and draping of the garment over the body for any design change on the garment patterns, this research study, proposes a new approach, offering a smart integration of the 2D pattern shape editor along with the 3D garment shape view to assess interactively the effect of any pattern shape edit or posture and measurement change on the virtual mannequin.

2.4 Communication Science Perspective

Theories from the social sciences and player-avatar relationship studies have examined factors that associate gamers' connection with virtual characters from being mere non-social objects, to developing one-way para social relationships to two-way social agent communications. Banks and Bowman (2016) explain how metrics of 'character attachment' as para social interaction, explore dimensions of identification, control, suspension of disbelief and responsibility. This describes the playstyle motivations, including tendencies toward prosocial (helping, cooperating) or antisocial (trolling, playing alone) playstyles (Bowman et al. 2012), and higher senses of gameplay enjoyment (hedonic/pleasurable response) and appreciation (eudaimonic/introspective response) (Bowman et al. 2013; Oliver and Raney 2011). Overall, the character attachment perspective considers the closest connection between player and avatar to be unification, in which the player and avatar are indistinguishable, occupying the same in-game space. While social science research focuses on this unification of player-avatar identification, there is very less focus on the human-like fashion attributes that could influence players to relate with virtual characters.

2.5 Animation as Performance

Virtual characters are also being studied for their performances. In the paper titled "Animation: The new performance?", Silvio outlines a general animation model, by first presenting some of the characteristics of animation that allows connections between social, technological, psychic structures; Silvio then examines some of the ways that the models of animation and performance interact in contemporary subcultural practices. "The practice of cosplay—dressing up as animated characters—can be seen as a remediation in the opposite direction, remediating digital animation into embodied performance" (Silvio 2010, pg. 433). The study refers to Susan Napier's ethnography of American manga and anime cosplayers, that reveals that young people tend to see cosplay as acting out roles, at times even using method acting techniques, like writing backstories for their characters, to get into character (Napier 2007).

In contrast, Silvio's fieldwork with Taiwanese cosplayers who dress as puppet characters, found that the vast majority saw cosplay as reanimating the characters by substituting the human body for the wooden one. Their performances consisted mostly of still posing for photographs, and they did not try to stay in character if a camera was not present. When they performed skits, they often maintained puppetry's striation of media, lip-synching, and posing to pre-recorded dialogue (Silvio 2006).

2.6 Theory-Practice Relationship

Ward (2006) examines theory-practice relationships in the field of animation studies via three conceptual frameworks. Animation is an intersecting, discursive field that needs to be studied through the concepts of 'legitimate peripheral participation', 'socially situated learning' and 'critical practice'. "Animation is far too diverse to be simply categorized as one single entity, and it is in the attention to the specific working practices, alliances, and recognitions between diversely situated people that the particular character of animation will emerge. Each of these concepts addresses the complex ways in which discourses and sets of knowledges overlap and interact. They openly acknowledge how different people might use the same discourse but do so in what appear to be entirely different contexts" (Ward 2006, pg. 244).

From the literature review that draws study details from different disciplines, it is inferred that virtual character design is a less explored topic in terms of design practices. Technical field of computer graphics focus on algorithms and simulation techniques that strive for realistic looks in virtual characters – be it the clothing, hair simulation or other physical attributes of the character. There is a gap in the literature when it comes to studying the process of designing CG characters, their cultural impact on the society and implications on fashion trends and virtual economy in the current entertainment industry.

3 Methodology

Our initial study objective was to understand the industry design practices of virtual character design. We reached out to professionals and educators who have industry experience designing virtual characters. We were able to introduce ourselves with the character designers and effects artists through emails and explain the objective of the research study and schedule one-to-one interviews.

Our analysis includes twelve interviews and two additional interview material with designers and CG artists who have played the roles of character designer, character modeler, look development artist, visual effects supervisor, character effects developer, fashion designer, theatrical costume designer and related roles in major entertainment studios, fashion studios and academic institutions. They have 7–25 years of work experience in industry design practices and some of them are also affiliated to academic institutions where they lecture courses on fashion design and costume designing for theatre. Semi-structured interviews were conducted that lasted for around 45–60 min each session. Designers were asked open-ended questions about their design process and the design factors that drive their creative decisions. We also asked the designers about the influence of fashion in styling their character's clothing, hair and other features. What are the similarities and differences in styling humans versus virtual characters? What are the research methodologies they follow and how the design of character's clothing and accessories affects the CG performance?

Hand-written notes and audio recordings were then transcribed, coded and interpreted. This information and the audio files were stored in a secure online location for storage and retrieval. In order to maintain the anonymity of the interviewees we chose to use numbers to refer to the designers e.g. designer #1, #2, #3.. All the quotes that appear in this paper are identified by the designer number that corresponds to the actual designer who was interviewed.

A thematic analysis approach helped us analyze the data from the interviews. After every interview, the data was transcribed and added to an online document. This was an iterative process in which we familiarized ourselves with the data and generated initial codes. Both the authors were involved in the coding and analysis process. After the interviews were completed, we started looking for common patterns, reviewing them and categorizing them into major themes. Grounded theory approach was employed to analyze the interview data.

Table 1 and 2 lists the interview questions that was used in the semi-structured interview sessions with the designers.

Table 1. Interview questions for designers

#	Interview questions
1	Can you broadly explain the process of how you design clothing, hair styles, body proportions and accessories for CG characters. What are some of your key design approaches?
2	What are the significant factors that contribute to the creative decisions that you make about your final design?
3	Does your CG character design process get its influence from the fashion industry and its practices? How similar or different are your design approaches to styling humans versus virtual characters?
4	What are some of the research methodologies that you use in fashion styling for character design?
5	What significant role does fashion styling and character effects have to play in bringing out the personality and performance of the virtual characters that you design?

Table 2. Modified interview questions for theatre & fashion industry designer

#	Interview questions
1	Can you broadly explain the process of how you design clothing, hair styles and accessories. What are some of your key design approaches?
2	What are the significant factors that contribute to the creative decisions that you make about your final design?
3	What are your observations of fashion styling in CG characters?
4	What are some of the research methodologies that you use in fashion styling for theatrical actors and real humans?
5	What is your opinion about the cultural role that fashion plays in bringing out the personality and performance of characters (real-life/onstage)?

4 Designer Stories

The main themes of our research work is to focus on (1) Character design process (2) Decision-making factors and (3) Human factors and designer motivation in virtual character styling. Based on these central themes, we looked for quotes and personal stories from the designers' interview data. Some of the personal experiences shared by the designers with the character design process are highlighted through quotes.

4.1 Character Design Process

The character design process is a very individualized process and has no set formula. One method as explained by [Designer #1] - "having a basic outline...creating small random thumbnails made of squiggly lines...selecting one or two depending on how it looks and if it has potential...incorporating story, history, physical characteristics, environment...scale it up and look at anatomy...gather references and curate visuals which have extra detail...stitching together a rough character in software".

In the character design process, factors of breathability, comfort, volume preservation, body anatomy and technical challenges are areas where styling differs between virtual and human characters. [Designer #1] adds -"Breathability and comfort take a back seat (in CG) as it is not a living being...virtual characters should have some anatomical characteristics similar to a living creature. e.g. longer limbs, bigger muscles or made of metal if it is a robot".

4.2 Decision-Making Factors

[Designer #2] - "There is a language of clothing that represents your character...your choice of color and comfort...it represents our origin". CG character design is first and foremost (mostly) a story driven process in the industry. It is inspired by the age, background, demography, timeline or era, story world, upbringing, personality traits, flaws, fashion/language trends of the time and even the effects of weather. Production cost, technology constraints and value addition to story and character appeal are the factors that drive creative decisions. [Designer #2] adds "If you run with layered clothes and a suitcase when a lion approaches you, your movement is restricted, but if you let the luggage go and run, you may save your life…this can save time and money on production too".

Fashion influences of color, silhouettes and composition play a major role in character design. [Designer #3] - "I'm personally impacted by color…synesthesia is the coming together of senses…sometimes you see color in music…color is very important because on stage you design the individual characters but also designing a composition that everyone is watching…so it has to work together".

4.3 Human Factors and Designer Motivation

Character design is an enjoyable process and designers have personal motivations that drive their design process. Adding the element of believability in storytelling through virtual characters and stretching the imagination of the audience are key motivating factors for designers. [Designer #3] - "Ultimately audience need to engage and have a suspension of disbelief. I want them to believe that the character believes this is real. If Juliet walks out and transforms into something crazy looking – if she believes that is what is right in her world, I want the audience to believe that".

Further [Designer #3] continues - "Important to leave some imagination – audience need to use imagination – grateful for things like digital media that have expanded acceptance of imaginative ideas by audience – 'You know they did not look like they belonged to that time period' – I don't like to hear that. If we are not asking our audience to stretch their imagination, then why do we even have… why are we doing what we do. It is a story for them. I like to imagine myself as the grandmother in the corner with all the grandkids… once upon a time there was this big frog and their minds going… imagining… each one has their own idea what this big frog is. What a book does".

5   Insights from Interview

In this section of the paper, we analyze the interview data based on the central themes of the paper. The highlighted designer stories from the previous section guided us in structuring the analysis into the following topics: (1) Design process (2) Fashion influence (3) Character performance (4) Challenges involved in virtual character design.

5.1   Design Process

Our interview data clearly indicated that the virtual character design process is a story-driven process (there could be instances where it is character-driven). Production costs also play a role when it comes to character design simplification and plot adjustments without losing the entertaining pace of the story. For example [Designer #4] says "Cloth dropped on floor all night and worn in the morning" – each wrinkle in the fabric has a story to tell about the character that adds value and interest to the scene.

Here is a list of factors that go into the design of virtual characters. Each factor is carefully selected by designers asking the fundamental question of "What can this design element of the character add to the story?" (Table 3):

Table 3. Design factors in virtual character design process

Cultural appropriateness	Demography	Fashion trends of the era
Emotional connection	Timeline or era of story	Flaws
Animation style	Family lineage	Personality traits
Age	Story world blending	Effects of weather
Trending language & accent	Tone of the film/franchise	Freedom of movement
Surface skin texture	Shapes & silhouettes	Technical challenges
Situation or context in story	Physical limitations	Weight
Budget	Functionality	Render efficient

Designers have their own individual approach to character design. Some create thumbnails, some go by the character outline or start off with templates and create generate rules for character behavior. [Designer #5] "Create templates of design…create general rules of movement for character…refine based on the animation style which could be cartoony, squashy/stretchy or life-like". It gets complex when working for a studio. The art department or the look development team comes up with the character outline or spec based on the director's creative vision and the script. Initial tests help look for technical issues that inform design changes. However, only when the digital characters reach the animators or the character effects designers do they actually get to see the efficiency of the designs, especially after lighting scenes. Minor dents near eye regions or penetrations that finally show up in lighting are expensive fixes that are difficult to redesign. Some studios focus more on previsualization to avoid these costs.

In terms of designing for live-action human characters versus virtual characters, designers find more freedom in live-action; Tangibility of fabric and the touch and feel of style in real-world make the process easier. The physical presence of character in live-set is one more reason to add. On the other hand, CG character design has its own advantages and challenges. Designers work on a wider design palette and digital tools help create believable hybrid creatures. [Designer #7] "If the character is human or humanoid it is easier to design, but if it is an animal or cartoony it gets tricky and at times requires some extra love and care to produce desired results". [Designer #7] adds "Stitching a trouser in real-world is simple. But then making the fabric of the trouser feel like cotton or denim takes a lot of effort in CG". Also, the lifecycle and preservation of costumes is very different between real-world and CG world. [Designer #3] says "Live-theatre only exists in the memory of the people who saw it. Its fleeting… like a rainy day or lovely rainbow…digital stays".

As part of research in character design and styling, designers study reference videos, search for images online, study movement, behavior, light interaction with objects and how things exist in real world. [Designer #5] - "for a frog-like monster studied lots of frogs, lizards, skin textures…study aesthetics of something that already exists and then incorporate in design…something that is unique but also familiar". Designers also start with sketches to make something completely new. They play with different shapes and see how it fits the design of the story world. While searching online, the basic outline of the character, purpose of the character in the story and the environment defines the final look of the design. One other exercise for digital stylists is to study pattern making and stitching. This helps them understand where the seams work, cuff length, fabric behavior, texture and stitches.

5.2 Fashion Influence

On the topic of fashion influence in virtual character design [Designer #6] says - "Everything we create is a mirror of what is going on in society and culture around…Color choices that are about mood, tone and sometimes the hue or tint or shade of hue…they (designers) are using because it is trending in society." [Designer #5] - "Making characters feel part of a world that audience can identify" - which indicates that it is important to observe the fashion trends of the time period in which the story is situated.

Studios tend to have a digital wardrobe or a generic library of costumes that artists mix and match to design characters. Designers even use a couple of common software overlapping fashion and entertainment industries. [Designer #1] says "I do take a look at the fashion industry when designing new characters…it helps in making the characters current, trendy and engaging, affecting the overall silhouette and color choice". Fashion does have a significant role in bringing out the personality and performance of the character. It helps to describe the character at first glance. Secondary design elements as [Designer #1] adds - "makeup…tattoos, 5 0'clock shadow, hair styling, freckles, skin color and skin tone (to signify where the character is from geographically) play a big part in silent storytelling".

Designers find that there is not much difference between CG world and the real one in terms of fashion styling characters. Virtual characters live in this digital world which is a digital reflection of us altogether. As media users, our eyes have got used to seeing high quality images, be it in smart phone or televisions. This requires designers to set new bench marks in each release. Designers follow steps similar to the fashion industry as [Designer #2] mentions - "sketching, pattern making, color palette, creating multiple sizes of pattern to fit each character, stitching and fitting clothes to characters digitally".

5.3 Character Performance

[Designer #5] - "What emotion does hair convey? A motionless character with only hair moving – CG industry takes tips from live-action. How clothing slides over character's body shows what the character feels…". [Designer #3] - "Costumes are sometimes the most important thing because it is like the skin of the character that the actor puts on". Advent of better software and technology helps designers get intricate with detailing in fabric and other character accessories for better visual appeal. [Designer #7] comments on adding life to 3D objects - "A 3D object can look like a sweater only when it moves in the wind with all the wrinkles". Character detailing plays a major role in silent storytelling. [Designer #1] "A skinny character with bags under the eyes could denote a brooding and depressed nature. A figure wearing all black could, (but not necessarily), signify a negative personality. Long limbs could mean that the character is a runner or is agile."

These personal quotes indicate the amount of intricate work that goes into the garment and accessories design for digital characters which is also an expensive deal. Choosing between a wet or dry look for a character's hair can be a major budget issue. However, the interviews indicate that this is an under-appreciated fact in CG storytelling. Clothing, hair and accessories design for characters is mostly for secondary emotions. The impact in character performance and storytelling is less studied.

On a side note, motion capture artists also contribute to the performance of digital characters as it is their movements that is transferred to these digital puppets. Motion capture artists need to keep in mind the timeline of the story and character history to deliver their best performance that is most appropriate for the digital character.

5.4 Challenges

"No script for motion" - [Designer #4] mentions that when working on character's garments and accessories - "there is lot of feeling involved than pure science". What does this creative note "add some extra love" mean to designers? What are some guidelines that designers are currently missing from their creative heads while working on blankets, extra heavy capes and tangled hair styles? Character designers are mostly part of the art department and the digital artists who work on character effects like clothing and hair seem to just follow the art references. How does this process of translation from physical sketches to efficient digital performances work in the pipeline? A lot of it comes through experience and close working with senior designers. However, from a research standpoint there are grey areas that are missing in the virtual character design process. Does a standardized process help designers or is it more disrupting to their individual approach to design?

Our interview analysis shows that fabric behavior is the most challenging in CG character design process and designers mostly rely on real-world references, field observations and live recordings of flowing capes of different material. For e.g. they end up stitching different capes to study fabric behavior. Are there better research methodologies that can help designers so that they spend lesser time in maintaining the consistency of character garments in the entire production work?

Again, another area that is a challenge for designers that lacks research work is to understand how 3D simulations and cloth dynamics influence character performance and emotions which is "very under-appreciated in the CG world". These challenges require further study in this area of virtual character design.

6 Discussion

The insights section has further extended into a discussion of what these explorative findings of the virtual character design process mean to the research community and how it all fits in the big picture.

Characters receive criticism when the design is not consistent with the fictional world. Designers observe that users' expectations are increasing and that they need to set a benchmark for every single digital release. This is one area where research can help support the virtual character design process by building tools that help designers get access to audience interests. It is important for designers to understand the trends of the world to make believable characters. Research into the fashion trends in terms of the language, pop culture and even the food of the time adds richness to the story. Also, animation studies of emotions in character performance can benefit from combining aspects of cloth styling and simulation dynamics for digital storytelling.

While some designers prefer using software for simulations others incline towards sculpting their detailed drapes on the character's garments. These challenges raise the question of whether there is a need for standardizing the process of CG character design. How can the existing research work and research terminologies about engaged player character interaction inform better character design practices and facilitate better design experiences?

Role in Culture. Cosplay is a tool of empowerment and a way to identify with characters that people love and can embody themselves. It breaks the barrier of the medium and audience become an embodiment of the character. It is a very important equation between character and audience. It also becomes a storytelling ritual and creates balance in this equation of audience, character and designer. Costumes keep the tradition alive. How can ethnographic research work help inform designers to make a bigger impact on their fan communities?

Fusion with Fashion Industry. Customer profiling and price point in fashion industry are terms picked up from the interviews for this study which is missing in CG fashion design. Trend forecasting is a major learning component for fashion designers who always need something new and fashion trends run interesting cycles influenced by economy. Do these practices from the fashion industry help digital character designers? Does the practice of buying skins and customizing individual digital characters in virtual worlds become the future of fashion industry? [Designer #6] – "We don't have to buy and waste all this… giant closets that will go in landfill… stop the waste…second hand clothing…recycling". Is going digital an alternative for fashion? Again, [Designer #6] continues "why in every movie … any futuristic world all clothing is in uniform? Do we become more homogeneous?". As gamers and virtual world users focus more on their digital characters, is it a better option for fashion industry to focus more on digital presence?

In general, the following diagram summarizes the focus area of designers and research. Further studies in this direction can benefit by overlapping designer and research focus to create more efficient virtual character designs (Fig. 1).

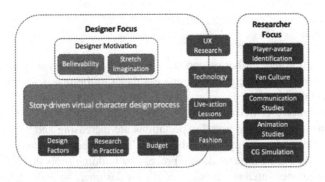

Fig. 1. Designer–research focus areas

7   Conclusion and Future Work

Klastrup and Tosca (2009), talk about the neglected area of clothing and fashion in computer games, which they claim as an important aspect of game-aesthetics and player perfrmance. This study has highlighted some key design practices in CG character development, influences of fashion, character performance and their challenges. The insights from this research work can lead to further studies that focus on the virtual character design's impact on game aesthetics, player experiences, online economy of virtual goods market and other larger implications in the fashion/entertainment industry.

References

Banks, J., Bowman, N.D.: Avatars are (sometimes) people too: Linguistic indicators of para social and social ties in player–avatar relationships. New Media Soc. **18**(7), 1257–1276 (2016)

Bowman, N.D., Rogers, R., Sherrick, B.I.: In control or in their shoes: how character attachment differentially influences video game enjoyment and appreciation. In: Paper Presentation at Broadcast Education Association Research Symposium, Las Vegas, NV, 6 April 2014 (2013)

Bowman, N.D., Schultheiss, D., Schumann, C.: I'm attached, and I'm a good guy/gal!: how character attachment influences pro- and anti-social motivations to play massively multiplayer online role-playing games. Cyberpsychol. Behav. Soc. Networking **15**(3), 169–174 (2012)

Bridson, R., Marion, S., Fedkiw, R.: Simulation of Clothing with Folds and Wrinkles (2005)

Castronova, E.: Synthetic Worlds. University of Chicago Press, Chicago (2005)

Creswell, J.: Qualitative Inquiry and Research Design: Choosing Among Five Traditions. Sage, Thousand Oaks (1998)

Fron, J., Fullerton, T., Morie, J.F., Pearce, C.: Playing dress-up: costumes, roleplay and imagination. In: Paper Presented at the Philosophy of Computer Games Conference, 24–27 January 2007 (2007). http://game.unimore.it/Papers/C_Pearce_Paper.pdf. Accessed 5 Jan 2009

Glaser, B.G.: Basics of Grounded Theory Analysis. Sociology Press, Mill Valley (1992)

Klastrup, L., Tosca, S.: "Because it Just Looks Cool!" Fashion as Character Performance: The Case of WoW (2009)

Miller, E., Kuhaneck, H.: Children's perceptions of play experiences and play preferences: a qualitative study. Am. J. Occup. Ther. **62**(4), 407 (2008)

Napier, S.: From Impressionism to Anime: Japan as Fantasy and Fan Cult in the Mind of the West. Palgrave MacMillan, New York (2007)

Oliver, M.B., Raney, A.A.: Entertainment as pleasurable and meaningful: identifying hedonic and eudaimonic motivations for entertainment consumption. J. Commun. **61**, 984–1004 (2011)

Rollings, A., Adams, E.: On Game Design. New Riders, Indianapolis (2003)

Seo, M.R., Kim, A.K.: Fashion styles and characteristics of game characters. J. Digital Convergence **13**(2), 343–349 (2015)

Silvio, T.: Informationalized affect: the body in Taiwanese digital-video puppetry and cosplay. In: Martin, F., Heinrich, L. (eds.) Embodied Modernities: Corporeality, Representation, and Chinese Cultures, pp. 195–217. University of Hawai'i Press, Honolulu (2006)

Silvio, T.: Animation: the new performance? J. Linguist. Anthropol. **20**(2), 422–438 (2010)

Volino, P., Cordier, F., Magnenat-Thalmann, N.: From early virtual garment simulation to interactive fashion design. Comput. Aided Des. **37**(6), 593–608 (2005)

Ward, P.: Some thoughts on practice-theory relationships in animation studies. Animation **1**(2), 229–245 (2006)

A System to Reduce Discomfort
of Taunted Player in Multiplayer
Online Games

Toshiki Goto and Yu Shibuya[✉] [ID]

Kyoto Institute of Technology,
Matsugasaki, Sakyo Ward, Kyoto City, Kyoto 6068585, Japan
shibuya@kit.ac.jp

Abstract. In recent years, online games have become widespread, however online games' taunting is one of the problems to be solved. In this study, we define taunting as a non-verbal redundant operation which makes fun of other players. According to our preliminary survey, it was found that 25 out of 26 college students had experienced to be taunted by opponents of multiplayer online games. Taunted players feel discomfort and cannot keep motivation to play with the taunting players. The purpose of this study is to reduce discomfort of taunted players. In our proposed system, user's PC detects automatically opponent's taunting by image processing in a multiplayer game. When the system detects opponent's taunting, the message mentioned above is shown to taunted user by notifications banner. We conducted an experiment to evaluate the proposed system. There were seven participants. Experimental results showed that our proposed system did not reduce discomfort of taunted players. The major reason was that our experimental design was not appropriate i.e. the experimenter, who was taunting, kept taunting after received warning message to increase the number of appearances of notification banner. However, in this situation, participants could not trust the proposed system.

Keywords: Computer games · Digital games/online games · Multiplayer games/MMORPGs · Netiquette · Communication support

1 Introduction

In recent years, online games have become widespread [1], however online games' taunting is one of the problems to be solved. In this study, we define taunting as a non-verbal redundant operation which makes fun of other players. One example of taunting in one-to-one fighting game is to keep kicking or punching the opponent avatar even after opponent lose a match. According to our preliminary survey, it was found that 25 out of 26 college students had experienced to be taunted by opponents of multiplayer online games. Taunted players feel discomfort and cannot keep motivation to play with the taunting players. Some

© Springer Nature Switzerland AG 2020
X. Fang (Ed.): HCII 2020, LNCS 12211, pp. 88–96, 2020.
https://doi.org/10.1007/978-3-030-50164-8_6

games, for example "Splatoon2" and "TEKKEN 7 FATED RETRIBUTION", take measures against taunting [2,3] but do not focus on discomfort of taunted players. The purpose of this study is to reduce discomfort of taunted players.

2   Related Work

Fuji & Yoshida examined the influences of online gaming on sociability and aggression in real life [4]. According to this study, desires and intentions for interpersonal relationships are easily expressed, and aggressive desires and intentions for other users are easily transferred to actions. However, Fuji et al. do not describe how to suppress aggressive desires.

Orengo, Abad, Alonso & Peiro describes that flaming present higher rates in computer mediated communication (CMC) than in face-to-face [5]. Consequently, it is need to suppress flaming in multiplayer online games.

Takahira, Ando, & Sakamoto mentioned that the more chat junior high school students use, the more they assert their opinion. In addition to, the more they play online games, the more they yield their opponents [6]. In our study, we focus on non-verbal taunting, however, it is need to reduce aggression.

3   Proposed System

To reduce discomfort of taunted players, we proposed a method to show the taunted player a message which mentions that the system warned the opponent player about taunting such as "Detect Taunting! Warned the Opponent!". We expected that this kind of message reduced discomfort of taunted player because the player felt the system supported her/him and warned the opponent instead of her/him.

Figure 1 shows our system configuration of our proposed system. At first, import game video from game system to PC. Secondly, user's PC detects automatically opponent's taunting by image processing [7] in a multiplayer online game. When the system detects opponent's taunting, the message mentioned above is shown to taunted user by notifications banner. In this study, we use Nintendo Switches [8] "Puyo Puyo Champions" [9] as the target game to detect opponent's taunting. "Puyo Puyo" is a series of tile-matching video games created by Compile in 1991 and Japan esports Union title [10]. Figure 2 show an A screen shot of participants game display and notification banner (under-right corner).

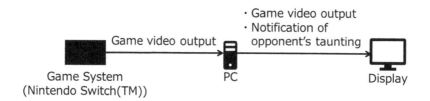

Fig. 1. System configuration of our proposed system

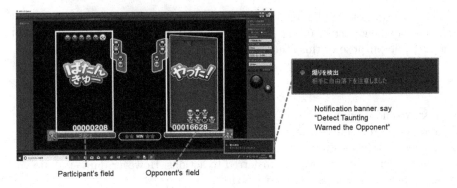

Notification banner say
"Detect Taunting
Warned the Opponent"

Participant's field   Opponent's field

Fig. 2. A screen shot of participantfs game display and notification banner (under-right corner)

3.1   Taunting Detection

Our proposed system detects three opponent's taunting in "Puyo Puyo Champions", Kasakasa Aori, Kakuteihakka, and Jiyurakka.

1. Kasakasa Aori
   Kasakasa Aori is excessive rotation of the operating block. At first, detect the outline of the operating block. Secondly, count the rotation of the operating block every 90° before fix the operating block. Finally, if the operating block turns more than seven times, our proposed system detects Kasakasa aori.
2. Kakuteihakka (Overkill)
   Kakuteihakka is making a further attack on the opponent, after the opponent defeat is confirmed. As shown in Fig. 3, taunted player's field leans left and right during kakuteihakka. Therefore, the outline of the taunted player's field leans left, our proposed system detects kakuteihakka.
3. Jiyurakka
   Jiyurakka is not to operate block, after the opponent defeat is confirmed. Our proposed system detects jiyurakka, when all of the following three conditions are true.
   - The taunting player's operating block falls freely
   - The taunting player's operating block does not move sideways
   - The screen of defeat (Fig. 4) appears in taunted player's field

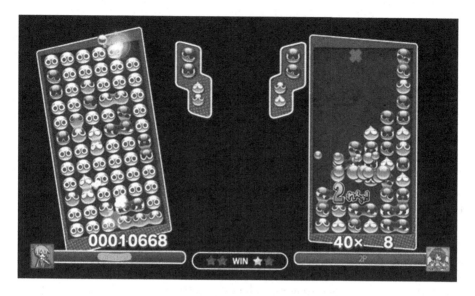

Fig. 3. The screen of kakuteihakka

Fig. 4. The screen of defeat

3.2 Implementation Environment

Our proposed system is implemented with following hardware and software.

- PC
  - Intel(R) Core(TM) i7 CPU
  - RAM: 8[GB]
  - OS: Windows10
- Display
  - Size: 21.5 type full HD
  - Window size: 1600[px] × 900[px]
  - Resolution: 1920 × 1080[dpi]

- Capture board
  - Ragno GRABBER2
- Game machine
  - Nintendo Switch
- Game software
  - Puyo Puyo Champions
- OpenCV version
  - 3.4.3.18
- Language
  - Python 3.7.3

4   Experiment

We conducted an experiment to evaluate the proposed system. There were seven participants (age 22–24). This experiment aimed to evaluate whether discomfort of taunted player was reduced by their opponents or not. Before the experiment, each participant was asked to answer the pre-experiment questionnaire and play "Puyo Puyo Champions" for 5 min to be familiar with its operation. Then each participant played "Puyo Puyo Champions" against the experimenter twice and answered the post-experiment questionnaire after each play. Three of seven participants firstly played the game without the proposed system and secondly played with the proposed system. Rest four participants firstly played the game with the proposed system and secondly without the proposed system. During the play, the experimenter did taunting act intentionally several times. In the experiment, participants played against the experimenter who is in a spatially separated room.

In the pre-experiment questionnaire, participants were asked whether their motivation to play games with the taunting opponent lose or not. Furthermore, they were asked whether their motivation to play the game have lose by taunting ever.

In the post-experiment questionnaire, participants were asked whether their discomfort against taunting reduced with the message or not. Furthermore, they were asked how much annoying of the message during the game.

5   Results

5.1   Pre-experiment Questionnaire

Results of the pre-experiment questionnaire are shown in Fig. 5 and Fig. 6. One participant (E) have not been taunted by opponents in multiplayer online games. Therefore, he did not answer pre-experiment questionnaire.

As shown in Fig. 5, two out of six participants answered "Lost motivation to play with the taunting opponent", two participants answered "Lost motivation to play with the taunting opponent slightly", one participant answered "Did not lose motivation to play with the taunting opponent slightly", and one participant answered "Did not lose motivation to play with the taunting opponent". According to this result, some people do not want to play with taunting opponents.

As shown in Fig. 6, one out of six participants answered "Lost motivation to play the game by taunting", one participant answered "Lost motivation to play with the taunting opponent slightly", one participant answered "Neither", two participants answered "Did not lose motivation to play with the taunting opponent slightly", and one participant answered "Did not lose motivation to play with the taunting opponent". From this result, less likely to quit the game by taunting.

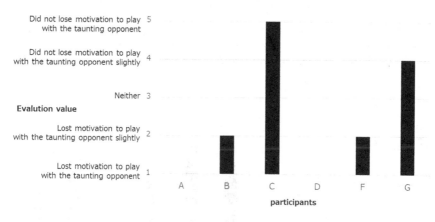

Fig. 5. Result of the pre-experiment questionnaire about motivation to play with the taunting opponent

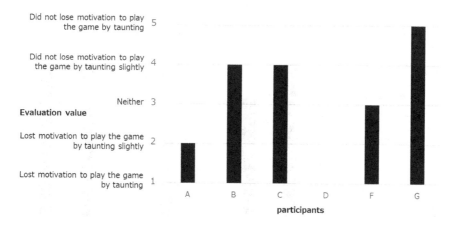

Fig. 6. Result of the pre-experiment questionnaire about motivation to play the game by taunting

5.2 Post-experiment Questionnaire

Results of the post-experiment questionnaire are shown in Fig. 7 and Fig. 8.

As shown in Fig. 7, two out of seven participants answered "Discomfort was reduced slightly", three participants answered "Neither", and two participants answered there was no effect of the proposed system. The average value of evaluation is 2.71. Therefore, experimental results showed that the proposed system did not reduce discomfort of taunted players. The major reason was that our experimental design was not appropriate i.e. the experimenter kept taunting after received warning message to increase the number of appearances of notification banner. However, in this situation, participants could not trust the proposed system.

As shown in Fig. 8, three out of seven participants answered "Not annoying", one participant answered "Not annoying slightly", one participant answered "Neither", and two participants answered "Annoying". The average value of

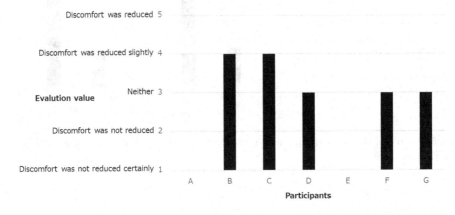

Fig. 7. Result of the post-experiment questionnaire about discomfort

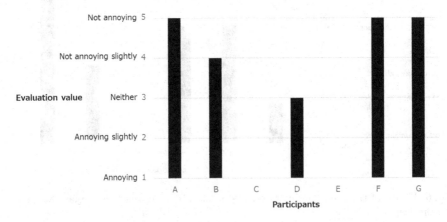

Fig. 8. Result of the post-experiment questionnaire about annoying

evaluation is 3.43. Thus, it could not be said that the proposed system was not annoying. There are too many notifications because of experimental design as mentioned above and the notification sound was loud. This caused the result.

6   Discussions

In this study, we use "Puyo Puyo Champions" as the target game to detect opponent's taunting. However, participants did not understand this game's taunting, because they have not played this game online. Therefore, we need to use major multiplayer online games.

In addition, some participants told that warning messages about the taunting opponent player were too small to understand contents of messages. Thus, it is need to enlarge messages.

Moreover, in the experiment, participants was only seven, additionally only experimenter did taunting act intentionally. It is need that the opponent player is also recruited like a participant of this experiment instead of experimenter. We are going to redesign the experiment. For example, we recruit more participants. furthermore, the opponent player is also recruited like a participant of this experiment instead of experimenter and evaluate the warning message to the taunting players too.

7   Conclusion

To reduce discomfort of taunted players, we proposed a method to show the taunted player a message which mentions that the system warned the opponent player about taunting. In the proposed system, user's PC detects automatically opponent's taunting by image processing in "Puyo Puyo Champions". When the system detects opponent's taunting, the message mentioned above is shown to taunted user by notifications banner.

We conducted an experiment to evaluate the proposed system. This experiment aimed to evaluate whether discomfort of taunted player was reduced by their opponents or not.

Experimental results showed that the proposed system did not reduce discomfort of taunted players. The major reason was that our experimental design was not appropriate i.e. the experimenter kept taunting after received warning message to increase the number of appearances of notification banner. However, in this situation, participants could not trust the proposed system. Moreover, it could not be said that the proposed system was not annoying. There are too many notifications because of experimental design as mentioned above and the notification sound was loud. This caused the result.

We are going to redesign the experiment. For example, we recruit more participants. Furthermore, the opponent player is also recruited like a participant of this experiment instead of experimenter and evaluate the warning message to the taunting players too. Moreover, participants did not understand "Puyo Puyo Champions" taunting, because they have not played this game online. We need to use major multiplayer online games.

References

1. Famitsu. https://www.famitsu.com/news/201806/11158825.html. Accessed 5 Jan 2020
2. PvP Game Blog. http://pvpgameblog.com/2018/01/13/post-4253/. Accessed 5 Jan 2020
3. Kakuge checker. https://kakuge-checker.com/topic/view/03833/. Accessed 5 Jan 2020
4. Fuji, K., Yoshida, F.: The influences of interaction during online gaming on sociability and aggression in real life. Jpn. J. Psychol. **80**(6), 494–503 (2010)
5. Orengo, V., Abad, A.M.Z., Alonso, F.P., Peiro, J.M.: The influence of familiarity among group members, group atmosphere and assertiveness on uninhibited behavior through three different communication media. Comput. Hum. Behav. **16**(2), 141–159 (2000)
6. Takahira, M., Ando, R., Sakamoto, A.: Estimation of causal effects through longitudinal study: an example of internet use and aggression. Jpn. J. Pers. **15**(1), 87–102 (2006)
7. OpenCV library. https://opencv.org/. Accessed 26 Jan 2020
8. Nintendo Switch. https://www.nintendo.com/switch/. Accessed 26 Jan 2020
9. SEGA. http://puyo.sega.jp/PuyoPuyo_eSports/. Accessed 26 Jan 2020
10. Japan esports Union. https://jesu.or.jp/contents/member_list/. Accessed 26 Jan 2020

InCuDe: Heuristics for Enhancing Spectator Experience in Streamed Games

Matthew Horton[1](✉), Janet C. Read[1], and Christopher Willitts[2]

[1] University of Central Lancashire, Preston PR1 2HE, UK
mplhorton@uclan.ac.uk
[2] Blackpool and the Fylde College, Blackpool FY2 0HB, UK

Abstract. Current video game titles are primarily designed for players rather than for the experience of those watching the play. Whilst there has been considerable work on understanding the needs of players and their experiences, much less has been done to understand video game 'audiences'. This paper describes how a Game Audience Experience Survey (GAES) was designed to determine the key aspects of design that would enhance audience experience of streamed games. The Game Audience Experience Survey was completed online by 257 viewers of streamed game content and the results are analyzed against five themes that inform the design of games for audience experience. From the analysis, and following an iterative conversation with five game developers, a ten-item heuristic set (InCuDe) is presented. This heuristic set highlights the need for attention to the interface, the possibilities for customisation and the design of the game and the. We present the survey findings and the heuristics as contributions.

Keywords: Surveys · Heuristics · Experience · Games

1 Introduction

User generated content platforms such as Twitch, Mixer & YouTube Gaming have changed how video game titles are showcased and played. Especially interesting is the rapidly growing and dominant area of streamed/watched online digital content.

The viewer of online streamed games is *"emerging as an important stakeholder in video games"* [6]. Alongside a growth in audiences, streamed content is now generating significant revenue [24] and a growing number of companies now award sponsorship deals to influential content creators on relevant platforms (YouTube/Twitch) in order to boost sales [2, 34]. Product engagement through viewing game play online is known to result in improved product sales. Additionally, as new technologies and avenues are created, greater numbers of consumers are being drawn to streamed content where they can evaluate games before making the decision to purchase titles [2, 23].

This activity around streamed video media has therefore created an interest in how best to attract large audiences in order that advertising and product engagement can be maximized.

© Springer Nature Switzerland AG 2020
X. Fang (Ed.): HCII 2020, LNCS 12211, pp. 97–116, 2020.
https://doi.org/10.1007/978-3-030-50164-8_7

The behaviors of game watchers have been studied using gratification theory [27] and a broad social angle [20] and activities resulting from such viewing have been considered from a marketing and commercial standpoint [1, 16] but there have, to date, been few attempts to understand the motivations and preferences of those watching streamed game content in order to consider their particular needs in the design of the games that they are watching.

This work advances knowledge in this area by developing a survey for use in examining the game audience experience (GAES), by presenting data from 257 respondents of the survey that outlines their preferences and concludes with InCuDe – a set of ten viewer experience game design heuristics.

2   Related Work

2.1   Online Platforms

Online video is immensely popular; CICSO (2018), [7], state that *"Internet video streaming and downloads are beginning to take a larger share of bandwidth and will grow to more than 82% of all consumer Internet traffic by 2022"*. This statistic takes into account various methods of video consumption online, from the most recognizable: Netflix, YouTube and Vevo, to sites which are less widely known like Twitch and YouTube Gaming (a dedicated streaming platform for games on YouTube).

Websites such as Netflix and YouTube excel in providing asynchronous content; video that has been created, edited and released, through certain channels to be consumed by users in their own time. Services like Twitch and YouTube Gaming offer synchronous content which is seen live (streamed at the same time as the content is being recorded). Whilst asynchronous content includes many millions of hours of video gaming footage, of the top fifty most subscribed asynchronous channels, only six are gaming related [29]; synchronous content, on the other hand, is a more recent trend in online content creation and is heavily consumed by gamers.

The vice-president of developer success at Twitch described, at the Game Developers Conference (GDC), the impact that having a game played by streamers has on the product's sales and user's engagement. She emphasized the correlation between games being streamed and being purchased through widely known digital distribution platforms such as Steam, noting that, as an example, following live streaming, Punch Club benefitted from a 25% increase in sales and also that those who had viewed the stream were 4.6 times more likely to purchase than people who had not [2]. This suggests that getting viewers to watch streamed games is financially beneficial for game producers and thus suggests that designing games in such a way that the streamed viewing experience is optimized is worthwhile.

2.2   Games Being Watched

Of the top twenty games watched on Twitch (based on the number of hours watched in January 2019), eighteen involve the streaming of PVP (player versus player) content [33]. PVP is a term that is broadly used to identify a game mechanic which allows competition between two live participants. PVP has been a staple of gaming since the arcade culture of the late 1970s [21] when PVP revolved primarily around players playing against their friends and other visitors at an arcade console while standing side-by-side with a shared screen, PVP today has many of the same hallmarks, but tends to be associated with an online environment.

Watching others play games has become increasingly popular and one major contributor to this rise has been the growth of eSports [3]. Oxford (cited by [18]), define eSports as being *"a computer game played in professional competitions, especially when it is watched by fans and broadcast on the Internet or on Television"*. It is important to see that this definition specifically refers to the spectator or audience engagement as an integral part of the game play.

MOBA (multiplayer online battle arena) games (occasionally referred to as *'Online Brawlers'*, or *'Hero Brawlers'*) are an extension of the PVP aesthetic in that players work in teams to eliminate the opposing team. Such games have also been described in terms of being a culmination of several different game genres, most notably Role-Playing Games (RPG) (for their progression/levelling systems and character archetypes), and Real Time Strategy (RTS) games (in their general interface, camera position, and control schemes) [14]. Electronic Entertainment Design and Research suggest that MOBA games, for spectators, provide the best 'visual experience' and that viewers are more drawn to team games rather than to one versus one play [13].

Massively Multiplayer Online (MMO) games are defined as being: *"huge online and persistent worlds filled with thousands of avatars, controlled by individual people, who interact with each other and with computer-controlled characters"* [25]. The template for games within the genre comes from Blizzard's (2004) World of Warcraft, which in turn took on many of its own interface elements and gameplay styles from earlier titles such as Ultima. Many of the games which adhere to these environments, where thousands of players play together, tend to be classified as Role Playing Games (RPG) [25]. As an MMO game, World of Warcraft has two different PVP modes that suit online streaming: Arena play, in which players fight other players in small teams of between two and five in fast-paced gameplay; and Battle-ground play in which much larger groups of players complete objectives and fight the opposing teams. Arena play is the more popular of the two and regularly sees tournaments take place at major events.

Collectible Card Games (CCG) are the least prevalent and perhaps the furthest away genre from MOBAs as well as being the least well known outside of experienced gaming enthusiasts. CCGs are defined as being titles in which *"players have a deck of cards at their disposal representing actors with different characteristics"* through which players have to manage a strategy wherein they collect cards which *"collectively provide synergy that allows robust attacking and defending plans to be carried out in various disparate situations"* [32]. In streamed media, Heroes of Warcraft is one CCG title that has presented itself as being a core game in the years it has been available with $1 Million in prize money available to the winner of the 2019 Hearthstone Championship – this being the largest prize for any CCG tournament. This prize money is a direct correlate of its attractiveness as viewed content in streamed play [8].

2.3 Games User Research

Games User Research (GUR) is defined by Seif el-Nasr et al. [26] as being *"a field concerned with developing a set of techniques and tools to measure the users' behaviors and ultimately improve their experiences as they engage with games"*. In most cases this work is concerned with the player's experience rather than the audience's experience. Notable work in Game User Research includes several heuristic sets for gameplay. Those most relevant to our work are briefly described here. The PLAY Heuristics [12], are an extension of interface heuristics that account for the non-standard interfaces and interaction methods that are found in computer games. Initially written as a revision of the HEP (Heuristics for Evaluating the Playability of Games) Framework [10], these account for game mechanics, game story and immersion in a way not covered by earlier frameworks. By the same authors and focusing on the initial game experience and any game tutorials, GAP [11] is intended to improve the initial experiences that players have within gaming. The aim is to improve the tutorial and initial elements within a game to improve its approachability and the friendliness of the interface. In 2005, Sweetser and Wyeth published their GameFlow heuristics [31] that were built on Csikszentmihalyi's work on Flow, [9]. The same heuristics have more recently been used to evaluate different game genres on different platforms [30].

Game researchers have acknowledged that whilst a game is built the same for all players, the game play is different for each player. Desurvire et al. [10] define gameplay as being *"the set of problems and challenges a user must face to win a game"*. This involves the mechanics of the game but also the way in which the player navigates the challenges. When audiences watch streamed media, these users are not experiencing the mechanics and challenges firsthand, but they are connected to the player's gameplay, often in a very intimate way [27, 28].

Uses and Gratification Theory UGT is the study of the development of motivations, gratification and improvement and is of primary interest within communications study [19]. In considering the watching of game play, and the connectedness that the viewers feel with the game play, UGT is important in understanding the motivations and actions of game viewers [27]. In a key study on motivation to view YouTube, users stated that they saw the platforms as a harbinger of what was to come, stating that the videos were incredibly useful for finding out information [15] much in the same way as Astromoff, [2], spoke of Twitch being a platform for users to discover new games and trends.

2.4 Studying and Designing Audience Experience

Audience motivation and experience has been studied from several different viewpoints in recent years. Understanding how the audience identify with the characters playing the game, and how viewing gives a sense of identity is the focus of a study in China which looked at two live streaming platforms and concluded that both personal and group identity played a central role in determining viewing behaviors [17]. A survey of 313 viewers responses – mapped against four key factors: flow, entertainment, social interaction, and endorsement – reported that the main motivations for viewing were to increase happiness and reduce stress [5].

Improving the viewer's experience by design has begun to generate some interest in the research space. One of the earliest such works is from 2016, in an MIT thesis on the design of a viewer interface for FPS games [35]. Improved communication channels have been proposed by [22], and dashboards for eSports spectating were described in 2018 by [4].

Design efforts to improve the viewer experience will continue to be suggested but our own work takes a step away from the detail needed for a single game experience to the more general question of how best to design a good audience experience for game viewers. We propose a Game Audience Experience Survey and use the results of that survey, with 257 respondents, to generate a set of Heuristics for Game Audience Design.

3   Designing the Game Audience Experience Survey

The Game Audience Experience Survey (GAES) was designed taking into account literature, previous game experience surveys, game design frameworks and heuristics. The aim of the survey was to explore the audience experience in the context of video game spectating. The survey was built in three sections; the first section (Qns 1–4) gathered demographics (gender, age, country and route to the survey). This was followed with a factual section (Qns 5–15) about viewing activity (platforms watched, games watched, and time spent), and then the main section, (Qns 16–47), which is the subject of this paper, that was concerned with the motivations and experiences of viewers.

3.1   Motivation and Experiences

The main section of GAES was made up of questions derived from existing frameworks and from questions that had emerged from the literature. The construction of questions is described in the next two sections.

Sjöblom's study [28] investigated the motivational factors behind the viewership of certain channels, and looked to some factors which may play a part in the reasoning behind watching certain games such as viewers watching streams as they would with more traditional television media or sports, increasing their knowledge about certain titles and playstyles (sometimes before playing the game themselves), enjoying the musical content (many streamers use a music play listing feature in order to play songs while they play), considering their nostalgia as many games that are played are not current titles, and seeking pure relaxation or to have on in the background while they accomplish other tasks (along the lines of a second screen experience) [27]. These themes can be seen in questions *18, 19, 20 and 21.*

The Game Approachability Principles, Gee (cited in [11]) identified several interface elements including on screen features which give information to the user on-demand (such as scoreboards or point tallies), allowance for customization of interfaces, and perception of movement and manipulation. These were considered to be core to the way in which a user gains knowledge from a video game interface. These elements are queried in questions *22, 23 and 24.*

The PLAY framework [12] is broken down into three major categories:

- Game Play,
- Coolness/Entertainment/Humour/Emotional Immersion,
- Game Usability.

The first category *(Game Play)* contains the widest selection of heuristics, including not being bored, and keeping the challenge going. The strategy involved, and the pacing of the game itself, is a consideration or audience experience due to the popularity of competitive play within streamed media so it is covered n GAES in questions *19, 20, 36*. Away from competitive gaming it could also be that a viewer watches a stream to reconnect with a story told within the game's world (particularly in games with multiple endings, paths through them or general sandbox titles), this is implemented in question *39*.

Coolness, entertainment and humor within the PLAY framework are entirely relevant to the present study especially as this category was designed by the researchers [12] in order to outline the general needs of the player away from gameplay and interface elements. For example; does the music and sound have to be visceral or could it be completely obsolete as found in Sjöblom's study [27]? or do graphics have an impact as seen in GameFlow? [30]. These elements are queried in questions *16, 17, 18, 38*.

The final PLAY Framework category (Usability & Game Mechanics), considers interface-based topics such as status and score including health, magic or ammunition meters alongside control schemes and their importance. This suggests questions to consider interface use within the secondary nature of the viewer as opposed to the player (Questions *22, 34, 35*). In a similar vein, Sweetser et al.'s [30] GameFlow framework (which, while being situated primarily in a single genre of game contains some potentially useful inclusions) considers the inclusion of level and game modification software (see Question *40*).

The motivation and experience section of GAES uses a Likert scale from 1–5 with 1 being *"Strongly Disagree"* and 5 being *"Strongly Agree"*. At the end of the scaled questions there were two additional, optional, open questions (Questions *46 and 47*) which collected qualitative results from the participants who wished to give them. For ease of reading, the questions are not listed here but are included only in the results section alongside each theme.

4 Survey Study

4.1 Procedure

The procedure for the study was that of a convenience sample, the survey itself was initially posted to Twitter and Reddit but sharing was expected to encourage a snowball sample. The procedure for each of the respondents was straightforward, they opened the link to the survey, consented, and then, clicked through the survey to completion.

4.2 Participants

The survey initially gained 259 responses from 29 different countries (from the UK and USA, to Australia, Hong Kong and the Philippines). The respondents came through a selection of routes, primarily: Twitter (179), Imgur (23), Twitch (22) and Reddit (21).

Of the 259 responses, two were corrupted and incomplete and as such were discarded. Thus, the results here are from the remaining 257 which were predominantly aged 18–27 (223) with the remainder aged 28–37 (26), 38–47 (5), and over 48 (3). The sample was gender mixed with 192 males and 65 females completing the survey. Most respondents watched content on Twitch and YouTube and over 45% of the respondents claimed they typically watched games for over an hour at a time. Tabletop games, MOOBA, RPG and FPS games made up over 75% of the games watched.

4.3 Results and Discussion

Examining the motivations of players, we consider five themes to frame the findings: Community, Pacing, Game Design, Interface Elements and AV content. This allows the salient points from the quantitative data to be examined and used to consider design.

Community. The first theme to be considered was that of community which is considered a key motivator from the literature [17]. Questions 15, 30, 31, 41 and 44 all pertain to channel communities, and their importance to the stream watchers. Given the low likelihood of respondents to want to engage in chat (Qn15 – Fig. 1), a study of community, and what it meant, was highly relevant.

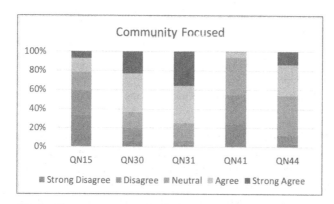

Fig. 1. The average scores for the community focused questions.

As can be seen in Fig. 1, one of the most positive responses within the study was for question 31 *(It is important that the streamer engage with the community while on the stream)* with an average rating of over 4. This speaks of the importance of the streamer being active within their channel, paying attention to the various avenues through which the community attempts interaction (be that through internal methods like the chat box, or external methods such as social media). In addition, another popular trend through the data, across all subsets of the data was found within question 44 *(I prefer to watch streams in which the player can play along with friends and/or audience members)* which could suggest that multiplayer titles in which the streamer plays along with their audience could play a part in maintaining that engagement.

The low ratings for question 41 *(I prefer streamers who are sponsored and run giveaways etc.)*, show the audience did not want to engage with streamers who ran contests and giveaways, meaning the focus should primarily be gameplay. Together, results suggest the audience were looking towards a community feel coming from the streamer, rating it quite highly in question 30 (The community around the channel is important to me), with less enthusiasm for themselves, as an audience, to have to actively interact.

Pacing. Considering the unpopularity (see Fig. 1) for breaks in streamed footage it's clear that pacing has a part to play within the reasoning for the successes of certain games within online streaming. As such, questions 28, 29 and 36 were considered together (see Fig. 2) in order to discover the influence pacing has on participant's selection in titles to view.

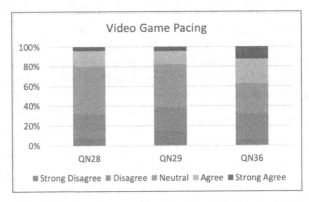

Fig. 2. The average scores for the pacing focused questions.

Question 36 *(It's important to me that the streamer is playing a game and not waiting for something to happen)* was the most positively received point in this section. Mapping the rankings for this question against favoured games to watch showed that those most keen on watching competitive content and eSports ranked this higher than others but those watching speedrunning were the most enthusiastic for pacing to align to gameplay. Clearly for these competitive customers, down time is VERY unappealing, with similar results and trends seen in the results of question 28 *(I prefer quick paced gameplay when watching a stream)*. Question 29 *(I prefer short-form games with multiple rounds over long-form games)* seems to indicate a preference for long play, which resonates with the play time of over an hour being the most reported by the respondents.

Game Design Elements. Several game design elements are summarized in Fig. 3. Here the results suggest some additional game design considerations to bear in mind when concerned with online streaming.

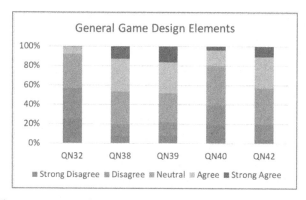

Fig. 3. The average scores for the specific game design elements focused questions.

Game difficulty (Question 42) *(I like watching streamers play games that are very difficult/challenging)* is an important subject within this particular topic in that across all participants the average score was above 3.0. This could also point to the popularity of speedrunning channels (which are seen as being a streamer who undertakes a very difficult task quickly) and eSports focused content. Despite often being mentioned in game design heuristics, tutorials (Question 32) *(The game the streamer is playing needs a tutorial or help system)* were not considered a popular option, neither was there support for modifications (Question 40) *(It is important that the game I am watching include support for modifications).* Notably within this theme seems to be that viewers want games that use humor well and have a good story (Questions 38, 39) *(It is important that the game I am watching uses humour well/It is important that the game I am watching has a good story to it).* Collectively, these results seem quite positive.

Interface Elements. Another key theme running through the questionnaire and pertaining to the experience felt by the viewer is that of the visibility of specific interface elements (see Fig. 4) on the viewed screen (and potentially beyond). These elements typically constitute on screen action buttons, pop ups, warnings and text boxes which appear on the screen throughout the course of a gaming session.

Questions 22 & 23 *(Understanding the score/status of the game being played is important/The score/status of the game is simple in its design and does not interfere with the overall look and feel of the game being played).* are both closely linked with the PLAY Framework heuristic regarding the visibility of score and status when playing a game [12], both of these were ranked as quite important with very few disagreeing with their importance. This theme of scores and status being visible was also mentioned by 21 respondents in the open questions that were at the end of the survey, with many saying that this was a priority in the output of the stream and that viewers *"find it intuitive"* and it *"allows the viewers to understand what they are looking at immediately"* meaning that their enjoyment of the stream is improved.

Question 26 *(I like to be able to see each button press and click the streamer makes appear on the interface of the game being played)* was rated quite low suggesting that such detailed interface elements are not always wanted by viewers. The qualitative data collected referred to the need for a simple interface, that included pertinent elements

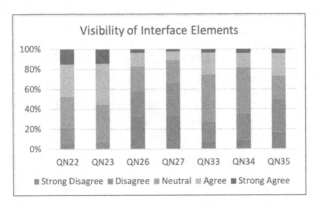

Fig. 4. The scores for the visibility of interface elements focused questions.

alone (43 positive responses in this area), this suggests that clarity, not clutter, improves the experience.

The question with the lowest scores in this area was question 27 *(I like to be able to see the physical movements of the streamer as they play the game)*. The physical movements of the player have been particularly popular when considering games with incredibly high actions per minute (APM) such as RTS and MOBA games like StarCraft and League of Legends as watching the player movement is core to understanding the skill shown by the players in eSports environments. It seems however with the responses received throughout the survey and the qualitative results in which one respondent mentioned that *"physical key presses are only something you want to see in balancing videos not on twitch"* (meaning that the respondent would only see that content when viewing developer created videos displaying the team balances within the titles) that this element is not an integral part of the interface the viewers want to see. Neither of the two questions 33 *(It's important that the game has a consistent control system much like that of other games within the same genre)*, and 34 *(It's important that I can see every bit of feedback that the game gives in an obvious manner)* scored especially high with a tendency towards neutrality suggesting these was not main themes.

Audio Visual Content. A trend has also become apparent, due to the very nature of online streaming media, of including a commentary over the game with sound from the streamer themselves. This begs the question as to the importance of the in-game audio on the stream and therefore on the game being played. When considering audio-visual content, graphics (Question 16) *(Graphics are important in the games I watch)*, seemed more important than in-game sound (Question 17) *(In-Game sound is important in the games I watch)* and adding music over the game audio (Question 18) *(I prefer streams in which the streamer plays music over the top of the game audio)* seemed to split the respondents almost equally into some for and some against but without a strong preference in either direction (Fig. 5).

A number of participants who contributed suggestions in the final two open questions added that there is a need for *"comprehensive volume control"* which could lead to having in-game options which balance the audio for streamed play.

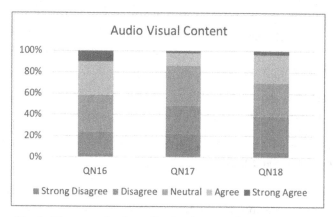

Fig. 5. The scores for the audio visual content focused questions.

Other Findings. The highest scoring response on the survey, with an average score greater than 4, was to question 21 (*I watch live-streams to relax*). This is corroborated with results from question 19 (*If you don't agree, what do you do while you watch?*) which highlighted that many viewers are doing much of their viewing as a secondary experience, while also concerning themselves with other activities, most popularly browsing the internet (36%), playing other games (35.1%) and working (17.5%).

Questions 24 (*The streamer having a customised interface is preferred*) & 25 (*I like streams more when the streamer uses a 'face-cam' on their stream*) considered the streamer and his/her ability to customize the experience for the viewer either by having their own '*skin*' to the interface or having a face cam and the importance of those '*front-end*' customizations for the viewers. While the idea of a streamer having a customized interface was well generally well received the idea of streamers using face-cams (a camera pointed at the streamer's face while they are streaming, and incorporated into the screen they broadcast) seemed to be particularly important (average score 3.7) to the vast majority of participants. Additionally, within the qualitative responses the inclusion of a face-cam on the interface was seen as being a very useful addition, with six respondents commenting on the major role they play in the experience. When considering these comments together, alongside the value of the feedback given by the interface, and the need to be aware of score and status within the games being played, it seems that the interface needs a space in which a face-cam (or similar) can be included without disruption to other on-screen elements.

Positives and Negatives. The most mentioned themes recorded in the final open-ended questions are summarized here with the number of individuals mentioning each theme in parentheses.

Positive themes

1. Simplicity of Interface (37)
2. Clarity of Interface Elements (21)
3. Interface Customisation (12)

4. Integration of Additional Elements (6)
5. Facecam (Specifically) (6)

Negative themes

1. Cluttered Interface (10)
2. Customised Overlays (8)
3. In-game chat (7)
4. Donation/Subscriber Alerts & Messages (5)
5. Score/Status Inclusion (5)

Clearly *simplicity* was important with both positive and negative reports stressing this. Twelve participants explained the need to allow streamers to *customize* their own interface in order that none of the key components of the interface were covered and this was also identified in the negative view of overlays that could get in the way of viewing. Clearly there is a need to design this in a more optimal way.

The need for *clarity in interface elements* in order that the streamer and the viewer could both identify courses of action to be taken, or the events that had previously transpired as and when required was highlighted.

In-game chat systems elicited only negative comments. Such chat systems were mentioned to contain *"spam messages"*, *"insults"*, and social notifications that those respondents found unnecessary to include on the interface.

5   InCuDe Heuristic Set

From the findings of the survey, a heuristic set was derived. This set (InCuDe) is made up of three categories, Interface, Customization and Design.

5.1   Validation of InCuDe

InCuDe v1 was taken to an internationally recognised games development company, and was presented to five members from their development, quality assurance and sound design teams, two of whom are also involved in their own online streaming channel. The meeting took place at a venue local to the game development company's venue and lasted two and a half hours.

Each participant was handed a copy of InCuDe v1, and then a two hour discussion ensued in which the themes were discussed in depth and wording scrutinized. After the meeting the comments and suggestions from the game developers were then applied to the heuristic set.

For ease of reading, the initial InCuDe is included here in italics against the salient points raised by the five experts.

Category One: Game Interface
In1. Clarity and suitability of audio/visual feedback
Games should give highly visible and audible feedback throughout play, this in-formation should be overt enough as to be clearly seen by a secondary viewer, but not overwhelm

wither participant in the viewing of game footage. Consider using these cues which are immediately recognisable and unique in order that the player needs only hear or see them to understand their purpose.

The statements particularly about the unique nature of particular feedback was a big topic of conversation concerning predominantly the method through which this was achieved. Overwatch was mentioned with regard to it having incredible sound design, and all elements of feedback subtly (and explicitly - when appropriate) dictating to the player the events and actions which surround their movement. This heuristic needed very little in the way of modifications and required only minor reinforcement of the issues raised.

In2. *Clarity of current player objectives and game mode*
Ensure that a player knows their objectives in play due to on screen elements at all times, meaning that at-a-glance they can understand the current situation they are in. Utilising this method also ensures that anyone tuning into streamed content after the game has begun can also very quickly understand the objectives the player must achieve and does not lose interest due to becoming lost.

There was little said about this. It was agreed almost immediately that although this is covered within other frameworks, they have had access to it bears mention within a study of this nature. As such this area needed very little in the way of modification.

In3. *Scaling and Inclusion of Appropriate Interface elements*
Ensure that the play area on screen (the players field of view) is the core focus of the interface, and that all elements are included and scaled appropriately. Consider additionally that should the game be streamed these elements may appear smaller, as such games should look to avoid text based icons on screen and instead look to include more idioms and metaphors to express certain element's purposes.

As well as the ability to rescale and modify the interface, the colour scheme of the in-game user interface was debated well within the focus group, concerning chiefly the crosshair (or reticule) on screen and the standard colour of white being used within current titles such as: Call of Duty: This colouration led the group to feel that their crosshair was constantly being *'lost'* within the interface, and many of the group choose to recolour (where they have access) in order to change the colour to something less common on the interface such as a bright green or pink. This change also impacts the streaming audience in the same way, and the allowance for these changes alongside those of customisable scaling and positioning may allow for a better experience for the viewer.

Category Two: Game Customisation
Cu1. *Allowance for the inclusion of overlay content*
The current trend in online streaming is that of face-cams and additional elements contained within third-party overlays. Ensure that the in-game interfaces make use of white space in order that these elements can be added without covering existing inter-face elements. Alternatively, games should either allow for interface customisation (which does not impact gameplay style) or include a further option in order to create a 'stream friendly' interface in which elements are slightly adjusted in placement in order to create space for third party elements.

The most animated conversation around this heuristic was when the group discussed the inclusion of additional content overlaid on top in game elements, in particular mini-maps. Despite that, no changes to this section were suggested by the group.

Cu2. Allowance for audio visual customisation to suit streaming content

Include a variety of customisation options with regards to audio and video settings. Video settings can be utilised in order to ensure the quality of streamed footage, in order that the game is well received by the audience. When considering audio settings consider their use with the growing streaming community, and which settings could be further customisable in order that they can be heard above them within elements of the game where it is deemed necessary.

The theme of audio customisation was seen as incredibly necessary in order to suit both players/streamers and audience alike. When concerning the audio customisation in particular, the sound design member of the group went into great depth as to the potential design issues which would come to light should the complete customisation of each element be utilized, as it could impact on the 'mix' (the levels of each sound which is tailored to each scene by the sound engineering teams) and overall negatively affect the atmosphere or mood of a particular scene or the game as a whole. Feedback came from the group concerning the ability for the streamer to be able to potentially customise their interface to include third party content and allow for a more controllable interface in order that both the streamer and audience had a similar experience. This customisation was also talked in terms of the audience's ability to make out elements on the screen, for example if the streamer had poor internet connection, elements may appear *'blurry'* however if they were made prominent enough on the interface this would not have as large an impact on the viewers.

Cu3. Availability of a spectator mode for tournament play

eSports are increasing in popularity and as such should the game include a competitive (PvP) mode, then allowances should be made for a spectator viewpoint, through which audiences can view the game live from a particular point of view (ensuring that this viewpoint could not be exploited). The game should also consider the development of a broadcaster viewpoint (which may only be in use during tournament content or similar) which will allow for the event team to have a broader over-view of the game and focus in on different players and zones in order to display this effectively to an audience.

The group agreed that for effective eSports content to be viewed by an audience member they benefit greatly from a *'caster'* (a person who commentates throughout the matches, telling the viewer of the various plays and tactics utilised, much like in non-eSports con-tent) who has access to a complete field of view which if given to everyone may un-fairly imbalance the play itself. The group felt that this heuristic should only concern games with eSports and competitive tendencies, however and should not be enforced in other games.

Category Three: Game Design

De1. Ensure the game has relatively fast pacing

The game should not rely upon long periods of in-game time being spent waiting for something to happen on screen (e.g. waiting for the other players to connect, or allowing too much time for players to make their way across the map in short-form gaming), there should almost always be something for them to engage in.

The group largely agreed with this heuristic when concerning streamed play, but also mentioned the *usage of slower elements of play* in order to cope with, what one member of the team termed, *"streamer fatigue"*; concerning the notion that streamers need to occasionally take small breaks from the stream in order to acquire refreshments. It was also agreed that the descriptor itself was perhaps misleading, in that *"waiting for additional players to join"* as probably more about downtime.

De2. *The game must strive to include a variety of playstyles*

Where possible games should include variety in the ways in which the user players the game, this could take the form of differentiation (for example, instead of the game being focused on purely team-deathmatch games in an FPS, there should also be the option to include some capture the flag gameplay), or multiple classes/roles to take on throughout play (consider the RPG mechanic of tank/DPS/support). This inclusion also reinforces the ability of the user to dictate their own pacing of pay throughout the game.

This was well discussed by the group, particularly concerning the language in that the term *"playstyles"* was misunderstood on first reading, and required the researcher to explain its' meaning. While the group agreed on the sentiment of the theme itself, they considered the linguistics used throughout to be ambiguous and in need of modification if it were to be completely understood by games development teams when reading it within the final toolkit. As such, the team discussed that instead of using playstyles, the term *'roles'* should be used as this better translates across academia and into development.

De3. *The game must look for as little downtime as possible*

As discussed games must have solid pacing and ensure where possible to involve the user in the titles primary gameplay at all times, however in moments of forced downtime for example matchmaking for a new round of action, or loading screens between maps etc., there should be an opportunity for them to engage in gameplay in order to keep the flow of the game high.

The theme of downtime was a particularly rich area for discussion amongst the group, particularly among the group members who partake in streaming themselves, as they considered the same issues as were brought up in the initial theme of pacing such as *"streamer fatigue"*. The title was the first element to be considered for modification, and the group agreed that while downtime could have adverse effects, allowing the player to make the best possible use of downtime was more in line with the purpose of the theme itself, secondly as this was then considered about the utilisation of a limited amount of downtime (between games or long loading screens) that the interface be set up to allow for the streamer to engage in communication with their community, while in periods of low interaction and not be punished by in-game mechanics (e.g. short periods of inactivity may incur penalties on the player). These issues led to an addition to the end of the descriptor itself in order to further clarify alongside additional titles for consideration, both implemented in order to better focus the theme.

De4. *The game must not take itself too seriously, and include humorous elements*

Elements of humour throughout a game help the game to become more accessible to a wider audience. Should a game have a serious tone, then consider using the elements of humour sparingly, however consider that more broadly speaking audiences who watch play and do not participate rank this feature highly within their stream viewing.

The theme of humour was the area of the framework which had the group most surprised, however after discussions regarding the games that they watched frequently, the notion that the majority of the games they watched included an element of humour intrinsically allowed the group to see the purpose for its' inclusion. As the study was focused on the game design elements as opposed to the potentially sociological inclusion suggested by investigating streamers and stream culture, the group agreed that due to humour being subtly or explicitly contained within many streamed titles that the theme was more than fit for the framework.

Summary. Finally, the group, when considering the framework as a whole were concerned with how the themes would be read when viewed by designers and developers and as such a change in language throughout could be used in order to allow the framework to feel like a list of elements a member of a game studio could look to implement. The group agreed that each section should come across in a similar manner to an aim or objective to be achieved, as opposed to a single statement which could potentially be taken out of context. With this in mind, the group suggested that each category would have an introductory sentence ending in *"the game should:"* which would allow for a more common use of language in the theme headings themselves.

5.2   Final Agreement

After these discussions the framework then underwent refinement in order to ensure a balanced, more focused direction for each of the individual categories and themes.

Category One: Game Interface. When considering the interface design process of a title being developed to engage with streamers and stream viewers it should:

In1. Emphasise the clarity, suitability and exclusivity of audio/visual feedback
Games should give highly visible and audible feedback throughout play, this information should be overt enough as to be clearly seen by a secondary viewer, but not overwhelm wither participant in the viewing of game footage. Consider using these cues which are immediately recognisable and unique in order that the player needs only hear or see them to understand their purpose.

In2. Ensure the clarity of current player objectives and game mode
Ensure that a player knows their objectives in play due to on screen elements at all times, meaning that at-a-glance they can understand the current situation they are in. Utilising this method also ensures that anyone tuning into streamed content after the game has begun can also very quickly understand the objectives the player must achieve and does not lose interest due to becoming lost.

In3. Include a simple, clean interface containing well scaled and included Interface elements
Ensure that the play area on screen (the players field of view) is the core focus of the interface, and that all elements are included and scaled appropriately. Consider additionally that should the game be streamed these elements may appear smaller, as such

games should look to avoid text based icons on screen and instead look to include more idioms and metaphors to express certain element's purposes.

Category Two: Game Customisation. When considering the interface design process of a title being developed to engage with streamers and stream viewers it should:

Cu1. Allow for the inclusion of overlay content
The current trend in online streaming is that of face-cams and additional elements contained within third-party overlays. Ensure that the in-game interfaces make use of white space in order that these elements can be added without covering existing inter-face elements. Alternatively, games should either allow for interface customisation (which does not impact gameplay style) or include a further option in order to create a 'stream friendly' interface in which elements are slightly adjusted in placement in order to create space for third party elements.

Cu2. Consider user-oriented audio visual customisation to suit streaming content
Include a variety of customisation options with regards to audio and video settings. Video settings can be utilised in order to ensure the quality of streamed footage, in order that the game is well received by the audience. When considering audio settings consider their use with the growing streaming community, and which settings could be further customisable in order that they can be heard above them within elements of the game where it is deemed necessary.

Cu3. Availability of a spectator mode for tournament play
eSports are increasing in popularity and as such should the game include a competitive (PvP) mode, then allowances should be made for a spectator viewpoint, through which audiences can view the game live from a particular point of view (ensuring that this viewpoint could not be exploited). The game should also consider the development of a broadcaster viewpoint (which may only be in use during tournament content or similar) which will allow for the event team to have a broader over-view of the game and focus in on different players and zones in order to display this effectively to an audience.

Category Three: Game Design. When considering the game design process of a title being developed to engage with streamers and stream viewers it should:

De1. Emphasise reasonably fast pacing
The game should not rely upon long periods of in-game time being spent waiting for something to happen on screen (e.g. waiting for ultimate/powerful abilities, or allowing too much time for players to make their way across the map in short-form gaming), there should almost always be something for them to engage in. It must be stated however that games that have a fast pace, must allow for slower moments in order for streamers to gain the ability to engage with their community.

De2. Strive to include a variety of in-game roles
Where possible games should include variety in the ways in which the user players the game, this could take the form of differentiation (for example, instead of the game being focused on purely team-deathmatch games in an FPS, there should also be the option to include some capture the flag gameplay), or multiple classes/roles to take on throughout

play (consider the RPG mechanic of tank/DPS/support). This inclusion also reinforces the ability of the user to dictate their own pacing of pay throughout the game.

De3. Make the most of downtime where required
Games are bound to be affected by downtime (loading maps, matchmaking etc.) and as previously discussed games must have solid pacing and ensure where possible to involve the user in the titles primary gameplay at all times, however in moments of forced downtime for example matchmaking for a new round of action, or loading screens between maps etc., there should be an opportunity for them to engage in alternative, optional gameplay in order to keep the flow of the game high. The reason for this is due to the streamers themselves occasionally needing breaks between/during games in order to deal with physical issues or engage further with the community.

De4. Include humorous elements
Elements of humour throughout a game help the game to become more accessible to a wider audience. Should a game have a serious tone, then consider using the elements of humour sparingly, however consider that more broadly speaking, audiences who watch streams and do not participate, rank this feature highly within their stream viewing.

6   Conclusion

This paper has studied the experiences of 257 viewers of streamed game content based on their experiences of, and their views around, watching streamed content. The survey that was used was developed from a combination of previous game user research sources and was specifically put together to enquire as to how better to design the experience for viewers of game content.

Game viewers were mainly shown to see viewing as relaxing, many multi tasked and most were unhappy with cluttered interfaces, in-game chat and interruptions in game streaming. Humour and customization were important themes as was the ability to see where the player/streamer was up to.

A set of ten design heuristics have been developed and iterated with game developers. These heuristics are currently being used in game development and further work will focus on their application in different settings.

References

1. Arantes, M., Figueiredo, F., Almeida, J.M.: Understanding video-ad consumption on YouTube: a measurement study on user behavior, popularity, and content properties. In: Proceedings of the 8th ACM Conference on Web Science. ACM (2016)
2. Astromoff, K.: 8 ways to succeed with broadcasters (the data may surprise you!) (2016)
3. Burroughs, B., Rama, P.: The eSports Trojan horse: twitch and streaming futures. J. Virtual Worlds Res. 8(2) (2015)
4. Charleer, S., et al.: Real-time dashboards to support esports spectating. in Proceedings of the 2018 Annual Symposium on Computer-Human Interaction in Play. ACM (2018)
5. Chen, C., Lin, Y.-C.: What drives live-stream usage intention? The perspectives of flow, entertainment, social interaction, and endorsement. Telemat. Inf. 35(1), 293–303 (2018)

6. Cheung, G., Huang, J.: Starcraft from the stands: understanding the game spectator. In: Proceedings of the SIGCHI Conference on Human Factors in Computing Systems. ACM (2011)

7. CISCO: Cisco Visual Networking Index: Forecast and Trends, 2017–2022 (2018)

8. Coates, D., Parshakov, P.: Team vs. Individual tournaments: evidence from prize structure in eSports (2016)

9. Csikszentmihalyi, C.: Flow: The Psychology of Optimal Experience. New York (1991)

10. Desurvire, H., Caplin, M., Toth, J.A.: Using heuristics to evaluate the playability of games. In: CHI 2004. ACM Press, Vienna (2004)

11. Desurvire, H., Wiberg, C.: Evaluating user experience and other lies in evaluating games. In: Computer Human Interaction Conference (2008)

12. Desurvire, H., Wiberg, C.: Game usability heuristics (PLAY) for evaluating and designing better games: the next iteration. In: Ozok, A.A., Zaphiris, P. (eds.) OCSC 2009. LNCS, vol. 5621, pp. 557–566. Springer, Heidelberg (2009). https://doi.org/10.1007/978-3-642-02774-1_60

13. EEDAR: eSports Consumer Analysis Whitepaper. EEDAR (Electronic Entertainment Design and Research): Carlsbag, CA, pp. 1–25 (2016)

14. Ferrari, S.: From generative to conventional play: MOBA and league of legends. In: Proceedings of DiGRA (2013)

15. Hanson, G., Haridakis, P.: YouTube users watching and sharing the news: a uses and gratifications approach. J. Electron. Publ. 11(3) (2008)

16. Holland, M.: How YouTube developed into a successful platform for user-generated content. Elon J. Undergr. Res. Commun. 7(1) (2016)

17. Hu, M., Zhang, M., Yu, J.: Computers in human behavior Wang, why do audiences choose to keep watching on live video streaming platforms? An explanation of dual identification framework. Comput. Hum. Behav. 75, 594–606 (2017)

18. Jin, D.Y.: Korea's Online Gaming Empire. The MIT Press, Cambridge (2010)

19. Katz, E., Blumler, J.G., Gurevitch, M.: Uses and gratifications research. Public Opin. Q. 37(4), 509–523 (1973)

20. Kaytoue, M., et al.: Watch me playing, i am a professional: a first study on video game live streaming. In: Proceedings of the 21st International Conference on World Wide Web. ACM (2012)

21. Kent, S.: The Ultimate History of Video Games: From Pong to Pokemon and Beyond… the Story Behind the Craze that Touched Our Lives and Changed the World. Three Rivers Press, New York (2010)

22. Lessel, P., Vielhauer, A., Krüger, A.: Expanding video game live-streams with enhanced communication channels: a case study. In: Proceedings of the 2017 CHI Conference on Human Factors in Computing Systems. ACM (2017)

23. Needleman, S.: Twitch's viewers reach 100 million a month, WSJ. http://blogs.wsj.com/digits/2015/01/29/twitchs-viewers-reach-100-million-a-month/. Accessed 17 July 2016

24. Newzoo: Top 25 Companies 2015 by Game Revenues Up 14% (2016). https://newzoo.com/insights/articles/game-revenues-top-25-public-companies-14-2015/. Accessed 16 Apr 2016

25. Poels, K., Ijsselsteijn, W.A., de Kort, Y.: World of Warcraft, the aftermath: how game elements transfer into perceptions, associations and (day) dreams in the everyday life of massively multiplayer online role-playing game players. New Media Soc. 17(7), 1137–1153 (2015)

26. Seif El-Nasr, M., et al.: Game user research. In: CHI 2012 Extended Abstracts on Human Factors in Computing Systems. ACM (2012)

27. Sjöblom, M.: Watching others play: a uses and gratifications approach to video game streaming motives (2015)

28. Sjöblom, M., Juho, J.: Computers in human behavior Hamari, why do people watch others play video games? An empirical study on the motivations of Twitch users. Comput. Hum. Behav. **75**, 985–996 (2017)
29. Socialblade: Top 100 YouTubers filtered by subscribers - socialblade YouTube stats I YouTube statistics (2016). https://socialblade.com/youtube/top/100/mostsubscribed Accessed 17 July 2016
30. Sweetser, P., et al.: GameFlow heuristics for designing and evaluating real-time strategy games. In: Proceedings of the 8th Australasian Conference on Interactive Entertainment: Playing the System. ACM (2012)
31. Sweetser, P., Wyeth, P.: GameFlow: a model for evaluating player enjoyment in games. Comput. Entertain. (CIE) **3**(3), 3 (2005)
32. Tryggvason, K.: Design and implementation of a collectable trading card board game and game AI (2016)
33. TwitchMetrics: The most watched games on Twitch (2019). https://www.twitchmetrics.net/games/viewership. Accessed 17 Dec 2019
34. Walker, Y.A.: Nintendo creators purgatory: why YouTubers should think twice before registering for the Nintendo creators program. Press Start **2**(2), 1–6 (2015)
35. Yeung, E.M.: Viewer interface for first person shooter streaming. Massachusetts Institute of Technology (2016)

Building Human-Autonomy Teaming Aids for Real-Time Strategy Games

Christianne Izumigawa$^{(\boxtimes)}$, Crisrael Lucero, Lena Nans, Kurt Frederiksen, Oliver Hui, Iovanni Enriquez, Seana Rothman, and Rebecca Iden

Naval Information Warfare Center Pacific, San Diego, CA, USA
{christianne.izumigaw,crisrael.lucero,lena.nans,kurt.frederiksen, oliver.hui,iovanni.enriquez,seana.rothman,rebecca.iden}@navy.mil

Abstract. StarCraft II (SC2) is a real-time strategy science-fiction video game developed by Blizzard Entertainment. Known for its complex state space and open-source environment [8], SC2 has become a popular domain for Artificial Intelligence (AI) research. This paper leverages the advances in AI research from SC2 to build human-autonomy teaming (HAT) aids, AI-driven software tools for human interactivity, for players to improve their skills. The human-machine interface (HMI) that houses these tools breaks the game into different components and visually represents each HAT aid to increase situational awareness and decrease response time.

Keywords: Human-autonomy teaming · Machine learning · StarCraftII · Real-time strategy games

1 Introduction

StarCraft II (SC2) is a real-time strategy game based on two opposing teams competing with each other to destroy all of their respective opponent's buildings. SC2 is played with *fog of war* meaning that each player can only see the units and buildings that belong to them and up to their units' level of visibility.

The major activities of SC2 can be grouped into four categories: resource gathering, attacking and defending, scouting, and deciding what to build and how to manage resources. At the start of each game, each player is given 1 home base and 12 worker units to collect resources with. Players use worker units to gather Vespene Gas from Vespene Geysers and Minerals from Mineral Patches on the map. Resources play an important role in the game as units have different Vespene and Mineral costs. After acquiring some resources, players can decide whether they want to implement lengthy, economic styles of game play or shorter, aggressive styles such as a unit rush. Unit rushes can be very effective against inexperienced players. However, seasoned players who aren't so easily defeated typically require a more economic strategy where players scout out enemy bases, carefully choose when and where to engage with their enemy, and manage their resources wisely.

© Springer Nature Switzerland AG 2020
X. Fang (Ed.): HCII 2020, LNCS 12211, pp. 117–127, 2020.
https://doi.org/10.1007/978-3-030-50164-8_8

With the recent advancements in SC2, AI agents outrank 99.8% of officially ranked players [7]. Rather than trying to create a better AI agent, this paper intends to create human-autonomy teaming aids that enhance a player's situational awareness and performance by expanding on a modular deep learning architecture for SC2 and applying visualization techniques and principles.

2   Background and Related Work

The inspiration of this work is previous research on using a flexible modular architecture for sharing decision responsibility among multiple agents [6]. In the previous work, each agent became their own module that had their output distinctly separated from the others, making a suite of battle management HAT aids nearly a one-to-one mapping to these agents. The proposed architecture had 5 key modules with the following responsibilities and designs:

1. **Worker Management:** Responsible for ensuring that resources are gathered at maximum efficiency; this module is scripted.
2. **Build Order:** Determines what unit or building to produce; this module uses a fully connected network.
3. **Tactics:** Determines where to send the army; this module uses a fully convolutional network.
4. **Micromanagement:** Manages units to destroy more opposing units; this module is scripted.
5. **Scouting:** Sends scouts for tracking opponent information; this module is scripted and uses a recurrent neural network.

Previous research has also been done on applying visualization techniques and principles to SC2. One study [4] focused on visualizing SC2 replays rather than visualizing the game in real-time to determine if they could teach players critical aspects of the game a posteriori. Because the focus of their study was on human interactions with games, the visualization systems were built to maintain immersion but were overloaded with information. While the systems were good at supporting the analysis of professional replays, the amount of information presented would easily overwhelm someone playing the game in real-time. This paper intends to maintain immersion for players without overwhelming them by removing non-essential content and visually representing essential content in an easy-to-digest manner.

3   Modular Architecture

There are three playable races in SC2. Each race comes with its own set of advantages and disadvantages as well as its own units and buildings. However, in order to reduce the complexity, this work will only focus on the *Protoss* race. To further reduce the complexity and stochasticity of the AI agent's environment,

Fig. 1. The *Ascension to Aiur* map is shown above. At the beginning of the game, one player will start in the upper left hand corner while their opponent starts in the lower right hand corner, opposite of them. The two starting bases are marked by green squares with circles in them. (Color figure online)

this work focuses solely on *Protoss* versus *Protoss* match-ups on the *Ascension to Aiur* map (Fig. 1).

From the set of five modules that were mentioned in previous work, the work in this paper expands the Build Order, Tactics, and Micromanagement modules and also introduces a Tactical Visualization module.

3.1 Build Order Agent

In SC2, the build order is the pattern of production aimed at achieving a certain goal. Build order is determined by several things such as current unit and building count, current capabilities, enemy capabilities, and resources at hand. From a command and control (C2) standpoint, this problem is akin to resource management, logistic and operational planning, and course-of-action recommendations. The approach taken for the build order module is based on work done in StarCraft: Brood War (the predecessor to SC2) [5]. In the aforementioned work, deep learning was used as opposed to goal-based AI due to its ability to adapt to the opponent at different states of the game.

This work presents a fully connected network that has 4 layers of rectified linear unit activation and 1 softmax output layer. The input layer to this network is a game state vector from a player's point-of-view, consisting of their active units, enemy units observed, technology depth/upgrades, and the state of their current resources. Table 1 below describes the input vector with greater detail. The output of the softmax layer is 1 of 64 potential outputs that represents what unit, building, or upgrade should be built next.

Table 1. Build order inputs

Input vector index	Input name
0	Time
1–41	Protoss units
42–83	Protoss units in progress
84–124	Protoss upgrades
125–166	Enemy units observed
167–171	Resources

The fully connected network was trained via supervised learning with replays from the winner's perspective of the match. By training the network to predict what unit should be built next based on a winner's build, we bias the agent to learn only winning build orders. Table 2 below shows the comparison of our build order agent's results to Justesen and Risi's work on StarCraft: Brood War. Our model organizes outputs by their probability of being correct; the top-1 choice of the model represents what the model thinks is the most probable output. Following this idea, the top-3 choice represents the model's 3 most probable outputs. The top-1 error rate in Table 2 represents the model's average percentage of error based on whether or not the true label of a test case matched the top-1 choice of our model. Likewise, the top-3 error rate in Table 2 represents the model's average percentage of error based on whether or not the true label of a test case was one of the model's top-3 choices. Because some versions of the same model can have slightly better accuracy than others, the results shown in Table 2 are from the best performing model.

Table 2. Build order agent results

Metric	Our results	Justesen and Risi
Pairs trained on	623,215	631,657
Pairs tested on	155,804	157,914
Top-1 error rate	38.35%	54.6%
Top-3 error rate	19.86%	22.92%

With statistically accurate results compared to previous work based on professional player actions, the build order agent is a prominent battle management aid that achieves its preliminary goal of mimicking human player builds. Future work for the build order agent includes increasing accuracy and exploring builds through deep reinforcement learning. User-centered future work for this module includes improving the content and presentation of information to users (e.g. remove extraneous content, visualize content with graphs) and adjusting the quantity and timing of suggestions to optimize reaction time.

3.2   Tactical Visualization

As previously mentioned, SC2 is played with *fog of war*, which means the map is only partially observable, and players are limited to knowing only their own units' and buildings' locations. This partial observability adds a layer of complexity to the game due to high levels of uncertainty in a player's situational awareness. To reduce the level of uncertainty for users, the tactical visualization module seeks to visually display predicted enemy unit locations and densities.

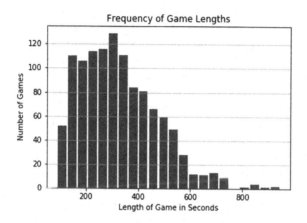

Fig. 2. This figure shows the frequency of game lengths pulled from the data used in this study.

To better understand the raw data that was collected from players' replays, preliminary analytics such as hard-coded heatmaps and histograms were used to find appropriate features and game timestamps. Outlaying trials were eliminated from the training and test data to streamline the process and to control for excessive zero-buffering that would skew experimental results. Varied game lengths (ranging from 1 min–27 min in this case) mean that agents cannot simply obtain an overall average at different phases throughout a game to determine an enemy's position. Different game lengths often result from different player styles and different quantities of units. To account for different player styles, this work trains on a wide range of game lengths. Histogramming, as seen in Fig. 2, illustrates one of the underlying issues in framing the analysis of tactics and strategy in this game. Using this graph to visualize the lengths of each game, data was extracted to maximize the information available to train the neural nets with 1248 games–encompassing most of the initial curve ranging from 90 s to 590 s. Each time-segment from 90 s to 590 s had greater than 20 trials which was our threshold for using the data in our experiment. The remaining game data was not used in this experiment because there were too few game trials that lasted long enough to justify incorporating them into the training data.

At the outset of each game, it is nearly impossible to anticipate the strategy that players will use or the length of the match. Therefore, a hard-coded algorithm will struggle with the accuracy of anticipating the quantities and placement of an adversary on a map. This problem is mitigated by using a smaller map, like *Ascension to Aiur*. Games on smaller maps tend to finish more quickly and encourage the agents to choose strategies that focus on winning as soon as possible.

[3] poses a more resilient solution to the above issue by implementing a convolutional Long Short Term Memory (LSTM) autoencoder architecture to "defog" the map. An LSTM is a type of Recurrent Neural Network (RNN) which, in this case, takes the player's observations as inputs. The "hidden state" of the LSTM is the defogged game which shows the enemy's position at the time of the observation. Using the player's observations, the neural net is trained with the hidden state as a desired output. After training and validation, the net will thereby learn to defog the game by predicting where the enemy lies. We intend to use the same encoder-decoder architecture as the [3] Brood War approach. The decoder then provides an output layer of predictions that range from unit types, number, and locations.

As implemented in StarCraft Broodwar, [3] has shown promise in predicting enemy positions. Inspired by these methods and their success, we have used the Keras API to implement three different architectures to compare their accuracies. All three architectures use an encoder-decoder setup with four stacked layers. The first and last modules of each architecture have the same number of filters, and the middle two modules contain one-half of those filters. Autoencoders set up with this kind of architecture are typically used to reduce the noise of inputs which we hope will increase the likelihood of correct defogging predictions.

The first architecture we implemented focuses on the temporal aspect of the data by using a LSTM. Using LSTMs exclusively has the potential downside of reducing the spatial data to one dimension before inputting it to the architecture. However, the sequential nature of game play in SC2 lends itself to LSTM architectures.

The second architecture we implemented focuses on retaining some of the spatial data by using stacked convolutional filters. Using the same approach as [3], we also step down the total resolution of the game space into one 16×16 field. This size helps the user conceptualize quadrants and sub-quadrants of proposed defogged enemy positions and it simplifies the input data. Within this space, the 256 squares are then grouped into three channels representing probes, troops, and buildings. This input setup helps both players and the AI agent discern the different types of enemy units occupying different areas on the map.

The last architecture incorporates both the spatial and temporal aspects of our game data. Using Keras's module, ConvLSTM2D, this architecture combines the convolutional neural nets with the LSTM algorithm. A very similar architecture was used in [1] where the authors applied unsupervised and semi-supervised learning to detect anomalous frames in video surveillance data. It is likely that this architecture will perform the best because it integrates all dimensions of the input data without reshaping it. By retaining the spatial and time data, this neural net is expected to discover certain patterns that are otherwise obscured when matrices are overly processed prior to their input into a network.

Once the above architectures are implemented, further work can be conducted on larger maps to study the resiliency of our approach. The map used in this study, for instance, begins with players at specific locations on the field. This effectively biases the data of the game by taking out some of the stochasticity present in other maps.

Fig. 3. After a neural net predicts the position of an adversary, a heatmap is generated with the position of the player included. The figure above shows an example of the output of the neural net. (Color figure online)

Outputs of the neural nets are used to build heatmaps which illustrate the statistical probability of enemy locations. Figure 3 depicts an example of neural net outputs where green represents probes, red represents units that can attack, and blue represents buildings. If a heatmap overlay is more transparent, there are less units occupying that part of the map. The work accomplished by visualizing SC2 [4] used heatmap information to build tactics directing where a player should be moving units based on enemy unit locations. The heatmaps produced by the tactical visualization module can provide key graphics to aid the player in partially observable situations while also directing a player's army placement.

3.3   Micromanagement and Scouting Agent

In the original modular architecture, the micromanagement module and scouting module were scripted [6]. Currently, they remain scripted in this work due to our limited time and resources. The automation of both scouting and micromanagement can be enabled and disabled during a game. The micromanagement module's main goal is to optimize the damage dealt to enemy units by rearranging friendly units' positions and attacking maneuvers. For example, a scripted action called *focus fire* involves searching for the enemy unit with the lowest amount of health remaining and dedicating the entire army's attack on that singular enemy.

The scouting agent's goal is to search the map for enemy units, buildings, and bases. Because SC2 is played with *fog of war*, and therefore enemy locations are unknown, scouting is essential to the goal of the game which is to destroy all enemy buildings. Scouting also plays a prominent role in determining what types of units to build. For example, if a player knew their enemy's army consisted mostly of air units, then the player would build the appropriate air unit counters.

Future work for both agents include using reinforcement learning techniques to optimize these strategies; however, improvements are still being tested because of the complexity of the problem.

4   Human-Machine Interface

The human-machine interface (HMI) we created is a web-based interface that houses the build order module, tactical visualization module, and micromanagement and scouting automation modules. To maintain player immersion while still allowing module recommendations to stand out, user-centered design considerations were applied to the HMI. For example, similar content was grouped into panels, and the panels were clearly separated from one another on the screen so players could easily find relevant information. Likewise, a color scheme similar to the color scheme used in SC2 was selected and used consistently throughout the HMI in order to maintain immersion while offering easily digestible information.

Figure 4 is a screenshot of the current web-based HMI design. The left side of the screen houses toggle switches to turn on and off the scouting and micromanagement automation and a text box to display hints about the tool or game state to players. In the middle of the screen, the minimap that is presented will display the tactical visualization module's predictions of where enemy units and buildings are on the map based on the current state of the game. Because the visualization module's outputs suggest the density and locations of enemy units, overlays of different colors will be placed on the minimap. Lastly, on the right side of the screen, the top 4 build order recommendations are listed with the most recommended unit at the top of the screen. Because the build order module outputs based on probabilities, the probability that a winning strategy would choose to build that recommended unit is also provided under the unit's or building's name.

Fig. 4. The human-machine interface that houses the modules and automation features.

Future work for the HMI includes conducting usability tests and adding supportive build functionality to the build order's recommendations. Usability testing will help ensure that key information is conveyed to players and determine if additional information is needed. Build functionality will allow players to auto-build recommended units by simply clicking on the build order's recommendations. Similar to the auto-build functionality given by toggle switches in the HMI, the auto-build for build order recommendations would allow units to be built and placed automatically by the system to help automate lower level work and free up a player's attention and mental resources for higher level decisions.

5   Experiment Design

An experiment was designed to test the impact of the battle aid system on player performance. The physical setup of the experiment will consist of two monitors put side by side; one monitor will display Blizzard's official SC2 game interface while the other monitor will display the HMI battle aid produced by this work. Figure 5 depicts what the physical setup for the experiment will look like.

While the battle aid is meant to help players regardless of their previous experience with SC2, the initial experiment will only include novice players with little to no experience with real-time strategy games. This will be done to avoid confounding the data and to ensure that we are testing the effects of our battle management aid rather than the effects of a participant's prior experience with real-time strategy games.

Participants will play four games in SC2: 2 with the HMI and 2 without the HMI. Participants will start the study by playing a short SC2 and tool tutorial that walks them through the basics of the game and its rules. Questionnaires to measure mental workload, trust, and usability of the HMI will be administered

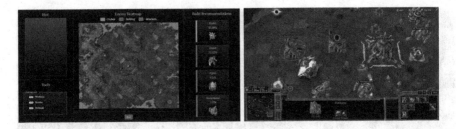

Fig. 5. The SC2 game screen put next to the HMI.

before and after each game. Participant preferences based on a win-loss record and a Blizzard score will be compared between games with the HMI and games without the HMI.

6 Discussion

A feature that is being explored but has not yet been incorporated in the current interface is a more explainable version of the build order module. While confidence scores and model sensitivity can be estimated from current battle aid modules, future implementations of the battle aid system will draw on not only traditional reinforcement learning concepts but also more causal and counterfactual reinforcement learning concepts in order to more easily convey suggestions to users. Work done within the recent year suggests that causality can play a role in increasing the understanding of human users [2] while counterfactual reasoning would give the system a better way to explain why actions were not selected though they seem to be correct in a user's eyes.

Though the work done in [2] does not seem to have a significant impact on the user's trust of an agent, the future iterations of this battle aid would hopefully see a different outcome. Because trust is something earned or gained rather than given all at once, over the course of a couple games, the HAT battle aid produced in this work would need to build up a reputation of good suggestions and therefore be deserving of a user's trust.

7 Summary

This paper presented a modular approach to creating deep learning agents for SC2 and an approach for converting agents into battle management aids. Although the modules are still being improved, the initial work that has already been accomplished is cohesive and offers users a tool that may help people understand and perform better on real-world strategy games.

References

1. Kiran, R., Thomas, D., Parakkal, R.: An overview of deep learning based methods for unsupervised and semi-supervised anomaly detection in videos (2018). https://arxiv.org/abs/1801.03149
2. Madumal, P., Miller, T., Sonenberg, L., Vetere, F.: Explainable Reinforcement Learning Through a Causal Lens (2019). https://arxiv.org/pdf/1905.10958.pdf
3. Synnaeve, G., Lin, Z., Gehring, J., et al.: Forward modeling for partial observation strategy games - a StarCraft defogger. In: Proceedings of the 32nd International Conference on Neural Information Processing Systems (NIPS 2018), pp. 10761–10771. Curran Associates Inc., Red Hook (2018)
4. Kuan, Y., Wang, Y., Chuang, J.: Visualizing real-time strategy games: the example of StarCraft II. In: 2017 IEEE Conference on Visual Analytics Science and Technology (VAST), pp. 71–80. https://doi.org/10.1109/VAST.2017.8585594
5. Justesen, N., Risi, S.: Learning macromanagement in StarCraft from replays using deep learning. In: 2017 IEEE Conference on Computational Intelligence in Games (CIG), pp. 162–169. https://arxiv.org/pdf/1707.03743.pdf
6. Lee, D., Tang H., Zhang, J., et al.: Modular Architecture for StarCraft II with Deep Reinforcement Learning (2018). https://arxiv.org/pdf/1811.03555.pdf
7. Vinyals, O., Babuschkin, I., Czarnecki, W.M., et al.: Grandmaster level in StarCraft II using multi-agent reinforcement learning. Nature **575**, 350–354 (2019). https://doi.org/10.1038/s41586-019-1724-z
8. StarCraft II Learning Environment. https://github.com/deepmind/pysc2
9. Blizzard StarCraft II Client. https://github.com/Blizzard/s2client-proto
10. Ascension to Aiur LE Map. https://liquipedia.net/starcraft2/File:Ascension_to_Aiur_LE.jpg

Multidisciplinary Iterative Design of Exergames (MIDE): A Framework for Supporting the Design, Development, and Evaluation of Exergames for Health

Yirou Li[1](✉), John Muñoz[1], Samira Mehrabi[2], Laura Middleton[2,3], Shi Cao[1], and Jennifer Boger[1,3]

[1] Department of Systems Design Engineering, University of Waterloo,
Waterloo, ON N2L 3G1, Canada
{yirou.li,john.munoz.hci,shi.cao,jboger}@uwaterloo.ca
[2] Department of Kinesiology, University of Waterloo,
Waterloo, ON N2L 3G1, Canada
{s4mehrab,lmiddlet}@uwaterloo.ca
[3] Research Institute for Aging, Waterloo, ON N2J 0E2, Canada

Abstract. Exercise video games (exergames) are increasingly being employed as a complementary intervention to promote physical activity engagement in response to the need for creating sustainable strategies for supporting health. While exergames have shown that they can have comparable effects to conventional human-guided training programs in certain situations, its adoption in healthcare applications are still limited. This is in part because of a disconnection between the technology/content producers, healthcare providers, and end-users. Many design frameworks have been proposed to guide the process of creating games for health, however, what is missing is an integrated and multifaceted approach that includes the preliminary research and evaluation stages that are needed to create plausible solutions for exergames. Furthermore, relevant stakeholders are often not included throughout the entire process, neglecting the importance of transdisciplinary collaborations when creating exergames for health. This paper presents the Multidisciplinary Iterative Design of Exergames (MIDE) framework as a comprehensive, integrative, and specific framework for exergame design, development, and evaluation following different research methods, techniques and tools. The MIDE framework is intended to support researchers, healthcare professionals, and industrial experts in identifying the stages, processes, techniques, and key roles needed to create novel exergames for exercise promotion. As older adults are a key user group, applicability of the framework is illustrated using considerations for older adults and immersive experiences (e.g., virtual reality). A specific use case is presented at the end of the paper to illustrate the use of the MIDE framework in the context of a project of using virtual reality exergames for promoting exercise in people living with dementia.

Keywords: Exergames · Framework · Game design · Game evaluation · Multidisciplinary · Iterative · Older adults · Virtual reality (VR)

© Springer Nature Switzerland AG 2020
X. Fang (Ed.): HCII 2020, LNCS 12211, pp. 128–147, 2020.
https://doi.org/10.1007/978-3-030-50164-8_9

1   Introduction

Research has shown that physical activity (exercise) is associated with better health outcomes and have been recognized as valuable part of preventative and therapeutic strategies for healthy living [5,37]. While playing video games has been considered a sedentary activity in the past [38,40], many commercial video games exist that require players to be physically active by encouraging them get up and move. Recent research has shown that interactive video games, in which human movements are integrated as the main interface to elicit physical activity similar to exercise (also known as exergames), are able to motivate people engage in physical activity by offering an appealing and fun game experience, compelling game challenges, and novel ways to meet and interact with others [29]. In fact, exergames have been used to provide long-term motivation to support physical activity engagement in different populations for different purposes including education [48], rehabilitation [27], and physical/cognitive training [26].

While there are several interventions under development, an area of rapid growth is virtual reality (VR) exergames for older adults. VR is showing promise as a way to provide a realistic, novel, and immersive environment that encourages game players to exercise [32,39,41]. Access to conventional exercise can become more difficult as people age. Exergames have shown potential to benefit older adults' functional fitness, improve older adults' mental health [8,39], increase social connections and encourage interactions with peers [12,39], and being mentally stimulating [19,43]. Even though Conventional screen-displayed VR exergames (e.g., Nintendo Wii, Microsoft Kinect) have been widely adopted to support aerobic, balance, and strength training in older adults to increase physical activity and promote health [17,26,44,52], head-mounted display (HMD) VR exergames are increasingly gaining attention as they present fully immersive 3-dimensional (3D) environments in a format that can be accessible and intuitive for older adults to use, which means they can provide more realistic and engaging gaming experience for the participants compared to the other mediums.

Exergames have shown comparable effects to conventional human-guided exercise programs [44,51], however, the rate of adopting both commercially available and customized exergames in rehabilitation settings is still low. Based on a survey carried out across Canada [28], this may in part be due to poor compatibility of the technology with end-user preferences. While exergaming frameworks exist (e.g., geronotoludic design [9], DDE framework [50]), they are mainly focused on specific game design elements, often neglecting other important stages/stakeholders required to elicit design requirements. Further evaluation of the exergames concerning end-users and healthcare professionals are also generally missed in these frameworks. In addition, the design of meaningful and playable experiences within exergames has remained a major challenge when targeting older adults considering variations in motor and cognitive abilities within the population. Although a number of frameworks for designing exergames targeting older adults [9,21] have been proposed, novel immersive HMD-VR exergames pose new challenges regarding interaction paradigms, game design elements, and human factors that are associated with the use of HMD-VR headsets (e.g., motion and simulation sickness). Therefore, a special considerations for both older adults and HMD-VR exergames are needed to foster an informed adoption of this technology for exercise promotion.

This paper outlines the Multidisciplinary and Iterative Design for Exergames (MIDE) framework, an exergaming framework that includes three stages: i) contextual research, ii) game design and development, and iii) system evaluation. The MIDE framework takes a generalizable approach that considers general research and evaluation phases, guides information transfer between different stages (inputs and outputs), integrates contributions from relevant stakeholders, and recommends research methods (e.g, user-centered design).

1.1 Existing Guidelines for Designing Accessible Games and VR for Older Adults

A review of the existing guidelines starts with guidelines for developing accessible games.

Specific considerations addressing accessibility pros and cons of using virtual environments have been proposed [2,25]. From a *mobility* perspective, advantages of using VR environments are: i) possibilities to overcome real world physical barriers, ii) fully immersed and stimulating environments, and iii) avatar's customization to fight stigma; on the other hand disadvantages can be listed as: i) players with mobility impairments may have difficulty using controllers, ii) interaction in virtual environments often requires precise click targets, iii) hygiene issues due to aroused physiological responses, iv) players with severe mobility impairments may find movements, such as reaching and grasping, or sensations, like haptic cues, are difficult to perform or interpret, and v) movements in lower limbs (i.e., walking, stepping, standing, etc.) are usually hard to include/track in VR environment. Also, the use of virtual environments poses advantages for players with *cognitive* limitations such as: i) after training, players can become proficient in virtual environments, ii) the vividness and synchronous interaction in VR can allow players to focus their attention more effectively, iii) VR can be designed to support error-free training, which can help alter the environment complexity into cognitive abilities, iv) the distraction provided in the virtual environments has been found to diminish pain perception in hospitalized patients [45]. However, disadvantages can be: i) the user interface can be difficult to learn, ii) input devices such as motion controllers can be difficult to master, iii) players may experience motion sickness, due partially conflicts between sensory cues, and iv) flashing or excessive moving objects may cause seizures or migraines.

With respect specifically to for physical activity promotion for older adults using HMD-VR, design guidelines that consider accessibility issues for games can be used to address some of the aforementioned disadvantages of VR. According to existing accessibility guidelines for game design [1,2], physical and cognitive changes of the population should be carefully considered when designing games for people with impairments or disabilities. Considerations for exergames design targeting older adults regarding *mobility* issues may include: i) allow controls or input devices to be reconfigured and adapted, ii) ensure interactive elements are large enough and well spaced with appropriate color contract, iii) provide alternatives to buttons that are required to be held down, iv) do not rely on motion tracking of specific body types, and v) do not make precise timing essentials to gameplay. Similar considerations from a *cognitive* perspective are: i) allow the game to start without the need of menus, ii) use simple, clear, readable text and language, iii) include contextual in-game guidance, iv) reinforce essential information through text, visual, and speech feedback, and v) avoid any sudden or unexpected movement or events.

1.2   Frameworks for Exergame Design

In this section, a brief review of the existing frameworks for designing exergames is presented, looking at elucidating important previous research carried out to better understand how exergames for health should be designed. Knowledge gaps and opportunities to create more complete and comprehensive frameworks are identified in order to facilitate the positioning of our MIDE framework.

In order to bridge the gap between relevant fields within game research and game development, the Mechanics, Dynamics, Aesthetics (MDA) framework [23] provides a structural approach to understand games and to facilitate discussion and knowledge translations amongst all different disciplines. The framework describes different layers of abstractions in the dynamics of a gaming system to better infer the design and development considerations of a user-centred experience-driven game. The framework, however, focuses on the game mechanisms and fails to provide a coherent approach for game design that is suitable for all types of games.

The gerontoludic design framework [9] extends the generic MDA framework by providing guidance in designing attractive digital entertaining games specifically for older adults. In addition to adapt the specific design interpretations for seniors using fundamental game elements such as mechanics and aesthetics, the gerontoludic framework emphasizes the importance of user-centered (more specifically player-centered) design approach towards the goal of meaningful play. Similar to MDA, geronotoludic design provide necessary considerations and suggestions when designing for older populations but lacks details on implementations during actual game design and development process.

In response to some criticisms and challenges about the MDA framework mentioned above, the Design, Dynamics, Experience (DDE) framework [50] aims to provide a more comprehensive guidance in the game design and development process. Transforming the three main components, DDE framework provides clarifications regarding each categories and their subcategories. Instead of connecting different game layers to formulate either player's perspective or designer's perspective, both parties have distinct relationships within each layer of the game in DDE framework. While DDE framework has provided more clear picture of different components of game layers and considers the experience of players in each game layer, players are not involved in the framework as part of the design process/component.

Inspired by the successful examples in serious games, or games for health, that are developed according to the best-practices in rehabilitation, an adaptive exergames design framework [21] has been proposed for elderly population to address the specific needs that are not considered in the commercial exergames. Additional to the generic architecture framework for rehabilitation games develop process, the detailed adaptive layer illustrates the relationships between user and sensors for adapting exergames training session according to individual performance and preferences. The conceptual architecture, however, fails to consider necessary stakeholders and their contribution to the system.

To guide the design of a gamified system for rehabilitation settings, the People, Aesthetics, Context, Technology (PACT) framework [7] presents a set of considerations for an inclusive rehabilitation game design. In particular, the framework emphasizes on involvement of all necessary stakeholders in addition to users and developers. By tailoring the game design to the specific context and technologies and incorporating stakeholders' suggestions, the developed product of the framework will better suit the need of healthcare system for larger scale deployments. Although the paper presents an example of using the framework in the process of gamifying a rehabilitation system, the framework only presents key components to be considered in the four areas.

Table 1 summarizes the exergames design discussed frameworks above, describing their target audience, game categories, design stages that are discussed, and whether VR considerations are discussed. Existing frameworks have focused on game elements or game development considerations but none have proposed a systematic process to guide other relevant stages, such as contextual research and system evaluation.

Table 1. Exergames design frameworks.

Framework	Target audience	Game category	Stages covered	VR considerations
Geronotoludic design [9]	Older adults	Entertainment games	Game design	No
DDE framework [50]	Not specified	Entertainment games	Game design	No
Adaptive exergames [21]	Older adults	Exergames	Game design	No
PACT framework [7]	Not specified	Games for health	Game design, game development	No
MIDE framework	Older adults	HMD-VR exergames	Game design, game development, system evaluation	Yes

2   MIDE Framework

This section introduces the MIDE framework (Fig. 1), which is intended to provide guidance in the design, development, and evaluation of HMD-VR exergames for promoting physical activity participation among older adults. The framework

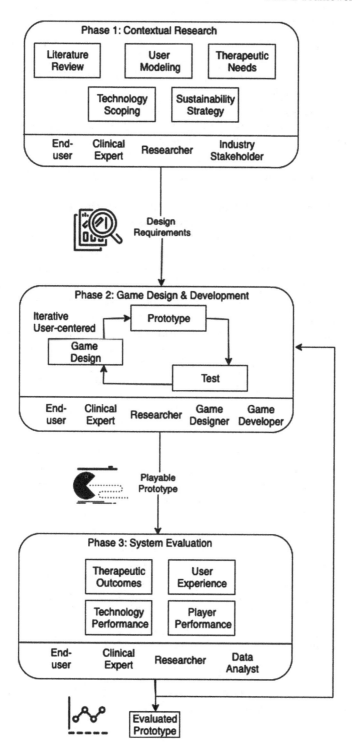

Fig. 1. The MIDE framework

is divided into three phases: contextual research, game design and development, and system evaluation. Key stakeholders are shown in the bottom portion of each Phase. While the framework can be used in exergames designed for health in general, specific elements that should be considered regarding HMD-VR and older adults have been described in the paper and should be used in part with the framework. While the framework is presented in sequential Phases, the developers should be aware of and planning for future stages and tasks to ensure activities performed in each Phase feed into the next.

2.1 Phase 1: Contextual Research

To develop appropriate exergaming solutions for the target user group, researchers need to be aware of the potential challenges and possible solutions by observing and interacting with older adults, healthcare professionals (such as physiotherapists, kinesiologists, clinical experts, nurses, etc.), industry stakeholders, and other possible parties (e.g., informal caregivers, family members, technicians, etc.) that can provide relevant information. In particular, researchers should carry out holistic reviews to define the problem and gaps, specify user preferences through user modeling, understand expected outcomes from therapeutic needs, understand the existing solutions and interventions via technology scoping, and manage distribution/deployment of the proposed exergaming solutions with sustainability strategies. The output of this phase is a set of design requirements that includes design considerations, accessibility recommendations, user modeling elements, and technological reflections to be followed in the design and development phase. Some of the aspects needed to carry out a contextually-informed model of end-users and exergames are:

Literature Review. A literature review is needed to understand the current knowledge about the proposed problem space from both research and industry perspectives as they usually complement each other by providing information from different aspects. In specific, there is a need for conducting reliable comprehensive literature reviews to understand the current theoretical and methodological contributions to the technology advancements, research methodologies, design considerations, and intervention evaluations. Examples of specialized academic conferences and journals include: Games for health (journal of Liebert), JMIR Serious Games (journal of JMIR), Serious Games and Applications for Health (conference of IEEE) and International Conference of Virtual Rehabilitation (conference of IEEE). It can be useful to explore non-academic information sources or grey literature (e.g., patents, industry networks) to better understand opportunities to create exergames that can transition from academic findings to potential marketable and accessible commercialized products. An example of a business to business (B2B) platform that showcase games for fitness promotion is https://www.fitness-gaming.com.

User Modeling. User models [18] should reflect the preferences and needs of the targeted user group from a multi-discipline perspective in order to optimize the exergaming experience. In addition to general aspects such as demographic, capability, characteristics, hobbies, and motivators for playing, exergames-specific user models should also include other attributes like the facilitators and barriers to physical activity engagement [49]. All these aspects help shape the game design elements such as mechanics and narrative. It has been shown that more familiar and plausible exergaming experience (e.g., prior experience, positive emotions) might be more effective in engaging older adults in physical activity. The detailed attributes in each aspect can be summarized from information-finding activities such as interviews, observations, and literature reviews. For example, hobbies and demographic information such as age, sex, and culture will highly influence the theme of the game [10]. Players with different characteristics, age, and backgrounds may prefer one game mode over another like enjoying cooperative games better than competitive games [24]. Specific physical and cognitive abilities should be considered to create more realistic player models capable to represent real users' capabilities. Finally, the user models can help to better categorize potential users into different player types [4] that can help in creating user archetypes (also called personas) that will facilitate the process of empathizing with the end-users [35].

Therapeutic Needs. The specific therapeutic needs of the population interacting with the exergames should be reviewed through existing evidence in exercise/exergames from the field and closely consulted with healthcare professionals in order to complement the existing training programs. The VR exergames will be adjusted based on individual needs and progress within the large scope of therapeutic requirement and best practice for the specific population. In conventional human-guided exercise training interventions, prescribed exercises are ideally tailored to the individual's unique health status, physical capability, interests, and exercise program goals. In this regard, exercise specialists are required to determine the core components of the training plan (e.g., type of exercise, target outcomes, based on FITT-VP: Frequency, Intensity, Type, Time, Volume, and Progression model) [20]. Periodic assessments are essential to adjust the exercise intervention according to the individual's training responses, progress and corresponding therapeutic needs. Following the same principles, in the exergames design and development process, researchers need to specify the users' fitness goals, training settings, and outcome measures beforehand. Individual clinical profiles and periodic assessments should also be considered in order to properly adjust the exergames training program in accordance with the individual's goals and progress. Taking the existing scientific evidence and best practice in exercise into consideration and acknowledging challenges and strengths of the exergames system are of prime importance when developing an individually tailored exercise regimen.

Technology Scoping. To deliver the solution with appropriate artifacts and equipment, the capacity of existing gaming technologies should be researched and scoped. By using techniques such as trend analysis and SWOT (Strength, Weakness, Opportunities, and Threats) matrix, appropriate technology interventions for the exergames should be identified by carefully comparing the existing technologies in the market. In consultation with industrial experts, hardware and software requirements for developing and deploying the exergames should be discussed and finalized especially for planning and budgeting purposes. For instance, the integration of existing fitness equipment, such as stationary bikes and treadmills, has been explored as a beneficial (e.g., engagement, user experience) technology integration approach for exergames [33]. Particularly in immersive VR, more sophisticated setups such as CAVE (Cave Virtual Environment) can be used to avoid hygiene issues (e.g., sweating by using the HMD) as well as to provide a more embodied experience which has boost the player experience [31]; however, this must be balanced against cost and the practicalities regarding implementation. Detailed strength and limitations of the VR system will come out from the stage to guide design process considering the needs of users and the capability of the system.

Sustainability Strategy. A shortcoming of the exergames for health that are designed and developed under research projects is their limited availability. Despite publishing scientific evidence of their impact, the majority of the final applications cannot be accessed or are not available beyond the duration of the project [30]. To tackle this issue, the technologies and games developed in academic contexts should consider strategies to be distributed/maintained outside of the research period so that they are available more widely and for longer-term by end-users and healthcare institutions. Examples of efforts towards creating digital libraries to facilitate the access to validated games for health can be found at: https://openrehab.org and https://seriousgames-portal.org.

2.2   Phase 2: Game Design & Development

To support appropriate development of exergames that meet expectations, older adults, healthcare professionals, and other stakeholders should be included in the game design process. This will enable meaningful and participatory contribution towards positively influencing the game design and development process. At the end of this phase, a fully functional prototype should be ready to playtest.

Design and Development Cycle. Following user-centered design approaches [47], the design and development cycle of the game should iterate until a qualified playable prototype is developed. In general, the cycle should start with a process, such as brainstorming as a multi-stakeholder group, to better understand the goal of the exergames and related training programs. Consequently, design sessions, where game concepts are discussed in light of the healthcare requirements and technological feasibility, should be carried out to establish a mutual exergames design expectation. The initial game elements such as game story and game mechanics should be discussed and analyzed on an ongoing basis by bringing examples from already existing exergames or other inspiring sources. Specific game concepts should then be evaluated and investigated through focus groups and individual interview sessions, with participation of older adults and healthcare professionals, later in the iterative cycle. Following the game design concepts, an iterative prototyping and playtesting process can be used to help estimate if the proposed game concepts (e.g., game mechanics, game theme) are suitable for the target population. When possible, the game content should be created with the interfacing hardware, allowing an early identification of possible modifications that have to be done in order to facilitate the interaction (e.g., removing the need of pressing buttons). The developed prototype should then be evaluated during test (or playtesting) sessions with both healthcare professionals and older adults. Through multiple playtesting and informal feedback sessions, specific game preferences and game elements will be modified based on the feedback from older adults and healthcare professionals during their one-on-one interactions with the prototype. The feedback and suggestions should be integrated in a new game design concept to improve existing limitations in the prototypes and the cycle starts again as many times as possible until a qualified prototype appears as suggested in conventional game design literature [42].

2.3   Phase 3: System Evaluation

The playable prototypes from game design and development phase are not the end product as they must be systematically evaluated with a representative sample of users to ensure the exergames meet their intended goals. The output of Phase 3 can be used in an iterative fashion as input into a continuation of Phase 2 as a part of a larger iterative cycle, supporting more extensive revisions and refinement. In particular, we propose four different domains to be evaluated for VR exergames.

Therapeutic Outcomes. Depending on the goals of the system, defined a priori, the exergames can be evaluated to better understand the targeted therapeutic outcomes and assess whether the individual therapeutic needs and goals are met. In this regard, physical, cognitive, and psychosocial aspects of the exergame can be some of the possible outcome areas:

- **Physical Aspect (Functional Fitness):** As a novel form of exercise, the impact of exergames on improving general fitness, and eliciting pre-specified physical outcomes can be evaluated. Increased cardiorespiratory fitness, range of motion, strength, and balance are of such physical outcomes depending on the training regimes (i.e., type of exercise, intensity, duration), fitness domain, and target muscle group. As a complementary and alternative training approach, evaluating the resulting energy expenditure and the exergames capacity in increasing exercise level can be important, in particular for those at higher risk of being sedentary, reluctant to exercise, or concerned about possible adverse events associated with physical activity [6,41]. Evaluating the system with respect to physical outcomes will help to adjust exergames parameters according to the individual therapeutic goals/needs and commodities to avoid physical overexertion as well as reducing the likelihood of unwanted or detrimental effects.

- **Cognitive Aspect:** Considering the existing evidence supporting exercise as a promising means to enhance cognition in aging adults or tackle some of the age-related cognitive declines [22,36], the impact of the exergames on cognition and the extent to which they can induce change in cognitive function among elderly can be assessed as an outcome of interest. The focus can be on global cognitive ability or domain-specific areas. Evaluation of the exercise-induced cognitive outcomes in relation to the physical load and cognitive demand during exergaming can help to further explore the effect of different training programs and exergames modalities on specific cognitive domains.

- **Psychosocial Aspect:** In addition to physical function and cognitive performance, psychosocial effects of the exergames, including psychological changes and social well-being, can be possible outcomes of the system. Concerning the psychosocial impacts of the exergames, changes in mood, depressive symptoms, and enjoyment can be assessed. Additionally, motivation level, perceived quality of life, and self-efficacy influenced by exergaming can be other outcomes to be evaluated. With social isolation being one of the major concerns for older adults, it can be beneficial to evaluate the social effects of exergames on this population, in particular its impact on reducing loneliness, improving socialization as well as bonding with peers and grandchildren. Considering lack of motivation is one of the main barriers to uptake exercise among the older population, opportunities of the social connection provided by exergaming may increase exercise participation and adherence among this population.

User Experience. To understand the usability and acceptability of the VR exergames, the perceptions of the game and technology will be evaluated from both players' and healthcare professionals' perspectives. For example, simulator sickness, specifically motion sickness, of the players during the exergames sessions should be investigated through specific questionnaires. To understand the feasibility of adopting VR exergames system for longer period of time in long term care facilities, both players' and healthcare professionals' perceptions/acceptance of the technology should be well documented. In addition, the game user experience and players perceptions of virtual environments are extremely helpful to improve the game design.

Technology Performance. In addition to the user experience, the technology intervention should also be evaluated on its intended behavior once compared with resulted behavior. The elicited physical and physiological responses during the exergames session should be monitored and compared against the recommended guidelines [46] for older adults as the exergames are intended to provide incentives for physical activity through gamified contents. For example, when a certain heart rate zone is a target outcome of a exergames as a key indicator of physical activity intensity, the exergames is a failure if it cannot elicit the target heart rate of the player during the gameplay sessions. On the other hand, the interactions of the exergames should be documented and compared to intended user behaviors to understand if the technology meets its expectations. For example, the technology controllers fail to meet the purpose and may need to be altered if the player cannot use it properly; the technology configuration when the audio instructions provide additional confusion to users rather than guiding them through the games at proper time.

Player Performance. Player performance can be evaluated at two levels: physical sensing and game data. Game data, including game interactions, game progress, game score, and game event, will be combined and interpreted to present player performance in a reasonable and easy-to-understand manner. VR sensors, physical activity monitors, and physiological sensors will be used in physical sensing part. The sensors in the VR system (e.g., acceleration, 3D position) can be used on their own to track the physical activities of the user or can be augmented by external physical activity tracking sensors can provide more accurate and validated information about the exergames sessions, such as physical intensity level and energy expenditure.

2.4   Other Key Considerations

In addition to the general process described above, many tools and concepts can be used to facilitate the design process for better adaptive VR exergames for health.

Intelligent Software Layer. Intelligent software layers based on computer algorithms (i.e., machine learning, data management, etc.) can significantly improve the way exergames impact people's health. Such layers can be created with a diversity of functionalities and objectives, but generally speaking they aim to maximize the healthcare benefits by configuring aspects of the software to provide customised and personalised support for people using the exergames or data from it as either the primary end-users or secondary users (such as healthcare professionals). This can be done by taking advantage of the data that can be captured during exergaming sessions as well as providing strategies for real-time adaptation based on physiological metrics. For example, adaptive modules such as kinematic adaptation layers [34] can be implemented to facilitate personalizing and adapting in-game difficulty to provide longer engagement with the exergames and elicit higher physical activity level. Data management modules can be included for in game-data logging purpose but additional connection blocks to external clinical electronic health record system or data visualization blocks are possibly necessary depending on the application of the exergames [11]. Efforts towards unifying the exergames ontology for publishing open game data are being created to facilitate the collaboration and to replicate results [3].

Rapid Prototyping Tools. Considering its emerging and disrupting nature, VR technologies are constantly evolving and staying updated with the knowledge is a challenging but necessary task for developing VR exergames. The most popular game engines (e.g., Unity3D, Unreal) are frequently releasing tutorials and software tools to facilitate the creation of content for VR. However, to be able to use these game engines, some specific technical skills may be required, thus limiting the creation of virtual environments and games to people with knowledge in 3D modeling, programming, and game design. Therefore, with the aim to aid a rapid adoption of VR in different ecosystems (e.g., education, training, healthcare), tools for rapid prototyping have been created to allow the development of low-fidelity prototypes by only investing a couple of hours of work without requiring specialized knowledge/skill for VR development. Some of the most useful tools for prototyping VR include:

- **Paper Prototyping:** From workshops and ideation/brainstorming sessions to game jams, the use of pencil and paper sketches and drawings is always highly recommended to rapidly show concepts and initial designs. VR is not an exception either. Sketching concepts by using distorted and spherical paper-based templates can help to materialize ideas in a quick and elegant fashion. Tools such as templates, perspective techniques and available prototypes can be found at: https://blog.prototypr.io.
- **Google Blocks:** Empowered by a diverse and extensive library of 3D objects that use computationally low-cost models (low-poly), Google Blocks allows people to create virtual environments by dragging-and-dropping pre-established objects into a scene. Google Blocks allows users to either to import already existent models or to create their own, but one of its most interesting characteristics is that it allows users to create models even when they are immersed in the virtual environments. Thus, spatial features of the scene and object positioning can be used to aid establishing realistic simulated environments since users act as architects in the virtual space in real-time. The tool is freely available to be used with state-of-the-art VR headsets.
- **BrioVR:** This online platform allows users to create visually compelling and interactive VR prototypes without professional training. Virtual scenes can be created using a drag-and-drop workflow that integrates a library of 3D objects, text edition tools, geometric primitives, and an entire library of tolls for interaction such as triggers and object behaviors. Results can be previewed in commercially available VR systems (e.g., HTC Vive, Oculus Rift) as well as mobile systems powered by mobile phones. BrioVR is freely available and runs in web explorers.
- **Varwin:** Powered by the most popular game engine, Unity3D, Varwin offers a middleware that is able to be integrated with professional VR projects. Varwin integrates a block-based visual programming language that simplifies the creation of interactions within the virtual environment. Varwin has a freely available version that can be used to create multiple VR projects.

3   Summary of MIDE Framework Contribution

The MIDE framework is different from other exergames design frameworks as it is:

- **Integrative:** In order to reach a holistic understanding of the complete process, all three stages (contextual research, game design and development, and evaluation) are required to truly establish the exergames product as a feasible and effective complement of the existing exercise training programs. The MIDE framework includes key representative stakeholders throughout each stage, reinforcing the idea that a multidisciplinary team is required to ensure that diverse, yet complementary, perspectives of various stakeholders (e.g., industry partners, data analysts, healthcare professionals) are considered in the process of designing and developing exergames.
- **Specific:** The MIDE framework includes specific information about research methods, game design practices and considerations, VR prototyping tools, and evaluation approaches to create novel customizable immersive HMD-VR exergames for older adults.
- **Comprehensive:** The MIDE is intended to support the process of planning and executing research in exergames, VR games, and serious games for health by illustrating both an overall picture of the process as well as individual strategies and considerations for each stage, specifying inputs and outputs of each stage, providing design tools, well-established techniques and protocols, and references for further research.

4   Illustrative Use Case of the MIDE Framework

To illustrate the application of the MIDE framework, we present a sample use case related to the authors' current work: the design, development, and evaluation of HMD-VR exergames to promote physical activity in older adults with mild cognitive impairment (MCI) or dementia. As it is a project in progress, we are currently at the game design & development phase. The proposed system evaluation study is structured and will be conducted in the near future. Aspects of the model from Fig. 1 are indicated by the use of *italics*.

During the contextual research period, we conducted multiple *literature reviews* to understand exergames for older adults with MCI/dementia, current HMD-VR technologies for exercise and well-being, as well as some specific design considerations in motion based technologies and games for older adults with dementia from both academic and industry perspectives. Observations were made through shadowing exercise therapists in our long term care facility partner (Schlegel Villages) to collect information that informed our *user modeling*. In our previous pilot research [13–16], we found out that using farm related activities in the exergames allow players complete the tasks in an intuitive fashion as they recognised the environment and tasks they were expected to do. Simple audio instructions were given in a narrative, story-telling fashion, which was found to be extremely important in supporting game players in understanding what they were expected to do. Together with existing literature about older adults with dementia, a user model was constructed to understand the preferred game design concepts. Key considerations in *therapeutic needs* around target exercise outcomes, intervention practice, and system capability were concluded through literature reviews on existing evidence of exergames/exercise for older adults with MCI/dementia and discussions with healthcare professionals within the research team. Based on literature reviews, our user model, and discussions with healthcare professionals at long term care facilities as well as within the research team, we decided the exergames should promote upper limb exercises (and, by proxy, core strength) in a seated position to ensure safety and the instructions of the game should be straight forward. The length of the games is restricted to a maximum of 20 min (including warm up and cool down) and the intensity of the exercise does not exceed 80% of users' target heart rate. The current suite of games are being created in collaboration with a VR game development company (VR Vision), as a *sustainability strategy*, to support the deployment of commercially exergames to market after *technology scoping*. Together with experts from the industry partner, demonstration sessions have been arranged with Schlegel Villages to collaboratively explore the design expectations and requirements on the actual device by explaining the technology and the design concept to therapists (Fig. 2).

Fig. 2. Working in collaboration: Demonstration sessions for HMD-VR exergames development with our industry partner (VR Vision) and our long-term care partner (Schlegel Villages)

We are currently in the design & development phase, where we have designed and developed an initial playable prototype (Fig. 3), in collaboration with VR Vision, based on our design expectations from contextual research stage. With the initial prototype, we will investigate the validity of initial design concepts by conducting focus groups and demonstrating the initial prototype to older adults with MCI/dementia from Schlegel Villages as well as their therapists. The conclusions from the focus group sessions will be sent to VR Vision to adjust the inital prototype. Following some fast iterative play-development cycles with playtesting sessions and informal feedback sessions, we will demonstrate the final prototype to older adults with MCI/dementia and their therapists to understand their perception and acceptance about the technology.

Fig. 3. HMD-VR exergames initial prototype. Rowing activity.

Future work involves a six-week long feasibility study of the developed final prototype from the design and development stage to be carried out in long term care facilities. The goal of the feasibility study is to explore the potential of proposed intervention for a future larger scale trial in understanding the efficacy of HMD-VR exergames in older adults with MCI/dementia. In specific, we look into the adherence of the proposed exergames program and the feasibility of the assessment methods. Pre-post assessments on participants' functional fitness, cognitive function, and wellbeing will be collected and compared to reveal the *therapeutic outcomes* of exergames program. The proposed exergames is also evaluated on its *user experience* and *technology performance* through focus groups with participants and therapists from Schlegel Villages, observations of participants during exergames sessions, and a shot survey at the end of each exergaming session probing participant's VR exergaming experience during the session. Lastly, we will validate the potential of HMD-VR exergames as a stand along system to provide accurate information about the exercise sessions and *player performance*. To reach this goal, we first compare the validity of raw data information collected in VR sensor with the physical activity tracking sensor for movement measurements. Then, we investigate possible algorithms to provide objective measures such as energy expenditure and physical activity intensity from VR sensors by correlating the referencing values of derived objective measures from both physical activity tracking sensor and heart rate sensor with VR sensor data. Lastly, we also investigate novel metrics to reflect useful information about the exergames sessions and player status. Through discussions with therapists, we will identify several novel metrics to represent the VR exergaming sessions using the game data and movement measurements data from VR sensors, which will presented as the example information shown in Fig. 3.

5   Conclusions

The MIDE framework aims to provide guidelines and considerations related to the process of designing, developing, and evaluating exergames. While we focus on the creation of exergames for supporting older adults using VR applications, the general process and principles can be applied to any possible type of serious games for health and rehabilitation. The MIDE framework integrates a multidisciplinary approach and that seeks to involve relevant stakeholders by acknowledging and capturing the unique and valuable contributions of each role in different phases. It emphasizes the necessity of a amalgamation of different phases and perspectives in order to produce exergames systems that are complement the contexts and populations they are intended to support. As the MIDE is a new guideline, further research and testing in real-world development situations needs to be done to validate and improve it.

Acknowledgement. We thank our collaborator Prof. Michael Barnett-Cowan for his input on the framework. We acknowledge the support from our industry partners, Schlegel Villages and VR Vision, in developing the HMD-VR exergames for older adults with MCI/dementia. This research was supported in part by NSERC – CREATE, Training in Global Biomedical Technology Research and Innovation at the University of Waterloo. [CREATE Funding 401207296].

References

1. Older users. https://www.unimelb.edu.au/accessibility/virtual-reality/older-users
2. A straightforward reference for inclusive game design. http://gameaccessibility-guidelines.com/
3. Bamparopoulos, G., Konstantinidis, E., Bratsas, C., Bamidis, P.D.: Towards exergaming commons: composing the exergame ontology for publishing open game data. J. Biomed. Semant. **7**(1), 4 (2016). https://doi.org/10.1186/s13326-016-0046-4
4. Bartle, R.: Hearts, clubs, diamonds, spades: players who suit muds. J. MUD Res. **1**(1), 19 (1996)
5. Canada, H.: Government of Canada, March 2011. https://www.canada.ca/en/health-canada/services/healthy-living/physical-activity.html

6. Chao, Y.Y., Scherer, Y.K., Montgomery, C.A.: Effects of using nintendo wii™ exergames in older adults: a review of the literature. J. Aging Health **27**(3), 379–402 (2015)
7. Charles, D., McDonough, S.: A participatory design framework for the gamification of rehabilitation systems. In: 10th International Conference on Disability, Virtual Reality and Associated Technologies, Gothenburg, Sweden, pp. 293–296 (2014)
8. Chen, S.T., Huang, Y.G.L., Chiang, I.T.: Using somatosensory video games to promote quality of life for the elderly with disabilities. In: 2012 IEEE Fourth International Conference on Digital Game and Intelligent Toy Enhanced Learning, pp. 258–262. IEEE (2012)
9. De Schutter, B.: Gerontoludic design: extending the MDA framework to facilitate meaningful play for older adults. Int. J. Gaming Comput.-Mediated Simul. (IJGCMS) **9**(1), 45–60 (2017)
10. De Schutter, B., Vanden Abeele, V.: Meaningful play in elderly life. In: Annual Meeting of the International Communication Association, 01 January 2008, Montreal, Quebec, Canada (2008)
11. Dimaguila, G.L., Gray, K., Merolli, M.: Person-generated health data in simulated rehabilitation using kinect for stroke: literature review. JMIR Rehabil. Assistive Technol. **5**(1), e11 (2018)
12. Dove, E., Astell, A.: The Kinect project: group motion-based gaming for people living with dementia. Dementia **18**(6), 2189–2205 (2019)
13. Eisapour, M.: Design and evaluation of virtual reality exergames for people living with dementia. Master's thesis, University of Waterloo (2018)
14. Eisapour, M., Cao, S., Boger, J.: Game design for users with constraint: exergame for older adults with cognitive impairment. In: The 31st Annual ACM Symposium on User Interface Software and Technology Adjunct Proceedings, pp. 128–130 (2018)
15. Eisapour, M., Cao, S., Domenicucci, L., Boger, J.: Participatory design of a virtual reality exercise for people with mild cognitive impairment. In: Extended Abstracts of the 2018 CHI Conference on Human Factors in Computing Systems, pp. 1–9 (2018)
16. Eisapour, M., Cao, S., Domenicucci, L., Boger, J.: Virtual reality exergames for people living with dementia based on exercise therapy best practices. In: Proceedings of the Human Factors and Ergonomics Society Annual Meeting, vol. 62, pp. 528–532. Sage Publications, Los Angeles (2018)
17. Fang, Q., et al.: Effects of exergaming on balance of healthy older adults: a systematic review and meta-analysis of randomized controlled trials. Games Health J. **9**(1), 11–23 (2019)
18. Fischer, G.: User modeling in human-computer interaction. User Model. User-Adap. Inter. **11**(1–2), 65–86 (2001). https://doi.org/10.1023/A:1011145532042
19. Foloppe, D.A., Richard, P., Yamaguchi, T., Etcharry-Bouyx, F., Allain, P.: The potential of virtual reality-based training to enhance the functional autonomy of Alzheimer's disease patients in cooking activities: a single case study. Neuropsychol. Rehabil. **28**(5), 709–733 (2018)
20. Gibson, A.L., Wagner, D., Heyward, V.: Advanced Fitness Assessment and Exercise Prescription, 8E. Human Kinetics, Champaign (2018)
21. Hardy, S., Dutz, T., Wiemeyer, J., Göbel, S., Steinmetz, R.: Framework for personalized and adaptive game-based training programs in health sport. Multimedia Tools Appl. **74**(14), 5289–5311 (2015). https://doi.org/10.1007/s11042-014-2009-z

22. Hsieh, C.C., et al.: The effectiveness of a virtual reality-based Tai Chi exercise on cognitive and physical function in older adults with cognitive impairment. Dement. Geriat. Cogn. Disord. **46**(5–6), 358–370 (2018)
23. Hunicke, R., LeBlanc, M., Zubek, R.: MDA: a formal approach to game design and game research. In: Proceedings of the AAAI Workshop on Challenges in Game AI, vol. 4, p. 1722 (2004)
24. Ijaz, K., Wang, Y., Milne, D., Calvo, R.A.: Competitive vs affiliative design of immersive VR exergames. In: Marsh, T., Ma, M., Oliveira, M.F., Baalsrud Hauge, J., Göbel, S. (eds.) JCSG 2016. LNCS, vol. 9894, pp. 140–150. Springer, Cham (2016). https://doi.org/10.1007/978-3-319-45841-0_13
25. Jerald, J.: The VR Book: Human-Centered Design for Virtual Reality. Morgan & Claypool, San Rafael (2015)
26. Kappen, D.L., Mirza-Babaei, P., Nacke, L.E.: Older adults' physical activity and exergames: a systematic review. Int. J. Hum.-Comput. Interact. **35**(2), 140–167 (2019)
27. Knols, R.H., Vanderhenst, T., Verra, M.L., de Bruin, E.D.: Exergames for patients in acute care settings: systematic review of the reporting of methodological quality, FITT components, and program intervention details. Games Health J. **5**(3), 224–235 (2016)
28. Levac, D., Glegg, S., Colquhoun, H., Miller, P., Noubary, F.: Virtual reality and active videogame-based practice, learning needs, and preferences: a cross-Canada survey of physical therapists and occupational therapists. Games Health J. **6**(4), 217–228 (2017)
29. Lieberman, D.A.: Dance games and other exergames: what the research says (2006)
30. Lu, A.S., Kharrazi, H.: A state-of-the-art systematic content analysis of games for health. Games Health J. **7**(1), 1–15 (2018)
31. Martin-Niedecken, A.L., Rogers, K., Turmo Vidal, L., Mekler, E.D., Márquez Segura, E.: Exercube vs. personal trainer: evaluating a holistic, immersive, and adaptive fitness game setup. In: Proceedings of the 2019 CHI Conference on Human Factors in Computing Systems, pp. 1–15 (2019)
32. McEwen, D., Taillon-Hobson, A., Bilodeau, M., Sveistrup, H., Finestone, H.: Two-week virtual reality training for dementia: single-case feasibility study. J. Rehabil. Res. Dev. **51**(7), 1069 (2014)
33. Mirelman, A., et al.: Addition of a non-immersive virtual reality component to treadmill training to reduce fall risk in older adults (V-TIME): a randomised controlled trial. The Lancet **388**(10050), 1170–1182 (2016)
34. Muñoz, J.E., Cao, S., Boger, J.: Kinematically adaptive exergames: personalizing exercise therapy through closed-loop systems. In: 2019 IEEE International Conference on Artificial Intelligence and Virtual Reality (AIVR), pp. 118–1187. IEEE (2019)
35. Munoz, J.E., Goncalves, A., Rúbio Gouveia, É., Cameirao, M.S., Bermudez i Badia, S.: Lessons learned from gamifying functional fitness training through human-centered design methods in older adults. Games Health J. **8**(6), 387–406 (2019)
36. Okamura, H., Otani, M., Shimoyama, N., Fujii, T.: Combined exercise and cognitive training system for dementia patients: a randomized controlled trial. Dement. Geriatr. Cogn. Disord. **45**(5–6), 318–325 (2018)
37. Penedo, F.J., Dahn, J.R.: Exercise and well-being: a review of mental and physical health benefits associated with physical activity. Curr. Opin. Psychiatry **18**(2), 189–193 (2005)
38. Robinson, T.N.: Reducing children's television viewing to prevent obesity: a randomized controlled trial. JAMA **282**(16), 1561–1567 (1999)

39. Meekes, W., Stanmore, E.K.: Motivational determinants of exergame participation for older people in assisted living facilities: mixed-methods study. J. Med. Internet Res. **19**(7), e238 (2017)
40. Rosenberg, D.E., Bull, F.C., Marshall, A.L., Sallis, J.F., Bauman, A.E.: Assessment of sedentary behavior with the international physical activity questionnaire. J. Phys. Act. Health **5**(s1), S30–S44 (2008)
41. dos Santos Mendes, F.A., et al.: Motor learning, retention and transfer after virtual-reality-based training in Parkinson's disease-effect of motor and cognitive demands of games: a longitudinal, controlled clinical study. Physiotherapy **98**(3), 217–223 (2012)
42. Schell, J.: The Art of Game Design: A Book of Lenses. AK Peters/CRC Press, Natick (2019)
43. Siriaraya, P., Ang, C.S., Bobrowicz, A.: Exploring the potential of virtual worlds in engaging older people and supporting healthy aging. Behav. Inf. Technol. **33**(3), 283–294 (2014)
44. Skjæret, N., Nawaz, A., Morat, T., Schoene, D., Helbostad, J.L., Vereijken, B.: Exercise and rehabilitation delivered through exergames in older adults: an integrative review of technologies, safety and efficacy. Int. J. Med. Inform. **85**(1), 1–16 (2016)
45. Spiegel, B., et al.: Virtual reality for management of pain in hospitalized patients: a randomized comparative effectiveness trial. PLoS ONE **14**(8), e0219115 (2019)
46. American College of Sports Medicine: ACSM's Exercise Testing and Prescription. Lippincott Williams & Wilkins, Philadelphia (2017)
47. Still, B., Crane, K.: Fundamentals of User-Centered Design: A Practical Approach. CRC Press, Boca Raton (2017)
48. Vaghetti, C.A.O., Monteiro-Junior, R.S., Finco, M.D., Reategui, E., da Costa Botelho, S.S.: Exergames experience in physical education: a review. Phys. Cult. Sport. Stud. Res. **78**(1), 23–32 (2018)
49. Vseteckova, J., et al.: Barriers and facilitators to adherence to group exercise in institutionalized older people living with dementia: a systematic review. Eur. Rev. Aging Phys. Act. **15**(1), 11 (2018). https://doi.org/10.1186/s11556-018-0200-3
50. Walk, W., Görlich, D., Barrett, M.: Design, dynamics, experience (DDE): an advancement of the MDA framework for game design. In: Korn, O., Lee, N. (eds.) Game Dynamics, pp. 27–45. Springer, Cham (2017). https://doi.org/10.1007/978-3-319-53088-8_3
51. Yeşilyaprak, S.S., Yıldırım, M.Ş., Tomruk, M., Ertekin, Ö., Algun, Z.C.: Comparison of the effects of virtual reality-based balance exercises and conventional exercises on balance and fall risk in older adults living in nursing homes in Turkey. Physiother. Theory Pract. **32**(3), 191–201 (2016)
52. Zeng, N., Pope, Z., Lee, J.E., Gao, Z.: A systematic review of active video games on rehabilitative outcomes among older patients. J. Sport Health Sci. **6**(1), 33–43 (2017)

Applying Social Gamification in a Gamified Point System

Boyang Liu$^{(\boxtimes)}$ and Jiro Tanaka

Waseda University, Fukuoka, Japan
waseda-liuboyang@moegi.waseda.jp, jiro@aoni.waseda.jp

Abstract. User engagement measures whether users find value in a product or service, which is highly correlated with overall profitability. If users choose to spend their time on a particular application or website, it means that they found value in it. This allows businesses to monetize products or services through advertising, subscriptions or sales. To increase user engagement, it is necessary to meet user needs to improve their experience. Recently, gamification has become increasingly popular because it applies game mechanics to non-gaming environment like education and shopping to attract and motivate participants. In this paper, we explore using social gamification in a gamified point system. In particular, we focus on two types of user interaction, namely competitive and non-competitive interaction. In preliminary experiments, we obtained positive results from the experimenters.

Keywords: Competitive and non-competitive interaction ·
Gamification · Social incentives · Motivation · User engagement

1 Introduction

User engagement is an assessment of an individual's response to a certain product (such as a product, service, or website), which is considered an important aspect of user experience [1]. An individual's degree of engagement may be determined directly through interaction or may be assessed through observation of the user's behaviors. A website user, for example, might click links, comment, download documents and watch videos, among other possibilities [2]. Highly engaged users are more likely to buy, return, and share the product or service with friends [3]. By improving engagement, the product's profitability can be improved. Therefore, user engagement is very important for commerce [9,10].

Some factors are considered important components to increase user engagement. One factor is to find out what users consider valuable [3]. For news sites, users may find value in the process of being knowledgeable, elated or outraged. For social media applications, it might be a hit of dopamine upon feeling socially connected. It is important to identify these critical moments and consider product changes that provide more variation.

© Springer Nature Switzerland AG 2020
X. Fang (Ed.): HCII 2020, LNCS 12211, pp. 148–161, 2020.
https://doi.org/10.1007/978-3-030-50164-8_10

Offer and incentive programs are also a frequently used method [4]. To increase engagement and retention, users need to be motivated to use the application. An example is reward program of Starbucks. Starbucks offers one of the most sought-after loyalty programs 'Starbucks Rewards' program that offers freebies and discounts to members giving them plenty of reasons to choose Starbucks over other players [5].

Financial incentives may not be the only reason that engages people. Social media marketing is a common way to increase user engagement nowadays. Since the dawn of social media, brands have been trying interact with potential customers in a two-way conversation [6]. Companies want to engage and interact by personalizing their consumers' online experience. Besides, previous research suggests that social incentives, such as a team weight-loss challenge and cash incentives based on group participation may keep participants engaged longer [7]. The peer pressure of being part of a team, desire to win in the competition, and encouragement from others are also motivating factors that can increase participation.

In summary, value, incentive program and social features are of great significance for user engagement.

A loyalty program is an example of user engagement designed to keep customers engaged to continue shopping or use the services associated with the program by providing financial rewards [8]. A very common type of loyalty program is the point system [11]. Customer purchases toward a certain amount of points to redeem the reward while retailers can collect personal data to profile the customers, maximizing the profitability of the promotional and pricing strategies [12].

Although they have proven to be valuable incentive programs, loyalty programs, including the point systems, need to be improved. According to The Loyalty Report 2017, customers belong to an average of 13.4 loyalty programs, but are active in only 6.7 programs [13]. Similarly, research finds that 54% of loyalty memberships are inactive with 28% of customers abandoning the loyalty programs without redeeming points [14]. One of the main reason is that these programs do not offer enough value to customers [15]. Offering customers 1% cash back on purchases, oftentimes does little to excite customers enough to change their buying behaviour and it was found the sweet spot when it comes to balancing business goals with high value rewards is around 5%. For preferred clients, 10% is often more than enough to motivate loyalty [15]. In addition, social feature is becoming increasingly important [16,17].

In our research, we explore social gamification, which uses social features and behaviors to amplify gamification effects, in a gamified point system to provide social connection between users [12]. Social connection is the experience of feeling close and connected to others [18]. It involves feeling loved, cared for, and valued, and forms the basis of interpersonal relationships. It is understood as a core human need, and the desire to connect as a fundamental drive [19] [20]. The purpose of the study is to explore whether social connections between users help promote user engagement. Specifically, we mainly focus on whether competitive and non-competitive interactions can positively impact user engagement.

For this purpose, we built a prototype of a gamified point system. The theme of raising pets was chosen in the proposed system because it can create a relaxing and pleasant environment for user interaction.

New input (mission) is added in the gamified point system. To reward users for value-creating activities in shopping, we have designed new feedback including value point, pet and virtual food as new outputs. When the user completes the mission according to the instructions, the user will get a certain value point, and the level of his pet will be improved. Value point can be used to exchange virtual food and can be used to help pets recover energy. After some time, the pet's status will decrease, which means that the user needs to feed it. This constitutes a simple cycle. Users need to constantly get value points in exchange for virtual foods to keep pets healthy. Based on these game elements, our system provides users with social connections, including competitive and non-competitive interactions, to stimulate user engagement. Users can interact with each other by giving away virtual food or competing with pets. After that, we conducted an experiment. Users experienced the gamified system and filled out a questionnaire. From the experimental results of the questionnaire, we got positive evaluation from the experimenters.

This article is organized as follows. In Sect. 1, the introduction is presented. Section 2 presents related work. Section 3 and Sect. 4 introduces the design and implementation of proposed system. In Sect. 5, we present our preliminary evaluation results. In Sect. 6, we make a conclusion and come up with some ideas about our future work.

2   Related Work

In this section, we discuss previous research in the areas of point system, social influence, gamification, and augmented reality game.

2.1   Point System

Enzmann et al. [21] think that users refuse to use point system because they may fear an invasion of privacy. Therefore, they present two variants of a privacy-friendly loyalty system to be used by online vendors for issuing points. In the study of Coskun et al. [22], the design of Near Field Communication (NFC) enabled loyalty system on smart cards of NFC mobiles and development details are presented. NFC technology is a short-range, high frequency, and low bandwidth wireless technology which occurs between two devices within few centimetres. With this model, loyalty and payment applications share and exchange valuable information through NFC Loyal Database system on smart card. Lim et al. [23] study online loyalty programs from a searchability perspective. The goal of their research is to explain how searchability can influence participation in loyalty programs. All above research aims at increasing user engagement through utilitarian motives such as improving the security, convenience and functionality of current point system. Our research focus on enhancing symbolic motives, which are related to needs for self-esteem and social approval.

2.2 Gamification

Gamification refers to the application of using game design elements and game mechanisms in a non-game contexts to enable users to solve problems and improve the contribution of users [28]. Commonly, gamification employs game design elements to improve organizational productivity, user engagement and more. Lots of research about gamification indicates that a majority of studies on gamification reveal that it exerts good effect on individuals. The gamification techniques are aiming at leveraging peoples natural desires for achievement, competition, socializing or simply their response to the framing of a situation as game or play. Li et al. [29] design a gamified multiplayer software tutorial system called CADament. Compared with existing gamified software tutorial systems, their system generates engaging learning experience through competitions. Their study shows that their system has an advantage over pre-authored tutorials for improving learners performance, increasing motivation, and stimulating knowledge transfer. In the paper of Dergousoff et al. [30], they think classic ways of gathering data on human behavior are timeconsuming, costly and are subject to limited participant pools. Therefore, they combine both gamification and crowdsourcing techniques into a smartphone-based platform to motivate voluntary participation and provide researchers with a framework that can be used to investigate multiple research questions without the need to develop costly specialized games. For the purpose of inspiring customers, some ideas of combining game and marketing are proposed to engage customers. Zichermann et al. [31] thought that traditional advertising is losing effectiveness as competition for consumer attention and game playing is on the rise and vying for customers attention. Gamification is also used in education and health. Arawjo et al. [32] present a puzzle game that builds student understanding of programming concepts. Their results from a lab study demonstrate that novices can learn programming concepts by playing the game and the game was well received. In the paper of Zhao et al. [33], they present the design and findings of a study on the motivational effects of using activity tracker based games to promote daily exercise. The results of their study show that participants preferred the gamified exercise experience over regular exercises and features related to social factors played a relatively more important role in this game experience. The above research shows that gamification is a universal and effective means to increase user engagement. Our system incorporates gamification elements to enhance user experience.

2.3 Social Impact

The social impact is particularly significant in commerce. For example, many people read what other people think about products by logging on to social media sites before making a purchase. Social media users trust what their friends, family, and even strangers say online about a brand or product. Instore shopping decisions are also affected, as customers use their mobile devices to look at reviews and ratings to reinforce their purchasing decisions [24]. Lee et al. [25]

proposed a multi-phased model for internet shopping, which fully takes the characteristics of the internet and cyber shopping into consideration in their paper. Their results indicate that diverse communication affects the level of trust. If customers share more values with other customers and if they have more diverse means of communication, they would intend to revisit the site more repeatedly. In the study of Zhu et al. [26], they designed and ran an experiment to measure social influence in online recommender systems. Their results show that social influence could sway peoples own choices significantly. Li et al. [27] found that emotion played a significant role in the mobile consumption experience in their research. They suggest that attention should be paid on the social communication process between humans to improve consumption experience. The above research shows that social influence has a positive effect in commerce. Our research is based on the combination of social influences and commerce. Specifically, we have designed two kinds of user interactions in our system to study how different social types affect user engagement.

3   System Design

3.1   System Overview

Our system is designed based on current point system: 1) Users can earn points by purchasing goods; 2) The redemption rate of the gamified system is the same as the current system. We propose a multi-user approach based on game design in the system to improve user engagement. A theme of keeping pets is selected in the proposed system, because 1) pets can be used to reflect the status of users; 2) as it is easier to exchange virtual food in the game, users can obtain satisfaction from accumulating value points; 3) the theme of pet raising can create a relaxing and pleasant social environment for multi-user interaction.

In the current point system, shopping is input and point is output. Point can be used as a financial incentive to motivate users to purchase, but they cannot support value creation in shopping. For example, environmental enthusiasts may want to buy energy saving lamps because it is good for the environment, not because it accumulates more points. Therefore, we design a gamified point system based on the current system framework. As shown in the Fig. 1, the solid line part represents the current system framework, and the dotted line part is our new design. Our system consists of several game elements including mission, value point, pet and virtual food. Mission is the goal for shopping. To motivate users to complete mission, value points, pets, and virtual food are designed.

The mission is to remind users to create value in shopping. It is given during shopping and confirmed at checkout. If a user selects one mission that requires the user to buy low-calorie food, the information obtained by scanning the barcode of the product will be used to confirm whether the mission is completed or not. Users are free to choose different mission they are interested in.

Feedback is designed based on the pet. In our system, every user can feed a pet. The pet will get experience value (EXP) if the user completes the mission. If the EXP of the pet reaches the threshold, the pet will level up. Therefore, the

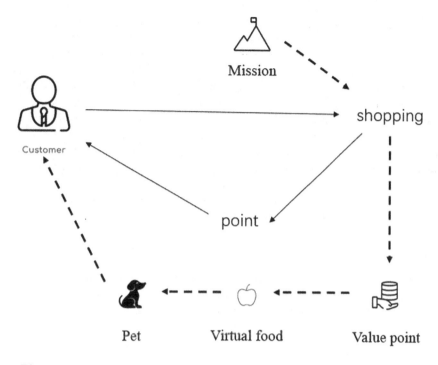

Fig. 1. The process of shopping when users use the gamified point system.

level of the pet reflects the status of the user. The pet also has energy and it gradually loses. The user needs to feed the pet with virtual food. Virtual food is purchased with value point. Value point comes from mission completion. This constitutes a loop that encourages users to complete mission.

3.2   User Interaction

In our design, we use user interaction to attract users and help them create value in shopping. We explore two modes to motivate users, competitive and non-competitive interactions.

3.3   Competitive Interaction

In the competitive interaction mode, users can compete with other users through the network. Figure 2 shows a scenario where three users participate in a competitive interaction. Each user has a smartphone with a gamified point system. When three users want to participate in the competitive interaction, they can join the competition room at different places. When everyone joins the room, the match result based on the level information will be displayed in the competitive interaction interface. It motivates users to continuously improve their pets to win the game.

To this end, we have designed user interfaces for competitive interaction across the network. In this interface, users can see their pets. When each user joins the competitive interaction room, the gamified system will obtain the level information from the database and display it as the pet level. In this interface, our system will give ranking results. Specifically, when the first user joins a room, a new room is automatically created and a pet with level information will be displayed. When subsequent users join the room, the room and pet information will be synchronized. When there is more than one user in the room, the system will give a ranking result based on their level. If there are two users in the room, the higher-level pet will have a golden crown over it head. If three or more users are in the room, the system will display golden, silver and bronze crowns on top of pets ranked first to third. Figure 3 shows a scenario where three users participate in a competitive interaction.

3.4 Non-competitive Interaction

Non-competitive interaction is important in social relationships. In some multiplayer games, users can engage in non-competitive interactions, such as collaboration, sharing resources, or sending gifts to friends. In our system, users

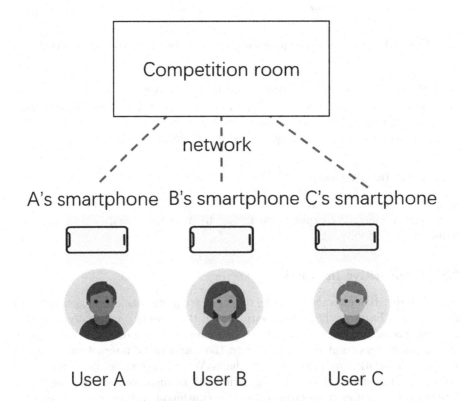

Fig. 2. Three users enter the competition room for cross-network competitive interaction.

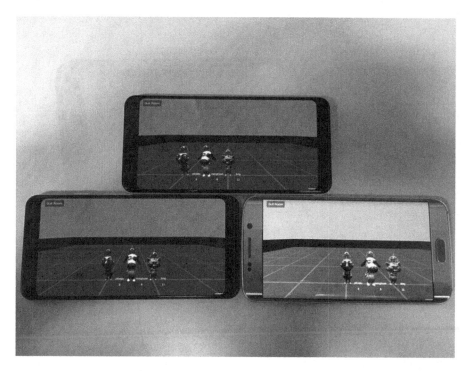

Fig. 3. Competitive interaction interface after three users join the competition room. The user name and pet level are displayed to the right of the pet. The system will give ranking result according to pet's level and display the crown with corresponding color on pet's head.

can socialize in a non-competitive way, in which users can give virtual food to friends (see Fig. 4). Value points can be used to buy virtual food, which is a reward for completing mission. Such a design motivates users to get satisfaction from exchanging rewards.

Users can purchase virtual food with value points in the non-competitive interaction interface by clicking the value points. When value points are spent, the volume decreases. The virtual food will be displayed in the interface. Users can click virtual food to feed their pets or give it to their friends. If the user chooses to feed his pet, the pet will get a certain amount of energy and do some action. If the user gives food to a friend, the virtual food will disappear. The recipient will be able to see a virtual food displayed on the interface with a label indicating who gave the gift.

Both designs attempt to engage users through interactions between users. In the competition mode, users can gain a sense of accomplishment from defeating other users. In the non-competitive interaction mode, users can gain the joy of accumulating value points by sharing the virtual food with their friends.

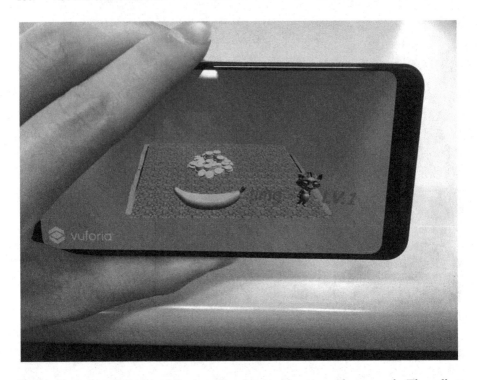

Fig. 4. Users can click virtual food and send it to others over the network. The yellow coins are value points. Banana is the virtual food. The user name is on the left of the pet, and level information is on the right. (Color figure online)

4   Implementation

The main hardware devices used for the development of our prototype system include a tablet PC and a smartphone. Windows 10 Home Edition is installed in the tablet PC. The processor is Intel(R) Core(TM) i7-6500U CPU @2.50 GHz 2.59 GHz. The RAM is 8.00 GB. The development software is Unity 2017.2.0f3 (64-bit), a cross-platform game engine. Unity 3D is used to build and render our threedimensional system. Vuforia SDK is used for augmented reality implementation, which uses computer vision technology to recognize and track images. After recognizing the image of point card on the smartphone, virtual objects created in Unity 3D will be superimposed on the smartphone. After that, users can see the 3D objects and interact with them. Photon Unity Networking is used to implement the competitive interaction. It is a Unity package for multiplayer games. Its matchmaking gets players into rooms where objects can be synced over the network. Models and text are synchronized across the network, enabling multiple users to compete at different place. As for the database, we used WampServer Version 3.0.6 32bit consisting of the Apache web server, OpenSSL for SSL support, MySQL database and PHP programming language. Apach and MySQL are always running on the server. Communication between the mobile devices and the server is implemented in PHP.

Our system is implemented based on client-server network structure. Gamified point system will be deployed on mobile device as a client. The retailers can manage and update user information in the server. Users access data when registering their own information and obtaining their information from database. We use the WWW class and the WWWForm class to send and receive data from Unity. When receiving from the database, the information is converted to JSON format and received. After receiving it on the Unity side, it is decoded into a string format.

5   Preliminary Evaluation

In this section, we introduce preliminary evaluation and analysis of results. We asked participants to do online shopping using our gamified point system. The main purpose of this research was to test whether our system can provide interesting feedback during shopping, thereby providing a good shopping experience for users, and whether the interaction of our system is easy to use because they are important factors to engage users. We will also discuss the feedback received from the survey.

5.1   Participants

We invited 5 participants (3 females and 2 males) from 20 to 27 years of age. All participants have basic computer skills. All of them have experience with online multiplayer games. All of them have experience using the current point system.

5.2   Methods

All participants were given a brief introduction of the system for approximately 5 min. Before each study, we introduced participants to the basic operating procedures of the system for approximately 10 min. First, users browsed the mission interface in the gamified system. Then they opened the shopping website through the link provided in the system. On the shopping website, users can complete the corresponding mission by purchasing products that meet the requirements. When users wanted to complete the mission of purchasing environmentally friendly products, they can choose products with an eco label. If users wanted to complete the mission of purchasing a local product, he can browse the information of the place where the goods are produced. Completing health-related mission required users to purchase products that meet health food standards. At checkout, the mission in the system was checked and the information in the database was updated. After that, users can use the point card and their smartphones to make user interaction in both competitive and non-competitive ways.

After the participants became familiar with the operation process, we asked them to use the gamified point system for approximately 15 min to make a complete shopping experiment.

After the shopping experiment, the participants were asked to fill in a questionnaire. The questionnaire has following 7 questions with 5-point Likert scale (1 - Strongly Disagree, 2 - Disagree, 3 - Neutral, 4 - Agree, 5 - Strongly Agree).

1. The system is easy to use.
2. The interaction with the pet is useful or interesting.
3. The feedback for shopping is useful or interesting.
4. I can easily interact with other users in the system.
5. I can easily understand my shopping target in the system.
6. I can feel the emotional connection in the system.
7. The system can provide a good shopping experience.

5.3   Results

The results are shown in Fig. 5. Question 1, 2 and 3 are used to test the ease of use and usability of the system. They mainly concern whether it's easy to use the system. The average score of question 1 is 4.8. The results prove that the system is easy to operate. Question 2 is used to test the usability of the pet-based interaction, The average score of question 2 is 4.4, the results shows that participants agree that interaction with pet is useful. Question 3 is used to test the usability of the feedback for shopping, The average score is 4.6. All the results show that the gamified system is still easy to use after adding new game elements.

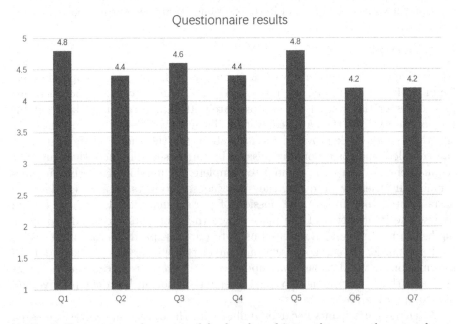

Fig. 5. Users can purchase virtual food and send it to others over the network.

Questions 4, 5, 6 and 7 are used to determine whether our system can give users a good shopping experience. The average score of question 4, 5, 6, 7 is 4.4, 4.8, 4.2 and 4.2. The results shows that participants agree that using our system can easily interact with other users, understand what they need to do and get a good shopping experience. The question 4 shows that our system supports user interaction well. The question 5 is about the guiding value of the mission. The results prove that users agree with the value of the mission. The question 6 shows that pet-based gamification design establishes an emotional connection between users and the system. The question 7 reflects that users recognize the value of the gamified system for improving the shopping experience. One participant believes that using our system can better promote user engagement compared to the current point system. Current point systems usually encourage users to spend through reward point, but it cannot establish a connection between the user and the system. Our gamification system uses pets as intermediaries to build a bridge between users and the system, and provides possibilities for user-to-user interaction.

Overall, we got a positive feedback through the preliminary user study.

6   Conclusion and Future Work

In this paper, a gamified point system on mobile devices is introduced. Gamified point system presents a method for engaging users using multiplayer game design. As an important advantage over current point system, each user can participate in a game experience to interact with others.

In the future, we want to investigate other important elements multiplayer games, such as collaboration and team work and further investigate the effects of each game element. In addition, we hope to further objectively evaluate the effectiveness of our gamified point system by conducting some experiments. First we will compare our gamified point system with baseline condition if our system increases engagement and duration by evaluating usage. We will then evaluate the game elements in the system. We will evaluate three mission (buying local goods, buying low-calorie food, and buying recyclable goods) by assessing the completion rate. Types of pets (cat, dog, turtle) will be evaluated to understand the impact of the pet. We will evaluate variation of user interactions to study the impact of different interactions.

References

1. Hung, Y.H., Parsons, P.: Assessing user engagement in information visualization. In: Proceedings of the 2017 CHI Conference Extended Abstracts on Human Factors in Computing Systems, pp. 1708–1717. ACM (2017)
2. User engagement. https://whatis.techtarget.com/definition/user-engagement. Accessed 8 Jan 2020
3. What is user engagement. https://mixpanel.com/topics/what-is-user-engagement/. Accessed 8 Jan 2020

4. 5 Methods for increasing app engagement & user retention. https://clearbridgemobile.com/5-methods-for-increasing-app-engagement-user-retention/. Accessed 9 Jan 2020

5. Starbucks rewards case study. https://zinrelo.com/loyalty-rewards-case-study-new-starbucks-rewards-program.html. Accessed 9 Jan 2020

6. Social media marketing: the importance of a two-way conversation. https://www.impactbnd.com/blog/social-media-marketing-the-importance-of-a-two-way-conversation. Accessed 9 Jan 2020

7. Increase participation with social incentives. https://blog.wellsource.com/increase-participation-social-incentives. Accessed 9 Jan 2020

8. Loyalty program, Wikipedia contributors, Wikipedia, The Free Encyclopedia. https://en.wikipedia.org/wiki/Loyalty_program. Accessed 10 Jan 2020

9. Practical tips to develop user engagement for e-commerce website. https://www.optimizesmart.com/practical-tips-develop-user-engagement-e-commerce-site/. Accessed 10 Jan 2020

10. What is customer engagement, and why is it important? https://blog.smile.io/what-is-customer-engagement-and-why-is-it-important. Accessed 10 Jan 2020

11. Magatef, S.G., Tomalieh, E.F.: The impact of customer loyalty programs on customer retention. Int. J. Bus. Soc. Sci. **6**(8), 78–93 (2015)

12. Liu, B., Tanaka, J.: Gamified point system based on mobile devices. In: The Twelfth International Conference on Advances in Computer-Human Interactions, pp. 174–180 (2019)

13. 17 Staggering customer loyalty stats that will change your perspective. https://www.claruscommerce.com/blog/17-staggering-customer-loyalty-stats-that-will-change-your-perspective/. Accessed 10 Jan 2020

14. How to set up an ecommerce loyalty program to improve retention, build community and drive 5X in sales. https://www.bigcommerce.com/blog/online-customer-loyalty-programs/#ideas-for-designing-a-great-ecommerce-loyalty-program. Accessed 10 Jan 2020

15. The reasons why loyalty programs fail. http://www.theloyaltybox.com/blog/step1-design-planning/why-loyalty-programs-fail/. Accessed 10 Jan 2020

16. Why the best loyalty programs use social media. https://www.socialandloyal.com/why-the-best-loyalty-programs-use-social-media/. Accessed 10 Jan 2020

17. How social media can enhance loyalty programs. https://makewebbetter.com/blog/seven-ways-enhance-social-media-loyalty-programs/. Accessed 10 Jan 2020

18. Social connection, Wikipedia contributors. Social connection. Wikipedia, The Free Encyclopedia. https://en.wikipedia.org/wiki/Social_connection. Accessed 10 Jan 2020

19. Baumeister, R.F., Leary, M.R.: The need to belong: desire for interpersonal attachments as a fundamental human motivation. Psychol. Bull. **117**(3), 497 (1995)

20. Lieberman, M.D.: Social: Why Our Brains Are Wired To Connect. Oxford University Press, Oxford (2015)

21. Enzmann, M., Schneider, M.: Improving customer retention in e-commerce through a secure and privacy-enhanced loyalty system. Inf. Syst. Front. **7**(4–5), 359–370 (2005)

22. Coskun, V., Ozdenizci, B., Ok, K., et al.: Design and development of NFC enabled loyalty system. In: Proceedings of the 6th International Conference of Advanced Computer Systems and Networks: Design and Application, Lviv, Ukraine, pp. 16–18 (2013)

23. Lim, S., Lee, B.: Online loyalty programs viewed from a searchability perspective. In: Proceedings of the 14th Annual International Conference on Electronic Commerce, pp. 255–262. ACM (2012)
24. Kim, Y., Srivastava, J.: Impact of social influence in e-commerce decision making. In: Proceedings of the Ninth International Conference on Electronic Commerce, pp. 293–302. ACM (2007)
25. Lee, J., Kim, J., Moon, J.Y.: What makes Internet users visit cyber stores again? Key design factors for customer loyalty. In: Proceedings of the SIGCHI Conference on Human Factors in Computing Systems, pp. 305–312. ACM (2000)
26. Zhu, H., Huberman, B., Luon, Y.: To switch or not to switch: understanding social influence in online choices. In: Proceedings of the SIGCHI Conference on Human Factors in Computing Systems, pp. 2257–2266. ACM (2012)
27. Li, M., Dong, Z.Y., Chen, X.: Factors influencing consumption experience of mobile commerce: a study from experiential view. Internet Res. **22**(2), 120–141 (2012)
28. Huotari, K., Hamari, J.: Defining gamification: a service marketing perspective. In: Proceeding of the 16th International Academic MindTrek Conference, pp. 17–22. ACM (2012)
29. Li, W., Grossman, T., Fitzmaurice, G.: CADament: a gamified multiplayer software tutorial system. In: Proceedings of the SIGCHI Conference on Human Factors in Computing Systems, pp. 3369–3378. ACM (2014)
30. Dergousoff, K., Mandryk, R.L.: Mobile gamification for crowdsourcing data collection: leveraging the freemium model. In: Proceedings of the 33rd Annual ACM Conference on Human Factors in Computing Systems, pp. 1065–1074. ACM (2015)
31. Zichermann, G., Linder, J.: Game-Based Marketing: Inspire Customer Loyalty Through Rewards, Challenges, and Contests. Wiley, New York (2010)
32. Arawjo, I., Wang, C.Y., Myers, A.C., et al.: Teaching programming with gamified semantics. In: Proceedings of the 2017 CHI Conference on Human Factors in Computing Systems, pp. 4911–4923. ACM (2017)
33. Zhao, Z., Arya, A., Whitehead, A., et al.: Keeping users engaged through feature updates: a long-term study of using wearable-based exergames. In: CHI, pp. 1053–1064. ACM (2017)

The Impact of Fulfilling a Desire for Idealism on Task Engagement and Enjoyment in Digital Games

Owen Schaffer[1]($\boxtimes$) and Xiaowen Fang[2]

[1] Computer Science and Information Systems, Bradley University, 1501 W Bradley Avenue, Peoria, IL 61625, USA
Owen.Schaffer@gmail.com

[2] College of Computing and Digital Media, DePaul University, 243 South Wabash Avenue, Chicago, IL 60604, USA
XFang@cdm.depaul.edu

Abstract. For practitioners and researchers who want to design for enjoyment, empirical research on what makes digital games enjoyable is critical. This is true for Game Design, Gamification of non-game applications, and Serious Games with a purpose beyond enjoyment. But existing theories are incomplete or lacking empirical support. A Desire Fulfillment Theory of digital game enjoyment is proposed, building on three established theories: Expectancy Disconfirmation Theory, Basic Human Desires Theory, and Flow Theory. Desire Fulfillment Theory suggests systems that fulfill users' basic human desires will maximize enjoyment. An online survey of 315 game players was conducted, focusing on the last digital game they played. Idealism, a desire to improve society, stood out as having the greatest impact (highest R^2) on the Task Engagement (flow not including enjoyment) factors Concentration and Sense of Control among the factors tested, and greater Task Engagement in turn increased Enjoyment. Multiple linear regression results support the proposed model with minor revisions. The revised model shows how Clear Proximal Goals, Immediate Progress Feedback, and Desire Fulfillment: Idealism lead to Task Engagement and Enjoyment. This is the first empirical evidence the authors are aware of that fulfilling a desire for Idealism leads to Task Engagement and Enjoyment in digital games. Implications for theory and practice are discussed.

Keywords: Enjoyment · Desire fulfillment · Idealism · Task engagement · Flow · Intrinsic motivation · Game design · Gamification · Serious games · Computer games · Digital games

1 Introduction and Related Work

The US video game industry reached record revenues of \$43.4 billion in 2018, up 20.5% from the year before [1]. Digital games are interactive, computer-based systems that present users with a series of goal-directed, challenging tasks to complete for the enjoyment the tasks provide. Digital games are games played on a computerized device,

© Springer Nature Switzerland AG 2020
X. Fang (Ed.): HCII 2020, LNCS 12211, pp. 162–178, 2020.
https://doi.org/10.1007/978-3-030-50164-8_11

such as a video game console, Personal Computer (PC), smartphone, or on the Internet. Enjoyment is the extent to which people positively evaluate their experience.

But there is little to no scientific consensus about what leads to that positive experience of enjoyment when people play digital games. Research on digital game enjoyment is still in its infancy, with scattered and incomplete theories that are either not supported by empirical research showing they lead to enjoyment such as Caillois's categories of games [2], Bartle's four player types [3], and Lazarro's Four Keys to Fun [4, 5], or do not provide a comprehensive model of what leads to enjoyment such as Self-Determination Theory [6], Player Experience of Needs Satisfaction (PENS) [7], Flow Theory [8], the Game Engagement Questionnaire [9], Yee's model of motivations to play online games [10, 11], Malone's model of intrinsically motivating educational games [12, 13], the Player Experience (PLEX) Framework [14], and the taxonomy of gameplay enjoyment from Quick et al. [15]. The proposed research aims to fill that gap in the literature.

A more extensive review of the literature on what makes games enjoyable has been conducted by the authors, summarizing 61 relevant peer-reviewed research articles and papers and categorizing them into 12 topic areas [16].

Understanding what makes digital games enjoyable is important not only for video and computer game designers, but also for practitioners of Gamification and designers of Serious Games as well. Gamification is "the use of game design elements in non-game contexts" [17], such as to make non-game systems more game like and enjoyable. Serious games are "full-fledged games for non-entertainment purposes" [17], such as education, exercise, or persuasion.

When users experience more enjoyment, which is by definition a more positive experience, it follows logically that they will be more likely to come back for more of that positive experience. This user behavior of coming back for more could translate into more sales, repeat sales, expanded market share, employee retention for a gamified business system, successful behavior change for a persuasive game, or better learning outcomes for an educational game. This is why design for enjoyment is so important.

Design for enjoyment is the common thread across Game Design, Gamification, and Serious Games. To engineer enjoyable systems, practitioners need empirical research on what makes digital games enjoyable. The present study will advance our knowledge of how to design for enjoyment, which is important to practitioners in the fields of Game Design, Human-Computer Interaction, and Information Systems.

The central research question guiding this research is: what leads to digital game enjoyment? A theory of desire fulfillment is proposed, hypothesizing that digital game enjoyment is a function of individual differences in desire to fulfill 16 basic human desires and how well the experience of playing the game fulfills each of those basic human desires. The more a game fulfills the basic human desires of players, the more that players will experience enjoyment. This Desire Fulfillment Theory is based on three established theories, Oliver's Expectancy Disconfirmation Theory [18, 19], Reiss's Basic Human Desires Theory [20], and Csikszentmihalyi's Flow Theory [8, 21]. A Desire Fulfillment Model of Digital Game Enjoyment is presented based on the proposed Desire Fulfillment Theory (see Fig. 1 below).

While all 16 of the basic desires Reiss proposed were investigated, the survey used in this study asked participants to indicate with checkboxes which desires were relevant to their experience and then answer only questions about the relevant desires. As a result, there was not enough overlap in the data to allow the desires to be analyzed together, and the desires had to be analyzed one at a time. Given the length limit, we chose to address one desire in detail in this paper.

This paper focuses on the desire for Idealism, the desire to improve society (including public service, altruism, and social justice), the desire that had the greatest impact (highest R^2) on the Task Engagement factors Concentration and Sense of Control, which in turn had the greatest impact on Enjoyment. Giving people a sense they are having a positive impact on society or making the world a better place leads to greater Concentration and Sense of Control, which in turn leads to greater Enjoyment. Fulfilling the Idealism desire had not only a statistically significant impact, but the greatest impact on Task Engagement among the factors tested. This suggests that a basic human desire for Idealism is rarely fulfilled when people play games, but when it is that desire fulfillment leads to more Task Engagement and thereby more Enjoyment. The present research contributes both to the theory and practice of designing interactive systems for enjoyment.

2   Framework, Model, and Hypotheses

Desire Fulfillment Theory is presented as a new theory to explain enjoyment of digital games, integrating concepts from Oliver's Expectancy Disconfirmation Theory [18, 19], Reiss's Basic Human Desires Theory [20], and Csikszentmihalyi's Flow Theory [8, 21]. The premise of Desire Fulfillment Theory is that human enjoyment results from the fulfillment of basic human desires. As a result, enjoyment is a function of individual desire or motivation and the experience of desire fulfillment for each basic human desire.

Expectancy Disconfirmation Theory states that Expectations and Disconfirmation of Expectations (which ranges from the experience being worse than expected to better than expected) are two separate independent factors, both positively related to Satisfaction. Satisfaction is synonymous with Enjoyment, with both terms meaning how positively a person evaluates their experience.

The relationships of Expectancy Disconfirmation Theory (EDT) were adapted to each of Reiss's 16 desires, and this was expanded on to create a Desire Fulfillment Model of Digital Game Enjoyment [22]. The version of the Desire Fulfillment Model as it is applied to the desire for Idealism is shown in Fig. 1 below.

Desire and Desire Fulfillment were hypothesized to have independent effects on Enjoyment, just as Expectation and Disconfirmation of Expectations have independent effects on Satisfaction.

Task Engagement is defined as all flow indicators (factors that indicate a person is in flow) not including Enjoyment. This was done to avoid the circular logic of Enjoyment leading to Enjoyment.

When Usability is high, there are less usability problems getting in the way of the user smoothly going from one task to the next, which is necessary to experience Task Engagement. So, it was hypothesized that users who perceive greater system Usability will be more likely to report greater Task Engagement. Flow Theory suggests that flow will be higher when Clear Proximal Goals and Immediate Progress Feedback are higher, and these were hypothesized to be sub-dimensions of Usability.

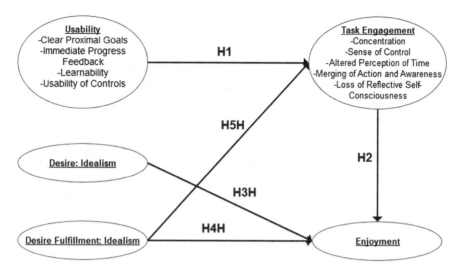

Fig. 1. Desire Fulfillment Model for Idealism showing hypothesized relationships.

Based on the above Desire Fulfillment Model for Idealism (Fig. 1), the following five hypotheses were proposed:

- H1: Usability is positively associated with Task Engagement
- H2: Task Engagement is positively associated with Enjoyment
- H3H: Desire for Idealism is positively associated with Enjoyment
- H4H: Fulfillment of Desire for Idealism is positively associated with Enjoyment
- H5H: Fulfillment of Desire for Idealism is positively associated with Task Engagement.

3 Method

An online survey of digital game players was conducted to test the proposed hypotheses. Previously validated Likert scale measures were adapted to test these hypotheses. Multiple linear regression was used to analyze the data.

3.1 Measures

The questionnaire measures used in this study ask participants about their experience playing the game they named as the last digital game they played for longer than thirty minutes. Participants were asked how much they agree with each statement on a seven-point Likert scale ranging from "Strongly Disagree" to "Strongly Agree" with each scale point labeled.

An 11-item *Enjoyment Questionnaire* was adapted from the authors' previous study of flow in games [23]. This measure includes five items adapted from the Interest-Enjoyment subscale of the Intrinsic Motivation Inventory (IMI), a previously validated measure of enjoyment [24]. Sample items include, "I enjoyed this game very much",

"Playing this game was rewarding in itself", and the reverse-scored "I wished I was doing something else".

A 33-item *Task Engagement Questionnaire* was adapted from the author's previous study of flow in games [23]. In that previous study, the factors that lead to flow, or the flow conditions, were separated from the factors that indicate how much a person is in flow, or the flow indicators. Task Engagement includes all flow indicators except for Autotelic Experience, which is synonymous with Enjoyment. This was done to avoid the circular logic of Enjoyment leading to Enjoyment. In addition, Task Engagement includes only flow indicators; it does not include any flow conditions, or the factors that lead to flow. This measure is made up of five sub-dimensions: Effortless Concentration, Altered Perception of Time, Loss of Self-Consciousness, Merging of Action & Awareness, and Sense of Control. Sample items include, "My attention was focused entirely on the game that I was playing", "It felt like time went by quickly", "I was not concerned with what others may have been thinking of me", "I played the game without thinking about trying to do so", and "I felt that I had everything under control".

A 25-item *Usability Questionnaire* was made up of three measures drawn from the literature and two measures from a previous study the author conducted. The factor structure and reliability of each of these measures has been validated by previous research. The 10-item System Usability Scale [25–27] was adapted to the context of digital games. The 4-item measure of Perceived Ease of Use was adapted from the Technology Acceptance Model [28]. The 3-item measure of Intuitive Controls was adapted from the Player Experience of Needs Satisfaction measure [7]. A 4-item measure of Clear Proximal Goals and a 4-item measure of Immediate Progress Feedback were adapted from the author's previous study on flow in games [23]. These two Flow Conditions are specific aspects of system usability that lead to flow or Task Engagement [8, 23]. Specifically, Clear Proximal Goals refers to how well players know what to do next throughout the game, and Immediate Progress Feedback is how much players know how well they are playing the game. Sample items from the 25-item Usability measure include, "I thought the controls of the game were easy to use" "I found it easy to get the game to do what I wanted it to do using the controls of the game" "My next steps were clearly defined" and "It was really clear to me how I was doing in the game."

A *Desire Fulfillment Questionnaire* and a *Desire Questionnaire*, each with 132 items, were adapted from the *Reiss Profile of Fundamental Goals and Motivation Sensitivities* [29]. Reiss and Havercamp [29, 30] validated the factor structure and reliability of Reiss's Profile. Sample items include, "Making the world a better place is one of my most important life goals". (Desire: Idealism) and, "Playing this game more than fulfilled my desire to feel like I was serving the public". (Desire Fulfillment: Idealism). To avoid fatigue, participants were only asked to fill out the desire questions for the desires that they indicated were relevant or applicable to their experience (see Procedure subsection below). The full measures are presented in the Appendices A-G of the first author's dissertation [22].

3.2 Instrument Validation

As described in the *Measures* subsection above, these measures were adapted from previously validated measures. No new measures or scales were constructed for this study. Instead, previously validated measures were adapted to fit the context of digital games and aims of this study. Factor analysis and reliability analysis were conducted to ensure and double-check the construct validity and internal consistency of the measures used since that the measures were adapted in this way.

Factor analysis was conducted with PROMAX rotation and Maximum Likelihood extraction using IBM SPSS. Items that did not load onto a single factor or that were split across multiple factors were dropped one at a time until a stable factor structure was found. The retained items had factor loadings above .4 and any cross-loadings were at least .2 less than the main factor loading.

In the factor analysis, four of the System Usability Scale items, two Ease of Use items, and three Intuitive Controls items converged into a single factor which was labeled Usability of Controls because these items measured the usability of the controls of the game. Two items from the System Usability Scale loaded onto their own factor which was labeled Learnability because they were about how easy it was to learn to play the game. Rather than converging with Usability of Controls or Learnability, the items for Immediate Progress Feedback and Clear Proximal Goals loaded onto their own separate factors.

In a previous study the authors conducted [23], items that represented Ease of Concentration had converged with Concentration to form Effortless Concentration. But in the present study, these Ease of Concentration items did not meet the criteria described above to survive instrument validation. So, Effortless Concentration was renamed to Concentration to reflect the meaning of the retained items. In addition to Learnability, two of the Task Engagement factors only retained two items each: Merging of Action and Awareness and Loss of Reflective Self-Consciousness. These two constructs from Flow Theory are difficult to capture, and many of the items intended to measure them were splitting into their own factors or loading onto unintended factors.

The factors that made up Task Engagement and Usability failed to converge into second-order factors, so the first-order factors that made up these higher-level, more abstract constructs were used in the analysis.

After identifying items for the non-desire factors, separate factor analyses were conducted with all of the non-desire variables and the Desire and Desire Fulfillment items for one desire at a time. In this way, items for each desire with sufficient construct validity were identified.

To test the internal consistency reliability of the measures, the Cronbach's Alpha was calculated for the items for each factor. Each scale had Alpha levels above .7 with two exceptions, Learnability and Loss of Reflective Self-Consciousness, which each had Alpha levels above .6 and only had two items. Most of the scales had Cronbach's Alpha levels above .8, indicating a high degree of internal consistency reliability. The factor loadings for each retained item and Cronbach's Alpha levels for each scale are presented in the Appendix H of the first author's dissertation [22].

3.3 Participants

Participants were recruited both online through social media and through fliers distributed on the campus of a Midwestern university with a diverse student body. There were 315 total valid responses to the online survey. The demographics and gameplay habits of the participants are summarized in Table 1 below.

Table 1. Summary of participant demographics and background

Total valid N	315 participants (100%)
Female	86 (27.35%)
Male	222 (70.5%),
Other (e.g. "Non-Binary", "undecided", etc.)	7 (2.2%)
Mean average age	24.07 years
Age range	18–49 years
English as only first language learned	220 (69.84%)
Other languages as first language learned	93 (29.52%)
Played digital games at least once per week	291 (92.38%)
Played digital games once per month or less frequently	24 (7.62%)
Played digital games every day or more frequently	141 (44.76%)
Mean average years playing digital games	15.59 years
Range of years played digital games	1–38 years

3.4 Procedure

An online survey of digital game players was conducted. Participants were presented with an information sheet on informed consent at the top of the survey.

Respondents were presented the following definition of a digital game: "A digital game is any game that you play on a computerized device, like a video game console, Personal Computer (PC), smartphone, or on the Internet". Then respondents were asked to name the last digital game they played for longer than thirty minutes. They were asked what genre the game is in, and then asked how long ago they played the game. Only respondents who played the game for longer than thirty minutes within the last six months were recruited to participate in the study. The question asking them to name the game asked about the last game they played for longer than thirty minutes, so only participants who go on to indicate that experience playing the game they named was within the last six months were recruited to participate. This screening was done to ensure that all participants had recently had the relevant experience to answer the survey questions.

Next, participants filled out a series of Likert scale questionnaires. Most of these questionnaires assessed their experience playing the game they identified as the last digital game they played for longer than thirty minutes, which will be referred to here as the game. The game that participant named and typed in as their answer to that initial question was inserted into the questions to ensure that participants knew that the questions were asking about their experience playing that particular game that they indicated they had played for longer than 30 min within the last six months.

The questionnaires assessed their Enjoyment and Task Engagement, then the perceived Usability of the game. Participants were then be asked which of the 16 basic human desires were fulfilled or satisfied by their experience playing the game, with checkboxes to select all desires that apply and short definitions of each desire. Then the questionnaires assessed how much playing the game provided Desire Fulfillment for each Desire the participant checked, then their level of Desire for each Desire the participant checked. Separate analyses were conducted for each basic human desire with the subset of participants who checked that desire. All of these questionnaires focused on their experience playing the game they identified except for the questionnaire about their individual level of Desire, which is about the participants themselves. The order of these questionnaires was chosen to ask about dependent or endogenous variables before independent or exogenous variables, to avoid the experience of answering questions about the independent variables priming or biasing their answers about the dependent variables.

Participants then filled out a demographics and digital game playing habits questionnaires. This questionnaire asks participants how many years they have been playing video or computer games, how often they play video games or computer games, and what genres of video games they typically play, with checkboxes allowing them to check all genres that they typically play. This information was collected to ensure a diverse sample of participants are recruited in terms of their experience playing digital games and their game-playing habits. Next, the questionnaire asked the first language participants learned or their native language, their age, and their gender. These questions were asked to ensure a diverse sample of participants were recruited in terms of their demographics and background.

Finally, participants provided their email address if they wish to be entered into a drawing to receive a prize. As an incentive to participate, eight participants who complete the study were randomly selected to receive either a gaming console system bundled with a game or a tablet computer (from \$237.99 to \$464.98 in value).

The time participants took to complete the survey was tracked. To reduce participant fatigue, a message at the top of each page of the survey told participants how they could complete the survey in multiple sessions.

The questionnaire data was analyzed using multiple linear regression, testing each part of the hypothesized model one dependent variable at a time.

4   Results

4.1   Hypothesis Testing: Idealism

Idealism is the desire to improve society (including public service, altruism, and social justice). Idealism was the desire twelfth most frequently checked as fulfilled or satisfied by participants, with 39/315 (12.4%) checking the box for Idealism and therefore answering the Desire and Desire Fulfillment Questionnaires for Idealism. However, Idealism showed the greatest significant impact (the highest R^2 among the factors tested) on Sense of Control and Concentration, the Task Engagement factors that in turn had a significant impact on Enjoyment (see Table 3 below). This means that it is uncommon for playing digital games to fulfill the desire for Idealism, but when Idealism is fulfilled it tends to make playing the game more engaging, and thereby more enjoyable.

Figure 1 above shows the proposed Desire Fulfillment Model for Idealism and its hypothesized relationships.

The analysis for Idealism began with stepwise multiple linear regression by testing each hypothesized relationship in the proposed model with separate analyses for one dependent variable at time. Mean average scores on each measurement scale were used for all regression analyses rather than weighting them by factor loadings so that each item was evenly weighted. The results of this analysis are shown in Table 2 below, with the separate analysis for each dependent variable in separate boxes.

Table 2. Results of stepwise multiple linear regression analysis of the Desire Fulfillment Model for Idealism.

Relationship	R^2 Change	Significance for this relationship (p-value from coefficients table t-tests)	Significance for the overall model (p-value from ANOVA table F test)
Sense of Control -> Enjoyment Concentration -> Enjoyment	.189 .104	.006 .027	.006 .002
Desire Fulfillment: Idealism -> Sense of Control Immediate Progress Feedback -> Sense of Control	.196 .121	.005 .016	.005 .001
Desire Fulfillment: Idealism -> Concentration Immediate Progress Feedback -> Concentration	.190 .079	.006 .056 (n.s.)	.006 .004

Looking at the results of the stepwise multiple linear regression, Sense of Control and Concentration both had significant impacts on Enjoyment ($p < .05$). This supports H2, that Task Engagement has a positive impact on Enjoyment. Desire Fulfillment: Idealism and Desire: Idealism did not have significant direct impacts on Enjoyment while controlling for effects of Sense of Control and Concentration on Enjoyment, meaning that H3H and H4H were not supported by the available evidence.

Desire Fulfillment: Idealism had significant impacts on both Sense of Control and Concentration, the two Task Engagement sub-dimensions that significantly impacted Enjoyment. This supports H5H, that Desire Fulfillment: Idealism has a positive impact on Task Engagement.

Immediate Progress Feedback had a significant impact on Sense of Control. This support H1, that Usability has a positive impact on Task Engagement. The impact of Immediate Progress Feedback on Concentration was nearly but not quite significant ($p = .056$).

Finally, the impact of Desire: Idealism on Desire Fulfillment: Idealism was not significant ($p = .278$). This result did not support the new relationship between Desire and Desire Fulfillment which was found significant for most of the other desires examined that had significant effects with the exception of Honor (see [22], Table 13, p. 167–168). This could mean that fulfilling desires for Idealism and Honor increase Task Engagement regardless of individual differences in Desire, or how much players wanted to experience fulfillment of Idealism and Honor.

It is possible that the relationships that were not significant could be found significant if a larger sample size was collected, as the sample size for this analysis consists of the 39 participants who checked the box to indicate that their recent experience playing the digital game they named satisfied or fulfilled a desire for Idealism. These results do not rule out these non-significant relationships, but the available evidence was not enough to support them.

Figure 2 shows the conceptual model visualizing the findings from the multiple linear regression analysis.

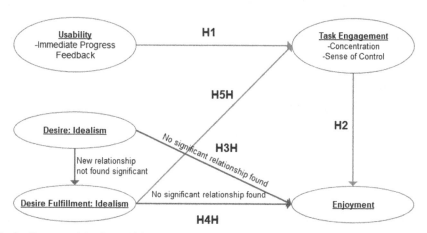

Fig. 2. Conceptual Desire Fulfillment Model for Idealism showing findings from multiple linear regression.

4.2 Comparing the Impact of Fulfilling Idealism to Other Desires

Fulfilling a desire for Idealism had a greater impact on the Task Engagement factors Concentration and Sense of Control than fulfilling any of the other desires examined, meaning the stepwise multiple linear regression analysis run separately for each desire on each dependent factor showed Desire Fulfillment: Idealism had the highest R^2 of any factor. Table 3 below compares the significant impacts of Desire and Desire Fulfillment on Enjoyment, Sense of Control, and Concentration from the separate analyses conducted for each desire.

Table 3. Significant impacts of desire and desire fulfillment on enjoyment, concentration, and sense of control from separate multiple linear regression analyses.

Relationship	R^2 Change	Significance for this relationship (p-value from coefficients table t-tests)	N
Desire Fulfillment: Curiosity -> Enjoyment	.117	<.001	200
Desire: Order -> Enjoyment	.037	.041	82
Desire Fulfillment: Independence -> Enjoyment	.018	.046	158
Desire Fulfillment: Idealism -> Concentration	.190	.006	39
Desire Fulfillment: Curiosity -> Concentration	.123	<.001	200
Desire Fulfillment: Order -> Concentration	.081	.007	82
Desire Fulfillment: Independence -> Concentration	.053	.002	158
Desire Fulfillment: Power -> Concentration	.040	.018	127
Desire Fulfillment: Tranquility -> Concentration	.039	.008	163
Desire Fulfillment: Saving -> Concentration	.029	.043	129
Desire Fulfillment: Idealism -> Sense of Control	.196	.005	39
Desire Fulfillment: Honor -> Sense of Control	.154	<.001	78
Desire Fulfillment: Independence -> Sense of Control	.035	.012	158
Desire Fulfillment: Tranquility -> Sense of Control	.033	.013	163
Desire Fulfillment: Curiosity -> Sense of Control	.031	.008	200

5   Discussion

Overall, the results from the online survey of digital game players supported the proposed model of Desire Fulfillment Theory for Idealism, with some revisions. The revised model based on the results from the analysis is presented in this section, and the implications of these findings are discussed.

The lower-level, first order factors intended to make up Usability and Task Engagement did not converge well onto higher-level, second-order factors, so the lower-level, first order factors were used for the analysis. When these lower-level factors were used, a consistent pattern emerged from the analysis. Clear Proximal Goals led to Concentration, which led to Enjoyment. Immediate Progress Feedback led to Sense of Control, which led to Enjoyment. These relationships are shown in Fig. 3 below.

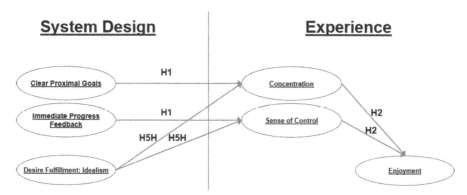

Fig. 3. Revised model of Desire Fulfillment Theory for Idealism.

Figure 3 above separates the factors into characteristics of the system or game design and the experience that results from the user using the system or the experience of the player playing the game.

This separation is useful because game designers and user experience professionals will have the most control over the system design factors. While the System Design factors have an impact on the Experience factors, designers do not directly control the Experience factors. Perhaps a design could distract players and decrease their Concentration, or take away control from players such as during a cinematic cut-scene and decrease their Sense of Control, but it is less tangible and useful to tell a designer to design for Concentration or a Sense of Control than to design for the System Design factors.

This means the primary focus for practitioners interested in designing for Enjoyment must be on three paths to game enjoyment: 1) Clear Proximal Goals: Clearly communicating the goal of the current next step throughout each step of the activity, 2) Immediate Progress Feedback: Clearly communicating how well the user is doing throughout the activity, and 3) Desire Fulfillment: Ensuring the activity fulfills the basic human desires of the user.

6 Implications

The present paper focuses on fulfillment of the desire for Idealism. Fulfilling a desire for Idealism involves improving society, advancing a social cause, or making things better for humankind. It is important to note that none of the games the participants listed were serious games with a pro-social purpose beyond enjoyment, so it appears that the fulfillment of the desire for Idealism was entirely within the fictional world of the digital game.

Saving the world or saving humankind may be a common theme or trope in digital games. But the present study provides evidence that feeling that your actions are improving society or making the world a better place satisfies a basic human desire, an underlying psychological motivation that drives human behavior.

This research has important implications for practitioners, designers, developers, and applied researchers. To design interactive experiences that are engaging and enjoyable, show users how their actions are having a positive impact on other people, on society, or on the environment. Use story, characters, and other game design elements to show that the user's actions are important because of that positive impact. In the call to action, show how needed the user's actions are. In the system feedback, show the positive impact of the user's actions, show how they made a difference. For example, show the people impacted by the user's actions (or characters representing them) and have them show their appreciation and celebrate the positive impact the user had on their lives.

This motivation to improve society or make the world a better place may be especially important for motivating people to play serious games, games with a positive purpose beyond enjoyment such as education, health-related behavior change, positive social change, or pro-environmental behavior change. Future research may investigate if the effects of feeling that one's actions are fulfilling a desire for Idealism are significantly greater or less when participants actions in the game have a real-world positive impact rather than being confined to a fictional game world.

This research also has important implications for basic research and theory. When the desire for Idealism is fulfilled, it may give players a sense of meaning, purpose, or significance. One of the categories of enjoyment sources in digital games identified by Schaffer and Fang [31] was "Significance, Meaning, Purpose, & Legacy", which is how much you know why your actions are important, significant, or meaningful or how much you feel that your actions are giving their life meaning or helping fulfill the purpose of your life.

So, perhaps fulfilling a desire for Idealism is so effective at increasing Concentration and Sense of Control because when players know that their actions are important, significant, or meaningful, they are more likely to focus their attention and concentrate. Because they are focused on what is important or gives their life meaning, as opposed to focusing on trivial, non-important tasks, perhaps this makes them feel more like they have everything under control. More research is needed to explore the role of Significance or Meaning in game enjoyment and task engagement.

The Idealism desire, this desire to improve society or make the world a better place, may be part of or connected to a basic human desire to do things that help others. Specifically, it is the perception that one's actions are improving society that makes those actions feel meaningful. Another category of enjoyment sources identified by Schaffer and Fang

[31] was "Friendship, Relationships, Love, Kindness, & Belonging". The kindness part of that category was defined as "Giving and receiving help and care, and seeing others help and take care of each other" [31]. Fulfilling a desire for Idealism, kindness, and pro-social behavior has been under-examined in the study of game enjoyment and task engagement. As far as the authors know, this paper is the first empirical evidence that fulfilling a desire for Idealism has a positive impact on Task Engagement, which in turn positively impacts Enjoyment.

As serious games present the possibility that playing games with a purpose beyond enjoyment can actually benefit society, one has to wonder if these benefits to society can themselves contribute to Enjoyment if they are presented to players in a way that makes their actions feel more meaningful and important. And that increased Enjoyment can then motivate people to play the serious game. Even in the fantasy context of digital games with no purpose beyond enjoyment, the basic human desire of Idealism, to contribute to the wellbeing of society, when fulfilled, showed the greatest impact on Concentration and Sense of Control (see Table 3 above).

Games that use their story and characters to give players a sense of meaning and purpose – a sense that their actions are important – by making them feel that their actions will serve the public, benefit humankind, or advance a social cause are more likely to get players into Task Engagement or a flow state by getting them to Concentrate on the task at hand and feel a Sense of Control, and this in turn leads to more Enjoyment.

Make users feel that their actions are important, that what they are doing will make the world a better place. This will increase Task Engagement, which leads to more Enjoyment.

7   Conclusion

Fulfilling a desire for Idealism has a positive impact on Task Engagement, which in turn has a positive impact on Enjoyment. As far as the authors are aware, no previous research has shown empirical evidence of how fulfilling a desire for Idealism impacts Task Engagement and Enjoyment in Digital games. The evidence presented in this paper supports the proposed Desire Fulfillment Theory of digital game enjoyment. Desire Fulfillment Theory builds on established theories, but is tested by doing research with actual game players.

The research presented above advances our knowledge of what makes games enjoyable and how designers and user experience practitioners can design for enjoyment. Designing interactive systems that give users clear proximal goals, immediate progress feedback and desire fulfillment will be more likely to lead to enjoyment. That means ensuring users know what to do next and how well they are doing throughout the activity. And it means identifying and fulfilling the basic human desires that motivate them.

Practitioners who want to fulfill the basic human desire for Idealism can show users how their actions are having a positive impact on other people, on society, or on the environment. Show the positive impact of user actions throughout the experience, from showing the need for user action in the call to action and through continuous feedback showing the impact of user action on the target of the pro-social actions the user is taking. These design guidelines apply for both fictional games and for serious games with a real-world impact.

Fulfilling a desire for Idealism has important theoretical implications for future basic research as well. When user tasks fulfill a desire for Idealism, this may help make user tasks more significant or meaningful, which may explain why fulfilling this desire increases users' Concentration and Sense of Control. Concentration and Sense of Control are the two Task Engagement factors or flow conditions [8, 23] that were found to positively impact Enjoyment. In addition, fulfilling a desire for Idealism, a desire to improve society, may be related to kindness and pro-social behavior, which are actions that help other people. With fulfilling a desire for Idealism standing out as having a greater impact than the other factors examined on Task Engagement and thereby Enjoyment in digital games (see Table 3 above), future research may explore the role of these related concepts of kindness and pro-social behavior in digital game enjoyment.

The present research also advances our understanding of how Task Engagement impacts Enjoyment, and the System Design factors that lead to Task Engagement. The results of this study showed that Clear Proximal Goals and Immediate Progress Feedback are the System Design factors that lead to the experience of Concentration and Sense of Control, which are the key Task Engagement factors that lead to Enjoyment.

Future research may focus on controlled experiments to test the causal linkages between the identified factors, and identifying other factors that impact enjoyment. Desire Fulfillment Theory can serve as a foundation for applied research as well, including studies of game mechanics, gamification of non-games, and serious games with a purpose beyond enjoyment. However, applied research must be informed by a solid foundation of empirical basic research. Desire Fulfillment Theory is a step forward. But more basic research must be done to fully understand what makes games enjoyable.

References

1. Entertainment Software Association: 2019 Essential Facts About the Computer and Video Game Industry (2019)
2. Caillois, R.: Man, Play, and Games. University of Illinois Press, Champaign (1961)
3. Bartle, R.: Hearts, clubs, diamonds, spades: Players who suit MUDs. J. MUD Res. 1, 19 (1996)
4. Lazzaro, N.: Why we play games: four keys to more emotion without story (2004)
5. Lazzaro, N.: Why we play: affect and the fun of games. In: Human-Computer Interaction: Designing for Diverse Users and Domains, pp. 155–176 (2009)
6. Ryan, R.M., Deci, E.L.: Self-determination theory and the facilitation of intrinsic motivation, social development, and well-being. Am. Psychol. 55, 68–78 (2000). https://doi.org/10.1037//0003-066X.55.1.68
7. Ryan, R.M., Rigby, S.C., Przybylski, A.: The motivational pull of video games: a self-determination theory approach. Motivat. Emot. 30, 344–360 (2006). https://doi.org/10.1007/s11031-006-9051-8
8. Nakamura, J., Csikszentmihalyi, M.: The concept of flow. In: Csikszentmihalyi, M. (ed.) Flow and the Foundations of Positive Psychology, pp. 239–263. Springer, Dordrecht (2014). https://doi.org/10.1007/978-94-017-9088-8_16
9. Brockmyer, J.H., Fox, C.M., Curtiss, K.A., McBroom, E., Burkhart, K.M., Pidruzny, J.N.: The development of the game engagement questionnaire: a measure of engagement in video game-playing. J. Exp. Soc. Psychol. 45, 624–634 (2009). https://doi.org/10.1016/j.jesp.2009.02.016

10. Yee, N.: Motivations for play in online games. CyberPsychol. behavior. **9**, 772–775 (2006)
11. Yee, N., Ducheneaut, N., Nelson, L.: Online gaming motivations scale: development and validation. In: Proceedings of the SIGCHI Conference on Human Factors in Computing Systems, pp. 2803–2806. ACM (2012)
12. Malone, T.W.: What makes things fun to learn? Heuristics for designing instructional computer games. In: Proceedings of the 3rd ACM SIGSMALL Symposium and the First SIGPC Symposium on Small Systems, pp. 162–169. ACM, New York (1980). https://doi.org/10.1145/800088.802839
13. Malone, T.W.: Toward a theory of intrinsically motivating instruction. Cogn. Sci. **5**, 333–369 (1981)
14. Korhonen, H., Montola, M., Arrasvuori, J.: Understanding playful user experience through digital games. In: International Conference on Designing Pleasurable Products and Interfaces. Citeseer (2009)
15. Quick, J.M., Atkinson, R.K., Lin, L.: Empirical taxonomies of gameplay enjoyment: personality and video game preference. Int. J. Game-Based Learn. **2**, 11–31 (2012)
16. Schaffer, O., Fang, X.: Digital game enjoyment: a literature review. In: Fang, X. (ed.) HCII 2019. LNCS, vol. 11595, pp. 191–214. Springer, Cham (2019). https://doi.org/10.1007/978-3-030-22602-2_16
17. Deterding, S., Dixon, D., Khaled, R., Nacke, L.: From game design elements to gamefulness: defining gamification. In: Proceedings of the 15th international academic MindTrek conference: Envisioning future media environments, pp. 9–15. ACM (2011)
18. Oliver, R.L.: Effect of expectation and disconfirmation on postexposure product evaluations: an alternative interpretation. J. Appl. Psychol. **62**, 480–486 (1977). https://doi.org/10.1037/0021-9010.62.4.480
19. Oliver, R.L.: A cognitive model of the antecedents and consequences of satisfaction decisions. J. Mark. Res. **17**, 460–469 (1980). https://doi.org/10.2307/3150499
20. Reiss, S.: Multifaceted nature of intrinsic motivation: the theory of 16 basic desires. Rev. Gener. Psychol. **8**, 179–193 (2004). https://doi.org/10.1037/1089-2680.8.3.179
21. Csikszentmihalyi, M.: Flow: The Psychology of Optimal Experience. Harper Perennial Modern Classics, New York (2008)
22. Schaffer, O.: A desire fulfillment theory of digital game enjoyment. Coll. Comput. Digit. Media Dissertat. **18** (2019). https://via.library.depaul.edu/cdm_etd/18
23. Schaffer, O., Fang, X.: Impact of task and interface design on flow. Presented at the HCI Research in MIS Workshop (SIGHCI) at the International Conference on Information Systems (ICIS), Dublin, Ireland (2016)
24. McAuley, E., Duncan, T., Tammen, V.V.: Psychometric properties of the Intrinsic Motivation Inventory in a competitive sport setting: a confirmatory factor analysis. Res. Q. Exerc. Sport **60**, 48–58 (1989)
25. Brooke, J.: SUS: a "quick and dirty" usability scale. In: Usability Evaluation in Industry, pp. 189–194. Taylor & Francis, London (1996)
26. Lewis, J.R., Sauro, J.: The factor structure of the system usability scale. In: Kurosu, M. (ed.) HCD 2009. LNCS, vol. 5619, pp. 94–103. Springer, Heidelberg (2009). https://doi.org/10.1007/978-3-642-02806-9_12
27. Bangor, A., Kortum, P.T., Miller, J.T.: An empirical evaluation of the system usability scale. Int. J. Hum.-Comput. Interact. **24**, 574–594 (2008). https://doi.org/10.1080/10447310802205776
28. Venkatesh, V., Davis, F.D.: A theoretical extension of the technology acceptance model: four longitudinal field studies. Manage. Sci. **46**, 186–204 (2000)
29. Havercamp, S.M.: The Reiss profile of motivation sensitivity: reliability, validity, and social desirability (1998)

30. Reiss, S., Havercamp, S.M.: Toward a comprehensive assessment of fundamental motivation: factor structure of the Reiss Profiles. Psychol. Assess. **10**, 97–106 (1998). https://doi.org/10.1037/1040-3590.10.2.97
31. Schaffer, O., Fang, X.: What makes games fun? Card sort reveals 34 sources of computer game enjoyment. Presented at the Americas Conference on Information Systems (AMCIS) 2018, New Orleans (2018)

Guidance Is Good or Avoid Too Much Hand-Holding? Proposing a Controlled Experiment on the Impact of Clear Proximal Goals on Digital Game Enjoyment

Owen Schaffer[⊠]

Computer Science and Information Systems, Bradley University, 1501 W Bradley Ave, Peoria, IL 61625, USA
Owen.Schaffer@gmail.com

Abstract. Empirical research on what makes digital games enjoyable is critical for practitioners and researchers who want to design for enjoyment. This is true not only for Game Design, but for Gamification of non-game applications, and Serious Games with a purpose beyond enjoyment. But existing theories are incomplete or lacking empirical support. Flow is the psychological state of "getting in the zone", of enjoying overcoming challenges for the sake of the enjoyment they provide. Flow theory suggests that Clear Proximal Goals, knowing what to do next throughout an activity, is a flow condition, or a factor that leads to the flow state. However, there is a popular notion among game designers and developers that it is better to avoid too much hand-holding, and to allow game players to figure out what to do themselves rather than guiding them each step of the way. These appear to be mutually exclusive assertions that cannot both be true. Does more guidance increase or decrease enjoyment? To resolve this controversy, an online controlled experiment with a 2 × 2 factorial design and a minimum of 280 total participants is proposed to test the impact of Clear Proximal Goals on Task Engagement (flow not including enjoyment) and Enjoyment. The presence or absence of on-screen text prompts and navigational assistance will be used to manipulate clear proximal goals. This study will advance the study of game enjoyment by testing how the clarity of players' next steps impacts game enjoyment using random assignment to different game designs.

Keywords: Enjoyment · Clear proximal goals · Controlled experiment · Task engagement · Flow · Intrinsic motivation · Game design · Gamification · Serious games · Computer games · Digital games

1 Introduction and Related Work

Is it better to avoid too much hand-holding, and to allow game players to figure out what to do themselves rather than guiding them each step of the way. Or is it better that the

---

The original version of this chapter was revised: the number of versions of the game was corrected. The correction to this chapter is available at https://doi.org/10.1007/978-3-030-50164-8_39

© Springer Nature Switzerland AG 2020, corrected publication 2020
X. Fang (Ed.): HCII 2020, LNCS 12211, pp. 179–185, 2020.
https://doi.org/10.1007/978-3-030-50164-8_12

game communicates player goals to ensure players know what to do next throughout the game? These are the central research questions driving the present research. Flow theory suggests knowing what to do next is critical for players to get "in the zone" when they play games, but there is also a popular notion among game designers and developers that it is better to avoid too much hand-holding, and to allow game players to figure out what to do themselves rather than guiding them each step of the way. These positions appear to be contradictory, suggesting they cannot both be true.

Flow is the experience of overcoming optimal challenges for the enjoyment they provide while continuously adjusting performance based on feedback. Unlike Self-Determination Theory which focuses on satisfying needs for autonomy, competence, and belonging [1, 2], flow theory focuses directly on the autotelic experience, enjoyment of an activity as the primary motivation for that same activity. Flow theory begins with this enjoyment a desirable end result rather than as a means to any other end, even if flow may have other benefits.

Much of the research on flow has attempted to measure how much people are in flow. For example, several flow measures consist of 9 dimensions from Csikszentmihalyi's [3, 4] popular books on flow (e.g. [5–7]). This approach of treating all of these factors as measures of flow how much a person is in flow may not be accurate because some of these factors are conditions that lead to flow, while others indicate how much the person is in flow.

Nakamura and Csikszentmihalyi [8] separated flow into two sets of factors: conditions, which are the factors that lead to flow and flow indicators, which are the factors that indicate how much a person is in flow. Most previous research on flow has failed to separate flow conditions from indicators [5, 7, 9].

The factors that measured the flow conditions identified by Nakamura and Csikszentmihalyi – clear proximal goals, immediate progress feedback, and optimal challenge – were separated from the factors that measured flow indicators: effortless concentration, sense of control, merging of action and awareness, loss of reflective self-consciousness, altered perception of time, and autotelic experience.

Three flow conditions lead to flow, which in turn leads to enjoyment: optimal challenge, clear proximal goals, and immediate progress feedback [8]. Optimal challenge is extent to which a person perceives the task they are doing has a level of task difficulty that is high enough to stretch their perceived skills without overwhelming them.

Clear proximal goals is how much the person feels they know what to do next throughout an activity. The word "proximal" emphasizes continuously receiving information about the goal of the next step rather than simply the overall goal, facilitating task engagement by providing step-by-step information about how to complete each task. As Csikszentmihalyi and Nakamura [10] explained, "What counts is not that the overall goal of the activity be clear but rather that the activity present a clear goal for the next step in the action sequence, and then the next, on and on, until the final goal is reached" (p. 187). The impact of game design elements that increase clear proximal goals by communicating the goal of "the next step in the action sequence" is the focus of the present study.

Immediate progress feedback is how much the person feels they know how well they are performing the activity or how well they are making progress through the activity. When the flow conditions are high, people experience flow, and enjoyment is a part of the flow experience.

If practitioners know what conditions lead to flow, designs can be engineered to meet the flow conditions. Controlled experiments have shown that optimal challenges lead to flow [11] and that immediate progress feedback leads to flow [12, 13]. However, the causal relationship between clear proximal goals and flow has yet to be demonstrated with a controlled experiment. This paper aims to fill this research gap.

The US video game industry earned record revenues of $43.4 billion in 2018, which was a 20.5% increase from the year before [14]. Digital games are interactive, computer-based systems that present users with a series of goal-directed, challenging tasks to complete for the sake of the enjoyment those tasks provide. Digital games are games played on a computerized device, such as a video game console, Personal Computer (PC), smartphone, or on the Internet. Enjoyment is the extent to which people positively evaluate their experience.

But there is little to no scientific consensus about what leads to that positive experience of enjoyment when people play digital games. Research on digital game enjoyment is still in its infancy, with scattered and incomplete theories that are either not supported by empirical research showing they lead to enjoyment such as Caillois's categories of games [15], Bartle's four player types [16], and Lazzaro's Four Keys to Fun [17, 18], or do not provide a comprehensive model of what leads to enjoyment such as Self-Determination Theory [1], Player Experience of Needs Satisfaction (PENS) [19], Flow Theory [8], the Game Engagement Questionnaire [20], Yee's model of motivations to play online games [21, 22], Malone's model of intrinsically motivating educational games [23, 24], the Player Experience (PLEX) Framework [25], and the taxonomy of gameplay enjoyment from Quick et al. [26]. The proposed research aims to fill that gap in the literature.

An extensive review of the literature on what makes games enjoyable has been conducted, which summarizes 61 relevant peer-reviewed research articles and papers and categorizes them into 12 topic areas [27].

Understanding what makes digital games enjoyable is important not only for video and computer game designers, but also for Gamification and Serious Games as well. Gamification is "the use of game design elements in non-game contexts" [28], such as to make non-game systems more game-like and enjoyable. Serious games are "full-fledged games for non-entertainment purposes" [28], such as education, exercise, research or persuasion.

Design for enjoyment is the common aim of Game Design, Gamification, and Serious Games. To reliably engineer enjoyable systems, practitioners need empirical research showing what makes digital games enjoyable.

Enjoyment is how positively users evaluate their experience. When users evaluate their experience more positively, it follows logically that they will be more likely to come back for more of that positive experience. When users come back for more, this could mean more sales, repeat sales, expanded market share, employee retention for a gamified business system, successful behavior change for a persuasive game, or better learning outcomes for an educational game. Increasing user enjoyment also has intrinsic value in its positive impact on the people whose enjoyment is increased. So, designing for enjoyment is important.

There is a popular notion among game designers and developers that it is better to avoid too much hand-holding, and to allow game players to figure out what to do themselves rather than guiding them each step of the way. This is incompatible with flow theory's notion of clear proximal goals, which suggests that it is best to ensure players know what to do next throughout the game. So, when it comes to conveying what the player is supposed to do next throughout a game, is guidance good or is it better to avoid too much hand-holding? Which leads to more task engagement and game enjoyment?

Popular games like *Elder Scrolls V: Skyrim* [29] and *World of Warcraft* [30] use text prompts to communicate the next step in the player's current task, quest, or mission and navigational aids like on-screen marks on a compass or map or paths indicating the direction the player needs to go to get to their next step. While games like the *Dark Souls* [31] series of games do not use these game design elements to communicate this information to players. Directly comparing these games would introduce too many confounding variables. By isolating these game design elements intended to increase Clear Proximal Goals in a controlled experiment, the present study explores the impact of including these game design elements on Task Engagement and Enjoyment.

The research question guiding this proposed study is: do games with more clear proximal goals lead to more or less digital game enjoyment? This study will contribute both to the theory and practice of designing interactive systems for enjoyment. This is an important aim for practitioners and researchers in the fields of Game Design, Human-Computer Interaction, and Information Systems.

2 Method

A between-subjects controlled experiment with a 2×2 factorial design will be conducted with random assignment of participants into four conditions. The conditions will consist of playing different versions of the same game, with the different versions designed to be identical except for specific design differences intended to manipulate Clear Proximal Goals, which is how much participants report knowing precisely what to do each step of the way.

The first independent variable or design difference will be the presence or absence of an on screen Text Prompt indicating the current proximal goal, meaning the goal of the next step in the sequence of actions the game requires players to do to complete the game. In the conditions where this Text Prompt is present, each time the player completes the current step they are on, the Text Prompt will be updated to show the next step that needs to be completed. The second design difference will be the presence or absence of an on screen Navigation Aid in the form of an on-screen arrow indicating the direction the player needs to move their character in the game to reach their current proximal goal, or the next step of the game. This 2×2 factorial design is illustrated in Fig. 1 below.

The Text Prompt is intended to convey information about what the player is trying to do, while the Navigational Aid is intended to convey information about where the player needs to go. By manipulating these two independent variables separately with a 2×2 factorial design, the present study will explore the impact of these two independent variables and how they interact.

		Independent Variable A: Text Prompt describing current proximal goal	
		Text Prompt	No Text Prompt
Independent Variable B: Navigational Aid, an on- screen arrow indicating direction of the current proximal goal	Navigational Aid	Text Prompt & Navigational Aid	No Text Prompt & No Navigational Aid
	No Navigational Aid	Text Prompt & Navigational Aid	No Text Prompt & No Navigational Aid

Fig. 1. 2 × 2 factorial design of experiment testing the impact of clear proximal goals on task engagement and enjoyment in digital games.

H1. Players in the Text Prompt condition will report greater Task Engagement and Enjoyment than players in the No Text Prompt condition.
H2. Players in the Navigational Aid condition will report greater Task Engagement and Enjoyment than players in the No Navigational Aid condition.
H3. There will be a positive interaction effect between the two independent variables such that players in the Text Prompt & Navigational Aid condition experience will report greater Task Engagement and Enjoyment.

The research games will be different versions of the same simple top-down 2D Role-Playing Game developed with the Unity game engine and C#, and built with WebGL to allow them to be posted online. This game type was chosen because it fits well with the design elements chosen as independent variables.

40 participants in the pilot study and then at least 240 participants in the main study will be recruited on the campus of a medium-size University in the Midwest region of the United States with flyers and social media. A total of 280 participants was chosen as the minimum sample size because a power analysis using G*Power showed 280 is the minimum total sample size required to detect a medium effect size ($f = .25$) with an ANOVA with a $p < .05$ and a Power $> .95$. This means there will be a minimum of 70 participants in each of the four experimental conditions.

Participants will be given information about informed consent and be randomly assigned to play one of the four versions of the research game. After playing the game for 30 min, participants will fill out a series of Likert scale questionnaire items to measure the extent to which they experienced enjoyment, task engagement (flow not including enjoyment itself), and clear proximal goals.

This length of time playing the game of 30 min was chosen based on previous experience to allow sufficient time for participants to experience the game while avoiding participant fatigue. The measure of how much participants experienced clear proximal goals will be used as a manipulation check to ensure the experimental manipulation had the intended impact on clear proximal goals.

These Likert scale questionnaire measures have been used in previous research, and were previously found to have sufficient validity and reliability [12, 13]. Participants will fill out a demographics and gaming habits questionnaire, and be thanked for their time.

The study will be conducted online, including the game play and filling out the survey measures after playing the game. Qualtrics, an online survey tool, will be used for the survey portion of the study. Conducting the study online will make it easier to collect a large sample size, which will increase the statistical power of the study. Participants who provide valid data will be entered into a drawing to receive a large prize as an incentive to participate.

References

1. Ryan, R.M., Deci, E.L.: Self-determination theory and the facilitation of intrinsic motivation, social development, and well-being. Am. Psychol. **55**, 68–78 (2000). https://doi.org/10.1037//0003-066X.55.1.68
2. Deci, E., Ryan, R.M.: Intrinsic Motivation and Self-Determination in Human Behavior. Plenum Press, New York (1985)
3. Csikszentmihalyi, M.: Finding Flow: The Psychology of Engagement with Everyday Life. Basic Books, New York (1997)
4. Csikszentmihalyi, M.: The Evolving Self: A Psychology for the Third Millennium. Harper-Collins, New York (1993)
5. Fang, X., Zhang, J., Chan, S.S.: Development of an instrument for studying flow in computer game play. Int. J. Hum.-Comput. Interact. **29**, 456–470 (2013). https://doi.org/10.1080/10447318.2012.715991
6. Jackson, S.A., Marsh, H.W.: Development and validation of a scale to measure optimal experience: the flow state scale. J. Sport Exerc. Psychol. **18**, 17–35 (1996)
7. Jackson, S.A., Eklund, R.C.: The Flow Scales Manual. Fitness Information Technology (2004)
8. Nakamura, J., Csikszentmihalyi, M.: The concept of flow. In: Csikszentmihalyi, M. (ed.) Flow and the foundations of positive psychology, pp. 239–263. Springer, Dordrecht (2014). https://doi.org/10.1007/978-94-017-9088-8_16
9. Sweetser, P., Wyeth, P.: GameFlow: a model for evaluating player enjoyment in games. Comput. Entertain. (CIE) **3**, 3 (2005)
10. Csikszentmihalyi, M., Nakamura, J.: Effortless attention in everyday life: a systematic phenomenology. In: Effortless Attention: A New Perspective in the Cognitive Science of Attention and Action, pp. 179–190 (2010)
11. Keller, J., Bless, H.: Flow and regulatory compatibility: an experimental approach to the flow model of intrinsic motivation. Pers. Soc. Psychol. Bull. **34**, 196–209 (2008). https://doi.org/10.1177/0146167207310026
12. Schaffer, O., Fang, X.: Finding flow with games: does immediate progress feedback cause flow? Presented at the Americas Conference on Information Systems (AMCIS), Puerto Rico (2015). https://doi.org/10.13140/RG.2.1.4236.8725
13. Schaffer, O., Fang, X.: Impact of task and interface design on flow. Presented at the HCI Research in MIS Workshop (SIGHCI) at the International Conference on Information Systems (ICIS), Dublin, Ireland (2016)
14. Entertainment Software Association: 2019 Essential Facts About the Computer and Video Game Industry (2019)
15. Caillois, R.: Man, Play, and Games. University of Illinois Press, Champaign (1961)

16. Bartle, R.: Hearts, clubs, diamonds, spades: players who suit MUDs. J. MUD Res. **1**, 19 (1996)

17. Lazzaro, N.: Why we play games: four keys to more emotion without story (2004)

18. Lazzaro, N.: Why we play: affect and the fun of games. In: Human-Computer Interaction: Designing for Diverse Users and Domains, pp. 155–176 (2009)

19. Ryan, R.M., Rigby, S.C., Przybylski, A.: The motivational pull of video games: a self-determination theory approach. Motivat. Emot. **30**, 344–360 (2006). https://doi.org/10.1007/s11031-006-9051-8

20. Brockmyer, J.H., Fox, C.M., Curtiss, K.A., McBroom, E., Burkhart, K.M., Pidruzny, J.N.: The development of the Game Engagement Questionnaire: a measure of engagement in video game-playing. J. Exp. Soc. Psychol. **45**, 624–634 (2009). https://doi.org/10.1016/j.jesp.2009.02.016

21. Yee, N.: Motivations for play in online games. CyberPsychol. Behav. **9**, 772–775 (2006)

22. Yee, N., Ducheneaut, N., Nelson, L.: Online gaming motivations scale: development and validation. In: Proceedings of the SIGCHI Conference on Human Factors in Computing Systems, pp. 2803–2806. ACM (2012)

23. Malone, T.W.: What makes things fun to learn? heuristics for designing instructional computer games. In: Proceedings of the 3rd ACM SIGSMALL Symposium and the First SIGPC Symposium on Small Systems, pp. 162–169. ACM, New York (1980). https://doi.org/10.1145/800088.802839

24. Malone, T.W.: Toward a theory of intrinsically motivating instruction. Cogn. Sci. **5**, 333–369 (1981)

25. Korhonen, H., Montola, M., Arrasvuori, J.: Understanding playful user experience through digital games. In: International Conference on Designing Pleasurable Products and Interfaces. Citeseer (2009)

26. Quick, J.M., Atkinson, R.K., Lin, L.: Empirical taxonomies of gameplay enjoyment: personality and video game preference. Int. J. Game-Based Learn. **2**, 11–31 (2012)

27. Schaffer, O., Fang, X.: Digital game enjoyment: a literature review. In: Fang, X. (ed.) HCII 2019. LNCS, vol. 11595, pp. 191–214. Springer, Cham (2019). https://doi.org/10.1007/978-3-030-22602-2_16

28. Deterding, S., Dixon, D., Khaled, R., Nacke, L.: From game design elements to gamefulness: defining gamification. In: Proceedings of the 15th International Academic MindTrek Conference: Envisioning Future Media Environments, pp. 9–15. ACM (2011)

29. Bethesda Game Studios: The Elder Scrolls V: Skyrim. Bethesda Game Studios (2015)

30. Blizzard Entertainment: World of Warcraft. Blizzard Entertainment (2004)

31. FromSoftware: Dark Souls. Namco Bandai Games (2011)

Gender Differences When School Children Develop Digital Game-Based Designs: A Case Study

Jeanette Sjöberg[1]([⊠]) [iD] and Eva Brooks[2] [iD]

[1] Halmstad University, Kristian IVs väg 3, 301 18 Halmstad, Sweden
jeanette.sjoberg@hh.se
[2] Aalborg University, Kroghstæde 3, 9220 Aalborg, Denmark
eb@hum.aau.dk

Abstract. With the increased emergence of digital technology in the school context it is important to be aware of the fact that children's use of digital technologies is conditioned by gender. In this paper we investigate how gender differences emerge in collaborative interactions between 9 to 10-year-old school children while collaboratively working on developing digital game-based designs. The unit of analysis is game design activities with a focus on children's gendered actions, positionings and agency while collaborating and working with problem solving activities. The research questions posed in the study are: (1) What gender-related patterns emerges in collaborative interaction exhibited by 9 to 10-year-old school children while collaboratively engaged in a digital game-based design workshop involving problem solving activities? (2) How do 9 to 10-year-old girls and boys position themselves while collaboratively engaged in a digital game-based design workshop involving problem solving activities? (3) How do 9 to 10 year-old girls and boys employ their agency while collaboratively engaged in a digital game-based design workshop involving problem solving activities? The results of this study imply that children's agency oscillate between individual freedom and the constraint of traditional gender patterns while collaboratively engaged in a digital game-based design workshop involving problem solving activities. As a consequence, this tends to affect the children's participation and contribution to the given task.

Keywords: Agency · Collaboration · Digital game-based design · Gender differences · Problem solving · School children

1 Introduction

1.1 Children, Technology and Gender

Since quite some time now, there is an increased presence of digital technologies such as digital game-based learning in classroom contexts [1, 2]. Given this fact, children are bound to encounter digital technologies as part of their learning activities [3]. With the introduction of digital technology in teaching situations, it would be desirable to create

© Springer Nature Switzerland AG 2020
X. Fang (Ed.): HCII 2020, LNCS 12211, pp. 186–201, 2020.
https://doi.org/10.1007/978-3-030-50164-8_13

awareness of gender differences in order to avoid reflecting and reproducing traditional gender patterns. However, since this transition is yet still in its initial phase, there is a need for research addressing the issues concerning gender differences [4, 5]. Rubegni et al. [6] claims that gender is a major variable affecting identity and life opportunities from a young age. Gender is present everywhere in society and affects our daily and social life, the use of digital technology is no exception. On the contrary, much research indicates that there is a pertinent gender difference in terms of technology use, which also includes different types of digital media [7–9]. For example, Admiraal et al. [8] claims that boys show a stronger preference for digital entertainment games than girls, which might have an impact on game-based learning as being more acceptable to boys than to girls. In their quasi-experimental study, however, they found that girls seemed to profit more from searching the Internet to complete assignments and boys from competing with others and in that sense they mean that game-based learning might improve the performance of both boys and girls, depending upon the instructional design [8]. Other studies show gender differences when it comes to game preferences [10, 11].

A decade ago, Jenson and de Castell [12] wrote: "It is difficult, if not outright impossible, to shake loose deeply ingrained, hegemonic normative discourses and practices that demarcate, delimit, and predominate everyday gendered subject positions, especially in relation to technologies" (p. 53). There is not much evidence that matters have changed for the better since then. One aspect of concern is that digital technology often is gendered as a male domain [13], and considering the fact that digital technology is increasingly being used within a school context this needs to be addressed. Wong and Kemp state that "There remains a particular concern that girls lack the aspirations to position themselves (and be positioned by others) as potential creators of digital technology" [13]. This evidently, becomes especially important to point out now when subjects such as programming and coding are being established in curriculum from an early age in school.

1.2 Children, Technology and Gendered Agency

The creative production of digital games and artefacts in learning activities has made it possible for children to engage in creative game development activities. Such productive activities have been linked to children's agency where a study by Petersen [14] shows how an understanding of children's agency may be expanded by investigating how children as designers make use of affordances of digital technologies as they act in new material and agentive ways. Correspondingly, research suggests that creative development activities raise awareness of technology, especially in female students [15]. Children's use of digital technologies is gendered [9], some researchers even conceptualize it as a gender digital divide which is the cause for a genuine concern [13], as do OECD [16] who discusses the matter in a recent report. Such circumstances reflect that an individual is not always free to choose an agentic position. Kinnula et al. [17] exemplifies this by describing how children's roles can be defined for them by adults, but how they also adopt various roles in situ by themselves in a technology design process. Positioning is considered as a linguistic practice producing the self in encounters. In terms of agency, this is how girls and boys "do" gender by taking specific positions.

While it is important to promote children's agentic processes in learning, it is only recently that agency in children has been acknowledged in educational practices. Baker-Sperry [18] investigated how children exert agency in a classroom setting. The findings showed that gender influence children's agency. Moreover, that gender is negotiated among peers, and is particularly evident when children engaged in actions associated with the opposing gender. In the present study, we investigate agency as relational and contextually situated, emerging from children's interaction with each other, and the social and material environment [19]. The analysis pays attention to children's doings and interactions; e.g. what is possible to do, what is not possible to do, what kind of position do the participants take on - or not, and what promotes or constrains this? There is however a problem regarding how concepts such as "children as social actors" and "children's participation" are transcribed into practice [20], hence children's agency is not always an easy concept to comprehend. It has to be put in relation to the constraints by the surrounding adult world. In this paper we are using the definition of agency as explained by Katsiada et al. [21], where children's agency means their capacity to make autonomous decisions and choices in all matters affecting them according to their dispositions.

1.3   Aim and Research Questions

The motivation behind this study lies within the concern of digital technology as a gendered domain [13], which can be argued having important educational implications [22], and the aligned need of creating awareness of such gender differences. Accordingly, this paper investigates how gender differences emerge in collaborative interactions between 9 to 10-year-old school children while collaboratively working on digital game-based designs. It departs from two separate studies involving two classes of third grade school children, from north Jutland, Denmark and from south-west Halland, Sweden. Each class was involved in a creativity workshop case designed to provide a playful and creative atmosphere inspiring children to collaborate to create ideas for new games and/or game designs. The following research questions have been formulated: (1) What gender-related patterns emerge in collaborative interaction exhibited by 9 to 10-year-old school children while collaboratively engaged in a digital game-based design workshop involving problem solving activities? (2) How do 9 to 10-year-old girls and boys position themselves while collaboratively engaged in a digital game-based design workshop involving problem solving activities? (3) How do 9 to 10 year-old girls and boys employ their agency while collaboratively engaged in a digital game-based design workshop involving problem solving activities?

In the following, we present the theoretical framework of the study focusing on collaboration and gender differences in relation to interaction and agency. Next, the methodology is described, which is based on a case study approach using video observations and interaction analysis. Thereafter, we introduce the findings of the study followed by a discussion and conclusion.

2   Theoretical Perspectives

This paper focuses on gender differences in children's collaborative interaction while collaboratively engaged in a digital game-based design workshop involving problem solving activities. Here, collaboration refers to the social dimension of collaborative learning situations, with a particular focus on gender. Research shows that gender is crucial to a child's everyday life [23]. In educational activities, gender influences, for example, children's performance at school. Theories on collaborative learning, however, have ignored social aspects of collaborative learning situations, such as gender [24, 25].

2.1   Collaboration and Gender Differences in Social Interaction

In line with Damsa et al. [26], we propose an understanding of collaboration, wherein aspects of social and relational issues while involved in a learning activity are taken into consideration. In doing so, social interaction becomes central to the analysis, where different types of knowledge, attitudes, and expectations characterize how collaboration is performed and, in turn, requires participants to align with the demands of a certain task. Research has shown that gender has an impact on how boys and girls interact in a classroom setting as well as on their conversations in small groups [27, 28]. In her book, Howe [27] identified three general conclusions regarding boys' and girls' classroom interaction, where the first was that, in general, boys contribute more than girls, for example by dominating discussions concerning curriculum content. The second referred to the predominance of boys' contribution, which the author found was a result of teachers' selection and, also, of student-initiated interactions. This is confirmed also by other studies that found boys more likely to initiate interaction than girls [29]. Howe's third general conclusion was that boys received more feedback, both positive and negative, compared to girls. Research by Leaper and Smith [28] has also found that gender influenced boys' and girls' ways of expressing themselves. They found that girls were slightly more talkative and used more affiliative speech (showing support, expressing agreement, or acknowledging others' contributions) compared to boys. Leman et al. [30] investigated the relationship between gender and children's conversational styles in problem-solving tasks. In their study, children were introduced to three different kinds of counters (triangles, squares, and circles), where each kind of counter had a different value. The task for the children was to, in pairs, add the counters together to arrive at the value of 100. However, the children had been told different values of the counters, which resulted in conflicts among the pairs of children. Here, Leman et al. [30] found that the children used gendered ways of communicating, for example, boys interrupted their co-partner more if their co-partner was a girl compared to if the co-partner was a boy. This resulted in that the conversational tone was more negative when a pair of children consisted of a boy and a girl.

Leman [22] argues that effects of gender in different settings have important educational implications. If boys are perceived as more experts related to a certain activity or task, they may dominate the interaction in mixed-gender group interactions and, conversely, girls may dominate the interaction if they are perceived as the experts. Joiner and Littleton [24] found that gender had an impact on children's conversations. More specifically it had an impact on the disagreements in problem-solving activities.

For example, female same-gender pairs disagreed more compared to male same-gender pairs in problem-solving activities. This is known to be important in children's learning. However, the authors underline that more research is needed to further study the impacts of gender on collaboration and how it eventually impacts on learning.

2.2 Collaboration and Gender Differences in Agency

When children work together on collaborative tasks they have to try to get on with doing the task. Consequently, the way that they do things together is dependent on interrelations between the task in question and socio-relational issues. We relate this to how children through interaction and circumstances offered in different settings, establish agency. One of the conditions had to do with the fact that the children were placed in groups by their teachers and were not allowed to form groups themselves. Their ability and willingness for collaboration was bound to the participants within these groups, as was their sense of personal agency [31]. Another condition was that in both cases there was a majority of boys in the classes. However, in line with Baker-Sperry [18], our approach to agency refers to how children, through interaction and conversation (verbal and non-verbal) negotiate meanings inherent to the problem-solving task they were engaged in. In other words, we did not expect that the children should accept what they were instructed to do, but based on their own standpoints and as familiar of their position in the group they were assigned to, we acknowledged that they were able to understand and influence the collaboration within the group. In this way, our interest was directed towards how the children engaged in meaning-making with others, like in relational agency [32]. Accordingly, the setup of the problem-solving activity included opportunities for the children to interpret and approach the game design problem as well as for reading the environment, for drawing on the resources available, and for being a resource for others. The question is how such relational agency is exerted by boys and girls respectively in collaborative situations.

According to Edwards [32] relational agency captures a capacity to work with others and to draw on the resources they offer. It recognizes the importance of pre-existing personal understandings gained in other situations in mediating interpretations of new situations and argues for attention to the negotiations that individuals make as they work in and with the social [33]. Thus, relational agency helps to understand how boys and girls negotiate and reconfigure the tasks involved in the game design activity. In particular, we are interested in how the children negotiate and reconfigure responsibilities in the activity and how the children's actions are elicited by their interpretations of and their engagement with the game design activity as such.

3 Methodology

The present paper is referred to as a case study and it includes two separate research cases involving two classes of third grade school children, one from Denmark and one from Sweden. The case study methodology is frequently used to obtain knowledge about phenomena connected to individuals, groups and organizations [34] and as such it plays a significant role in research related to educational and social issues [35].

The purpose of a case study approach is to explore contemporary real-life phenomenon within its context and the relationships of a limited number of events or conditions through detailed contextual analysis [34]. Even though this study is not able to make any claims for generalizations (due to the moderate sample of empirical material), the results can however provide important indications within a limited area of interest. In this case, the aim of the study was to investigate how school children 'do' gender while collaboratively designing games. Thus, it is interesting to take a closer look at how children communicate with each other in game design activities and, moreover, how these activities are framed by the context. We are aware of that when approaching the issue of gender in our research, we are ourselves influenced by a range of factors including, amongst others, personal experience, gendered identities, and theoretical beliefs [36].

3.1 Participants

Case 1 included a class of 28 children from a third grade school in north Jutland, Denmark, north Jutland. The participants were divided between 19 males and 9 females between 9–10 years of age. Case 2 included a class of 22 children from a third grade school in south-west Halland, Sweden. Here, the participants included 16 males and 6 females between 9–10 years of age. Each class was involved in a creativity workshop case designed to provide a playful and creative atmosphere inspiring children to collaborate to create ideas for new games and/or game designs. Both workshops were carried out in research laboratory settings, and the participants were supplied with a wide range of analogue materials (in both cases) as well as digital technology (in Case 2) for creating stop-motion videos of the children's game design solutions. The two workshop cases were carried out in the form of a design experiment [37] in the sense that it was designed to control some variables emphasizing the availability of resources that the children can draw on and use, as well as allowing for situated interpretations related to the chosen theoretical framing. The authors of this paper designed the set-up of the study and the sessions were conducted by two research assistants to make it possible for the authors to observe the game design activities (the procedure is further elaborated below, Sect. 3.3). In Case 1 the workshop session took place in one room (approximately 90 m^2), which created a lively and slightly loud environment. In Case 2, the groups were divided into two rooms, which created a more calm atmosphere compared to the other case.

In both cases the children's teachers participated in the activity, which helped to create a safe learning environment; in Case 1, there were three teachers and in Case 2, there were two teachers. In addition, the two authors of this paper participated in both cases together with three assistants who assisted when the children needed help, kept an eye on the cameras, and supplied the children with water and fruit during the session. The teachers had on beforehand divided the children into six groups of either 5–6 (Case 1) or 3–4 (Case 2) children and each group had their own work station. Each of these work stations was equipped with a video camera, recording the whole game design session; what happened around the table as well as between the group members, other members and material available.

3.2 Video-Observations and Data Collection

To get access to as much multifaceted empirical material as possible, we chose to employ video-observations in this study. To record videos is especially useful when social interactions are in focus [38] and, also, an effective way to catch details that otherwise would have been missed out [39], since video recordings offer opportunities to review social actions and interactions. As mentioned previously, each of the work stations in both workshop cases was equipped with a video camera, recording the whole game design sessions. Accordingly, both cases used six cameras, which were operated by the research assistants, and produced empirical data consisting of 12 video observations (in total 25.8 h). In addition to the video observations, casual conversations with teachers and children, and field notes have continuously been recorded during the course of the study. In this way, our study included different types of knowledge representations (written, spoken as well as visual forms of text), which we put in relation to one another to represent various but interwoven stories of the research. This enabled a deeper insight into the context of our study.

Compared to more structured methods, such as interviews, video observations can capture complexity and nuance of people's interaction to a higher extent [40]. Video observations are also useful when it comes to analyzing verbal and nonverbal contexts in which a study takes place. Without video recorded material, it can be problematic to reliably analyze nonverbal communication, such as body language, gestures, posture, gaze, and mimicry [41]. This was especially important in this study as we were looking into how children communicate with each other through verbal as well as non-verbal interaction such as intonations and positioning. Video recording as a methodological tool can thus be seen as a reliable tool, but at the same time it is possible to question objectivity as video recording always includes a range of choices among different possible and interesting situations in an activity. The present study was set up in the form of a workshop carried out in two research laboratory settings, where the participants were divided into groups and supplied with creative material and digital equipment to produce stop-motion videos.

3.3 Procedure and Ethical Considerations

The present study is presented as a qualitative study where game design workshops were applied to enhance opportunities for collaboration and communication among the participating children. The game design workshop was structured in different phases intended to offer space for the children to express and position themselves, individually and as a group and in this way influence the collaboration with their peers in the group. The structure was there to motivate the participants' minds to exercise the collaborative game design process.

The workshop ran for half a day between 09:00–12:00 h and was divided into two distinct phases following the timings and activities depicted in Fig. 1, below.

In both cases, the research assistant introduced the game design activities to the children by telling them that they were going to be game designers and in groups create games based on a specific theme. The game design task was grounded in a narrative approach, where the authors, on beforehand, prepared six different themes locating the

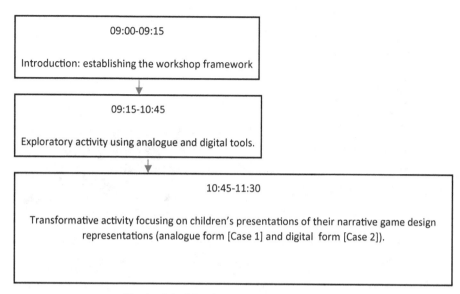

Fig. 1. Schedule of the game design workshop.

game design in different settings: Desert; Jungle; Woods; City; Under water; Space (one theme to each of the groups). The narrative as such, i.e. the game design, was developed by the children and, here, we also framed the activity for them. Each group received an A4 sheet of paper where the theme was written together with open space for the children to develop classical narrative content [42, 43], namely the plot, characters involved in the gameplay, and objects/props (Fig. 2, left) (storyboarding). The children were then introduced to the creative material (Fig. 2, right), for instance foam clay, modelling clay, crayons, markers, LEGO, cardboard, different kinds of papers, yarn, glue, tape, scissors, and post-its. The Case 2 children were also introduced to the stop motion equipment. The children were told that they were free to explore and use all materials at hand; there were no rights or wrong.

All teachers and parents were informed about the study in writing and the parents agreed to let their child participate by signing informed consent forms. The children were informed that they could withdraw from participation in the game design workshop at any time if they e.g. felt uncomfortable in any way. In line with ethical guidelines, all the names of the children as well as of the school are anonymized and, thereby, no identifying information is provided.

3.4 Analytical Approach

The analytical method applied for this study is interaction analysis [44]. This analytical approach is especially appropriate when working with human interaction, including verbal and non-verbal expressions (such as facial expressions, gestures and postures) as well as para-verbal expressions (where elements of speech such intonation, tone, stress, and rhythm are used). Jordan and Henderson writes: "Another topic of inherent interest for Interaction Analysis concerns the extent to which co-present individuals share

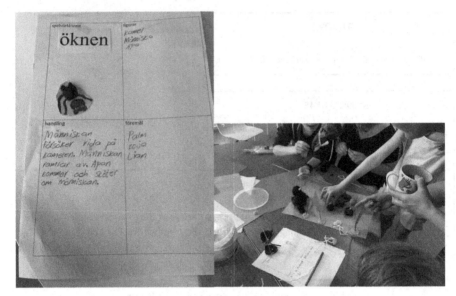

Fig. 2. The storyboard: instructional material provided in the initial phase of the workshop (left). Some of the creative material available for the children (right).

a common task orientation and attentional focus" (p. 67). Parts of the video recordings have been transcribed and analyzed in accordance with the theoretical principles of participation structures in interaction analysis [44]. Prior this process, the video recordings were repeatedly reviewed by both authors in order to identify recurring patterns of gendered interaction in verbal and non-verbal actions and interactions between the children and the analogue and digital game-based design activities. The transcriptions were then organized in different categories focusing on participation structures specifically related to gender differences. In total, four analytical steps were conducted throughout the process (see Table 1). From this analysis we identified three overall themes: (1) Gender-related patterns; (2) Gendered positionings; and (3) Gendered agentic actions, which are presented in the next section.

Table 1. Analytical steps in interaction analysis.

Steps	Activities undertaken	Foci guided by analysis
Step 1	Repeatedly reviewing video recordings	Overall view of the material
Step 2	Transcription of specific excerpts	Identifying recurring patterns of gendered differences
Step 3	Organization of excerpts into categories	Analyzing excerpts in accordance to participation structures
Step 4	Checking the categories guided by questions regarding the participation	Deciding which excerpts to include

4 Results

4.1 Gender-Related Patterns

Excerpt 1.

Actor	Verbal	Nonverbal
Alice	Cars, coins and a treasure chest	Writes on the storyboard
Ben	But we must also have houses!	Leans towards the storyboard
Alice	Houses, you don't have to have houses?!	Makes a frown, putting her arm between the storyboard and Ben
Carl	Yes, but we do!	
Alice	But how is it (all) going to fit?	Throws a skeptical glance at the table where they have placed a large sheet of paper
Ben	They (the houses) are up there, but in the background	Gesticulates on the sheet of paper on the table
Carl	They are here, you are filming up there, and they are driving like this	Showing on another piece of paper
Alice	But can't you just have a small house in a corner or something like that?	
Carl	I want quite a few houses	
Alice	But we write, like, two houses, because otherwise we will not have enough room for the roads, because the roads cannot be too narrow	Starts to write on the storyboard again

A recurring gender-related pattern was that in mix-gender groups, girls became leaders in the group, either by choice or by the others in the group appointing them to the task. Most often the leadership was initiated by the girl's way of expressing her beliefs effectively to influence the others. Excerpt 1 represents an interaction in a mix-gender group consisting of two boys and a girl discussing what their game's background should look like. Their game design theme is "the city" and they are filling in the storyboard. The girl was in charge of the pencil and the one who wrote details into the storyboard sheet of paper. The girls as leaders applied an assertive participation structure rather than an affiliative. As is shown in Excerpt 1, Alice expresses directive statements in her attempts to convince Ben and Carl that just a few houses are possible in order to have enough room for wide roads, which she considered more important than many houses. Through these assertive participation, Alice is reluctant to Ben and Carl's ideas and finally rejects their viewpoint by informing them what she wrote into the storyboard.

Another recurrent pattern of interaction related to gender in mix-gender groups was that girls were appointed as administrators of the group work, and as such responsible for the administrative part of the work, e.g. to fill out the storyboard for the task (like in Excerpt 1), to keep track of time, and to ensure that all the steps in the task were carried out.

4.2 Gendered Positioning

Excerpt 2.

Actor	Verbal	Nonverbal
Charlie	Should we make a tree out of clay?	Looking at Mary, working with clay, making a tiger
Tom	Nope	
Charlie	No. Couldn't we come up with another character so we can…or do you need…	Looking at both Tom and Mary
Tom	No, it's going to be too hard, this is enough	Looking at Charlie
	But it's enough with one tiger, that's enough!	Turning towards Mary, sharp glance
Mary	The only thing strange about just having one (tiger), because there are two monkeys and it can only chase after one at a time and in that case…	Looking at Tom
Charlie	Can't we make a jaguar?	Looking at both Mary and Tom
Tom	But we only have one	Facing Mary, ignores Charlies question
Mary	Now, but then that sort of can only be one monkey as well, otherwise it will be really weird because it can't chase both	Also ignoring Charlie
Tom	Yes, but it will chase both and, but, then you can see who is taken by it and they win…	Pointing at the material on the table
Mary	A but it will be a bit strange because it will say "victory" in the end and…	Pointing at the storyboard

In Excerpt 2, Tom and Mary have slightly different views on what to do regarding the characters to include in the game. According to their particular game design, a two-player design, there should be two tigers chasing two monkeys (player 1 and player 2) but Tom does not seem to want to do more than one tiger. Charlie very much wants to make something out of clay. The interaction shows how the participants by having different views, position themselves, in particular Tom and Mary, by trying, more or less strongly, convince the other person to agree with their specific standpoint. These positioning interactions lean towards a competing discourse where Tom and Mary try to come up with arguments to become the most powerful by controlling and decide what kind of and how many characters the game should include. However, they do this without stepping out of what could be considered as correct participation behavior. One reason why the interaction between Tom and Mary does not lead to a conclusion, is that both of them know what to do to produce their game idea and are prepared to lead the necessary actions to complete it. Clearly, Charlie had difficulties in gaining a constructive position in the group. One explanation to this is that his input to the interaction, by proposing the making of a jaguar, was totally outside the scope of conversation that engaged Tom and Mary.

4.3   Gendered Agentic Actions

Excerpt 3.

Actor	Verbal	Nonverbal
Alan		Drawing a tree on a piece of paper
Sarah		Is studying Alans drawing
Sarah	Remember not to draw too far out for you are also to do that banana bunches. You can think like two bunches on each tree	
Alan	No, one!	Looks up from the drawing, irritated look
Rick	No, we're just doing one bunch	
Sarah	But, like one bunch here and one there	She shows with her hand on the drawing
Alan	But it will be too much, with those lianas as well	Points in the air, towards the drawing
Sarah	But can't we have that, then you can, like, swing in them and it's just great fun!	Again, shows with her hands on the drawing, gesticulates and smiles
Alan	But not bunches of bananas, I mean lianas. We are going to have lianas. And bunches as well	Continues to draw on the tree
Rick	No bunches of bananas, that will be too hard, can't we skip bananas?!	Shakes his head
Sarah	But can't we have one (tree) with lianas and one with bananas	
Rick	But no, you should have lianas on all of them so you can swing from tree to tree, like this. See?	Showing with body movements how it should be done
Sarah	Okay, we take lianas then	Leans back heavily on her chair

In the specific context of this study, with its explorative and creative setting, the children's agency seemed to oscillate between individual freedom and the constraint of traditional gender patterns (as well as the set conditions for the task itself). In Excerpt 3, one of the groups, consisting of two boys and a girl, has "the jungle" as the theme for their game. They have jointly come up with a game narrative, the storyline (i.e. what will happen in the game), and are developing the background material. Initially, before the conversation taking place in Excerpt 3, the three participants of the group have discussed what makes trees significant for a jungle and concluded different standpoints whether lianas or bunches of bananas are most characteristic of jungle trees.

In their interaction, Sarah, Alan, and Rick are at the borderline of a conflict, but by the end of the conversation Sarah reaffirmed her understanding of a jungle tree and the conflict was avoided. At the start of the interaction, Sarah expresses her own standpoint about what a jungle tree should look like; it should be represented by both lianas and a couple of bunches of bananas. She instructs Alan, slightly assertively, by correcting his way of drawing the tree. Alan and Rick reply to this correction according to a gender-expected conversation style. For example, their argumentation tended to become assertive by closing rather than opening up for negotiation about the look of a jungle tree. However, all three children were eager to utilize their agency. This can be explained by the fact that the task, to produce a game design, offered both genders opportunities to contribute with their individual experiences in the field of game play. Sarah, in a gendered way, indicated collective agency by, from the start of the interaction in Excerpt 3, applied an affiliative interaction style where she targeted a mutual affirmation ("But can't we have one [tree] with lianas and one with bananas") and ended up with a willing submission ("Okay, we take lianas then").

We could identify that gendered agentic actions and participation structures may be influenced by different processes, such as negotiation, non-verbal meanings, routine actions, and relational aspects of agency. For example, when Sarah by being affiliative, introduced alternatives and negotiated meanings to address more than one possibility to represent a jungle tree.

5   Discussion

5.1   Emergent Gender Differences

In this paper, we set out to investigate how gender differences emerge in collaborative interactions between 9 to 10-year-old school children while collaboratively working on developing digital game-based designs. The results show that the participating girls, even though being in minority in both cases, put on a leading role in the groups where they secured an effective working structure so that the production process kept on track, as well as contributed practically in all phases of the design process. In some groups their role was negotiated and in some groups it was not acknowledged, but rather an obvious social contract in no need for negotiation. This corresponds to traditional gendered inter-action in school settings where girls tend to take a responsible role, either by their own choice or ascribed by others. In either case it is a socially rooted phenomena. However, the participation culture within the group work also included incidents showing non-expected gender differences. While Wong and Kemp [13] state that girls lack aspirations to position themselves, our study showed the opposite. This could be explained by the setup of the workshop and the material available (creative as well as technology-based) where we had considered children's pre-existing experiences of playing games. This kind of workshop design seemed to promote both boys' and girls' aspirations of contributing to fulfilling their game design ideas as well as influencing the collaboration in the group while engaged in meaning-making with each other. This is in line with Edwards [19, 32] who states that relational agency should capture a capacity to work with others by being attentive in and with the social. The relational agency was exerted in expected gendered participation structures, but in some instances also with non-expected interactions. For example, the girls as leaders used a combination of assertive and affiliative interaction patterns. In part this follows Leman et al. [30] who found that children use gendered ways of communicating in group-based problem solving activities, but it is also different from it as we could see that, in particular girls' gendered participation structures showed instances of unexpected gendered ways of interaction within their groups. Further, the participating girls contributed slightly more than the boys, for example through their leadership but also by dominating the content discussions concerning the game's storyline. This differs from Howe [27], who found that boys contribute more than girls in small group interactions and confirms Leaper and Smith's [28] study, stating that girls were slightly more talkative compared to boys in group-based interaction.

5.2 Conclusion and Implications for the Field

The ambition of this study is to contribute to the research field of children's learning conditions by highlighting gender differences in collaborative settings orchestrated by the school. Gender is ever present [6] and predominated everyday gendered subject positions are hard to overlook [12]. In addition, we hope to contribute to the field of human-computer-interaction (HCI), by illustrating how gender differences within the field of design and digital technologies with school children as actors might unfold. The results in this study imply that children's agency oscillate between individual freedom and the constraint of traditional gender patterns while collaboratively engaged in a digital game-based design workshop involving problem solving activities. As a consequence, this tends to affect the children's participation and contribution to the given task. In our case, we argue that the organization of the workshop, with creative elements and a large measure of freedom within a given framework, was beneficial for how the interactions between the children unfolded. By allowing the children, together in groups, to design digital games based on a given structure, where digital games are considered an interest for mainly boys [8], both boys and girls were allowed to exercise their personal agency [31], which had positive effects on participation on both parts. For example, in the groups that worked with the creation of stop-motion films to visualize their digital games (Case 2), both girls and boys clearly exercised their personal agency [31] by adopting the digital material. Even though technology is seen as a male domain [13], it was evident in the present study that the girls saw it as natural for them to interact with and use the digital technology, as did the boys. Pedagogically, the study challenges designers and teachers to rethink how they design learning activities in order to strengthen children's sense of personal agency [31] and to raise an awareness of gender differences that might have an impact on those. Considering that HCI becomes increasingly important in a school context (e.g. related to programming and computational thinking), this study aims to emphasize the importance of a gender conscious approach.

References

1. Camilleri, D.: Minding the gap. Proposing a teacher learning-training framework for the integration of robotics in primary schools. Inf. Educ. **16**(2), 165–179 (2017)
2. Nousiainen, T., Kangas, M., Rikala, J., Vesisenabo, M.: Teacher competencies in game-based pedagogy. Teach. Teach. Educ. **74**, 85–97 (2018)
3. Brooks, E., Sjöberg, J.: Evolving playful and creative activities when school children develop game-based designs. In: Brooks, A.L., Brooks, E., Sylla, C. (eds.) ArtsIT/DLI -2018. LNICST, vol. 265, pp. 485–495. Springer, Cham (2019). https://doi.org/10.1007/978-3-030-06134-0_51

4. Dele-Ajayi, O., Strachan, R., Pickard, A., Sanderson, J.: Designing for all: exploring gender diversity and engagement with digital educational games by young people. In: 2018 IEEE Frontiers in Education Conference (FIE), San Jose, CA, USA, pp. 1–9 (2018)
5. Lukosch, H., Kurapati, S., Groen, D., Verbraeck, A.: Gender and cultural differences in game-based learning experiences. Electron. J. e-Learn. **15**(4), 310–319 (2017)
6. Rubegni, E., Landoni, M., De Angeli, A., Letizia, J.: Detecting gender stereotypes in children digital StoryTelling. In: IDC 2019: Proceedings of the 18th ACM International Conference on Interaction Design and Children, pp. 386–393, June 2019
7. Spinner, L., Cameron, L., Calogero, R.: Peer toy play as a gateway to children's gender flexibility: the effect of (counter)stereotypic portrayals of peers in children's magazines. Sex Roles **79**, 314–328 (2018). https://doi.org/10.1007/s11199-017-0883-3
8. Admiraal, J., Huizenga, J., Heemskerk, I., Kuiper, E., Volman, M., ten Dam, G.: Gender-inclusive game-based learning in secondary education. Int. J. Incl. Educ. **18**(11), 1208–1218 (2014)
9. Chaudron, S., Di Gioia, R., Gemo, M.: Young children (0-8) and digital technology. A qualitative study across Europe. In: JRC Science for Policy Report, European Commission (2018)
10. Tatli, Z.: Traditional and digital game preferences of children: a CHAID analysis on middle school students. Contemp. Educ. Technol. **9**(1), 90–110 (2018)
11. Romrell, D.: Gender and gaming: a literature review. Paper presented at the annual meeting of the AECT International Convention, Hyatt Regency Orange County, Anaheim, CA (2014)
12. Jenson, J., de Castell, S.: Gender, simulation, and gaming: research review and redirections. Simul. Gaming **41**(1), 51–71 (2010)
13. Wong, B., Kemp, P.E.J.: Technical boys and creative girls: career aspirations of digitally skilled youths. Camb. J. Educ. **48**(3), 301–316 (2018)
14. Petersen, P.: "That's how much I can do" - children's agency in digital tablet activities in a Swedish preschool environment. Nordic J. Digit. Lit. **10**, 145–169 (2015)
15. Giannakos, M.N., Jaccheri, L.: From players to makers: an empirical examination of factors that affect creative game development. Int. J. Child-Comput. Interact. **18**, 27–36 (2018)
16. OECD: Bridging the digital gender divide. Include, upskill, innovate. OECD report (2018)
17. Kinnula, M., Iivari, N., Isomursu, M., Kinnula, H.: Socializers, achievers or both? Value-based roles of children in technology design projects. Int. J. Child-Comput. Interact. **17**, 39–49 (2018)
18. Baker-Sperry, L.: Gendered agency: power in the elementary classroom. Women Lang. **29**(2), 38–46 (2006)
19. Edwards, A.: Relational agency: learning to be resourceful practitioner. Int. J. Educ. Res. **43**(3), 168–182 (2005)
20. Vandenbroeck, M., De Bie, M.: Children's agency and educational norms: a tensed negotiation. Child. – Glob. J. Child Res. **13**(1), 127–143 (2006)
21. Katsiada, E., Roufidou, I., Wainwright, J., Angeli, V.: Young children's agency: exploring children's interactions with practitioners and ancillary staff members in Greek early childhood education and care settings. Early Child Dev. Care **188**(7), 937–950 (2018)
22. Leman, P.J.: Gender, collaboration and children's learning. In: Littleton, K., Howe, C. (eds.) Educational Dialogues: Understanding and Promoting Productive Interactions, pp. 216–239. Routledge, London (2010)
23. Lloyd, B., Duveen, G.: Gender Identities and Education: The Impact of Starting School. Hemel Hempstead: Harvester Wheatsheaf (1992)
24. Joiner, R., Littleton, K.: Paper and computers. Gender differences in children's conversations in collaborative activities. In: Baker, M., Andriessen, J., Järvelä, S. (eds.) Affective Learning Together. Social and Emotional Dimensions of Collaborative Learning, pp. 120–135. Routledge. Taylor & Francis Group, London (2013)

25. Joiner, R., Messer, D., Light, P., Littleton, K.: The effects of gender, expectations of success and social comparison on children's performance on a computer-based task. Educ. Psychol. **18**, 319–325 (1998)

26. Damşa, C., Ludvigsen, S., Andriessen, J.: Knowledge co-construction—epistemic consensus or relational assent? In: Baker, M., Andriessen, J., Jaarvela, S. (eds.) Affective Learning Together: Social and Emotional Dimensions of Collaborative Learning. New Perspectives in Learning and Instruction Series, pp. 97–119. Routledge, London (2013)

27. Howe, C.: Peer Groups and Children's Development. Wiley/Blackwell, London (2010)

28. Leaper, C., Smith, T.A.: A meta-analytic review of gender variations in children's talk: talkativeness, affiliative speech, and assertive speech. Dev. Psychol. **40**, 993–1027 (2004)

29. Duffy, J., Warren, K., Walsh, M.: Classroom interactions: gender of teacher, gender of student, and classroom subject. Sex Roles **45**, 579–593 (2001)

30. Leman, P.J., Ahmed, S., Ozarov, L.: Gender, gender relations, and the social dynamics of children's conversations. Dev. Psychol. **41**, 64–74 (2005)

31. Sirkko, R., Kyrönlampi, T., Puroila, A.: Children's agency: opportunities and constraints. IJEC **51**, 283–300 (2019)

32. Edwards, A.: Relational agency in professional practice: a CHAT analysis. Actio: Int. J. Hum. Activity Theory **1**, 1–17 (2007)

33. Billett, S.: Relational interdependence between social and individual agency in work and working life. Mind Cult. Activity **13**(1), 53–69 (2006)

34. Yin, R.: Case Study Research: Design and Methods, 2nd edn. Sage Publishing, Beverly Hills (1994)

35. Alnaim, F.: The case study method: critical reflection. Glob. J. Hum. Soc. Sci.: Arts Humanit. Psychol. **15**(7), 29–32 (2015)

36. Pink, S.: Doing Visual Ethnography, 2nd edn. SAGE Publications Ltd, London (2010)

37. Krange, I., Ludvigsen, S.: The historical and situated nature of design experiments: implications for data analysis. J. Comput. Assist. Learn. **25**(3), 268–279 (2009)

38. Hatch, A.: Doing Qualitative Research in Education Settings. State University of New York Press, New York (2002)

39. Knoblauch, H.: Videography: focused ethnography and video analysis. In: Knoblauch, H., Schnettler, B., Raab, J., Soeffner, H.-G. (eds.) Video Analysis: Methodology and Methods, pp. 69–84. Peter Lang, Frankfurt am Main (2009)

40. Cohen, L., Manion, L., Morrison, K.: Research Methods in Education, 7th edn. Routledge, New York (2011)

41. Heath, C., Hindmarsh, J., Luff, P.: Video in Qualitative Research. Analysing Social Interaction in Everyday Life. Sage, London (2010)

42. Greimas, A.J.: Actants, actors, and figures. On meaning: selected writings in semiotic theory. In: Theory and History of Literature, vol. 38, pp. 106–120. University of Minnesota Press, Minneapolis (1973/1987)

43. Ropp, V.: Morphology of the Folktale, 2nd edn. University of Texas Press, Austin (1928/1968)

44. Jordan, B., Henderson, A.: Interaction analysis: foundations and practice. J. Learn. Sci. **4**(1), 39–103 (1995)

Virtual Tourism in a Game Environment: Untangling Judged Affordances and Sense of Place

Ingvar Tjostheim[1]([⊠]) [iD] and John A. Waterworth[2] [iD]

[1] Norwegian Computing Center, P.O. Box 114, Blindern, 0314 Oslo, Norway
Ingvar.Tjostheim@nr.no
[2] Umeå University, Main Campus, 901 87 Umeå, Sweden

Abstract. The present study enriches and deepens understanding of the concepts of telepresence and sense of place, by examining their relevance to capture a place experience evoked in 3D environments through a research design that includes the affordance concept in virtual tourism. Many previous presence studies concern the in-the-moment experience without modeling the relationship with response variables that can help explain behavior in the digital or the material space. In this paper we tested affordance as the response variable in two different research models. The participants in our experiment explored the city of Los Angeles in a virtual environment (VE). Often, though not always, the participants had a feeling of "being there." The results indicated that both concepts – telepresence and sense of place – can be used to measure the user experience in a VE. Telepresence appears to be a more reliable predictor than the alternative concept sense of place, but its meaning aspect is generally less well known, particularly with regard to a tourist's intended activities and relevant affordances during a visit to a place.

Keywords: Virtual tourism · Telepresence · Sense of place · Affordance

1 Introduction

A place can be defined as a spatial environment that exists in the physical world. Tourists visit places and tourism researchers seek to capture and understand how tourists experience place, typically referred to as 'destination.' Most video games feature fantasy places, but there are many examples of well-known cities in games. Salmond and Salmond [1] observe that some videogames represent environments that encourage touristic behavior. This has not gone unnoticed by researchers studying geography, travel and tourism. The geographer Leigh Schwartz (2006) [2: 315] quotes a player of the video game *Grand Theft Auto*: "*You feel as if you're in a real town/city with other people*" (p. 315). According to Widyarto and Latiff [3] a virtual application works well in a travel context as a tool for getting to know a place. Is it possible that gamers visit and explore a game space in a similar manner to tourists?

The tourism industry uses different media-channels in order to attract visitors to a destination. A tourist may not be satisfied with a virtual substitute for a physical visit, but

© Springer Nature Switzerland AG 2020
X. Fang (Ed.): HCII 2020, LNCS 12211, pp. 202–217, 2020.
https://doi.org/10.1007/978-3-030-50164-8_14

the virtual experience might increase their desire to visit the actual place [4]. Lombard and Weinstein [5], in their study of technology-mediated presence experiences, quote a participant as writing: *"I completely felt that I was a part of the world and the characters and settings were all real and **places I have been** (our emphasis)", (p. 6).* This raises the question of whether an experience in a video game is only about the *here and now* of playing the game, or is it also about going to the place as a tourist, in other words a virtual tourism experience?

To illuminate this question in the present study, we formulated the following research questions; what is the relationship (if any) between the telepresence experience and affordances in the virtual environment, and what is the relationship (if any) between the sense of place experience and affordances?

From a theoretical point of view, how should we understand and empirically investigate the activities of a tourist through there actions at a destination in a virtual environment? In this paper, we draw attention to Gibson's affordance concept and the notion of action possibilities. According to Jonietz and Timpf [6], the affordance concept emphasizes the central role of action potentials for spatial perception and ties together the afforded action, geospatial objects and the subjective element of human perception. Jonietz and Timpf's context is geography. To these authors, places are predominantly perceived as action spaces. As a research field, tourism is closely related to geography [7].

The remainder of the paper is organized as follows. The next section is a review of previous research with relevance for understanding the experience of place in VEs and why we have chosen affordance as the dependent variable in the research models. Then, based on the review of the literature, research models and hypotheses are derived, followed in subsequent sections by an outline of the research method and measurements, data analysis and results. Finally, we conclude with a discussion of the results and their implications for theory and practice.

2 Perspectives on Virtual Places, Virtual Tourism and Game Environments

The concept of place is one of the core constructs in human geography [8]. Tourists visit places, and it is therefore reasonable that destinations and attractions represent a core subject in tourism research terminology [9]. Virtual reality (VR), film, graphics and many types of multimedia can be used to replicate a place and present it with a high degree of realism. Guttentag [10] argues that new technologies such as VR will create many opportunities for the tourism sector. Some videogames have created environments that encourage touristic behavior [1]. Virtual tourism and VR for tourism purposes can be traced back to the early 1990s [4, 11–14] when virtual tourism research was primarily conducted by information technology researchers. They anticipated virtual tourism becoming a mainstream knowledge domain for adoption by the tourism industry. Some also investigated the relationship between virtual tourism and actual travel. Fencott [15, 16] argued that the longer visitors linger overall in virtual tourism environment, the more likely they are to find the virtual experience memorable and perhaps retain the desire to actually visit the place the VE is modeling.

Slater and Sanchez-Vives [17] discuss virtual travel with reference to Cheong's (1995) [13] visions for virtual tourism in the mid-1990s, because "virtual reality offers numerous distinct advantages over the actual visitation of a tourist site." According to Slater and Sanchez-Vives this vision has not been fulfilled, and they speculate that: "Perhaps, VR is not meant to be a substitute for real travel but just **another form of travel** (our emphasis), no less valid in its own terms than all that physically boarding the real airplane entails". Acosta et al. [18], focused on mobile devices and technologies such as HTC VIVE, Oculus Rift and GearVR Headset as tools for the exchange of information and presenting atmospheric aspects of the experience. Tussyadiah et al. [19] found that virtual environment can increase enjoyment and produce a stronger liking and preference for a destination. They conclude that VR can an effective marketing tool and that their study "provides empirical evidence from the field of tourism to support previous research suggesting the positive consequences of presence in VR on attitude and behavior" (p. 152). According to Beck et al. [20] there are studies that suggest that VR, regardless of whether it is non-, semi- or fully immersive, is capable of positively influencing the individual motivation to actually visit a place.

Schwartz [2] argues that realism and attention to details allow gamers to experience game spaces as real. He cites a player of the video game entitled *Grand Theft Auto* as an example in which "you feel as if you're in a real town/city with other people" [2]. Therefore, it can be inferred that some gamers visit and explore the game space in a similar manner to tourists. Schwartz concludes that video game environments afford the blending of fantastic and realistic aspects into a believable, attractive place for players to visit, just as tourists may conjure up images of faraway places when reading stories about foreign countries.

We can also find examples of researchers who have approached game-worlds as ethnographer/tourists [21]. Martin [22] reviewed a number of video-games, 258 in total. Many of them included actual places in the USA. Quite often, racing games have reproductions of real tracks or cities. Liberty City in the game GTA IV is based on New York city. Martin [22] makes a detailed list of the names of places and streets in the game, and the equivalent names in the actual city. Although it is not a task in the game, a player of the game can explore the city as a tourist. Schweizer [23] give more detailed examples of tourist activities in games. In N.Y.C: The Big Apple, the game-player is a tourist seeking Manhattan landmarks and visiting places. In a number of games, sightseeing is an option, an alternative to explore the (game) place. In Driver San Francisco, monuments and landmarks "become essential for conveying the San Francisco-ness" of the city. Examples of landmarks are the Transamerica Pyramid, the Ferry Building, Union Square, Fisherman's Wharf and Lombard Street [23].

The authors of the publications from the Benogo project linked tourism and telepresence, and also human geography, to experiences in VEs [24–27]. The paper by Hyun and O'Keefe [28] builds on telepresence. There is a connection between the two; the term virtual tourism is related to telepresence because both concern the feeling of *being there*. In tourism research some refer to the telepresence concept, but there remains a dearth of empirical work, including telepresence measurements, in the context of virtual tourism.

3 Telepresence

In 1420 the Venetian engineer Giovanni Fontana designed the *castellum umbrarum*, the castle of shadows. Codognet [29] describe this apparatus as a pre-cave installation and probably one of the first examples of VR. Today the term telepresence is used to describe technology that allows a person to feel as if they were present at a place other than their physical location. According to Marvin Minsky [30], Patrick Gunkel at Hudson Institute coined the term "telepresence" in 1979. The term refers to tele-operation technology that provides the user with a "remote presence" in a different location via feedback systems that allow her to "see and feel what is happening." But the concept of telepresence is older. It emerged in an academic context beginning over a half a century ago in film theory [31] and sociology [32]. The first experimental three-dimensional TV set was built in the 1920s [33]. In the 1960s, Sutherland [34] wrote about *the ultimate display*. He describes the display as a technical system with interactive graphics, force-feedback devices, audio, smell and taste, which serves as one of the early empirical VR examples.

Telepresence refers to experiences that cover a wide range of phenomena involving interaction within a real, yet physically remote, environment. It is a rich concept with several components. It represents remote presence, i.e., a mediated (or medium-induced) experience [35, 36], and is usually designed to alter a given psychological state or subjective perception [37]. The highly cited definition by Lombard and Ditton [38] is of telepresence as the illusion of non-mediation. The media available to render this experience are not necessarily high-tech.

Some researchers describe the sense of presence as a function of our experience of a given medium [38–45]. According to this view, the level of presence is reduced by the experience of mediation. The question of why humans can feel presence when they use media or simulation technology is seldom addressed by researchers that advocate this view of media presence.

Other researchers consider presence as 'inner presence', a psychological phenomenon not necessarily linked to the experience of a medium [36, 46–53]. Presence is, according to this view "the intuitive perception of successfully transforming intentions into action" [54]. According to Waterworth et al. [55], this view reflects an understanding of the evolutionary function of presence, that of distinguishing internal events (such as daydreaming) from current external events in the physical world (which must often have priority for survival of the individual). Because of this, these authors suggest that immersion in a book or in a daydream should not be seen as an example of presence. Presence requires mental engagement with an external world (whether the physical world or a VR). Baños et al. [56] tested this interpretation by comparing reported sense of presence in imagined space versus VR. They found that participants in the former experienced a decrease in their sense of presence, compared to a control condition, whereas the opposite occurred for participants in VR.

By both these views, the sense of presence in a place produced by media will be less if the experience of mediation is greater. By the second view, the sense of place produced via technology is essentially the same kind of experience as that produced by visiting an actual physical location.

Turner, Turner and Carroll [27] comment that the users of a virtual environment need a meaningful narrative in order to create an engaging experience and a sense of place. The contextual factor plays a role that goes hand in hand with a compelling narrative. For testing and research purposes Turner and Turner [26] used the botanical garden and the technical university in Prague as two virtual environments. In the tests the participants were given specific roles and tasks. One of the tasks was to conduct surveillance and watch people use a staircase to come and go from a particular place in a virtual environment. These two quotes show that the participants experienced the environment differently: *"It was very empty I think,... very... very impersonal feeling..."* *"I think it took a lot of my attention just looking down, if anybody were coming in or going and then of course I was listening to all these... these voices around ..."* [26: 213]. The authors write *"Did the technology recreate the sense of being seated at a desk on a staircase in Prague?" the answer is again—not proven."* (p. 214). Turner et al. (2006) [27] assert that *"Relph's discussion of insideness and outsideness offers a compelling insight for contextualizing the VR experience."* [27: 291]. In a similar way, Shamai [57] argues that Relph's distinction between seven different degrees of outsideness and insideness in ways of sensing a place is quite suitable because it takes into account the strength of the relationship, the level of intensity of the experience in relation to the place. He writes that "each different way of sensing the place can be seen as a different level on an ordinal scale; that is, starting with the lowest level of sense of place and 'climbing' up six more steps to reach the most intense and deepest way of sensing a place" [57: 349]. Based on this it can be hypothesized that for a place experience the insideness types have a better fit with residents than for visitors, and that the outsideness types have a better fit with visitors than residents.

Biocca [58, 59] writes that the problem of presence, especially perception mediated by technology, or more generally telepresence, is most fruitfully conceptualized as a subset of the mind-body problem. For Biocca presence is motivated by the desire to transcend the body "to move beyond the limits of the body and the sensory channels" [58: 13] and he calls attention to what he calls the cyborg's dilemma: the extension of the human senses through technology [60]. Merleau-Ponty writes, in *Phenomenology of Perception* [61] that only through our lived bodies do we have access to what he describes as the primary world. He argues that consciousness is necessarily intentional. To him the most immediate and essential aspects of the lived dimension of space are sensory experience and bodily movement. His thinking has not gone unnoticed in telepresence, a field that often emphasises the visual sense. For instance, Turner et al. [27] write, after reviewing Merleau-Ponty's theory, "instead we argue that the role of the body in virtual environments can be attenuated by recognizing that a tourist's corporeality may be less important than their visual sense" [27: 11].

4   Affordance, Perception and Action

Gibson [62], a perceptual psychologist, introduced the term affordance in *The Ecological Approach to Visual Perception*. Since then the affordance concept has been used in a number of disciplines other than psychology. One example is human computer interaction [63, 64]. Affordance refers to something seen to be response-dependent, namely, instantiated by virtue of a behavioral response (e.g., a catching, a throwing) a subject would have relative to the property bearer. Affordances are independent of whether or not they are perceivable or eventually directly or indirectly perceived [65].

One type of affordance is a perceptual or *perceptible affordance* [66]. User interfaces can offer perceptual affordances because they can offer information about objects that can be acted upon. A perceptual affordance is a perceptual cue to the function of an object that causes an action. For instance, a visual presentation contains visual information about the behavioral possibilities afforded to the user. It is this action and behavioral aspect that the affordance concept captures.

There are a number of actions that provide perceptual affordances in sightseeing when it takes place in a virtual environment. A perceptual affordance queries what activity a particular sightseer would like to engage in at a particular moment in time. Consider an attraction on the screen, for instance, a tourist who gazes at a historic monument and at that moment thinks "I will walk to the front-door and enter the building through that door." A video game context can simultaneously enable the perception of action when watching images on a screen, while sitting passively in a chair. An example might be a website for a destination developed for marketing purposes. What is the effect of this website? An interview may reveal that the website-user considers the portrayed destination to be beautiful. Whilst another person who looks at the same website may decide it is time to book accommodation; find out how to get there, and search for events and what to do upon arrival. It is this second example that corresponds to the notion of perceptual affordance. Flach and Holden [67] were among the pioneering scholars to investigate affordance and presence and emphasized the necessity to understand the effect of interaction with objects in virtual environments.

In this paper we argue that affordance, a concept emphasizing behavioral possibilities, seems relevant as a response variable in an empirical study on virtual tourism. We developed and tested two research models in order to investigate sightseeing experiences in a VE. The first is a model with a telepresence measurement instrument, the second model with a sense of place measurement instruments from human geography. Affordance, a perceptual possibility for action, is our choice for the response variable in both models.

5   Research Models and Hypotheses

We derived three constructs from our literature review presented above, each concerning experience of place, with affordance as the response variable. The telepresence perspective emphasizes mediated experience(s), for instance how an environment in a game is perceived. The constructs from human geography underscore the relationship between individuals and a place, and also what the place means to a person. These were not developed with new technology in mind, but still the concepts might also be relevant to use in a mediated environment. Affordance incorporates the active element, not only passive viewing but the behavioral as well.

In both research models we posited a positive association between the independent variables and the response variable affordance. Prior research on telepresence indicates a positive relationship; a high level of presence is more strongly associated with affordance than a weaker level of presence. Figure 1 presents the two research models investigated in this study. We hypothesised that we would also find a positive relationship with affordance in these models.

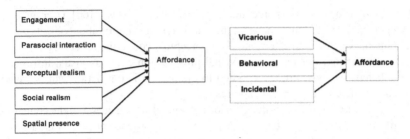

Fig. 1. Research model 1 (left) and Research model 2 (right)

6 Method

The research design was a within-subject design, meaning that all participants had the same sightseeing experience which was measured with the same scales. For pre- and post-questionnaires, paper and pencil testing was used. Before an individual session was completed, the interviewer checked that the participant's two questionnaires had been fully completed.

6.1 Participants

A total of 60 students took part in the study. They were recruited from a class of international summer students (19), from classes at two different business schools (25) and through an electronic billboard for university students (16). Of the 60 participants, 60% were female and 40% were male, 48% were between 19 and 24 years old, 27% between 25 and 29, and 25% were 30 years or older. Of the participants, 75% answered that they used video or computer games approximately once a month or more seldom and 25% weekly or daily. The students were offered 5 euros for participating in the study.

6.2 Materials

This study applied video gaming, specifically a *Playstation* game, with the purpose of creating an immersive and lifelike 3D environment for sightseeing. The game *Midnight club LA,* containing sections of Los Angeles, was chosen for this purpose. Many tourists go sightseeing and, although the game does not contain a sightseeing tour as such, it enables users to sightsee. In order to achieve ecological validity by creating a sightseeing experience in the VE corresponding to physical sightseeing in the city, the music that comes as a game component was turned off and replaced by an audio clip taken from the *Tourcaster* production *Hollywood Audio Tour.* As a consequence, the audio came from a laptop computer placed in front of the participant and not the game itself. The guide on the audio is a storyteller. For the participants, the visuals, the interaction through the steering wheel and the story told by the guide, became one experience. Tourists share their experiences with others and good stories are persuasive [68, 69]. To cite Weick [70], they think narratively [71]. A sightseeing experience is thus more than just a visual experience.

6.3 Procedure

The same procedure was used for all participants. First the interviewer explained that the participant was going to visit a city on the screen after s/he had filled in a pre-study questionnaire. The session with introduction, pre-study questionnaire, sightseeing, and post-study questionnaire lasted 45 min of which the sightseeing lasted 15–20 min. The name of the city was not explicitly mentioned before the participant filled in the pre-study questionnaire, but the participant could see a view from Los Angeles (LA) on the screen. The invitation had pictures from Los Angeles and a short text about sightseeing in LA. After the pre-study questionnaire was completed, the interviewer gave a short demo and explained to the participants how to use a Playstation with a steering wheel. The interviewer said *"you are now going to do sightseeing in LA on the screen in front of you."* In order to synchronize the visuals and the sound, the interviewer gave instructions such as "now please stop and listen to the guide", "please continue on Hollywood Blvd to the traffic light in front of the Highland center", "please stop in front of the shop opposite the Graham Chinese Theater and listen to the guide", so on. The participants used a steering wheel with the option "bumper view" which means that the participant did not see the car, but only the street, that is the environment in front of the car. Although the sound was not fully integrated in the game, the visual and the narrative fitted well together.

Only after the task and surveys were completed were the participants shown the cover of the game. The post-study questionnaire revealed that none of the participants had actually played the game *Midnight club LA* before participating in this study.

6.4 Measurement Instruments and Structural Modeling

We applied different measurement instruments on the dependent side for each of the two research models, and the affordance measurement for the response measurement, as shown in Fig. 1. The Temple Presence Inventory (TPI) was used to measure telepresence [38]. The TPI uses a 7-points Likert scale and prior research has validated the scale [38, 72]. The measurement for Relph's three types of sense of place, was made by Tjostheim and Go [73, 74]. Finally, affordance was measured with a three-item scale developed by the first author.

Partial least square (PLS) was used to verify the two measurement models and test the research hypotheses. PLS is a structural equation modeling technique, which can simultaneously estimate measurement components and structural components that are the relationships among these constructs [75, 76]. PLS is appropriate to use when assumptions of multivariate normality and interval scaled data cannot be made, and when the primary concern is with the prediction of dependent endogenous variables [77]. As a structural equation-modeling tool PLS can handle formative and reflective constructs, and compared to other SEM tools such as LISREL and AMOS, it does not require a large sample size [76, 78]. With PLS it is not a prerequisite that the research models are based on comprehensive theories [76, 79]. A research model should have a theoretical foundation, but might contain exploratory aspects. This is particularly relevant if the research purpose aims to expand a model or theory. In this study, scales from established theories were applied in a setting in which 3D technology was used to create a mediated experience. As a consequence, the study contained an exploratory aspect.

The minimum sample size required by PLS is seven to ten times the larger number of paths leading to an endogenous construct when, as in this study, all constructs are reflective [79]. Furthermore, the guidelines and quality criteria for PLS and measurement modeling were followed. The first step was to assess the convergent validity, reliability and discriminant validity of all latent constructs before testing the research model. Discriminant validity is suggested if all measurement items load more strongly on their respective construct than on other constructs. Convergent validity is suggested if factor loadings are 0.60 or higher [80] and each item loads significantly on its latent construct [81]. Some items were lower than 0.6, see for example place dependency, but without having a negative effect on the discriminant and convergent validity of the research models. For spatial presence, the item with a loading below 0.6 it is easy to explain and as expected, because the voice of the narrator was not integrated with the game, but came from a laptop computer. The perceived lack of control with para-social interaction can be related to the fact that the sightseer did not interact with the avatar. The avatar moved out of the way when the sightseer came close, but this just happened without direct interaction from the participant. For place dependency, it is the item "no other place can be compared to Los Angeles" that did not load on the construct.

Some researchers delete items with a low loading, but in this study these three items were not removed. When a construct has five to seven items to capture the completeness of the construct as in this case, the fact that one does not load satisfactorily on all items is not a substantial problem. Also, the square root of AVE of each construct should be higher than the correlations between that construct and any other constructs [75]. All constructs in the two research models satisfied these two criteria for discriminant validity with one exception. There was a correlation between spatial presence and parasocial interaction. For all latent variables, the composite reliability and Cronbach's alpha exceeded the recommended thresholds for exploratory research of 0.7 and 0.6 respectively, and the average variance extracted (AVE) was above the recommended 0.5 threshold, indicating a satisfactory level of convergent validity. Therefore, the four measurement models are considered reliable and valid, and able to support further analysis of the research hypotheses.

7   Results

Partial least squares (PLS) analysis was used to interpret data from the study and to test the hypotheses.

7.1   Results of the Hypothesis Testing

The first hypothesis states that there is a positive association between telepresence and affordance. The telepresence instrument, the TPI, contains five sub-constructs. The paths between engagement, perceptual realism presence and parasocial interaction were significant; see Fig. 2. Affordances concern interaction and as expected there was a significant relationship with engagement and parasocial interaction. From a theoretical point of view the user could have a high or low experience of 3D space and this can be unrelated to affordance. The lack of a significant relationship between spatial presence and affordance is therefore not surprising. In sum, there was a significant path between the feeling of being there and affordance. Chin [82] describes R^2 as above 0.67 as substantial, and above 0.33 as moderate. The analysis shows that the overall R^2 was 0.59 for model 1. This is an indication that there was a medium to strong association between telepresence with affordance.

The TPI has a theoretical foundation [38] and the result can be regarded as an expected result. The TPI sub-constructs capture nuances that will be missed if a scale based on a simple question such as "to what extent did you have a feeling of being there" is applied. In Table 1 we present detailed information of the four models with sub-constructs. We conclude that research model 1 is supported.

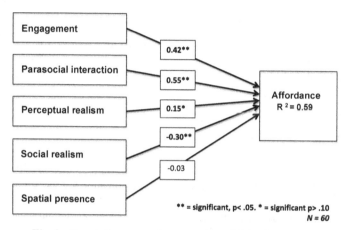

Fig. 2. Correlation scores for research model 1 subconstructs

Table 1. PLS results of the two models

Hypothesis	Path coefficient β	T-values	Conclusion
Model 1 - telepresence			Supported
Engagement -> affordance	0.42	3.18**	
Perceptual -> affordance	0.15	1.89*	
Parasocial -> affordance	0.55	5.12**	
Social Realism -> affordance	−0.30	2.10**	
Spatial presence -> affordance	−0.03	0.16 ns	
Model 2 - sense of place			Supported
Vicarious -> affordance	0.33	3.44**	
Behavioral -> affordance	0.45	4.85**	
Incidental -> affordance	−0.09	0.80 ns	

* p < 0.1** p < 0.05, ns non-significant

For the second research model based on Relph's theory of sense of place, the explained variance was on a moderate level [82]. In the model the direct path for incidental outsideness and affordance was not significant (see Fig. 3 and Table 1), but for vicarious outsideness and behavioral outsideness the paths were significant. We also conclude that the data supports research model 2.

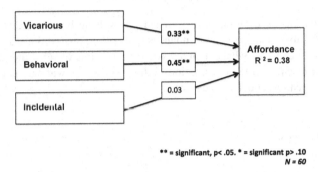

Fig. 3. Correlation scores for research model 2 subconstructs

8 Discussion

In the physical world, place experience is a multifaceted phenomenon. That is to say, a place such as a city represents many offerings and meanings. One single measurement cannot capture all aspects and nuances of such offerings and meanings. A scale made to capture the experiential character of place, by necessity, would have to emphasize certain aspects and nuances at the expense of others. As a consequence, specific experiential aspects and nuances of place that might be relevant for some individuals in a particular situation or context are likely to be excluded. A multi-theoretical and multi-methodological approach is thus justified in the present study, because it affords comparison by contrasting the results of the scales employed.

In the present study, telepresence is a key concept. The study was designed as a personal sightseeing experience, which takes place in a VE, rather than in physical place in real time. Telepresence researchers would refer to this place as *there*. However, the other theories employed in this study emphasize the *place* concept to a stronger degree. For example, human geography and leisure science are concerned with what meaning the concept of place and the bonds to the place might have for the resident or visitor. With affordance as the dependent (response) variable structural modeling showed that the telepresence concept performs well with a relatively high variance explained, followed by sense of place, in explaining the effect of the VE experience. Many scholars have taken to using the telepresence construct, because it rests on a sound theoretical foundation and as expected worked well for city sightseeing in a VE.

Edward Relph [83] writes that he has limited knowledge about technology and virtual reality. However, Benyon et al. [84]; Smyth et al. [25]; Turner et al. [27], and the empirical data from this study attest that Relph's theory seems to be an appropriate foundation for capturing and exploring a virtual environment in a travel and tourism context. Semantically, vicarious sense of place and telepresence are related. Depending on the purpose of a study, Relph's theory can be used either together with telepresence or separately. There is a significant risk that a single scale or a one-size-fits-all approach will omit relevant information by not taking into account important factors. One goal of behavioral studies is to understand and predict how people behave. It is essential to understand tourists' needs, motives and attitudes and in this regard the behavioral aspect of this study, particularly its emphasis on behavioral outsideness, represents a good fit.

When someone is sightseeing in a VE of a city that actually exists, it is primarily a visual experience, but the place is perceived as real [85]; or, to paraphrase the telepresence terminology, that person may have the feeling of *being there*. Some authors use the term real as an antonym for the term virtual. However, as this can be misleading, Lee [37] suggests that it is more appropriate to use the term *actual*. Following Etzioni and Etzioni [86] we suggest that *face-to face* may be an even more fitting term than *actual* or *real*. As Chalmers [87: 309] argues *"...virtual reality is a sort of genuine reality, virtual objects are real objects, and what goes on in virtual reality is truly real."*

In all, the answer to the question of which method and theories to use and under what circumstances is not simple. Statistical analysis is no panacea and cannot replace salient theories and critical ideas that have stood the test of time. No doubt today's technologies will be further improved and refined, especially their capacity to replicate places and aid tourists to imagine what activities they might be able to experience while visiting a particular place. Technologies are expected to play a role of significance in processes of replicating places and supporting tourists by boosting their powers of imagination. In this regard, visual and immersive technologies have the potential to bring about a new arena for interaction and competition, particularly in tourism marketing [88].

9 Concluding Remarks

Chris Ryan [89: 46] writes *"The tourist experience is shaped by many things, motive, past experience, knowledge of place, persons with whom that place is shared, and patterns of change at the place, the images induced about place and activities, individual personalities."* Today, technology plays a key role in all phases of traveling, from planning, the travel itself, and on to the post-visit phase. Our study emphasized the subjective experience; how our participants judged affordances, the sense of presence when sightseeing in a virtual environment. The feeling of being there is not necessarily something that happens all the time during sightseeing in a VE. Engagement, which also has to do with the narrative and not only the visual and interactive element, contributes significantly to the feeling. Gottlieb [90] argues that the vacationer's experience is real, valid and fulfilling, no matter how superficial it may seem to a social scientist. Sightseeing via a screen might be described as superficial, but in the moment it can be perceived as a real.

References

1. Salmond, M., Salmond, J.: The gamer as tourist: the simulated environments and impossible geographies of videogames. In: Morpeth, N.D. (ed.). Tourism and the Creative Industries: Theories, Policies and Practice, pp. 151–163. Routledge, London and New York (2016)

2. Schwartz, L.: Fantasy, realism, and the other in recent video games. Space Cult. **9**(3), 313–325 (2006)
3. Widyarto, S., Latiff, M.S.A.: The use of virtual tours for cognitive preparation of visitors: a case study for VHE. Facilities **25**(7/8), 271–285 (2007)
4. Dewailly, J.M.: Sustainable tourist space: from reality to virtual reality? Tourism Geogr. **1**(1), 41–55 (1999)
5. Lombard, M., Ditton, T.B., Weinstein, L.: Measuring telepresence: the validity of the temple presence inventory (TPI) in a gaming context. In: Fourteenth International Workshop on Presence (ISPR 2011), October, Edinburgh (2011)
6. Jonietz, D., Timpf, S.: On the relevance of Gibson's affordances for geographical information science (GISc). Cogn. Process. **16**(Suppl. 1), 265–269 (2015)
7. Lew, A.: Editorial: a place called tourism geographies. Tourism Geogr. **1**, 1–2 (1999)
8. Kaltenborn, B.P.: Effects of sense of place on responses to environmental impacts—a study among residents in Svalbard in the Norwegian High Arctic. Appl. Geogr. **18**(2), 169–189 (1998)
9. Tribe, J.: The indiscipline of tourism. Ann. Tourism Res. **24**(3), 638–657 (1997)
10. Guttentag, D.: Virtual reality: applications and implications for tourism. Tourism Manag. **31**(5), 637–651 (2009)
11. Bauer, C., Jacobson, R.: Virtual travel: promoting tourism to unfamiliar sites through pre-trip experience. In: ENTER 1995: Information and Communication Technologies in Tourism, pp. 17–21. Springer, Vienna (1995)
12. Benjamin, I., Cooper, M.: Virtual tourism - a realistic assessment of virtual reality for the tourist industry. In: ENTER 1995: Information and Communication Technologies in Tourism, pp. 135–143. Springer, Vienna (1995)
13. Cheong, R.: The virtual threat to travel and tourism. Tourism Manag. **16**(6), 417–422 (1995)
14. Williams, P., Hobson, J.S.P.: Virtual reality and tourism: fact or fantasy? Tourism Manag. **16**(6), 423–427 (1995)
15. Fencott, C.: Content and creativity in virtual environments design. In: Proceedings of Virtual Systems and Multimedia 1999, pp. 308–317. University of Abertay Dundee, Dundee (1999)
16. Fencott, C., Ling, J., van Schaik, P., Shafiullah, M.: The effects of movement of attractors and pictorial content of rewards on users' behaviour in virtual environments: an empirical study in the framework of perceptual opportunities. Interact. Comput. **15**, 121–140 (2003)
17. Slater, M., Sanchez-Vives, M.: Enhancing our lives with immersive virtual reality. Front. Robot. AI **3**, 74 (2016)
18. Acosta, A.F., et al.: Tourism marketing through virtual environment experience. In: Proceedings of the 2017 9th International Conference on Education Technology and Computers, pp. 262–267. ACM, December 2017
19. Tussyadiah, I.P., Wang, D., Jung, T.H., tom Dieck, M.C.: Virtual reality, presence, and attitude change: empirical evidence from tourism. Tourism Manag. **66**, 140–154 (2018)
20. Beck, J., Rainoldi, M., Egger, R.: Virtual reality in tourism: a state-of-the-art review. Tourism Rev. **74**(3), 586–612 (2019)
21. Miller, K.: The accidental carjack: ethnography, gameworld, tourism, and grand theft auto. Game Stud. **8**(1), 147 (2008)
22. Martin, P.: Space and place as expressive categories in videogames. Unpublished thesis, Brunel University (2011)
23. Schweizer, R.T.: Videogames cities in motions. Dissertation, Georgia Institute of Technology (2014)
24. O'Neill, S.J., McCall, R., Smyth, M., Benyon, D.R.: Probing the sense of place. In: Proceedings of the Seventh Annual International Workshop Presence 2004, Universidad Politecnica de Valencia, Spain (2004)

25. Smyth, M., Benyon, D.R., McCall, R., O'Neill, S.J., Carroll, F.: Patterns of place – a toolkit for the design and evaluation of real and virtual environments. In: Ijsselsteijn, W., Biocca, F., Freeman, J. (eds.) The Handbook of Presence. Lawrence Erlbaum, Mahwah (2006)
26. Turner, P., Turner, S.: Place, sense of place, and presence. Presence: Teleoperators Virtual Environ. **15**(2), 204–217 (2006)
27. Turner, P., Turner, S., Carroll, F.: The tourist gaze: towards contextualised virtual environments. In: Turner, P., Davenport, E. (eds.) Spaces, Spatiality and Technology, pp. 1–14. Kluwer, Dordrecht (2006)
28. Hyun, M.Y., O'Keefe, R.M.: Virtual destination image: testing a telepresence model. J. Bus. Res. **65**(1), 29–35 (2012)
29. Codognet, P.: Artificial Nature and Natural Artifice. http://pauillac.inria.fr/~codognet/VR.html. Accessed 27 Jan 2020
30. Minsky, M.: Telepresence. Omni (June) 45–51 (1980)
31. Bazin, A.: What is Cinema? (H. Gray, Trans.). University of California Press, Los Angeles (Original work published 1951) (1967)
32. Goffman, E.: The Presentation of Self in Everyday Life. Doubleday, Anchor Books, New York (1959)
33. Pourazad, M.T., Nasiopoulos, P., Ward, R.K.: Generating and depth map from the motion information of H.264-encoded 2D video sequence. EURASIP J. Image Video Process. **2010**(1), 108584 (2010). https://doi.org/10.1155/2010/108584
34. Sutherland, I.E.: The ultimate display. In: Proceedings of International Federation for Information Processing (IFIP) Congress 1965, New York, pp. 506–508, May 1965
35. Bolter, J.D.: Literary texts in an electronic age: scholarly implications and library services. In: Sutton, B. (ed.) Proceedings the Clinic on Library Applications of Data Processing, pp. 7–20, 10–12 April 1994
36. Fisher, S.S.: Recent developments in virtual experience design and production. In: Fisher, S.S., Bolas, M.T., Merritt, J.O. (eds.) Stereoscopic Displays and Virtual Reality Systems. Proceedings of SPIE, vol. 2409 (1995)
37. Lee, K.M.: Presence, explicated. Commun. Theory **14**(1), 27–50 (2004)
38. Lombard, M., Ditton, T.B.: At the heart of it all: the concept of presence. J. Comput.-Mediat. Commun. **3**(2), JCMC321 (1997)
39. IJsselsteijn, W.A., de Ridder, H., Freeman, J., Avons, S.E.: Presence: concept, determinants and measurement. In: Proceedings of the SPIE, Human Vision and Electronic Imaging V, San Jose, CA, January 2000
40. Loomis, J.M.: Distal attribution and presence. Presence: Teleoperators Virtual Environ. **1**(1), 113–119 (1992)
41. Marsh, T., Wright, P., Smith, S.: Evaluation for the design of experience in virtual environments: modeling breakdown of interaction and illusion. Cyberpsychol. Behav. **4**(2), 225–238 (2001)
42. Sadowski, W.J., Stanney, K.M.: Measuring and managing presence in virtual environments. In: Stanney, K.M. (ed.) Handbook of Virtual Environments Technology. Lawrence Erlbaum Associates, Mahwah (2002)
43. Schloerb, D.: A quantitative measure of telepresence. Presence: Teleoperators Virtual Environ. **4**(1), 64–80 (1995)
44. Sheridan, T.B.: Musing on telepresence and virtual presence. Presence: Teleoperators Virtual Environ. **1**, 120–125 (1992)
45. Sheridan, T.B.: Further musing on the psychophysics of presence. Presence: Teleoperators Virtual Environ. **5**, 241–246 (1996)
46. Baños, R.M., Botella, C., Perpiña, C.: Virtual reality and psychopathology. Cyberpsychol. Behav. **2**(4), 283–292 (1999)

47. Mantovani, G., Riva, G.: "Real" presence: how different ontologies generate different criteria for presence, telepresence, and virtual presence. Presence: Teleoperators Virtual Environ. **8**(5), 538–548 (1999)

48. Riva, G., Davide, F., IJsselsteijn, W.A. (eds.) Being There: Concepts, Effects and Measurements of User Presence in Synthetic Environments. IOS Press, Amsterdam (2003)

49. Schubert, T., Friedmann, F., Regenbrecht, H.: The experience of presence: factor analytic insights. Presence Teleoperators Virtual Environ. **10**, 266–281 (2001)

50. Spagnolli, A., Gamberini, L.: Immersion/emersion: presence in hybrid environments. Paper presented at the Presence 2002: Fifth Annual International Workshop, Porto, Portugal, 9–11 October 2002 (2002)

51. Waterworth, J.A., Waterworth, E.L.: Focus, locus, and sensus: the three dimensions of virtual experience. Cyberpsychol. Behav. **4**(2), 203–213 (2001)

52. Waterworth, J.A., Waterworth, E.L.: The meaning of presence. Presence-Connect **3**(2) (2003)

53. Zahoric, P., Jenison, R.L.: Presence as being-in-the-world. Presence: Teleoperators Virtual Environ. **7**(1), 78–89 (1998)

54. Riva, G., Waterworth, J.A., Waterworth, W.L., Mantovani, F.: From intention to action: the role of presence. New Ideas Psychol. **29**, 24–37 (2011)

55. Waterworth, J.A., Waterworth, E.L., Riva, G., Mantovani, F.: Presence: form, content and consciousness. In: Lombard, M., Biocca, F., Freeman, J., IJsselsteijn, W., Schaevitz, R.J. (eds.) Immersed in Media, pp. 35–58. Springer, Cham (2015). https://doi.org/10.1007/978-3-319-10190-3_3

56. Baños, R.M., Botella, C., Guerrero, B., Liaño, V., Alcañiz, M., Rey, B.: The third pole of the sense of presence: comparing virtual and imagery spaces. PsychNology **3**(1), 90–100 (2005)

57. Shamai, S.: Sense of place: an empirical measurement. Geoforum **22**, 347–358 (1991)

58. Biocca, F.: The cyborg's dilemma: progressive embodiment in virtual environments. J. Comput. Mediat. Commun. **3**(2), JCMC324 (1997)

59. Biocca, F.: Inserting the presence of mind into a philosophy of presence: a response to Sheridan and Mantovani and Riva. Presence: Teleoperators Virtual Environ. **10**(5) 546–556 (2001)

60. Mennecke, B.E., Triplett, J.L., Hassall, L.M., Conde, Z.J.: Embodied social presence theory. In: 43rd Hawaii International Conference on System Sciences (HICSS), Hawaii, USA, pp. 1–10 (2010)

61. Merleau-Ponty, M.: Phenomenology of Perception (trans. C. Smith). Routledge, New York (Original work published in 1945) (1962)

62. Gibson, J.J.: The Ecological Approach to Visual Perception. Houghton Mifflin, Boston (1979)

63. Norman, D.A.: Affordances, conventions, and design. Interactions **6**(3), 38–41 (1999)

64. Hartson, H.R.: Cognitive, physical, sensory and functional affordances in interaction design. Behav. Inf. Technol. **22**(5), 315–338 (2003)

65. Scarantino, A.: Affordances explained. Philos. Sci. **70**, 949–961 (2003)

66. Gaver, W.W.: Technology affordances. In: Robertson, S.P., Olson, G.M., Olson, J.S. (eds.) Proceedings of the ACM CHI 91, Human Factors in Computing Systems Conference, New Orleans, Louisiana, 28 April–5 June 1991, pp. 79–84 (1991)

67. Flach, J.M., Holden, J.G.: The reality of experience. Presence Teleoperators Virtual Environ. **7**, 90–95 (1998)

68. McKee, R.: Storytelling that moves people; a conversation with screenwriting coach. Harvard Bus. Rev. **80**, 51–55 (2003)

69. Woodside, A.G., Megehee, C.M.: Advancing consumer behavior theory in tourism via visual narrative art. Int. J. Tourism **12**(5), 418–431 (2010)

70. Weick, K.E.: Sensemaking in Organizations. Sage, Thousand Oaks (1995)

71. Woodside, A.G., Cruickshank, B.F., Dehuang, N.: Stories visitors tell about Italian cities as destination icons. Tourism Manag. **28**(1), 162–174 (2007)

72. Nunez, D.: A capacity limited, cognitive constructionist model of virtual presence. Unpublished Ph.D. thesis, Department of Computer Science, University of Cape Town, South Africa (2007)
73. Tjostheim, I., Go, F.M.: Sense of place in a virtual environment. Edward Relph's place theory, vicarious and behavioral outsideness. In: Proceedings TTRA Europe, Rotterdam-Breda, 22–23 April 2009, pp. 337–351 (2009)
74. Tjostheim, I., Go, F.M.: Place marketing and experience of place in a virtual environment. In: Go, F., Govers, R. (eds.) International Place Branding Yearbook 2011. Managing Reputational Risk. Palgrave Macmillan (2012)
75. Fornell, C., Larcker, D.F.: Evaluating structural equation models with unobservable variables and measurement error. J. Mark. Res. **18**(1), 39–50 (1981)
76. Barclay, D.C., Higgins, C., Thompson, R.: The partial least squares approach to causal modeling: personal computer adoption and use as an illustration. Technol. Stud. **2**(2), 285–308 (1995)
77. White, J.C., Varadarajan, P.R., Dacin, P.A.: Market situation interpretation and response: the role of cognitive style, organizational culture, and information use. J. Mark. **67**(3), 63–79 (2003)
78. Fornell, C., Bookstein, F.L.: Two structural equation models: LISREL and PLS applied to consumer exit-voice theory. J. Mark. **19**, 440–452 (1982)
79. Chin, W.W., Marcolin, B.L., Newsted, P.R.: A partial least squares latent variables modeling approach for measuring interaction effects: results from a monte carlo simulation study and an electronic-mail emotion/adoption study. Inf. Syst. Res. **14**(2), 189–217 (2003)
80. Bagozzi, R.P., Yi, Y.: On the evaluation of structural equation models. J. Acad. Mark. Sci. **16**(1), 74–94 (1988)
81. Gefen, D., Straub, D.: A practical guide to factorial validity using PLS-Graph: tutorial and annotated example. Commun. AIS **16**(5), 91–109 (2005)
82. Chin, W.W.: The partial least squares approach to structural equation modeling. In: Marcoulides, G.A. (ed.) Modern Methods for Business Research, pp. 295–358. Lawrence Erlbaum Associates, Mahwah (1998)
83. Relph, E.: Spirit of place and sense of place in virtual realities. Res. Philos. Technol. Special Issue: Real and Virtual Places, Techne **10**(3), 17–24 (2007)
84. Benyon, D., Smyth, M., O'Neill, S., McCall, R., Carroll, F.: The place probe: exploring a sense of place in real and virtual environments. Presence: Teleoperators Virtual Environ. **15**(6), 668–687 (2006)
85. Slater, M.: Measuring presence: a response to the Witmer and Singer Presence Questionnaire. Presence: Teleoperators Virtual Environ. **8**(5), 560–565 (1999)
86. Etzioni, A., Etzioni, O.: Face-to-face and computer-mediated communities. A comparative analysis. Inf. Soc. **15**(4), 241–248 (1999)
87. Chalmers, D.J.: The virtual and the real. Disputatio **9**, 309–352 (2017)
88. Yung, R., Khoo-Lattimore, C.: New realities: a systematic literature review on virtual reality and augmented reality in tourism research. Current Issues Tourism **22**, 1–26 (2017)
89. Ryan, C.: Ways of conceptualizing the tourist experience. A review of literature. Tourism Recreat. Res. **35**(1), 37–46 (2010)
90. Gottlieb, A.: American's vacations. Ann. Tourism Res. **9**, 165–187 (1982)

Wizard of Oz and the Design of a Multi-player Mixed Reality Game

Niklas Torstensson[✉], Tarja Susi, Ulf Wilhelmsson, and Mikael Lebram

University of Skövde, Högskolevägen, 54128 Skövde, Sweden
niklas.torstensson@his.se

Abstract. This paper describes the use of the WOz method in the development of a prototype for a multi-player mixed reality game for children. It is an adventure game with hidden treasures, clues to hiding places, and information that should not be revealed. The game design, however, includes deceptive elements aimed at luring players to give up information. The game's underlying intent is to raise children's online risk awareness. The WOz was used in the early developmental stage to evaluate and explore the game concept, and to find a way to synchronise and integrate different in-game processes. We describe four central game mechanics for which the wizarding proved to be highly useful. We also discuss some ethical aspects related to the method a such as well as to the game design. In sum, we found the WOz method as such to be very useful for game design and development.

Keywords: Wizard of Oz method · Mixed reality game · Game development

1 Introduction

Wizard of Oz (WOz) is a well-known method in human-centered design, human factors, and other fields for exploring user interfaces in complex systems (Dow et al. 2005a). The perhaps earliest uses of the WOz approach include a natural language understanding system (Bobrow et al. 1983) and a simulated listening typewriter for speech recognition (Gould et al. 1983), although the term 'Wizard of Oz' was not coined until the 1980s (Kelley 1984). When WOz is used, users are usually lead to believe they interact with a fully functioning system, while in reality the system is controlled by a human, a 'wizard'. The WOz method is powerful in iterative design processes for evaluation and testing of concepts and designs before completing a whole system. This method can help designers not to get locked into a particular design, and for evaluating a design before investing too much time in the development of a prototype, with the benefit of saving time and money (Dow et al. 2005a, 2005b).

WOz studies have been in many different contexts, with technology ranging from lo-fi to hi-fi prototyping. In Human-robot interaction research WOz is commonly used since robots cannot interact in socially appropriate ways, and there is even reporting guidelines aimed at rigour in experiments and reporting (Riek 2012). In the context of mixed reality and games, it seems the WOz has not been used extensively, although there is a number

© Springer Nature Switzerland AG 2020
X. Fang (Ed.): HCII 2020, LNCS 12211, pp. 218–232, 2020.
https://doi.org/10.1007/978-3-030-50164-8_15

of reportings. To provide some examples, WOz was used in a study on "The voices of Oakland", an audio-based tour based on a historic cemetery in Atlanta, with focus on story telling (Dow et al. 2005b). Paelke and Sester (2010) explored augmented paper maps, an integration of paper maps and mobile devices. Paavilainen (2008) describes the evaluation of implementing mobile use context in a multi-player casual quiz game, while Bernhaupt et al. (2007) explored "Capture the Flag", a location-based multi-player game for mobile devices, using GPS positioning of game players. In a study by Vahdat et al. (2013) the WOz method was used for exploring a serious game for collaborative learning on city traffic rules and signs. Marco et al. (2012) designed a farmer game with tabletop toys combined with a virtual farm for young children, and Höysniemi et al. (2004) designed a computer vision based action game for children, both using the WOz method. These studies point out different merits of the WOz method and its usefulness, for instance, concept evaluation, flexibility and cost effectiveness.

Yet, despite the benefits of using WOz, there are some limitations. One of them, as pointed out by Dow et al. (2005a, p.18), is the "effort required to engineer a success-ful WOz interface and integrate it with an incomplete system". Höysniemi and Read (2005) point other potentially problematic methodological issues, summarised in three categories. The first concerns technology, for instance, designing systems that cannot be realised. The second concerns the method's deceptive nature, which can lead to unethical research since, for instance, children may not understand what they are participating in. The third category is wizard problems, that is, their capability and effect on a study. We will return to limitations and ethics in the last section of this paper.

In this paper we describe the use of the WOz method during the iterative development of a hi-fi game prototype. The game is a multi-player mixed reality game, aimed to raise children's online risk awareness. The WOz method was used for evaluation and exploration of the game concept and some of the game mechanics that needed to be integrated and synchronised. The work described in this paper is part of a larger project that also included basic research on online interactions between children and adults, and later on, game evaluations (Susi and Torstensson 2019; Susi et al. 2019).

The next sections describe the game more in detail and the WOz setup. The follow-ing sections describe the exploration of four main in-game mechanics and the WOz-techniques used in this project. The paper concludes with a discussion, including the benefits and limitations of the Woz-approach, and ethical aspects.

2   A Multi-player Mixed Reality Game

Hidden in the Park. (Parkgömmet© in Swedish, The Change Attitude Foundation 2019) is a multi-player mixed reality game intended for children 8–10 years old. It is a hide and seek adventure game for 2–4 players, where the goal is to find another player's hidden treasure to win the game. The game design also creates a shared game experience, which provides a social dimension of interaction, competition, and discussion about different game events. The game includes analogue and digital game components. It comprises a cardboard tabletop game board with squares along the outer edges, where game pieces are moved forward, similar to Monopoly. The tabletop game board also has AR Tags to support augmented reality. There is a tablet computer equipped with AR-technology, which allows players to view the tabletop game board as a three dimensional animated world, in which treasures are hidden by pointing and touching the screen. As a player hides a treasure, she gets a set of four clue cards to the hiding place in return. The tablet contains a digital dice and after each roll the player moves her physical game piece ahead on the tabletop game board. At the same time, the tabletop gameboard is represented on the tablet, where a digital version of the player's game piece moves along with each roll of the dice, to help players keep track of their correct positions. The game includes digital mini-games and surprise elements that provide an extra dimension of fun game events. Besides being a fun game, the game's underlying purpose is to raise young childrens' risk awareness during online interactions. For this end, the aforementioned clue cards are considered as personal information that should be minded to avoid them being exposed to the other players.

The game design, however, also contains four deceptive unknown characters (UCs), one for each player, that communicate with the players through text messages (SMS) that appear on the tablet. These UCs try to lure players to take pictures of their clue cards, using the tablet's camera and send them in return. The UCs use different strategies aimed at gaining information (pictures of clue cards) from the players, and if they succeed they will expose the information at some point. When a player's clue cards are exposed the other players may find her hidden treasure. Players can choose whether or not to take a picture, but if they do take a picture, they will also face the consequences of having complied; the sudden insight of having been deceived as the information is exposed to all other players. The strategies implemented in the game's UCs are based on research on real online interactions, where adults try to gain personal information from young people (cf. Susi and Torstensson 2019; Susi et al. 2019). We chose four main strategies that were transferred to and implemented in the game; flattery, bribes, coercion, and threats. Regardless wether players take pictures or not, clue cards have to be revealed at some point, to progress the game play. When clues are revealed the players get the opportunity to look for a hidden treasure by viewing the 3D view on the tablet, and when a treasure is found, the game ends. The game events then create a basis for a pedagogical follow-up discussion centered on online risk awareness.

3   The WOz Setup

For an overview of the setup of our study, we use the taxonomy formulated by Höysniemi and Read (2005), which includes a number of points of variability and the setup for each such point. The taxonomy is here summarised as a table, in which the first two columns include points of variability and the setup for each point (Table 1). The third column adds information about the setup of our study. In this paper we mainly focus on the first points of variability, that is, the technology and wizard interventions. Further details are provided in the following sections.

Table 1. Taxonomy of Wizard of Oz studies (Höysniemi and Read 2005), with the setup of the present study in the third column.

Point of variability	Setup	Setup of our study
1 Functionality of the technology	• Fully functional prototype • Low-tech prototype • Non-tech prototype	Fully functional prototype
2 Discretion of the wizard	• Free to do whatever • Constrained to a set of options • Pre-programmed response (robot-of-oz)	From free to do whatever, to sets of options
3 Wizard control	• Sole provider of functionality • Wizards some interactions	From provider to wizarding some interactions
4 Visibility of the wizard	• Seen or unseen • Known/unknown to be wizarding	Seen but unknown to be wizarding
5 User knowledge (level of deception)	• Believes all is done by a functional UI • Knows the wizard does it all • Knowledge that lies in between the above extremes	Users believed all was done by a functional user interface
6 Experimental design	• Controlled experiment • Free exploration	Free exploration
7 Number of wizards	• One or several wizards • Wizard exchanged during study	One wizard
8 User understanding (level of understanding the process, the risks, and the deception)	• The user is part of the team • The user has little knowledge	The users had little knowledge
9 Wizard knowledge (brought to the domain of the experiment)	• System developer or designer • Brought in on an ad hoc method	System developer, programmer

The WOz sessions were set up with children playing the game, researchers and the wizard all in the same room (Fig. 1). There were eight children who participated by playing the game in groups of 3–4 players in different constellations, on five different occasions. Written consent for participation was gathered from both the children themselves and their parents. The researchers included a wizard, two observers and a game master who provided instructions. The only instructions provided were that each player had to hide a treasure using the tablet, and that the tablet would tell them what to do.

Since all people were in the same room, the participants could see the wizard but they did not initially know he was wizarding and thereby controlling the game.

The children were not informed about the wizard setup, until after the third play session (after that all participants were informed about the wizard). Interestingly, the children's game play was not visibly affected once they knew there was a wizard; they were absorbed by the game play and the game's competitive elements, and they fully ignored the wizard. At the time, the game was a fully functional but not completed prototype. The wizard could control most of the game mechanics in real-time and modify computer responses to players' actions.

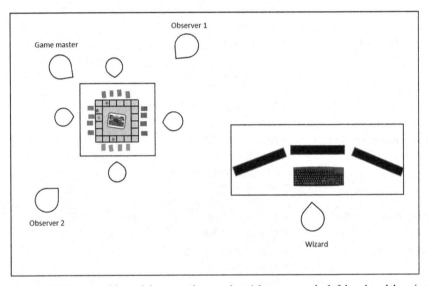

Fig. 1. The WOz setup with participants and researchers/observers on the left hand, and the wizard and controls on the right hand.

Both the tabletop game board and its digital representation on the tablet had rudimentary graphics and symbols (Fig. 2). The game board layout and the graphics were subject to changes and further refinement as a consequence of the WOz approach. Changes were continuously implemented in several iterations of the game during the 10-week period of WOz-testing.

Fig. 2. A group of children playing an early version of the game prototype with rudimentary graphics and symbols. (©Niklas Torstensson). (Color figure online)

4 The Wizard at Work

This chapter describes the wizard's role in the development process, the tools developed for the task, the nature of the interventions made by the wizard and how this affected the game development process.

4.1 The Technology and the Wizard's Role

The game prototype and the technology for wizarding was setup by a research engineer, highly skilled in programming and system development. A basic game prototype was developed in Unity 5 (Unity Technologies 2015), with all the required game mechanics. The game was then installed on a computer tablet (Samsung Galaxy Note 10.1 2014 Edition). The wizard system was implemented as a local web server, facilitated by a WampServer (a software stack for Windows, including the Apache web server, MySQL database, and PHP programming language). The wizard's browser based graphical interface was programmed in PHP and javascript. The wizard's computer and the game computer tablet had a WLAN connection to the server for data exchange.

There was a number of interconnected processes that needed to be implemented in order to make the game work as intended, and to make them work in parallel for two, three or four players. Also, to find a balance between fun and the game's more serious intention was in itself another challenge. With the uncertainty of how to fit everything within one coherent game concept, the WOz approach was the wiser option during the prototyping stage, which went from an initial prototype with basic coding, to a finalised fully coded prototype.

During this process, the wizard assumed different roles during the exploration and evaluation of the game mechanics. As described by Dow et al. (2005a) the wizard's role can change, from a controller to a moderator, and then to a supervisor. As a controller, the wizard fully simulates an unbuilt system component whereas the supervisor instead oversees a working system, with the possibility of overriding system or user decisions. The third role, the moderator, lies somewhere between the former two. The moderator can e.g., intercept output from a working system component before it is sent as input to the rest of the system. In our study, the wizard assumed all these roles as the game development progressed, but not in a linear way. Instead, the wizard's role continously shifted back and forth depending on which part of the game system that needed wizarding. Initially, no game event processes were pre-programmed in the game system. Instances like what number would come up with the rolling of the digital dice, how often to get a chance to play a mini-game, and monetary gains and losses were individually coded, and their appearance was randomised. After a few rounds of game play, the wizard took control over game responses to player interactions. On an overall level, there were five iterations of the game, since it was further developed between each of the five game sessions where the children played the game. However, there were also on the fly iterations during the actual game play, as the wizard implemented changes that came into effect during the next round of rolling the dice.

Gradually, as the game mechanics, processes and game progression fell into place, the wizard's manual operations were coded into sets of options and sets of sequences to choose from. The wizard could however, still override the coding and choose different responses. Finally, when all parts were balanced the coding was completed. The whole process of exploration and testing with the WOz method lasted 10 weeks.

4.2 The Wizard's Graphical Interface

For the WOz method to work, and as a tool of control, a graphical interface (GUI) for wizard intervention was created. Because of the real-time setting and the need for quick responses, this GUI has to be detailed, but at the same time very clear and easy to survey. The wizard's GUI shows a representation of the state of the game – present, past and future – for all players. Each player is assigned a colour; red, yellow, blue, or green. The

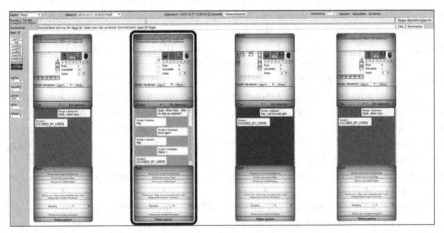

Fig. 3. The wizard's GUI where each player is represented individually (©Mikael Lebram). (Color figure online)

controls in the GUI are colour-mapped accordingly. In the game, players' actions are interconnected, but each player is individually represented on the Wizard's GUI (Fig. 3).

The wizard can see the over-all state of the game through the GUI and, for each players, a representation of the tabletop gameboard and the player's position, and the state of their clue cards (revealed or not) (Fig. 4).

Fig. 4. The wizard's GUI for player yellow (©Mikael Lebram). (Color figure online)

In closer detail, Fig. 5a shows an event and text message log, and below the log is a representation of the tabletop gameboard as little squares with yellow player's current position, and clue cards. There is also information about the treasure hiding place, and number of coins. In Fig. 5b we se see the flow of text messages and player responses, while Fig. 5c shows the wizard's options for input to the system, e.g., messages using free writing, send a yes/no question, send a photo request, or make player gain or lose coins. The wizard can oversee and override decisions made by the system and instead try alternative scenarios.

Another important feature that proved valuable for analysis, development and follow-up is that the Wizard application saves a complete log of every game round when the tablet has been connected to the server. This makes it possible to both back-track problematic situations and to get statistical data from the different game rounds. Being able to analyse and understand game events in retrospect proved a vital part of the development process. The game logs show, for instance, the time spent on different game events and how many coins a player had at an instance when a bribe had no effect.

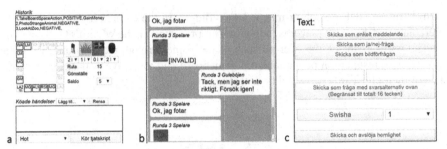

Fig. 5. a–c. The wizard's GUI with details of a player yellow (©Mikael Lebram). (Color figure online)

5   Exploration and Evaluation of Game Mechanics

There were a number of interconnected processes that needed to be implemented in order to make the game work as intended. The focal point, for the game to fulfil its main purpose of enhancing the players' risk awareness, is that at least one of the players actually fall into the trap of taking and sending a picture of a clue card, so that the picture/clue gets revealed and the hidden treasure is found. There had to be a progression, causing game events to unfold, to drive the game play forward so the game would come to an end. The SMSs, prompting players to make choices, like sending pictures of clue cards, must fit in the on-going game play context. There was also a need for a monetary system, partly with the function of rewarding players, but more importantly as an incentive to make players comply with requests in SMSs in order to acquire more coins. Furthermore, if no player would agree to take a picture, it would still be necessary to somehow reveal clues to push the game play forward. Yet another dimension to consider was the time it would take to play the game. Since the game is intended for elementary school settings there needed to be a time constraint for game play that fits well into an ordinary school day in Swedish elementary schools. Lessons in schools are typically 40 min, and ideally the game play should fit within one lesson.

The major game mechanics we focused on were 1) progression of game play, 2) timing and sequences of text messages intended to lure players to reveal clues to the hiding place of a treasure, 3) the appropriate number of coins to motivate players to take actions to gain more coins, and 4) when and how clues should be exposed, to forward game progression so the game would end within a certain time frame. These four aspects are described in the following subsections.

5.1   Progression of Game Play

The first aspect to consider was *progression of game play*. Depending on which squares on the tabletop gameboard the players reach, the outcome can vary considerably. The game is event-based, and every square on the gameboard is assigned to a certain event that concerns either the player who ends up on that square, or it may concern all the players. Examples of such events are to re-roll the dice and move forward or backward, to lose or gain coins, to play a mini-game or to use the tablet to visually search for a treasure. It was important to find a proper balance between mere fun (e.g., to play mini-games), and progression from a revealed clue to a hiding place, to the state of experiencing the consequences of having revealed too much information.

Initially, the rolling of the dice was not controlled, but programmed to be random. This led to an overrepresentation of mini-games and gaining of coins, long game play times, and it hampered the desired progression leading to the escalation of events and, finally, bringing the game to an end.

The wizard software was then designed to allow control of the game's progression by manipulating the dice, to decide what kind of a game event square a player would reach. The wizard could also use the interface to see and manipulate queued and upcoming game events from a dynamic list of game events. By this level of control, the wizard could influence the game play progression and find a balance between the level of fun and game play progression.

5.2   Timing and Sequences of SMS

The second aspect to consider was the *timing and sequences of the text messages* that intentionally should lure players to reveal clues to the hiding places of their treasures. The unknown characters' SMSs represent different strategies to gain access to players' clue cards; flattery, bribes, coercion, and eventually threats. These strategies constitute four of the behaviours found in the underlying research on online interactions between adults and children (Susi and Torstensson 2019). The first three types of SMSs appear in various orders, but once a player has taken and sent a picture the UC gains a leverage and escalates the process to threats, as in "If you don't send another one I'll show your previous picture to everyone". Since every player has four clue cards, they can comply and send more pictures, but they do not initially know why the UC asks for pictures or what he or she will do with them.

The challenge was to set the timing of SMSs correctly in relation to game events but also in relation to the overall progression of the game play. The SMSs needed to appear occasionally but at the right time for each player. The messages also had to be related to what had just taken place. For instance, if a player scores well in a mini-game, there could be an SMS saying "You're doing well!", but it could not be followed by a coercive message saying "please, just one more" (begging for a another picture) since that would not fit the context and it would be confusing and meaningless to the player.

There were some issues with the SMSs as they appeared too rarely and their timing with other events was off. For instance, messages were not synchronised with the frequency of different kinds of events. There were also too many rounds of play without any messages at all, and players gained too much coins. The SMSs with bribes and coercion were essential, for instances to bribe a player with coins for a mini-game, and for a picture in return. In case a player declines the bribe, the next step should be to coerce the player to agree. However, it became clear that when players had a lot of coins neither bribes nor coercion had any effect, which stalled the game play progression. Having noticed these issues, the wizard began to control what SMSs should appear, and when they should appear. He could override the system and send a certain pre-coded SMS, or write messages of his own choice. The WOz-approach made it possible to experiment with these techniques in order to find the most efficient way of timing the messages without actually implementing them in code.

5.3 The Monetary System

The third aspect concerned *the appropriate number of coins* to gain or lose, to motivate players to take actions to gain some more. Coins are used e.g., to pay for mini-games, so coins should provide enough incentive to get players to take pictures of their clue cards, in order to gain more coins. For that to work, there has to be a proper amount of coins; with too many coins there is no need to agree with bribing, while having no coins would exclude a player from taking part in anything that has to be paid for, and the player could fall outside the socially shared game experience.

Initially, actual physical metal coins were introduced in the game, but that soon proved to be one element too much to handle. The coins drew too much attention away from the game play, and it was also hard to keep the coins in place on the table since the young players tended to move around the table. Yet, this gave a clue to the amount of coins or currency needed in the game, and the amount turned out to be 0–6 coins, which was less than initially estimated. The physical coins were replaced with virtual coins in the game system, and by controlling the dice, the wizard was also able to control whether a player would lose or gain coins. Gains and losses were decided in relation to the amount of coins a player had at the time. The amount of money also had to be set in relation to SMSs – if a player had little or no money she should be asked to take a picture, be offered a bribe, and be coerced to accept. If a player instead had many coins she should lose some, to set the stage for bribes etc. The coins turned out to provide a competitive element to the game where the main attraction lied in whether a player had *more* or *less* coins than another player, rather than the exact number of coins someone actually had. By altering gains and losses, and setting them in relation to the proper messages, the monetary system could be set in balance.

5.4 Exposure of Clue Cards

The fourth aspect concerned *the exposure of clue cards to forward game progression and end the game within a certain time frame*. The main point with the clue cards is that they represent where a player has hidden her treasure, so it is comparable to personal information that should not be revealed. At the same time, their exposure leads to someone winning the game. Assuming that the flattery, bribes etc. would work, players would take pictures. When a picture has been taken, the UC should request more pictures and coerce the player to comply, and also threaten to reveal a previous picture unless the player sends another one. This process is a mimicking of real world online events.

The clue cards contain symbols, like flags, grass, and barrels. The symbols on the physical clue cards are black and white and each player has four cards with different symbols. There is no need to hide the cards since they all look pretty much the same. The game system however, assigns the symbols with different colours. Once a clue card is exposed (shown on the tablet), the players see e.g., that there is green grass where player red has hidden her treasure. When a player gets the opportunity to look for red player's treasure in the 3D-view of the gameboard, the player has to find green grass.

When two or more clues have been revealed, the players need to find the place where all the exposed clues are gathered. When a player finds the right spot she wins the game. In essence then, players want to see the other players' clues but would not want to expose their own. But, here the UCs enter the scene and lure players to take pictures and send them in return. What the players do not know is that the UCs will deceive them, and at some point expose the pictures to all players.

To get players to take pictures, the wizard had to make the players lose money, as described in the previous section. The players were very eager to play mini-games and even though there are five different mini-games, all players tended to choose the same one; they competed for the highest score and with a good score they also gained coins. With little or no money the players received messages saying for instance, "Would you like to get two coins?". If the players responded with a 'yes', the next message would be "Then take a picture".

Initially there was no control of the sequence of SMSs, except that threats could not appear until a player had taken a picture. Hence there was no control of when an UC should request pictures of clue cards or when clues should be exposed, which meant that the game did not progress as expected, and nothing much happened except rolling the dice and moving game pieces. The fact that the text message sequences were just random meant that requests for pictures of clue cards appeared solely on chance. At the same time, players could be in possession of so many coins that it rendered any attempt of a bribe useless. This seriously affected the game play time, and play-rounds simply took too long. The wizard had to take control by overriding the game system and control the number of coins a player would have and decide when to send which SMS. By exploring different combinations and sequences of game events, the wizard could intertwine different game events into o coherent game system.

We also had to find a clever way of exposing clues in case no player actually would agree to take any picture. The solution became to make a message appear saying "Oh no, someone saw you hide your treasures and will reveal a clue for each player", and one clue for each player would be shown on the tablet. This mechanism of 'automated exposure' is triggered if a certain time of game play has elapsed with no pictures taken. Players may also become more wary of taking any pictures once they see that the pictures can be exposed, which could lead to very long play time. In that case, the same time trigger mechanism comes into effect to forward the game progression.

When the monetary system, the SMSs, and incentives for taking pictures and the following threats of exposure were set in balance, the game progression and game play time also fell in place. With all processes properly balanced the play time is 20–45 min. This is suitable for Swedish elementary schools where a lesson usually lasts 40 min.

Once all the game elements were balanced and synchronised the prototype was coded and finalised.

6   Discussion

To summarise this WOz study, there are four main processes at the core of the game, that have to work in unison to make the game function as intended; the progression of game play, the timing and sequencing of SMS, the monetary system and lastly the exposure of the clue cards. It was a complex process to interweave all the game events, and to synchronise them for each player within one and the same game context. We found the WOz method highly appropriate for creating the integration of the different processes, but the method also has inherent limitations and ethical issues.

Höysniemi and Read (2005) raise some interesting concerns regarding WOz, for instance, that the method in itself is deceptive which may lead to unethical research, and that it is questionable whether children have the ability to give informed consent to participate in WOz experiments. First of all, we did not conduct experiments but instead explored and evaluated the design concept. The participating children gave their consent to participate, although it is near impossible to say what their understanding of the situation was, except that they would play a new game that was being developed. The children's parents were informed about the study and they also gave their consent for their children's participation. We did not find the issue of consent to be problematic. We would instead rather agree with Marco et al. (2012, p.159), that it is "important to remember that children are not really 'testing' our prototypes; they are in fact playing, and they will only do so for fun" (Marco et al. 2012). Our impression is that the children played for fun and nothing else. We did not want to affect the game play by revealing the setup in advance, so the children were told only after a while that the wizard had been controlling parts of the game play. The fact that they had been subjected to the 'deceptiveness' of the WOz approach did not trigger any negative reactions. On the contrary, they described the experience as "cool" and they were excited to be the first players/end users of a new game.

Höysniemi and Read (2005) also discuss some pitfalls when the users in WOz experiments are children. One such is developmental stage effects when using technology, difficulties with reading and "differing ability to understand the setup or deception" (p.3). Understanding can certainly be a problem, but the game discussed here is specifically adapted to a level of understanding that can be expected at the ages of 8–10 years. Adaptations include for instance, reading, instructions, and interaction styles. The WOz setup, or deception, was no serious issue, as discussed above. A more serious and important issue is the dimension of real world deception, which was here transformed into game mechanics, and the game's design that intentionally deceives players by bribing them to give up their clue cards. Is it fair game to do so? We argue it is. The realisation that maybe an 'unknown character' is not who she or he may seem to be provides an opportunity for learning about risk awareness. This is learning not just 'in theory', but through first-hand experience of deception and potential consequences of sharing too much personal information, and all this under safe off-line conditions. Related to this is also the subject of exposing clue cards even when no one has taken a picture during game play. The truth is that in reality, pictures can easily be shared without the photographed subject's knowledge.

One of the major challenges with the WOz method was the obvious need for high technical competence, which has been pointed out before. As such competence was available in-house, it was possible to explore different solutions without spending resources on coding and, possibly, an elaborate prototype that would have to be discarded. Even though testing is time consuming, it proved a considerable advantage to be able to let the wizard switch between the different roles of controller, moderator, and supervisor, and control different parts of the game before final coding. Another advantage was the many iterations that could take place, both during game play and between play sessions. In sum, the need for both technical and programming competence can be a highly limiting factor in the use of the WOz approach, but we found the method highly useful in the process of developing a fully functional prototype with intricate game mechanics. This approach allowed us to explore the game concept, to save time and costs, and it led to important improvements before completion of the game prototype. The prototype was then finalised into a complete and distributable game by a game development company. The finalised game is now distributed free of charge to all ca 5000 Swedish elementary schools (from 2019 and onwards).

Acknowledgements. The game *Hidden in the Park* was developed by a team of researchers at the University of Skövde, Sweden, on commission and in collaboration with the Change Attitude Foundation. The project was funded by Sten A Olsson Foundation for Research and Culture. The final game production was conducted by IUS Innovation AB, Sweden, in a following, separate project. The game is available for download at www.parkgommet.se (in Swedish).

References

Bobrow, D.G., Kaplan, R.M., Kay, M., Norman, D.A., Thompson, H., Winograd, F.: GUS, a frame-driven dialog system. Artif. Intell. **8**, 155–173 (1983)

Bernhaupt, R., Jenisch, S., Keyser, Y., Will, M.: Capture the flag: simulating a location-based mobile game using the Wizard-of-Oz method. In: Proceedings of the International Conference on Advances in Computer Entertainment Technology, pp. 228–229 (June 2007)

Dow, S., MacIntyre, B., Lee, J., Oezbek, C., Bolter, J.D., Gandy, M.: Wizard of Oz support throughout an iterative design process. IEEE Pervasive Comput. **4**(4), 18–26 (2005)

Dow, S., Lee, J., Oezbek, C., MacIntyre, B., Bolter, J.D., Gandy, M.: Wizard of Oz interfaces for mixed reality applications. In: CHI 2005 Extended Abstracts on Human Factors in Computing Systems, pp. 1339–1342. ACM (2005b)

Gould, J.D., Conti, J., Hovanyecz, T.: Composing letters with a simulated listening typewriter. Commun. ACM **26**(4), 295–308 (1983)

Höysniemi, J., Hämäläinen, P., Turkki, L.: Wizard of Oz prototyping of computer vision based action games for children. In: Proceedings of the 2004 Conference on Interaction Design and Children: Building a Community, pp. 27–34. ACM (2004)

Höysniemi, J., Read, J.: Wizard of Oz studies with children. In: Proceedings of Interact 2005 Workshop on Child Computer Interaction: Methodological Research (September 2005)

Kelley, J.F.: An iterative design methodology for user-friendly natural language office information applications. ACM Trans. Inf. Syst. (TOIS) **2**(1), 26–41 (1984)

Marco, J., Cerezo, E., Baldassarri, S.: Tangible interaction and tabletops: new horizons for children's games. Int. J. Arts Technol. **5**(2–4), 151–176 (2012)

Paelke, V., Sester, M.: Augmented paper maps: exploring the design space of a mixed reality system. ISPRS J. Photogram. Remote Sens. **65**(3), 256–265 (2010)

Paavilainen, J.: Mobile game prototyping with the Wizard of Oz. In: Proceedings of Dream 2008 (2008)

Riek, L.D.: Wizard of Oz studies in HRI: a systematic review and new reporting guidelines. J. Hum. Robot Interact. **1**(1), 119–136 (2012)

Susi, T., Torstensson, N.: "Who's texting?" – playful game experiences for learning to cope with online risks. In: Fang, X. (ed.) HCII 2019. LNCS, vol. 11595, pp. 427–441. Springer, Cham (2019). https://doi.org/10.1007/978-3-030-22602-2_32

Susi, T., Torstensson, N., Wilhelmsson, U.: Can you send me a photo? A game-based approach for increasing young children's risk awareness to prevent online sexual grooming. In: DiGRA 2019, the 12th Digital Games Research Association Conference, Kyoto, Japan (2019)

The Change Attitude Foundation. Hidden in the Park [Parkgömmet©, Adventure game]. IUS Innovation (2019)

Unity Technologies. Unity game engine. Unity Technologies (2015)

Vahdat, M., George, S., Serna, A.: Wizard of Oz in designing a collaborative learning serious game on tabletops. Int. J. Inf. Educ. Technol. 3(3), 325–329 (2013)

Gender and Genre Differences in Multiplayer Gaming Motivations

Donghee Yvette Wohn[1]([✉]), Rabindra Ratan[2], and Leticia Cherchiglia[2]

[1] New Jersey Institute of Technology, Newark, NJ 07102, USA
wohn@njit.edu
[2] Michigan State University, East Lansing, MI 48824, USA

Abstract. This study examines gaming motivations for two different genres of multiplayer games—casual social network games (SNGs) and massively multiplayer online (MMO) games—and tests for gender differences in motivation after considering genre. We conducted a survey of 515 SNG players and 505 MMO players in the U.S. through Mechanical Turk, asking about their motivations for play and basic gaming behavior such as frequency and length of play. Using a self-determination theory approach to categorize motivations, we looked at how game genre and gender are associated with six types of motivation. We find that hypotheses of gender differences from previous games research are contradicted or unsupported—for example, female players for both SNGs and MMOs reported higher levels of external game regulation than males, contradicting previous studies of men being more achievement oriented than women. There are also major genre differences in relation to different motivations. Results reflect a cultural shift in gaming away from gender stereotypes, supporting the importance of reconsidering previous scholarship in this area. Future research should account for both the affordances and culture associated with different game genres rather than generalizing gender effects to all games.

Keywords: Multiplayer games · Gender · Genre · Motivation

1 Introduction

Many studies have examined gaming motivations, but few have compared gaming motivations in more than one genre at a time. The assumption that motivations to play games are uniform across different genres does not consider the complexities in narrative, mechanics, and social interactions that differ across genres. Moreover, although gender demographics have been found to differ across genres, little research has examined the role of motivation in such gender differences across genres.

In this study, we examine two genres of multiplayer games: massively multiplayer online (MMO) games and social network games (SNGs). These two genres differ on various levels, such as game design and game aesthetics, but this study distinguishes between these two genres primarily because of theoretically relevant factors in understanding motivation and habit. These include communication factors—such as speed

© Springer Nature Switzerland AG 2020
X. Fang (Ed.): HCII 2020, LNCS 12211, pp. 233–248, 2020.
https://doi.org/10.1007/978-3-030-50164-8_16

of communication (asynchronous/synchronous) and connectivity with a social network site (high/low anonymity)—as well as frequency of game play (high/low) and gender differences. The study's goal is not to test the effect of these specific factors, but to acknowledge that these two game genres have features that should be considered when hypothesizing and interpreting how theories of motivation operate in these similar, yet different contexts.

MMOs are persistent virtual environments that host thousands of people concurrently (Yee 2006b). A persistent world is a digital environment that exists independent of the players, much like the offline physical world. All players access the same world. While MMOs can be played alone, the most popular mode is multiplayer, possibly because socialization is one of the main motivational factors for MMO players (Fuster et al. 2012). Further, players usually organize themselves into groups (or guilds) because many of the missions in the games require collaboration as each individual has a specific, unique set of skills that complement other players' skill sets. Thus, MMOs are designed to require the skills of others to perform specific tasks, resulting in synchronous interactions between players, usually in groups (Yee 2006b).

SNGs differ from MMOs because the players are also connected outside of the game through network data from social network sites (Wohn et al. 2011; Wohn and Lee 2013). SNGs do not have a single world that is persistent; usually individuals have their own worlds and can visit others'. Because the connection to a social network site is reflective of one's actual identity, people are hindered in their ability to remain completely anonymous (although some SNGs support anonymous play). SNGs often "force" players to interact with each other in order to progress in the game (Wohn et al. 2010; Wohn 2016). Unlike MMOs, however, this interaction is mostly asynchronous and dyadic. For example, players usually make requests of each other through private messages within the game (e.g., "Player A would like you to send a virtual gift!") or by posting requests on social media that others can respond to (e.g., "Player A needs more resources, click here to help them out!"). These requests are usually automatically generated by the system even if they are directly sent from one user to another, so the communication is less intimate and usually related to requesting goods or sending gifts.

2   Self-determination Approach to Understanding Motivation

Self-determination theory (SDT; Ryan and Deci 2000) has been used extensively to explain gaming behavior. SDT maintains that humans have an innate psychological need for competence, autonomy, and relatedness, and when these needs are met the behavior becomes more enjoyable, which leads to increased engagement and persistence in behavior (Deci et al. 1999; Deci and Ryan 1991; Ryan and Deci 2000).

SDT identifies different types of motivation that lie on a continuum from extrinsic to intrinsic. This concept of gaming motivations as lying on a spectrum from extrinsic (external goal-driven) to intrinsic (internal satisfaction-driven) relates to player styles in educational games (Heeter 2008). Further, this intrinsic-to-extrinsic gaming motivations spectrum is distinct from the typologies of motivations used in most game motivation research (e.g., Hamari and Tuunanen 2014; Kahn et al. 2015; Yee 2006a) because it is based on a theory of fulfilling fundamental psychological needs rather than affordances of the medium (Ryan et al. 2006).

The departure of intrinsic and extrinsic as a dichotomy to one that is a continuum is conceptually important in SDT as there can be varying degrees to which the individual can transform external factors into inner values that he or she personally endorses. This proactive process is known as internalization (Deci et al. 1994). Within extrinsic motivation, SDT presents four different forms of regulation to differentiate degrees of internalization: external, introjected, identified, and integrated.

External regulation occurs when behavior is contingent on external stimuli, such as rewards or punishment. It is considered to be the most extrinsic of the four regulation types and is the type of reinforcement-based motivation that is described in operant conditioning. In a gaming context, for example, players who are extrinsically motivated are interested in activities such as getting points, leveling up, completing quests, and collecting items (Heeter 2008). SDT posits that this type of regulation allows for very little autonomy, thus resulting in weak maintenance of behavior once the contingencies of reinforcement are removed. Players of social multiplayer games can similarly be externally reinforced via in-game mechanics and events, but have the potential to be motivated by extrinsic social factors as well. For example, a guild's core player may feel unsatisfied with a new update, but keeps playing because they feel doing otherwise would let down the rest of the guild.

Introjected regulation occurs when individuals are driven by reinforcement – rewards or punishment – that they administer on themselves. The behavior is still influenced by the contingencies of immediate reward or punishment, but is self-administered. For example, individuals who want to eat healthfully can reward themselves with a movie after eating vegetables, or punish themselves with chores after eating a candy. Although there is some internalization because the individual is in control of the contingencies, the behaviors that result from introjected regulation are still low on the self-determination continuum because the behaviors are still relatively detached from the internal values. Introjected regulation, however, does not make much sense in the context of wanting to play games, although it may be a mechanism to discourage gaming behavior.

Identified regulation occurs when the individual poses a longer-term goal that is consistent with an underlying understanding of the value of the behavior, such as playing a game to improve a relationship, communication or collaboration skills. Identified regulation is extrinsic because the behavior is a means to the end goal, but the individual still chooses to engage in the behavior, which is internally endorsed. In other words, the individual performance is identified behavior because it is valuable and important to the individual (Levesque et al. 2008). In the context of multiplayer online games, people may want to play the game to achieve positive relationship outcomes and develop social skills (Wohn et al. 2011).

Integrated regulation occurs when an individual engages in a behavior that supplements internal values. For example, an individual may want to play online multiplayer games because experiencing new entertainment technologies is perceived as valuable. Integrated regulation is different from intrinsic motivation because it may not necessarily be enjoyable, but it is the most internalized of the four types of extrinsic motivation because it is not associated with a specific goal. Many empirical studies, however, did not find support for this construct as being distinct from intrinsic motivation (e.g., Markland and Tobin 2004; Vallerand and Bissonnette 1992).

Finally, intrinsic motivation occurs when the behavior itself is enjoyable on its own. For example, people who explore new territories in virtual worlds simply for the enjoyment of that activity are intrinsically motivated (Heeter 2008). This would be considered a hedonic intrinsic motivation. Alternatively, accomplishment-oriented intrinsic motivation is based on the individual's desire to accomplish or fulfill something (Vallerand and Bissonnette 1992). Accomplishment-oriented intrinsic motivation has mainly been studied in the context of education and is somewhat similar to identified regulation, except for the fact that there is no specific goal—the individual just has an abstract tendency to want to better themselves (Vallerand and Bissonnette 1992).

While SDT has been used in games research, no research of which we are aware has examined differences across genres. This is a potentially fruitful area of inquiry given that different game genres tend to offer different mechanics and experiences that likely influence extrinsic and intrinsic motivation. As this is a pioneering research endeavor, we begin with a general open research question that descriptively compares the motivation factors across two gaming genres:

RQ1. Are there differences in self-determined motivations between MMOs and SNGs?

3 Gender Differences in Game Playing Motivation

Many studies have documented gender differences in playing games (e.g., Cassell and Jenkins 1998; Hartmann and Klimmt 2006; Lucas and Sherry 2004). In summary, scholars have found that males and females tend to prefer different game genres, are motivated to play for different reasons, and significantly differ in terms of how much time they spend playing games. Although these differences have been found across numerous studies, few studies have provided a theoretical explanation for why these gender differences may exist. Here, we take a communication perspective, following Lucas and Sherry (2004), to explain gender differences through the understanding of social norms and stereotypes. However, the landscape of game player demographics has substantially changed in the past ten years, given the rise of "casual" games and with it, the increase of female players (Wohn and Lee 2013). As of 2017, 41% of all game players are female (Entertainment Software Association 2017), and the biggest participation gap happens on the categories of under 18 years old (18% male vs. 11% female) and 18–35 years old (17% male vs. 10% female).

Although many females are playing games, they are not necessarily playing the same ones as males. Industry and research statistics suggest that there are major demographic differences in terms of game genres. For example, MMOs have more male than female players as supported by Williams et al. (2008) who found that the gender distribution in the MMO EverQuest II was 80.8% male. SNGs cater more to female players: the average casual game player is a woman between 35 and 44 years old (Casual Games Association 2012) and 69% of match-three and farm simulation games are played by women, compared to 7% in first-person shooters (Quantic Foundry 2017). Thus, there is reason to believe that gender differences in motivation do not persist in this genre where females are just as likely to be game players as males.

3.1 Social Motivation

Numerous studies, both in the context of games and other types of media, have found that females prefer social interaction over males. In a study of girls and women in Germany, Hartmann and Klimmt (2006) asked participants to rate fictional video games and found that females disliked games that lacked meaningful social interaction. Another study suggests that girls who play online "pink games" (i.e., games designed to target girls) tend to seek social interaction (Van Reijmersdal et al. 2013). In the context of SNGs, another study (Sung et al. 2010) also found that females were more likely than males to engage in social interactions such as exchanging gifts. While not interaction per se, Yee (2006a) found that female players of MMOs were significantly more likely than males to be driven by relationship-related motivations. This could explain why players of action-oriented MMOs with minimal social interaction (e.g., First Person Shooter Games) are more likely to be male and to spend less time playing when compared with players of narrative-oriented MMOs in which social interactions are essential to gameplay (e.g., Role Playing Games; Nagygyörgy et al. 2013). From an SDT perspective, these types of positive social motivations would fall under identified regulation. We would thus expect female players be more motivated by identified regulation than male players.

However, people may also feel socially pressured to play games. This type of social pressure has been identified particularly in SNGs, where players feel obliged to respond to others' requests for help in game (Wohn et al. 2011; Wohn 2016). Social pressure could be seen as an external force in SDT. The literature is unclear about whether this type of social pressure would be considered similar to social interaction desires documented in previous studies. Thus, we examine this issue through an open question:

RQ2. Are there gender differences in social motivations, namely, identified regulation and external social motivation?

3.2 Achievement Motivation

There has been significant scholarly interest in how specific gameplay motivations—such as achievement—are influenced in specific player attributes, such as gender or nationality (e.g., Bialas et al. 2014; De Grove et al. 2017; Yee et al. 2012). Substantial evidence suggests that adult women tend to avoid competition (e.g., Niederle and Vesterlund 2007; Vandegrift and Brown 2005). Many of the studies examining gender differences in competition in a game-playing context are consistent with these theories. Literature from the 1990s to early 2000s pointed to men enjoying competitive games more than women (Lucas and Sherry 2004). Similarly, Yee (2006b) found that male MMO players were significantly more likely than female players to be driven by achievement-oriented motivations. Building on this, we pose the following general expectation across genres.

H1. Male players have higher achievement motivations than female players across genre.

Similar to Yee's findings, Hartmann and Klimmt (2006) found that females were less attracted to competitive elements in videogames; games that had time pressure and any kind of conflict or threat in the narrative were defined as being competitive. Further, males reported higher desire to win and higher desire to compete. However, in predicting use of different genres, the authors found that the desire to compete was only a significant predictor for first-person shooter games and strategy games—not for action-adventure games or sports games. The need to win was only a significant predictor for first-person shooters. Further, other research has found gender differences in competitive gameplay motivations dissipate with age; competition is more important for male teenagers than female teenagers, but by the age of 45, there is no longer a significant difference (Yee 2016). This is especially notable given general age differences between SNG and MMO players. Additionally, for SNGs, competition and reward systems embedded in the game equally increase the likelihood that men and women will play (Omori and Felinto 2012).

Together, these findings suggest that gender differences in achievement motivation may not be as strong in SNGs as in MMOs. One reason for this might be the differences in salience of gender stereotypes between these contexts. According to the theory of Stereotype Threat, reminders of stereotypes about an individual's demographic group will detract from that individual's performance on activities related to the stereotype (Steele and Aronson 1995). There is a common stereotype that female are less skilled than male players (Fox and Tang 2014; Vermeulen et al. 2014). Consistent with Stereotype Threat theory, previous studies have found that reminders of such gender stereotypes hinder gaming performance and, in some cases, cause a disassociation from games in general (Kaye and Pennington 2016; Richard and Hoadley 2013).

Gender stereotypes about achievement ability may be more salient in MMOs than SNGs for multiple reasons. First, the proportion of women who play SNGs is higher than the proportion who play MMOs and this is common knowledge. In fact, this very knowledge may be the basis for the general stereotype that female players are more casual and less capable in gaming in general (Fox and Tang 2014). Further, interpersonal interactions within SNGs are mostly asynchronous reducing the feeling of immediate threat relative to MMOs, where many social interactions occur in real time. Additionally, SNGs players usually play with people they already know (Wohn and Lee 2013), also reducing the likelihood of threat relative to MMOs, which are often played with others who are unknown to the player prior to the shared gaming experience. Thus, although the general stereotype that women are less capable in gaming is expected to hinder women's achievement motivations relative to men's, this gender difference is expected to be larger in MMOs than SNGs. Building on this line of thought, we ask:

RQ3. Are there gender differences in achievement-oriented motivations?

4   Methods

Participants were recruited through Mechanical Turk (MTurk). MTurk is an online task-completion system that allows participants to perform tasks and receive compensation for their time. Demographic surveys suggest that recruiting participants from MTurk yields similar results in terms of sample distribution when compared to traditional subject pools across a variety of research domains and that retention rates for panel surveys are high (Shapiro et al. 2013). In particular, a 2011 study found that MTurk users are slightly more diverse than the standard Internet sample demographic and significantly more diverse than a typical American college sample (Buhrmester et al. 2011). All MTurk participants in this particular study were given $.75 for their participation.

Participants were recruited to two separate surveys: one for MMOs and the other for SNGs. These two genres were chosen so we could recruit a variety of different players, as males are more likely to play MMOs and females are more like to play SNGs (Entertainment Software Association 2017). For both surveys, participants were limited to those who indicated that they have played an MMO or SNG and they were adults age 18 or older. The sample was also restricted to participants living within the United States to prevent possible scamming activity and control for possible cultural differences that have been found to exist within the subject population (Lee and Wohn 2012). Reported gender was used to "block" participants as to obtain a similar number of male and female participants.

Once participants met these criteria, they were directed to an online consent form and asked to note their favorite MMO or SNG. If the participant's favorite game was not among the ten examples given, they could type in the game name. The questions of the survey were thus tailored specifically to each participant based on their favorite game. For example, participants would be asked, "Think of your favorite game, [NAME OF GAME]" before answering sets of questions, and response items were also tailored ("Playing [NAME OF GAME] is part of who I am"). This customization was intended to help participants focus on the same game throughout the survey.

4.1 Measures

A self-determination gaming motivations scale was developed based on scales regarding general MMO (Yee 2006a; Yee et al. 2012) and SNG motivations (Wohn et al. 2010; Wohn and Lee 2013). Items were reworded to mirror existing self-determination motivation scales (Lafrenière et al. 2012) whenever relevant. The items addressed the different regulatory types. Social external regulation ($\alpha = .93$) pertained to reinforcement received from other players within the game (similar to the external regulation of physical activity behaviors; (Gardner and Lally 2013)) while game external regulation was related to reinforcement via game mechanics ($\alpha = .90$). Identified regulation ($\alpha = .94$) was related to wanting to have a social connection.

Intrinsic motivation was separated into two, following Vallerand and Bissonnette (1992). Intrinsic accomplishment ($\alpha = .90$) was related to one's feeling of pleasure when improving one's own performance, while intrinsic hedonic ($\alpha = .94$) was a measure of pure enjoyment—this intrinsic hedonic construct was the measure of intrinsic motivation used by Przybylski et al. (2010) in their study of self-determination in the context of MMOs. Amotivation ($\alpha = .83$) referred to complete absence of motivation. Please see the appendix for a full list of items.

Participants also answered a number of questions about themselves, such as gender, age, race, education level, and household income. Participants also provided descriptive information related to their current favorite game, such as time spent playing their favorite game per session, how many people they actively play with in the game, and how long they had been playing the game.

5 Results

We surveyed a total of 1018 players of MMOs (N = 503) and SNGs. At the time of data collection for MMOs, the most popular game participants reported as being their favorite was World of Warcraft (39.1%), followed by League of Legends (12.7%), Star Wars: The New Republic (6.9%), Guild Wars (5.8%), and Maple Story (3.8%). Several game titles that were "multiplayer" but not "massively multiplayer," such as League of Legends, Halo online, and Team Fortress, were removed from analysis to be consistent with the conceptual definition of MMOs.

For SNGs, Words With Friends (28%) was reported as being the most popular with participants, followed by Candy Crush Saga (25.9%), Draw Something (11.9%), Farmville (8%), Texas Hold'em Poker (7.2%), Tetris Battle (4.7%), and Plants vs. Zombies Adventure (4.3%). Compared to MMOs, SNGs were more diverse in subgenre, ranging from simple arcade games to word, card, strategy, and simulation.

SNG players were an average age of 39 (SD = 9.31) while MMO players were 28 years on average (SD = 7.92). Most respondents were white (79% for SNGs and 84% for MMOs). The average years of formal education completed (excluding kindergarten) were 16 years for both SNG and MMO players.

5.1 Descriptive Differences Between SNGs and MMOs

Frequency. There were statistically significant differences between casual SNG players and MMO players in terms of how frequently they played the game in a typical week ($t(1016) = 3.81$, $p < .001$) and how frequently they played the game in the previous week ($t(1016) = 4.36$, $p < .001$). Casual SNG players reported higher frequency of game play in a typical week than MMO players but spent less time per session than MMO players. Almost half of all MMO players (49.3%) played three or less times a week. In contrast, in a typical week, 27% of casual SNG players played more than seven times, 10.9% played six or seven times, and 21.2% played four or five times (Table 1).

Time. The time spent per session was significantly different between SNGs and MMOs ($t(1016) = -30.51$, $p < .001$). When asked how much time they spend playing the game in a typical session, which was explained as the time between when the player logs on and off, most MMO players said they spent more than an hour but less than 2 h (34.9%), followed by those who played more than two hours but less than three hours (29.7%). About 15% said they played more than 30 min but less than an hour, 2% played more than 10 min but less than 30 min. There were also 39 players (9.2%) who said they played between three and four hours, and 37 players (8.7%) who played four hours or more. On the other hand, most casual SNG players (42.2%) spent more than 10 min but less than 30 min during each game session, with the majority (88.7%) of players spending less than one hour per session. There were 45 individuals (8.8%) who played more than one hour but less than two hours, seven who played between two and three hours, two who played between three and four hours, and four individuals who played four hours or more (see Table 1).

Table 1. Differences in basic game-play variables between SNGs and MMOs.

	Casual SNG ($n = 515$)	MMO ($n = 503$)
Frequency of game play in past week	$M = 2.88, SD = 1.45$	$M = 2.48, SD = 1.31$
Frequency of game play in a typical week	$M = 3.11, SD = 1.40$	$M = 2.78, SD = 1.28$
Time spent per session	$M = 2.30, SD = 1.05$	$M = 4.54, SD = 1.20$
How long they have been playing the game	$M = 6.38, SD = 2.13$	$M = 7.66, SD = 2.01$

Length of Play. SNG and MMO players were also significantly different in how long they have been playing their favorite game ($t(1016) = -9.37$, $p < .001$). On average, MMO players had been playing their favorite game for a longer period than casual SNG players. For the MMO players, about 62.8% said they had been playing their favorite game for a year or more. In comparison, about 54% of casual SNG players had been playing their favorite SNG for less than six months; 17% had been playing the game between six months and one year, and about 29% had been playing for more than one year (see Table 2).

Table 2. How long user has been playing their favorite game (percentage).

	SNGs	MMOs
1 week or less	1.0	.5
More than 1 week but less than 2 weeks	2.3	.9
At least 2 weeks but less than 4 weeks	6.2	2.4
At least 1 month but less than 2 months	9.7	9.0
At least 2 months but less than 4 months	18.9	7.5
At least 4 months but less than 6 months	15.8	5.2
At least 6 months but less than 8 months	11.9	6.8
At least 8 months but less than 1 year	5.4	5.9
1 year or more	28.8	61.8
Total	100.0	100.0

5.2 Genre Differences in Motivation

Our first research question inquired into the differences in self-determined motivations based on genre. A t-test comparison of means showed that all motivations were significantly different between the two genres. MMO players had higher intrinsic hedonic motivations ($t(1016) = -4.48$, $p < .001$), higher intrinsic accomplishment ($t(1016) = -5.38$, $p < .001$), higher social identified ($t(1016) = -5.91$, $p < .001$), and higher external game (t(1016) = −13.36, p < .001) than casual SNG players. However, SNG players had higher external social (t(1016) = 3.07, p = .002) and higher amotivation (t(1016) = 5.35, p < .001) than MMO players. Table 3 shows the means and standard deviations for each motivation type.

Table 3. Means and standard deviations of motivations by genre.

	Casual SNG players	MMO players
Intrinsic hedonic	5.88 (1.06)	6.17 (.94)
Intrinsic accomplishment	4.52 (1.51)	5.00 (1.28)
Identified social	3.21 (1.67)	3.83 (1.70)
External social	2.57 (1.54)	2.27 (1.43)
External game	3.63 (1.86)	5.03 (1.44)
Amotivation	3.23 (1.55)	2.72 (1.44)

5.3 Gender Differences in Motivation

RQ2 and RQ3 inquired into gender differences in self-determined motivations while taking also into consideration potential genre differences. To test effects of gender, a series of 2 × 2 factorial ANOVAs examining main effects for gender as well as interaction effects of gender and genre, was conducted on four different motivations: identified regulation (desire to be social) and external social motivation (pressure to play by others) were considered "social" motivation (RQ2). Intrinsic accomplishment and external game motivation were considered achievement-related motivations (RQ3).

For identified regulation, there was a significant genre effect (F(1, 1014) = 4.37, p < .05). MMO players had higher identified motivation than SNG players. There was no main gender effect, but there was an interaction (F(1, 1014) = 4.4, p < .05): with casual SNG players, males had higher identified motivation than females but the difference was not significant for MMO players. For external social motivation (motivated because others require you to play), there was a main effect of genre (F(1, 1014) = 9.36, p < .001), but no main gender effect (F(1, 1014) = .29, p = .60). There was also no gender by game interaction (F(1, 1014) = 1.59, p = .21). Opposite of the results of identified motivation, SNG players had higher external social motivation than males. These results shed light on RQ2.

RQ3 examined gender differences in two different achievement motivations. Intrinsic accomplishment and external regulation motivations were used to assess achievement motivation. For intrinsic accomplishment, there was only a main effect of genre (F(1, 1014) = 28.81) and no main effect of gender (F(1, 1014) = 2.24, p = .14), nor interaction effect (F(1, 1014) = 2.22, p = .14). For external regulation related to game mechanics, there was a significant main effect of genre (F(1, 1014) = 179.14, p < .001). This indicates that MMO players were far more driven by game mechanics than casual SNG players. There was also a significant main effect of gender ($F(1, 1014) = 6.57, p < .05$). Female players for both SNGs and MMOs reported higher levels of external game regulation than males. These results provide no support for H1 and thus contradict some previous studies of males being more achievement oriented than females. Means and standard deviations are reported in Table 4.

Table 4. Means and standard deviations of self-determined motivations by genre and gender

Motivation type	SNG		MMO	
	Male ($n = 260$)	Female ($n = 255$)	Male ($n = 255$)	Female ($n = 248$)
Intrinsic hedonic	5.77 (1.12)	6.01 (.97)	6.19 (.90)	6.14 (.98)
Intrinsic accomplishment	4.39 (1.50)	4.66 (1.52)	5.00 (1.20)	5.00 (1.36)
Identified social	3.41 (1.65)	3.01 (1.66)	3.82 (1.63)	3.85 (1.76)
External social	2.65 (1.53)	2.48 (1.55)	2.25 (1.43)	2.31 (1.44)
External game	3.46 (1.77)	3.81 (1.94)	4.94 (1.51)	5.12 (1.36)
Amotivation	3.28 (1.58)	3.17 (1.52)	2.82 (1.44)	2.62 (1.43)

6 Discussion

The present study utilized a framework of gaming motivations – built on self-determination theory to examine gender differences within two distinct genres of gaming, social network games (SNGs) and massively multiplayer online games (MMOs). Results from a survey of 1018 SNG and MMO players were not consistent with gendered expectations derived from previous literature, namely, that women have higher social motivations and are less achievement-oriented than men. Although numerous motivation differences were found between genres, these differences were not gendered. Instead, across both SNGs and MMOs, women reported more achievement motivation than men and no gender differences were found in social motivation. These results may reflect a cultural shift in videogame participation that is consistent with the understanding that gender differences found in gaming are driven more by malleable social norms than by innate biological abilities.

The culture of gaming – just as in most areas of our society – is evolving. Most studies on gender differences in gaming were conducted over ten years ago and the patterns found in such research may no longer hold. As the proportion of women gamers has increased over the past decade, play motivations may have changed as well. Specifically, the notion that women tend to play games primarily to socialize instead of accomplish success, may no longer be supported empirically. On the contrary, the present study offers evidence that women are more motivated than men by game achievement (operationalized as completing missions, unlocking game elements, and collecting items or badges). Further, women were not found to differ from men in their social motivations to play. While a failure to reject the null hypothesis generally does not indicate support for it, given the present study's large sample and methodological consistency with previous similar studies that did find gender differences in social motivation, we choose to cautiously interpret both findings in tandem. Namely, together, these results may suggest that over the past decade, the population of female gamers has become more achievement-oriented and less socially-oriented while these orientations have not changed much for their male counterparts.

This inference is consistent with the argument articulated in previous research that gender differences in gaming are driven primarily by the amount of previous gaming experience, of which male players tend to have more. For example, multiple studies have found that skill and resources in online games are accrued at the same rate for male than female players when (statistically) controlling for the amount of time played, but without such a consideration of previous time played, male players appear to achieve at a faster rate than female players (Lehdonvirta et al. 2014; Ratan et al. 2015; Shen et al. 2016). Of course, such statistical controls are not available to the casual observer and thus gender stereotypes have persisted in the face of such empirical evidence. However, as the population of female players grows, so does their amount of experience. If the gender gap in experience is decreasing, then the stereotypical perception that female players are less adept than male players should also be decreasing, according to this previous research. This suggests that stereotype threat should be less salient, which means that female players would feel more motivated by achievement in videogames. In other words, the present study helps support the claim that the gender gap in videogames is diminishing.

An alternative explanation would suggest that the gap is further widening and self-selecting to accommodate only certain types of female players. In other words, we do not know if female gamers individually have become more achievement oriented or if the types of games on the market are attracting more achievement-oriented females. Given much documentation of harassment of female players in social games, there is also a potential that current female gamers are more achievement-oriented and less socially-oriented—not by choice but to survive in hostile social gaming environments. Further research is required to unpack the cultural implications of our quantitative results, as statistics indicate what is going on but not why.

This conclusion should be corroborated by additional empirical evidence and interpreted in light of this study's limitations. For one, the study's recruitment methods should be considered. Most large-scale studies of motivation used in-game incentives, while we used Mturk, which provides a small monetary incentive that is not associated with the game itself. Using in-game virtual items may attract more players who are achievement-oriented or less socially oriented, which could help explain the inconsistency between the present study and previous studies.

Because we used a theory-driven approach, another limitation is the lack of consistency between the conceptualization and measures of motivation used in this study and those used in previous studies. As noted in the literature review, many game motivation studies conceptualized motivations as categorical variables rather than a continuum of motivations ranging from intrinsic to extrinsic. Even those that used an SDT framework did not examine the full spectrum of motivations, which makes it difficult to directly compare our results. However, all previous game studies identified social and achievement motivations—which is why we focused on these two specifically. Furthermore, our study explicated social and achievement in two dimensions and found significantly different patterns; we suggest that this theoretically-driven division provides a more nuanced understanding of player psychology.

A final limitation is that generalizing the effects of gender may be problematic as a whole. Gender is at least in part a social construct and is heavily dependent on the contextual norms of a particular virtual environment, which include the culture of the game as well as the mechanics, or affordances, of the game. The results also showed significant motivation differences between the two genres of SNG and MMO. This suggests that a blanket "gaming motivation" approach may ignore the nuances of context, content, and mechanics that differ by genre. However, although this study looked at genre-based differences, genre may even be broad a lens. Not all games are alike, even within the same genre, so taking a more granular affordance-focused perspective to understanding games might increase validity. For example, comparing games based on specific game mechanics, design, and/or reward structure would enable researchers to make claims about specific game features rather than broader genres.

7 Conclusion

This study examined gaming motivations for two different genres of multiplayer games—casual social network games (SNGs) and massively multiplayer online (MMO) games—and examined whether there are gender differences in motivation after taking genre into consideration. Using a self-determination theory perspective to categorize motivations, we found that gender differences from previous games research were not supported and that player motivations widely differed between genre. These results support the importance of considering both the affordances and culture associated with different game genres rather than generalizing gender effects to all games. Further, this study suggests that the field should reconsider previous findings about gender differences, accounting for shifting cultural norms and player landscapes.

References

Bialas, M., Tekofsky, S., Spronck, P.: Cultural influences on play style. In: 2014 IEEE Conference on Computational Intelligence and Games, pp. 1–7. IEEE, August 2014

Buhrmester, M., Kwang, T., Gosling, S.D.: Amazon's Mechanical Turk: a new source of inexpensive, yet high-quality, data? Perspect. Psychol. Sci. 6(1), 3–5 (2011). https://doi.org/10.1177/1745691610393980

Cassell, J., Jenkins, H. (eds.): From Barbie to Mortal Kombat: Gender and Computer Games. Cambridge, MIT Press (1998)

Casual Games Association: Casual Games Association report (2012)

Deci, E.L., Eghrari, H., Patrick, B.C., Leone, D.R.: Facilitating internalization: the self-determination theory perspective. J. Pers. 62(1), 119–142 (1994)

Deci, E.L., Koestner, R., Ryan, R.M.: A meta-analytic review of experiments examining the effects of extrinsic rewards on intrinsic motivation. Psychol. Bull. 125(6), 627–68–700 (1999). http://www.ncbi.nlm.nih.gov/pubmed/10589297

Deci, E.L., Ryan, R.M.: A motivational approach to self: integration in personality. In: Dienstbier, R. (ed.) Nebraska Symposium on Motivation. Perspectives on Motivation, vol. 38. University of Nebraska Press (1991). http://www.mendeley.com/research/a-motivational-approach-to-self-integration-in-personality/

De Grove, F., Breuer, J., Hsueh Hua Chen, V., Quandt, T., Ratan, R., Van Looy, J.: Validating the digital games motivation scale for comparative research between countries. Commun. Res. Rep. **34**(1), 37–47 (2017)

Entertainment Software Association: Essential facts about the computer and video game industry (2017). http://essentialfacts.theesa.com/mobile/

Fox, J., Tang, W.Y.: Sexism in online video games: the role of conformity to masculine norms and social dominance orientation. Comput. Hum. Behav. **33**, 314–320 (2014)

Fuster, H., Oberst, U., Griffiths, M., Carbonell, X., Chamarro, A., Talarn, A.: Psychological motivation in online role-playing games: a study of Spanish World of Warcraft players. Anales de Psicología/Ann. Psychol. **28**(1), 274–280 (2012)

Gardner, B., Lally, P.: Does intrinsic motivation strengthen physical activity habit? Modeling relationships between self-determination, past behaviour, and habit strength. J. Behav. Med. **36**, 488–497 (2013). https://doi.org/10.1007/s10865-012-9442-0

Hamari, J., Tuunanen, J.: Player types: A metasynthesis. Trans. Digit. Games Res. Assoc. **1**(2), 29–53 (2014)

Hartmann, T., Klimmt, C.: Gender and computer games: Exploring females' dislikes. J. Comput.-Mediated Commun. **11**(4), 910–931 (2006)

Heeter, C.: Playstyles and learning styles. In Handbook of Research on Effective Electronic Gaming in Education. IGI Global (2008). http://gel.msu.edu/carrie/publications/playstyleANDlearninghandbook2008.pdf

Kahn, A.S., et al.: The Trojan Player Typology: a cross-genre, cross-cultural, behaviorally validated scale of video game play motivations, 354–361 (2015). https://doi.org/10.1016/j.chb.2015.03.018

Kaye, L.K., Pennington, C.R.: 'Girls can't play': the effects of stereotype threat on females' gaming performance. Comput. Hum. Behav. **59**, 202–209 (2016)

Lafrenière, M.A.K., Verner-Filion, J., Vallerand, R.J.: Development and validation of the gaming motivation scale (GAMS). Personality Individ. Differ. **53**(7), 827–831 (2012)

Lee, Y.-H., Wohn, D.Y.: Are there cultural differences in how we play? Examining cultural effects on playing social network games. Comput. Hum. Behav. **28**(4), 1307–1314 (2012). http://www.sciencedirect.com/science/article/pii/S0747563212000568

Lehdonvirta, V., Ratan, R., Kennedy, T.L.M., Williams, D.: Pink and blue pixel$: gender and economic disparity in two massive online games. Inf. Soc. **30**, 243–255 (2014). https://doi.org/10.1080/01972243.2014.915277

Levesque, C., Copeland, K.J., Sutcliffe, R.A.: Conscious and nonconscious processes: implications for self-determination theory. Can. Psychol. **49**(3), 218–224 (2008). https://doi.org/10.1037/a0012756

Shen, C., Ratan, R., Leavitt, A., Cai, Y.D.: Do men advance faster than women? Debunking the gender performance gap in two massively multiplayer online games. J. Comput. Mediat. Commun. **21**, 312–329 (2016). https://doi.org/10.1111/jcc4.12159

Lucas, K., Sherry, J.L.: Sex differences in video game play: a communication-based explanation. Commun. Res. **31**(5), 499–523 (2004). https://doi.org/10.1177/0093650204267930

Markland, D., Tobin, V.: A modification of the behavioral regulation in exercise questionnaire to include an assessment of amotivation. J. Sport Exerc. Psychol. **26**, 191–196 (2004)

Nagygyörgy, K., et al.: Typology and sociodemographic characteristics of massively multiplayer online game players. Int. J. Hum. Comput. Interact. **29**, 192–200 (2013)

Niederle, M., Vesterlund, L.: Do women shy away from competition? Do men compete too much?. Q. J. Econ. **122**(3), 1067–1101 (2007)

Omori, M.T., Felinto, A.S.: Analysis of motivational elements of social games: a puzzle match 3-games study case. Int. J. Comput. Games Technol. **2012**, 9 (2012)

Przybylski, A.K., Rigby, C.S., Ryan, R.M.: A motivational model of video game engagement. Rev. Gen. Psychol. **14**, 154–166 (2010). https://doi.org/10.1037/a0019440

Quantic Foundry: Beyond 50/50: Breaking Down The Percentage of Female Gamers by Genre (2017). http://quanticfoundry.com/2017/01/19/female-gamers-by-genre/

Ratan, R., Taylor, N., Hogan, J., Kennedy, T.L.M., Williams, D.: Stand by your man: an examination of gender disparity in League of Legends. Games Cult. **10**, 438–462 (2015). https://doi.org/10.1177/1555412014567228

Richard, G.T., Hoadley, C.M.: Investigating a supportive online gaming community as a means of reducing stereotype threat vulnerability across gender. In: Proceedings of Games, Learning & Society 9.0, pp. 261–266. ETC Press (2013)

Ryan, R., Deci, E.: Intrinsic and extrinsic motivations: classic definitions and new directions. Contemp. Educ. Psychol. **25**, 54–67 (2000). https://doi.org/10.1006/ceps.1999.1020

Ryan, R.M., Rigby, C.S., Przybylski, A.: The motivational pull of video games: a self-determination theory approach. Motiv. Emot. **30**(4), 344–360 (2006). https://doi.org/10.1007/s11031-006-9051-8

Shapiro, D.N., Chandler, J., Mueller, P.A.: Using Mechanical Turk to study clinical populations. Clin. Psychol. Sci. **1**, 213–220 (2013). https://doi.org/10.1177/2167702612469015

Steele, C.M., Aronson, J.: Stereotype threat and the intellectual test performance of African Americans. J. Pers. Soc. Psychol. **69**(5), 797 (1995)

Sung, J., Bjornrud, T., Lee, Y., Wohn, D.Y.: Social network games: audience traits. In: Proceedings of the 28th of the International Conference Extended Abstracts on Human Factors in Computing Systems - CHI EA 2010, pp. 3649–3654. ACM Press, New York (2010). http://doi.org/10.1145/1753846.1754033

Vallerand, R., Bissonnette, R.: Intrinsic, extrinsic, and amotivational styles as predictors of behavior: a prospective study. J. Pers. **60**(3), 599–620 (1992). http://onlinelibrary.wiley.com/doi/10.1111/j.1467-6494.1992.tb00922.x/abstract

Vandegrift, D., Brown, P.M.: Gender differences in the use of high-variance strategies in tournament competition. J. Socio-Econ. **34**, 834–849 (2005)

Van Reijmersdal, E.A., Jansz, J., Peters, O., Van Noort, G.: Why girls go pink: game character identification and game-players' motivations. Comput. Hum. Behav. **29**(6), 2640–2649 (2013)

Vermeulen, L., Castellar, E.N., et al.: Challenging the other: exploring the role of opponent gender in digital game competition for female players. Cyberpsychol. Behav. Soc. Netw. **17**, 303–309 (2014)

Williams, D., Yee, N., Caplan, S.E.: Who plays, how much, and why? Debunking the stereotypical gamer profile. J. Comput.-Mediated Commun. **13**, 993–1018 (2008). https://doi.org/10.1111/j.1083-6101.2008.00428.x

Wohn, D.Y.: From faux-social to pro-social: the mediating role of copresence in developing expectations of social support in a game. Presence Teleop. Virt. Environ. **25**(1), 61–74 (2016)

Wohn, D.Y., Lampe, C., Wash, R., Ellison, N., Vitak, J.: The "S" in social network games: initiating, maintaining, and enhancing relationships. In: 2011 44th Hawaii International Conference on System Sciences, pp. 1–10. IEEE (2011). http://doi.org/10.1109/HICSS.2011.400

Wohn, D.Y., Lee, Y., Sung, J., Bjornrud, T.: Building common ground and reciprocity through social network games. In: Proceedings of the 28th of the International Conference Extended Abstracts on Human Factors in Computing Systems - CHI EA 2010, pp. 4423–4428. ACM Press, New York (2010). http://doi.org/10.1145/1753846.1754164

Wohn, D.Y., Lee, Y.-H.: Players of Facebook games and how they play. Entertain. Comput. **4**(3), 171–178 (2013). https://doi.org/10.1016/j.entcom.2013.05.002

Yee, N.: Motivations for play in online games. CyberPsychol. Behav. **9**, 772–775 (2006a). http://online.liebertpub.com/doi/abs/10.1089/cpb.2006.9.772

Yee, N.: The demographics, motivations, and derived experiences of users of massively multi-user online graphical environments. Presence Teleop. Virt. Environ. **15**, 309–329 (2006b)

Yee, N.: As gamers age, the appeal of competition drops the most. strategy is the most age-stable motivation. Quantic Foundry (2016). http://quanticfoundry.com/2016/02/10/gamer-generation/

Yee, N., Ducheneaut, N., Nelson, L.: Online gaming motivations scale: development and validation. In: Proceedings of the SIGCHI Conference on Human Factors in Computing Systems, pp. 2803–2806. ACM (2012)

User Engagement and Game Impact

Customer Inspiration via Advertising Value of Pop-Up Ads in Online Games

Amir Zaib Abbasi[1(✉)], Ali Hussain[2], Helmut Hlavacs[3], Muhammad Umair Shah[4], Ding Hooi Ting[2], and Umair Rehman[5]

[1] Faculty of Management Sciences, Shaheed Zulfiqar Ali Bhutto Institute of Science and Technology (SZABIST), Islamabad, Pakistan
aamir.zaib.abbasi@gmail.com

[2] Department of Management and Humanities, Universiti Teknologi PETRONAS, Bander Seri Iskander, 32610 Tronoh, Perak, Malaysia

[3] Research Group Entertainment Computing, University of Vienna, Vienna, Austria

[4] Department of Management Sciences, Faculty of Engineering, University of Waterloo, Waterloo, Canada

[5] Systems Design Engineering Department, University of Waterloo, Waterloo, Canada

Abstract. Pop-up ads in online gaming is an emerging phenomenon on the internet that provide massive opportunities for business enterprises. Despite its importance for any businesses, do gamers get inspired by pop-up ads? To answer the query, we develop the conceptual model predicting customer inspiration through perceived advertisement value of pop-up ads in the context of online games. Based on the conceptual model, we first aim to highlight the factors that can motivate gamers to interact with pop-up ads in online games and gain perceived advertisement value of pop-up ads. After that, we intend to understand the impact of perceived advertisement value of pop-up ads on customer inspiration. Our study makes several notable contributions to the literature. First, we apply and extend Ducoffe model of advertisement value in pop-up ads, especially in online games. Second, we add audio and visual aesthetic factors in the existing Ducoffe model. Third, we primarily focus on predicting customer inspiration through perceived advertisement value of pop-up ads in online games.

Keywords: Pop-up ads · Online games · Ducoffe advertising model · Conceptual model

1 Introduction

It has been observed that due to the rapid proliferation of technology, the ways of entertainment have also changed dramatically in the last few decades. According to Chaney, Hosany [1], the television is not a popular source of entertainment anymore, and games are rapidly becoming one of the favourite pastimes among people of all age groups. More than 164 million adolescents in the United States play video games, and after tremendous revenue generation of $43.4 billion by the gaming industry in 2018 now it is a need of time to study the lifestyle of these individuals to better understand

© Springer Nature Switzerland AG 2020
X. Fang (Ed.): HCII 2020, LNCS 12211, pp. 251–259, 2020.
https://doi.org/10.1007/978-3-030-50164-8_17

their interest and hobbies [2]. It also forecasts that the revenue of the gaming industry will increase from \$4034 million in 2018 to \$4654 million in 2020 [3].

Now this billion-dollar industry attracts the attention of the marketers, advertising agencies and game developers, they are keenly observing new research and development activities on the advertising through the online games [4]. It has been also observed that games have a long shelf life because once the player gets involved in the game, then the player will play that game again and again [3].

Past studies mainly focused on the In-game advertising effects and people attitude towards these In-game ads [5–7]. Little attention is given to measure the advertising value of the online game pop-up ads, and what is the influence of this advertising value on user inspiration from that specific advertisement, thus the following research questions emerged;

RQ1- What are the factors that influence the advertising value of pop-up ads?
RQ2- Do gamers get inspired by the perceived advertisement value of pop-up ads?

To answer these research questions, the present study employs a framework by Ducoffe [8], that is used to measure advertising value. Specifically, this study addresses the value of online pop-up ads in video games. Ducoffe's model was the first to propose the concept of the advertising effectiveness with the antecedents of informativeness, entertainment, and irritation [9]. Later, studies have added additional variables like credibility, incentives, and personalization [10–13]. Beyond applying Ducoffe's model to the relevant gaming industry, the current study also includes two new antecedents, namely visual aesthetic and audio aesthetic, to better understand the perceived advertising value of pop-up ads in online games and its effect on gamers' inspiration.

2 Literature Review

2.1 Ducoffe Advertising Model

Ducoffe [8] developed a model (with three antecedents comprising informativeness, irritation, and entertainment) for assessing the perceived advertising value of an ad. Brackett and Carr [14] added the credibility factor in the Ducoffe advertising value model. Xu [11] conducted a study on mobile advertising and included the personalization factor in determining perceived advertising value of mobile ads. Whereas, Kim and Han [12] also applied the Ducoffe advertising model to examine the value of mobile ads. However, use many researchers have contributed to the Ducoffe model through studying the effect of perceived incentives in mobile ads and its influence on creating the perceived advertising value of mobile ads.

Even though the gaming industry is a vibrant and entertaining medium that increases the emerging importance of online games advertising, we still lack understanding about the influential factors for the effectiveness of online games advertising [15]. Ducoffe advertising model is widely discussed to measure the advertising value of different advertising medium, like SMS [16], Facebook [17], Twitter [18], and mobile advertising [11]. However, to the best of our knowledge, no study has applied Ducoffe's approach to the context of pop-up ads via online games and how it can further impact on gamers' inspiration. Therefore, the present study further extends the Ducoffe model by including the visual and audio aesthetics to assess the perceived advertising value of pop-up ads in online games and its influence on gamers' inspiration. In particular, the visual aesthetics refer to the combination and interplay of colors and themes, whereas audio aesthetics include the sound and music in the advertisement [19].

2.2 Gamers' Inspiration

Inspiration is defined as motivational state that compels individuals to bring ideas into actualization [20]. According to the [21], inspiration is basically intrinsic motivation because and it is stimulated by external sources. Although it is always challenging to describe what is the state of inspiration and how does it trigger? However, few researchers have easily explained there inspiration level by some action or by words. Thus, inspiration can be increased with consumers perceive emotional gratification from an external source, but because inspiration reveals new possibilities or the realization of new ideas, inspiration is also positively influenced by utilitarian value [22]. Inspiration can trigger though ads [23]. An ad is a source through which individuals get inspired. Similarly, when gamers experience a pop-up ad in online game context then they gain the perceived advertisement value, which in turn inspires the gamers (such inspiration can include a videogame app installation, wom, and etc.).

2.3 Conceptual Model and Hypotheses

Advertisement-Related Informativeness Value. According to Ducoffe [24] advertisement related Informativeness is defined as the extent to which the advertising medium provides users with resourceful and helpful information. Accordingly, information delivered to them via online game pop up ads also needs to show qualitative features like accuracy, timeliness, and usefulness for the consumer [25]. Game ads cannot be avoided, thus reach of and exposure to the gamers is guaranteed. Games have a long 'shelf life' since many players repeatedly play them over long periods of time [3]. As online game pop-up advertisements are transmitted via the internet, consumers can confirm immediately whether the information in the advertisements is correct or not [13]. This means that the more informative a consumer feels advertising is, the greater is the value advertising will hold in that consumer's mind. Thus:

H1: Informativeness of an online game advertising message is positively correlated with advertising value.

Advertisement-Related Entertainment Value. Entertainment of the ads is refers to its ability to fulfill audiences' needs for escapism, diversion, aesthetic enjoyment or emotional release; a view which is also extended from the UGT [26]. In the advertising context, entertainment is pleasurable, enjoyable, and fun to watch [9]. Ducoffe [24] also confirmed that the ability of advertising to entertain can enhance the experience of advertising exchanges for consumers. Previous studies have confirmed the growing influence of entertainment, while the main advertising channel has changed from paper advertising to online advertising [13]. Entertainment is also a crucial factor for online game marketing. Consumers, in general, rely on the games and other mass media for escapism, diversion, enjoyment and emotional release [1]. Thus:

H2: Entertainment of an online game pop-up advertising message is positively correlated with advertising value.

Advertisement-Related Irritation. While Informativeness and entertainment are positive predictors of the advertising value model, irritation serves as a negative indicator. Irritation refers to the extent to which consumers perceive that online game pop-up advertisements are irritating or annoying, involving negative feelings toward the advertisements [24]. Consumers may feel a sense of irritation from advertisements, as they may feel annoyed or insulted while viewing them [14]. Similarly, when an ad is perceived as intrusive, this can result in negative attitudinal responses because it interrupts the gameplay and deviate the attention of the player [27]. According to [28], consumers then feel confused about the advertising and react negatively to it, and irritation caused by incomprehensible or unwanted online game pop-up advertising messages may reflect negatively on the perceived value of online game pop-up advertising. Thus:

H3: Irritation of an online game advertising message is negatively correlated with advertising value.

Advertisement Credibility. The credibility of the advertisement refers to as truthfulness and believability of professing about brands in message content of advertisement in general [9]. Previous studies have also indorsed that credibility of the advertisement has a notable effect on the advertising value [17, 29, 30]. Advertising credibility depends not only on the content of the ad, but it also influenced by other factors like the com pany's credibility and the holder of the message [31]. Based on these arguments, we conclude that the credibility of the online game pop-up ads has positive influence on the advertisement value of the game pop-up ads. Thus:

H4: Credibility of an online game advertising message is positively correlated with advertising value.

Advertisement-Related Incentives. According to Varnali, Yilmaz [32] incorporation of incentives in the advertising can leads towards more favorable evaluation of the campaign. Previous studies also indorsed that people who received advertisement with some incentive significantly more responsive then those who received traditional advertisement [33, 34]. In the online game ads context incentives can be in the form of monetary benefits like discounts, coupons, free gifts and non-monetary benefits such as addition of point scores, promotion to next level and bonus life points for the players. Therefore, based on prior studies, we propose the following hypothesis:

H5: Incentives of an online game advertising message is positively correlated with advertising value.

Advertisement Personalization. Earlier researches in marketing found that customers are more leaned towards ads that are customized and pertinent to their demographic, user preferences, context, and content factors [35]. According to Malheiros, Jennett [36] personalization of the online game pop-up advertisement enhance the appeal of the ad, the reason behind this is customer perceived that there is a match between his/her self and product. Personalized messages has positive effect in traditional marketing channels on advertising value [37]. In the same way personalization in the online games, pop-up ads also enhance the effectiveness of the advertising. Therefore, we propose the following hypothesis:

H6: Personalization of an online game advertising message is positively correlated with advertising value.

Advertisement-Related Visual Aesthetic. It has been observed that the visual aesthetic of the advertisement is considered to be a significant predictor of user satisfaction and pleasure [38]. The term visual aesthetic generally associated with fine art and different researcher explore this area with different approaches such as beauty, responses to product and appeal [39, 40]. The visual quality of the online game pop-up ads actually attracts the attention of the user when the user is also getting pleasure and satisfaction while watching game pop-up advertisement. Thus, it is hypothesized as follows:

H7: Visual aesthetic of an online game advertising message is positively correlated with advertising value.

Advertisement-Related Audio Aesthetic. The use of music in advertising has a long history, and it is viewed as a strong platform for creating moods in advertising The use of rich media, particularly in the advertisement leads toward the better customer experience with the ad and thus create much more favorable attitude of the customer toward the ads and enhance the effeteness of the ads [41]. According to Fernández-Martínez, Hernández-García [42] audio content (sound and music) of the online game pop-up advertisement in general help most of the time to attract the attention and further leads towards creating particular response as well. Thus, we postulate that:

H8: Audio aesthetic of an online game advertising message is positively correlated with advertising value.

Pop-Up Advertisement Value. Advertising value defines as "a subjective evaluation of the relative worth or utility of advertising to consumers" [8]. Advertising value is an actual measure of advertising efficiency, such that specific advertisements provide sufficiently, for example, information and entertainment to the customer according to their need and desire [43]. According to Logan, Bright [44], the advertising value of online game pop-up ad is also associated with uses and gratifications theory: For example, players watch an advertisement for different gratification seeking motives like entertainment, informativeness, and incentives. An ad is a source of inspiration for individuals [23]. Gamers experience a pop-up ad in online gaming environment and gain the perceived advertisement value from the ad, which in turn becomes a source of inspiration for gamers (it may match with their needs and desires that can further influence them to download the videogame or any behavioral action). Thus, we hypothesize in Fig. 1 that;

H9: A positive association exists between the advertisement value of an online video-game pop-up ad and gamers' inspiration.

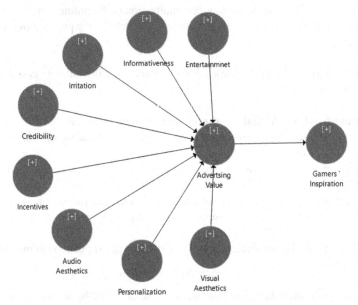

Fig. 1. Advertising model for pop-up ads in online games

3   Discussion

In this study, we have witnessed the importance of pop-up ads in online games. However, prior studies on pop-up ads in videogame environment lacks the implementation of advertising model to assess the role of factors affecting the perceived advertisement value of pop-up ads in online games, which in turn influences the gamers' inspiration. In this study, we initially proposed two research questions; what are the factors that influence the advertising value of pop-up ads? Do gamers get inspired by the perceived advertisement value of pop-up ads? To answer these questions, we have reviewed prior studies on Ducoffe model since the year 1995. We have found its implications in various platforms like Facebook, twitter, YouTube, smartphones etc. [9, 17, 18, 45]. Besides, these researchers have extensively used informativeness, irritation, entertainment factors and also added the importance of credibility, personalization, and incentives to assess the advertising value of an ad.

Our critical evaluation of prior studies on Ducoffe model, revealed that no study has yet investigated the factor affecting perceived advertisement value of pop-up ads in online games and its further effect on gamers' inspiration. Therefore, we apply the Ducoffe model and further extend the model through the addition of audio and visual aesthetic dimensions. Such dimensions have potential to examine the perceived advertisement value of pop-up ads in online games, which in turn contributes to gamers' inspiration. Gamers' inspiration is state which can compel any players to convert ideas (gain through pop-up ads) into action (that can include, videogame app installation, word-of-mouth, referrals etc.)

4   Contribution and Future Research

This study contributes to the theoretical knowledge in several ways. For instance, we extend the use of Ducoffe model to assess the advertising value of pop-up ads in online games [8, 24]. Audio and visual aesthetic variables are added in the Ducoffe advertising model, especially in the context of pop-up ads in online games [8, 24]. We further assess the role of perceived advertising value of pop-up ads in predicting gamers' inspiration and we also extend the notion of inspiration that inspiration comes from the source i.e., pop-up ads in online games [23]. This study is conceptual in nature and there is a dire need for another study that can empirically extend the study model. The concept of inspiration can be applied to other advertising avenues like youtube, social media sites, and vehicle ads.

Author Disclosure Statement. No competing financial interest exists.

References

1. Chaney, I., et al.: Size does matter: Effects of in-game advertising stimuli on brand recall and brand recognition. Comput. Hum. Behav. **86**, 311–318 (2018)
2. Entertainment Software Association (2019)
3. De Pelsmacker, P., Dens, N., Verberckmoes, S.: How ad congruity and interactivity affect fantasy game players'attitude toward in-game advertising. Journal of Electronic Commerce Research **20**(1), 55–74 (2019)
4. Lewis, B., Porter, L.: In-game advertising effects: examining player perceptions of advertising schema congruity in a massively multiplayer online role-playing game. J. Interact. Advert. **10**(2), 46–60 (2010)
5. Hansson, L.: Dynamic in-game advertising: how important is it that ads are dynamic and capable of changing? (2017)
6. Morillas, A.S., Cansado, M.N., Sastre, D.M.: New business models for advertisers: the video games sector in Spain. Advergaming Vs Ingame Advertising. Revista ICONO14 Revista científica de Comunicación y Tecnologías emergentes **14**(2), 256–279 (2016)
7. Rizk, W., Miriam, R., Englander, S.: Systems and methods for providing non-disruptive in-game advertising and identifying target knowledge. Google Patents (2019)
8. Ducoffe, R.H.: How consumers assess the value of advertising. J. Curr. Issues Res. Advert. **17**(1), 1–18 (1995)
9. Martins, J., et al.: How smartphone advertising influences consumers' purchase intention. J. Bus. Res. **94**, 378–387 (2019)
10. Elms, A.C.: Influence of fantasy ability on attitude change through role playing. J. Pers. Soc. Psychol. **4**(1), 36 (1966)

11. Xu, D.J.: The influence of personalization in affecting consumer attitudes toward mobile advertising in China. J. Comput. Inf. Syst. **47**(2), 9–19 (2006)
12. Kim, Y.J., Han, J.: Why smartphone advertising attracts customers: a model of Web advertising, flow, and personalization. Comput. Hum. Behav. **33**, 256–269 (2014)
13. Lee, E.-B., Lee, S.-G., Yang, C.-G.: The influences of advertisement attitude and brand attitude on purchase intention of smartphone advertising. Ind. Manage. Data Syst. **117**(6), 1011–1036 (2017)
14. Brackett, L.K., Carr, B.N.: Cyberspace advertising vs. other media: consumer vs. mature student attitudes. J. Advert. Res. **41**(5) 23–32 (2001)
15. Seo, Y.-N., et al.: Attention to eSports advertisement: effects of ad animation and in-game dynamics on viewers' visual attention. Behav. Inf. Technol. **37**(12), 1194–1202 (2018)
16. Haghirian, P., Madlberger, M., Tanuskova, A.: Increasing advertising value of mobile marketing-an empirical study of antecedents. In: Proceedings of the 38th Annual Hawaii International Conference on System Sciences. IEEE (2005)
17. Hamouda, M.: Understanding social media advertising effect on consumers' responses: an empirical investigation of tourism advertising on Facebook. J. Enterp. Inf. Manage. **31**(3), 426–445 (2018)
18. Murillo, E., Merino, M., Núñez, A.: The advertising value of Twitter Ads: a study among Mexican Millennials. Revista Brasileira de Gestão de Negócios **18**(61), 436–456 (2016)
19. Phan, M.H., Keebler, J.R., Chaparro, B.S.: The development and validation of the game user experience satisfaction scale (GUESS). Hum. Factors **58**(8), 1217–1247 (2016)
20. Oleynick, V.C., et al.: The scientific study of inspiration in the creative process: challenges and opportunities. Front. Hum. Neurosci. **8**, 436 (2014)
21. Thrash, T.M., Elliot, A.J.: Inspiration as a psychological construct. J. Pers. Soc. Psychol. **84**(4), 871 (2003)
22. Bulearca, M., Tamarjan, D.: Augmented reality: a sustainable marketing tool. Glob. Bus. Manage. Res. Int. J. **2**(2), 237–252 (2010)
23. Böttger, T., et al.: Customer inspiration: conceptualization, scale development, and validation. J. Mark. **81**(6), 116–131 (2017)
24. Ducoffe, R.H.: Advertising value and advertising on the web-Blog@ management. J. Advert. Res. **36**(5), 21–32 (1996)
25. Haghirian, P., Madlberger, M.: Consumer attitude toward advertising via mobile devices-an empirical investigation among Austrian users. In: ECIS 2005 Proceedings, p. 44 (2005)
26. Yang, K.-C., et al.: Consumer attitudes toward online video advertisement: YouTube as a platform. Kybernetes **46**(5), 840–853 (2017)
27. Edwards, S.M., Li, H., Lee, J.-H.: Forced exposure and psychological reactance. In: Stafford, M.R., Faber, R.J. (eds.) Advertising, Promotion, and New Media, pp. 215–237. ME Sharpe, New York (2005)
28. Sinkovics, R.R., Pezderka, N., Haghirian, P.: Determinants of consumer perceptions toward mobile advertising—a comparison between Japan and Austria. J. Interact. Mark. **26**(1), 21–32 (2012)
29. Haq, Z.: E-mail advertising: a study of consumer attitude toward e-mail advertising among Indian users. J. Retail Leisure Property **8**(3), 207–223 (2009). https://doi.org/10.1057/rlp.200 9.10
30. Yang, B., Kim, Y., Yoo, C.: The integrated mobile advertising model: the effects of technology- and emotion-based evaluations. J. Bus. Res. **66**(9), 1345–1352 (2013)
31. Bidmon, S., Röttl, J.: Advertising effects of in-game-advertising vs. in-app-advertising. In: Cauberghe, V., Hudders, L., Eisend, M. (eds.) Advances in Advertising Research IX. European Advertising Academy, pp. 73–86. Springer, Wiesbaden (2018). https://doi.org/10.1007/978-3-658-22681-7_6

32. Varnali, K., Yilmaz, C., Toker, A.: Predictors of attitudinal and behavioral outcomes in mobile advertising: a field experiment. Electron. Commer. Res. Appl. **11**(6), 570–581 (2012)
33. Kalakota, R., Robinson, M., Kalakota, D.R.: M-business: The Race to Mobility. McGraw-Hill, New York (2002)
34. Unni, R., Harmon, R.: Perceived effectiveness of push vs. pull mobile location based advertising. J. Interact. Advert. **7**(2), 28–40 (2007)
35. Martí Parreño, J., et al.: Key factors of teenagers' mobile advertising acceptance. Ind. Manage. Data Syst. **113**(5), 732–749 (2013)
36. Malheiros, M., et al.: Too close for comfort: a study of the effectiveness and acceptability of rich-media personalized advertising. In: Proceedings of the SIGCHI Conference on Human Factors in Computing Systems. ACM (2012)
37. Saadeghvaziri, F., Hosseini, H.K.: Mobile advertising: an investigation of factors creating positive attitude in Iranian customers. Afr. J. Bus. Manage. **5**(2), 394–404 (2011)
38. Lavie, T., Tractinsky, N.: Assessing dimensions of perceived visual aesthetics of web sites. Int. J. Hum. Comput. Stud. **60**(3), 269–298 (2004)
39. Tuch, A.N., et al.: The role of visual complexity and prototypicality regarding first impression of websites: Working towards understanding aesthetic judgments. Int. J. Hum. Comput. Stud. **70**(11), 794–811 (2012)
40. Bhandari, U., Chang, K., Neben, T.: Understanding the impact of perceived visual aesthetics on user evaluations: an emotional perspective. Inf. Manage. **56**(1), 85–93 (2019)
41. Appiah, O.: Rich media, poor media: the impact of audio/video vs. text/picture testimonial ads on browsers' evaluations of commercial web sites and online products. J. Curr. Issues Res. Advert. **28**(1), 73–86 (2006)
42. Fernández-Martínez, F., et al.: Combining audio-visual features for viewers' perception classification of Youtube car commercials (2014)
43. Liu, W.-L., Jang, H.-Y.: Factors affecting consumer's perceived advertising value and attitude toward mobile advertising: focus on company-factors and consumer-factors. Asian J. Bus. Manage. Sci. **3**(2), 44–55 (2011)
44. Logan, K., Bright, L.F., Gangadharbatla, H.: Facebook versus television: advertising value perceptions among females. J. Res. Interact. Mark. **6**(3), 164–179 (2012)
45. Young, N.L., et al.: Passive Facebook use, Facebook addiction, and associations with escapism: an experimental vignette study. Comput. Hum. Behav. **71**, 24–31 (2017)

A Warning: Potential Damages Induced by Playing XR Games

Jakub Binter[1,2](✉), Daniel Říha[1], and Hermann Prossinger[3]

[1] Department of Anthropology, Faculty of Humanities, Charles University, Prague, Czech Republic
jakub.binter@fhs.cuni.cz
[2] Department of Philosophy and History of Science, Faculty of Science, Charles University, Prague, Czech Republic
[3] Department of Evolutionary Biology, University of Vienna, Vienna, Austria

Abstract. This article focuses on psychological safety while playing XR (VR + AR) games, and the development of safe-guards ('fuses') to avoid possible negative impacts incurred during virtual experiences. VR and AR have moved from hi-tech development laboratories and design studios into the homes of otherwise conventional users. XR technology has been repeatedly proven to be beneficial for supportive treatment of phobia, PTSD (post-traumatic stress disorder), training of complex behaviors in harsh environments, and education related applications.

Gaming applications are in high demand and financially successful, but are insufficiently supervised by professionals with regard to user safety. Immersion and quality of the technology has increased markedly, resulting in the emergence of arenas that look and feel increasingly realistic, and hence can trigger and impact human affectual states, notably fear and sexual pleasure, more easily. The tendency to create super-stimuli is in the minds of the creators with little (we argue: insufficient) regard to deleterious side effects.

Motion sickness has been considered a negative side-effect of VR gaming, but the possible damage to emotional and psychological well-being of users has been overlooked. Other media platforms, such as movies, have documented the impact on the human psyche of pre-disposed individuals, especially when their psychological state is affected by psychoactive substances. We argue the necessity of programming psycho-physiological response-based 'fuses' that limit possible negative impacts on individuals with pre-existing or pre-generated conditions.

We do not criticize XR development trends or claim that XR is dangerous outright, and we suspect that various benefits could far outweigh the risks. The warning call we publish here should help establish safety measures while not diminishing the enjoyment during XR gaming.

Keywords: Virtual reality · Augmented reality · VR gaming · Gamer safety and gamer wellbeing · PTSD · Psychoactive substances · Neural networks · Decision trees · Kernel density estimation

© Springer Nature Switzerland AG 2020
X. Fang (Ed.): HCII 2020, LNCS 12211, pp. 260–270, 2020.
https://doi.org/10.1007/978-3-030-50164-8_18

1 Introduction

1.1 Overview

Welcome to a near future that is actually upon us already. Virtual reality (VR) and augmented reality (AR; oftentimes, VR and AR together are labeled XR) games keep developing at a breath-taking pace. Their quality has improved tremendously, while currently available state-of-the-art and next generation hardware promises almost flawless implementation. These mass-produced gaming arenas offer such a high degree of immersion that oftentimes during the gaming session it is (intentionally!) well-nigh impossible to distinguish between what is real and what is virtual. In addition to these developments, the cost of hard- and software for gaming keeps decreasing, making consoles increasingly widely available.

Since triggering sensations in humans is easy to achieve in certain psychological domains, developers have become spectacularly imaginative in mastering scenarios that force the delivery of the very last possible drop (as it were) of adrenaline so as to trigger experiences of sexual arousal, fear, panic, and so on. From a psychological perspective (not a peripheral aspect for the game developer), the reality of these experiences is not debatable; it is the gaming environment that is virtual [1]. Herein, we deal with the psycho-medical issues involved in these very real experiences; the psychological domains that are characterized by high activation of affective states [2]. Typically, they trigger the above-listed stressful responses—just what the game developer intends.

In this article, we do not deal with psychological issues involving erotica; instead, we focus on the other scenarios in which humans exhibit a high resemblance to the real environment response. Vertigo, fear-inducing animals, and scary scenarios with villains unpredictably appearing with the intention to harm—these are typically used in gaming plots to provoke adrenaline rush. Typically, the fight-or-flight response, a primal adaptation, is triggered [3].

1.2 A Scenario

A woman is wearing a goggle set and playing an XR game—a horror game. She is motivated to challenge herself more and more as the game progresses. She stayed awake longer than usual and drank, prior to gaming, a few energy drinks to achieve a higher state of alertness. In the game's plot, she is on the verge of being attacked by an opponent and she believes she has no more resources at her disposal to avert her ultimate death.

In the next moment, this woman perceives herself to be eaten alive by a gigantic spider-resembling monster that has jumped on her from apparently nowhere. There is no one to help her, and she hears her bones crack as massive teeth bite into her flesh. The whole sequence of terror-inducing events resembles a nightmare she had for several months after having seen a horror movie as a child.

In this proof-of-concept essay, we desist from continuing with the plot and its (programmed) outcome, especially the outcome for the gamer. Rather, we discuss a plethora of issues that occur during the crescendo up to the moment we described above.

1.3 Horror Plot Issues

There are several issues in horror and comparable VR games:

(a) the psychic stability of and the psychological risks to the gamer;
(b) whether the programmers have devised an AI (artificial intelligence) support so that an imminently dangerous course of events can be averted or 'de-fused' when the above scenario or a similarly dangerous one arises;
(c) whether VR gamers should be wearing appropriate devices that monitor, perhaps independently (i.e. not all using the same device) heart-beat-rate, oxygen consumption, breathing amplitudes, galvanic skin response, etc.;
(d) what algorithmically derived combination of monitoring device outputs can be used to reliably predict the imminent psychic crisis of the gamer;
(e) whether VR games of this horror and violence severity should incorporate a suite of augmented predictor algorithms designed to anticipate the moment when 'de-fusing' is to be triggered.

These issues we have listed pose considerable challenges for the game developer. We address their algorithmic challenges here and elaborate technical details below. Plots, far from having a linear progression, must be designed with tree structures along their evolvement. The branching points we are referring to must be of a safety fuse nature: on at least one branch, the plot must de-escalate and evolve further without referral to the experiences that may have induced panic, etc. that was on the verge of causing potentially far-from-trivial psychological (and perhaps physiological—think of an exorbitantly excessive heart beat rate!) harm.

Even more challenging for the game developer is the predictive nature of issue (d). There is little research on how to regress or cluster psychological and physiological crisis states from the device exports. Technically, this is a far from straightforward problem. The inputs we have listed are continuous variables, and the regressed prediction is a categorical variable; if the predicted categorical variable has the two states 'continue'/'de-escalate' then it is tempting to consider a logistic regression [4]. However, psychologists can quite often list risk states that are not binary, and emergency physicians can list many more such non-binary risk states, because many physiological parameters are interdependent via feedback cycles. For non-binary branching scenarios, one-hot encoding [5] is necessary and the seemingly-attractive multi-level logistic regression [6] is ill-advised; we describe alternatives.

2 Psychology

2.1 Fight-or-Flight Response

In natural environments, there is a linkage between emotional stress and sympathetic activation—the so called "fight-or-flight" response. Psychologically: individuals then feel anxious or aggressive. In certain individuals, namely those with existing pre-dispositions, this may lead to emotional instability or even "freezing" (described as extreme condition of panic [7]). These symptoms lead to future alterations of behavior. Psychologically, fight-or-flight response is characterized by an increased activation that prepares the body for strenuous actions that consume the body's glycogen reserves.

Physiologically, fight-or-flight response is characterized by increased heart beat rate, sweating, heavy breathing, tunnel vision, and muscle tension. Increased levels of cortisol, testosterone, and neurotransmitters—adrenaline, dopamine, and serotonin—cause these characterizing reactions. Perceived control over the situation is altered, but to what degree depends on each individual's mental level and previous relatable experience that may have positively—but sometimes perhaps very negatively—impacted the overall outcome. We note that this suite of reactions is what gaming programmers intend to precipitate. A XR horror or fear game necessitates such reactions, if commercial success is to be ensured. The gamer wants to experience such reactions, otherwise he/she would choose a different type of game.

2.2   Ingestion of Psychoactive Substances

To what intensity these reactions are experienced is further modified whenever psychoactive substances impacting the balance within the homeostatic system are (literally) incorporated. Legal substances such as caffeine, taurine, and alcohol but also illegal ones ('drugs' in common parlance) are such modifiers. We need to address this aspect, actually a concern, because it can be considered common knowledge that players often ingest some of them prior to gaming. Professional players are not permitted to incorporate any of these substances prior to gaming competitions and transgressions are controlled by anti-doping agencies, but there are no restrictions for amateur gamers. We, the authors, are debating among ourselves whether to insist that a warning to gamers be displayed in the title frame of the game, but we currently remain undecided. We are aware of many experts and professionals debating the possibilities of impact on human mental health; and that some deny the possibility of negative impact on wellbeing and mental health. We disagree with the deniers—our position will be elaborated below. Consumption of psychoactive substances makes the algorithmic inclusion of where to place branching points in the demanded tree structure within the plot extraordinarily challenging (see below).

Our concern for psychological risks, which is one *raison d'être* for this paper, cannot be overstated. The issue of consumption of psychoactive substances prior to gaming sessions becomes more and more urgent as XR is becoming better and better (both in quality and immersion intensity), more popular (more time spent gaming), and more widespread (more and more gamers enter the market as consumers).

2.3   Virtual Reality and Psychological Reality

In VR, psychological systems are affected differently from in RR ('real reality'). In RR scenarios humans have evolved adaptations and calibrations for these systems. Thus, in VR, the individual 'knows' (or, rather: 'should know') that the experienced horror, terror, or other fearful scenario is not real. For remedial therapies that use VR, knowledge of the difference between 'reality' in VR and RR seem to be the reason these therapies are successful [8, 9].

The differential impact on the systems under control of the solely sympathetic system (GSR), or in combination with the parasympathetic system (HRV) could serve as proxy for the stress experienced by the individual, irrespective of whether he/she is a therapy client or an (avid) gamer of horror plots. GSR and HRV are related to the Behavioral Inhibition System (BIS) and the Behavioral Activation System (BAS) scales [10, 11] that can be tested on every user and aid in predicting the future physiological responses [12].

2.4 Physiological (Continuous) Random Variables

Electro-dermal, cardiovascular, and breathing intensity changes are measures that have been commonly used in the past studies focused on affective state processing. Galvanic skin response (GSR) predominantly indicates sympathetic activity, and heart beat rate variability (HRV) has been closely linked to parasympathetic activity [13].

The heart beat rate increases in reaction to sympathetic activation and decreases with parasympathetic activation [14].

The arousal dimension is quantifiable by the combined readings of GSR, HRV, and other physiological measures. In particular, combinations of multiple measures should yield better predictions of discrete affective states. Therefore, the chosen psychophysiological measures are a valuable way to assess affective state processing and judgment.

2.5 Psychological (Categorical) Random Variables

To address individual profiles of categorical variables, standardized questionnaire responses are an option.

Behavioral Inhibition (BIS) and Activation System (BAS): BIS is thought to be related to sensitivity to punishment as well as to avoidance motivation, while BAS to sensitivity to reward as well as to approach motivation [10]. BIS is more activated during VR gaming than BAS.

Furthermore, even though registrations of two motivational systems are not only differently distributed between the two sexes [10] but also the multivariate distributions vary within each, systematically affecting ratings, behavioral responses, and psychophysiological responses [15]. Women were shown to have stronger inhibitory systems then men [15].

2.6 Potentially-Harmful Experiences During Computer Gaming

Parallel to the inclusion of branching points by game developers, we list the following categories of the VR gaming environment to mitigate risk-controlled, potentially-harmful psychical experiences in VR gaming:

- a 'simple' VR arena with limited interaction options based on ferocious antagonists;
- an interactive VR arena with standard peripherals and game controllers (game pad, etc.);

- an interactive VR arena with realistic and artificial (experimental) locomotion;
- an interactive VR arena with extended peripherals (haptic, endless pavement, etc.).

Those attempting to develop 'fuses' that trigger branching should also consider adapting some previous 'extreme' computer game scenarios that are no longer *en vogue*. Although current levels of photorealism in computer (horror) gaming do not (as of this writing: yet) fully match reality, we list several pre-VR gaming experiences that have offered already near-reality authentic state of mind alteration and extreme decision making in the potentially harm-generating gameplay situations. As early as 2001, in *Return to Castle Wolfenstein*, a gamer was thrust into a dreadful situation upon being astonished by a sudden zombie attack in the (dark) castle subterranean vaults. In *Postal 2* (2003), the gamer could use different urinating strategies both as a weapon and as a fire extinguisher. In *Manhunt 2* (2007), the gamer is forced to kill an enemy by stabbing his neck with a pencil whereupon he could progress to the next game level. In *RapeLay* (2006) the gamer adopts the role of the rapist stalking a mother and her daughter in a subway/underground environment. In *Silent Hill: Homecoming* (2008) the gamer proceeds to experience numerous torture scenes. More recently: in *Hatred* (2015) the gamer is portrayed as a suicidal mass murderer shooting innocent civilians; in *Agony* (2018), the gamer is a tormented soul not remembering his or her past while being possessed by various demons. While this list of controversial game products cannot be considered comprehensive, the aforementioned 'experience game' designs serve as a quite impressive set of examples of potentially harmful experiences by gamers. By specifically referring to the horror features in this list, we argue that in a VR environment such game designs lead to situations with an increased potential for psychologically harming the players; therefore, game producers need to implement certain types of branching options to be the harm-avoiding 'fuses'.

In all the above mentioned scenarios, we can perceive another potential beyond instilling fear and inducing harm, namely the violation of moral codes. This twist, surely intentionally designed by the game developer, may again impact some gamers more than others and inflict damage because the gamer is forced to behave in a very brutal and sadistic manner, against their will (we hope!). So, while some will enjoy the freedom—and we do not doubt that there exists compensatory mechanism in human psyche that will benefit some players—others may find this frame extremely harmful and bothering to their persona [12].

3 Algorithms

3.1 Regression Algorithms: Generalities

In modern machine learning environments, a prediction based on the analysis of numerical random variables is called a regression and a prediction that is based on categorical variables is called a clustering [5].

There has been some research into how the change in several physiological parameters is indicative of altered psychological states that are brought about by horror/terror games. Most of this research is based, however, on reports of observed effects experienced by clients undergoing VR exposure therapy [12, 17].

The reported results have two serious shortcomings:

1. Healthy individuals' responses (i.e. those who do not need anxiety disorder treatments—at least not prior to a damaging experience in a VR game) have not been monitored during gaming (and not controlled for the ingestion of psychoactive substances).
2. Many reported results rely on (i) fallacious statistical approaches (NHST—null hypothesis significance testing, for example [18], rather than calculating Bayes Factors); (ii) assumptions about the normality of the continuous variables, and the attendant ANOVA (rather than using maximum likelihood methods to determine the ML distributions); (iii) assigning numerical values to categorical variables (rather than using one-hot encoding).

In order to avoid a dangerous psychological state from arising, the gaming algorithm should continuously evaluate the state (a vector including the real-number-valued physiological parameters) and create a branch whenever a certain (vector) state indicating a dangerous level is predicted by the algorithm to be imminent. This algorithmic approach may, of course, require a time series analysis of several prior readings while the gamer is gaming. The knowledge of what constitutes a dangerous state is wherein one of the challenges lies. We see no other option other than running many learning algorithms on many personality types of gamers using the conventional training/test set paradigm of AI (artificial intelligence), possibly using neural networks. Other options, when attempting to determine boundaries between 'continue' and 'de-escalate' can include clustering algorithms of multi-variate categorical variables (among these: the BIS and BAS scales).

3.2   Regression Algorithms: Specifics

The description of algorithm details assumes that large data sets have been collected in order to construct predictions based on machine learning techniques [4], preferably those using AI [5]. The AI paradigm requires the repeated, random splitting of each data set into a training and a test set, perhaps necessitating the acquisition of still larger—or at least many more—data sets.

The components of the input vector for each gamer are realizations of two types random variables; some, such as age, and all the physiological variables (heart beat rate, skin conductivity, etc.) are continuous, real-valued, while others, such as sex (or gender, if the gamer is willing to reveal not only his/her chromosome-23 count, but also his/her sexual orientation) and a host of psychological scores, are categorical. The data matrix of the gamers used to determine the thresholds for branching points is therefore a formidable 'animal' (formidable for the programmer, not for the threatened gamer). The categorical variables, including binary, need to be one-hot encoded, increasing the dimensions of each gamer's vector considerably. One consequence of this increase is, of course, the need to increase the sample size. (This makes sense, because, irrespective of the complexity of the statistical techniques of the algorithm, the more options for some categorical variable, the larger the number of 'guinea pig' gamers for this variable, so as to ensure an adequate number for each option).

Building algorithms that output predictions from a data matrix that contains a mixture of continuous and categorical variables is a task comparable to the *Titanic Challenge* (www.Kaggle.com): use the passenger lists of the eponymous passenger ship (containing names, class, age, family size, sex—but not gender—, fare paid, title: 3 categorical and 3 continuous random variables), and the inventories of who was rescued, to predict the survival chance for each line in the data matrix (i.e. for each passenger). Currently, there are more than 16 thousand teams that have submitted almost 81 thousand algorithms.

Spiegelhalter [19] describes one algorithmic approach: using (binary) classification trees while suppressing greediness. At each step in building the tree, the algorithm decides which of the two branches a passenger is assigned.

Another approach is based on constructing contingency tables and using KDE (kernel density estimation) to predict which cluster a passenger belongs to. Each cluster has a survival probability. The challenge therefore involves finding KDE algorithms and cluster detection methods so that, optimally, all passengers in a cluster are either survivors or not.

The third approach involves using NN (neural networks), a method that appears to be very promising. Build a neural net with several layers and let the NN (literally) learn which entries generate a prediction of survival or not. There are several flexibilities available for the design of NN.

The implementation of one of these three AI approaches to avoiding serious psychological harm are clear. During the gaming session, the continuous random variable inputs are constantly being updated (the categorical variables presumably stay constant). Based on the trained algorithm, the output switches from 'continue' to 'de-escalate' based on the prediction generated by the algorithm.

We warn against simplifying the data set used for generating predictions as a matrix of continuous variables and using a simpler regression algorithm. This simplification would require an enormous number of algorithms, one for each combination of categorical variable realizations (combinatorics would show how the number of possibilities explodes). If, for example, there are n_{BIS} BIS states, n_{BAS} BAS states, n_{SIS} SIS states, and n_{gender} gender states, then the number of data matrices of continuous variables would be

$$n = n_{BIS} \times n_{BAS} \times n_{SIS} \times n_{gender}$$

Assuming the number of states in each categorical variable is 5 (a conservative assumption), then $n = 5^4 = 625$ data matrices would be needed, each with roughly 1000 gamer entries. Because no gamers can be in two different data matrices, considerably more than half a million 'guinea pig' gamers must be surveyed and analyzed with one suitable, or, better yet, several de-fusing algorithms.

On the other hand, it would be highly unusual for the states (except gender, perhaps) to be independent. Because the AI paradigm results in highly optimized outcome prediction, interdependencies will automatically be accounted for, reducing the computational load.

A further optimization can be achieved by finding higher-dimensional manifolds which are close to the registrations post one-hot encoding. Applying dimension-reduction algorithms, prior to AI learning, will most likely (pun intended!) be possible.

More detailed descriptions of algorithm development strategy we cannot supply, because strategies depend on the population profile of the gamers, including their psycho-active substance consumption habits. In any case, including the categorical variable(s) in the data matrix and then applying AI learning promises to improve performance, efficiency and tractability.

Much to the chagrin of psychology researchers, AI learning approaches do not offer insight into what is 'going on' in the mind of the gamer. But, for the game developer, this lack of insight is of minor concern, as long as prediction reliability is ensured (and the scariness to be instilled in the gamer retained). The reliability is the necessity we are arguing for: it protects the gamer from psychological and physiological harm.

4   Conclusion

We have argued that induced psychological harm is a health risk that should not be under-estimated and, in particular, be addressed with both a device-reliant and an algorithmic approach to be developed using AI.

Devices: Prior to rigorous multivariate statistical analysis of physiological data involv-ing dimension reduction, learning and prediction algorithms, gamers should play only while being equipped with suitable devices that measure at least heart beat rate, galvanic skin response, blood pressure, and respiratory pattern. Modern technology has developed such data acquisition devices that are small, reliable, and neither physically constrain nor distract the gamer.

Algorithms: Gaming plots must be based on a tree structure (not necessarily a binary tree) so that the program can pre-emptively side track a gamer before dire scenarios cause psychological damage to him/her. Algorithms must employ state-of-the art AI statistical learning tools, such as kernel density estimation, decision trees, or neural networks tuned and trained on to-be acquired data sets with suitably distributed (i.e. non-biased) categorical variable realizations.

We expect the protection of gamers from being psychologically harmed will be dramatically enhanced by implementation of the algorithms we demand.

We fear the industry and the gamers will resist proposed solutions that avoid harm; yet we insist on 'fuse'-mechanism being included in gaming arenas. It may be that the industry will fear considerable extra investment in programming, and gamers might fear losing the chance to experience the 'ultimate kick'. We point out that the same devices and algorithmic tools can be used to track the state of any individual and therefore create appropriate vector descriptions in other situations. They have already been successfully implemented in (remedial) treatment-cum-gaming scenarios. The future of VR is promis-ing, as long as it can benefit from additional safety by including the above described tools. As many physiological measurements can be collected during the gaming session, we suspect that the prediction accuracy will increase when machine-learning algorithms are included in the gaming package.

We know that our safety approach has a speculative aspect, due to the fact that we cannot let several players experience a physical and mental state that would lead to harm and deduce data-based algorithms from these extreme cases. Game developers do not solely rely on reliability progress through amassing data sets. Prior to mature, 'fuse'-based algorithms, gamers could volunteer to wearing both head-mounts and bracelets with detectors that could be used to signal when they are exhausted, frightened, and so on. A mechanical option, such as a simple switch, could also be supplied as a last resort. Such provisional measures would allow for using gamers' physiological profiles as stepping stones for AI development schemes.

We are aware that it is almost impossible to forbid or prevent gamers at home to ingest substances that alter their psychological dispositions and the physiology of their body (most notably the legal ones). Thus, physiological measures could be used to infer that an alarmingly harmful situation is imminent. There are recorded cases in which people have hurt themselves because of their inability to retain their posture/balance due to the demanding action in VR [9]. If individuals already become stressed while not under the influence of a psychoactive substance, imagine what can happen after the consumption of, say, ethyl alcohol and/or taurine. We do not delude ourselves to believe that we can forbid gamers from ingesting psychoactive substances and so we resign ourselves to knowing they will. These changes of homeostasis will occur and algorithms must monitor the individual's physiological state and save him/her from harm.

We know that the needed *devices* are already available and claim that the appropriate *algorithms* can be developed, allowing for even better—and harm-free—gaming arenas in the brave new worlds of XR gaming.

Acknowledgements. JB & DR are funded by the Czech Science Foundation (Grant No. 19-12885Y "Behavioral and Psycho-Physiological Response on Ambivalent Visual and Auditory Stimuli Presentation") and DR is further funded by the Ministry of Education, Youth and Sports, Czech Republic and the Institutional Support for Long-term Development of Research Organizations, Faculty of Humanities, Charles University, Czech Republic (Grant PROGRES Q21 "Text and Image in Phenomenology and Semiotics").

References

1. Martens, M.A., Antley, A., Freeman, D., Slater, M., Harrison, P.J., Tunbridge, E.M.: It feels real: physiological responses to a stressful virtual reality environment and its impact on working memory. J. Psychopharmacol. **33**(10), 1264–1273 (2019)
2. Badia, S.B., et al.: Toward emotionally adaptive virtual reality for mental health applications. IEEE J. Biomed. Health Inform. **23**(5), 1877–1887 (2018)
3. McCarty, R.: The fight-or-flight response: a cornerstone of stress research. In: Stress: Concepts, Cognition, Emotion, and Behavior, pp. 33–37. Academic Press, Cambridge (2016)
4. Kuhn, M., Johnson, K.: Applied Predictive Modeling. Springer, New York (2016). https://doi.org/10.1007/978-1-4614-6849-3
5. Murphy, K.P.: Machine Learning. A Probabilistic Perspective. MIT Press, Cambridge (2012)
6. Agresti, A.: An Introduction to Categorical Data Analysis. Wiley, Hoboken (2019)
7. Roelofs, K.: Freeze for action: neurobiological mechanisms in animal and human freezing. Philos. Trans. R. Soc. B Biol. Sci. **372**(1718), 201–206 (2017)
8. Holly, J., Bridgewater, C., Lambert, A.M.: The use of virtual reality as a treatment medium for autonomic dysfunction across three diagnostic groups: Case studies. In: 2017 International Conference on Virtual Rehabilitation (ICVR), pp. 1–3. IEEE (2017)

9. Widdowson, C., et al.: Virtual reality applications in assessing the effect of anxiety on senso-rimotor integration in human postural control. In: 2016 38th Annual International Conference of the IEEE Engineering in Medicine and Biology Society (EMBC), pp. 33–36. IEEE (2016)

10. Carver, C.S., White, T.L.: Behavioral inhibition, behavioral activation, and affective responses to impending reward and punishment: the BIS/BAS scales. J. Pers. Soc. Psychol. **67**(2), 319 (1994)

11. Singh, A.K., et al.: Visual appearance modulates prediction error in virtual reality. IEEE Access **6**, 24617–24624 (2018)

12. Wilhelm, F.H., Pfaltz, M.C., Gross, J.J., Mauss, I.B., Kim, S.I., Wiederhold, B.K.: Mechanisms of virtual reality exposure therapy: the role of the behavioral activation and behavioral inhibition systems. Appl. Psychophysiol. Biofeedback **30**(3), 271–284 (2005). https://doi.org/10.1007/s10484-005-6383-1

13. Cacioppo, J.T., Berntson, G.G., Larsen, J.T., Poehlmann, K.M., Ito, T.A.: The psychophysiology of emotion. In: Handbook of Emotions, vol. 2, pp. 173–191 (2000)

14. Storbeck, J., Clore, G.L.: Affective arousal as information: how affective arousal influences judgments, learning, and memory. Soc. Personal. Psychol. Compass **2**(5), 1824–1843 (2008)

15. Brenner, S.L., Beauchaine, T.P., Sylvers, P.D.: A comparison of psychophysiological and self-report measures of BAS and BIS activation. Psychophysiology **42**(1), 108–115 (2005)

16. Russell, P.S., Giner-Sorolla, R.: Bodily moral disgust: what it is, how it is different from anger, and why it is an unreasoned emotion. Psychol. Bull. **139**(2), 328 (2013)

17. Tsai, C.F., Yeh, S.C., Huang, Y., Wu, Z., Cui, J., Zheng, L.: The effect of augmented reality and virtual reality on inducing anxiety for exposure therapy: a comparison using heart rate variability. J. Healthc. Eng. **2018**, 8 (2018)

18. Gigerenzer, G., Krauss, S., Vitouch, O.: The null ritual. In: The Sage Handbook of Quantitative Methodology for the Social Sciences, pp. 391–408 (2004)

19. Spiegelhalter, D.: The Art of Statistics. Learning from Data. Penguin Random House, New York (2019)

Games

20. *Return to Wolfenstein.* Activision (2001)
21. *Postal 2.* Running with Scissors (2003)
22. *Manhunt 2.* Rockstar Games (2007)
23. *RapeLay.* Illusion Soft (2006)
24. *Silent Hill: Homecoming.* Double Helix Games (2008)
25. *Hatred.* Destructive Creations (2015)
26. *Agony.* Man Mind Studio (2018)

Impact of Competitive Versus Cooperative Exergame Play on Releasing Anxiety Among Male University Students

Boyang Fan, Xueni Cao, Jingran He, and Ting Han[⊠]

School of Design, Shanghai Jiao Tong University, Shanghai, China
{boyangfan,hanting}@sjtu.edu.cn

Abstract. Exergames appear to have great potential in releasing anxiety and two ubiquitous elements of exergames are competition and cooperation. However, less is known about effects of competition and cooperation in exergames on anxiety state. Thus, the aim of this study was to examine and compare possible anxiolytic impacts of the two game modes in male university students. Twenty-four healthy male students were recruited and randomly assigned to competitive exergame, cooperative exergame or control conditions. All participants' state anxiety, trait anxiety or skin conductance were accessed before and after the interventions. During the experiment, the competition and cooperation groups played the exergame in different modes respectively, while the control group was asked to do traditional exercises. Results showed that cooperative exergame significantly improved the state anxiety as well as the physiological behavior. No significant changes of self-report anxiety or physiological response occurred in the competition and control group. Exergames, especially played cooperatively, can be an effective tool for anxiety management.

Keywords: Exergame · Competition · Cooperation · Anxiety

1 Introduction

Anxiety is a burdensome emotional state characterized by nervousness, apprehension, and pervasive thoughts of worry and pessimism [1]. It is one of the most prevalent mental health complaints [2] affecting individual's physical and psychological behavior, cognitive function and quality of life [3]. This prevalence is more apparent in young adults like university students, who have been reported to be one of the highest risk groups for anxiety [4, 5] and experience some form of academic, economic and social pressures on a daily basis.

Physical exercise has been shown to be associated with benefits both to physical and mental health [6]. Mounting evidence suggests that exercise can be an instrumental nonpharmacologic means to release anxiety [3]. However, many university students failed to meet recommended weekly physical activity [6] due to the limitation of time, equipment and space as well as the lack of exercise motivation and social support.

© Springer Nature Switzerland AG 2020
X. Fang (Ed.): HCII 2020, LNCS 12211, pp. 271–281, 2020.
https://doi.org/10.1007/978-3-030-50164-8_19

As a combination of exercise and gameplay, exergames provide a more accessible, enjoyable and engaging setting to motivate participation in physical activity. It has been proved that playing exergames has significant reductive effects on anxiety state [3]. A well-designed exergame can be a promising tool for anxiety management.

Two ubiquitous design elements in exergames are competition and cooperation. In competitive exergame play, personal success is inversely related to the success of others while in cooperative play, players succeed through their team's achievement of team goals [7]. Past studies have shown their influence on exercise performance, exertion, motivation and enjoyment, but few investigated whether they have an impact on player's anxiety state.

2 Related Work

Within exergame research, social psychology theories have been utilized to explain how competition and cooperation modes influence players' behavior. Cognitive Evaluation Theory (CET) and Social Cognitive Theory postulate the relationship between competition and motivation. As a sub theory of Self Determination Theory, CET proposes that competition can affect individual's intrinsic motivation levels, which are determined by levels of autonomy and competence [8]. Autonomy reflects an individual's perceived locus of causality, while competence influence intrinsic motivation through social-contextual events such as winning or losing [9]. Social Cognitive Theory further posits that in a social context, people tend to self-monitor the outcomes of their actions and make referential comparisons [7]. A competitive game setting doesn't only provide win-loss feedback to affect individual's competence, but also creates an environment to make comparisons between players' performances, leading to changes in levels of autonomy and intrinsic motivation.

The impact of cooperative gameplay is associated with the Kohler Effect. Groups often contain members with diverse competencies, including some stronger and some weaker members [7]. The Kohler Effect purports that the least capable group member exhibits a motivation gain when they feel being indispensable for the group's success on conjunctive tasks [10]. Driven by unfavorable social comparisons, they are motivated to perform better in order not to let down their fellows. Feltz et al. [10] conducted a study with university students to test the effect in exergames. Participants were asked to complete a series of plank exercises using a specially developed exergame. Results showed that when being told that their game score will be decided by the partner who stopped the exercise first and their partner had performed better than them previously, participants performed significantly better than when playing alone.

Based on different psychological mechanisms, there are also differences between the outcomes of competition and cooperation in exergaming. Marker and Staiano [7] suggest that competition appears particularly useful for increasing energy expenditure and aggression in short bouts of exergame play, while cooperative exergaming has been found to increase motivation, promote continued play, enhance self-efficacy and increase prosocial behaviors. In a 20-week study conducted by Staiano et al. [11], 54 overweight and obese African-American adolescents were randomly assigned to competitive exergame, cooperative exergame or control conditions. It was found that cooperative exergame players lost significantly more weight than the other groups. Yet, compared to the control group, both exergame conditions significantly increased peer support. Cooperative exergame players also significantly increased their self-efficacy. Staiano et al. further point out that the competitive condition required participants to compete individually, which may have been too challenging and elicit negative moods.

Consistent with the findings of Staiano et al., there have been some research focusing on the emotional impact of competition and cooperation. Evolutionary psychology suggests that humans have evolved positive emotions to facilitate survival through cooperation, and negative emotions to defend against those who do not cooperate and to compete for resources [12]. Accordingly, competition may arouse more negative emotions than cooperation. Yet researchers have also pointed out that people actually seem to derive great enjoyment from competition during game and physical activities [12]. This could probably be explained by the CET and Social Cognitive Theory mentioned above that a challenging activity also increase feelings of autonomy and competence, resulting in higher enjoyment and motivation. Siefken et al. [6] looked at possible effects of the two modes in daily physical activities. It was reported that the anxiety and depression scores of indoor team athletes were lower than individual athletes. However, few studies investigated the anxiolytic impacts of competition and cooperation in exergames.

On the basis of what has been discussed above, the aim of this study is to examine the physiological and psychological effects of competitive and cooperative exergame play on the anxiety state of university students and compare their possible anxiolytic impacts with traditional physical exercise.

3   Materials and Methods

3.1   Participants

Twenty-four healthy male university students (23.3 ± 1.3 years; 70.71 ± 21.32 kg; 1.74 ± 0.05 m) from different departments of Shanghai Jiao Tong University were recruited. In order to eliminate the interference of gender, physical strength and other factors, only male participants were recruited in this stage. All participants were not currently clinically diagnosed with anxiety or other mental disorders and students who have answered "yes" to one or more questions in the Physical Activity Readiness Questionnaire [13] were excluded. Informed consent was obtained from all subjects prior to testing.

3.2   Stimuli

An online mobile game named FightingFit was specially modified for this study. The game used an Arduino-based pressure sensor installed on a yoga mat to record the number of user's push-ups, sent data through Bluetooth and provided visual interactive feedback on the mobile phone screen placed in front of the participant. Two game modes were developed: the competition mode required the player to beat the opponent by doing more push-ups within one minute, while in the cooperation mode, the player worked with a teammate online to compete with another team, and the team's total number of push-ups determined final win or loss (see Fig. 1). As individual's behavior can't be controlled, the game pre-set virtual opponents or partners with same game performance based on average exercise abilities of college male students in a pilot study, as it has been suggested that a computer-controlled partner can provide a substitute for human partners in previous studies [10, 14]. The stimuli ran on a five-inch screen of a mobile phone with 1920 px*1080 px resolution.

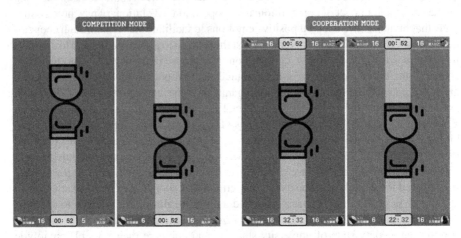

Fig. 1. User interfaces of different game modes.

3.3 Procedure

Participants were randomly assigned to competitive exergame (n = 8), cooperative exergame (n = 8) and control conditions (n = 8). Upon arrival, participants were asked to complete consent forms and State-Trait Inventory to evaluate their baseline subjective anxiety state. Next, finger electrodes were attached to the forefinger and the fourth finger of the left hand and the participants sat quietly for a 1-min baseline measure of skin conductance. Tasks in the upcoming experiment were fully debriefed afterwards. Participants in two exergame groups were told that they were playing with real people online and given time to familiarize with the game. During the experiment, the competition and cooperation groups played the exergame in different modes respectively, while the control group was asked to do traditional push-ups. Each exercise session lasted for one minute with a two-minute break and repeated three times. The number of push-ups and the win-loss performance of the participants were also recorded. After 10 min of seated rest, subjective anxiety and physiological behaviors were assessed again. At the end of the procedure, participants were interviewed about their feelings or suggestions for the game or experiment and thanked with a $5 gift.

Fig. 2. Collection of skin conductance data.

3.4 Measures

State and Trait Anxiety. Subjective anxiety levels were assessed using the State Anxiety Inventor (SAI) and the Trait Anxiety Inventory (TAI) [15], which have been proved to be valid and reliable [16]. SAI evaluates the immediate emotional experience or feelings of the participant while TAI is related to more stable anxiety and tense personality [17]. Each inventory consists of 20 items and uses a 4-point Likert scale ranging from "not at all" to "very much so". High scores usually reflect high anxiety levels of the participants.

Skin Conductance. Skin conductance (SC) was also recorded as an indicator of physiological behavior changes related with anxiety state [18]. Physiological instrument (Psytech-10) was used to collect Skin Conductance/Galvanic Skin Response (SC/GSR) data. Real time analysis of all the data was accomplished by the software (BioTrace+) run on a laptop (see Fig. 2).

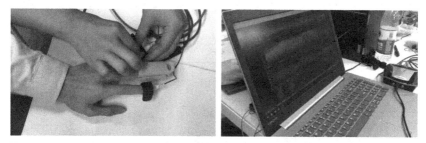

Fig. 3. Box plot of the difference between the SAI, TAI and the total scores before and after the exercise sessions.

Game Performance. To examine whether the game result (winning or losing) will affect anxiety levels of participants in competition and cooperation groups, the final win-loss performance was recorded in each exergame session.

4 Results

One-way ANOVA analysis demonstrated the SAI, TAI and SC data collected before and after the experiment were comparable. Paired T test (Table 1) revealed that cooperative exergame players' state anxiety decreased significantly ($p = 0.042 < 0.05$) after the intervention. While the mean scores of trait anxiety also decreased, it was not statistically significant ($p = 0.063$). The analysis of the competitive exergame group data told a different story. Nonsignificant increase in both SAI and TAI scores were observed ($p = 0.485$, and $p = 0.512$, resp.), reflecting slightly negative impacts of competitive elements on the participants' subjective anxiety. As for the control group, traditional push-up exercise produced a small, nonsignificant decrease in SAI and TAI scores ($p = 0.351$, and $p = 0.239$, resp.), suggesting possible improvements on anxiety state though not as strong as what was shown in the cooperation group (see Fig. 3).

Table 1. Paired T test of the SAI and TAI scores in all three groups

Conditions	Scores	Pre ($\bar{x} \pm s$)	Post ($x \pm s$)	t	p
Control	S-AI	39.75 ± 7.72	36.88 ± 9.75	1.000	0.351
	T-AI	45.13 ± 9.23	43.25 ± 8.75	1.287	0.239
	Total	84.88 ± 14.63	80.13 ± 15.90	1.492	0.179
Competition	S-AI	32.75 ± 6.94	34.5 ± 7.63	−0.737	0.485
	T-AI	38.75 ± 4.68	40.13 ± 7.38	−0.691	0.512
	Total	71.50 ± 11.17	74.63 ± 14.11	−0.779	0.461
Cooperation	S-AI	34.75 ± 7.76	27.62 ± 4.81	2.489	0.042
	T-AI	40.36 ± 7.46	36.38 ± 6.52	2.207	0.063
	Total	75.12 ± 14.79	64.13 ± 9.05	2.438	0.045

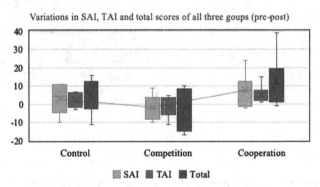

Fig. 4. Box plot of the difference between the SC/GSR data before and after three exercise sessions of all three groups.

As an objective evidence of mood changes, data of skin conductance were also analyzed with paired T test to evaluate the participants' physiological changes (Table 2). Reductions in SC/GSR were seen immediately following cooperative exergame interventions ($p = 0.024 < 0.05$), representing a more peaceful mind. The competitive exergame and control conditions also resulted in slightly lower skin conductance levels, though not evident ($p = 0.149$, and $p = 0.209$, resp.). The differences between different groups are shown in Fig. 4.

Table 2. Paired T test of SC/GSR data in all three groups

Conditions	Pre ($\bar{x} \pm s$)	Post ($\bar{x} \pm s$)	t	p
Control	4.66 ± 1.43	3.80 ± 1.72	1.384	0.209
	6.33 ± 2.70	4.87 ± 3.41	1.622	0.149
	6.96 ± 3.00	4.52 ± 3.31	2.874	0.024
Competition	4.66 ± 1.43	3.80 ± 1.72	1.384	0.209
	6.33 ± 2.70	4.87 ± 3.41	1.622	0.149
	6.96 ± 3.00	4.52 ± 3.31	2.874	0.024
Cooperation	4.66 ± 1.43	3.80 ± 1.72	1.384	0.209
	6.33 ± 2.70	4.87 ± 3.41	1.622	0.149
	6.96 ± 3.00	4.52 ± 3.31	2.874	0.024

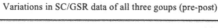

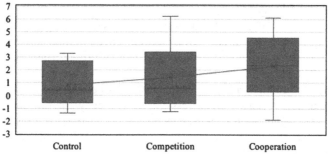

Fig. 5. Box plot of the difference between the SC/GSR data before and after the exercise sessions of all three groups

Taking the participants' performance into consideration, the SAI, TAI and SC data were further classified and examined by the independent t-test based on whether or not the win streak was achieved in three exergame sessions. No apparent link was found between the win streak and the objective or subjective anxiety changes.

5 Discussions

5.1 Effects of Influencing Factors

The purpose of this study was to investigate and compare the effects of competitive and cooperative exergame gameplay on both subjective and objective behaviors of anxiety state. While some of the outcomes were statistically nonsignificant, the key findings of this study indicate that exergames, especially played cooperatively, can be an effective means of releasing state anxiety. Viana et al. [3] have reported that single session of aerobic exergame can significantly reduce state anxiety of healthy young women. Our results show that exergames in the form of resistance exercise may also be a viable tool for anxiety management. This is in agreement with evidence in Silver's [19] study that both aerobic and resistance training are positively related with anxiety reduction. However, in a study conducted by Hill et al. [4], no significant reductions were found in participants with completions of three sets of resistance exercises. We attribute such a contradict to that compared to traditional exercises, exergames can provide participants with more enjoyment [3] and therefore arouse more positive mood changes.

The state anxiety of participants from competition and control group didn't elicit significant variations in our study. A possible explanation may be that as the exergame activates the nervous system, it may engender transient physiological response that contributes to a false representation of anxiety due to the wording in the State Anxiety Inventory such as "I am tense" or "I am jittery". This kind of short-term misattribution of arousal may lead participants to score higher on the SAI [4].

According to Petruzzello et al. [20], physical training programs need to exceed 10 weeks before significant changes in trait anxiety occur. This could possibly explain why the trait anxiety didn't improve significantly in all three conditions. Further research should include long-term interventions to evaluate the influence of competition and cooperation on anxiety state.

The analysis results of SC/GSR data were in in consistent with the findings in subjective anxiety in some way. It gave a view on objective physiological behaviors that cooperative exergame gameplay could effectively release anxiety. There were also small reductions of SC/GSR in the competition and control group, though not as significant as the cooperation group. While skin conductance has been used as a valid indicator in anxiety evaluation, it is also directly associated with body arousal. Lim and Reeves [21] have reported higher arousal (skin conductance and heart rate) during competition, which may explain the difference between competition and cooperation conditions. Consequently, we postulate that compared with conventional exercises and competitive exergames, cooperative exergames may elicit more positive changes in physiological responses related to anxiety.

5.2 Improvements to the Current Game

While the FightingFit exergame achieved positive results, there were some elements not designed optimally. The study has collected some feedbacks from participants through interviews. The most frequently mentioned issue was about the game difficulty. Some participants reported that they consciously paid less efforts to the push-up exercises when they felt at overwhelming advantage in last seconds of the game. One possible solution can be matching the players with opponents of same or higher skill levels [22] to elicit unfavorable social comparisons. Previous studies showed that exercising with a more capable, virtually present partner led to a 24% improvement on persistence at plank exercises and a 125% improvement in aerobic exercise on a stationary bike [10]. Additionally, a "ghost" partner can be utilized for self-competition. "Ghost" refers to the replay of individual's previous exergame session. Shaw et al. [14] have developed a cycling exergame with a "ghost racer", in which the participants see a non-interactive replay of their past attempt on the track as they play. And it was reported that when competing with a "ghost", the participants travelled significantly further than playing with a virtual trainer.

Apart from adaptive game difficulties, players' personal preference should also be taken into consideration. Zhao [23] suggest that a "one-size-fits-all" approach does not work well for exergame design. Players with different personalities should have options to choose their favorable game modes. Song et al. [9] investigated the outcomes of competitive exergame gameplay in individuals with competitive and non-competitive personalities. While non-competitive players reported lower enjoyment of the game than competitive players, they were more motivated to participate in voluntary additional play. Further studies need to be conducted to figure out whether such differences can affect participants' anxiety levels.

5.3 Implications for Health Interventions

The current study has contributed to the body of research highlighting the benefits of exergames for health improvement. The findings indicate that cooperative exergame may be more effective in releasing anxiety than competition exergame. This is in agreement with evidence in previous literature that cooperation has higher recognition than competition in exergame design. According to Marker et al. [7], cooperative play is thought to facilitate stronger benefits and feeling of achievement as it allows more opportunities for success than are available individually. Wu et al. [24] suggest that a personal goal in competition may reduce the sense of empathy and elicit fear of failure, which can lead to loss of playing motivations and rises in anxiety levels. Yet we can not draw the conclusion that competitive exergames couldn't be applied in health interventions, as previous studies also show that competition is critical for enjoyment, motivation [25] and produces greater levels of physical exertion [26]. Our findings call for more future research to look at the impacts on anxiety, motivation, enjoyment and other factors together in order to design suitable exergames for health interventions.

5.4 Limitations

In addition to those limitations discussed throughout, there are some other limitations worth mentioning. First, the sample size was not big enough and some results are likely to occur only sporadically. Second, during the experiment, the performance of the participant was watched by researchers standing by, which might have an influence on the participants' anxiety state [27]. Lastly, further studies need to be conducted to generalize the findings to other types of exergames in different contexts and more general population as the present study only focused on a convenient healthy university male student sample.

6 Conclusions

In conclusion, the current study compared two types of exergames (competitive exergame and cooperative exergame) with conventional exercises in male university students and found that cooperative exergames can be a more promising tool for releasing anxiety. The study showed that single bouts of cooperative exergame gameplay could significantly improve state anxiety and physiological behaviors related to anxiety. Competitive exergames, while relieving players' physiological anxiety-related behaviors in some way, had no significant effect on subjective anxiety reduction, which makes its anxiolytic impacts worth to be further discussed. These preliminary findings provide support for the feasibility and efficacy of exergames as an anxiety management tool for healthy populations.

Acknowledgement. The research is supported by National Social Science Fund (Grant No. 18BRK009).

References

1. Stubbs, B., Koyanagi, A., Hallgren, M., Firth, J., Vancampfort, D.: Physical activity and anxiety: a perspective from the world health survey. J. Affect. Disord **208**, 545–552 (2017)
2. Sigfúsdóttir, I.: Physical activity and sedentary behavior among university students: association with anxiety and stress (Doctoral dissertation) (2019)
3. Viana, R.B., et al.: Anxiolytic effects of a single session of the exergame Zumba® fitness on healthy young women. Games Health. J. **6**(6), 365–370 (2017)
4. Hill, M.D., Gibson, A.M., Wagerman, S.A., Flores, E.D., Kelly, L.A.: The effects of aerobic and resistance exercise on state anxiety and cognitive function. Sci. Sports **34**(4), 216–221 (2019)
5. Xu, F., Liu, W., Rose Chepyator-Thomson, J., Schmidlein, R.: Relations of physical activity and stress vulnerability in university students. Coll. Stud. J. **52**(1), 65–73 (2018)
6. Siefken, K., Junge, A., Laemmle, L.: How does sport affect mental health? An investigation into the relationship of leisure-time physical activity with depression and anxiety. Hum. Mov. **20**(1), 62–74 (2019)
7. Marker, A.M., Staiano, A.E.: Better together: outcomes of cooperation versus competition in social exergaming. Games Health J. **4**(1), 25–30 (2015)
8. Ryan, R.M., Deci, E.L.: Self-determination theory and the facilitation of intrinsic motivation, social development, and well-being. Am. Psychol. **55**(1), 68 (2000)
9. Song, H., Kim, J., Tenzek, K.E., Lee, K.M.: The effects of competition and competitiveness upon intrinsic motivation in exergames. Comput. Hum. Behav. **29**(4), 1702–1708 (2013)
10. Feltz, D.L., Forlenza, S.T., Winn, B., Kerr, N.L.: Cyber buddy is better than no buddy: a test of the Köhler motivation effect in exergames. Games Health Res. Dev. Clin. Appl. **3**(2), 98–105 (2014)
11. Staiano, A.E., Abraham, A.A., Calvert, S.L.: Adolescent exergame play for weight loss and psychosocial improvement: a controlled physical activity intervention. Obesity **21**(3), 598–601 (2013)
12. Kivikangas, J.M., Kätsyri, J., Järvelä, S., Ravaja, N.: Gender differences in emotional responses to cooperative and competitive game play. PloS one **9**(7), e100318 (2014)
13. Adams, R.: Revised physical activity readiness questionnaire. Can. Fam. Physician **45**, 992 (1999)
14. Shaw, L.A., Buckley, J., Corballis, P.M., Lutteroth, C., Wünsche, B.C.: Competition and cooperation with virtual players in an exergame. PeerJ. Comput. Sci. **2**, e92 (2016)

15. Spielberger, C.D., Sydeman, S.J., Owen, A.E., Marsh, B.J.: Measuring anxiety and anger with the State-Trait Anxiety Inventory (STAI) and the State-Trait Anger Expression Inventory (STAXI). Lawrence Erlbaum Associates Publishers, Hillsdale (1999)
16. Barnes, L.L., Harp, D., Jung, W.S.: Reliability generalization of scores on the Spielberger state-trait anxiety inventory. Educ. Psychol. Meas. **62**(4), 603–618 (2002)
17. Li, X., Li, R., Han, T.: Effect of gamification of exercise therapy on elderly's anxiety emotion. In: Zhou, J., Salvendy, G., (eds.) HCII 2019. LNCS, vol. 11593, pp. 533–544. Springer, Cham (2019). https://doi.org/10.1007/978-3-030-22015-0_41
18. Najafpour, E., Asl-Aminabadi, N., Nuroloyuni, S., Jamali, Z., Shirazi, S.: Can galvanic skin conductance be used as an objective indicator of children's anxiety in the dental setting? J. Clin. Exp. Dent. **9**(3), e377 (2017)
19. Silver, R.: The relationship between physical activity levels and health anxiety. Senior honors diss., University of North Carolina at Chapel Hill (2019)
20. Petruzzello, S.J., Landers, D.M., Hatfield, B.D., Kubitz, K.A., Salazar, W.: A meta-analysis on the anxiety-reducing effects of acute and chronic exercise. Sports Med. **11**(3), 143–182 (1991)
21. Lim, S., Reeves, B.: Computer agents versus avatars: responses to interactive game characters controlled by a computer or other player. Int. J. Hum. Comput. Stud. **68**(1–2), 57–68 (2010)
22. Novak, D., Nagle, A., Keller, U., Riener, R.: Increasing motivation in robot-aided arm rehabilitation with competitive and cooperative gameplay. J. Neuroeng. Rehabil. **11**(1), 64 (2014)
23. Zhao, Z.: Personalization of wearable-based exergames with continuous player modeling. PhD diss., Carleton University (2019)
24. Wu, Z., Li, J., Theng, Y.L.: Examining the influencing factors of exercise intention among older adults: a controlled study between exergame and traditional exercise. Cyberpsychol. Behav. Soc. Netw. **18**(9), 521–527 (2015)
25. Kivikangas, J. M.: Emotion and social context in a digital game experience. Institute of Behavioural Sciences, Studies in Psychology (2015)
26. Peng, W., Crouse, J.: Playing in parallel: the effects of multiplayer modes in active video game on motivation and physical exertion. Cyberpsychol. Behav. Soc. Netw. **16**(6), 423–427 (2013)
27. Murray, E.G., Neumann, D.L., Moffitt, R.L., Thomas, P.R.: The effects of the presence of others during a rowing exercise in a virtual reality environment. Psychol. Sport Exerc. **22**, 328–336 (2016)

The Role of Parenting Styles and Parents' Involvement in Young Children's Videogames Use

Heqing Huang⬤, You Zhou, Fangbing Qu, and Xiaocen Liu⁽⊠⁾ ⬤

Capital Normal University, Beijing, People's Republic of China
cindyliu@cnu.edu.cn

Abstract. With growing numbers of younger children engaging in videogame use, and children using videogames at an increasingly younger age, parents' responses are becoming increasingly complex. The sample in the present study were 699 parent–preschooler dyads. Subjective reports were used in this research to examine children's videogame use, parents' involvement in this, and related parenting styles. Among them, the objective and motivational aspects were measured with the Video Game Status Questionnaire and the Survey of Children's Engagement with Videogames, respectively. The parents related factors were measured with the Questionnaire of parenting styles and the Parents' Involvement in the Children's videogame use. The results find the separate and interactive predictions of the parents' related factors, and the parenting styles predicted the children's videogame use partly through the parents' involvement in the children's videogame use. In addition, these results suggest that parents' involvement benefits young children by protecting them from excessive use or by enhancing their positive experience during videogame use. Moreover, democratic parenting was found to have the healthiest influence on children's use of videogames.

Keywords: Videogame use · Parenting styles · Young children

1 Introduction

1.1 Preschoolers' Videogame Use

In contemporary society, digital products have invaded our lives. An especially prominent example is videogames, which growing numbers of young children are beginning to use [1]. Although only little research has investigated young children, the nascent literature suggests that there are relations between family-related factors and children's videogame use [2].

Both extensive and premature exposure to videogame use are known to cause various problems. There is increasing public and scientific concern regarding the long-term behavioral effects of videogame use in children. When children lose control over time spent gaming or game excessively, impairment of their physical [3] and mental health [4] can result. The age at which children begin to engage in excessive use of videogames also

© Springer Nature Switzerland AG 2020
X. Fang (Ed.): HCII 2020, LNCS 12211, pp. 282–294, 2020.
https://doi.org/10.1007/978-3-030-50164-8_20

appears to be dropping. Significant relations among videogame exposure and problem behaviors have been found in preschoolers [5], and research also indicates that the younger a child begins gaming, the greater their likelihood of developing internet game disorder [6].

Current understanding of young children's videogame use is limited. Most studies have used objective indexes, such as average playing time and play frequency, to examine young children's videogame use. However, while playing videogames, there are also individual differences in motivational and arousal aspects, which can reflect children's engagement in the game. Thus, this study seeks to fill this knowledge gap.

1.2 Parents' Involvement in Children's Videogame Use

Research indicates that parenting factors play important roles in young children's videogame use [7]. A myriad of studies has examined the relationship between family-related factors and children's videogame playing. A recent review proposed poor parent–child relations as the most prominent family-related risk factor for problem videogame use [8]. Family-related factors are complex and can have different effects on children's videogame use. For example, family can influence a child through direct or indirect paths.

The first path includes parents' specific and contextual behaviors with respect to their children's videogame playing [9]. Today, parents have no choice but to deal with videogame-related issues, whether actively or passively. The various videogames impose strain on parents of young children, and parents' videogame-related behaviors are becoming increasingly complicated. On the one hand, parents report that they may use videogames as tools for care or education [10]; on the other hand, parents have various worries about videogames and use strategies to control children's videogame playing, with respect to both content and time.

Each family also has general features, including the core feature of parenting style, which affects every aspect of a child's life through direct and indirect paths, including their use of videogames [11]. According to Baumrind, there are five types of parenting styles: permissive, democratic, uninvolved, authoritarian, and inconsistent. Researchers more recently identified distinct "digital parenting styles" that resemble general parenting styles [12].

The direct and indirect factors identified above influence children's videogame use in an integrated way. Accordingly, this study assumes that different parenting styles have different effects on preschoolers' videogame use, and that parents' actions with respect to their children's videogame use may mediate this relationship.

1.3 The Present Study

This study has two general aims. First, we will examine the situation of Chinese young children's videogame use, including both objective and emotional aspects. Second, we will investigate how direct and indirect family-related factors are related to children's videogame use. In this study, the family-related factors include both parenting styles and parents' contextual attitudes and behaviors regarding their children's videogame use [13]. Our research frame and hypotheses are set out in Fig. 1.

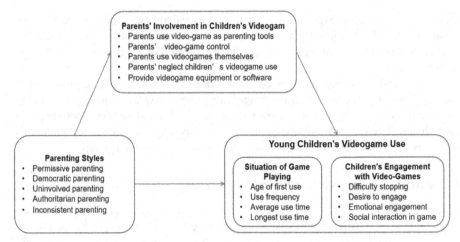

Fig. 1. The study's hypotheses and variables.

As Fig. 1 indicates, this study aims to investigate the relations between young children's videogame use, their parents' involvement in this, and related parenting styles.

2 Methods

2.1 Participants

We initially recruited 884 parents from an urban preschool in north China. After deleting the data from participants whose preschool children have not played videogames, the final sample comprised 699 parent-preschooler dyads. The preschoolers (471 boys and 228 girls) were aged from 2.08 to 7.18 years, $M_{age} = 4.76$, $SD_{age} = 0.96$. Among the children, 194 (27.75%) were in the first grade, 263 (37.63%) were in the second grade, and 242 (34.62%) were in the third grade. The participating parents comprised 622 mothers (88.98%) and 77 fathers (11.02%).

The parents completed a series of questionnaires. Responses to the brief income and education questionnaire revealed that household income was less than \$50,000 for 14% of participating families, between \$50,000 and \$80,000 for 25%, and more than \$80,000 for 47%. The highest level of education achieved in the household was high school or some postsecondary education. We used a formula to compose an integrated index of participants' socioeconomic status (SES): $M_{ses} = 0.032$, $SD_{ses} = 1.01$, $Range_{ses} = -5.05$ to 2.60.

2.2 Materials and Procedure

Background Information. Background information on the children (e.g., birthday, gender) and their parents (e.g., age, roles, education, and annual household income) were collected.

The Videogame Status Questionnaire. Four items from our self-designed eight-item Videogame Status Questionnaire were used in this study. They are all objective indexes of children's videogame use: age of first use, use frequency, average use time, and longest use time.

Survey of Children's Engagement with Videogames. A self-designed questionnaire was used to investigate children's motivation and arousal during videogame use. After item collection and expert evaluation, the original questionnaire comprised 28 items. Following exploratory factor analysis and the exclusion of eight items, the final questionnaire comprises 20 items organized in four sub-scales: *difficulty stopping, desire to engage, emotional engagement,* and *social interaction in game.* The sub-scales' Cronbach's alphas are 0.91, 0.85, 0.83, and 0.83, respectively, in this study.

Questionnaire of Parents' Involvement in Children's Videogame Use. A self-designed questionnaire was used to investigate how the parents act with respect to videogames. After item collection and expert evaluation, the original questionnaire comprised 21 items. Exploratory factor analysis led to the exclusion of one item, leaving a final questionnaire comprising 20 items organized in five sub-scales: parents use videogames as a parenting tool; parents exercise control over children's videogame use; parents use videogames themselves; parents ignore children's videogame use; and parents provide videogame equipment or software. The sub-scales' Cronbach's alphas are 0.872, 0.879, 0.867, 0.828, and 0.741, respectively, in this study.

Questionnaire of Parenting Styles. We used the Questionnaire of Parenting Styles [11] developed by Yang and Yang [14] with Chinese young children. It comprises 40 items covering five parenting styles: permissive, democratic, uninvolved, authoritarian, and inconsistent. The instrument's Cronbach's alpha is 0.81, and its test-retest reliability is 0.87. This questionnaire uses a 5-point Likert scale.

3   Results

Besides the descriptive analysis (results reported in Table 1), three stages of analyses were used in this study. In the first and second stages, sets of multivariate analyses of variance (MANOVAs) were used to examine whether gender and age are related to videogame use in Chinese young children. In the third stage, to explore the relationship between parental factors and children's videogame use, a series of *Pearson* correlation and regression analyses were conducted.

3.1   Age, Gender, and Videogame Use

To explore the characteristics of Chinese young children's videogame use, two sets of MANOVAs were conducted.

In the first set of MANOVAs, age group (3, 4, and 5 years old) and gender (boys and girls) were the independent variables, and the four objective indexes of children's videogame use (age of first use, use frequency, average use time, and longest use time) were the dependent variables. For age of first use, a significant age effect was found, $F(2, 451) = 76.77$, $p < 0.001$, $\Delta\eta2 = 0.221$, $d = 1.0$, and post-hoc analysis suggests there are significant differences between each age groups, the younger children also use video game at an earlier age, and this result revealed that children's first exposure to videogames is now coming at an earlier age. For average use time, both age and gender differences were found, $F(2, 451) = 2.891$, $p = 0.056$, $\Delta\eta2 = 0.011$, $d = 0.565$; $F(1,$

Table 1. Descriptive analyses of the children's usage of video-games and the parental characters.

	Age		3 years old			4 years old			5 years old		
	Gender		Boys	Girls	Total	Boys	Girls	Total	Boys	Girls	Total
Situation of game playing	Age of first use	M	2.56	2.55	2.56	2.89	2.99	2.94	3.64	3.90	3.75
		SD	0.76	0.72	0.74	0.83	0.85	0.84	1.03	1.04	1.04
	Use frequency	M	6.71	4.91	5.83	3.31	4.32	3.80	2.94	3.32	3.10
		SD	14.55	12.31	13.47	4.29	9.99	7.59	2.95	3.36	3.12
	Average use time	M	22.41	19.40	20.93	24.77	20.21	22.57	24.32	24.81	24.52
		SD	12.62	8.76	10.95	14.04	12.80	13.61	13.74	17.27	15.25
	Longest use time	M	39.83	33.02	36.48	43.13	34.66	39.04	42.40	44.35	43.20
		SD	25.14	21.36	23.51	31.44	22.65	27.81	23.01	31.34	26.70
Children's engagement with video-games	Difficulty stopping	M	2.60	2.32	2.47	2.34	2.07	2.21	2.23	2.29	2.25
		SD	0.82	0.92	0.88	0.84	0.82	0.84	0.87	0.92	0.89
	Desire to engage	M	2.99	2.64	2.83	2.70	2.35	2.54	2.60	2.65	2.62
		SD	0.89	1.03	0.97	1.02	0.93	1.00	0.92	0.99	0.95
	Emotional engagement	M	3.28	3.21	3.25	3.33	3.06	3.21	3.26	3.28	3.27
		SD	0.99	0.99	0.99	1.01	1.10	1.06	1.08	0.98	1.03
	Social interaction in game	M	2.72	2.62	2.67	2.60	2.57	2.58	2.60	2.79	2.68
		SD	0.92	1.01	0.96	0.97	0.95	0.96	0.97	1.04	1.01
Parents' involvement in children's videogame use	Parents use video-game as parenting tools	M	2.47	2.48	2.48	2.60	2.43	2.52	2.72	2.61	2.67
		SD	0.66	0.90	0.78	0.85	0.80	0.83	0.79	0.97	0.87
	Parents' video-game control	M	3.41	3.19	3.30	3.40	3.26	3.33	3.41	3.47	3.43
		SD	0.87	1.15	1.02	0.92	1.04	0.98	0.83	1.00	0.91
	Parents use videogames themselves	M	2.11	2.27	2.19	2.38	2.14	2.27	2.36	2.31	2.34
		SD	0.92	1.06	0.99	0.91	0.90	0.91	0.86	1.02	0.93
	Parents' neglect children's videogame use	M	2.44	2.58	2.51	2.64	2.52	2.58	2.75	2.60	2.69
		SD	1.01	1.06	1.03	1.05	0.89	0.98	1.05	1.15	1.09
	Provide videogame equipment or software	M	2.16	2.25	2.20	2.23	2.18	2.21	2.33	2.29	2.31
		SD	0.99	1.07	1.03	0.84	1.00	0.92	0.85	1.03	0.93

(*continued*)

Table 1. (*continued*)

		Age	3 years old			4 years old			5 years old		
		Gender	Boys	Girls	Total	Boys	Girls	Total	Boys	Girls	Total
Parenting styles	Permissive parenting	M	1.72	2.02	1.87	1.95	1.92	1.93	2.00	1.80	1.91
		SD	0.66	0.84	0.77	0.65	0.64	0.65	0.72	0.60	0.68
	Democratic parenting	M	3.67	3.39	3.53	3.52	3.48	3.50	3.53	3.50	3.52
		SD	0.67	0.87	0.78	0.71	0.75	0.73	0.75	0.88	0.80
	Uninvolved parenting	M	2.02	2.08	2.05	2.09	2.10	2.09	2.16	2.01	2.10
		SD	0.56	0.75	0.66	0.57	0.67	0.62	0.66	0.60	0.64
	Authoritarian parenting	M	2.65	2.58	2.62	2.68	2.65	2.67	2.75	2.67	2.72
		SD	0.58	0.63	0.60	0.42	0.50	0.46	0.51	0.51	0.51
	Inconsistent parenting	M	2.54	2.54	2.54	2.55	2.55	2.55	2.63	2.59	2.61
		SD	0.60	0.78	0.69	0.65	0.70	0.67	0.64	0.72	0.67

451) $= 5.166, 3.530, p = 0.023, 0.061, \Delta\eta2 = 0.009, 0.006, d = 0.621, 0.466$. Post-hoc analyses suggest that 5-year-olds have a significantly longer average use time than 3-year-olds, and that boys have a longer average use time than girls. For longest use time, there were also age and gender differences, $F(2, 451) = 5.166, p = 0.023, \Delta\eta2 = 0.009, d = 0.621$, for the age difference; $F(1, 451) = 3.530, p = 0.061, \Delta\eta2 = 0.009, 0.006, d = 0.466$, for the gender difference, respectively. Post-hoc analysis revealed that 5-year-olds' longest use time was significantly longer than that of 3- and 4-year-olds. Moreover, boys' longest use time was longer than that of girls.

In the second set of MANOVAs, age group and gender were again the independent variables, and the four dimensions of the children's engagement in videogame use (difficulty stopping, desire to engage, emotional engagement, and social interaction in game) were the dependent variables. Significant age and gender differences were found for difficulty stopping, $F(2, 659) = 2.788, p = 0.062, \Delta\eta2 = 0.008, d = 0.549, F(1, 659) = 4.005, p = 0.046, \Delta\eta2 = 0.006, d = 0.515$. The 5-year-olds scored marginally higher on this index than the 3-year-olds, and boys scored higher than girls. Boys also scored higher than girls on desire to engage, $F(1, 659) = 5.031, p = 0.025, \Delta\eta2 = 0.008, d = 0.610$.

Results of the above analyses indicate that children play more videogames and become more engaged in videogame use as they grow older, and that boys' play videogames more and are more engaged in videogame use compared to girls.

3.2 Parents Involvement in Children's Videogame Use

To explore the parenting-related factors, three set of analyses were conducted.

First we explored parenting styles by conducting a repeated design ANOVA, Mauchly's $W(9) = 0.234, p < 0.001, \chi^2 = 949.932$. The results indicated that there were significant interactions between age, gender, and parenting style, $F(8, 656) =$

1.936, $p = 0.05$, $\Delta\eta2 = 0.006$, $d = 0.813$. Subsequent analyses indicated that for different gender and age groups, albeit with slight differences, parents scored highest on democratic parenting and lowest on permissive parenting, all $Fs > 66$, all $ps < 0.001$.

We also investigated parents' involvement in children's videogame use. MANOVAs were conducted with the five dimensions of involvement as the dependent variables and children's age group and gender as the independent variables; the results indicated that parental involvement in children's videogame use did not differ across gender and age, all $ps > 0.05$.

3.3   Relationship Between Family-Related Factors and Children's Videogame Use

To explore the relationship between children's demographic variables, family-related factors, and children's videogame use, *Pearson* correlations were conducted; the results are reported in Table 2.

Table 2 shows there were various correlations between the variables for children's videogame use and the parental factors. To determine which family-related factors predict young children's videogame use, eight hierarchy regressions were conducted in which both the four objective indexes and the five indexes of videogame engagement were dependent variables. Independent variables were entered into the regression in three steps. The background variables, including children's age and gender and family SES, were entered in the first step; next, parenting styles were entered; finally, family-related factors related to videogame use were entered. The results are reported in Table 3.

In the first model, children's age was significantly correlated with the age of first use and longest use time, which suggests that children become more engaged in videogames as they grow older. Moreover, children's gender was negatively correlated with longest use time, difficulty stopping, and emotional engagement during videogame use, which indicates that boys are more engaged than girls in videogames. These results accord with the MANOVA results.

Parenting styles and parents' involvement in their children's videogame use were entered at the second and third steps, respectively. The results suggest that these two sets of variables have both separate and interactive effects on children's videogame use.

First, the dimensions of parents' involvement have different correlations with children's videogame use. Using videogames as a parenting tool positively predicted children's videogame use frequency, desire to engage, and social interaction in game during videogame use. Exercising control over videogame use negatively predicted children's videogame use frequency and difficulty stopping, but positively predicted children's emotional engagement when using videogames. It seems that parental control decreases children's desire to use videogames but enhances their emotional engagement during use. Parents using videogames themselves positively predicted children's average use time, but negatively predicted children's social interaction in game during videogame use. This latter finding suggests that when children and their parents both engage in videogame use, children's desire to share the videogames with their parents is met, consequently lowering the intensity of their desire to connect. Ignoring children's videogame use positively predicted children's difficulty stopping and use desire. Parents providing

Table 2. Correlations between the variables.

		1	2	3	4	5	6	7	8	9	10	11	12	13	14	15	16	17	18	19	20
Background Information	1 Age	1.00	-0.04	.44**	0.01	0.07	.10*	.10*	.11**	0.02	0.05	0.02	0.02	0.00	0.00	-0.01	-0.02	-0.03	-0.02	0.02	-0.01
	2 Gender		1.00	0.01	-0.05	-.10*	-.09*	-.09*	-.11**	-0.03	0.05	-0.02	-0.01	0.01	-0.02	0.02	0.01	0.00	-0.01	-0.03	0.00
Situation of Children's Video Game Use	3 Initial using age			1.00	-.18**	0.07	0.05	0.02	0.02	0.06	0.06	-0.01	.10**	-0.03	0.00	-0.07	-0.05	.08*	-0.02	-0.01	-.08*
	4 Frequency				1.00	.18**	.26**	.23**	.30**	0.06	0.06	.24**	-0.04	.23**	.16**	.21**	.19**	-.10*	.20**	.10*	.13**
	5 Average playing time					1.00	.69**	.15**	.25**	.13**	0.05	.15**	0.05	.18**	0.07	.10*	0.02	0.02	0.07	.08*	.10*
	6 Longest playing time						1.00	.21**	.26**	.09*	0.07	.12**	0.01	.14**	.09*	0.06	0.05	-0.02	.12**	.10*	.13**
Children's Engagement in Game Use	7 Difficulty stopping							1.00	.61**	.39**	.36**	.35**	0.00	.38**	.29**	.34**	.37**	-.10*	.39**	.25**	.34**
	8 Desire to engage								1.00	.53**	.38**	.39**	.14**	.31**	.35**	.31**	.22**	.14**	.26**	.27**	.34**
	9 Emotional engagement									1.00	.42**	.29**	.41**	.16**	.20**	.14**	0.07	.41**	.09*	.23**	.21**
	10 Social interaction in game										1.00	.31**	.18**	.12**	.24**	.29**	.10**	.10**	.12**	0.05	0.07
Parents' Interaction with Children in Games	11 Using game as tools											1.00	.38**	.57**	.50**	.58**	.34**	.17**	.34**	.30**	.34**
	12 Video-game control												1.00	.19**	.20**	.25**	0.00	.53**	-0.02	.21**	.12**
	13 Parents' engagement													1.00	.40**	.48**	.42**	0.01	.44**	.32**	.38**
	14 Neglect due to game use														1.00	.45**	.22**	.12**	.25**	.24**	.31**
	15 Material providence															1.00	.34**	0.00	.36**	.26**	.28**
Parenting Styles	16 Permissive parenting																1.00	-.10*	.76**	.48**	.48**
	17 Democratic parenting																	1.00	-0.07	.33**	.28**
	18 Uninvolved parenting																		1.00	.52**	.56**
	19 Authoritarian parenting																			1.00	.57**
	20 Inconsistent parenting																				1.00

Table 3. The predictions of parents' related factor to children's video game use.

Models		Age of first use B	β	t	Use frequency B	β	t	Average use time B	β	t	Longest use time B	β	t	Difficulty stopping B	β	t	Desire to engage B	β	t	Emotional engagement B	β	t	Social interaction in game B	β	t
Model 1	Age	.53	.48	12.37**	.01	.03	.60	1.20	.08	1.87*	3.37	.12	2.61**	.10	.12	2.76**	.15	.15	3.54**	.09	.10	2.38*	.10	.10	2.44*
	Gender	.06	.03	.74	-.05	-.06	-1.38	-1.82	-.07	-1.52	-5.51	-.10	-2.26*	-.18	-.11	-2.52*	-.22	-.12	-2.87**	-.01	.00	-.10	.07	.04	.89
	SES	.03	.03	.76	-.09	-.23	-5.18**	-1.89	-.13	-3.11**	-3.85	-.15	-3.19**	-.07	-.09	-2.05*	-.07	-.07	-1.71+	.02	.03	.65	.00	-.01	-.11
Model 2	Age	.52	.47	12.32**	.01	.02	.54	1.31	.09	2.04*	3.31	.12	2.57**	.11	.12	3.12**	.14	.15	3.52**	.08	.09	2.03*	.10	.10	2.44*
	Gender	.05	.03	.67	-.04	-.05	-1.25	-1.86	-.07	-1.55	-5.44	-.10	-2.25*	-.16	-.10	-2.47*	-.21	-.12	-2.86**	.00	.00	-.04	.07	.04	.88
	SES	.02	.02	.53	-.08	-.22	-5.07**	-1.84	-.13	-3.00**	-3.77	-.14	-3.12**	-.05	-.06	-1.64	-.07	-.07	-1.78*	.00	-.01	.00	-.01	-.01	-.32
	Permissive parenting	-.14	-.09	-1.41	.05	.09	1.36	-2.57	-.12	-1.77*	-6.19	-.16	-2.08*	.19	.15	2.46*	.11	.08	1.24	.16	.13	1.89*	.17	.12	1.82*
	Democratic parenting	.13	.09	1.86	-.01	-.02	-.36	-1.18	-.06	-1.09	-2.55	-.07	-1.18	-.17	-.15	-2.98**	.01	.01	.12	.32	.27	4.97**	.18	.15	3.00**
	Uninvolved parenting	.18	.10	1.53	.01	.02	.22	2.39	.10	1.39	7.67	.17	2.15*	.11	.08	1.17	.00	.00	.02	-.08	-.06	-.75	.16	.11	1.46
	Authoritarian parenting	.01	.00	.09	.00	.00	.08	.43	.02	.27	2.30	.04	.72	-.01	-.01	-.14	.11	.06	1.09	.01	.01	.15	-.20	-.11	-2.02*
	Inconsistent parenting	-.23	-.14	-2.82**	.07	.12	2.19*	1.34	.06	1.11	3.93	.09	1.59	.22	.17	3.45**	.25	.18	3.36**	.06	.05	.86	-.14	-.10	-1.81*
Model 3	Age	.52	.47	12.23**	.00	.01	.18	1.29	.09	2.01*	3.21	.11	2.47*	.10	.12	3.04**	.13	.13	3.31**	.06	.07	1.69*	-.01	-.01	-.33
	Gender	.06	.03	.70	-.03	-.04	-.94	-1.81	-.07	-1.51	-5.15	-.10	-2.12*	-.14	-.09	-2.31*	-.18	-.10	-2.58*	.01	.01	.16	.08	.06	.95
	SES	.02	.02	.53	-.08	-.20	-4.81**	-1.66	-.12	-2.70**	-3.54	-.13	-2.91**	-.04	-.05	-1.36	-.05	-.06	-1.41	.02	.02	.44	.15	.12	2.30*
	Permissive parenting	-.12	-.08	-1.22	.02	.03	.39	-3.28	-.16	-2.23*	-7.02	-.18	-2.32*	.14	.11	1.80*	.03	.02	.29	.12	.09	1.36	.10	.07	.96
	Democratic parenting	.09	.06	1.14	.00	.00	-.03	-.66	-.03	-.56	-1.65	-.05	-.70	-.13	-.12	-2.15*	.01	.01	.15	.21	.17	3.00**	-.24	-.13	-2.51*
	Uninvolved parenting	.19	.11	1.64	-.01	-.02	-.20	2.11	.09	1.22	7.38	.17	2.05*	.06	.05	.67	-.05	-.03	-.46	-.09	-.07	-.92	-.17	-.12	-2.31*
	Authoritarian parenting	.01	.00	.09	-.01	-.01	-.17	.19	.01	.12	2.13	.04	.66	-.04	-.02	-.43	.07	.04	.69	-.03	-.02	-.32	.21	.19	3.30**
	Inconsistent parenting	-.21	-.13	-2.48*	.05	.08	1.44	.77	.04	.62	2.82	.07	1.09	.16	.12	2.44*	.17	.12	2.36*	.07	.06	1.01	.01	.01	.26
	Use as parenting tools	-.02	-.02	-.33	.09	.19	3.11**	1.60	.09	1.51	1.98	.06	.92	.09	.09	1.62	.18	.17	2.96**	.09	.09	1.43	.16	.17	3.25**
	Videogame control	.07	.06	1.31	-.03	-.07	-1.37	-.86	-.06	-1.06	-1.52	-.05	-.93	-.09	-.09	-2.02*	-.05	-.05	-.97	.18	.19	3.85**	.10	.10	2.44*
	Use videogames themselves	-.03	-.03	-.54	.02	.04	.77	1.74	.12	2.06*	2.42	.08	1.37	.08	.08	1.52	.03	.03	.59	.03	.03	.60	.07	.04	.89
	Parents' neglect	.03	.03	.66	.02	.05	.94	-.72	-.05	-1.03	-.08	.00	-.08	.07	.08	1.81*	.16	.19	4.00**	.07	.08	1.71	.00	-.01	-.11
	Provide equipment	-.06	-.05	-1.08	.03	.08	1.49	-.12	-.01	-.14	-1.08	-.04	-.62	.10	.11	2.20**	.07	.07	1.40	-.06	-.06	-1.19	.10	.10	2.44*

videogame equipment positively predicted children's difficulty stopping and their social interaction in game.

Second, parenting styles were found to differently predict children's videogame use, either directly or via the effects of parents' involvement in their children's videogame use. In the second model, democratic parenting positively predicted children's age of first use, but negatively predicted children's difficulty stopping. It thus seems that democratic parenting could protect against children's excessive videogame use. Moreover, democratic parenting positively predicted children's emotional engagement and their desire for social sharing and connection when using videogames; these results suggest that democratic parenting may increase children's positive experience during videogame use. In the third model, when parents' involvement with children's videogame use was entered into the regression, the above predictions of democratic parenting remained significant. This means that democratic parenting directly predicts children's videogame use and that these predictions are not mediated by parents' involvement in children's videogame use.

Uninvolved parenting also positively predicted children's longest use time and difficulty stopping, and neither of these predictions was mediated by parents' involvement. Permissive parenting appears to be a protective factor for children's videogame use as it negatively predicted children's longest use time and difficulty stopping. These predictions remained significant even after parents' involvement was entered into the regression, which suggests that parents' involvement did not mediate the effects of permissive parenting on children's videogame use. Inconsistent parenting may also be a risk factor for children's videogame use, as it positively predicted use frequency, difficulty stopping, and use desire. These predictions were partly mediated by parents' involvement in their children's videogame use: when the indexes of parents' involvement were entered into the regression, inconsistent parenting became a non-significant predictor of use frequency and its prediction of difficulty stopping decreased to common significance.

Finally, authoritarian parenting did not predict children's time and degree of videogame use, but especially negatively predicted children's desire for social sharing and connection during videogame use, regardless of parental involvement. It seems that as the level of authoritarian parenting rises, children's desire to share and connect with others during videogame use decreases.

4 Discussion

The results support our assumption that each parenting style has different effects on young children's videogame use, and that parents' involvement sometimes mediates these relationships. The results will be discussed in relation to the three main aspects on which this study focused.

4.1 The Role of Parents' Involvement in Children's Videogame Use

This study examined parents' ways and degrees of involvement in their children's videogame use. Whereas most previous studies focus on parents' control over children's videogame use [15], this study explored the different aims and approaches of parental involvement, and found them to be associated with different aspects of children's videogame use.

The results suggest that parents using videogames as a parental tool, playing videogames themselves, ignoring children's videogame use, and providing videogame equipment or software all positively predict the time children spend playing videogames. An interesting result was that parental control over children's videogame use positively predicted children's emotional engagement while playing: this suggests that the more parents control children's videogame use, the more engaged children are when using them. Social interaction in game, which reflects children's wish to personally interact with others while playing videogames, was negatively predicted by parents using videogames themselves, unrelated to parents exercising control over children's sharing intention, and positively predicted by the other three parental involvement variables.

4.2   The Role of Parenting Styles in Children's Videogame Use

This study found that five parenting styles differently predicted young children's videogame use. Consistent with previous studies [16], our results suggest that democratic parenting style benefits children most: for example, it not only helped children to avoid excessive videogame use but also increased their positive experiences, in terms of emotional engagement and the desire for social sharing and connection, during videogame use. Moreover, these effects were not mediated by contextual parental involvement. These findings may be explained by the previously identified contribution of democratic parenting to individuals' self-regulation [17], leading to children being better able to control themselves when using videogames.

The study also found that permissive parenting negatively predicted children's videogame longest use time and difficulty stopping. Although previous studies found that permissive parenting is a risk factor for children's excessive videogame use, this study found that permissive parenting may have a protective effect. Cultural differences in the performance of each parenting style [18] may explain these results: in western culture, the core characteristic of permissive parenting is low control of and demands on children, whereas its core characteristic in Chinese culture is parents' too much care and replacing children to do their job [19]. This result accords with the finding in previous studies that permissive parenting may harm a child's self-regulation [19]. in case of the young children's videogame use, the permissive parents are more likely to regulate their children's videogame use, therefor a likeable consequence is that the children's self-regulation ability is not developed. This can partly explain why permissive parenting could help to decrease children's excessive videogame use when parents are involved. More research is needed to determine the exact mechanism.

Uninvolved and inconsistent parenting styles were found to significantly predict children's excessive videogame use, even when the effects of parents' involvement were controlled. It seems that the children whose parents employed uninvolved and inconsistent parenting styles neither exhibited self-regulation nor accepted their parents' control. These findings support the previously identified link between these two parenting styles and children's problem behavior [20].

Although the core feature of authoritarian parenting is high control, this study did not find any relationship between authoritarian parenting and any index of children's videogame use. Conversely, authoritarian parenting negatively predicted children's social interaction in game during videogame use. It seems that children subjected to a more authoritarian parenting style are more likely to use videogames alone, instead of playing with others. This result supports the prior finding that authoritarian parenting is negatively related to children's social abilities [21].

4.3 Contributions, Limitations, and Future Directions

By investigating how children use videogames and how parents can influence this, our study provides valuable insights into how family-related factors affect children's videogame use. Furthermore, the study's Chinese sample broadens understanding about this important problem by adding evidence from a non-Western culture. From a practical perspective, the study also reveals that parental characteristics are potential prevention and treatment targets.

However, this study has two main limitations. In this research, data on children's videogame use and the family-related factors were all self-reported, and so could have been biased by societal stereotypes, and future studies should include multiple measures, such as behavior indexes. In addition, the cross-sectional design prevents causal inferences regarding how family-related factors influence children's videogame use, a longitudinal design or intervention research would enable better identification of the underlying mechanism.

Acknowledgments. This study was funded by the National Social Science Fund of China (18BSH130). Moreover, we appreciate the support from the Infant and Child Development Laboratory and all the individuals who provided assistance or participated in our study.

References

1. Ofcom: Children and parents: Media use and attitudes report (2015). http://stakeholders. ofcom.org.uk/market-data-research/other/research-publications/childrens/children-parents-nov-15/
2. Duch, H., Fisher, E.M., Ensari, I., Harrington, A.: Screen time use in children under 3 years old: A systematic review of correlates. Int. J. Behav. Nutr. Physi. Acti. **102** (2013). https://doi.org/10.1186/1479-5868-10-102
3. Carson, V., et al.: Systematic review of sedentary behavior and cognitive development in early childhood. Prev. Med. **78**, 115–122 (2015). https://doi.org/10.1016/j.ypmed.2015.07.016
4. Reid-Chassiakos, Y, Radesk, J., Christakis, D., Moreno, M.A, Cross, C.: Council on Communications and Media. Children and adolescents and digital media. Pediatrics **138**, e20162593 (2016)
5. Linebarger, D.L.: Contextualizing video game play: the moderating effects of cumulative risk and parenting styles on the relations among video game exposure and problem behaviors. Psychcol. Popul. Media Cult. **4**, 375–396 (2015). https://doi.org/10.1037/ppm0000069
6. Beard, C.L., Haas, A.L., Wickham, R.E., Stavropoulos, V.: Age of initiation and internet gaming disorder: the role of self-esteem. CyberPsychcol. Behav. **20**, 397–401 (2017). https://doi.org/10.1089/cyber.2017.0011

7. Nathanson, A.I.: Media and the family: reflections and future directions. J. Child Media **9**, 133–139 (2015). https://doi.org/10.1080/17482798.2015.997145

8. Schneider, L.A., King, D.L., Delfabbro, P.H.: Family factors in adolescent problematic internet gaming: a systematic review. J. Behav. Addict. **6**, 321–333 (2017)

9. Cesur, M.S., Odluyurt, S.: An investigation of the opinions and suggestions of parents and teachers about the teaching of play skills to children with autism spectrum disorders. Int. J. Early Child Spec. Educ. **11**, 128–140 (2019). https://doi.org/10.20489/intjecse.670469

10. Masud, H., Shakil, A.M., Cho, K.W., Fakhr, Z.: Parenting styles and aggression among young adolescents: A systematic review of literature. Commun. Mental Health J. (2019). https://doi.org/10.1007/s10597-019-00400-0

11. Levin, E.: Baumrind's Parenting Styles. Springer, New York (2011). https://doi.org/10.1007/978-0-387-79061-9

12. Konok, V., Bunford, N.N., Mikllor, A.: Associations between child mobile use and digital parenting style in Hungarian families. J. Child Media (2019). https://doi.org/10.1080/17482798.2019.1684332

13. Steinkuehler, C.: Parenting and video games. J. Adolesc. Adult Lit. **59**, 357–361 (2016). https://doi.org/10.1002/jaal.455l

14. Jiang, J., Xu, Y., Jiang, B., Yu, S., Zheng, F.: The reliability and validity of a Chinese version of the parental bonding instrument (in Chinese). Psychol. Sci. **32**, 1193–1196 (2009). CNKI:SUN:XLKX.0.2009-01-053

15. Hwang, Y., Choi, I., Yum, J.Y., Jeong, S.H.: Parental mediation regarding children's smartphone use: role of protection motivation and parenting style. Cyberpsychcol. Behav. Soc. Netw. **20**, 362–368 (2017). https://doi.org/10.1089/cyber.2016.0555

16. Spera, C.: A review of the relationship among parenting practices, parenting styles, and adolescent school achievement. Educ. Psychol. Rev. **17**, 125–146 (2005). https://doi.org/10.2307/23363898

17. Azhar, H., Baig, Z., Koleth, S., Mohammad, K., Petkari, E.: Psychosocial associations of emotion-regulation strategies in young adults residing in the United Arab Emirates. Psychcol. J. **8**, 431–438 (2019) https://doi.org/10.1002/pchj.272

18. Murray, A.D., Bornstein, M.H.: Cultural approaches to parenting. Parenting **12**, 212–221 (2012). https://doi.org/10.1080/15295192.2012.683359

19. Bahrami, B., Dolatshahi, B., Pourshahbaz, A., Mohammadkhani, P.: Parenting style and emotion regulation in mothers of preschool children. J. Pract. Clin. Psychol. **6**, 3–8 (2018). https://doi.org/10.29252/nirp.jpcp.6.1.3

20. Aunola, K., Nurmi, J.E.: The role of parenting styles in children's problem behavior. Child Dev. **76**, 1144–1159 (2005). https://doi.org/10.2307/3696624

21. Chao, R.K.: Beyond parental control and authoritarian parenting style: understanding Chinese parenting through the cultural notion of training. Child Dev. **65**, 1111–1119 (1994). https://doi.org/10.1111/j.1467-8624.1994.tb00806.x

The Relation Between Video Game Experience and Children's Attentional Networks

Hui Li[1(✉)], Muyun Long[1], and Kaveri Subrahmanyam[2]

[1] Central China Normal University, Wuhan 430070, Hubei, People's Republic of China
huilipsy@mail.ccnu.edu.cn, muyun_long@foxmail.com
[2] California State University Los Angeles, Los Angeles, CA 90032, USA
ksubrah@exchange.calstatela.edu

Abstract. Video games are popular in children's lives. Previous studies suggest that video games are related to children's attention. In order to further characterize this relation, especially in early childhood, we used the Child Attentional Network Test (Child-ANT), which uses reaction time to assess the three subsystems of attention, including alerting, orienting and executive control networks. Participants included 60 child video game players (VGPs) and non-video game players (NVGPs). The results showed that children's experience with video games was related to their orienting network and their executive control network. The results have implications for parents and educators, who make decisions regarding children's use of games and game-like learning technologies.

Keywords: Video games · Children · Attention · Attentional Network Test

1 Introduction

With the development of technology, video games have become an integral part in the lives of children around the world. Previous research suggests that children spend much time playing video games on computers or mobile devices, such as iPads or smartphones every day [1–3]. According to the latest *Chinese Child Development Report (2019)*, Children aged 3- to 15-years spend 43.24 min on electronic devices at school, and this number is even higher on weekends. Importantly, nearly all (98%) children under eight have some type of mobile device at home, which suggests that video games have become popular among Chinese children [3].

Prior studies suggest a relation between video games and attention, during childhood, adolescence and adulthood, with findings suggesting both positive and negative associations. One research study focusing on the efficiency of visual search found that adult video game players (VGPs) had faster stimulus-response mapping [4]. Action video game players (AVGPs) also showed better spatial resolution of visual ability that could be trained to resist the disturbance when a distractor comes close to the target [5]. Among young adults, females benefit more from action video games in spatial attention and rotation after video games training leading to a decrease in the gender disparity in spatial cognition [6]. However, in a cognitive task for 45 Italian teenagers, the drop

© Springer Nature Switzerland AG 2020
X. Fang (Ed.): HCII 2020, LNCS 12211, pp. 295–304, 2020.
https://doi.org/10.1007/978-3-030-50164-8_21

in performance in a sustained attention task over time was more significant for AVGPs compares to the NAVGPs group, showing that playing action video games had a negative association on sustained attention [7]. However, some researchers have found that the effect of video games on some aspect of attention is not significant [8–10]. When it comes to children, video games appear to help improve attention for differently abled children [11–13, 17]. For typically developing children as young as 7 years old, VGPs have faster response rates without sacrificing accuracy [14].

Attention is regulated by three different networks: alerting, orienting, and executive control, each of which is based on anatomically separate systems, and have different biochemical mechanisms [15]. Based on initial neuroimaging image evidence, Posner and Peterson [15] suggest that alerting is the ability to produce and maintain alertness to process high priority signals. The orienting network is focused on shifting priority, mostly visually, to another modality or location [15, 16]. Finally, executive control involves solving conflicts between thoughts, feelings and responding [11]. Anatomically, they have different neural structural foundations and are controlled by separate regions in the brain which also regulate different functions [12]. However, they also interact with each other, and studies have found that alerting enhancing orienting processes and exclusive control was restricted by alerting networks [13, 17, 18]. A similar result was also observed in childhood as alerting cues accelerate attention shifts, which indicate better performance in orienting processes. This interaction is age-related and stems from childhood, and is more fully developed in adulthood [19].

The Attention Networks Test (ANT), which was designed by Fan et al. [12, 20], aims to evaluate the three different functions of attention. It can evaluate the efficiency of three individual attention networks by measuring people's reaction time to different visual cues, and it has shown to be proved reliable by many studies [10, 14, 21]. Procedurally, in the ANT, a central fixation point is first shown on the screen, and remains on the screen during the entire session. Before the target appears, cues are shown both above and below the fixation point (Fig. 1-**Double cue**), or appears to one place as a hint for where the target occurs (Fig. 1-**spatial cue**). A blank control (Fig. 1-**No cue**), in which no cue will be shown is also be set. Then the target, an arrow, occurs either above or below the fixation point. Participants are required to point out where the target points to (right or left) by pressing the right or left button. There are three conditions for the target's appearance (Fig. 2): Neutral, in which only an arrow appears, Congruent-in which participants see a row of same-direction arrows, and Incongruent – in which participants see arrows on both sides of the central target all pointing to the opposite direction.

The time between the target's appearance and the participants pressing of the button is recorded, and it is then processed in order to measure the efficiency of the three subsystems. First, the efficiency of the alerting network is calculated by subtracting the Reaction Time (RT) of the double-cue condition where the cues are shown in both locations from the no-cue condition. This is because when no cue is shown, participants' attention is regarded to be distracted, however, it will then alert when the double cues appear. The higher result means better performance in alerting. Second, orienting network is measured by comparing spatial cue condition and the center cue condition, which encourages orientation attention to the center, but only the spatial cue predicts where the target will appear. This is because even either cue attract participants' attention, spatial cue also suggests where the target appears. Finally, the executive control system is calculated by subtracting the response time of the congruent flanking conditions (or neutral conditions) from incongruent flanking conditions. When the target points to the opposite direction compared with the rest of the arrows, individuals need to process the central target effectively regardless of other disturbances, which is the executive control networks' responsibility. This means more time is required when processing conflict. However, with better performance of executive network, differences between these two-target conditions will be reduced. As a result, the lower the value is, the better executive control network ability the participants have. In order to make children understand the test easily, we used the adapted version, Child-ANT [22], which provides a story and clear feedback. The most apparent adaption is that arrows are replaced by an image of a cartoon fish and it faces either left, or right with animated feedback. In the present quasi experimental study, we explore the relation between video game playing on children, especially on their attention by comparing attentional networks of child VGPs and no game control.

Each trial lasted for 4000 ms in total (Fig. 3). The central fixation point is first shown on the screen for 400–1600 ms depending on the time spent on the prior trial, followed by the presenting of the cue (100 ms). The cue then will then be removed and 400 ms later, the target appears. The child is then required to judge the direction by pressing the left or the right button within 1700 ms. When 4000 ms run off, another trial is initiated again.

The development of children's attention is also a gradual process. Young children are less able to search for targets than young adults and the elderly [23, 24]. Besides, the processes of the three subsystems of attention develop separately. The development of alerting systems mainly starts in infancy and early childhood and then gradually becomes steady till late childhood. Studies which have used the Child-ANT, show that children (aged < 7) benefit more when an alerting cue is presented. Similarly, the efficiency of the orienting attention network increases from middle- to late-childhood [19]. As for executive control, a study has found considerable improvement in the ability to resolve conflicts between 2 and 7 years, and then it continues improving until adulthood [25].

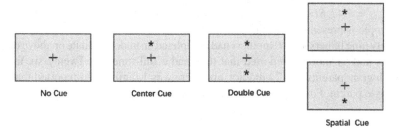

Fig. 1. Four types of Cue

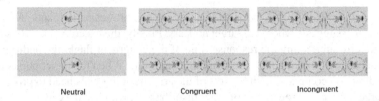

Fig. 2. Four types of Target

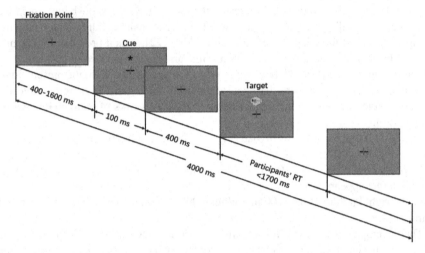

Fig. 3. Children's version of Attentional Network Test

2 Methods

2.1 Participants

Participants included 263 children who were recruited from a large preschool affiliated with a University, which was located in the central part of China, all were ethnically Chinese. Based on children's video game play experience, sixty children (27 boys and 43 girls) ($M_{age} = 5.47$, $SD_{age} = 0.68$) finally participated in this study. Descriptive statistics of the sample is presented in Table 1.

Twenty nine fathers and 40 mothers had completed an undergraduate or above degree. 46 fathers and 51 mothers reported that they had a full-time job. Twenty-six families lived with grandparents and 24 did not, and there was 1 family who reported that there was a single parent. Forty-seven children were without siblings.

2.2 Tools and Materials

The version(Child-ANT) used in this study was downloaded from the website for free (https://sacklerinstitute.org/cornell/assays_and_tools/ant/jin.fan/) [25]. Similar to the ANT, the Child version requires children to feed the fish in the middle by pressing the left or the right button depending on which side the fish face. A single fish or a row of fish was presented as the stimulus, and the one in the middle either faces the same direction or the opposite direction as the others. In each trial, a fixation point is first shown in the central part of the screen before the cue appears. There are four types of cues. The first one is the central cue, which appears at the same place of fixation point. The second one is the double cue appearing simultaneously above or below the fixation point. The next one is the spatial cue, which appears either above or below the fixation point, and located at the same place where the upcoming stimuli are. The final one is no cues. Shortly after the cue appears, fish then appear as the target above or below the central fixation point.

According to the design of Fan et al., the levels of the three attention networks can be measured by comparing the VGPs and NVGPs' reaction time in the task [12]. Specifically, for alerting and orienting, higher score shows a higher attention level: Alerting $RT_{no\ cue} - RT_{double\ cues}$; Orienting $RT_{central\ cues} - RT_{spatial\ cues}$. On the contrary, Executive attention $RT_{target\ stimulation\ \&\ inconsistent\ directions} - RT_{target\ stimulation\ \&\ consistent\ directions}$. As individuals need more time processing conflict when the target is not consistent, the lower value indicates better performance in executive control.

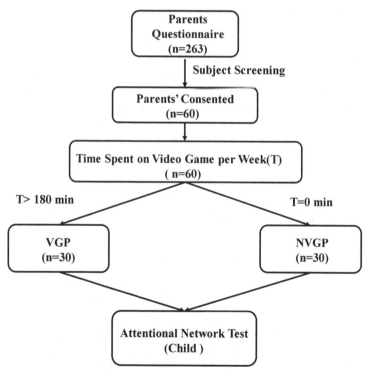

Fig. 4. Preocedure

Parent Questionnaire. In this study, parental reports were used to collect information about children's time spend on Video Game on weekends and weekdays in the past six months. Time (T) playing video games every week $T_{\text{playing video games every weekday}} \times 5 + T_{\text{playing video games every weekend}} \times 2$. The result is used as a quantitative indicator of the time that children played video games over the course of a week.

2.3 Procedure

After we got parents' consent, we asked them to complete a questionnaire which included their children's basic information, such as gender, age and time spent on playing video games on weekdays and weekends on average (Fig. 4. Procedure). Each child was supervised individually by a trained psychology postgraduate student during the task which lasted about 20 min. The test was provided in Chinese. The experimenter first talked with the children to establish rapport and build trust. For example, he/she would say: "How are you? What is your name? How old are you? Do you want to play games? Today we will play a game called 'feed the fish'". After the participant quietened down in front of the computer, the experimenter would start to introduce the tasks. "This is a hungry little fish, and we will feed the little fish later. Look (the experimenter presents the Fig. 5. Example of the task for attention network test on the computer), when the fish faces to the left, we press the left button to so the small fish will be fed; when the small fish faces to the right, we press the right bottom. If there is a row of fish, then you should only look at the middle one, and press the bottom where that one faces to" (Fig. 6. Example of the task for attention network test). To make the child familiar with the instruction, a practice block was provided shortly after the introduction: "Let's try it out. If you see such a little fish like this, which key should you press? If the little fish gets fed successfully, it will make an "oh ho" sound; if it doesn't, it will make a "beep" sound". Then a 3-min practice test containing 24 trials was presented to the child. If the

Fig. 5. Example of the task for attention network test

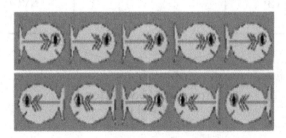

Fig. 6. Example of the task for attention network test

child already understood the instruction and successfully passes the practice task, then he/she started the formal experiment immediately; otherwise, the experimenter repeated the instruction above again. Each child participated in three blocks, with 48 trials in each block.

2.4 Results

According to parents' report, children's descriptive data was indicated in Table 1. Parents of 263 children filled out the questionnaire including reporting children's time spent playing video games per week. The results suggest that children spent 139.26 min on video games every week. The highest number was 840 min, and there were also children who never played any video games.

Based on the parents' responses to the questionnaire, children who played at least 180 min of video games per week in the past six months, and children who never played action video games were divided into VGP group and NVGP group separately.

Table 1. Descriptive data of children

	N	Minimum	Maximum	Mean	SD
Overall	263	0	840	91.79	139.206
NVGP	30	0	0	0	0
VGP	30	180	840	369.33	180.07

The results indicated that the orientation network of the Video Game Player group ($t = -3.01$, $p < 0.01$) and the executive control network ($t = -2.99$, $p < 0.01$) were significantly lower than the control group, comprising children who did not play video games. The result was further calculated to account for the alertness, orientation, and efficiency of executive control (Table 2). Overall, the results suggest that video game players performed better in executive control network, however, their orienting network performance was not as good.

Table 2. Children's ANT between VGPs and NVGPs

Group	Alerting	Orienting	Executive control
VGPs	83.14 ± 48.35	59.59 ± 39.26	85.66 ± 43.19
NVGPs	105.52 ± 77.98	99.06 ± 59.57	138.94 ± 86.41

3 Discussion

The results suggest that video game playing had a negative association on children's orienting network, but a positive association to the executive network. The orienting network led the attention to the spot where the stimuli accrue. Executive network focuses on task-related stimuli and suppresses distraction [14]. Green and Bavelier's research [26] shows that experience with video games had a positive relation to attention, in other words, VGPs have a more substantial visual attention capacity than the NVGPs. Other researches about perceptual load also provide evidence that videogames players had a higher attentive distribution. Load theory of attention shows that when attention is engaged into a low-load task, the remaining attention resources will be used to process distractors. A coordination effect appears when people process tasks with a distractor with both the same identity and incongruent response, which means they make more mistakes [27, 28]. Dye, et al. found that coordination effects of VGPs was significantly higher than NVGP [5, 14, 26]. This means that VGPs had more attentional resources that can be distributed to the adjacent area to manufacturing information. One thing that should be noticed, the results are still ambiguous, and gamers will process irrelevant stimuli, as indicated by the poor executive control of VGPs.

This study suggests that the relation between video games playing experiences and children's attention networks are different. This may be caused by this reason. The positive association of video games shown in the previous studies may be strategic rather than due to changes in basic cognition or perception. The positive relation of video games could be strategical rather than changes on basic cognition or perception [29]. However, we searched for the differences between the VGPs and NVGPs from the perspective of long-term associations, which may be a change in basic cognitive ability. The results of this study indicated that video games may have a negative long-term relation on children's orienting and executive control networks. The result should attract considerable attention from both society and parents. However, it is important to point out that we have only found the correlation between playing video games and children's attentional skills. There is another possibility that children with different levels of attentional networks may also have different preferences for video games. Therefore, further correlational research should explore whether children with higher attentional networks play video games more than those with lower attentional networks.

Acknowledgments. This research was funded by the National Natural Science Foundation of China Grants (31700968).

References

1. Center, C.N.C.: Children's blue book china child development report. In: Yuan (ed.) (2019)
2. Lixin, Y.: Blue book: Chinese children development report (2019)
3. Census, C.S.: He Common Sense Census: Media Use by Kids Age Zero to Eight 2017 (2017). https://www.commonsensemedia.org/research/the-common-sense-cen sus-media-use-by-kids-age-zero-to-eight-2017. Accessed Nov 30 2019

4. Castel, A.D., Pratt, J., Drummond, E.: The effects of action video game experience on the time course of inhibition of return and the efficiency of visual search. Acta Psychologica **119**(2), 217–230 (2005)

5. Green, C.S., Bavelier, D.: Action-video-game experience alters the spatial resolution of vision. Psychol. Sci. **18**(1), 88–94 (2007)

6. Feng, J., Spence, I., Pratt, J.: Playing an action video game reduces gender differences in spatial cognition. Psychol. Sci. **18**(10), 850–855 (2007)

7. Trisolini, D.C., Petilli, M.A., Daini, R.: Is action video gaming related to sustained attention of adolescents? Q. J. Exp. Psychol. **71**(5), 1033–1039 (2018)

8. Schubert, T., Finke, K., Redel, P., Kluckow, S., Müller, H., Strobach, T.: Video game experience and its influence on visual attention parameters: an investigation using the framework of the Theory of Visual Attention (TVA). Acta Psychologica **157**, 200–214 (2015)

9. Boot, W.R., Kramer, A.F., Simons, D.J., Fabiani, M., Gratton, G.: The effects of video game playing on attention, memory, and executive control. Acta Psychologica **129**(3), 387–398 (2008)

10. Williams, R.S., Biel, A.L., Wegier, P., Lapp, L.K., Dyson, B.J., Spaniol, J.: Age differences in the Attention Network Test: Evidence from behavior and event-related potentials. Brain Cogn. **102**, 65–79 (2016)

11. Posner, M.I., Rothbart, M.K.: Research on attention networks as a model for the integration of psychological science. Annu. Rev. Psychol. **58**, 1–23 (2007)

12. Fan, J., McCandliss, B.D., Sommer, T., Raz, A., Posner, M.I.: Testing the efficiency and independence of attentional networks. J. Cogn. Neurosci. **14**(3), 340–347 (2002)

13. Weinbach, N., Henik, A.: The relationship between alertness and executive control. J. Exp. Psychol. Hum. Percept. Perform. **38**(6), 1530 (2012)

14. Dye, M.W., Green, C.S., Bavelier, D.: The development of attention skills in action video game players. Neuropsychologia **47**(8–9), 1780–1789 (2009)

15. Posner, M.I., Petersen, S.E.: The attention system of the human brain. Annu. Rev. Neurosci. **13**(1), 25–42 (1990)

16. Petersen, S.E., Posner, M.I.: The attention system of the human brain: 20 years after. Annu. Rev. Neurosci. **35**, 73–89 (2012)

17. Fuentes, L.J., Campoy, G.: The time course of alerting effect over orienting in the attention network test. Exp. Brain Res. **185**(4), 667–672 (2008)

18. Callejas, A., Lupianez, J., Funes, M.J., Tudela, P.: Modulations among the alerting, orienting and executive control networks. Exp. Brain Res. **167**(1), 27–37 (2005)

19. Pozuelos, J.P., Paz-Alonso, P.M., Castillo, A., Fuentes, L.J., Rueda, M.R.: Development of attention networks and their interactions in childhood. Dev. Psychol. **50**(10), 2405 (2014)

20. Cooper, N.R., Uller, C., Pettifer, J., Stolc, F.C.: Conditioning attentional skills: Examining the effects of the pace of television editing on children's attention. Acta Paediatrica **98**(10), 1651–1655 (2009)

21. Dye, M.W., Green, C.S., Bavelier, D.: Increasing speed of processing with action video games. Curr. Dir. Psychol. Sci. **18**(6), 321–326 (2009)

22. Rueda, M.R., Fan, J., McCandliss, B.D., Halparin, J.D., Gruber, D.B., Lercari, L.P., Posner, M.I.: Development of attentional networks in childhood. Neuropsychologia **42**(8), 1029–1040 (2004)

23. Trick, L.M., Enns, J.T.: Lifespan changes in attention: the visual search task. Cogn. Dev. **13**(3), 369–386 (1998)

24. Schul, R., Townsend, J., Stiles, J.: The development of attentional orienting during the school-age years. Dev. Sci. **6**(3), 262–272 (2003)

25. Rueda, M.R., Posner, M.I., Rothbart, M.K.: The development of executive attention: contributions to the emergence of self-regulation. Dev. Neuropsychol. **28**(2), 573–594 (2005)

26. Green, C.S., Bavelier, D.: Action video game modifies visual selective attention. Nature **423**(6939), 534 (2003)
27. Lavie, N.: Distracted and confused?: selective attention under load. Trends Cogn. Sci. **9**(2), 75–82 (2005)
28. Lavie, N., Hirst, A., De Fockert, J.W., Viding, E.: Load theory of selective attention and cognitive control. J. Exp. Psychol. Gen. **133**(3), 339 (2004)
29. Nelson, R.A., Strachan, I.: Action and puzzle video games prime different speed/accuracy tradeoffs. Perception **38**(11), 1678–1687 (2009)

Can Video Game Training Improve the Two-Dimensional Mental Rotation Ability of Young Children?
A Randomized Controlled Trial

Xiaocen Liu[1]([⊠]) [ID], Heqing Huang[1] [ID], Kai Yu[1], and Donghui Dou[2]

[1] Capital Normal University, Beijing, People's Republic of China
cindyliu@cnu.edu.cn
[2] Central University of Finance and Economics, Beijing, People's Republic of China

Abstract. Mental rotation skill has been constantly shown to reliably predict science, technology, engineering, and mathematics (STEM) achievements, and is a major component of spatial ability. Previous studies have documented that mental rotation capacity develops rapidly in early years and can be enhanced through training. However, few studies have estimated the training effects of video games on the mental rotation performance of preschoolers, particularly with respect to gender differences and ability levels. This study, therefore, aimed to examine whether video game training can facilitate the mental rotation development of young children, and whether gender- or ability-based discrepancies can be moderated via intervention. We randomly assigned 40 five- to six-year-olds to one of two treatment conditions: an intervention group (playing *My Little Pony Rotate Puzzle*) or a control group (receiving no training). The former played the allocated video game for six min/day for five consecutive days, while the control group continued with their routine activities. Video game training led to significant improvements in mental rotation ability, and the training effects gradually became larger as the degree of rotation increased. Boys outperformed girls at pre-test but gender differences were remarkably lessened by training. Initial ability differences in the intervention group also disappeared after training, and children who scored low at pre-test improved most through the intervention. Our findings imply that video game training can reduce gender and ability disadvantages in mental rotation, and may serve as an effective alternative to traditional intervention programs.

Keywords: Video game · Mental rotation · Young children · Spatial ability · Gender differences · Randomized controlled trial

1 Introduction

1.1 Spatial Ability and Mental Rotation

Spatial ability or visuospatial ability is the capacity to perceive, reason, retrieve, and transform visual images. It plays an indispensable role in people's daily life and academic performance [1]. In particular, spatial ability is exceedingly associated with students' achievements in science, technology, engineering, and mathematics (STEM) disciplines. Conversely, limited spatial ability may lead to impaired STEM performance

© Springer Nature Switzerland AG 2020
X. Fang (Ed.): HCII 2020, LNCS 12211, pp. 305–317, 2020.
https://doi.org/10.1007/978-3-030-50164-8_22

[2]. Therefore, spatial ability is an essential foundation for children to succeed in STEM fields.

Among various types of spatial ability, mental rotation is one of the most studied skills [3] and is the most frequently documented predictor of STEM accomplishment [4]. Mental rotation refers to the capacity to rotate a mental representation of a two- or three-dimensional object to align it with another reference object [5]. Given the importance of this ability, there has been increasing interest in the emergence and development of mental rotation skill. Recent evidence suggests that mental rotation develops rapidly in early childhood [6].

1.2 Video Game Training

A number of studies have identified that mental rotation ability may be improved through training, thereby potentially enhancing an individual's STEM performance [7]. Some effective training, such as ghost stimuli, can even be applied to preschool-aged children [8]. Recently, the up-to-date intervention approach of video game training has increasingly grabbed researchers' attention. Considerable literature has reported improved performance on mental rotation tasks among people who received video game training [9].

Nowadays, children are raised in a media-saturated digital era. Video game playing has already become an inevitable activity for the generation of digital natives [10]. According to Granic *et al.* [11], video games have become increasingly complex, diverse, realistic, and social in nature. Games provide players with immediate feedback, positive emotions, and flow experiences; they are ideal training tools for mastering cognitive skills. However, we still lack comprehensive understanding of how video game training contributes to young children's mental rotation ability.

1.3 Gender Differences and Ability Changes

The gender differences in mental rotation and training-related effects on gender discrepancies are much-debated topics [9]. Some studies have shown that boys outperform girls in mental rotation tasks before training [12, 13], but others have demonstrated that no sex differences exist in children's mental rotation ability [6, 14]. Research on gender-relevant training effects has also yielded mixed results: some studies suggest that intervention is more beneficial for boys than for girls [14], whereas others report greater improvements among girls [12, 15]. Therefore, the gender differences in mental rotation are worthy of scholarly attention.

Another notable aspect of the training-triggered concerns the role of children's mental rotation ability level. Several intervention studies indicate that children who initially score low in mental rotation tasks make the greatest improvements after training [6, 12]. This finding implies that mental rotation intervention may be most effective for children with lower ability. Regarding the amount of training time, a typical mental rotation intervention usually takes several weeks to take effect [12, 16]. However, a recent study by Liu *et al.* [17] suggests that preschoolers' behavior could be intensely fostered through 5 days of video game training, owing to the imperative function of play for young children. Further work is required to confirm this finding.

1.4 The Present Study

In light of the above considerations, this study aims to investigate: (1) whether video game training could enhance young children's mental rotation ability in a short time period; (2) whether gender differences exist in mental rotation performance and, if so, whether they could be reduced by intervention; and (3) whether training could moderate the effect of ability level.

Previous evidence leads us to hypothesize that: (1) video game training improves preschoolers' mental rotation capacity within 5 days; (2) boys outperform girls at pre-test, but original gender differences disappear after training; and (3) children with lower mental rotation ability gain more from the intervention.

2 Method

2.1 Participants

Forty young children (20 boys; mean age $M = 6.11$ years, $SD = 0.21$) participated in this study. Informed parental consent was obtained prior to the experiment. All the children were right-handed and had normal visual acuity.

2.2 Mental Rotation Assessment

The Windows Test (WT), designed by Tzuriel and Egozi [15], was utilized to evaluate young children's mention rotation ability. The original test comprised three difficulty levels: WT1, WT2, and WT3. We only administered WT1 because we considered this test most suitable for young children.

The assessment materials (Fig. 1) comprised two types of houses, namely the upright houses (left) and the rotated houses (right). Windows of the houses were arranged in a 3×3 pattern, with 9 windows on each house. Children were asked to identify which windows should be open (blackened) on each rotated house to match its accompanying upright houses. WT1 comprised 18 tasks with varying complexity (2, 3, and 4 open windows) and degree of rotation ($45°$, $90°$, and $180°$). The tasks in the pre-and post-test phases were parallel.

We awarded 1 point for each correctly matched response. Thus, the maximum score for each rotation degree was 6. Cronbach's alpha for this test was 0.80.

2.3 Video Game Training

My Little Pony Rotate Puzzle (CloudFlare Inc.) was used as the video game training program (Fig. 2). The game can be downloaded from the iTunes App Store. It requires the player to rotate puzzle pieces by clicking on them, with the goal of achieving the correct image. Each child in the intervention group was instructed to play the game individually on an iPad device (Apple Inc.) for 6 min per day for 5 consecutive days.

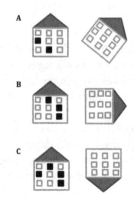

Fig. 1. Example items of mental rotation tasks from the Windows Test (WT). House A with 2 open windows rotated 45°; House B with 3 open windows rotated 90°; House C with 4 open windows rotated 180°.

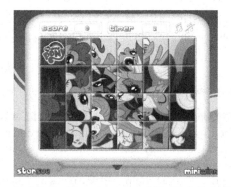

Fig. 2. Screenshot of the video game named *My Little Pony Rotate Puzzle*.

2.4 Procedure

Figure 3 illustrates the procedural steps of this experiment. After obtaining written informed consent from their parents, we asked all children to provide information on their video game experiences. None of the participants had played the allocated game before.

In the pre-test stage, 2 days before the intervention, all participating children completed the WT1 tasks independently. We then randomly assigned the children into either of two treatment conditions: (a) video game training and (b) non-treatment. Gender was balanced across conditions. The intervention group received 5 consecutive days of training (6 min/day), while the control group received no intervention. In the post-test stage, 2 days after the intervention, all children completed an alternative set of WT1 tasks. All the tests and intervention sessions were conducted individually in a quiet kindergarten room. Every child completed all phases of the experiment.

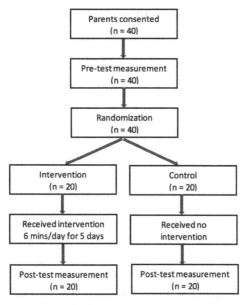

Fig. 3. Study flow chart.

3   Results

3.1   Training Effects

Table 1 shows pre- and post-test performance on mental rotation (*M*, *SD*) in the control and intervention groups for each degree of rotation.

Table 1. Descriptive statistics (*M*, *SD*) of pre- and post-test mental rotation scores between treatment groups for each degree of rotation.

Measure	Pre-test		Post-test	
	Control	*Intervention*	*Control*	*Intervention*
45°	5.95 (0.22)	5.95 (0.22)	5.90 (0.31)	6.00 (0.00)
90°	4.30 (1.03)	4.30 (1.03)	4.80 (0.77)	5.70 (0.47)
180°	1.75 (0.64)	1.70 (0.92)	1.45 (0.76)	4.15 (0.88)

Note: Standard deviations in parentheses.

To assess the training-related changes, a 2 (Group: control, intervention) × 2 (Time: pre-test, post-test) × 3 (Degree: 45°, 90°, 180°) repeated-measures ANOVA was conducted, with Time and Degree as within-subjects variables, and mental rotation score as the dependent variable. A summary of all significant main and interaction effects is presented in Table 2.

Table 2. Summary of ANOVA of Time, Group, and Degree.

Effect	df, df_{error}	F	η^2
Time	1, 38	93.94***	0.71
Group	1, 38	24.61***	0.39
Degree	1, 38	612.34***	0.94
Time × Group	1, 38	80.54***	0.68
Time × Degree	1, 38	18.52***	0.33
Group × Degree	1, 38	18.34***	0.33
Time × Group × Degree	1, 38	24.75***	0.39

Note: *** $p < 0.001$.

The analysis yielded significant main effects for Group, with the intervention group outperforming the control group; for Time, with higher scores in the post-test than in the pre-test; and for Degree, with scores dropping as the degree of rotation increased.

As expected, the interaction between Time and Group was significant. In the intervention group, there was a significant improvement in children's mental rotation performance [$t(1, 19) = 10.18$, $p < 0.001$, $d = 3.12$]; in the control group, by contrast, there was no change in children's performance from pre- to post-test [$t(1, 19) = 0.9$, $p > 0.05$, $d = 0.09$]. This suggests that training led to improved performance in the mental rotation task. Furthermore, the effect of Time interacted with Degree: children's performance at 45° did not change over time [$t(1, 39) = 0$, $p > 0.05$], whereas their performance at 90° [$t(1, 39) = 5.21$, $p < 0.001$, $d = 0.67$] and 180° [$t(1, 39) = 4.07$, $p < 0.001$, $d = 0.68$] notably improved from pre- to post-test. Moreover, there was an interaction between Group and Degree: further analysis showed significant differences between treatment groups at 90° [$t(1, 38) = 2.13$, $p < 0.05$, $d = 0.67$] and 180° [$t(1, 38) = 6.37$, $p < 0.001$, $d = 2.01$], but not at 45° [$t(1, 38) = 0.83$, $p > 0.05$, $d = 0.26$].

An intriguing finding is the significant three-way interaction of Time × Group × Degree (Fig. 4). Simple interaction analyses revealed interactions between Time and Group at 90° [$F(1, 38) = 7.03$, $p < 0.05$, $\eta^2 = 0.16$] and 180° [$F(1, 38) = 86.69$, $p < 0.001$, $\eta^2 = 0.70$], but not at 45° [$F(1, 38) = 2.00$, $p > 0.05$, $\eta^2 = 0.05$]. This implies that the divergence between the control and intervention groups in the post-test session incrementally increased as the degree of rotation became higher.

3.2 Gender Differences

As our sample size was small we considered it inappropriate to run a five-way repeated-measures ANOVA. Therefore, we analyzed gender and ability effects in separate ANOVAs in the following analyses. Gender differences and training-triggered changes were analyzed by a four-way repeated-measures ANOVA of Gender × Group × Time × Degree (2 × 2 × 2 × 3), with Time and Degree as within-subjects variables, and mental rotation score as the dependent variable. The pre- and post-test mental rotation scores for boys and girls in the intervention and control groups are summarized in Table 3.

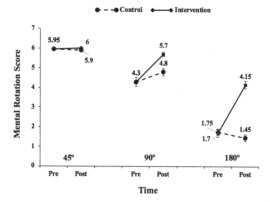

Fig. 4. Pre- and post-test mental rotation scores by time and training condition for each degree of rotation. Error bars represent standard errors.

Table 3. Means and standard deviations for pre- and post-test mental rotation scores between boys and girls for each degree of rotation.

Measure	Control		Intervention	
	Boys	*Girls*	*Boys*	*Girls*
Pre-test				
45°	6.00 (0.00)	5.90 (0.32)	6.00 (0.00)	5.90 (0.32)
90°	4.80 (0.92)	3.80 (0.92)	4.30 (1.16)	4.30 (0.95)
180°	2.00 (0.00)	1.50 (0.85)	2.00 (0.67)	1.40 (1.07)
Post-test				
45°	6.00 (0.00)	5.80 (0.42)	6.00 (0.00)	6.00 (0.00)
90°	5.10 (0.74)	4.50 (0.71)	5.70 (0.48)	5.70 (0.48)
180°	1.70 (0.82)	1.20 (0.63)	4.00 (0.94)	4.30 (0.82)

Note: Standard deviations in parentheses.

For brevity, only significant gender effects are elaborated here. Unsurprisingly, the analysis revealed a main effect of Gender on mental rotation performance [$F(1, 36) = 6.02, p < 0.05, \eta^2 = 0.14$], suggesting that boys outperformed girls in mental rotation ability. Additionally, the interaction between Gender and Group was marginally significant [$F(1, 36) = 3.45, p = 0.07, \eta^2 = 0.09$]. As illustrated in Fig. 5, boys scored higher than girls in the control group but not in the intervention group. Moreover, intervention-group girls outperformed control-group boys on the 180° task at post-test [$t(1, 38) = 13.78, p < 0.001, d = 4.36$]. This suggests that girls could benefit more from the intervention, and that gender differences could be substantially lessened by training.

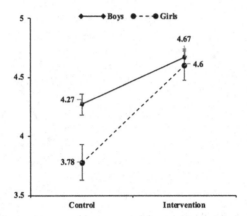

Fig. 5. Means and standard errors of mental rotation scores by gender and treatment group. Error bars represent standard errors.

3.3 Ability Changes

The mean total score on the mental rotation pre-test was 11.98, and the median and mode scores were 12.20 and 12.00, respectively. Thus, we classified young children into three mental rotation ability groups: low ability for those scoring below 12 (n = 10); median ability for those scoring exactly 12 (n = 15); and high ability for those scoring above 12 (n = 15). The means and standard deviations of the pre- and post-test mental rotation scores for low-, median-, and high-ability children in the intervention and control groups are displayed in Table 4.

Based on this classification scheme, 2 of 20 boys and 8 of 20 girls were categorized as having low mental rotation ability; 9 boys and 6 girls had median ability; and 6 girls and 6 girls had high ability. Ability levels differed between boys and girls [$\chi^2(2, 40) = 4.80, p = 0.09$]. Further chi-square independence tests revealed that more girls were considered to have low mental rotation ability than boys [$\chi^2(1, 10) = 3.60, p = 0.06$]. However, no gender differences were found in the median- and high-ability groups [$\chi s^2(1, 15) = 0.60, ps > 0.05$].

To distinguish the effects of ability levels on the training-related improvements in children's mental rotation performance, a four-way repeated-measures ANOVA was performed, with Ability (3) and Group (2) as between-subjects variables, Time (2) and Degree (3) as within-subjects variables, and mental rotation score as the dependent variable. Table 5 reports all the significant interaction effects of ability levels.

The results reveal three significant two-way interactions: between Ability and Time, Ability and Degree, and Ability and Group. The findings suggest that ability differences at pre-test [$F(2, 37) = 80.62, p < 0.001, \eta^2 = 0.81$] disappeared at post-test [$F(2, 37) = 1.23, p > 0.05, \eta^2 = 0.06$]; that ability differences peaked at 90° [$F(2, 37) = 16.29, p < 0.001, \eta^2 = 0.47$], were smaller at 45° [$F(2, 37) = 5.05, p < 0.05, \eta^2 = 0.21$], and became less obvious at 180° [$F(2, 37) = 2.99, p = 0.06, \eta^2 = 0.14$]; and that the control group [$F(2, 17) = 55.05, p < 0.001, \eta^2 = 0.87$] had greater discrepancies in ability than the intervention group [$F(2, 17) = 9.58, p < 0.01, \eta^2 = 0.53$].

Table 4. Means and standard deviations for pre- and post-test mental rotation scores among different ability groups for each degree of rotation.

	Measure	Ability		
		Low	Median	High
Control	*Pre-test*			
	45°	5.75 (0.50)	6.00 (0.00)	6.00 (0.00)
	90°	3.00 (0.82)	4.11 (0.33)	5.29 (0.76)
	180°	0.75 (0.50)	1.89 (0.33)	2.14 (0.38)
	Post-test			
	45°	5.50 (0.58)	6.00 (0.00)	6.00 (0.00)
	90°	4.00 (0.00)	4.78 (0.83)	5.29 (0.49)
	180°	0.75 (0.50)	1.33 (0.71)	2.00 (0.58)
Intervention	*Pre-test*			
	45°	5.83 (0.41)	6.00 (0.00)	6.00 (0.00)
	90°	3.50 (0.55)	4.00 (0.89)	5.13 (0.83)
	180°	0.83 (0.75)	2.00 (0.89)	2.13 (0.64)
	Post-test			
	45°	6.00 (0.00)	6.00 (0.00)	6.00 (0.00)
	90°	5.67 (0.52)	5.83 (0.41)	5.63 (0.52)
	180°	4.17 (0.98)	4.00 (0.89)	4.25 (0.89)

Note: Standard deviations in parentheses.

Table 5. Interaction effects of Ability.

Effect	df, df_{error}	F	η^2
Ability × Time	2, 34	11.82^{***}	0.41
Ability × Degree	4, 68	4.78^{**}	0.22
Ability × Group	2, 34	7.53^{**}	0.31
Ability × Time × Degree	4, 68	3.78^{**}	0.18
Ability × Time × Group	2, 34	3.54^{*}	0.17

Note: For brevity, only significant interaction effects of Ability are presented. $* p < 0.05, ** p < 0.01, *** p < 0.001$.

The analysis also yielded two critical three-way interactions: Ability × Time × Degree and Ability × Time × Group. As illustrated in Fig. 6, an interaction between Ability and Degree was found in the pre-test phase [$F(2, 17) = 14.41, p < 0.001, \eta^2 = 0.44$] but not in the post-test phase [$F(2, 17) = 0.92, p > 0.05, \eta^2 = 0.05$]. Furthermore,

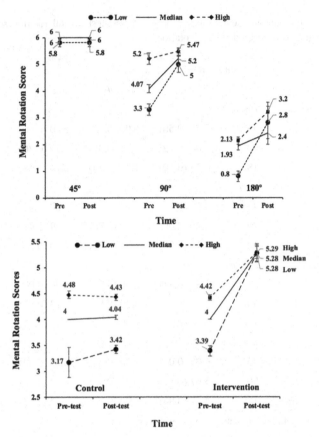

Fig. 6. Pre- and post-test mental rotation scores of different ability groups for each degree of rotation (above) and in the intervention and control conditions (below). Error bars represent standard errors.

in the intervention group, pre-test ability differences [$F(2, 17) = 63.78, p < 0.001, \eta^2 = 0.88$] disappeared at post-test [$F(2, 17) = 0.003, p > 0.05, \eta^2 < 0.001$], whereas ability discrepancies in the control group remained stable from pre-test [$F(2, 17) = 31.17, p < 0.001, \eta^2 = 0.79$] to post-test [$F(2, 17) = 65.07, p < 0.001, \eta^2 = 0.88$]. These findings indicate that children considered to have low mental rotation ability can profit most from the intervention, and that ability differences in mental rotation can be lessened by training.

4   Discussion

4.1   Training Effects

Consistent with our hypotheses, this research found that video game training was able to improve preschoolers' mental rotation ability within a short intervention time of 5 days (30 min in total). This result is in line with those of previous studies. According to Spence and Feng [18], compared to conventional training programs, video game training can produce generalized and long-lasting training effects. Granic *et al.* [11] contend that video games are an ideal cognitive training tool. A possible explanation is that video games' customized and immediate feedbacks motivate gamers to keep devoting themselves to playing. In other words, instantaneous and specific feedbacks serve as rewards for children to conquer their frustration and promote their optimal progress toward the "zone of proximal development" [19]. In addition, video games place gamers in a multi-functional, problem-based learning environment. By provoking players' positive emotions, flow experiences, and repetitive practices, video games assist players to perform competently in their discovery learning [20].

A notable finding from this study is the effects of angular disparities on young children's mental rotation performance and training outcomes. Specifically, we found that discrepancies between the two treatment groups increased with the enlargement of angular disparities at post-test. Moreover, discrepancies in ability were found to be extreme at 90°, smaller at 45°, and non-existent at 180°. These results may reflect the rise in difficulty level as the degree of rotation increased, with preschoolers' mental rotation scores declining as angular disparities became larger. Thus, due to the celling and floor effects, it is unsurprising to find the largest ability discrepancies at 90°.

4.2 Gender Differences

Consistent with many previous results, boys scored higher than girls in mental rotation tasks, and more girls than boys were classified as having low mental rotation ability. There are conflicting interpretations of what causes the gender differences in mental rotation ability. Parsons *et al.* [21] speculate that they might relate to the generation of mental representations, which are mediated by the left hemisphere. As a result of prominent left hemisphere processing of rotational objects, men tended to outperform women in mental rotation tasks [21]. Sanchis-Segura *et al.* [22] argue that males' superior mental rotation ability might result from gender-related stereotypes: their research showed that self-confidence was a mediating factor of gender-science associations. In contrast, some researchers contend that gender differences are caused by the characteristics of the stimuli. For instance, Fisher *et al.* [23] found that the gender differences in mental rotation ability were linked to the artificiality of the stimuli. Alternatively, Boone and Hegarty [24] reported that strategy use, including the piecemeal strategies adopted by women and the global-shape strategies utilized by men, comprise additional sources of gender differences. Similarly, Tzuriel and Egozi [15] suppose that global-local processing strategies might be a moderating factor between mental rotation and gender. In their research, boys outperforming girls in mental rotation was largely due to the former relying more on a global-holistic strategy.

Further crucial findings of this study are that boys only scored higher than girls in the control group, and that intervention-group girls outperformed control-group boys on the 180° task at post-test. These results indicate that girls may benefit more than boys from the video game training. This is likely related to young children's gaming experiences. Experienced players have previously been found to outperform non-experienced players in mental rotation tasks [25]. Also, because males and females spend different amounts of time playing computer games, there might be a link between video game playing and learning, and mental rotation capacity may be enhanced by minimal video game practice [20]. This conclusion is consistent with that of Feng *et al.* [26], who found that action video game training could help to reduce gender discrepancies in mental rotation ability.

4.3 Ability Changes

Our hypothesis that children with lower mental rotation ability would benefit more from video game training than their counterparts was supported by the study's results. We speculate that ability-based changes cannot be interpreted on the basis of statistical regression effects because these changes were only seen in the intervention group and not in the control group. Conversely, these changes may be associated with both the training and the ceiling effects. In the intervention condition, the three ability groups scored almost identical average mental rotation scores at post-test (5.28, 5.28, and 5.29), which were all very close to the highest score of 6. By contrast, the three ability groups in the control condition made very little progress and huge discrepancies persisted, with post-test scores of 3.42, 4.04, and 4.43.

In conclusion, despite the small sample size, this study strengthens three ideas: (1) preschoolers' two-dimensional mental rotation ability can be enhanced through video game training; (2) boys have superior mental rotation ability compared to girls, but the original gender differences can be reduced via intervention; and (3) young children considered to have low mental rotation capacity can improve most after training. Given the ubiquity of video games and the importance of mental rotation skill to STEM study and career opportunities, a key implication of these findings is that video game training constitutes a promising alternative to conventional mental rotation training programs for young children.

Acknowledgments. This research was funded by the National Social Science Fund of China (18BSH130).

References

1. Shriki, A., Barkai, R., Patkin, D.: Developing mental rotation ability through engagement in assignments that involve solids of revolution. Math. Enthusiast **14**, 541–562 (2017)
2. Kell, H.J., Lubinski, D.: Spatial ability: a neglected talent in educational and occupational settings. Roeper Rev. **35**, 219–230 (2013). https://doi.org/10.1080/02783193.2013.829896
3. Fernández-Méndez, L.M., Contreras, M.J., Elosúa, M.R.: From what age is mental rotation training effective? Differences in preschool age but not in sex. Front. Psychol. **9**, 753 (2018). https://doi.org/10.3389/fpsyg.2018.00753
4. Stieff, M., et al.: Operational constraints on the mental rotation of STEM representations. J. Educ. Psychol. **110**, 1160 (2018). https://doi.org/10.1037/edu0000258
5. Shepard, R.N., Metzler, J.: Mental rotation of three-dimensional objects. Science **171**, 701–703 (1971). https://doi.org/10.2307/1731476
6. Fernández-Méndez, L.M., Contreras, M.J., Elosúa, M.R.: Developmental differences between 1st and 3rd year of early childhood education (preschool) in mental rotation and its training. Psychol. Res. 1–9 (2018). https://doi.org/10.1007/s00426-018-1104-6

7. Sanchez, C.A.: Enhancing visuospatial performance through video game training to increase learning in visuospatial science domains. Psychonom. Bull. Rev. **19**, 58–65 (2012). https://doi.org/10.3758/s13423-011-0177-7
8. Frick, A., Hansen, M.A., Newcombe, N.S.: Development of mental rotation in 3-to 5-year-old children. Cogn. Dev. **28**, 386–399 (2013). https://doi.org/10.1016/j.cogdev.2013.06.002
9. Latham, A.J., Patston, L.L., Tippett, L.J.: The virtual brain: 30 years of video-game play and cognitive abilities. Front. Psychol. **4**, 629 (2013). https://doi.org/10.3389/fpsyg.2013.00629
10. Prensky, M.: Digital natives, digital immigrants. Part 1. On the Horizon. **9**, 1–6 (2001)
11. Granic, I., Lobel, A., Engels, R.C.: The benefits of playing video games. Am. Psychol. **69**, 66 (2014). https://doi.org/10.1037/a0034857
12. De Lisi, R., Wolford, J.L.: Improving children's mental rotation accuracy with computer game playing. J. Genet. Psychol. **163**, 272–282 (2002). https://doi.org/10.1080/00221320209598683
13. van Tetering, M., van der Donk, M., De Groot, R.H.M., Jolles, J.: Sex differences in the performance of 7–12 year olds on a mental rotation task and the relation with arithmetic performance. Front. Psychol. **10** (2019). https://doi.org/10.3389/fpsyg.2019.00107
14. Rodán, A., Gimeno, P., Elosúa, M.R., Montoro, P.R., Contreras, M.J.: Boys and girls gain in spatial, but not in mathematical ability after mental rotation training in primary education. Learn. Ind. Differ. **70**, 1–11 (2019). https://doi.org/10.1016/j.lindif.2019.01.001
15. Tzuriel, D., Egozi, G.: Gender differences in spatial ability of young children: the effects of training and processing strategies. Child Dev. **81**, 1417–1430 (2010). https://doi.org/10.2307/40800682
16. Moreau, D.: Differentiating two-from three-dimensional mental rotation training effects. Q. J. Exp. Psychol. **66**, 1399–1413 (2013). https://doi.org/10.1080/17470218.2012.744761
17. Liu, X., Liao, M., Dou, D.: Video game playing enhances young children's inhibitory control. In: Fang, X. (ed.) HCII 2019. LNCS, vol. 11595, pp. 141–153. Springer, Cham (2019). https://doi.org/10.1007/978-3-030-22602-2_12
18. Spence, I., Feng, J.: Video games and spatial cognition. Rev. Gener. Psychol. **14**, 92–104 (2010). https://doi.org/10.1037/a0019491
19. Vygotsky, L.S.: Mind and Society: The Development of Higher Mental Processes. Harvard University Press, Cambridge (1978)
20. Gecu, Z., Cagiltay, K.: Mental rotation ability and computer game experience. Int. J. Game-Based Learn. (IJGBL) **5**, 15–26 (2015). https://doi.org/10.4018/ijgbl.2015100102
21. Parsons, T.D., et al.: Sex differences in mental rotation and spatial rotation in a virtual environment. Neuropsychologia **42**, 555–562 (2004). https://doi.org/10.1016/j.neuropsychologia.2003.08.014
22. Sanchis-Segura, C., Aguirre, N., Cruz-Gómez, A.J., Solozano, N., Forn, C.: Do gender-related stereotypes affect spatial performance? Exploring when, how and to whom using a chronometric two-choice mental rotation task. Front. Psychol. **9**, 1261 (2018). https://doi.org/10.3389/fpsyg.2018.01261
23. Fisher, M.L., Meredith, T., Gray, M.: Sex differences in mental rotation ability are a consequence of procedure and artificiality of stimuli. Evol. Psychol. Sci. **4**, 124–133 (2018)
24. Boone, A.P., Hegarty, M.: Sex differences in mental rotation tasks: not just in the mental rotation process! J. Exp. Psychol.: Learn. Mem. Cogn. **43**, 1005 (2017). https://doi.org/10.1037/xlm0000370
25. Sims, V.K., Mayer, R.E.: Domain specificity of spatial expertise: the case of video game players. Appl. Cogn. Psychol.: Off. J. Soc. Appl. Res. Mem. Cogn. **16**, 97–115 (2002). https://doi.org/10.1002/acp.759
26. Feng, J., Spence, I., Pratt, J.: Playing an action video game reduces gender differences in spatial cognition. Psychol. Sci. **18**, 850–855 (2007). https://doi.org/10.1111/j.1467-9280.2007.01990.x

Relationship Between Young Children's Problematic Behaviors, Videogaming Status, and Parenting Styles

Fangbing Qu, Changwei Gu, Heqing Huang, Aozi Zhang, Meng Sun,
and Xiaocen Liu[✉]

College of Preschool Education, Capital Normal University, Beijing, People's Republic of China
cindyliu@cnu.edu.cn

Abstract. A growing number of studies have been focusing on the impact of videogame use on children's psychology and behaviors. This study contributes by examining the relationships between videogaming status, parenting styles, and problematic behaviors. We used bivariate correlations to analyze a cross-sectional sample of 728 young children (3–5 years old) recruited from different regions (urban, town, and rural) in two large Chinese cities. The results revealed that young children's average and longest videogaming time per week and the parenting styles they encountered were significantly correlated with their problematic behaviors. A series of linear regressions were then conducted to further investigate how different dimensions of videogame use and different parenting styles affect problematic behavior. The results highlight the critical importance of examining the relationships among these three factors in family contexts.

Keywords: Young children · Videogaming status · Problematic behaviors · Parenting style

1 Introduction

With the rapid development of technology, videogames are successfully marketed to and easily obtained by young children. A growing number of studies have expressed concerns regarding the effects of videogame use on children's behavior and mental health; in particular, problematic gaming can increase the likelihood of aggressive and violent behavior, or cause depression and attention problems (Mazurek and Engelhardt 2013; Tortolero et al. 2014; Lobel et al. 2017). The association between children's problematic behavior and parenting styles has also been discussed (Aunola and Nurmi 2005). However, to what extent young children's videogaming use and parenting styles influence children's problematic behaviors still needs to be investigated.

Researchers have noted that, compared with other activities, videogames seems more interesting, provide more fun and excitement, and include more attention-attracting cues (e.g., color, sound, and violence). Most videogames effectively exploit features that trigger an orienting response, such as edits, sounds effects, and flickering light levels (Gentile et al. 2012). Frequent use of videogames might elevate young children's

© Springer Nature Switzerland AG 2020
X. Fang (Ed.): HCII 2020, LNCS 12211, pp. 318–329, 2020.
https://doi.org/10.1007/978-3-030-50164-8_23

expectations about other daily activities. The greater the contrast between videogames and daily activities, the greater the difficulty for young children to get away from the former. Therefore, children as young as 2–3 years old may start to be attracted by videogames and spend increasing amounts of time playing them.

Instead of spending time on activities that may enhance their attention and behavioral qualities, young children are attracted to spend more time on videogames. According to the strength model of self-control, compared with other activities such as work and school, videogame use requires less self-control resources and may weaken ability to exert self-control. Therefore, the time spent on videogames may be a predictor of behavior and attention problems (Gentile et al. 2012), although this relationship needs further analysis. Young children's videogame use might predict their problematic behaviors.

As the main interaction subjects of young children, the home environment may exert considerable influence on their daily activities. Among the most important elements of the home environment is parenting style, which is known to play a key role in young children's development. Parenting style was initially considered to have two dimensions: demandingness and responsiveness (Aunola et al. 2000). Both refer to parents' interaction with their children: demandingness concerns the extent to which parents exhibit high control, maturity demands, and supervision, whereas responsiveness concerns the extent to which they exhibit affective warmth, acceptance, and involvement.

Based on these two dimensions, a model of four parenting styles was developed, comprising authoritarian, permissive, democratic, and uninvolved parenting. Authoritarian parenting is demanding but unresponsive. Parents that employ this style show a low level of trust in their children, seldom engage with them, discourage open communication, and exert strict control that is more adult- than child-centered. By contrast, permissive parenting is responsive but undemanding. Parents adopting this style usually exhibit warm acceptance and a child-centered attitude toward their children; (Maccoby and Martin 1983; Baumrind 1989), they also exert little parental control (Aunola et al. 2000), and allow their children to behave autonomously and independently. Democratic parenting entails more acceptance/involvement, demands for maturity, and the granting of psychological autonomy (Baumrind 1989). By contrast, uninvolved parenting (also called neglectful parenting) is neither responsive nor demanding; parents employing this style usually show no support or encouragement to their children, and often fail to monitor or supervise their children's behavior (Maccoby and Martin 1983).

Studies have shown different effects of parenting styles on children's behavior. Authoritarian parenting has been shown to detract from learning by discouraging active exploration and problem solving, and by encouraging dependence on adult control and guidance (Hess and McDevitt 1984). The element of excess control has been proved to be associated with children's passivity and lack of interest in school (Aunola et al. 2000). Meanwhile, permissive and uninvolved parenting styles have been shown to be negatively related to self-regulation in children, and may leave them more impulsive (Barber 1996). Consequently, both styles have been associated with children's and adolescents' underachievement. However, research is still needed on the relationship between parenting style, videogame use, and young children's behaviors.

This study aims to investigate the following research questions:

1. What is the present status of videogame playing among young children (aged 3–5) in China?
2. To what extent is videogame use associated with young children's problematic behaviors?
3. To what extent are parenting styles associated with young children's problematic behaviors?
4. What are the contributions of videogame use and parenting styles to young children's problematic behaviors?

2 Methods

2.1 Subjects

We initially recruited 819 young children–parent dyads from two cities in China (Beijing and Taiyuan). All children were aged 3–5 years old ($mean_{age} = 4.25$, $SD_{age} = 1.00$). Valid responses were collected from 728 dyads, representing a final effective rate of 89%. Informed consent was obtained from all parents for both their own and their children's participation. The sample's demographic information is reported in Table 1.

Table 1. Basic information on the young children in our sample.

Variable	Group	Beijing (%)	Taiyuan (%)	Total (%)
Sex	Male	391 (47.7)	40 (4.9)	431 (52.6)
	Female	329 (40.2)	59 (7.2)	388 (47.4)
	Total	720 (87.9)	99 (12.1)	819
Age	3	378 (48.3)	37 (4.7)	415 (53)
	4	211 (26.9)	38 (4.9)	249 (31.8)
	5	99 (12.6)	20 (2.6)	119 (15.2)
	Total	688 (87.9)	95 (12.1)	783
Kindergarten region	Urban	497 (61)	0	497 (61)
	Town	187 (22.9)	99 (12.1)	286 (35.1)
	Rural	32 (3.9)	0	32 (3.9)
	Total	716 (87.9)	99 (12.1)	815

Notes: Of the 819 young children initially enrolled, 20 were under 3 years old, 2 were over 5 years old, and 14 had parents unwilling to supply their age; this left valid age data on 783 children. Also, as 4 children were not enrolled in school, we collected region data on 815 children.

2.2 Measures

Demographic Data Collection. Parents reported young children's sex and age, the family's current residence region (city, town, or rural), and the family's socioeconomic status (see Table 1).

Parenting Styles. Parents also completed a 40-item parenting styles questionnaire (Lizhu and Chunqing 1998), which measures the types of interaction between parent and child, covering five different types of parenting style: permissive, democratic, uninvolved, authoritarian, and inconsistent. Each question is answered on a 1–5 point Likert scale (never, rarely, sometimes, often, always). The validity and reliability values for this questionnaire are 0.875 and 0.929, respectively.

Videogaming Status. To investigate young children's daily exposure to videogames and their gaming behavior, we devised the Videogaming Status Questionnaire, which includes the age of first use of videogames, the average and longest time spent playing videogames, and children's performance during gaming, measured on four dimensions: difficulty stopping, desire to engage, emotional engagement, and social interaction in game). The Cronbach's alphas for the four dimensions during gaming are 0.86, 0.815, 0.8, and 0.856, respectively.

Problematic Behaviors. Young children's teachers completed the Chinese version of the Conners Teacher Rating Scale, a 28-item measure of young children's conduct problem, hyperactivity, and inattention. This measure requires teachers to indicate how often each child shows each of the listed symptoms. Each question is answered on a 0–3 point Likert scale (never, sometimes, often, very often).

Teachers also completed the Chinese version of the Rutter Teacher Questionnaire, a 26-item measure of antisocial behavior (Type-A behavior) and neurotic behavior (Type-N behavior). This measure requires teachers to indicate how often each child shows each of the listed symptoms. Each question is answered on a 0–2 point Likert scale (never, sometimes or less than once a week, very often or at least once a week). A child can be classified as exhibiting problematic behaviors if their score is above 9. If a child's Type-A (Type-N) score is greater than the Type-N (Type-A) score, then they can be classified into Type-A (Type-N) behavior.

2.3 Data Analyses

To investigate the relationships between young children's problematic behaviors, parenting styles, and videogame use status, bivariate relationships between continuous variables were examined using Pearson's correlations. The problematic behaviors were indicated by items in the Videogaming Status Questionnaire.

Linear regression analyses were then conducted to examine the relative contributions of videogame use variables and parenting styles to the cross-sectional prediction of problematic behaviors. Separate regression models were computed for each dependent variable of interest (including conduct problem, inattention, hyperactivity, antisocial (Type-A) behavior, and neurotic (Type-N) behavior), controlling for children's age. The independent variables included sex, residence region, age of first use of videogames, average and longest time spent using videogames, and parenting styles (permissive, democratic, uninvolved, authoritarian, and inconsistent).

3   Results

3.1   Descriptive Statistics on Young Children's Videogaming Status, Parenting Styles, and Problematic Behaviors

Videogame Use. Table 2 reports data on children's age of first use, average use time, and longest use time. The results indicate that young children in our sample began to use videogames at a very early age of 2 years old. Children living in villages and towns started to use videogames relatively later than those living in urban or rural communities. Across the whole sample, young children spent an average of 26.13 h per week playing videogames, and children living in villages and towns spent more time playing videogames than children in urban or rural communities.

Table 2. Means and standard deviations of young children's videogame use.

Videogame use		Age group 3		Age group 4		Age group 5	
		Male	Female	Male	Female	Male	Female
Age of first use	Urban	2.75 (0.80)	2.75 (0.74)	2.75 (0.74)	2.75 (0.74)	3.49 (1.19)	3.73 (1.07)
	Town	3.24 (0.97)	3.24 (0.97)	3.71 (1.22)	3.71 (1.22)	4.25 (1.29)	4.78 (1.26)
	Rural	2.79 (0.70)	3.24 (0.97)		3.71 (1.22)		3.50 (0.71)
Average use time	Urban	24.15 (12.30)	20.56 (9.57)	27.31 (15.23)	21.73 (12.44)	24.22 (13.66)	25.19 (23.76)
	Town	28.91 (16.82)	24.91 (12.60)	25.31 (13.19)	24.07 (10.48)	30.28 (18.82)	34.12 (21.88)
	Rural	20.71 (7.87)	42.37 (31.73)		19.25 (13.50)		25.00 (7.07)
Longest use time	Urban	45.38 (32.05)	42.37 (31.73)	43.11 (24.08)	33.03 (23.18)	58.59 (40.33)	55.42 (43.84)
	Town	65.00 (47.43)	52.14 (47.95)	60.29 (38.04)	45.73 (27.33)	47.22 (24.48)	48.24 (29.21)
	Rural	45.71 (35.05)	52.14 (47.95)		97.50 (65.51)		48.24 (29.21)

Parenting Style. Table 3 reports parents' ratings of their interaction with their children in terms of the five dimensions of parenting styles. The results indicate that democratic parenting is the most common style, followed by authoritarian and inconsistent parenting styles. Uninvolved and permissive parenting styles were relatively rare in our sample.

Table 3. Descriptive statistics of parents' self-reported parenting styles

	Min	Max	Mean	SD
Permissive parenting	1.00	5.00	1.90	0.64
Democratic parenting	1.00	5.00	3.47	0.79
Uninvolved parenting	1.00	4.56	2.07	0.60
Authoritarian parenting	1.13	4.38	2.67	0.50
Inconsistent parenting	1.00	4.83	2.52	0.67

Problematic Behaviors. Table 4 reports teachers' ratings of young children's problematic behaviors while in kindergarten using both the Conners and the Rutter questionnaires. The results indicate that children showed more inattention than hyperactivity or misconduct, and that Type-A and Type-N problems were most common.

Table 4. Descriptive statistics for teachers' reports on young children's problematic behaviors.

	Dimensions	Mean	SD
Conners	Conduct problem	0.55	0.57
	Hyperactivity	0.61	0.61
	Inattention	0.66	0.57
Rutter	Type-A	1.64	2.63
	Type-N	5.39	5.38
	Mixed (A = N)	7.00	2.68

Table 5 reports descriptive statistics for young children's problematic behaviors by age, sex, and residence region.

Table 5. Descriptive statistics for young children's problematic behaviors by sex, age, and residence region.

		Region	3 years old		4 years old		5 years old	
			Male	Female	Male	Female	Male	Female
Conners	Conduct problem	Urban	0.54 (0.58)	0.54 (0.56)	0.60 (0.63)	0.42 (0.38)	0.69 (0.59)	0.58 (0.45)
		Town	0.72 (0.68)	0.48 (0.57)	0.56 (0.73)	0.35 (0.50)	0.66 (0.68)	0.51 (0.63)
		Rural	0.51 (0.33)	0.55 (0.16)	0.75 (0.32)	0.70 (0.49)		0.88 (0.88)
	Hyperactivity	Urban	0.70 (0.64)	0.60 (0.59)	0.64 (0.60)	0.41 (0.49)	0.71 (0.63)	0.58 (0.46)
		Town	0.84 (0.71)	0.47 (0.57)	0.67 (0.80)	0.36 (0.52)	0.80 (0.63)	0.47 (0.53)
		Rural	0.49 (0.45)	0.45 (0.29)	0.71 (0.23)	0.63 (0.39)		0.79 (0.30)
	Inattention	Urban	0.81 (0.57)	0.62 (0.46)	0.63 (0.45)	0.48 (0.48)	0.86 (0.66)	0.68 (0.53)
		Town	0.81 (0.57)	0.65 (0.64)	0.60 (0.70)	0.39 (0.52)	0.61 (0.46)	0.51 (0.63)
		Rural	0.74 (0.50)	0.61 (0.33)	0.83 (0.17)	0.78 (0.30)		1.00 (0.18)
Rutter	Type-A	Urban	1.65 (0.62)	1.64 (2.62)	1.99 (2.98)	0.98 (1.57)	2.05 (2.72)	2.47 (3.59)
		Town	1.78 (0.55)	1.35 (2.37)	2.00 (3.75)	0.77 (1.63)	2.71 (3.26)	1.17 (2.04)
		Rural	1.92 (2.53)	1.00 (1.29)	2.00 (3.08)	2.40 (2.79)		4.00 (5.66)
	Type-N	Urban	5.54 (5.54)	5.94 (5.45)	5.18 (4.77)	3.38 (3.92)	7.24 (6.59)	7.41 (7.55)
		Town	6.57 (6.23)	4.89 (4.47)	5.05 (5.42)	3.14 (3.82)	4.76 (4.61)	4.57 (4.47)
		Rural	5.00 (3.32)	5.43 (4.31)	6.20 (8.26)	10.80 (5.63)		15.50 (6.36)
	Mixed (A = N)	Urban	5.00	8.00	5.50 (0.71)			
		Town			9.00 (4.24)			
		Rural						

3.2 Correlations Between Young Children's Videogame Use, Parenting Styles, and Problematic Behaviors

Correlations were computed between the variables of videogame use, parenting styles, and problematic behaviors (see Table 6). The results reveal several significant correlations between parenting style and young children's videogaming use. Uninvolved parenting was positively related to average use time and longest use time per week ($r = .0.09$, $p < 0.05$; $r = .13$, $p < 0.05$). Authoritarian parenting was also positively related to average use time per week ($r = .0.1$, $p < .05$). Inconsistent parenting was positively related to both average use time and longest use time per week ($r = .0.14$, $p < .05$; $r = .0.16$, $p < .05$). However, no significant correlation was found between permissive or democratic parenting and young children's videogame use (all $ps > 0.05$). All four dimensions of young children's performance during videogame playing were significantly correlated with parenting styles (all $ps < 0.05$). However, there was no significant correlation between children's difficulty stopping and democratic parenting ($p > 0.05$).

The results also reveal several significant correlations between young children's videogame use and their problematic behaviors. Average use time per week was significantly correlated with conduct problem and hyperactivity ($r = 0.13$, $p < 0.05$; $r = 0.11$, $p < 0.05$); longest use time per week was also significantly correlated with conduct problem, hyperactivity, inattention, and Type-N behaviors (all $ps < 0.05$).

Regarding the relationship between parenting styles and behavioral problems, the results reveal different correlation patterns. Both permissive and uninvolved parenting was significantly positively correlated with all the Conners and Rutter dimensions (all $ps < 0.05$). Authoritarian parenting was significantly positively correlated with conduct problem, hyperactivity, and inattention (all $ps < 0.05$), but not with Type-A and Type-N behaviors (all $ps > 0.05$). Inconsistent parenting was positively correlated with all the problematic behavior dimensions except for Type-N behavior. However, democratic parenting was not significantly correlated with conduct problem, hyperactivity, or inattention (all $ps > 0.05$), and was significantly negatively correlated with Type-A and Type-N behaviors ($r = -0.17$, $p < 0.05$; $r = -0.19$, $p < 0.05$).

3.3 Contributions of Videogame Use and Parenting Styles to Problematic Behaviors

To examine the contributions of videogame use and parenting styles to young children's problematic behaviors, five linear regression models were constructed after deleting non-significant predictors. As reported in Table 7, both young children's residence region and longest use time significantly predict conduct problem, hyperactivity, inattention, and neurotic (Type-N) behavior (all $ps < .01$), but not antisocial (Type-A) behavior. Difficulty stopping significantly predicts all the five problematic behaviors (all $ps < .01$). Permissive parenting significantly predicts young children's inattention, antisocial (Type-A) behavior, and neurotic (Type-N) behavior (all $ps < .01$). Uninvolved parenting only significantly predicts inattention ($p < 0.01$).

Table 6. Correlations of videogame use, parenting styles, and problematic behaviors

	1	2	3	4	5	6	7	8	9	10	11	12	13	14	15
1 *Average use time*															
2 *Longest use time*	.67**														
3 Permissive parenting	.04	.07													
4 Democratic parenting	.03	−.03	−.034												
5 Uninvolved parenting	.09*	.13**	.75**	.00											
6 Authoritarian parenting	.10*	.08	.39**	.55**	.45**										
7 Inconsistent parenting	.14**	.16**	.52**	.28**	.62**	.59**									
8 *Desire to engage*	.29**	.31**	.25**	.12**	.28**	.26**	.35**								
9 *Social interaction in game*	.07	.05	.11**	.19**	.12**	.12**	.12**	.49**							
10 *Emotional engagement*	.15**	.09*	.12**	.35**	.12**	.28**	.24**	.59**	.58**						
11 *Difficulty stopping*	.18**	.25**	.39**	−.05	.46**	.26**	.36**	.68**	.39**	.49**					
12 Conduct problem	.13**	.19**	.21**	−.00	.28**	.12**	.19**	.23**	.08*	.09*	.29**				
13 Hyperactivity	.11*	.18**	.16**	−.00	.14**	.10**	.19**	.23**	.08*	.13**	.28**	.81**			
14 Inattention	.05	.17**	.19**	.02	.14**	.08*	.14**	.17**	.06	.14**	.23**	.66**	.70**		
15 *Antisocial behavior*	.00	.08	.19**	−.17**	.15**	.00	.09*	.16**	.02	.00	.26**	.71**	.65**	.53**	
16 *Neurotic behavior*	−.02	.13**	.19**	−.19**	.13**	−.03	.03	.12**	.04	.01	.26**	.65**	.64**	.66**	.74**

* $p < .05$, ** $p < .01$, *** $p < .001$. Videogame use variables are italicized.

Table 7. Contributions of videogame use and parenting styles to problematic behaviors: linear regression analyses.

	Conduct problem			Hyperactivity			Inattention			Antisocial behavior			Neurotic behavior		
	B	R^2	F	B	R^2	F	B	R^2	F	B	R^2	F	B	R^2	F
Sex	–	.09	12.02***	-.12		11.63***	–	.12	11.62***	-.06	.09	17.34***	–	.12	10.13***
Residence region	.08			.11			.08			–			.08		
Age of first use	-.09			–			–			–			–		
Average use time	–			–			-.15			–			-.19		
Longest use time	.12			.10			.15			–			.19		
Difficulty stopping	.21			.20			.21			.22			.20		
Permissive parenting	–			–			.10			.13			.10		
Uninvolved parenting	–			–			-.17			–			–		

$* p < .05, ** p < .01, *** p < .001.$

4   Discussion and Conclusion

This study aimed to identify the relationships between young children's problematic behaviors, aspects of their videogame use, and parenting styles. Consistent with previous research, we found videogame playing to be associated with young children's problematic behaviors. The average use time per week was significantly correlated with conduct problem and hyperactivity, while the longest use time per week was significantly correlated with conduct problem, hyperactivity, inattention, and Type-N behaviors. These results support prior evidence that playing violent videogames can uniquely predict inattention and other problems (Fling et al. 1992; Funk et al. 2002), and that the total time spent playing videogames robustly predicts attention problems and impulsiveness (Gentile et al. 2012).

This study also found significant relationships between parenting styles and problematic behaviors. The regression models indicated that the most reliable predictors of young children's problematic behaviors were videogame use and residence region. Specifically, young children's difficulty stopping significantly predicts five different problematic behaviors, while longest use time and residence region both significantly predict four problematic behaviors (the exception being antisocial behavior). Meanwhile, permissive parenting style significantly predicts young children's inattention and their antisocial and neurotic behaviors. These results provide important new information about the relationship between young children's daily videogame use, parenting styles, and possible problematic behaviors.

Several study limitations should be considered when interpreting the results. First, the relationships between young children's problematic behaviors, their videogame use, and parenting styles were mainly identified using bivariate correlations and linear regressions. More variables and sophisticated moderation models should be considered in future research. Second, we mainly considered young children's behavior problems in kindergarten, which was measured using reports from their teachers. Future research should also consider children's behaviors at home, which can be reported by their parents. Third, the underlying mechanisms of the relationships identified by our results need to be explored in future research.

Acknowledgment. This research was partially supported by grants from Capacity Building for Sci-Tech Innovation – Fundamental Scientific Research Funds (19530050186) and the Social Science General Project (SM202010028010). We also express our appreciation to the staff of the Infant and Child Learning and Developmental Lab at the College of Preschool Education, Capital Normal University.

References

Aunola, K., Nurmi, J.E.: The role of parenting styles in children's problem behavior. Child Dev. **76**(6), 1144–1159 (2005)

Aunola, K., Stattin, H., Nurmi, J.E.: Parenting styles and adolescents' achievement strategies. J. Adolesc. **23**(2), 205–222 (2000)

Barber, B.K.: Parental psychological control: Revisiting a neglected construct. Child Dev. **67**(6), 3296–3319 (1996)

Baumrind, D.: Rearing competent children. In: Damon, W. (ed.) Child Development Today and Tomorrow. Jossey-Bass, San Francisco (1989)

Fling, S., Smith, L., Rodriguez, T., Thornton, D., Atkins, E., Nixon, K.: Videogames, aggression, and self-esteem: a survey. Soc. Behav. Pers. Int. J. **20**(1), 39–45 (1992)

Funk, J.B., Hagan, J., Schimming, J., Bullock, W.A., Buchman, D.D., Myers, M.: Aggression and psychopathology in adolescents with a preference for violent electronic games. Aggressive Behav. Official J. Int. Soc. Res. Aggression **28**(2), 134–144 (2002)

Gentile, D.A., Swing, E.L., Lim, C.G., Khoo, A.: Video game playing, attention problems, and impulsiveness: evidence of bidirectional causality. Psychol. Popular Media Cult. **1**(1), 62 (2012)

Hess, R.D., McDevitt, T.M.: Some cognitive consequences of maternal intervention techniques: a longitudinal study. Child Dev. **55**, 2017–2030 (1984)

Lizhu, Y., Chunqing, Y.: The relationship between the temperament of young children and parenting styles. Psychol. Sci. **01**(011), 1671–6981 (1998)

Lobel, A., Engels, R.C., Stone, L.L., Burk, W.J., Granic, I.: Video gaming and children's psychosocial wellbeing: A longitudinal study. J. Youth Adolesc. **46**(4), 884–897 (2017). https://doi.org/10.1007/s10964-017-0646-z

Maccoby, E.E., Martin, J.A.: Socialization in the context of the family: parent–child interaction. In: Mussen, P.H. (ed.) Handbook of Child Psychology, vol. 4, pp. 1–101. Wiley, New York (1983)

Mazurek, M.O., Engelhardt, C.R.: Video game use and problem behaviors in boys with autism spectrum disorders. Res. Autism Spectr. Disord. **7**(2), 316–324 (2013)

Tortolero, S.R., et al.: Daily violent video game playing and depression in preadolescent youth. Cyberpsychol. Behav. Soc. Networking **17**(9), 609–615 (2014)

Non-intrusive Measurement of Player Engagement and Emotions - Real-Time Deep Neural Network Analysis of Facial Expressions During Game Play

Dines Rae Selvig[1]($\boxtimes$) ⃝iD and Henrik Schoenau-Fog[2]($\boxtimes$) ⃝iD

[1] Selvig Consultancy, Copenhagen, Denmark
dines@dinesselvig.com
[2] Aalborg University, Copenhagen, Denmark
hsf@create.aau.dk

Abstract. Prior research suggests and reveals that there is a correlation between human emotional responses and the subjective qualities of digital interactive experiences. Using facial analysis done by deep neural networks presents a true non-intrusive way of measuring emotional responses and engagement assessed as the desire to continue playing. This paper proposes a tool to measure emotional responses across eight different emotions and in real time of any game. The emotional recognition system achieves an accuracy of 98% and the continuation desire system achieves 93.3% accuracy in a pilot test with a two player game and 78.5% accuracy in a single player game. This forms a strong tool that shows a correlation between emotions and the continuation desire of a player, which can be used to evaluate engagement in games and digital interactive experiences, e.g. in critical stages of development of said content.

Keywords: Continuation desire · Conation · Emotion · Machine learning · Facial expressions · Design tools/technologies · Game and flow · Game immersion · Player engagement assessment

1 Introduction

The Game industry is a billion dollar industry, with video game revenue predicted to exceed over 180 billion US dollars by 2021 [60] and it is an industry, where content quality often dictates the revenue. It is estimated that with an improved infrastructure for testing and removal of bugs or low quality scenes, millions of dollars can be saved [44]. The QA (Quality Insurance) department needs more tools at hands for testing, not only for game mechanic bugs that makes a game unplayable but also for narrative bugs, which is an increasingly

Supported by Samsung Media Innovation Lab for Education (SMILE Lab).

X. Fang (Ed.): HCII 2020, LNCS 12211, pp. 330–349, 2020.
https://doi.org/10.1007/978-3-030-50164-8_24

part of every game. In the current research, a vast majority of interactive experience testing revolves around using interviews and observation of play testers to evaluate games and interactive experiences in terms of fun and engagement. Few attempts have been made to develop a non-intrusive framework for a more reliable testing using different data gathering techniques. Such data could give a deeper understanding of what a user experience during a test session. Many techniques rely on heavy equipment and complicated setups, which is not always applicable for smaller studios to use, or it is complicated to replicate a specific scientific method from an academic paper. As the rise of Machine Learning and computational power, it is now more accessible to use algorithms to find correlations in high dimensional data signals and give a better understanding of what these signals mean. Other than for testing purposes, such data could also be used for adaptive experiences in a real-time setting, such as changing the narrative or character behaviour or even lighting mood inside an interactive experience, to create a more tailored experience to the user.

When evaluating interactive experiences, one can measure, flow [10,12], presence [31], immersion [29] or enjoyment [27], but one method of measure specifically developed for evaluating engagement in interactive experiences is the concept of continuation desire [45–47,50]. Continuation desire is the desire to continue playing/watching digital content, which evaluate the real metric for content to be engaging and popular, namely retention [15,58].

Emotion recognition is the process to identify an affective state of a person, and is getting increasing attention from researchers in human-computer interaction [52]. Such as the use for gaming experience evaluation [25], mental diagnosis [57], driving safety [56]. There is a vast amount of different data measures that can be used for emotion recognition such as audio, video and physiological measures. Using audio as emotion recognition have been used by researchers in different works, using spectral analysis as features to predict emotions in speech [7]. In terms of visual based recognition, different approaches have been explored such as older systems using binary patterns [34,53], and image processing techniques to track landmark points [55] and newer methods such as convolutional neural networks [6,21]. Typically individual researchers achieve high accuracies, in the area of 90–95%, within their own testings, but it is usually a result of sparse data, and commonly systems learn specific individuals which is used in the experiment, rather than a generalised solution [28,30,38,61].

In this paper, the scope and focus is to develop such a tool to measure emotions and continuation desire both during development of interactive experiences and finished productions such as games. The measured data from a test session is then visualised as graphs to pinpoint emotional spikes and changes in continuation desire, these points can show elements in the interactive experience which spark these spikes.

The tool is equally relevant and applicable in adaptive game balancing or interactive experiences, as an input to control certain aspects of the environment such as the narrative, character behaviour and mood lighting. The developed emotion recognition system achieves an accuracy of 98% trained on two million images, moreover a continuation desire system is developed which achieves 95.1% accuracy trained on 2.6 million samples, when used in a co-op two player game session and 78.5% in a single player game session.

Furthermore, an expert interview with a game company reveals that a tool to measure emotions and continuation desire such as the system suggested in this paper is applicable in the production phase of a game, and can give great value to the developers in early stages as well as later in the production phase.

2 Related Works

Creating adaptive video games is drawing more attention from both players and game studios, as the research have found that stimulating the mind, with signals that create an emotional response is an import component of game design [13,37].

Machine learning have also been used to predict emotions from different kind of physiological signals, such as heart rate, video data, galvanic skin response, electroencephalogram (EEG), eye tracking etc. [59,62]. It is a promising way for seamless and accurate measures of emotions during game play in real time.

When working with different measures, both physiological and video feeds, one has to choose a subjective measure which best fit the way of evaluating the experience of play. Different models exist to evaluate the experience of play, but one model for evaluating engagement as continuation desire, proves as a useful tool for game design and analysis of games [45,48,49]. As of now, the connection between continuation desire and different physiological signals have not been explored in any academic sense to its fullest, apart from [51]. Which used Galvanic skin response, eye tracking and heart rate to determine the level of continuation desire a user was feeling, during game play, the project achieved an respectable accuracy of 75%.

Outside of academia, there are multiple products related to emotion recognition, especially targeted at affective gaming, and product analysis. A common denominator is using physiological signals and a processing method, either in terms of signal processing or using neural networks to model the data to an emotion. Typically in this space, arousal and valence is used to describe each emotion, instead of the actual emotion itself. This is due to the fact that valence and arousal are continuous values which in theory can map any combination of values to a direct emotion, as seen on the circumplex model of affect [41].

Most companies accept different input modalities from heart rate to electroencephalography. The most complete and complex setup is from Sensum [3], where it is possible to provide tailored emotion recognition setups for a specific project, and use almost any kind of input, and output various data. Only one of the companies focus on testing within games and experiences, which is Modl.ai [2], and their products is within the field of player experience and retention. However, they use player behaviour telemetry inside the game, and do not measure any physiological signals. Therefore it seems that there is no company which specifically focuses on player and user experiences in the games or film industry, by utilising the concept of continuation desire. Based on the current research specific areas are extracted and elaborated upon in more detail in the following literature review, explicitly Engagement, Continuation Desire, Emotions and Machine Learning.

3   Literature Review

3.1   Engagement

Engagement is an element of the player experience which is highly important, and it is of utter importance for games to be engaging to be considered a good game. It is not enough to only motivate players to keep playing, they have to be engaged to keep playing a game [46]. Player engagement is one facet of the player experience, and can be related to flow [10,12], presence [31], immersion [29], enjoyment [27], affective dimensions, and satisfaction [5]. With these dimensions one can fully define and attempt to measure engagement. This can play a large role in evaluating video games, as engagement, enjoyment and immersion arise from a volition to experience the game.

Engagement is thus an intertwined concept and can further be defined as:

"A value of user-experience that is dependent on numerous dimensions, comprising aesthetic appeal, novelty, usability of the system, the ability of the user to attend to and become involved in the experience and the user's overall evaluation of the salience of the experience." [35]

In relation to player engagement, the concept of continuation desire is essential to include, as for a player experience to be engaging, the player must have the desire to continue. According to Brown et al. [9], in the context of play, the desire to keep playing is a product of play and that the pleasure of the experience makes a player continue playing. In [46] we set the desire to continue in the context with player engagement, and we elaborate which characteristics of a players engagement that makes a player want to continue playing.

3.2   Continuation Desire

When evaluating engagement as the desire to continue, the term Conation can be used as a foundation to give an overview of the topic. Conation was first defined in the eighteenth century, as one of three parts of the mind: Affection, Cognition and Conation (Continuation Desire) [23]. Conation was then and still is defined as the desire and will to strive for a goal, and as this connection between knowledge and affection which leads us to act [26]. Huitt describes conation as the following:

"The personal, intentional, planful, deliberate, goal-oriented, or striving component of motivation, the proactive (as opposed to reactive or habitual) aspect of behaviour" ([26], p.1).

This means that conation is the intrinsic motivation that is displayed when attempting to achieve a goal through volition. In [45,50], we redefine conation in the context of digital media, more explicitly video games as continuation desire, and formalise it as the player engagement process framework (PEP) [46].

Continuation desire is a way to describe a player's engagement based on different triggers which cause players to engage in or disengage from an interactive experience. The player engagement process presents a comprehensive connection between four components which forms continuation desire: objectives, activities accomplishments and affect [47]. The relationship between these components can be seen on Fig. 1.

Fig. 1. Causes of continuation desire add to the level of conation. Source: [48]

The objective(s) of an interactive experience is the extrinsic and intrinsic motivations to reach a goal or overcome a challenge a player experiences during play. These includes the extrinsic objectives which are set up by the game as well as any intrinsic objectives that a player brings to or forms during the experience.

The activities describe the ways a player can become engaged with the experience while pursuing the objective(s). The accomplishments are defined as receiving achievements, experiencing progression in the narrative or levelling up as well as completing objectives.

The activities, objectives and accomplishments of a game thus comes from either the conscious design of the developer, which have designed the experience, from specific items, narratives, or it can come from the preconceived expectations of the game that players can have, or objectives set up by the players themselves.

Lastly the affect is defined as the emotions which are experienced during play as well as the absorption of the player into some activity. The affect can also be described as the conscious or sub conscious emotional response experienced by the player. This response can cause a physiological, cognitive and behavioural reaction, such as facial expressions, increase/decrease in heart rate and higher/lower conductance with electrodermal activity [8,47].

The affect can then be translated into the positive or negative emotions which makes or breaks the experience, or in other words pull the player in or out of the experience.

These four components of the Player Engagement Process in combination can add to the level of conation a player is currently experiencing.

The components interacts sequentially with each other in cyclical rotation. This cycle is the player engagement process, and the process may begin with the affect of the player. The reason is that the player will initially have a form of intrinsic motivation to start the game before the experience begins.

The experience provides the player with different objectives, which can be accomplished through defined activities. The accomplishments, (or merely performing the activities) can then result in the player becoming absorbed and/or lead to a negative or positive affect which makes the player want to continue or disengage from the experience [46].

Fig. 2. The relation between objectives, accomplishments, activities and affect (The OA3 framework). Source: [46]

The emotions which relate to affect can cover the whole spectrum of emotional responses, from low to high arousal and low to high valence. These changes in human behaviour can be measured and there is therefore potential to classify them using machine learning [28]. When using such a method it is thus possible to obtain continuation desire without using subjective measures, as the affective space of elements of the continuation desire can be measured through emotions.

This is also supported by [16], who found that there is a significant correlation between physiological measures and self reported measures revolving a players experience in a FPS (First Person Shooter) game.

Continuation desire is a combination of many facets and it can be argued that all actions will lead to a affective response, as seen on Fig. 2, therefore we suggest that it is possible to use the affective state of a player to measure continuation desire.

In summary, the feeling of the desire to continue, can be described by affect or emotions, as a person often react to content with an emotional response. The next section will therefore focus on emotions, and how to measure a persons emotional state and which cognitive processes and state can influence a persons emotional response.

3.3 Emotions

Almost 150 years ago in 1872, Charles Darwin wrote in his book called 'The Expression of the Emotions in Man and Animals',

> "Facial expressions of emotion are universal, not learned differently in each culture" [14].

Today, this is still a statement that has been much debated. However, psychologist Paul Ekman, proposed six universal emotions, sadness, disgust, fear, anger, surprise and happiness [17,18,39].

In both the field of psychiatric and neuroscience research, there is a general consensus that through evolution, humans have been supplied with a range of basic emotions [18,39]. Each of the emotions is unique in the physiological and behavioural expression, and each of them emerges from an activation within particular neural pathways in the central nervous system.

The emotional system is complex, and it can be described by the emotional continuum, see Fig. 3. A human has three orders of emotion, the first order is the automatic processes within the human body, such as appetites. As it is bodily responses, which is an automatic process, that is hard to control by cognitive processes, and is a responses or reaction to a stimuli and is therefore categorised as uncontrollable responses.

The second order is basic emotions, which as mentioned, are the universal emotions: emotions, sadness, disgust, fear, anger, surprise and happiness. These emotions can also be translated to high/low arousal and positive/negative valence [39].

The third order is higher order emotions which requires cognitive process to be activated, these are emotional responses which are activated by complex neural signals. Higher order emotions can be pride, anxiety, remorse, etc. As these emotional responses are produced by complex signal and cognitive processes makes them significantly more subjective than the basic emotions. The third order is also tertiary emotions, which means that they require higher level cognitive processing, as the emotions are usually self-conscious, and require self reflection and evaluation.

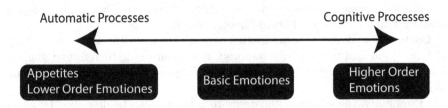

Fig. 3. Figure showing the emotional continuum and the different emotion orders.

There exists six different states, which cover the phenomena concerning the emotional responses, as many emotions and responses is depended on the state of mind a person [41,42]. The states are: emotion, feelings, moods, attitudes, affective style and temperament. These states could and in many cases will affect the measuring of emotional responses, both with self reported measures or measured with physiological measures [41,42].

As mentioned emotions can be segmented into arousal and valence, and by using the two axes a model can be made to plot emotions on a two dimensional system. Such as model was described by Russell [41], and depicted as the "circumplex model of affect". The model describes how emotions have both arousal and valence properties which relate to the neural circuitry.

Being able to concise emotions in a visual way and compare emotions on a mapped figure makes it more accessible to compare emotions. According to [39,41,42], is it possible to sub serve all emotions on the model, as valence and arousal cover all affective states.

There has been much research in the difficulties people have in assessing the describing their emotions [43]. When conducting self reported measures of emotions, people tend to either not experience the emotion or recognise emotions when isolated from each other. Cacioppo describes that the psycho physiology as a field that is based on a assumption that emotion and cognition are embodied phenomenon rooted deep in the physical substrate of the body and brain [11]. It must then be possible to measure characteristics of the human body to elucidate and infer the understanding of the structures of third order cognitive functions.

From this section it is found that emotion have roots in the physiological state of mind, and that basic emotions is close to uncontrollable, meaning that it is possible to measure an emotional response. The basic emotions is also referred as universal emotions, which makes it possible for one system to measure emotions from every human on earth, as emotional responses should be largely identical.

Closely related to emotions is the facial expression, and the next section will focus on the visual emotional responses that occurs when a person reacts to stimuli.

3.4 Facial Expressions

As Darwin wrote, all facial expressions are universal, and even the debate that some could be culturally different, the basic emotions is universal to a high degree. From newborns to blind persons to the average person, all show the basic emotions in the exact same way [32]. This study concur with Darwin in some manner, that most facial expressions is universal, especially macro expressions, but micro expressions might have a slight variance depending on the cultural background of a subject. The two different kinds of expressions, macro and micro-expressions, denotes both the duration and the area of the facial musculature that is used. Macro-expressions often last 0.5–4 s and involves the entire face [19]. Macro-expressions is mostly single emotional responses and last said duration when the emotion is not being concealed, by higher cognitive functions. Macro-expressions occur mostly when we are alone or with friends or family, when we feel most open and familiar.

Micro-expressions are however different, as they last as little as 1/30 of a second and involves only small parts of the face. Micro-expressions are therefore arduous to see, especially for a human. They are often categorised as concealed emotions as they occur when two parts of the brain, the cortical motor strip and subcortical areas, oppose over the neural pathways to take control over the facial expression. This ends with quick fleeting micro expressions.

An evaluation test developed by Matsumoto & Hwang concludes that humans can on average classify micro-expressions and subtle macro-expressions with a 48% accuracy, and when both joy and surprise is removed, which are the easiest to recognise, the recognition falls to 35%. This means that most people are not very good at recognising facial expressions, when the emotional response is short.

Several researchers have investigated how high cognitive load affects the response of an emotional expression, and usually high cognitive load tends to suppress emotional responses yielding a more neutral expression or of lower intensity. This means that, in relation to games, that during a challenging level, players might not express high intensity emotions in the moment, or even any. Expressions can be enforced by being in a social setting, when people playing a game together, expressions occur more often than when alone. This means that being in a social setting, amplifies your emotional expressions as the context is more appropriate to express emotional responses [20]. Measuring emotions from facial expressions can introduce challenges as expressions is depended on the environment and setting around the person. It is therefore important to create an environment and setting that facilitate responses in a safe manner.

4   Machine Learning

Classifying and predicting human emotions is a hard task, even for humans. Creating a machine learning algorithm which can predict and classify such emotions is equally hard. As the era of machine learning is upon us, research in this area is moving at enormous speeds, also within predicting and mimicking human behaviour.

When working with images, or image sequences (video), convolutional layers is commonly used to extract features of each image. As images are 2D, having a width and height, 2D convolutional layers is used, which takes a kernel and literately processes the image. The essence of a convolutional layer is to extract feature patterns from a picture. In terms of Facial Expression Recognition (FER), the kernel will learn to look for specific lines in the face, such as eye placement, eyebrow angle, mount width and angle, as these landmarks usually relates to a specific expression.

A study by T. Zhang et al. used EEG data and a LSTM model to predict emotions with a 90% accuracy [62]. The network was constructed with a quad-directional spatial LSTM layer, after this layer a bi-directional temporal RNN layer is used to spot more subtle emotion patterns, lastly a softmax layer creates probability for each class.

A study using only a video feed for facial recognition to classify emotions, have achieved high accuracy (+80%) [36]. It is stated that it would be possible to use in real time, but no such tests is conducted in the studies. A common factor is that the dataset is often small, and consists of only a few people, meaning that the algorithm is learning specific responses relating to the person. This means that the algorithm is not learning a generalised way of predicting emotions, which will make the algorithm useless in a real environment. Therefore it is important to have as many different samples as possible in the data set.

Our study bases its algorithm on a shallow but deep architecture, using both residual connections [22,54], high-way layers [24] and shared parameter states to create a novel architecture which is highly optimised and achieves state of the art results on emotion classification. The developed emotion recognition system was trained on 2 million samples and achieved a high accuracy of 98% on the test set.

The continuation desire algorithm is a sequence based model of LSTMs, as conation is a feeling that is time based. The algorithm will ingest data from the emotion system both in terms of facial embeddings, but also softmax scores. With this rich feature set, it is possible to accurately predict a users conation level. The algorithm was trained on 2.6 million samples and achieved a high accuracy of 95.2% on the test set, which is more than previous work in this area [51].

To get an indication of the speed of the algorithms, the inference time for the emotion recognition system, a single frame takes 0.002 s to process making it indeed quick enough to run along side multiple other high load systems, such as a game. For the continuation desire predictor, it processes 18000 samples in 0.1 s, as this algorithm runs every five minutes, the slightly larger overhead is not significant, and would still be able to run alongside a game. This means that both algorithm are able to run in real time, even simultaneously with a complex graphical 3D game.

5   Experiment

When designing engaging experiences, levels of conation is a good measure of player experience as the PEP is a cohesive model, rooted in affect. Affect correlates closely with valence and arousal which makes up emotions described by the circumplex model. Therefore if measuring emotions, either with physiological data, or a video feed, it is possible to determine levels of continuation desire through the use of said data. To measure emotions truly unobtrusive, using a camera to capture facial expressions is the optimal way, since other physiological signals such as heart rate and galvanic skin response require equipment attached to the test participant. The setup can quickly become complex and expensive, and the scope of this project is concerned with creating and testing a software system which is accessible and applicable for e.g. smaller development studios.

In terms of facial expressions during high cognitive loads, where faces usually become very neutral, this study is founded on the co-operational play style in two player games to enforce interaction, even through challenging play levels. A neutral face may occur, and this could also relate to conation. The expressions are determined usable to infer conation from said data.

Using faces as features, it is optimal to use machine learning, especially deep learning to extract deep facial features during experiencing digital content, these deep features can both be used for emotion recognition but also to determine the level of conation. This could be a powerful tool for both affective and adaptive gaming, for changing narrative behaviour, but also for game or film evaluation, to investigate the underlying emotions and continuation desire during a game or film. The use such a system for adaptive system, the developed recognition system should be able to process data in real-time, therefore the developed system needs to be lightweight in terms of compute power needed, and usable cross platforms for PC, Unix based systems and mobile operating systems.

Two machine learning algorithms is developed in this study, namely the emotion recognition system, and the continuation desire predictor. The emotion recognition system was developed by using Deep Learning trained on two million images across eight different emotions. The continuation desire predictor system was developed by creating a downstream task on the emotion recognition system, using rich feature vectors. The data for training this system was gathered by pilot testing the game "Little Big Planet"[1] for Play Station 4. The game is a platformer in semi 3D, which can be played in a co-op setting. The test persons played for at least 30 min, and reported their desire to continue every five minutes during play on a scale from 1 to 7. This resulted in 2.6 million data points.

The systems has then been validated to access its accuracy in other domains from where it was developed. This validation was done by using the game "This is the Only Level"[2], which is a lightweight 2D graphics game where one player have to complete stages of the same level where small mechanics change from stage to stage.

The method for the test will be for test players to complete 15 stages of "This is the Only Level", after each stage completed the test persona will report their current desire to continue on a scale from one to seven.

Cross validation between the reported continuation desire and the predicted values will be done, to analyse the true accuracy of the system. To analyse the true accuracy of the emotion recognition system, sequences of images of the session will be validated to see if they correspond to the recognised emotion of the system.

The validation test was conducted over three days, all in all 18 participants were tested (n = 18), resulting in a mean play length of 8.2 min and a variance of 1.43 $x = 8.2, \sigma = 1.43$. This aggregates to 147 min of game play video. All participants completed all 15 stages of the game.

The age distribution of all participant had an age range from 22–30 $x = 25.61, \sigma = 1.94$. The sampling method for the test is convenience sampling. This means that the distribution of ages is much the same as in the continuation desire test session. Most participants were about 25–26 years of age, while a couple of participants were in their early twenties or late twenties.

---

[1] https://www.playstation.com/en-us/games/littlebigplanet-3-ps4/.

[2] John Cooney, 2009 (jmtb02) http://www.jmtb02.com/this-is-the-only-level.

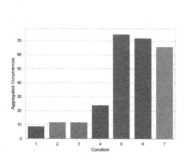

Fig. 4. Continuation desire levels reported from the test on the game

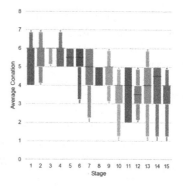

Fig. 5. Reported continuation desire at each stage from the game test.

The participants also reported the weekly hours spent on gaming. The reported average was 9 h per week and this indicates that the general skill level of the participants is higher than the average, so it was expected that most participants would complete all stages in a quickly manner.

On Fig. 4, the aggregated occurrences of the reported continuation desire levels can be seen (x axis/Conation levels: 1 = low, 7 = high). The aggregated occurrences of conation/continuation levels in the test of "this is the Only Level" ranges from 1 = low, 7 = high. In the test, the conation levels created a negative skewed distribution being that over 70% of the occurrences were above level 4.

On Fig. 5 a box plot show the mean continuation desire values reported from each participant. It shows all 15 stages at the x-axis, and there is a tendency for the continuation desire to decrease over stages. This is assumed as the game is quite repetitive, and can become boring after several levels. It is also seen that in the first seven stages the reported continuation desire is stable, and does not contain much variance. Towards to end stages, the variance becomes larger, and here the players preferred game genre might come in to play. Some players do like the repetitive game play, where others do not, and if you are not too fond of the repetitive game style, the game will become boring, and thus feel disengaging. Overall it can be seen that the level of continuation desire decreases over time.

During the test, three emotions was not spotted by the algorithm, namely surprise, calm and disgust. It is not surprising that these emotions were not captured, as the game play does not actively stimulate those emotions. Happy and sad were the most captured emotions by 80%. Neutral and angry accounted for 10% each, while fearful was 2%.

The sad response is surprising as the game does not create situations where a sad response makes sense. The distribution however is different from the emotion distribution from the pilot test on "Little Big Planet", where the most captured emotion was angry (as players were sometimes frustrated).

The emotion recognition system was validated by taking every 30th frame from the video taken of each participant and manually tagging the frame with the emotion which the validator believes is fitting. The whole test have 132,387 frames with faces, every 30th of that is 4,412 frames which have been analysed, to see if the recognition algorithm predicted correctly. The investigation revealed that the emotion recognition system predicted correctly 91.28% of the time, making the algorithm well generalised from the training. It was also noticed that, as mentioned in the 1st iteration result section, that the background, light and shadows was producing significant noise in the predicting, indicating that the algorithm is sensitive to the environment in which it is operating.

Moreover as sad is also identified almost as much as happy, it was noticed that the facial expressions when sad was predicted, looked more like it was supposed to be neutral or frustration over the current stage in the game.

On Fig. 6, the graph shows the play-through analysis of the 15 stages of "This Is The Only Level" for one participant. In this particular session, the continuation desire predictor have mostly low continuation desire through out the session, but the participant had high continuation desire the first seven stages (until around frame 1000) and thereon after low continuation desire. It also shows two strong periods of happiness, in between the two spikes, sadness rises. In this sadness spike, the participant had problems with completing a level. The participant looked frustrated which at times can look like a sad or angry facial expression, this frustration is something that the emotion recognition algorithm does not account for, and therefore subjects can be classified wrongly in certain situations.

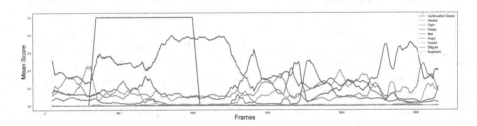

Fig. 6. Graph showing a play through analysis for all 15 stages from the validation test on the game "This is the only level", the y-axis show the aggregated probability of the emotions. The x-axis depicts frames after start (1 frame = 1/30 s).

To analyse how well the continuation desire predictor performed on the test, the reported values were compared to the predicted values. A comparison of the percentages of low/high continuation desire level from the algorithm and the participants' own reported level was conducted. The percentages from the algorithm's levels are depicted in Fig. 7 and for the reported levels from the participants in Fig. 8. The figures were based on the game "This is the only level" and made by calculating the percentages on high/low continuation desire of both the reported and predicted levels. The reported levels from participants were converted from seven levels to high/low by binning them. Continuation desire level 1, 2, 3, 4 is low, while 5, 6, 7 is high. In the comparison analysis the algorithm predicted correctly 78.48% of the time, which is lower than observed during training on the test set. One reason why the accuracy is lower is that the domain in which the algorithm was used is not where it was meant to be used, as this is not a co-operational game or multiplayer game as in the pilot test. This means that there is no interaction between players which does increase a subject's will to express emotional responses. Taken that into account the algorithm does perform quite well for a real scenario even if the applied environment is out of context.

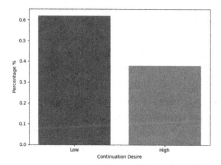

Fig. 7. Barplot showing the algorithm's predicted continuation desire percentages from the test.

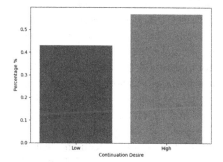

Fig. 8. Barplot showing the reported high/low continuation desire percentages by participants from the test.

It can be seen that the algorithm does predict less 'high' level of continuation desire relative to the true reported level from the subjects (38% high predicted versus 58% high reported), this can be explained with that the subjects had more periods with neutral or sad, which the continuation desire predictor takes as low continuation desire. This supports the hypothesis about that the subjects does not express as many reactions when playing single player games. This is also discussed in the literature review, where it is mentioned that when a person is alone, emotional expression is far more uncommon than when interacting with other persons. Moreover the game is also a puzzle game, which can introduce high cognitive load, which does suppress facial expressions as well.

6 Discussion

In the following section a discussion of the study as a whole, what results and new knowledge have been created, and what could have been done to enhance the method, development and test. The goal of the study is to investigate to which extend it is possible to infer a players continuation desire and emotions during an interactive experience. This had to be done by only using a video feed, and do this analysis in real time as well.

The developed emotion recognition system achieved a high accuracy of 98% on validation test set which is, compared to other algorithms in the research [6, 21, 34, 40, 53, 55], a significant increase to a point where it is (at least theoretically) significantly better than humans. Humans can recognise micro-expressions 47% of the time [1, 32], and macro-expression to a degree of 84% [1, 32] in real life scenarios. The algorithm was validated in the 2nd iteration, and ended at a 91.28% accuracy in a real world test, which is excellent performance compared to 80.17% [34], 86.9% for [53], 78% for [55], 66% for [6], 71.16% for [21], 88.8% [4] and 74.15% for [40]. For the mentioned papers, they all have data quality and sufficient data set in common, as mentioned in the analysis many papers use data set which consist of less than 1000 samples, and with even fewer different persons, this means that the algorithms learns the data, and only the persons in the data set. This is a significant bias, which is common for papers that are not published recently. This introduced a bias to the accuracies, meaning that the proposed earlier solutions only worked on internal data sets, and not in real scenarios. The current study has used 2,000,000 images on 500,000+ different persons, which makes the final results more valid than tests on smaller data sets. However, the results between studies are not directly comparable as no benchmark data set has been made for emotion recognition as of yet, and this is a problem for comparing different approaches and algorithms. This is a common practise in other fields within machine learning, such as natural language and image processing.

During development of the emotion recognition system, it was observed that image quality and lighting could interfere with the algorithms predictions. To account for this, more work needs to be done with the pre-processing of the input features, so light and shadows do not bias the image to such a degree that facial expressions are being mis-classified. A thorough investigation should have been conducted on data from the data gathering test to see the actually cause of the errors.

The data used for the emotion recognition system, is of high quality, but observed from the data, many of the expression are of high intensity, meaning that some expression are over exaggerated to a degree that would not occur in a real environment, this was mostly from the FER data set, which had 35,000 samples [21]. A data set formed from playing subjects emotional responses would be of greater value and possibly create a more specialised algorithm for interactive experience emotion recognition.

The continuation desire algorithm achieved high accuracy as well, 95.2% was the final accuracy on the two player pilot test set from training, which is higher than previous work done in this area. In the out of context testing of the single player game "This is the Only Level", an accuracy of 78.48% was achieved. Because the algorithm was trained on data from the data gathering test from the 1st (two player) iteration, where bias in the test environment have made the data biased in terms of predicted emotions, the algorithm may have learned wrong underlying relations between emotions and continuation desire. This error in the data could implicate the continuation desire algorithm to an extend were the output is inaccurate. But the real world test on "This is the Only Level" shows that it still perform relatively well in an out of sample environment to an extend where it is acceptable, but it is not as close to the original pilot test set accuracy as seen with the emotion recognition algorithm. Further testing needs to be done to verify the in-sample environment accuracy of the continuation desire algorithm, as it is predicted that it will perform better on a multiplayer or interactive game.

The continuation desire algorithm is trained on only 12 subjects' data, which is to a degree sufficient, but with more data, the algorithm would be able to accommodate more player types and expression styles. More data would also make the algorithm more robust to different emotional changes which happens in games, as games have different flows and tempo which affects the emotional response. Capturing this data is time consuming but it is needed to create an even better performing algorithm. Using one type of game also comes with risk, as each game produces different emotional curves, testing on different games should also be done to minimise the classification bias which is introduced by only using one game.

The eight emotions that have been used as output from the emotion recognition model, was chosen because of the basic emotions, happiness, fear, sad, surprise, anger and disgust, these emotions are the most occurring ones, but humans are not expressing emotions at all times, therefore neutral and calm was added to accommodate this behaviour. However, from investigating hours of video data from game playing, it becomes more apparent that those expressions might not be enough, as frustration and focus are facial expressions, that are very frequent during game play, especially in single player games, and this typically means that the player is engaged. But these emotions are very close to other emotions as well, such as frustration to sadness and anger, and focus to calm and neutral, distinguishing between these expressions are difficult. This could possibly be done by another approach such as outputting arousal/valence values instead, so that each emotion have a numerical value, which could create more detailed incremental steps between emotions. An intensity index on each emotions could also enhance the interpretability of the predicted emotion, to see if the person is very angry or less angry.

Gathering these two algorithms and using them to infer emotions and continuation desire from video data was done in a case study with the indie game company Invisible Walls based in Copenhagen. The overall points from the interview were that although the company was still in early stages of their development of their next game, they could see that a data driven approach like the one suggested in this study could give great value in their tests, even in their short usability tests. Due to the only requirement for the system being a video camera, no additional equipment for an expensive and complex setup is needed, it becomes attractive to smaller studios as well. This use case is only based on one interview with one game studio, but the information gathered leads to larger game studios benefiting from a system like this as well. This approach is also largely seen in the marketing sector where emotion recognition is used extensively to see responses from test groups regarding a commercial or product.

In summation, the developed algorithms and evaluation framework proves that it is indeed possible to predict emotions and continuation desire in real time using only video. The system is usable in its core, and with different tweaks and additional features it could work as a method for testing and evaluation of a variety of interactive experiences.

7   Conclusion

The purpose of this study was to investigate the possibility to measure and classify emotions and continuation desire during game play from a video stream in real time by using state of the art and novel machine learning approaches. The proposed solution is an emotion recognition system which perform better than state of the art algorithms and (theoretically) humans which achieves 48% on facial expression recognition tasks [33]. Furthermore the system is trained on the currently (as of June 2019) largest publicly known emotion recognition data set.

The results of this study is an emotion recognition algorithm which performs in static test sets 98% accuracy and in a real two-player scenario 91.28%, which is quite high, even with the problems in the emotion recognition data. A continuation desire algorithm which performed 95.2% of accuracy and 78.48% in an out of environment test with a single player game, suggesting an algorithm which is well generalised and use-able on different game genres and styles. The case study furthermore shows that such a system is also usable in a game company.

It can therefore be concluded that we successfully created an emotion recognition and continuation desire predictor algorithm which is usable in real time and usable for game testing which creates value for game testing teams during development. With minor changes the algorithms could perform better and achieve higher accuracies, while making them more robust to changes in the environments surrounding the participants.

References

1. Nonverbal Communication: Science and Applications AU - Matsumoto, David AU - Hwang, Hyi Sung. SAGE Publications, Inc., Thousand Oaks (2013). https://doi.org/10.4135/9781452244037. http://sk.sagepub.com/books/nonverbal-communication
2. Modl.ai (2019). http://modl.ai/
3. Sensum (2019). https://sensum.co/
4. Albanie, S., Nagrani, A., Vedaldi, A., Zisserman, A.: Emotion recognition in speech using cross-modal transfer in the wild. arXiv preprint arXiv:1808.05561 (2018)

5. Amir Zaib Abbasi, D.H.T., Hlavacs, H.: Engagement in games: developing an instrument to measure consumer videogame engagement and its validation. Int. J. Comput. Games Technol. **2017**, 1–10 (2017)

6. Arriaga, O., Valdenegro-Toro, M., Ploger, P.: Real-time convolutional neural networks for emotion and gender classification. CoRR abs/1710.07557 (2017)

7. Bitouk, D., Verma, R., Nenkova, A.: Class-level spectral features for emotion recognition. Speech Commun. **52**(7), 613–625 (2010)

8. Brett, A., Smith, M., Price, E., Huitt, W.: Overview of the affective domain. Educ. Psychol. Interact, 1–21 (2003)

9. Brown, S., Vaughan, C.: Play: How it Shapes the Brain, Opens the Imagination, and Invigorates the Soul. Avery (2009). https://books.google.dk/books?id=ESQDsgqfgusC

10. Buchanan, R., Csikszentmihalyi, M.: Flow: the psychology of optimal experience. Des. Issues **8**(1), 80-1 (1991)

11. Cacioppo, J.T., Tassinary, L.G., Berntson, G.: Handbook of Psychophysiology. Cambridge University Press, Cambridge (2007)

12. Chen, J.: Flow in games (and everything else). Commun. ACM **50**, 31–34 (2007)

13. Christy, T., Kuncheva, L.I.: Technological advancements in affective gaming: a historical survey. GSTF Int. J. Comput. (JoC) **3**(4), 32–41 (2013)

14. Darwin, C.: The Expression of the Emotions in Man and Animals. D. Appleton and Co., New York (1872)

15. Debeauvais, T.: Challenge and Retention in Games. UC Irvine. ProQuest ID: Debeauvais_uci_0030D_13948. Merritt ID: ark:/13030/m53n6r1p (2016). https://escholarship.org/uc/item/6k3357qx

16. Drachen, A., Nacke, L.E., Yannakakis, G., Pedersen, A.L.: Correlation between heart rate, electrodermal activity and player experience in first-person shooter games. In: Proceedings of the 5th ACM SIGGRAPH Symposium on Video Games, pp. 49–54. ACM (2010)

17. Ekman, P.: Body position, facial expression, and verbal behavior during interviews. **68**, 295 (1964). https://doi.org/10.1037/h0040225

18. Ekman, P.: An argument for basic emotions. Cogn. Emot. **6**(3–4), 169–200 (1992)

19. Ekman, P.: Emotions revealed. **12** (2004). https://doi.org/10.1136/sbmj.0405184

20. Frith, C.: Role of facial expressions in social interactions. Philos. Trans. R. Soc. Lond. B Biol. Sci. **364**(1535), 3453–3458 (2009)

21. Goodfellow, I.J., et al.: Challenges in representation learning: a report on three machine learning contests. In: Lee, M., Hirose, A., Hou, Z.-G., Kil, R.M. (eds.) ICONIP 2013. LNCS, vol. 8228, pp. 117–124. Springer, Heidelberg (2013). https://doi.org/10.1007/978-3-642-42051-1_16

22. He, K., Zhang, X., Ren, S., Sun, J.: Deep residual learning for image recognition. CoRR abs/1512.03385 (2015). http://arxiv.org/abs/1512.03385

23. Hilgard, E.R.: The trilogy of mind: cognition, affection, and conation. J. Hist. Behav. Sci. **16**(2), 107–117 (1980)

24. Huang, G., Liu, Z., Weinberger, K.Q.: Densely connected convolutional networks. CoRR abs/1608.06993 (2016). http://arxiv.org/abs/1608.06993

25. Hudlicka, E., Broekens, J.: Foundations for modelling emotions in game characters: modelling emotion effects on cognition, pp. 1–6 (2009). https://doi.org/10.1109/ACII.2009.5349473

26. Huitt, W., Cain, S.: An overview of the conative domain. Educ. Psychol. Interact., 1–20 (2005)

27. Ijsselsteijn, W., et al.: Measuring the experience of digital game enjoyment. In: Proceedings of Measuring Behavior (2008)

28. Jang, E.H., Park, B.J., Kim, S.H., Eum, Y., Sohn, J.H.: Identification of the optimal emotion recognition algorithm using physiological signals, pp. 1–6, November 2011

29. Jennett, C., et al.: Measuring and defining the experience of immersion in games. Int. J. Hum.-Comput. Stud. **66**(9), 641–661 (2008)

30. Lee, C., Yoo, S., Park, Y., Kim, N., Jeong, K., Lee, B.: Using neural network to recognize human emotions from heart rate variability and skin resistance. In: Engineering in Medicine and Biology 27th Annual Conference (2005)

31. Lombard, M., Ditton, T.: At the heart of it all: the concept of presence. J. Comput. Mediat. Commun. **3**(2), 0 (1997)

32. Matsumoto, D., Willingham, B.: Spontaneous facial expressions of emotion of congenitally and noncongenitally blind individuals. J. Pers. Soc. Psychol. **96**, 1–10 (2009). https://doi.org/10.1037/a0014037

33. Matsumotol, D., Hwang, H.S.: Reading facial expressions of emotion. Psychol. Sci. **115**, 541–558 (2011)

34. Moore, S., Bowden, R.: Local binary patterns for multi-view facial expression recognition. Comput. Vis. Image Underst. **115**(4), 541–558 (2011)

35. O'Brien, H.L., Toms, E.G.: What is user engagement? A conceptual framework for defining user engagement with technology. J. Am. Soc. Inform. Sci. Technol. **59**(6), 938–955 (2008). https://doi.org/10.1002/asi.20801

36. Ouellet, S.: Real-time emotion recognition for gaming using deep convolutional network features. CoRR abs/1408.3750 (2014)

37. Picard, R.W.: Emotion research by the people, for the people. Emot. Rev. **2**(3), 250–254 (2010)

38. Pollreisz, D., TaheriNejad, N.: A simple algorithm for emotion recognition, using physiological signals of a smart watch. In: 2017 39th Annual International Conference of the IEEE Engineering in Medicine and Biology Society (EMBC), pp. 2353–2356 (2017)

39. Posner, J., Russell, J.A., Peterson, B.S.: The circumplex model of affect: an integrative approach to affective neuroscience, cognitive development, and psychopathology. Dev. Psychopathol. **17**(3), 715–734 (2005)

40. Rashid, M., Abu-Bakar, S.A.R., Mokji, M.: Human emotion recognition from videos using spatio-temporal and audio features. Vis. Comput. **29**(12), 1269–1275 (2012). https://doi.org/10.1007/s00371-012-0768-y

41. Russell, J.A.: A circumplex model of affect. Pers. Soc. Psychol. **39**, 1161 (1980)

42. Russell, J.A., Barrett, L.F.: Core affect, prototypical emotional episodes, and other things called emotion: dissecting the elephant. J. Pers. Soc. Psychol. **76**, 805 (1999)

43. Saarni, C.: The Development of Emotional Competence. Guilford Series on Social and Emotional Development. Guilford Publications, New York (1999)

44. Sagi, B.R., Silvestrini, R.: Application of combinatorial tests in video game testing. **29**, 745–759 (2017). https://doi.org/10.1080/08982112.2017.1300919

45. Schoenau-Fog, H.: Hooked! – evaluating engagement as continuation desire in interactive narratives. In: Si, M., Thue, D., André, E., Lester, J.C., Tanenbaum, J., Zammitto, V. (eds.) ICIDS 2011. LNCS, vol. 7069, pp. 219–230. Springer, Heidelberg (2011). https://doi.org/10.1007/978-3-642-25289-1_24

46. Schoenau-Fog, H.: The player engagement process - an exploration of continuation desire in digital games. In: DiGRA - Proceedings of the 2011 DiGRA International Conference: Think Design Play. DiGRA/Utrecht School of the Arts, January 2011

47. Schoenau-Fog, H.: At the Core of Player Experience: Continuation Desire in Digital Games, pp. 388–410. Wiley (2014). https://doi.org/10.1002/9781118796443.ch14

48. Schoenau-Fog, H.: Designing and evaluating conative game-based learning scenarios. In: Busch, C. (ed.) Proceedings of The 8th European Conference on Games Based Learning – ECGBL 2014, pp. 512–518. Academic Conferences and Publishing International, October 2014

49. Schoenau-Fog, H., Birke, A., Reng, L.: Evaluation of continuation desire as an iterative game development method. In: Proceeding of the 16th International Academic MindTrek Conference, MindTrek 2012, pp. 241–243. ACM, New York (2012). https://doi.org/10.1145/2393132.2393185

50. Schoenau-Fog, H., Louchart, S., Lim, T., Soto-Sanfiel, M.T.: Narrative engagement in games-a continuation desire perspective. In: FDG, pp. 384–387 (2013)

51. Selvig, D., Stovring, N., Sjoblom, A., Korsholm, J.: Continuation desire and its physiological underpinnings - unpublished (2018)

52. Seng, K.P., Ang, L., Ooi, C.S.: A combined rule-based amp; machine learning audio-visual emotion recognition approach. IEEE Trans. Affect. Comput. **9**(1), 3–13 (2018)

53. Shan, C., Gong, S., McOwan, P.W.: Facial expression recognition based on local binary patterns: a comprehensive study. Image Vis. Comput. **27**(6), 803–816 (2009)

54. Szegedy, C., Ioffe, S., Vanhoucke, V.: Inception-v4, inception-resnet and the impact of residual connections on learning. CoRR abs/1602.07261 (2016)

55. Tawari, A., Trivedi, M.M.: Face expression recognition by cross modal data association. IEEE Trans. Multimedia **15**(7), 1543–1552 (2013)

56. Tawari, A., Trivedi, M.M.: Audio visual cues in driver affect characterization: issues and challenges in developing robust approaches, pp. 2997–3002 (2011). https://doi.org/10.1109/IJCNN.2011.6033615

57. Tokuno, S., et al.: Usage of emotion recognition in military health care, pp. 1–5 (2011). https://doi.org/10.1109/DSR.2011.6026823

58. Vyvey, T., Castellar, E.N., Van Looy, J.: Loaded with fun? The impact of enjoyment and cognitive load on brand retention in digital games. **18**, 72–82 (2018). https://doi.org/10.1080/15252019.2018.1446370

59. Wang, C., Pun, T., Chanel, G.: A comparative survey of methods for remote heartrate detection from frontal face videos. Front. Bioeng. Biotechnol. **6**, 33 (2018)

60. Xerfi: Global video game turnover between 2011 and 2019 (2019). https://www.statista.com/statistics/862278/global-video-game-revenues-worldwide/. Accessed 19 Mar 2019

61. Yu, S.N., Chen, S.F.: Emotion state identification based on heart rate variability and genetic algorithm, pp. 538–541, August 2015. https://doi.org/10.1109/EMBC.2015.7318418

62. Zhang, T., Zheng, W., Cui, Z., Zong, Y., Li, Y.: Spatial-temporal recurrent neural network for emotion recognition. IEEE Trans. Cybern. **49**(3), 839–847 (2018)

Brain-Controlled Drone Racing Game: A Qualitative Analysis

Dante Tezza[✉], Derek Caprio, Sarah Garcia, Blanche Pinto, Denis Laesker, and Marvin Andujar

University of South Florida, Tampa, FL 33620, USA
dtezza@usf.edu

Abstract. Brain-Computer Interfaces (BCI) provides a direct path of communication between the human brain and electronic systems. With the evolution of BCI hardware and software, the realm of BCI applications is expanding. An emerging field is the integration of BCI and video-games. In addition to providing a new user experience, brain-controlled games also allow users with physical disabilities to join the gaming community and compete at the same level as all players. Recently, drone racing has emerged as a popular sport, and analogously to car racing, it is natural that drone racing games will also rise in popularity. This paper presents a brain-controlled drone racing video game where users can control a racing drone using a non-invasive BCI headset by performing a motor imagery task. Additionally, it presents a qualitative analysis of a user study performed with 54 participants to understand users' perceptions towards brain-controlled games and gain insight on the future of brain-controlled games from the users' perspective. Results from this study indicate a high level of excitement from players regarding brain-controlled drone games. This paper also provides suggestions for genres of BCI games as well as a discussion of possible future directions for research in this field.

Keywords: BCI · Brain-controlled drones · Brain-controlled games · Games · Motor imagery

1 Introduction

The use of video game technologies has drastically increased over the last two decades, they are now ubiquitous and part of the mainstream media culture [22]. In the United States, 91% of children and teenagers between the ages of 2 and 17 play video-games [7]. The emerging of electronic sports, also known as e-sports led the gaming industry to grow considerably, attracting large investments as well as new research opportunities. Traditionally, hand-held controllers have been used to control video games, however, more recent technological advancements have allowed researchers to explore new interaction and control modalities for video games such as body gestures (e.g. Microsoft Kinect and Playstation Move). However, both hand-held and gesture controllers present limitations for users with physical disabilities (e.g. upper limb differences or those

X. Fang (Ed.): HCII 2020, LNCS 12211, pp. 350–360, 2020.
https://doi.org/10.1007/978-3-030-50164-8_25

in a wheelchair). Brain-Computer Interfaces (BCI) provides a direct path of communication between the human brain and electronic systems, which can be explored to create brain-controlled games. BCIs are capable of decoding users' brain activity and converting it directly into game commands, without the use of muscle movements. Therefore, BCIs allow users with physical disabilities to play video-games they might not have been able to otherwise. Additionally, BCIs also interest able-bodied gamers as a new control modality capable of creating different gaming experiences.

Video-games can be categorized as a form of art [15], therefore brain-controlled games fall under the category of Artistic BCI. In artistic BCI applications, the user manipulates a physical or audiovisual digital environment with their brain-waves to build a creative work [21]. Additionally, these applications offer a new modality for humans to express themselves creatively [21], and gamers are known to use creativity during the game-play to compete against others, solve puzzles, and pass obstacles [2]. The artistic aspect of brain-controlled games allows players not only to express themselves by actively controlling an avatar but also from an affective BCI perspective. For example, the game might change its audiovisual features (e.g. sky color) depending on the player's affective state measured with a BCI. As BCIs become more robust, affordable, and make their way from research laboratories into users' homes, the video game community is expected to be among the first to embrace this technology for entertainment purposes as gamers are known to be early-adopters of new technologies [13].

A well-known game genre is racing games, such as car racing. Recently, a new form of racing has emerged in the form of drone racing [3]. Additionally, integrating racing drones and BCIs has been a focus for researchers, with brain-drone race competitions being held at various universities [18]. As brain-drone racing grows as a sport, it is expected that brain-drone racing video-games and simulations will also grow in popularity. Analogous to popular car racing games, a simulation can be used to overcome potential hassles of racing physical drones. For example, players are able to practice at a lower cost, without the risk of crashes, and does not require special authorizations for flying unlike physical drones (e.g. FAA regulations in the USA). This paper presents a brain-controlled drone racing game built with the Unity engine. The game allows users to control specific movements of a racing drone using an electroencephalography (EEG) headset while performing motor imagery. Figure 1 shows a player wearing the EEG headset while playing the game. Motor imagery is the imagination of muscle movement, resulting in signals from the motor cortex area of the brain allowing the use of BCI devices to infer the user's intent [11]. The game allows the selection of different drones to be used as the racing avatar, types of races (e.g. lap-based vs. drag), and customization of distractions (e.g. sound and visual). As the game requires the user to focus to perform a motor imagery task, customized distractions can be used to increase the difficulty and improve players' ability to focus. The current version of the racing simulation is integrated with the Emotiv Insight BCI, a non-invasive 5-channel EEG headset that reads electrical signals from the scalp using semi-dry electrodes.

Fig. 1. Player controlling brain-controlled drone racing game.

The main contribution of this paper is a qualitative analysis of a user study conducted with 54 participants. It provides a discussion of users' perceptions towards brain-controlled games, an analysis of how much users would pay for brain-controlled games, and insights in the future of the technology.

2   Related Work

Previous research found that non-invasive EEG headsets are the most suitable BCI technology for gaming due to high temporal resolution, low cost (compared to other BCI's), safety, and portability [11]. Active control using BCIs has been used for a variety of game genres: action, simulation, puzzle, strategy, and role-playing games [11]. Both traditional games, such as Pacman and Pong [9], as well as modern role-playing games (e.g. World of Warcraft) [10] have been integrated with brain-control. Additionally, the passive use of BCI to detect and evaluate the players' cognitive activity during game-play has also been explored [12]. Passive control can be used to create an additional information channel between the user and the game, allowing the software to adapt the experience according to the user's current brain activity. This is beneficial, as adapting the game to the user's affective state allows for adjustments to the flow of information, providing a more effective and pleasant experience for the player [6]. Other researchers have made use of motor imagery-based BCIs to create video games such as *Pinball* [16] and a two-player football game [5].

Brain-controlled drones is a concept that has existed for almost a decade with studies dating back to 2010 [1]. More recently, the sport of drone racing has increased its popularity as it has been on mainstream television (ESPN) since 2016. Integrating drone racing with BCI technology allows for the creation of a universal sport, in which all participants compete fairly, independent of body type, gender, or disabilities; such brain-drone racing competitions have been implemented at the University of Florida [17], University of South Florida [20], and University of Alabama [14]. Analogous to racing games that simulate real car racing, it is natural that as brain-drone racing increases in popularity, the trend will follow with simulations. The first brain-drone racing game is described in [19], where the authors describe the game and how the game-play increased the players' positive affective states. This study differs from the above, as it collects and analyzes qualitative data in regard to users' perceptions towards BCI, to gain insight into the future of brain-controlled games.

3   Methodology

3.1   Study Design

This study presents a qualitative analysis of an exploratory user study. During the experiment, participants controlled a virtual racing drone in a video-game using a non-invasive 5-channel EEG headset. Each participant attended one session, which lasted approximately 30 min. First, the participant completed a pre-survey containing questions related to demographics, handedness, gaming background, coffee and energy drink consumption, and how many hours participants slept the night prior. With these questions researchers are able to explore possible correlations between these factors and how they participant interacted with the game (e.g. time required to complete the lap). Following, participants completed a training lap around the race track to get familiar with the BCI and the game. Each participant than completed three additional laps, allowing them to experience the game for a longer period. Each lap time was recorded for post-analysis. Additionally, to understand users' perception towards brain-controlled drone racing games and user experience while playing it, participants were asked to answer the following questions in a post-survey:

1. Do you envision any specific use for BCI devices for gaming?
2. Did you feel uncomfortable during the experiment? Please specify.
3. How much would you pay for a Brain Controlled Game (device and software bundle)?
4. Do you have any additional comments about the experiment or the idea of using BCI devices for controlling video games?

3.2   Procedures

At the beginning of each session, a member of the research team explained the experiment and acquired informed consent from the participant to take part in the study. Following, participants were provided a laptop where they filled-out a pre-questionnaire using Qualtrics Survey software. Following, participants were instructed on how to perform motor imagery and were assisted with wearing the BCI headset; a member of the research team ensured good electrode-skin contact and signal quality before proceeding. Each participant went through a training phase, where electrical activity was acquired during a relaxation (baseline) state and during a motor imagery task. This training phase is necessary by the Emotiv software to later detect and decode player's brain activity into commands in real-time. At this stage, each participant had a trained profile with two states that were translated into two game commands: accelerate and decelerate the drone. Following this, the participant controlled the drone to perform four laps around the race track. At the end of each lap, the time required to complete that lap was recorded in an electronic table. Lastly, each participant was asked to complete a post-experiment questionnaire and provide feedback through the Qualtrics Survey.

3.3 Participants

A total of 54 participants (33 males and 21 females) were recruited from the University of South Florida to participate in the experiment. From these, 45 participants were between 18 and 24 years old, 8 were between 25 and 34, and 1 participant was between 35 and 44. Additionally, 33 participants stated that they play video-games on a regular basis, while 21 participants do not.

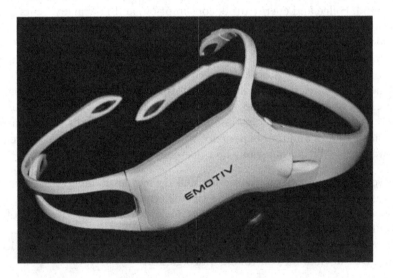

Fig. 2. Emotiv Insight EEG headset used to control the game.

3.4   Equipment

The Emotiv Insight brain-computer interface showed in Fig. 2 was used in the experiment. This device is a non-invasive 5-channel EEG headset that reads the electrical activity from the user's scalp through the use of semi-dry electrodes. The channels are located at the AF3, AF4, T7, T8, and Pz locations according to the 10–20 International System [8]. Additionally, the Emotiv official software suite was used to interface the headset and the game. First, the Emotiv ControlPanel was used to read and decode the brain activity while the participant performed motor imagery into either a neutral(drone hovering) and a command (drone flying forward) state. Following, the Emotiv Emokey software interprets the ControlPanel output (neutral vs command) and emulates keyboard strokes to control the game accordingly to the current participant's brain activity.

3.5   User Interaction

The brain-controlled drone racing game, displayed in Fig. 3, was developed using the Unity engine and allows players to control the drone avatar using their brain-activity. To interact with the game, players perform a motor imagery task. In other words, they must imagine a muscle movement without physically performing it. Although the current game version offers different tracks, the one used in this experiment allows the participant to control the speed of the drone only, and not the direction in which the drone flies. This approach was used to facilitate the game control, as users are not familiar with controlling a video-game with their brain-waves. Instead, the drone follows a pre-programmed path, while the player can accelerate the drone by performing motor imagery or decelerate by not imagining muscle movements. In this game, the player's objective is to increase their focus on the motor imagery task, this allows the drone to fly faster and complete laps in the shortest time possible.

4   Results and Discussion

4.1   User Perception Towards BCI in Gaming

Overall, participants provided positive feedback regarding the concept of brain-controlled video games. Many expressed highly enthusiastic responses after the experiment. Additionally, many participants also stated that they believe BCIs will become popular in the gaming industry. Following are examples of the feedback (quotes) provided by players:

- Very interesting and the game was fun!
- It was an enjoyable experience, I can see this taking off in a decade or so from now similar to how VR games came into existence.
- It is very interesting, I think it is the future of gaming.
- I believe it is incredible and very accurate. This kind of technology could open the doors for VR or AR-Brain Controlled interactions and many different experiences, not just in gaming.

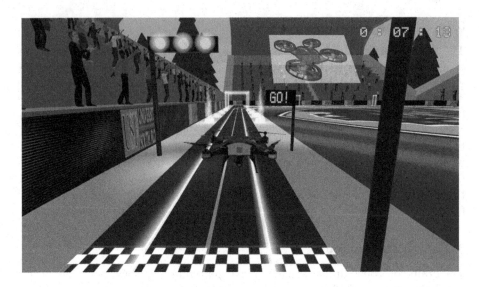

Fig. 3. Brain-controlled drone racing game.

- It was a lot of fun!
- It was a good game, and using BCI for video games can become very popular.
- The game was impressive.
- I'm not much of a video game player, but it seems to be as attractive as VR.
- I thought it was fun and interesting to use your brain to control devices.

The excitement demonstrated in these responses indicates that brain-computer interfaces have the potential to become the next generation game controller. Moreover, only 4 out of 54 participants said they would not buy a brain-controlled game, and some added comments such as "I would definitely buy one if the technology got to a point where it was very accurate and reasonably priced". As shown in Fig. 4 and Fig. 5, most participants stated that they would pay between $200 and $500 US dollars for a gaming bundle (device + software). One possible shortcoming for the technology is that brain-controlled games require the use of a BCI headset, which can possibly cause discomfort to players. However, in this experiment only 1 out of 54 participants expressed physical discomfort while wearing the BCI headset, suggesting that discomfort will not be a problem for most players. Combined, the above results show that BCIs can be used for gaming purposes and that users have a positive perception towards this concept. BCIs will lead to a new game modality, providing a different user experience in which they are not only entertained, but can also exercise their brain.

4.2   Future of Gaming BCI

Gaming Genres. Participants were asked if they envisioned any specific use of BCIs in the gaming industry. Sixteen participants stated that they would like to

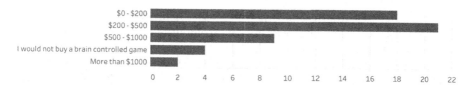

Fig. 4. Monetary value all participants would pay for a brain-controlled video game.

Fig. 5. Monetary value participants would pay for a brain-controlled video game by gender.

see BCIs integrated with specific game genres. The most commonly mentioned genre was first person shooting games mentioned by 6 players, followed by racing (n = 4), Massive Multiplayer Online Role-Playing Games (MMORPG) (n = 3), and puzzle games (n = 2). Other game genres were mentioned by a single participant each: fighting and combat, aircraft simulators, strategy, and adventure games. The variety of responses demonstrate that users expectations towards brain-controlled games goes beyond drone racing. Additionally, it also serves as a guide for future researchers, specifying which game genres players are most interested in. Future studies can further explore some of the more popular genres mentioned. This would include focus group studies to discuss with users in more detail what they look for in their preferred games.

Virtual Reality. Participants expressed their desire to see brain-computer interfaces integrated with virtual reality (VR) technologies. Various of them stated that BCIs integrated with the immersion provided by VR would create enjoyable user experiences. Their feedback can be summarized by the statement of a participant: "It would be really cool to be able to use brain computer interface devices along with virtual reality to create a more immersive gaming experience." The proliferation of virtual reality technologies in the last decade has increased the development of VR games. Consumer devices such as the Oculus' Rift and GO, as well as the HTC Vive, allow users to immerse themselves into virtual environments while remaining at home. Currently, BCI-VR integration is possible by combining these VR headsets with BCIs. Additionally, there are few dedicated headsets providing both BCI and VR capabilities (e.g. Neurable DK1), however, the options are limited. In the near future, it is expected to see a variety of new BCI devices incorporated into VR headsets thus giving rise to a new gaming experience. Researchers can explore the immersive capabilities of VR, coupled with the novelty and challenging aspects of controlling games with brain waves to create new user experiences, which is an appealing idea to the gaming community. Furthermore, due to the current popularity of VR games, researchers can also use its integration with BCIs to increase the popularity of brain-controlled games.

Increased Accessibility. Participants also provided their remarks on how this technology can be used to include people with severe physical disabilities in the gaming hobby. They remarked that BCIs would allow players with paralysis and other types of disabilities to play games, which would not be viable using standard game controllers. Therefore, inclusivity is a main benefit of brain-controlled games as players can control games using their brain-waves without muscle movements, even users with severe physical disabilities can experience games that they may not otherwise be able to. Furthermore, this type of game allows every player to compete at an equal level, regardless of whether or not they have physical disabilities, another advantage not provided by other types of control modalities. In addition to these ethical considerations, according to [4] there are also financial and legal reasons why accessible games are beneficial. Future studies conducted with brain-drone racing games and users with physical disabilities such as upper limb differences could give further insight into the requirements necessary for BCI games to be successful in regard to accessibility.

Improving Attention. Participants reported an increased level of focus while playing the game with comments such as "It actually allowed me to focus which made me feel good". They also commented that they would like to see BCI games specifically designed to help improve attention in the future. These responses support the claim that brain-controlled games can be useful as a form of brain exercise, where users can play the games while exercising their abilities to focus on motor imagery tasks. Furthermore, such comments are aligned with the finding from [19], where the authors found that brain-controlled games increase attention levels of participants. This characteristic of brain-controlled games can be further explored to create brain exercises. Future research to evaluate brain-controlled game capability as a fun form of therapy for ADHD users is suggested, such as long-term studies measuring the effects of BCI games on user concentration.

5   Conclusion

This paper presents a brain-controlled drone racing game and the results of a qualitative study performed with 54 participants. The qualitative analysis suggests that users feel excited about BCI technology incorporation with video games, and that there is a positive future for their commercialization and use. The majority (50 out of 54) of participants stated that they would purchase a brain-controlled game, and most of them would pay between $200 and $500 for it.

The findings also demonstrate that participants would like to see the integration of brain-controlled games with virtual reality. Additionally, the most desired brain-controlled game genres are first-person view shooting, followed by racing and MMORPG. Users also expressed their belief that BCIs have the potential to increase entertainment in gaming as well as further physical disability inclusion initiatives in the gaming industry, as they allow users to experience games with only the use of their brain waves.

References

1. Akce, A., Johnson, M., Bretl, T.: Remote teleoperation of an unmanned aircraft with a brain-machine interface: theory and preliminary results. In: 2010 IEEE International Conference on Robotics and Automation, pp. 5322–5327. IEEE (2010)
2. Andujar, M., Crawford, C.S., Nijholt, A., Jackson, F., Gilbert, J.E.: Artistic brain-computer interfaces: the expression and stimulation of the user's affective state. Brain-Comput. Interfaces 2(2–3), 60–69 (2015)
3. Barin, A., Dolgov, I., Toups, Z.O.: Understanding dangerous play: a grounded theory analysis of high-performance drone racing crashes. In: Proceedings of the Annual Symposium on Computer-Human Interaction in Play, pp. 485–496. ACM (2017)
4. Bierre, K., Chetwynd, J., Ellis, B., Hinn, D.M., Ludi, S., Westin, T.: Game not over: accessibility issues in video games. In: Proceedings of the 3rd International Conference on Universal Access in Human-Computer Interaction, pp. 22–27 (2005)
5. Bonnet, L., Lotte, F., Lécuyer, A.: Two brains, one game: design and evaluation of a multiuser BCI video game based on motor imagery. IEEE Trans. Comput. Intell. AI Games 5(2), 185–198 (2013)
6. Gilleade, K., Dix, A., Allanson, J.: Affective videogames and modes of affective gaming: assist me, challenge me, emote me. In: DiGRA 2005: Changing Views-Worlds in Play (2005)
7. Granic, I., Lobel, A., Engels, R.C.: The benefits of playing video games. Am. Psychol. 69(1), 66 (2014)
8. Klem, G.H., Lüders, H.O., Jasper, H., Elger, C., et al.: The ten-twenty electrode system of the international federation. Electroencephalogr. Clin. Neurophysiol. 52(3), 3–6 (1999)
9. Krepki, R., Blankertz, B., Curio, G., Müller, K.R.: The Berlin brain-computer interface (BBCI) – towards a new communication channel for online control in gaming applications. Multimed. Tools Appl. 33(1), 73–90 (2007). https://doi.org/10.1007/s11042-006-0094-3
10. van de Laar, B., Gürkök, H., Bos, D.P.O., Poel, M., Nijholt, A.: Experiencing BCI control in a popular computer game. IEEE Trans. Comput. Intell. AI Games 5(2), 176–184 (2013)
11. Marshall, D., Coyle, D., Wilson, S., Callaghan, M.: Games, gameplay, and BCI: the state of the art. IEEE Trans. Comput. Intell. AI Games 5(2), 82–99 (2013)
12. Nijholt, A.: BCI for games: a 'state of the art' survey. In: Stevens, S.M., Saldamarco, S.J. (eds.) ICEC 2008. LNCS, vol. 5309, pp. 225–228. Springer, Heidelberg (2008). https://doi.org/10.1007/978-3-540-89222-9_29
13. Nijholt, A., Bos, D.P.O., Reuderink, B.: Turning shortcomings into challenges: brain-computer interfaces for games. Entertain. Comput. 1(2), 85–94 (2009)

14. Reynolds, K.: University of Alabama students use mind control to fly drones, April 2019. https://www.wbrc.com/2019/04/04/university-alabama-students-use-mind-control-fly-drones/
15. Smuts, A.: Are video games art? Contemp. Aesthet. **3**(1), 6 (2005)
16. Tangermann, M.W., et al.: Playing pinball with non-invasive BCI. In: Proceedings of the 21st International Conference on Neural Information Processing Systems, pp. 1641–1648. Citeseer (2008)
17. Tepper, F.: University of Florida held the world's first brain-controlled drone race, October 2016. http://tcrn.ch/1Wm18eQ
18. Tezza, D., Andujar, M.: The state-of-the-art of human-drone interaction: a survey. IEEE Access **7**, 167438–167454 (2019)
19. Tezza, D., Garcia, S., Hossain, T., Andujar, M.: Brain eRacing: an exploratory study on virtual brain-controlled drones. In: Chen, J.Y.C., Fragomeni, G. (eds.) HCII 2019. LNCS, vol. 11575, pp. 150–162. Springer, Cham (2019). https://doi.org/10.1007/978-3-030-21565-1_10
20. Verdina, N.: USF students control drones with their brains using electronic headbands, February 2019. http://www.fox13news.com/news/local-news/usf-students-control-drones-with-their-brains-using-electronic-headbands
21. Wadeson, A., Nijholt, A., Nam, C.S.: Artistic brain-computer interfaces: state-of-the-art control mechanisms. Brain-Comput. Interfaces **2**(2–3), 70–75 (2015)
22. Williams, D.: Structure and competition in the US home video game industry. Int. J. Media Manag. **4**(1), 41–54 (2002)

An Analysis of Engagement Levels While Playing Brain-Controlled Games

Dante Tezza[(⊠)], Derek Caprio, Blanche Pinto, Isabella Mantilla,
and Marvin Andujar

University of South Florida, Tampa, FL 33620, USA
dtezza@usf.edu

Abstract. This paper presents a brain-controlled game that allows players to fly a virtual drone using their brain-waves, while the game measures their engagement levels using a BCI. The active BCI element in the game allows players to accelerate and decelerate the virtual drone by performing a motor imagery task (imagining a muscle movement). The passive BCI element processes the EEG signal from the players' frontal lobe to calculate their engagement in the game. Optionally, the player can see their engagement level as a feedback in the game. This study aims to evaluate (1) the correlation between players' engagement and performance in brain-controlled games, (2) users' perception towards receiving feedback on their engagement levels, and (3) the impact of providing engagement level feedback on players' engagement and performance. A within-subject study with 10 participants was conducted to explore such research questions. Results demonstrate a strong correlation between engagement and performance, measured by the time it took participants to complete each lap in the game. Higher engagement levels resulted in significantly better performance, while low engagement levels led to significantly worse performance. Additionally, qualitative data collected from participants demonstrate a positive attitude towards using engagement level feedback to improve their attention during gameplay.

Keywords: Active BCI · Brain-computer interfaces · Drone racing · Engagement · e-Sports · Passive BCI · User experience

1 Introduction

In recent years, there has been an increasing interest in the use of BCIs for gaming purposes [10]. Research focusing on video-games is leading to more inclusive, immersive and enjoyable user experiences. Especially, new control modalities are being explored, such as the integration of games with brain-computer interfaces (BCI). BCIs acquire the player's brain signals, which can be decoded by software algorithms directly into game commands, without the use of muscle movements. Brain-controlled games allow both able-bodied users and those with physical disabilities to control the game using their brain activity, such as by performing a motor imagery task (imagination of a muscle movement). Although

© Springer Nature Switzerland AG 2020
X. Fang (Ed.): HCII 2020, LNCS 12211, pp. 361–372, 2020.
https://doi.org/10.1007/978-3-030-50164-8_26

brain-controlled games have been previously explored by researchers [10,11,17], there is little research evaluating the correlation between players' engagement levels measured with a BCI and how they interact with the brain-controlled games. Therefore, this paper presents a brain-controlled drone racing game and the results of a user study conducted to evaluate the correlation between users' engagement and their performance, which is measured by the time required to complete each lap around the race track.

Brain-computer interfaces are divided into two categories: active and passive BCIs. Active BCI allows users to control a system by purposefully manipulating their brain signals to control an application [15]. For instance, in the game presented in this paper, the player can perform a motor imagery task to control the speed of the virtual drone. On the other hand, passive BCIs are used to detect changes in a cognitive state and measure the affective state of a user during the execution of a task [15]. In this game, passive BCI is used to measure and quantify the users' engagement during the game play experience.

The brain-controlled drone racing game presented in this paper can be seen in Fig. 1. Players can accelerate and decelerate the virtual drone by performing a motor imagery task. Additionally, the game calculates a score that indicates players' engagement using the formula $E = (\beta/(\alpha + \theta))$ [2] where E represents engagement and α, β, and θ represent the alpha, beta, and theta EEG frequency bands in the frontal lobe. Optionally, the player can select to receive their engagement score as feedback in the game. The hypothesis is that such feedback will encourage players to increase their focus in the game and consequently perform better. The game is integrated with a non-invasive EEG headset (Emotiv Insight), which is used to measure the electrical activity in the player's scalp (brain signals). These signals are decoded into game commands and used to calculate a score indicating the player's engagement levels.

The main contribution of this paper includes an analysis of a user study performed with 10 participants aimed to evaluate (1) the correlation between engagement levels acquired from the brain and motor-imagery based game performance, (2) user perception towards receiving engagement score as feedback, and (3) if providing engagement score feedback increases participants' engagement. Results shows a strong correlation between the calculated engagement score and participants' performance in the game, measured by the time required to complete a lap around the race track. Additionally, qualitative results indicate that receiving feedback encouraged participants to try harder in the game. However, the results of this paper do not show any significant increase in the measured engagement score when the engagement level feedback was provided.

2   Related Work

The use of BCIs in human-computer interaction has been increasing in the last few years [11,12]. Consequently, BCI applications are emerging in different fields, including gaming. Gamers are known as early adopters, they are open to trying new technologies, and are willing to put great efforts to gain an advantage in the game (even if it is minimal) [10]. Such a factor is appealing for BCI researchers

Fig. 1. Player controlling virtual drone with a BCI.

who can use gamers' interest to test cutting-edge BCI applications, and attract investments from the gaming industry. Companies can also benefits from gamers' interest in BCI, as the first company to introduce a novel type of game or gaming element can generate large profits [10]. Both active and passive elements of BCIs can be explored in games, which are discussed below.

In games integrated with an active BCI element, the players must voluntarily manipulate their brain activity to control an element of the game (e.g. move an avatar). Active BCI games can rely on external stimuli (e.g. P300, SSVEP) or the user's own conscious control of their thoughts (e.g. motor imagery). Motor imagery has been used to control first-person shooter games [13], Google Earth [14], flight simulators [8], and more. Emotiv, the developers of the BCI used in this study, have developed a demonstration game in which the player is able to rebuild Stonehenge using motor imagery to lift, push, and rotate stones into place [10]. These are some examples of how motor imagery BCIs can be used to interact with video games.

Brain-controlled games can also include a passive BCI element. In this approach, the player does not need to manipulate their thoughts to control the game. Instead, the BCI is used to measure the players' mental state (e.g. boredom, stress, engagement) and adapt accordingly. For instance, researchers integrated the popular World of Warcraft game with the Emotiv Epoc BCI to create αWoW [7]. In this game, the players' avatar changes its form (e.g. druid, vs animal form) according to the players' EEG activity in the alpha (8–12 Hz) spectrum as measured with the BCI. Additionally, a characteristic of a game is the 'immersion' or 'flow' [4], meaning that the player feels deeply immersed in the game and forgets about the real world. Researchers have attempted to measure a player's immersion using physiological information (e.g. heart rate, sweat, respiration, blood pressure) [5] and body language [3]. Feedback from a passive BCI measuring the players' affective state might also be useful to measure their engagement and immersion in the game. Additionally, the game can be adapted using such feedback, for example by changing the environment to increase immersion when a low engagement is measured.

In addition to creating new experiences and allowing players with physical disabilities to play games, brain-controlled games can also be explored for medical applications. For instance, brain-controlled games can potentially be used as an alternative treatment for Attention-Deficit/Hyperactivity Disorder (ADHD). This can be achieved by using the game as a fun and engaging tool to teach players how to increase their attention or relaxation. For instance, in [9] "The Harvest Challenge" is presented, a game designed for attention training in children diagnosed with ADHD. The game, which simulates a Colombian coffee farm, aims to train ADHD patients in 4 aspects: (1) waiting ability, (2) planning ability, (3) ability to follow instructions, and (4) ability to achieve objectives.

Drone racing is emerging as a popular racing sport. Integrating drone racing with BCIs allows participants to compete against each other at the same level, independent of body type, gender, or physical disabilities. Researchers have been exploring brain-controlled drones since 2010 [1]. Furthermore, brain-drone racing competitions have been hosted by several research universities [16]. A video-game version of brain-drone racing gives players the opportunity to practice at lower cost and risks of crashes. A brain-controlled drone racing game is presented in [17], with the results of an exploratory user study (n = 30). The authors found that the game significantly increased the participants' positive affective states, which were measured by using the standard "Positive And Negative Affect Schedule" (PANAS) [18]. They concluded by suggesting future research in brain-controlled drone games, such as an investigation on which factors impact a player's performance. This study differs from previous as it aims to expand the study described in [17] to evaluate the impact of providing visual feedback of the players' engagement score measured with a BCI while performing motor imagery in a video game environment.

3   Brain-Controlled Game Overview

3.1   BCI Hardware and Software

Participants used the Emotiv Insight EEG headset shown in Fig. 2 to fly virtual drones with their brains (hands-free) within the game. This device is a semi-dry, non-invasive headset with five EEG channels at locations AF3, AF4, T7, T8, and Pz according to the 10–20 International System [6]. To be able to control the game, the player must first create and train a user profile using the EmotivBCI software. During training, the user is asked to train two commands: neutral and push. During neutral training, the user relaxes and clears his mind, during push training the user performs a motor imagery task (imagination of muscle movement). After training the profile, the EmotivBCI software is able to classify the user mental activity into the trained states (neutral or push) in real-time. To integrate the device with the game, the Emotiv Cortex API V1.0 was used. Once the game connects to the Cortex services, a periodical JSON object is returned from the Cortex stating if the user is performing a neutral (relaxation) which is interpreted as a decelerate command, or push (motor imagery) task which is interpreted as a command to accelerate the virtual drone. Additionally the Cortex services also provides a periodical JSON object containing the α, β, θ EEG band powers, which are used to calculate engagement. The alpha wave frequency ranges from 7 to 13 Hz and is related to the state of relaxation and consciousness [2]. The beta wave ranges from 13 to 30 Hz and is associated to relaxed but focusing thinking and alertness [2]. Finally the theta waves ranges from 4 to 7 Hz and represents creativeness and dreams [2]. The ratio of $\beta/(\alpha+\theta)$ is a known equation to calculate user engagement with a BCI.

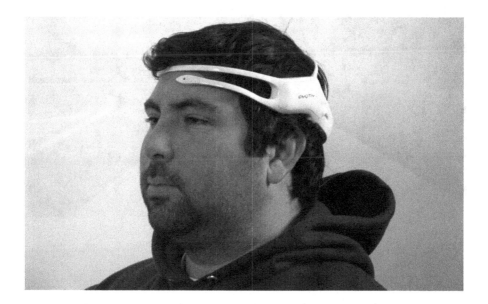

Fig. 2. Emotiv Insight EEG headset.

3.2   User Experience

The game consists of a drone racing environment, where the goal is complete the race track as fast as possible. The player is able to customize the game by selecting different drone avatars and racing tracks. Additionally the players can select if they would like to see their engagement score (measured with the BCI) at the end of each lap. Once the game has started, the virtual drone follows a programmed path, but the player is able to control its acceleration using the BCI.

Brain-controlling a system requires practice and concentration, and most users are not familiar with controlling systems using their brain-waves. Therefore, in this study, the player is able to control only one degree of freedom (virtual drone acceleration). The player performs a motor imagery task to accelerate the drone and relax their mind to decelerate. A motor imagery tasks consist of imagining a muscle movement, for example, if players imagine opening and closing their hands.

The game has both active and passive BCI elements, which can be seen in Fig. 3. The EEG headset measures the brain signals generated by the player performing a motor imagery task (active BCI). These signals are then classified into game commands using the Emotiv software machine learning algorithms. Additionally, the EEG signals measured in channels AF3 and AF4 are used to calculate the α, β, and θ band powers, necessary to calculate engagement (passive BCI). The engagement score is then displayed to the user at the end of each lap, completing the game cycle.

Fig. 3. Brain-controlled drone racing game.

4   Methodology

4.1   Study Design

The conducted experiment was within subject design in which each participant receives feedback on their engagement levels acquired from the brain after four of the eight laps. Five of the 10 participants received feedback for their first four laps, and the other five received it on their last four laps. A single engagement score was calculated for each lap as: $E = \beta/(\alpha + \theta)$ averaged over the time to complete the lap where E represents engagement and α, β, and θ represent the alpha, beta, and theta EEG frequency bands (Fig. 4).

A pre-experiment survey was administered to gather general demographic information, as well as study-specific information such as gaming experience,

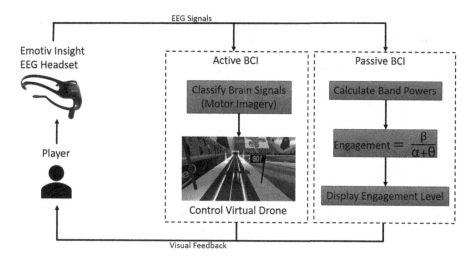

Fig. 4. Game cycle with a BCI.

caffeine consumption, and whether or not the participant has been diagnosed with any attention disorder. With these questions researchers are able to explore possible correlations between these factors and how they participant interacted with the game (e.g. time required to complete the lap). Also, the standardized Positive and Negative Affects Schedule (PANAS) [18] was completed twice by each participant, once before and once after their gaming experience, allowing analysis of how the gameplay impacted participants' affective state. Finally, a short post-experiment questionnaire was also included to give participants the opportunity to provide any open-ended feedback.

4.2 Procedures

Each participant attended one session that lasted approximately 30 min. After obtaining the participant's informed consent, a member of the research team administered the pre-experiment survey to the participant, followed by the first PANAS questionnaire. After this, the participant was aided in properly mounting the BCI device and training a profile using the Emotiv BCI software. Each participant trained two commands: a neutral state which corresponds to the drone hovering still and the participant being relaxed, and a push state which corresponds to the drone accelerating forward and the participant performing motor imagery.

Following this, the participant is ready to begin the gameplay. Each participant completed eight consecutive laps around the track and their lap times and engagement scores were recorded by a researcher. As previously mentioned, half of the participants were able to see their engagement scores for the first four laps, while the other half saw these scores for their last four laps. Lap times were presented after every lap. This information was presented after each lap was finished and before the next began.

After completing the eight laps, participants removed the EEG headset and completed another PANAS questionnaire. Lastly, each experiment was concluded with the participant providing their open-ended feedback about the experience in the post-experiment questionnaire.

4.3   Participants

A total of 10 participants were recruited from a local university to participate in the study, 4 of them being males and 6 females. Out of these, 6 were between the ages of 18 and 24 and 4 were between 25 and 34 years old. Additionally, all participants were right-handed, 6 reported to be gamers, 2 consumed caffeine prior to the experiment, and 1 participant was previously diagnosed with ADHD.

5   Results and Discussion

5.1   Engagement and Game Performance Correlation

Results of the user study indicate a strong negative correlation between participants' engagement levels and their lap times. In other words, participants took a longer time to complete a lap around the race track when their engagement score was low, and when their engagement score was high, they completed the track faster. The Pearson R correlation value between the time it took participants to complete a lap and their engagement score was calculated to quantify the correlation. Results varied from $-.53$ and -0.91, with an average p value of 0.011, showing a strong negative correlation. A breakdown of each participant's results can be seen in Table 1. A further breakdown with each participant's time and corresponding engagement level can be seen in Table 2. Results should be analyzed within subject, a comparison of the engagement score across different participants is not possible due to the uniqueness of each individuals' brain waves. Such results demonstrate that players' performance is dependent on their engagement in the game, therefore, it can be beneficial and important to evaluate approaches to increase users' engagement when playing motor-imagery based brain-controlled games.

5.2   Impact of Providing Engagement Feedback

This study hypothesis was that providing the engagement level as a feedback would encourage participants to try harder to increase their engagement in the game. However, the results did not show any significant indications of an increase in players' performance or engagement level when providing engagement level feedback in the game. Such results, however, are contrasting to the qualitative responses received on the post-survey. Participants indicated that seeing their engagement score impacted their gameplay experience with comments such as

Table 1. Correlation between time required to complete a lap and engagement score.

Participant	Pearson r-value	t statistic	p-value
001	−0.5371	−1.5599	0.0849
002	−0.9112	−5.4179	**0.0008**
003	0.9248	−5.9551	**0.0005**
004	−0.5696	−1.6974	0.0703
005	−0.8427	−3.8334	**0.0043**
006	0.7215	2.5522	**0.0217**
007	−0.8211	−3.5241	**0.0062**
008	−0.6832	−2.2920	**0.0309**
009	−0.5770	−1.7307	0.0671
010	−0.7481	−2.7030	**0.0177**

Table 2. Completion time (T) and engagement score (S) for each participant (P) for each lap (1–8).

P	T1	S1	T2	S2	T3	S3	T4	S4	T5	S5	T6	S6	T7	S7	T8	S8
P01	23.1	50.0	73.2	13.1	29.7	234	42.9	113	34.2	194	49.7	74.0	18.4	150	26.2	103
P02	68.0	6.0	120	2.9	37.2	13.0	75.6	4.7	119	3.6	120	2.7	54.9	8.1	120	3.2
P03	17.9	89.2	120	6.7	17.2	87.6	16.9	69.4	25.5	41.3	115	3.7	120	4.3	58.1	33.1
P04	110	19.3	42.4	166	113	107	33.9	445	55.5	264	118	23.1	23.9	74.7	69.9	43.3
P05	60.4	42.6	120	32.0	115	28.3	41.2	85.7	83.8	50.6	19.1	255	22.2	175	118	23.3
P06	25.4	37.3	24.3	78.8	17.9	161	29.4	58.6	90.2	3.2	19.9	149	18.8	161	23.6	108
P07	24.1	34.5	29.3	27.3	69.1	8.5	120	7.3	64.8	11.6	52.0	14.9	96.0	16.9	117	5.3
P08	26.9	16.7	28.2	19.7	26.7	22.2	32.3	21.6	47.3	6.9	111	2.69	36.8	13.0	34.8	33.1
P09	16.9	5.2	106	3.3	18.1	11.6	17.7	17.3	17.4	26.4	17.4	27.0	20.7	26.6	17.6	25.2
P10	16.9	25.0	18.1	31.5	18.0	19.6	33.0	19.8	30.4	25.3	24.6	21.3	21.8	34.2	45.5	7.0

"It made me want to try harder" and "I felt it improved my focus". Therefore, future work is suggested to further explore this matter. For instance, a future work could evaluate different approaches to providing engagement level feedback, such as continuous display instead of providing an engagement score at the end of each lap only.

The post-survey included questions to allow researchers to better understand the study population. Participants were asked if they considered themselves to be easily distracted, if they have trouble maintaining focus, and if they would use engagement level feedback to improve their attention levels. Their responses can be seen in Fig. 5. As shown, 4 out of 10 participants strongly agreed and another 4 agreed that they could use the feedback to improve their attention. Additionally, participants also demonstrated a positive attitude towards the use of engagement score feedback in the open ended questions, and suggested its use for various other activities, such as while studying, driving, during yoga and while playing sports.

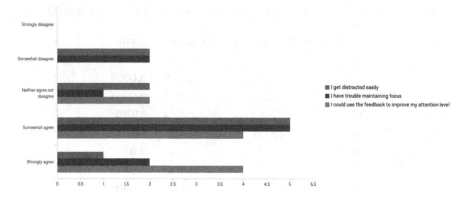

Fig. 5. Participants response towards using engagement level feedback

5.3 Impact of External Factors and PANAS

This study also evaluated if external factors impacted participants' performance in the game, measured by the time required to complete each lap. However, results show that neither gaming experience or caffeine consumption impacted the lap times in a statistically significant manner. Only one participant declared a previous attention disorder diagnosis, therefore, analysis of this factor was not possible. Additionally, the analysis of the PANAS survey did not result in any statistically significant change in the participant's affective state during the experiment.

6   Conclusion

As BCIs continue to gain popularity within the gaming community, it becomes important to explore new use-cases in which they can enrich the user's gaming experience. This paper presented a brain-controlled drone racing game that involves both passive and active BCI elements. Players are able to control the virtual drone using their brain-waves (active BCI), while having their engagement measured and displayed (passive BCI). Results of a user study with 10 participants demonstrated a strong correlation between players' engagement and performance in the game with statistically significant values ($p < 0.05$). Additionally, qualitative data suggests that players would like to have engagement feedback in brain-controlled games, and that it encouraged them to improve their focus. However, quantitative results did not show a significant improvement in players' performance or an increase in engagement levels when feedback was provided. The strong correlation between engagement and performance found in this study, together with the participants' positive attitude toward the concept, demonstrates the relevance of future research in the topic. One specific future study could evaluate continuous feedback and different visual displays (e.g. bar graph), as in the current study the feedback was displayed at the end of each lap only as a numerical representation.

References

1. Akce, A., Johnson, M., Bretl, T.: Remote teleoperation of an unmanned aircraft with a brain-machine interface: theory and preliminary results. In: 2010 IEEE International Conference on Robotics and Automation, pp. 5322–5327. IEEE (2010)
2. Andujar, M., Gilbert, J.E.: Let's learn!: enhancing user's engagement levels through passive brain-computer interfaces. In: CHI 2013 Extended Abstracts on Human Factors in Computing Systems, pp. 703–708. ACM (2013)
3. Cairns, P., Cox, A.L., Berthouze, N., Jennett, C., Dhoparee, S.: Quantifying the experience of immersion in games. In: CogSci 2006 Workshop: Cognitive Science of Games and Gameplay (2006)
4. Czikszentmihalyi, M.: Flow: The Psychology of Optimal Experience. Harper & Row, New York (1990)
5. Gilleade, K., Dix, A., Allanson, J.: Affective videogames and modes of affective gaming: assist me, challenge me, emote me. In: DiGRA 2005: Changing Views-Worlds in Play (2005)
6. Klem, G.H., Lüders, H.O., Jasper, H., Elger, C., et al.: The ten-twenty electrode system of the international federation. Electroencephalogr. Clin. Neurophysiol. **52**(3), 3–6 (1999)
7. Van de Laar, B., Gürkök, H., Bos, D.P.O., Poel, M., Nijholt, A.: Experiencing BCI control in a popular computer game. IEEE Trans. Comput. Intell. AI Games **5**(2), 176–184 (2013)
8. Middendorf, M., McMillan, G., Calhoun, G., Jones, K.S.: Brain-computer interfaces based on the steady-state visual-evoked response. IEEE Trans. Rehabil. Eng. **8**(2), 211–214 (2000)
9. Muñoz, J.E., Lopez, D.S., Lopez, J.F., Lopez, A.: Design and creation of a BCI videogame to train sustained attention in children with ADHD. In: 2015 10th Computing Colombian Conference (10CCC), pp. 194–199. IEEE (2015)
10. Nijholt, A., Bos, D.P.O., Reuderink, B.: Turning shortcomings into challenges: brain-computer interfaces for games. Entertain. Comput. **1**(2), 85–94 (2009)
11. Nijholt, A., Tan, D., Allison, B., del R. Milan, J., Graimann, B.: Brain-computer interfaces for HCI and games. In: CHI 2008 Extended Abstracts on Human Factors in Computing Systems, pp. 3925–3928. ACM (2008)
12. Nijholt, A., et al.: Brain-computer interfacing for intelligent systems. IEEE Intell. Syst. **23**(3), 72–79 (2008)
13. Pineda, J.A., Silverman, D.S., Vankov, A., Hestenes, J.: Learning to control brain rhythms: making a brain-computer interface possible. IEEE Trans. Neural Syst. Rehabil. Eng. **11**(2), 181–184 (2003)
14. Scherer, R., Schloegl, A., Lee, F., Bischof, H., Janša, J., Pfurtscheller, G.: The self-paced Graz brain-computer interface: methods and applications. Comput. Intell. Neurosci **2007** (2007)
15. Tan, D., Nijholt, A.: Brain-computer interfaces and human-computer interaction. In: Tan, D., Nijholt, A. (eds.) Brain-Computer Interfaces. HCIS, pp. 3–19. Springer, London (2010). https://doi.org/10.1007/978-1-84996-272-8_1

16. Tezza, D., Andujar, M.: The state-of-the-art of human-drone interaction: a survey. IEEE Access **7**, 167438–167454 (2019)
17. Tezza, D., Garcia, S., Hossain, T., Andujar, M.: Brain eRacing: an exploratory study on virtual brain-controlled drones. In: Chen, J.Y.C., Fragomeni, G. (eds.) HCII 2019. LNCS, vol. 11575, pp. 150–162. Springer, Cham (2019). https://doi.org/10.1007/978-3-030-21565-1_10
18. Watson, D., Clark, L.A., Tellegen, A.: Development and validation of brief measures of positive and negative affect: the PANAS scales. J. Pers. Soc. Psychol. **54**(6), 1063 (1988)

Serious Games

A Cooperative Storytelling Card Game for Conflict Resolution and Empathy

Byung-Chull Bae[✉] and Hyun-Jee Kim

School of Games, Hongik University, 2639 Sejong-ro, Sejong, South Korea
{byuc,luluhyunjee}@hongik.ac.kr

Abstract. In this paper we present a prototype for a cooperative story-telling card game focusing on the resolution of conflict and empathy in a narrative. The story-making process in the proposed prototype design is based on Maslow's hierarchy of needs, and consists of five types of story cards(characters, setting, objects/actions, goals, and emotions) as its story elements. We have developed and tested a prototype game using Unity3D game engine on an Android platform with two play modes - single-player and multi-player. In the multi-player mode, three players can play together: each player is assigned the role of an initiator, a conflictor and a mediator in wireless network environments. Our ultimate goal is to encourage players to empathize with other players by letting them create and resolve (or mediate) emotional conflicts through the process of perspective-taking in a collaborative storytelling game.

Keywords: Storytelling card game · Conflict resolution · Empathy

1 Introduction

Storytelling has many beneficial effects on learning and training. While reading novels or watching movies, the reader can see the story world through the eyes of the characters in the narrative rather than his or her own perspectives. With this narrative experience, the reader can feel various narrative emotions including character identification or narrative empathy [16,24]. Keen, in particular, defines narrative empathy as "the sharing of feeling and perspective-taking induced by reading, viewing, hearing, or imagining narratives of another's situation and condition" [16].

Emotion is also crucial to game design, which is often associated with the notion of fun [20] and the Flow-like immersion [13]. Aarseth [6] suggests four dimensions - world (linear or open), objects (dynamic, user-created, or static), agents (flat or round), and events (open, selected, or plotted)- as common aspects between game design and narrative design. Inspired by Aarseth's theory, Sullivan and Salter [32] analyzed a dozen of analog storytelling board and card games, claiming two dimensions - ordering (dynamic vs. static) and events (game-specified vs. player-centered) - for the taxonomy of narrative-centric games.

© Springer Nature Switzerland AG 2020
X. Fang (Ed.): HCII 2020, LNCS 12211, pp. 375–384, 2020.
https://doi.org/10.1007/978-3-030-50164-8_27

In narrative theories, narrative is often described as having either two layers (story and discourse) [10,15] or three layers (fabula, syuzhet, and text/media) [17]. In the two-layer model, story refers to the content of narrative, while discourse denotes a representation of the story. In the three-layer model, fabula incorporates story events in chronological order; syuzhet rearranges the ordering and selection of the events in fabula; text/media denotes how to represent the fabula through a specific medium. Nowadays, narrative is represented across various media - from text and films to digital media such as hypertext and virtual environments [23,28].

In general, interactive storytelling refers to nonlinear storytelling, where the reader (or the player) can influence the story unfolding with a sense of agency to some degree [9,12]. Research on computer-based story generation and interactive storytelling has been extensively conducted based on AI techniques such as planning [26] and machine learning [19,21]. Recently, interactive storytelling is also applied in the form of interactive digital narrative video in Netflix, a commercial video streaming platform [27].

Empathy, according to studies on emotion, can be divided into two types: emotional empathy and cognitive empathy [31]. Emotional empathy refers to feeling the same emotions of another person by mirroring or reflecting his or her emotions into one's mind, while cognitive empathy refers to understanding someone else's emotions or feelings by putting oneself into his or her shoes. In a different vein, the OCC emotion model [25] defines two types of empathy-relating emotions: (1) happy-for in "feeling pleased when a desirable event occurs to someone else"; (2) sorry-for in "feeling displeased when an undesirable event occurs to someone else". While the OCC emotion model does not provide emotion-specific parameters in detail, numerous studies have been conducted based on this model. In narrative, empathic narrative techniques can include "character identification" (e.g., naming, indirect implication of traits, change of character personality during the story progression, etc.) and "narrative situation" via perspectives [16].

In this study, we present a prototype for a storytelling card game, focusing on conflict resolution and empathy. We particularly employ simple image cards representing narrative elements such as characters, objects, actions, settings (locations and time), goals, and emotions. Our ultimate goal is to build an emotional storytelling system that is particularly designed for perspective-taking and empathy in narrative.

2   Background

Diverse attempts have been made to embrace narrative or storytelling in games. Particularly, story making with other players can be a fun activity in itself as well as serve educational purposes. Several collaborative storytelling board games such as Dixit (Libellud, 2008) [4] and Once Upon A Time (Atlas Games, 1994) [2] have been very popular for a long time, with continuous updates. Rory's Story Cubes (The Creativity Hub Ltd., 2005) [3], a dice-based storytelling game using pictogram, is designed particularly for children to foster their creativity. Motivated by Rory's Story Cube, Bae and his colleagues [8] had players design their own story cubes for a procedural story generation.

In digital games, Reigns by Devolver Digital [5] employs a card-style storytelling game play, in which a player can select either 'yes' or 'no' option to rule a country as king. Eladhari and her colleagues, inspired by previous works such as Once upon a time [2] and Rory's Story Cube [3], designed a collaborative story-making prototype game called '4Scribes' and conducted an ad-hoc playtest [14]. In 4Scribes, players cooperate in story-making, using three types of cards or 'narrative tokens' (scene cards for representing emotions or events, character cards, and myth cards for symbolizing "dramatic story changing events"), while at the same time, competing with one another to win the game by inducing a secret ending that each player has in mind.

Conflict and its (proper) resolution is a key element both in narratology and in ludology for the creation of tension or suspense in stories and games. Designed as a rather serious game, dealing with the issue of bullying in elementary schools, Fearnot! [7] focused on evoking a player's empathy towards the victims. Village Voices [11] is another collaboratively-playing video game, concentrating on possible conflict and its resolution: this game targeted young children age 9–12. "Tappetinna's Empathy Game", a relatively recent storytelling project, also aims to promote a player's empathy by playing a collaborative storytelling game [29,30].

In this paper we utilize the concept of *Charactergram*, a "new illustrative and representational method which suggests certain messages without text, and it creates various interpretations with rearrangement by audiences" [18]. In charactergram, *character* symbolizes "the model of a person, an animal, or an object"; *gram* stands for "the message, and communications as Telegram and Pictogram" [18]. We utilize the feature of charactergram, where basic elements (such as time, space, characters, events, and objects) are rearranged for the design of a storytelling card game.

3   Design

As mentioned in the previous section, there are several good references for storytelling card games, such as 'Dixit' and 'Once upon a time'. Most of those storytelling card games include some structural features containing conflicting situations among players, such that the players can continue to tell a story together. In this study, we employ the concept of *charactergram* as a pictorial language medium for communicating with the players. While pictograms convey direct meaning of straightforward messages rapidly to all ages, charactergram itself can convey a certain story element or emotions intended by its designers. Unlike pictogram, charactergram can be arranged in both linear and non-linear structures by the players [18]. Then, the players can control the entire storyline and conclusions. In our card game design, we develop a method of visualization with charactergram, having multiple players communicate interactively to create various patterns of story structures. We also adopt the concept of Maslow's hierarchy [22] of needs in order to help players set up a story goal and to create possible conflicts occurring from different needs or goals.

3.1 Overall Play Design

Our prototype storytelling card game requires three players and includes five different types of charactergram cards - characters, setting (time and location), goals, objects/actions, and emotions. The three players are assigned to play distinct roles as follows:

- Player 1: The role of the first player is '*initiator*' who creates a (possibly) coherent simple story to achieve a character's goal. The first player can choose a character (i.e., protagonist) and his or her goal from the given set of goal cards. The player then chooses additional charactergram cards to elaborate the story including time, location, and a sequence of actions for the protagonist to achieve the chosen goal.
- Player 2: The role of the second player is '*conflictor*' who adds possible conflict that is intertwined with the story created by the first player. Like the first player, the second player can select a character (i.e. antagonist or villain) and his or her goal to create an adversary plan to obstruct or stop the protagonist's plan of the first player.
- Player 3: The role of the second player is '*mediator*' or '*resolver*' who concludes the story by mediating or resolving the conflict created by the second player. The mediation or resolution of the conflict hereby can include various endings regardless of the protagonist's achievement/failure in the conflicted situation. The third player may come up with a novel solution which can resolve the conflict without harming the goal achievement of both the protagonist and the antagonist.

Figure 1 illustrates overall play design of the proposed storytelling card game with three players.

3.2 Five Types of Storytelling Cards

The prototype storytelling cards contain five different types - characters, setting, objects/actions, goals, and emotions. The character card (e.g., human figure, animal) works as an avatar of the player. The setting card shows a specific time in a day, season, or era. The setting card can also include a specific location using national flags or iconic scenes. The goal card symbolizes each need or goal specified in Maslow's hierarchy of needs [22]. Events could be represented as actions performed by the characters or happenings occurred by accident (or by nature), which is represented by the action/object card. Finally, the emotion card includes various emotion types from basic emotions (e.g., joy, sadness, anger, fear) to complicated emotions (e.g., love, shame, etc.). Here are the five types of story cards in our prototype game:

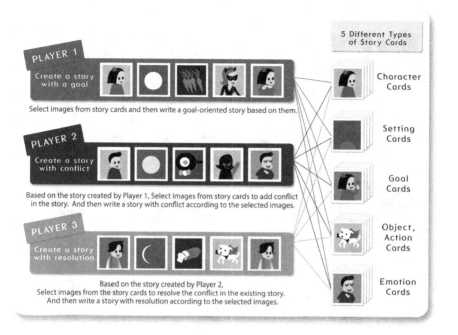

Fig. 1. Overall play design of the proposed storytelling card game using chractergram. Player 1 creates a basic story with a character's goal; Player 2 modifies the story by adding a conflict in it; Player 3 finalizes the game by presenting a resolution to the conflict.

1. **Character cards** symbolize gender (e.g., male, female, not specified), age (e.g., child, adolescent, adult, senior), personality (e.g., extrovert vs introvert), and social status (e.g., teacher, doctor, artist, musician, judge, priest).
2. **Setting cards** stand for time and location for story background: e.g., specific time in a day such as morning, afternoon, night; a season - spring, summer, winter, and fall; a span of period; an era from Jurassic to modern, place, physical space using national flags or iconic scenes.
3. **Goal cards** present epitomized, categorized human needs based on Maslow's hierarchy of needs [22] - physiological (food, water, rest), safety (health), intimate relationships (e.g., friendship, family, love), esteem (respect), and self-actualization (e.g., creative activities).
4. **Action/object cards**, at current stage, only include superpower-related theme: e.g., teleportation, time travel, psychokinesis, super strength, medusa, underdog, Darth Vader.
5. **Emotion cards** illustrate six basic emotions (joy, sadness, anger, fear, surprise, disgust), additional emotions (respectful, shameful, guilty, spiritless, etc.) and other complex emotions (ironic smile, love and hatred at the same time, etc.).

Figure 2 shows selected samples from the five types of storytelling cards.

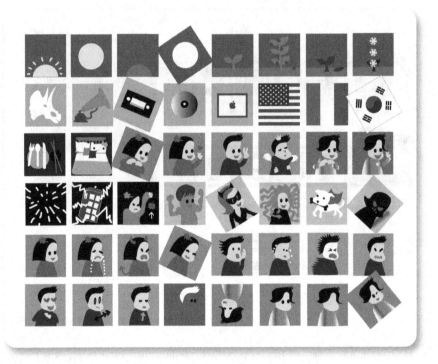

Fig. 2. Selected samples of charactergram cards (the first and second rows: setting (time & location); the third row: goals based on Maslow's hierarchy of needs; the fourth row: actions (with superpower-related theme); the fifth and sixth row: emotions (from basic to complicated)

3.3   Rules

Several simple rules for the storytelling card game are presented below:

- Rule 1: The player can describe a story based on a keyword which is related to each image in the story card.
- Rule 2: The player can state, at most, three sentences with one story card; also, multiple story cards can be used to address just one sentence.
- Rule 3: The game can be played either in a single-player mode or in a three-player mode. In the three-player mode, a player's story coherence is judged by the other two players. The other two players can choose 'accept' if they think the created story makes sense: otherwise they can choose 'reject'. If a created story is rejected at least by one player, then the story writer can roll a dice that has two options - 'retry' or 'pass'. If the 'retry' side comes out, the story writer needs to rewrite his or her story. If the dice shows a 'pass' side, the game continues without rewriting, despite an objection from one of the players.

It is noted that Rule 3 is necessary in case a player writes a story in a more or less careless manner. This rule can also prevent possible situations where two other players collaborate to intentionally disagree with the other player's story.

Fig. 3. Prototype storytelling game using charactergram cards

4 Implementation

4.1 Prototype Development

We are currently implementing and testing a prototype using Unity3D game engine on an Android platform (Oreo 8.0). And for the hardware platform, we are testing on Samsung Galaxy tablet S3 (4 GB RAM, 32 GB Memory). Our prototype includes the following features:

- **Mode of play:** The prototype currently features two modes of play: single-player and multi-player. In a single-player mode, a player can freely create a story using the charactergram cards. In a multi-player mode, three players can collaborate on a thee-stage storyline: i) a goal-oriented initiating story; ii) a story with conflict against the presented goal; iii) a story proposing a resolution of the conflict.
- **Voice-to-text:** After selecting a set of five charactergram cards, the player can write a created story either by typing in or by using the voice-to-text (Google Voice) feature supported in Android OS.

– **Networking:** For developing a multi-player game, we are currently using Photon Unity networking framework plugin [1]. While it is free and easy to use, it also has some disadvantages from the absence of a server for the management of saved text/image data.

4.2   Discussion

While testing the initial version of our digital prototype (see Fig. 3), we found several issues.

First, the Initiator (Player 1) needs to come up with a goal-oriented story using the given charactergram cards. While some players may create stories with ease, it is not so easy to build a complete goal-oriented story from scratch. Thus, a set of charactergram cards need to be intentionally designed to help the first player conceive a goal-oriented story.

Second, similar to the Initiator, the Conflictor (Player 2) and the Mediator (Player 3) need to provide a (creative and coherent) story, either with conflict or with resolution, respectively. Our initial test showed that the second player's role (i.e., creating a conflict followed by the first player's story) is the hardest. We presume that it is mainly because there are no conflict cards with explicit explanations that can assist Player 2. In the next version, we plan to design conflict in action/object cards to be added to the game.

Through the proposed game, we expect that the players can solve given missions (that is, creating a goal-oriented story in a coherent manner: weaving a possible conflict into a story: resolving the conflict in the story) by coming up with some interesting and novel ideas. This three-stage process may even reflect our real world, in that we (i.e., characters or agents in the story world) often face unexpected conflicts with others, and there could exist a mediator who can solve the conflicts in a wise manner. By exchanging the roles, the players may have a chance to ponder on other players' different situations, goals, and emotions through a change of perspectives. We believe that it can be a small step to understanding and enhancing perspective-taking or empathy by taking turns and having different roles in story-making.

5   Conclusion

In this paper we presented our prototype design for a storytelling card game with five different types of story cards - characters, setting (time and place), objects/actions, goals, and emotions - using the notion of charactergram. The proposed storytelling game can be either crafted with pen and paper or implemented as a digital storytelling game. This paper is focused on a digital storytelling game on a mobile platform.

One of our ultimate goals is to gather data on how we handle any conflicting situations and resolve such conflicts with the given charactergram cards or constraints. As further work, we will consider two issues - i) designing charactergram cards associated with conflict; ii) conducting a user-study to collect story data on conflicts and their resolutions.

Acknowledgement. This work was supported by Institute for Information & communications Technology Promotion (IITP) grant funded by the Korea government (MSIT) (No.2017-0-01772, Development of QA systems for Video Story Understanding to pass the Video Turing Test) and Basic Science Research Program through the National Research Foundation of Korea (NRF) funded by the Ministry of Science and ICT (2017R1A2B4010499). This work was in part supported by 2019 Hongik University Research Fund.

References

1. Pun (photon unity networking). https://www.photonengine.com/en/pun. Accessed 31 Jan 2020
2. Once upon a time (1994). https://www.atlas-games.com/onceuponatime/
3. Rory's story cube (2005). https://www.storycubes.com
4. Dixit (2008). https://www.libellud.com/dixit
5. Reigns (2016). https://www.devolverdigital.com/games/reigns
6. Aarseth, E.: A narrative theory of games. In: Proceedings of the International Conference on the Foundations of Digital Games, FDG 2012, pp. 129–133. ACM, New York (2012). https://doi.org/10.1145/2282338.2282365
7. Aylett, R.S., Louchart, S., Dias, J., Paiva, A., Vala, M.: Fearnot! - an experiment in emergent narrative. In: Panayiotopoulos, T., Gratch, J., Aylett, R., Ballin, D., Olivier, P., Rist, T. (eds.) IVA 2005. LNCS, vol. 3661, pp. 305–316. Springer, Heidelberg (2005). https://doi.org/10.1007/11550617_26
8. Bae, B.C., Seo, G., Cheong, Y.G.: Towards procedural game story creation via designing story cubes. In: Nack, F., Gordon, A.S. (eds.) ICIDS 2016. LNCS, vol. 10045, pp. 399–402. Springer, Cham (2016). https://doi.org/10.1007/978-3-319-48279-8_35
9. Cavazza, M., Young, R.M.: Introduction to interactive storytelling. In: Nakatsu, R., Rauterberg, M., Ciancarini, P. (eds.) Handbook of Digital Games and Entertainment Technologies, pp. 1–16. Springer, Singapore (2016). https://doi.org/10.1007/978-981-4560-52-8_55-1
10. Chatman, S.: Story and Discourse: Narrative Structure in Fiction and Film. Cornell University Press, Cornell Paperbacks (1978)
11. Cheong, Y.G., Khaled, R., Holmgård, C., Yannakakis, G.N.: Serious games for teaching conflict resolution: modeling conflict dynamics. In: D'Errico, F., Poggi, I., Vinciarelli, A., Vincze, L. (eds.) Conflict and Multimodal Communication. Computational Social Sciences, pp. 449–475. Springer, Cham (2015). https://doi.org/10.1007/978-3-319-14081-0_21
12. Crawford, C.: Chris Crawford on Interactive Storytelling. Pearson Education, London (2012)
13. Csikszentmihalyi, M., Abuhamdeh, S., Nakamura, J.: Flow. In: Michalos, A.C. (ed.) Encyclopedia of Quality of Life and Well-Being Research, pp. 227–238. Springer, Dordrecht (2014). https://doi.org/10.1007/978-94-007-0753-5
14. Eladhari, M.P., Lopes, P.L., Yannakakis, G.N.: Interweaving story coherence and player creativity through story-making games. In: Mitchell, A., Fernández-Vara, C., Thue, D. (eds.) ICIDS 2014. LNCS, pp. 73–80. Springer, Heidelberg (2014). https://doi.org/10.1007/978-3-319-12337-0_7
15. Genette, G.: Narrative Discourse: An Essay in Method. Cornell University Press, Cornell Paperbacks (1980)

16. Keen, S.: Narrative empathy. In: Hühn, P., et al. (eds.) The Living Handbook of Narratology. Hamburg University, Hamburg (2013). Accessed 31 Jan 2020

17. Kenan, R.S.: Narrative Fiction: Contemporary Poetics. Routledge, London (1983)

18. Kim, H.J.: Development on visualization as storytelling: focusing on character-gram. In: Proceedings of the International Association of Societies of Design Research 2009, IASDL 2009, pp. 3451–3461. Korean Society of Design Science, Korea (2009)

19. Kybartas, B., Bidarra, R.: A survey on story generation techniques for authoring computational narratives. IEEE Trans. Comput. Intell. AI Games 9(3), 239–253 (2017). https://doi.org/10.1109/TCIAIG.2016.2546063

20. Lazzaro, N.: Why we play games: four keys to more emotion without story. In: Game Developers Conference, March 2004

21. Martin, L.J., et al.: Event representations for automated story generation with deep neural nets. In: Proceedings of the Thirty-Second AAAI Conference on Artificial Intelligence, New Orleans, Louisiana, USA, 2–7 February 2018 (2018). https://www.aaai.org/ocs/index.php/AAAI/AAAI18/paper/view/17046

22. Maslow, A.: A theory of human motivation. Psychol. Rev. 9(50), 370–396 (1980)

23. Miller, C.: Digital Storytelling: A Creator's Guide to Interactive Entertainment. CRC Press, Boca Raton (2014)

24. Oatley, K.: A taxonomy of the emotions of literary response and a theory of iden-tification in fictional narrative. Poetics 23(1–2), 53–74 (1995). https://doi.org/10.1016/0304-422X(94)P4296-S

25. Ortony, A., Clore, G., Collins, A.: The Cognitive Structure of Emotions. Cambridge University Press, Cambridge (1990)

26. Riedl, M.O., Young, R.M.: Narrative planning: balancing plot and character. J. Artif. Intell. Res. 39(1), 217–268 (2010)

27. Roth, C., Koenitz, H.: Bandersnatch, yea or nay? Reception and user experience of an interactive digital narrative video, August 2019. https://doi.org/10.1145/3317697.3325124

28. Ryan, M., Thon, J.: Storyworlds Across Media: Toward a Media-Conscious Narra-tology. Book collections on Project MUSE, UNP - Nebraska Paperback (2014)

29. Skaraas, S.B., Gomez, J., Jaccheri, L.: Playing with empathy through a collabo-rative storytelling game. In: Clua, E., Roque, L., Lugmayr, A., Tuomi, P. (eds.) ICEC 2018. LNCS, vol. 11112, pp. 254–259. Springer, Cham (2018). https://doi.org/10.1007/978-3-319-99426-0_26

30. Skaraas, S.B., Gomez, J., Jaccheri, L.: Tappetina's empathy game: a playground of storytelling and emotional understanding. In: Proceedings of the 17th ACM Con-ference on Interaction Design and Children, IDC 2018, pp. 509–512. Association for Computing Machinery, New York (2018). https://doi.org/10.1145/3202185.3210765

31. Smith, A.: Cognitive empathy and emotional empathy in human behavior and evolution. Psychol. Rec. 56(1), 3–21 (2006). https://doi.org/10.1007/BF03395534

32. Sullivan, A., Salter, A.: A taxonomy of narrative-centric board and card games. In: Proceedings of the 12th International Conference on the Foundations of Digital Games, FDG 2017, pp. 23:1–23:10. ACM, New York (2017)

A Self-adaptive Serious Game for Eye-Hand Coordination Training

Leonardo Cardia da Cruz[1,2](✉) , César A. Sierra-Franco[2] ,
Greis Francy M. Silva-Calpa[2] , and Alberto Barbosa Raposo[1,2]

[1] Department of Informatics, Pontifical Catholic University of Rio de Janeiro
(PUC-Rio), Gávea, Rio de Janeiro 22451-900, Brazil
[2] Tecgraf Institute, Pontifical Catholic University of Rio de Janeiro (PUC-Rio),
Gávea, Rio de Janeiro 22451-900, Brazil
{lccruz,casfranco,greis,abraposo}@tecgraf.puc-rio.br

Abstract. In this study, we propose a self-adaptive game aiming auxiliary in eye-hand coordination and short-term training. The game requires a player to pop specific balloons appearing in a screen aiming to prevent that they fly. The game uses the Dynamic Difficulty Adjustment (DDA) technique for verifying reaction time, pragmatic six-step plan for implementing adaptive difficulty proposed, and a Leap Motion controller as an input device. The adaptive difficulty of the game is implemented through Q-Learning, a Reinforcement Learning algorithm. We conducted experimental tests with ten participants (ages between 16 and 23 years). We evaluated the game's learning effect by comparing velocity by episodes and accumulated reward by episodes for each player. We also evaluated the user experience using the System Usability Scale (SUS). Experimental results suggest that players accumulated positive rewards according to the velocity of the game adjusted to the profile of the user, taking it to a level of adequate and challenging difficulty at the same time. The SUS score per player shows that the game adapted dynamically difficulty being satisfactory. The study shows that the game implemented can contribute to eye-hand coordination training positively.

Keywords: Serious game · Adaptive · Eye-hand coordination training · Reinforcement learning · Dynamic Difficulty Adjustment · Usability

1 Introduction

Hand-eye coordination is one of the essential steps of the human learning process. It consists of the ability to coordinate and track hand movements with the eyes, which is essential to reading and writing skills. The performance of various activities requires careful eyes for the brain to know the accuracy of space, along with the use of hands for visual capture. Some examples of hand-eye coordination include writing, driving a car, playing sports, locking and unlocking a door, and so on.

© Springer Nature Switzerland AG 2020
X. Fang (Ed.): HCII 2020, LNCS 12211, pp. 385–397, 2020.
https://doi.org/10.1007/978-3-030-50164-8_28

However, some individuals (children, adults, and older people) have difficulties with hand-eye coordination, showing problems in performing specific tasks. There are clinical exercises for stimulating cognitive action as a treatment stage to improve people's hand-eye coordination. Among these, in the *Grooved Pegboard Test (PegB)*, a patient should insert 25 cylindrical pins as quickly as possible into each of the 25 holes of a plate, one at a time. The time to complete the task is twice each hand. The *stick capture test (StickC)* is another clinical exercise where the reaction time is checked [5].

With the advancement of technology, traditional clinical exercises can be improved so that their use does not become something monotonous for the participant; instead, the user feels engaged in carrying out the tasks, such as serious games [3,13]. Serious games can be classified as a playful interactive tool capable of addressing different thematic areas and concepts through its resources, becoming a facilitator in the teaching process [14]. Studies on eye-hand coordination are explored through gamification in serious games, where the exercise environment can adapt to players, depending on their age group and the intensity of the problem.

Serious games can help to develop motor coordination, attention, memorization, among other physical and cognitive skills. Their intrinsic characteristics, such as rewards, assets, sounds, goals, and achievements, allow players to engage and stimulate their senses. However, to create a serious game that meets players' skills is a big challenge, as each user has a different skill level [7]. Offering a challenging game can cause players to be frustrated and disinterested. By contrast, leaving a more accessible level can bore and displease others [6]. One way to solve the difficulty adjustment problem in a game is to employ the Dynamic Difficulty Adjustment (DDA) technique. It consists of making modifications to parameters, scenarios, and game behaviors in real-time to avoid the player's frustration when facing the game challenges [2].

Studies have shown that employing the DDA approach in games generates a high level of overconfidence in the player [7]. Therefore, using it for visual-haptic attention training, for example, ensures comfortable training with significant improvements for training participants [17]. In [18], the authors analyzed executive function skills training with both adaptive and non-adaptive methods, obtaining that DDA was more effective than the non-adaptive method.

In this study, we propose an adaptive serious game using the DDA technique. The adaptive difficulty of the game is implemented through a Reinforcement Learning algorithm. Our game is based on Stick Catching test [5], which consists of verifying the reaction time of players during the task of collecting the corresponding color balloons to prevent that they fly. Players use a Leap Motion controller for interaction with the game. We evaluate the game's adaptivity by comparing velocity by episodes and accumulated rewards for each player. We also conducted experimental tests involving ten participants for usability evaluation.

The rest of this paper is organized as follows. In Sect. 2, we present the related work. In Sect. 3, we detail the proposed solution, which includes a description of the DDA technique, the steps followed for implementing adaptive difficulty, and the Leap Motion Controller. The evaluation and results are described in Sect. 4. Finally, in Sect. 5, we present the conclusions of this study.

2   Related Work

We found in the literature several studies using serious games, such as a tool to assist in therapeutic processes that involve coordination as well as works that include DDA techniques.

Stavros et al. [20] present a study on how to design serious games for individuals with intellectual disabilities (ID) from existing design frameworks. The authors structure a survey into two categories. In the first category, they presented the structure of serious games, suggesting the essential elements and principles for their construction. The second category presents design guidelines for serious games intended for people with ID. The authors conducted a survey identifying the elements needed to create an SG for people with ID. The authors conclude that no design framework includes all design guidelines from the literature for implementing an SG for DI. Still, it is possible to make some changes in the construction of such games. Although our work is not focused on designing SG for people with DI, we have adopted two features presented in that study: Graphical Interface and Game Difficulty, which use machine learning techniques to create a Game with a self-adaptive difficulty adjustment.

The study by Hendrix et al. [10] shows how games can dynamically adapt according to the player's ability. The authors propose a six-step method for implementing a game with adaptive difficulty. They evaluated that method with users through experimentation in two games. The results show that the pragmatic six-step plan presents a relatively good and straightforward set of steps that a game developer can follow regardless of the genre and style of the game as well as the tool used. In our work, we use the pragmatic six-step plan for implementing adaptive difficulty showing from the above authors.

Hidalgo et al. [11] propose a serious game to support therapy for children with motor difficulties. The game consists of associating different figures-colors of their environment, and with each new level of play, the difficulty is increased so that the child works yet more his hand-eye concentration. The game uses a Leap motion controller as an input device. The accompanying therapist adjusts the difficulty level of the game. The authors evaluated their work with 20 participants. They evidenced that the game was surprising among some children. They were able to adapt quickly within the space and depth of the virtual game.

The study by Lin et al. [13] present a serious game to encourage physical and cognitive functions in the elderly. The serious game consists of a rhythm game where each phase works some cognitive ability such as response speed, short term memory, or working memory. User interaction with the game is via a motion sensor controller. This device is like a set with some buttons scattered around it, and when the user wears them, these buttons line upon his body. To interact, one need to press these buttons that also estimate acupuncture points. Therefore, the player must observe in the game interface, the position and the colors of the notes and then press the buttons of the corresponding motion sensor controller. During gameplay, player data collected for analysis of cognitive skills. To validate the game, the authors conducted experiments with older individuals (age between 63–93 years) that presented a viable game with improvement points.

Regarding studies that use DDA techniques, Zohaib [21] reports that in the last decade (2009–2018), several research studies have been carried out on DDA, both to develop new methods, improve methods, and to apply them in several areas. There are several approaches to working with DDA, being the reinforcement learning one of them. For digital games the creation of an adaptive game allows a more exceptional experience for each style of player. As there are players with different profiles, static challenges sometimes do not take into account the player's reality. Some work shows that using reinforcement learning with the DDA technique, players feel comfortable in a balanced environment, as parameter adjustments are made in real-time in response to their skills. In addition, studies are presented that create adaptive algorithms using concepts of evolutionary computing and reinforcement learning. We use the DDA technique in the implementation of the game presented in the present work. Details can be seen in the section below.

3   Proposed Solution

Our method consists of the combination of three different elements: the Dynamic Difficulty Adjustment method to create a game where the difficulty levels are adjusted according to the player's skills; pragmatic six-step plan to implement adaptive difficulty and the Leap Motion controller as interaction device with the game interface.

3.1   Dynamic Difficulty Adjustment (DDA)

Dynamic Difficulty Adjustment (DDA) allows adjusting the entire scenario of the game, including design, gameplay, features, components, behaviors, and the different elements that compose the game. This adjustment is made at runtime according to the performance of each player. The modeling of the scenario must take place in real-time according to the player's abilities so that it presents a challenging difficulty to the point of not frustrating him, and which do not be so easy as to disappoint him. We use the DDA technique in the game, aiming to keep the players engaged in a task with an appropriate level of difficulty according to their performance. We follow the recommendations by Andrade and colleagues [1] to apply the DDA technique in our game. The authors [1] suggest that DDA must comply with three basic needs, as follows:

- The game needs to automatically track the player's ability and rapidly adapt to it.
- The game must follow the player's improving or falling level and maintain a balance according to the player's skill.

– The players must not perceive the process of adaptation, and successive game states need to have coherence with the earlier ones.

Csikszentmihaly [15] proposes the flow channel for creating the DDA (Fig. 3). This model indicates how the difficulty level of a task directly implicates the player's perception. The flow channel prevents frustration under challenging tasks and boredom under simple ones (Fig. 1).

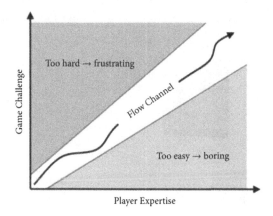

Fig. 1. Flow channel model. Source: Image from [21]

We adopted the above flow channel to create an adaptive game that is not difficult to the point of being frustrating and not easy to the point of being boring.

3.2 Pragmatic Six Step Plan for Implementing Adaptive Difficulty

The primary key for a game to be adaptable is through user performance. We use the method proposed by Hendrix et al. [10] for creating an adaptive game. It consists of the following six steps:

1. Identify variables in the game that are good indicators of the player's performance.
2. Determine variables that influence the difficulty of the game, and that can be changed.
3. If an implementation of the game exists, locate the performance and difficulty indicating variables.
4. Consider whether the game features multiple mechanics and if so, to which mechanic do performance and difficulty variables relate.
5. Decide how the performance variables will be used to calculate difficulty.
6. Decide upon sensible starting values for the identified variables, impacting the difficulty balancing.

3.3 Leap Motion Controller

In this work we use the Leap Motion Controller[1]as the user interaction device. Leap Motion is a device that connects to a computer and allows one to track gestures with hands and thus interact with virtual objects intuitively and naturally. It consists of two cameras and three infrared LEDs, forming an area of interaction, as shows Fig. 2. It has been used in several fields, such as virtual simulations, learning environments, rehabilitation, entertainment, among others. This device allows creating a more natural and intuitive interaction, contributing, thus, to motor coordination required in the eye-hand coordination training.

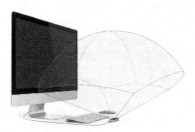

Fig. 2. Leap Motion interaction area. Source: Image from [9]

To fit our game, we used the leap motion interaction area divided into two zones, one for the player to navigate using the hands through the environment and thus position the hands on the objective and one other that detects the user's interaction with the game objects.

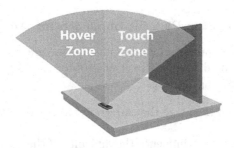

Fig. 3. Interaction space is split into two zones. Source: Image from [16]

---

[1] https://www.leapmotion.com/.

3.4 Implementation

In this section, we present the proposed game implementation process, including the game design principles, the adaptive difficulty process, and the reinforcement learning algorithm implementation for the self-adaptive game difficulty functionality.

Proposed Game. Using the Unity 3D engine[2], we construct our proposed game in two dimensions (2D). The goal of the game is popping balloons the same color that appears in the indicative panel, as shows Fig. 4.

Fig. 4. Game Interface with points and hands for the interaction of balloon (Color figure online)

The colors used are the basics of the RGB (Red, Green, Blue) additive color system. The difficulty level of the game is given by speed the balloons to rise, forcing the player to memorize the color and pop the balloons quickly. The users use a leap motion controller as the input device.

Implementation of the DDA Technique. We mapped our game by following the six implementation steps suggested by Hendrix et al. [10] to make it adaptive game difficulty.

Initially, We identified the following: *number of the score, number of losses,* and *total of balloons* as variables in the game that are good indicators of player performance.

As second step, we identify variables that influence the difficulty of the game, and that can be changed: *speed of balloons* and *Quantities of balloons.*

In the third step, we identify the variables *score, loss, performancePlayer and balloon.velocity* in the script denoted AgentScript.

In the fourth step, we define the game design by including a single mechanic.

---

[2] https://unity.com/.

In the fifth step, we used the reinforcement learning (RL) technique for that rewards are obtained according to the performance variable [19] explains, RL is a technique that allows learning what should be done, mapping situations to actions, aiming to maximize rewards obtained by actions. The agent does not know which steps to take, so he must find out the steps that bring the most rewards.

Finally, in the sixth step, we chose to empirically the starting variables. The default values can be adjusted if required.

Reinforcement Learning Approach to Include Game Self-adaptive Functionalities. We implemented the adaptive difficulty of the game through Q-Learning, a Reinforcement Learning algorithm. Q-Learning is an off-policy temporal difference algorithm that focuses on state-action values. The action value in each state is obtained using a table that is updated in each interaction with the environment, denoted Q-values, as shown in the Eq. (1).

$$Q(s,a) = Q(s,a) + \alpha[r + \gamma.maxQ(s',a') - Q(s,a)], \tag{1}$$

where s is the current state and a is an action taken in this state. When each action a is taken, a new s' state is selected, and a reward issued for that pair of (s, a). For the new selected state, a new action a' is taken, chosen randomly using a predefined probability (a method called Epsilon-Greedy Policy). α is the learning rate, r is the reward for an action taken in a given state and γ and the factor of discount. We are working with the velocity v of the balloon as a parameter for game difficulty. Therefore, the states are the respective velocities that the balloon can assume:

$$S_{velocity} = \{v_1, v_2, v_3, v_4, v_5, v_6, v_7, v_8, v_9, v_{10}\} \tag{2}$$

The three possible actions that change the game's difficulty are increasing, decreasing, and keep up speed.

$$A = \{v_{+1}, v_{-1}, v_=\} \tag{3}$$

We chose to implement our RL algorithm, using the ML-Agents toolkit as a facilitator for game design and communication with the algorithm through the Python API (Fig. 5).

An agent observes the environment so that he can make a better decision. Our agent is the entire game environment, including heads-up display (HUD), balloons, and color panel.

The brain is linked to one or several agents. He receives remarks and rewards from the agent and returns an action. Our brain is connected to the game environment. It has a vector of observation with space size two, allowing the observation of the current balloon speed as well as the player's performance. It also has a vector with the branches size of two, so that the agent receives two possible actions, balloon velocity increase and decrease.

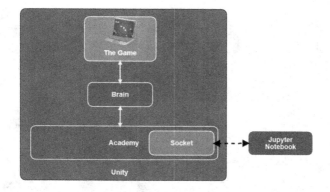

Fig. 5. Block diagram of ML-Agents toolkit adapted for our work.

For communication between the Python API part and Unity, it is necessary to use the academy, which will orchestrate all of the Agent and Brain objects in a Unity scene, including observations, decisions, rendering quality, and other features. This communication is accomplished through external communicator (feature called broadcasting).

4   Evaluation and Results

We evaluated the adaptive of the game through experiments involving ten participants (ages between 16 and 23 years). These users are all-male, whose selection was carried out at random. Each participant performs a ten-minute experiment to assess the perception of the use of the proposed game and whether the environment is adjusted according to their capacity. For each participant, the game was adapted according to their ability, presenting a difficulty that was challenging and achievable. The tests sessions were conducted using a notebook of 1 TB HD, 8 GB of RAM, processor of 2.70 GHz intel core i5 and Intel HD Graphics 620. Each test session consisted of one participant interacting with the game through Leap Motion (Fig. 6). The test for each participant lasted between 10 min. Before the tests, we introduce participants to the use of the device and provide them the game instructions.

During each test, information was collected from each player's virtual environment, such as rewards earned and balloon speed. We use the SUS (System Usability Scale) questionnaire [4] model to check the usability of the game. It consists of the following 10 item questionnaire that each participant answered after the test:

1. Frequency of using the game.
2. Complexity in interacting with the environment.
3. Facility of use.
4. Constant support from someone to instruct in the use.
5. Well-integrated interaction device;

Fig. 6. Example of participants playing the proposed game.

6. Inconsistency in the game.
7. Quick learning ability.
8. Complicated to use the interaction device.
9. Confidence when playing.
10. Need to learn several things before playing.

The SUS questionnaire uses the Likert scale [12] to verify the level of agreement in each statement. The scale used in this model is five levels: 5 (strongly agree), 4 (agree), 3 (neutral), 2 (disagree), and 1 (strongly disagree). Obtain the global SUS value, which ranges from 0 to 100, is necessary to calculate the questionnaire score. Thus, odd questions (1, 3, 5, 7, and 9) subtract one less from the value marked on the scale. In the even questions (2, 4, 6, 8, and 10), subtract by five. After calculating the value of each question, it is necessary to sum all the values and multiply by 2.5 to obtain the overall result. As stated by *Cunha* [8], scores below 60 represent dissatisfaction to the user, while above 80 have a high level of satisfaction.

The results are described according to both the adaptivity of the game and the user experience playing the game.

According to the adaptivity of the game, Fig. 7 (top) shows the velocity by episode for the players 1 and 6. Figure 7 (bottom) shows the cumulative reward for each player indicating the performance of reinforcement learning algorithm. We selected two players (1 and 6) to show the learning environment at two different times. For player 1, it maintains a lower speed, while player 6 at a faster velocity. We can see that the game learn to adjust the velocity that allows the player to accumulate increasing positive rewards, according to its performance in that particular difficulty.

Considering an average of SUS of 68 scores, our system presented an average of 74 scores, which results in a usable and satisfactory environment for the user, as shown in Fig. 8.

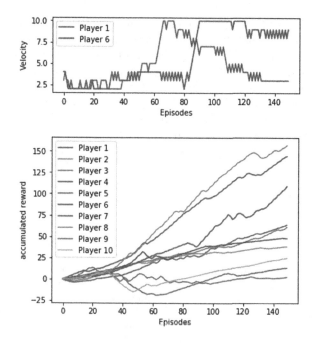

Fig. 7. Result of the experiment with speed being adjusted as the player advanced in the game (top); Result of the performance of the algorithm per player throughout the experiment (bottom).

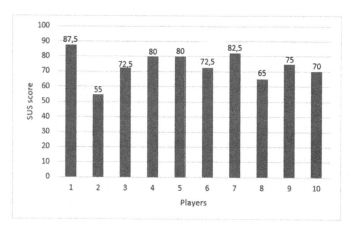

Fig. 8. SUS score per players.

5 Conclusions

We presented a serious game with a self-adaptive difficulty level to the player's profile. We implemented the self-adaptive process through a reinforcement learning approach maximizing the users' success according to their skills. This self-adaptive process occurs in real-time when the player interacts with the game. Here, a central intelligent process modifies the player environment while observing the user actions and performance results. Experimental results shows the effectiveness of our solution for the self-adaptive process, increasing user satisfaction and game engagement. This feature brings direct benefits to users contributing to the eye-hand coordination training skills. As the next steps, we intend to explore interactive RL approaches, where an external adviser speed up and enhances the game self-adaptive learning process. We also intend to explore new deep RL techniques to develop more complex games, manipulating state variables with a higher degree of dimensionality.

References

1. Andrade, G., Ramalho, G., Santana, H., Corruble, V.: Extending reinforcement learning to provide dynamic game balancing. In: Proceedings of the Workshop on Reasoning, Representation, and Learning in Computer Games, 19th International Joint Conference on Artificial Intelligence (IJCAI), pp. 7–12 (2005)
2. de Araujo, B., Feijó, B.: Evaluating dynamic difficulty adaptivity in shoot'em up games. In: Proceedings of the XII Brazilian Symposium on Games and DigitalEntertainment-SBGames 2013, pp. 229–238 (2013)
3. Binaee, K.: Study of human hand-eye coordination using machine learning techniques in a virtual reality setup. Ph.D. thesis, Rochester Institute of Technology (2019)
4. Brooke, J., et al.: Sus-a quick and dirty usability scale. Usabil. Eval. Ind. **189**(194), 4–7 (1996)
5. Carmeli, E., Bar-Yossef, T., Ariav, C., Levy, R., Liebermann, D.G.: Perceptual-motor coordination in persons with mild intellectual disability. Disabil. Rehabil. **30**(5), 323–329 (2008)
6. Cechanowicz, J.E., Gutwin, C., Bateman, S., Mandryk, R., Stavness, I.: Improving player balancing in racing games. In: Proceedings of the First ACM SIGCHI Annual Symposium on Computer-human Interaction in Play, CHI PLAY 2014, pp. 47–56. ACM, New York (2014). https://doi.org/10.1145/2658537.2658701
7. Constant, T., Levieux, G.: Dynamic difficulty adjustment impact on players' confidence. In: Proceedings of the 2019 CHI Conference on Human Factors in Computing Systems, p. 463. ACM (2019)
8. CUNHA, M.L.C.: Redes sociais dirigidas ao contexto das coisas. Ph.D. thesis, Dissertação (Mestrado)–Pontifícia Universidade Católica, Rio de Janeiro (2010)
9. Dobosz, K., Mazgaj, M.: Typing braille code in the air with the leap motion controller. In: Gruca, A., Czachórski, T., Harezlak, K., Kozielski, S., Piotrowska, A. (eds.) ICMMI 2017. Advances in Intelligent Systems and Computing, vol. 659, pp. 43–51. Springer, Cham (2017). https://doi.org/10.1007/978-3-319-67792-7_5
10. Hendrix, M., Bellamy-Wood, T., McKay, S., Bloom, V., Dunwell, I.: Implementing adaptive game difficulty balancing in serious games. IEEE Trans. Games **11**(4), 320–327 (2018)
11. Hidalgo, J.C.C., Bykbaev, Y.R., Delgado, J.D.A., Coyago, T.P., Bykbaev, V.R.: Serious game to improve fine motor skills using leap motion. In: 2018 Congreso Argentino de Ciencias de la Informática y Desarrollos de Investigación (CACIDI), pp. 1–5. IEEE (2018)

12. Likert, R.: A technique for the measurement of attitudes. Arch. Psychol. (1932)
13. Lin, Y.H., Mao, H.F., Tsai, Y.C., Chou, J.J.: Developing a serious game for the elderly to do physical and cognitive hybrid activities. In: 2018 IEEE 6th International Conference on Serious Games and Applications for Health (SeGAH), pp. 1–8. IEEE (2018)
14. Mainieri, B.O., et al.: Dificuldade adaptativa em jogo para o ensino da matemática (2019)
15. Nakamura, J., Csikszentmihalyi, M.: Flow theory and research. In: Handbook of positive psychology, pp. 195–206 (2009)
16. Pambudi, R.A., Ramadijanti, N., Basuki, A.: Psychomotor game learning using skeletal tracking method with leap motion technology. In: 2016 International Electronics Symposium (IES), pp. 142–147. IEEE (2016)
17. Peng, C., Wang, D., Zhang, Y., Xiao, J.: A visuo-haptic attention training game with dynamic adjustment of difficulty. IEEE Access **7**, 68878–68891 (2019)
18. Plass, J., Homer, B., Pawar, S., Brenner, C., MacNamara, A.: The effect of adaptive difficulty adjustment on the effectiveness of a game to develop executive function skills for learners of different ages. Cogn. Dev. **49**, 56–67 (2019)
19. Sutton, R.S., Barto, A.G.: Reinforcement Learning: An Introduction. MIT Press, Cambridge (2018)
20. Tsikinas, S., Xinogalos, S.: Designing effective serious games for people with intellectual disabilities. In: 2018 IEEE Global Engineering Education Conference (EDUCON), pp. 1896–1903. IEEE (2018)
21. Zohaib, M.: Dynamic difficulty adjustment (DDA) in computer games: a review. Adv. Hum.-Comput. Interact. **18**, 1–12 (2018)

Serious Game Design for and with Adolescents: Empirically Based Implications for Purposeful Games

Barbara Göbl[1]([✉]), Dayana Hristova[2], Suzana Jovicic[3], and Helmut Hlavacs[1]

[1] Faculty of Computer Science, University of Vienna, Vienna, Austria
barbara.goebl@univie.ac.at
[2] Department of Philosophy, University of Vienna, Vienna, Austria
[3] Department of Social and Cultural Anthropology,
University of Vienna, Vienna, Austria

Abstract. Serious games have been successfully implemented in many fields in recent years. Along the way, the call for audience specific solutions rose within the game community. In the course of a project focusing on fostering social media literacy among adolescents, we have developed a design for a serious game tailored to this specific age group. We present the results of a survey conducted among Austrian youths ($N = 86$) in which the participants reported on their gaming preferences and habits. The results are supplemented with data from participatory design workshops. Considering prospective players, their resources, play environments, and the game's characteristic goal, we provide general directions for serious game design for adolescents and address ethical questions.

Keywords: Serious games · Player personality · Characteristics and demographics · Game based learning · Mobile games · Development methodology

1 Introduction

Digital games have become an ubiquitous phenomenon - their diverse technical implementations reaching all ages and genders. Drawing from the motivational potential of such games, various areas have integrated gameful solutions to achieve other, non-entertainment purposes. Summed up by the term *serious games*, these solutions have been reported to positively impact many fields [5]. Especially among adolescents, serious games have helped in diverse areas reaching from dietary education [8,23] to the support of psychotherapeutical goals [6,26].

As they are applied in various fields and settings, serious games involve highly heterogenous user groups. Therefore, one-size-fits-all solutions are hardly feasible, underlining the need for specifically tailored solutions [2,34]. With regard to these customizing efforts, the various motivational types among gamers need to be accounted for. Following a player type analysis by Bartle [1], several authors

Supported by a DOC-team fellowship of the Austrian Academy of Sciences.

have analyzed the various motivations for playing games [16, 33, 37, 38]. Nevertheless, most of these studies have, not surprisingly, only focused on gamer populations, who are not necessarily representative of serious game audiences. Another upcoming trend, gamification, has somewhat ensured an integration of non-gamers in the analysis of suitable game elements [35], but related research still lacks more systematic approaches. For example, suitable technical implementation - based on resources and user skills -, interfaces or consideration of technology usage patterns have been underrepresented in scientific analysis.

This paper aims to fill these gaps by discussing future directions for serious games for adolescents, based on empirical data and literature-based research. Data was gathered in the course of a project that focuses on social media literacy as well as transparency about attention economy and related business practices. We present the results of a quantitative study among adolescents, with further input stemming from workshops held in school classes in Vienna. In this, an analysis of gathered data demonstrates the potential of participatory methods to inform game design. We will address the following research questions:

RQ 1: How can serious game design decisions be best tailored to accommodate technology usage patterns among adolescents?
RQ 2: What game elements and interaction patterns currently best address adolescent preferences?

In this paper, we will outline our methodology and, subsequently, our results. Following this, our research questions and findings will be discussed with the help of an exemplary case study, thus contextualizing our project and its practical application.

2   Methodology

2.1   Quantitative Survey

We conducted a quantitative online survey among our prospective player group of Austrian adolescents. In total, 88 participants ($f = 36, m = 50$) filled in the survey between November 2018 and February 2019. Our sample ($N = 86$) consisted mostly of Austrians ($n = 85$), aged 12–19 ($M = 15.0$, $SD = 1.40$), and a majority lived in Vienna ($n = 72$) at the time. Most participants were high school students ($n = 74$), one participant was currently pursuing an apprenticeship, and one participant attended university. The survey was completed in German. Previously gathered data, as presented in [14, 15, 19], and online privacy guides tailored specifically to adolescents [30] served as a basis for the design of our survey questions which are presented in the following sections.

Gaming Preferences and Habits. To support subsequent game development, we gathered data on our prospective players' gaming preferences and self-reported practices, such as the amount of their overall weekly time investment in games (PC/console based and mobile gaming) or duration of the gaming sessions. We asked for weekly time spent with gaming (open format) and duration of gaming sessions providing a range from: 0–15 min, 15–30 min, 30 min–1 h, more than 1 h. The survey also asked for a ranking of preferred player interaction patterns, based on Fullerton [12]: Single Player vs. Game, Player vs. Player (One vs. One), Multilateral Competition (All vs. All), Team Competition, Cooperative Play (All vs. Game), Unilateral Competition (One vs. All). To accommodate players with less well-established preferences, a "not sure" option was also provided. Furthermore, participants were asked to list situations (open format) in which they prefer to play mobile games.

Gamification User Types. The questionnaire included the Gamification User Type Hexad scale [35], which consists of 24 non-gaming related statements. Building on gamification types as developed by Marczewski [24], the scale is especially suitable to include non-gamers' preferences and analyses motivational aspects. Participants are asked to indicate their agreement on a 7-point Likert scale from "strongly agree" to "strongly disagree" and are subsequently categorized into several types: *Philantropists* are considered to be altruistic and drawn to supporting and helping others, while not expecting rewards. A *Socialiser's* motivation is framed as based on creating connections and interacting with others - even competitively. *Free Spirits* are characterized by their interest in exploring and creating, while *Achievers* enjoy learning new things, overcoming challenges and improving themselves. *Disruptors'* main motive is change, both positive and negative. Finally, *Players* are regarded as extrinsically motivated, striving for rewards, and acting accordingly in order to collect many of them.

2.2 Workshops

Following the methodology presented in [14], we held a workshop combining a variety methods to gather participatory data on the game's design. The workshop took place in a 10th grade class of a Viennese highschool and was attended by 23 pupils ($f = 11, m = 12$). Pupils were split into 5 teams and took part in quizzes, intermixed with group discussions, in order to introduce and discuss the topic of social media practices. Subsequently, game prototyping sessions took place, in which every team created their own, social media-related, prototype. Special focus was paid to character design and development. Game prototyping consisted of a phase of idea generation, which was then followed by a modified version of world café to discuss ideas with members of other teams, and then culminated in paper prototyping and sketching sessions. The prototypes were presented in a final team challenge and subsequently analyzed by the research team. Previously gathered data [14] had already determined the game's genre (jump 'n' run) and storyline: the player's character and their companion are trapped in a digital world inside a smartphone after agreeing to an app's dubious Terms of Service. They have to master several challenges to find a way out. Participants of this workshop were asked to think about and create characteristics, abilities and the appearance of the player character and their in-game companion.

3 Results

3.1 Quantitative Survey

Gaming Preferences and Habits. According to our data, 84% ($n = 72$) of the participants play digital video games, either on a PC, console or on a mobile device. This group will henceforth be referred to as gamers. Two thirds of female participants play digital video games in any form, compared to 96% of male participants. More specifically, 61% of the female participants play *mobile* games, as well as 82% of the male participants. As Fig. 1 shows, about a third (34%) of the latter reports playing on the mobile platform daily, compared to 8% of female participants. Notably, 19% of participants whose parents don't have higher education never play mobile games, compared to 10% of those with one parent with higher education and 3% among those with two parents with higher education. Similarly, 22% of participants with immigration background never play mobile games, in contrast to only 5% of participants with Austrian background. Figure 2 displays weekly video game play time. On average, participating gamers play for more than 14 h weekly (all platforms combined), but tend to invest more time on PC and console based games (9.1 h) rather than mobile based games (5.2 h). This is mostly due to a strong preference of male gamers towards non-mobile gaming, as female gamers report a total score of 6 hours per week evenly split between 3 h of mobile and 3 h of non-mobile games. In general, male gamers invest more hours in gaming, with a total mean score of 18.5 h per week.

Results on player interaction patterns are displayed in Table 1. The favored approach was team competition, as a total of 38% of gamers ($n = 33$) ranked this pattern first. This interaction pattern was the most popular with both male (44%) and female gamers (31%). Single player mode scored second in general, with 22% of overall votes, 22% of male votes and similarly, 22% of female votes. Female gamers were more undecided concerning interaction patterns, as "Not sure" ranked second in their preferences (25%). Among male gamers, 4% could

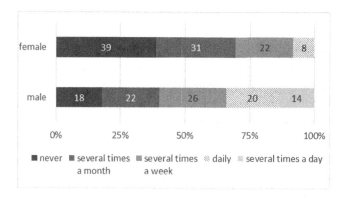

Fig. 1. Frequency of playing mobile games among participants (in percent)

Table 1. Favored player interaction patterns

	Overall	Female	Male
Team competition	38%	31%	44%
Single player	22%	22%	22%
Not sure	13%	25%	4%
Cooperative play	9%	14%	6%
Player vs. player	8%	6%	10%
Multilateral competition	6%	0%	10%
Unilateral competition	4%	3%	4%

not decide on a specific interaction pattern as well and ranked "Not Sure" in first place. Cooperative play (overall: 9%, f: 14%, m: 6%), player vs. player (overall: 8%, f: 6%, m: 10%), multilateral competition (overall: 6%, f: 0%, m: 10%) and unilateral competition (overall: 4%, f: 3%, m: 4%) were less frequently ranked in first place, with multilateral competition receiving no female votes at all.

Participants reported the length of their gaming sessions as follows: among mobile gamers ($n = 63$), the most frequent duration for one session is up to 15 min (37%). About a third (30%) play 15–30 min and 27% report playing 30 min–1 h. Only a small margin of participants (3%) play more than an hour per session. This might be related to the most commonly reported situations, which we summarized into following categories: when waiting or during breaks ($n = 14$), in public transport or during commute ($n = 14$), before going to sleep ($n = 6$), at school ($n = 5$), when they're bored ($n = 4$) or while in the bathroom ($n = 3$).

Gamification User Types. Based on the data from the HEXAD questionnaire items, *Philantropist* received the highest score among user types. It was closely followed by *Socialiser*, *Free Spirit* and *Player* types. *Achiever* received a rather

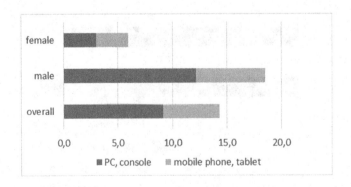

Fig. 2. Weekly video game play time (in hours)

Table 2. Gamification user types

User type	Mean score	S.D.
Philantropist	21,07	4,50
Socialiser	20,84	5,19
Free spirit	20,70	3,77
Player	20,14	4,22
Achiever	19,78	4,61
Disruptor	14,31	4,51

similar mean score of 19.78, with *Disruptor* being the only notably lower mean score of 14.31 (see Table 2).

3.2 Workshops

The 5 groups in the workshop consisted of 2 all-male teams, each having 5 members, while one team was mixed ($f = 2, m = 2$) and 2 teams were all-female, consisting of 4 and 5 members, respectively. All teams created a player character and a companion character. A large majority of player characters was designed as humans, with the exception of one all-female team, who designed an animal player character. Companions, on the other hand, where more diverse: 2 human characters (both stemming from all-male teams), 2 animal characters (all-female teams) and companion with a more abstract appearance (a fireball), designed by the mixed team. Two teams included customization of the player character in the beginning of the game, while all 3 teams changed the companion's looks according to the progress of the game, considering the required in-game development of the companion. Only one team also included the improvement of abilities of the companion character, who learned new forms of movements and attacks to fight against enemies in later stages of the game. One team portrayed player character progress by providing new and stronger weapons. While several teams included hostile non-player characters (NPC) in the presentations of their game, none specified their appearance in more detail. They were, quite contrary to the player and companion character, mostly closely related to the game's setting inside a digital world: 2 teams presented viruses, one team referred to a Trojan (horse) and one included "Twitter birds" as enemies.

4   Serious Game Design for Adolescents

The following sections will discuss possible future directions for serious game design, considering several crucial aspects: 1) characteristics of prospective players, 2) play environments, i.e. the setting in which the game will be played, 3) player resources, referring to both available hardware and a player's skill (physical or cognitive), and lastly, 4) the game's characteristic goal, which refers to the defining, non-entertainment goal of the game [7]. Based on our empirical data, we compiled a list of recommendations that help to tailor serious games for adolescents and address RQ 1 and RQ 2 as posed above.

4.1 Considerations for Serious Game Design for Adolescents

Technical Considerations. Intended deployment platforms and their specifications should be closely considered as design choices might limit the possibilities of prospective players to participate. Especially outside of formal education settings, in cases where no hardware is typically provided, both hardware availability and skills of our prospective players may present constraints. Mobile platforms are by far the most widespread among the examined demographic [10]. Additionally, while adolescents are savvy smartphone users [13], research reports that they experience difficulties using desktop computers and related software [4]. The latter has also been indicated by our own research [19]. However, consoles, desktop computers and other platforms are a suitable option when availability, training and support are provided or when the characteristic goal, e.g. for exergames involving physical movement, calls for it. In other cases, the mobile platform appears as the most suitable and also necessary choice.

User Interface (UI) and Controls. General guidelines in user interface design call for the use of simple and common UI elements [36]. The latter refers to familiarity, which, again brings up the issue of inclusive design considering non-gamers and their knowledge, or lack thereof, regarding common game interaction elements. Research has shown that natural user interfaces may engage users more in comparison to conventional approaches [27,39]. The advent of messaging platforms, especially among our prospective players [28], for example, suggests natural language interaction as a promising solution.

Session Design. Several smartphone practices indicate a strongly habitualized use of the device and installed apps, be it triggered at certain times of the day or by certain situations, e.g. traveling to school, or feelings like boredom [17, 19]. While many app designers make use of these persuasive techniques [11,18], serious game designers should consider the use of these triggers from an ethical standpoint. Since heavy smartphone use can potentially lead to stress among adolescents [29], building habit-forming products, might not always be advisable in a serious game setting. While progress-indicators are certainly important from a learning perspective, and also a popular feature among adolescents [14,18], measures should be taken to ensure that these games do not foster addictive tendencies - by e.g. limiting play time [25]. Providing statistics about play time or implementing warnings when a certain threshold of play time is reached would also help to create transparency in these matters. Beside ethical considerations, prospective player's practices should be taken into account, such as average duration of game sessions. This is relevant for the design of some game elements, for example: subgoals (e.g. time to complete a level or challenges) or check points in order to save a game's progress. More than a third of our participants report an average length of up to 15 min for their mobile gaming sessions, another 30% play between 15 and 30 min. This would be mitigated by splitting the game into sections with less than 15 min duration, using short puzzles, levels, or checkpoints for appropriate segmentation.

Gaming Motivations and Player Interaction. Previous work identified challenge and, even more so, competition as major motivators for teenage gamers [16,33]. These findings are only partly mirrored in our survey's data: *Achievers*, which are drawn to a game because of its challenging aspects, have not been represented prominently in our sample, ranking 5th out of 6. Also, the *Philantropist* user type scored highest among our participants, characterized by people motivated by cooperation and helping others. This is in line with our findings about adolescent workshop participants, who readily opened up about their social media usage when considered experts, as in our game design workshops [14]. *Socializers* scored second highest, a category which includes those enjoying competition. This is also supported by team competition as the highest ranked interaction mode. Nevertheless, multiplayer scenarios might restrict playability by e.g. asking for a minimum amount of active players or internet connection. In some situations, it might also be inappropriate for the learning goals, e.g. in psychotherapeutical settings [32]. Single player mode is an appropriate player interaction in such cases, especially considering that it was among the favorite play modes, thus also catering to player preferences.

Story and Character Design. Story and character design can be addressed by a more creative and exploratory approach, supported by participatory and co-design methods [9,20,31]. Especially when designer and intended user groups differ in main characteristics, e.g. age, gender or cultural background, participatory design can support suitable design choices [7]. Insights can be gained on familiar metaphors, graphical styles or storylines in the context of the game's characteristic goal. Results presented above suggest that adolescent players might prefer human avatars for player characters but are more open towards animal or abstract companion characters. Prototypes, developed in the aforementioned workshop, also suggest that the design of NPCs is preferably closely related to the game's learning goals and game setting: in our case, the player encounters Twitter birds, viruses and Trojans in a digital world set in a smartphone.

The 4 above mentioned criteria can of course not be viewed separately but always interact with each other: e.g. the play environment might determine what hardware is available and what kinds of interfaces are the most appropriate. In the following sections we will provide an example of how these factors can interact and how they can be taken into consideration for the design of a serious game.

4.2 Case Study

The following section presents the design of a serious game project supporting social media literacy among adolescents. Participatory methods accompanied the

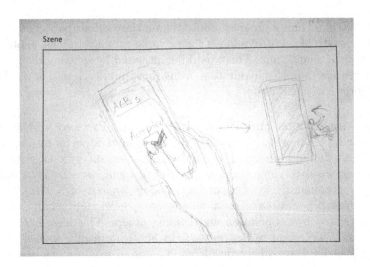

Fig. 3. Storyboard displaying the player's companion agreeing to questionable terms of use

development process and are the foundation for story and character design [14]. In terms of the above mentioned criteria, the prospective players are adolescents aged 14–19. As the game is intended for non-formal education purposes, the play environment is not specified. Evaluation of technical resources and player's relevant skillsets are based on previous research [4, 10, 19] and on the survey presented above. The game aims to provide transparency about attention economy and related gamification practices as well as data privacy. This characteristic goal is another determining factor for game design decisions.

The story of the game, developed in previous workshops [14], revolves around the player character and their animal companion, a caterpillar. After agreeing to dubious Terms of Service (see Fig. 3), they get sucked into a digital world representing the insides of a smartphone. The player is introduced to the game's map, consisting of several little villages the duo has to visit to reach the final level before being able to exit the smartphone. Each village represents one level, which covers a topic from the field of social media and related practices. By completing the levels, the player will gain both knowledge and related in-game items necessary to access and play through the final level. Based on adolescents' prototypes [14], it will be a jump 'n' run game intercepted with puzzles and quizzes. The characteristic goal of the game was introduced in the design sessions beforehand to facilitate the development of relevant stories and prototypes.

Considering available technical resources among our game's audience, the game is developed for a mobile platform, given that 97% of adolescents aged 12–19 own a smartphone, according to studies in the region [10]. As several of our research participants reported to not have regular access to the internet [19], the game, once installed, does not rely on an internet connection to ensure playability, especially in many of the gaming situations mentioned in our

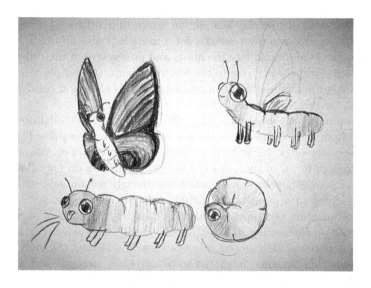

Fig. 4. Companion's optical development as designed in a participatory session

questionnaire. Despite suggestions from participants to include e.g. motion sensors, controls are based solely on touch input to accommodate a larger variety of smartphones, including older models.

The interaction with the companion (Fig. 4) will be supported by a text-based dialogue system, or chatbot, for various reasons: it is one of the most-familiar interaction methods for adolescents on a mobile phone [28] and it holds a great potential for reflective learning [21], e.g. by asking questions and allowing free text input. Spoken language interfaces will not be implemented, since most reported situations for mobile gameplay do not allow for uninterrupted interaction. While multiplayer settings would accommodate findings regarding team competition as popular interaction mode, single player game mode was selected due to the need for offline play.

The large number of *Philanthropists* among our users will be addressed by establishing a teacher-student relationship between the player and their companion. Based on the protégé pattern [3], the player will learn by discussing their knowledge with their game companion and answering their questions.

5   Discussion

The presented findings lay out current issues in serious game design for adolescents, based on empirical data. While there is a large body of research discussing the various motivational factors of gaming, we address some of the issues that come into play when drawing on these findings. Serious games need to include the characteristics of non-gamers as well, a group that has been largely neglected so far in these studies. According to our results, participants with parents with no higher education degree play less mobile games than others, as do female participants. This underlines the necessity for a more inclusive approach, to ensure that serious games accommodate the needs and preferences of their diverse audience members. Nevertheless, due to the non-representative sample of our survey, further investigation will be necessary to address this issue and consider further implications for inclusive game design.

Furthermore, we are aware that the criteria presented as guidelines for game design decisions and requirements do not represent an exhaustive list. Serious game projects are often subject to additional restrictions. For example, available resources, in terms of time, staff or budget oftentimes do not allow the free pursuit of all possible options. Also, while we strongly recommend participatory methods in order to appropriately include prospective players and stakeholders, the generalization of results is limited. Ultimately, specifics of participatory design depend on the setting, the participant group's characteristics and previous gaming experience [22], among other factors. In addition, the materials used during prototyping sessions, might have, in our case, strengthened a focus on development of characters' appearances instead of their abilities.

6   Conclusion and Outlook

Our survey as well as qualitative data gathering indicate several further directions for research. While this paper focuses on adolescents, presented methodology can be applied among other age groups to shed further light on the intricacies of serious game design. Our team intends to conduct additional workshops in order to discuss and further develop our serious game prototype in an interactive process, thus evaluating requirements presented in this paper. As our results point to the differences in gaming practice, based on gender and socioeconomic variables, we conclude with a call for further serious games research seeking to understand and involve diverse audiences.

References

1. Bartle, R.: Hearts, clubs, diamonds, spades: players who suit MUDs. http://mud.co.uk/richard/hcds.htm. Accessed 21 Jan 2020
2. Busch, M., et al.: Personalization in serious and persuasive games and gamified interactions. In: Proceedings of the 2015 Annual Symposium on Computer-Human Interaction in Play, pp. 811–816. ACM, New York (2015)
3. Chase, C.C., Chin, D.B., Oppezzo, M.A., Schwartz, D.L.: Teachable agents and the protégé effect: increasing the effort towards learning. J. Sci. Educ. Technol. 18(4), 334–352 (2009). https://doi.org/10.1007/s10956-009-9180-4
4. Comber, O., Motschnig, R., Mayer, H., Haselberger, D.: Abschlussbericht Sparkling Science Projekt: learn to proGrAME - Programmieren lernen durch Computerspieleentwicklung (in preparation)
5. Connolly, T.M., Boyle, E.A., MacArthur, E., Hainey, T., Boyle, J.M.: A systematic literature review of empirical evidence on computer games and serious games. Comput. Educ. 59(2), 661–686 (2012)

6. Coyle, D., Matthews, M., Sharry, J., Nisbet, A., Doherty, G.: Personal investigator: a therapeutic 3D game for adolecscent psychotherapy. Interact. Technol. Smart Educ. **2**(2), 73–88 (2005)
7. Dörner, R., Göbel, S., Effelsberg, W., Wiemeyer, J.: Introduction. In: Dörner, R., Göbel, S., Effelsberg, W., Wiemeyer, J. (eds.) Serious Games, pp. 1–34. Springer, Cham (2016). https://doi.org/10.1007/978-3-319-40612-1_1
8. Dunwell, I., Dixon, R., Morosini, D.: A mobile serious game for lifestyle change: conveying nutritional knowledge and motivation through play. In: 2015 International Conference on Interactive Mobile Communication Technologies and Learning (IMCL), pp. 259–263, November 2015
9. Falcão, T.P., de Andrade e Peres, F.M., de Morais, D.C.S., da Silva Oliveira, G.: Participatory methodologies to promote student engagement in the development of educational digital games. Comput. Educ. **116**, 161–175 (2018)
10. Feierabend, S., Rathgeb, T., Reutter, T.: JIM-Studie 2018. Jugend, Information, Medien (2018). https://www.mpfs.de/fileadmin/files/Studien/JIM/2018/Studie/JIM_2018_Gesamt.pdf. Accessed 2 Jan 2020
11. Fogg, B.J.: Persuasive Technology: Using Computers to Change What We Think and Do. Morgan Kaufmann, San Francisco (2003)
12. Fullerton, T.: Game Design Workshop: A Playcentric Approach to Creating Innovative Games. CRC Press, Boca Raton (2014)
13. Gardner, H., Davis, K.: The App Generation: How Todays Youth Navigate Identity, Intimacy, and Imagination in a Digital World. Yale University Press, Maple Ridge (2013)
14. Göbl, B., Hristova, D., Jovicic, S., Chevron, M.F., Slunecko, T., Hlavacs, H.: Fostering social media literacy through a participatory mixed-methods approach: discussion of workshop findings. In: IEEE International Conference on Serious Games and Applications for Health (SeGAH) (2019)
15. Göbl, B., Hristova, D., Jovicic, S., Slunecko, T., Chevron, M.-F., Hlavacs, H.: Towards a more reflective social media use through serious games and co-design. In: Göbel, S., et al. (eds.) JCSG 2018. LNCS, vol. 11243, pp. 229–234. Springer, Cham (2018). https://doi.org/10.1007/978-3-030-02762-9_23
16. Greenberg, B., Sherry, J., Lachlan, K., Lucas, K., Holmstrom, A.: Orientations to video games among gender and age groups. Simul. Gaming **41**(2), 238–259 (2010)
17. Hristova, D., Dumit, J., Lieberoth, A., Slunecko, T.: Snapchat streaks: how adolescents metagame gamification in social media. In: 4th International GamiFIN Conference (in press)
18. Hristova, D., Göbl, B., Jovicic, S., Slunecko, T.: The social media game? How gamification shapes our social media engagement. In: Dillon, R. (ed.) The Digital Gaming Handbook. CRC Press, Boca Raton (in press)
19. Jovicic, S., Hristova, D., Göbl, B.: Verspielte Grenzen des Digitalen: Relationalität und Verhandlung gamifizierter Räume in Wiener Jugendvereinen. In: Mitteilungen der Anthropologischen Gesellschaft in Wien (MAGW). Verlag der Anthropologischen Gesellschaft, Wien (2019)
20. Kayali, F., Schwarz, V., Götzenbrucker, G., Purgathofer, P.: Learning, gaming, designing: using playful participation to create learning games together with high school students. Conjunctions Transdiscipl. J. Cult. Particip. **3**(1), 1–10 (2016)
21. Kerly, A., Hall, P., Bull, S.: Bringing chatbots into education: towards natural language negotiation of open learner models. Knowl.-Based Syst. **20**(2), 177–185 (2007)
22. Khaled, R., Vasalou, A.: Bridging serious games and participatory design. Int. J. Child-Comput. Interact. **2**(2), 93–100 (2014)

23. Majumdar, D., Koch, P.A., Lee, H., Contento, I.R., Islas-Ramos, A.d.L., Fu, D.: "Creature-101": a serious game to promote energy balance-related behaviors among middle school adolescents. Games Health Res. Dev. Clin. Appl. **2**(5), 280–290 (2013)

24. Marczewski, A.: Even Ninja Monkeys Like to Play: Gamification, Game Thinking and Motivational Design. CreateSpace Independent Publishing Platform, Scotts Valley (2015)

25. Orji, R., Vassileva, J., Mandryk, R.L.: LunchTime: a slow-casual game for long-term dietary behavior change. Pers. Ubiquit. Comput. **17**(6), 1211–1221 (2013). https://doi.org/10.1007/s00779-012-0590-6

26. Radkowski, R., Huck, W., Domik, G., Holtmann, M.: Serious games for the therapy of the posttraumatic stress disorder of children and adolescents. In: Shumaker, R. (ed.) VMR 2011. LNCS, vol. 6774, pp. 44–53. Springer, Heidelberg (2011). https://doi.org/10.1007/978-3-642-22024-1_6

27. Rego, P.A., Moreira, P.M., Reis, L.P.: Natural user interfaces in serious games for rehabilitation. In: 6th Iberian Conference on Information Systems and Technologies (CISTI 2011), pp. 1–4, June 2011

28. Saferinternet.at: Jugend-Internet-Monitor (2019). https://www.saferinternet.at/jugendinternetmonitor. Accessed 7 Apr 2019

29. Saferinternet.at: Neue Studie: Immer mehr Jugendliche im digitalen Zeitstress (2019). https://www.saferinternet.at/news-detail/immer-mehr-jugendliche-im-digitalen-zeitstress/. Accessed 12 Mar 2019

30. Saferinternet.at: Stay online, stay safe! (2019). https://www.saferinternet.at/zielgruppen/jugendliche/. Accessed 4 Apr 2019

31. Sanders, E.B.N., Stappers, P.J.: Co-creation and the new landscapes of design. Co-design **4**(1), 5–18 (2008)

32. Schrammel, A., et al.: Mind Book – a social network trainer for children with depression. In: De Gloria, A. (ed.) GALA 2014. LNCS, vol. 9221, pp. 152–162. Springer, Cham (2015). https://doi.org/10.1007/978-3-319-22960-7_15

33. Sherry, J.L., Lucas, K., Greenberg, B., Lachlan, K.: Video game uses and gratifications as predictors of use and game preference. In: Playing Video Games: Motives, Responses, and Consequences, vol. 24, no. 1, pp. 213–224 (2006)

34. Streicher, A., Smeddinck, J.D.: Personalized and adaptive serious games. In: Dörner, R., Göbel, S., Kickmeier-Rust, M., Masuch, M., Zweig, K. (eds.) Entertainment Computing and Serious Games. LNCS, vol. 9970, pp. 332–377. Springer, Cham (2016). https://doi.org/10.1007/978-3-319-46152-6_14

35. Tondello, G.F., Wehbe, R.R., Diamond, L., Busch, M., Marczewski, A., Nacke, L.E.: The gamification user types hexad scale. In: Proceedings of the 2016 Annual Symposium on Computer-Human Interaction in Play, pp. 229–243. ACM, New York (2016)

36. Usability.gov: User interface design basics (2020). https://www.usability.gov/what-and-why/user-interface-design.html. Accessed 23 Jan 2019

37. Yee, N.: Motivations for play in online games. CyberPsychol. Behav. **9**(6), 772–775 (2006)

38. Yee, N.: As gamers age, the appeal of competition drops the most. Strategy is the most age-stable motivation (2016). https://quanticfoundry.com/2016/02/10/gamer-generation/. Accessed 3 Apr 2019

39. Zadrozny, W., Budzikowska, M., Chai, J., Kambhatla, N., Levesque, S., Nicolov, N.: Natural language dialogue for personalized interaction. Commun. ACM **43**(8), 116–120 (2000)

Games for Cybersecurity Decision-Making

Atif Hussain[1]([✉]), Kristen Kuhn[1], and Siraj Ahmed Shaikh[1,2]

[1] Systems Security Group, Institute for Future Transport and Cities (IFTC),
Coventry University, Coventry CV1 5FB, UK
{atif.hussain,kristen.kuhn}@coventry.ac.uk
[2] Security, Risks Management and Conflict (SEGERICO) Research Group,
Universidad Nebrija, 28015 Madrid, Spain

Abstract. Decision-makers are often confronted with cybersecurity challenges, which they may not fully comprehend but nonetheless need to critically address. Efficient preparation through cybersecurity games has become an invaluable tool to better prepare strategy and response to cyber incidents. Such games offer the potential for capacity building of decision-makers through a controlled environment, often presenting hypothetical scenarios that are designed to invoke discussion, while decision-making skills are put to the test. While games are acknowledged to be an effective method for such situations, many rely on technical capabilities to address these challenges. However, a key challenge is to understand the factors that influence cybersecurity decision-making. Further, game effectiveness for developing these skills is often not validated. This paper surveys cybersecurity games and compiles a dataset of 46 games to investigate how effective cybersecurity games are for assessing decision-making skills, and determines the state-of-the-art game. Through critical review and analysis of the data-set, a criteria to assess games for decision-making skills is presented. Furthermore, the criteria is applied to ten games, which determined Cyber 9/12 to be the state-of-the-art cybersecurity game for decision-making. The paper concludes with insights into how the assessment criteria can support the development of better decision-making skills through games.

Keywords: Cybersecurity games · Decision-making ·
Capacity-building · Human-computer interaction

1 Introduction

1.1 Motivation

Cyber incidents often pose monumental threats, yet the scope and scale of their impact is not always immediately evident. Indeed, if an organisation experiences a cyber incident, the costs can carry over for years. According to a Ponemon Institute survey in 2019 [1], 507 organisations across 16 geographies and 17

© Springer Nature Switzerland AG 2020
X. Fang (Ed.): HCII 2020, LNCS 12211, pp. 411–423, 2020.
https://doi.org/10.1007/978-3-030-50164-8_30

industries, the average cost of a data breach was USD 3.92 million – with 67% of costs occurring in the first year – and the average time it took to identify and contain a breach was over nine months.

To those charged with cyber-incident response – usually on behalf of government agencies [2], stakeholders, committees, or the public – nine months to manage a breach is difficult to justify. Those responsible are under extreme pressure to contain a breach as soon as it is discovered. If urgent response to an incident is overlooked, delayed, or compromised, then the incident may escalate into a crisis, which can be exacerbated by factors including media attention and unrest by those affected.

Decision-makers are often confronted with cybersecurity challenges they may not understand, but nonetheless need to address. Uncertainty is a key component of a crisis [3] and decision-makers must frame it as a consideration, rather than an obstacle, to respond. While cyber-incidents and their impact cannot be predicted, decision-makers can prepare strategy and response to plausible incidents, thus in turn building muscle memory to effectively react.

Efficient preparation through cybersecurity games has become an invaluable tool to improve readiness for cybersecurity decision-making. Such games offer the potential for capacity-building of decision-makers through a controlled environment, often presenting hypothetical scenarios that are designed to invoke discussion, while decision-making skills are put to the test.

1.2   Research Objectives

Human Computer Interaction (HCI) is a key element in the design of systems [4], and also in the design of games. Increasingly, manual games of all kinds, including cybersecurity games, are run on software and their parameters can be defined by computer-based tools. The processing power of a computer, along with its increased availability, means computer games are challenging manual games-especially when the topic of the game is cybersecurity [5]. HCI is redefining the meaning and the scope of games. Consequently, this study takes a multidisciplinary approach, centering on human and technology issues.

The human dimension is of particular interest in cybersecurity games as decision-makers have to make judgements about threats, risks and consequences of their actions. One challenge is to understand the factors that influence cybersecurity decision-making. In this context, this research is motivated by two research questions:

1. How effective are cybersecurity games for assessing decision-making skills?
2. What is the state-of-the-art for cybersecurity games for decision-making?

In order to answer these questions, this study develops a qualitative evaluation criteria to assess cybersecurity games for decision-making. In addition to providing a tool to conduct this study, the criteria informs the development of characteristics for strategic games, through which alignment to this criteria offers insights into how to quantify game effectiveness. The criteria is then applied to sample of cybersecurity games.

1.3   Research Contributions

This study adds to understanding of cybersecurity games five-fold: (1) It examines cybersecurity games in the context of decision-making, (2) it develops a criteria to measure game effectiveness, (3) it examines how certain observation methods are better matched to evaluation methods, (4) it identifies the state-of-the-art cybersecurity game and (5) it provides insights into how the assessment criteria can advance the development of better decision-making skills through games.

Much scientific literature on cybersecurity games [6–8] focuses on a single challenge - that of communicating abstract information to players who are not cyber-savvy. Cybersecurity is *"viewed as a niche technical subject requiring a computer science degree just to grapple with its impenetrable jargon"* [5]. While technical command of cybersecurity is an acknowledged issue amongst boards [9], policymakers [10], and public [11], it is inadequate measure of effectiveness of cybersecurity games as it overlooks a key factor: decision-making.

Cybersecurity games are a great tool to test and challenge both cybersecurity skills and decision-making skills. While previous work has surveyed cybersecurity games according to technical skills [7], no work has focused on decision-making. The starting point for this study is the assertion that cybersecurity games should not be assessed in isolation from decision-making. Therefore, this research provides unique insights into whether games are effective in developing cybersecurity decision-making skills.

This study critically reviews and analyses a range of cybersecurity games. Further, it develops a criteria to measure game effectiveness with regards to decision-making, which is a tool for the cybersecurity games community to improve games. It also examines how observation methods are better matched to certain evaluation methods. Lastly, the application of this tool is demonstrated to identify the existing state-of-the-art cybersecurity game.

1.4   Rest of this Paper

The rest of this paper is organised as follows. Section 2 presents the methodology of this study. Section 3 includes a game survey and provides a critical review and analysis of the data-set. It explains various game objectives, characteristics of scenario injects, and pairs of observation methods and evaluation methods that are effective in assessing decision-making skills. Section 4 demonstrates how the criteria can be applied to a selection of games to determine effectiveness of decision-making skills. Section 5 discusses the results and provides insights into how cybersecurity decision-makers can be better supported. Section 6 concludes this paper and outlines future work.

2   Methodology

This paper surveys cybersecurity games, and compiles a data-set by reviewing related work such as European Union Agency for Network and Information Security (ENISA), which examined 200 cyber exercises that were executed between

2002 and 2015 [12,13]. Desk-based research is carried out to identify additional games executed between 2016 and 2019. By grouping multiple editions of the same game, this data-set contains 67 distinct cybersecurity games. Some of the games did not provide information which was necessary for further data analysis. In order to improve the quality and reliability of results, this list is further reduced to 46 games for data analysis. Then, a qualitative approach is used to investigate this data-set by reading through available information on the games, such as game highlights, presentation and after action reports. The critical review and analysis of the data-set focuses on game objectives, scenario injects, observation methods and evaluation methods. This leads to two outcomes: (1) a criteria to assess cybersecurity games for decision-making skills which is developed through analysis of 46 games in the data-set, and (2) a conclusive finding on the state-of-the-art game, which is demonstrated by applying the criteria to a sample of ten games, which involve cybersecurity decision-making (Fig. 1).

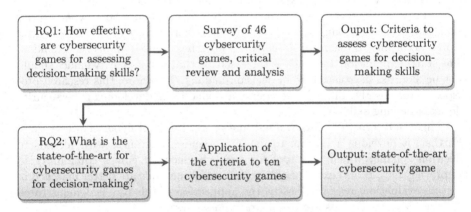

Fig. 1. The figure shows the research flow of this study. RQ1 is addressed through the survey of 46 games, which leads to a criteria. RQ2 is addressed through the application of this criteria to a sample of ten games, which leads to the state-of-the-art game.

3   Criteria to Assess Cybersecurity Games for Decision-Making Skills

The critical review and analysis of 46 cybersecurity games is based on four main areas of typical cybersecurity game format [14–16], which includes: Game objectives, scenario injects, observation methods and evaluation methods. These provide grounds to address the research questions; and therefore, are the focus of the results presented in the subsequent section.

In response to the first research question, which asks how effective cybersecurity games are for assessing decision-making skills, a criteria is developed to score the games. The qualitative analysis of the data-set identified (1) five key themes of the game objectives, (2) characteristics of scenario injects, (3) six observation methods, and (4) four evaluation methods. The criteria is composed of these elements, and is presented in Fig. 5. The 'lessons learnt' can feed into 'game design' for next edition and have the potential to improve the overall quality of the game. These two groups were not included in the criteria due to the fact that they exist outside of game-play.

3.1 Game Objectives

Game objectives were collated in a text file, which was fed into NVivo qualitative data analysis software [17] for word frequency analysis. The word grouping was matched 'with synonyms'. This matching algorithm matches words such as 'building', when it appears as build, building, established or making. The analysis returned 50 most frequent words from which five themes emerged, as shown in Table 1.

Games that include *capacity-building* are used for training or practice, and provide an environment for participants to develop skills and awareness. A focus on *decision-making* generally invokes critical thinking, and asks participants to make decisions and judgement calls. Games that have *engagement* promote cooperation and coordination internally and among other responsible organisations, often through the means of information sharing and communication outlets. Further, games with *incident management* can incite response and ask participants to manage risk factors. Finally, games that include *testing* are used to gauge preparedness by asking participants to apply procedures, processes, plans and identify areas for improvement.

Table 1. Themes emerged from game objectives analysis of 46 cybersecurity games.

Capacity-building	Skills, training, awareness, practice
Decision-making	Critical
Engagement	Cooperation, information sharing, communication, coordination
Incident management	Incident response, risk management
Testing	Plans, procedures, processes, identify, preparedness, improve

3.2 Scenario Injects

During game-play, information from a wide range of sources is provided to participants, which is a scenario inject. This can include supporting cybersecurity evidence such as technical advisory, media items, non-confidential government or agency reports, confidential intelligence briefing, industry analysis and academic research [10]. Scenario injects can have certain characteristics such as time pressure, escalation, reputation and resource allocation, which challenges decision-making, and are shown in Fig. 2.

Escalation is an increase in the severity of an incident. Cyber incidents have the potential to quickly escalate from localised incident into national emergency [18]. *Time pressure* prompts an urgent response in a timely fashion. It can be a challenge to respond effectively under pressure. *Reputation* refers to the opinions generally held about someone or something. In this context, it implies the loss or damage incurred due to a cyber incident. *Resource Allocation* refers to effective distribution of available resources.

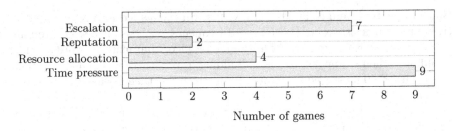

Fig. 2. Frequency of characteristics of scenario injects in 46 cybersecurity games.

3.3   Observation Methods

Observation methods are used for data collection in the form of computer-based observation, discussion, human observer, presentation, questionnaire and written submission. These are shown in Fig. 3.

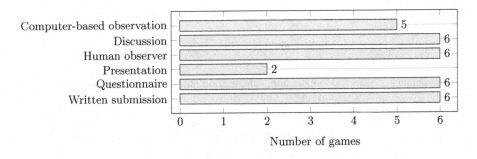

Fig. 3. Frequency of observation methods in 46 cybersecurity games.

Computer-based observation is the use of computers to record, calculate, and report on data collected from systematic observation, such as the use of score-bot which is a computer program that keeps track of points. *Discussion* allows participants to talk about specific topics in order to share ideas, explore various options, or reach a decision. *Human observers* are individuals or groups, who monitor game activities but do not participate in game-play. Generally, this provides game exposure to observers. Organisers may solicit feedback from observers, which can be used for game evaluation. *Presentation* involves verbally sharing experiences or results to an audience such as other participants or experts. *Questionnaire* is a survey used to gather participant feedback. *Written Submission* is a statement the participants submit to organisers in response to a scenario during game-play, such as a policy document or media engagement strategy prepared by the participants in response to a cyber incident.

3.4 Evaluation Methods

Evaluation methods are used to gauge effectiveness of the game in the form of challenge solving, computer-based evaluation, expert judgement and participant self-reflection. These are shown in Fig. 4.

Challenge solving includes a call to participate in a competitive situation where individuals or groups compete towards an objective. For instance, a challenge can be to secure a vulnerable server, and participants have to provide a solution to secure it. *Computer-based evaluation* includes a software which keeps track of win or loose conditions, for example, in Capture The Flag (CTF) competitions the software can evaluate whether the submitted flag is correct and award points. *Expert judgement* include expert opinion or evaluation as a mode of feedback. For instance, a panel of judges may score a submission. *Participant self-reflection* includes a self-assessment. For example, an after-game survey may ask their perception of how confident they feel their skills improved from participation in the game.

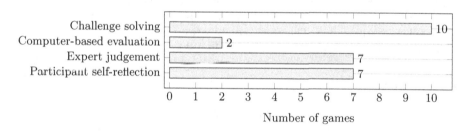

Fig. 4. Frequency of evaluation methods in 46 cybersecurity games.

From the above analysis of the 46 cybersecurity games, a criteria to assess decision-making skills in cybersecurity games is established, which is shown in Fig. 5. The next section applies this criteria to ten games to determine the state-of-the-art.

4   State-of-the-Art Cybersecurity Game

In response to the second research question, which asks what is the state-of-the-art for cybersecurity games for decision-making, the criteria is applied to ten games listed in Table 2. These games were selected as they represent the diversity of games in the data-set with regards to game objectives, scenario

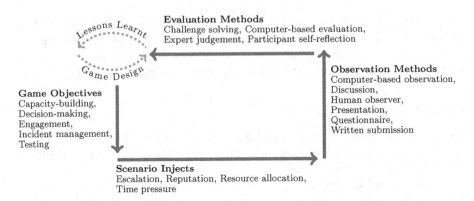

Evaluation Methods
Challenge solving, Computer-based evaluation,
Expert judgement, Participant self-reflection

Observation Methods
Computer-based observation,
Discussion,
Human observer,
Presentation,
Questionnaire,
Written submission

Game Objectives
Capacity-building,
Decision-making,
Engagement,
Incident management,
Testing

Scenario Injects
Escalation, Reputation, Resource allocation,
Time pressure

Fig. 5. The criteria to assess cybersecurity games for decision-making skills.

injects, observation and evaluation methods. Game highlights, presentation and after action reports of ten cybersecurity games are examined to confirm the presence of each characteristic of the game criteria, as identified in Fig. 5. For instance, if a game includes capacity-building, then it is noted (✓) in Table 3.

The criteria examines how certain observation methods are better matched to evaluation methods. Observation methods are used for data collection and feed into evaluation methods. This paper argues that specific observation methods are better matched with particular evaluation methods, e.g. computer-based observation and computer-based evaluation. This allows an effective evaluation of the cybersecurity game. Therefore, combinations of effective observation and evaluation methods are presented together in Table 3.

5   Discussion

While this study assesses decision-making skills in cybersecurity games, the analysis of game objectives have revealed decision-making as an objective. This was an interesting finding. Generally, technical and strategic decision-making are distinguished, but more often than not both are needed to develop a sufficient understanding of cybersecurity challenge to form an effective decision. Because technical and strategic decision-making happens simultaneously, there is no need to discern between them. This represent the complexities when exploring the human dimension of cybersecurity decision-making.

Much consideration was given in the design of scenario injects, with specific regard to the inclusion of evidence. Evidence plays significant role in the development of a scenario, providing facts that can inform a response. However, there is more to scenario injects in terms of its characteristics that triggers critical thinking and challenges decision-making, including time pressure, escalation, reputation and resource allocation. For evidence, this could extend to include conflicting or misleading information which is structured and unstructured. However, the scope of this paper includes only general characteristics of scenario injects.

Table 2. A brief description of ten cybersecurity games that are selected from data-set to demonstrate the application of the criteria.

Baltic Cyber Shield: Strengthens comprehension of global cyber environment and enhances international cooperation for technical handling of incidents [19].
Blue Cascades II: Tests plans and procedures to raise awareness of infrastructure inter-dependencies, related vulnerabilities and gaps in preparedness, identifying impacts and potential solutions [20].
Cyber 9/12 Strategy Challenge: Strengthens comprehension of policy challenges relatde to cyber crisis; asks teams to respond to a hypothetical, evolving cyber-incident and analyse the national, global, and private sector threats posed [21].
Cyber Atlantic: Explores EU and US engagement and cooperation amidst cyber-attacks on their critical information infrastructures through simulated scenarios [22].
Cyberstorm: Exercises inter-agency coordination and strategic decision making to respond to an incident in accordance with state procedures and policy. [23].
GridEx: Invites industry executives and government officials to share the actions they would take and issues they would face in response to a scenario [24].
MIT Cybersecurity Simulation Game: Tests the success of decision-makers in building cybersecurity capabilities despite potential delays in capability development and in predicting cyber incidents with respect to uncertainty [25].
OZON Crisis Exercise: Tests procedures, internal collaboration and escalation processes of participants in response to technical attacks and moral dilemmas. Makes it possible to experience what its like to be targeted by a hacker group [26].
Quantum Dawn: Improves the ability of financial sector to coordinate and respond to a systemic cyber-attack, by prompting a response to a wide-scale cyber-attack [27].
White Noise: Tests coordinated central government response to a range of threats facing the UK. This programme is designed to ensure best possible response to various emergency scenarios [28].

It is also interesting to see that games include various aspects of decision making. While the objectives create an environment which frames decision-making, it is actually the scenario injects which trigger a response and critical thinking and challenge players to make decisions. However, of the ten games examined, almost all of them included game objectives centred around the themes that emerged, but incorporated less scenario injects. There should be greater focus on the use of diverse scenario injects to provide more opportunities for cybersecurity decision-making.

The games have their own metrics to evaluate performance. This includes both observation for data collection and evaluation. Some of these observations are easy to evaluate, such as a proof or flag could indicate a winning condition,

Table 3. The criteria is used to score game effectiveness for decision-making skills. It is applied to ten games and a score out of 24 is calculated to determine state-of-the-art.

The criteria to assess cybersecurity games for decision-making skills	Baltic Cyber Shield	Blue Cascades II	Cyber 9/12	Cyber Atlantic	Cyberstorm	GridEx	MIT	OZON	Quantum Dawn	White Noise
Game objectives										
Capacity-building	✓	✓	✓			✓	✓	✓	✓	
Decision-making	✓		✓	✓	✓	✓	✓	✓	✓	
Engagement	✓	✓	✓	✓	✓	✓		✓	✓	✓
Incident management	✓	✓	✓	✓	✓	✓	✓	✓	✓	✓
Testing		✓	✓	✓	✓	✓	✓	✓	✓	✓
Scenario injects										
Escalation	✓		✓	✓		✓	✓	✓	✓	
Reputation		✓						✓		
Resource allocation		✓	✓		✓		✓			
Time pressure	✓		✓			✓				
Observation & evaluation methods										
Computer-based observation							✓			
Computer-based evaluation							✓			
Discussion		✓	✓	✓	✓	✓		✓		
Expert judgement		✓	✓	✓	✓					
Participant self-reflection		✓				✓				
Human observer	✓		✓	✓		✓		✓	✓	
Expert judgement	✓		✓					✓	✓	
Presentation			✓							
Expert judgement			✓							
Questionnaire	✓		✓	✓	✓	✓		✓		✓
Participant self-reflection	✓		✓	✓	✓	✓		✓		✓
Written Submission			✓			✓		✓		
Expert judgement			✓			✓				
Challenge solving			✓							
Score	10	8	16	11	9	14	8	13	8	5

Key finding - Table 3 score suggests that 'Cyber 9/12' is the state-of-the-art cybersecurity game for decision-making with a score of 16 points.

whereas in open ended responses, judgement can be challenging. This study has captured commonly used methods and suggests how observation methods are better suited to a specific evaluation methods. When applying the criteria, it was interesting to note that no mismatch was found. This validates the proposed combinations in the template given in Table 2. The majority of observation methods include expert judgement as evaluation method, where judgement often includes assessment of observation carried out through discussion and written submission.

When the criteria was applied to ten games, the 'Cyber 9/12 Strategy Challenge' was found to be state-of-the-art for assessing decision-making skills of the participants. This is a two-day game, which presents cybersecurity scenarios in three rounds and asks teams to formulate a policy document. Each team presents their statement to experts, who critically review and question the teams about their written submission. Experts judge the presentation and written submission and score it. Successful teams qualify for the next round. At the end of final round, teams are given ten minutes to prepare their response, replicating time pressure faced in real-world cyber incidents. Cyber 9/12 is an effective cybersecurity game for decision-making because it incorporates a wide range of the characteristics identified in the criteria. For instance, Cyber 9/12 includes all characteristics of scenario injects, in this case because the game includes diverse evidence items.

While the novelty of this study is most clearly pronounced in the development and identification of a state-of-the-art cybersecurity game, many other innovative findings have been established: From compiling a data-set and investigating cybersecurity games in the context of decision-making to not only developing a criteria to measure game effectiveness, but examining how certain observation methods are better matched to effective evaluation. In looking at the state-of-the-art, it also provides further insights into how assessment criteria can advance the development of better decision-making skills through games. This leads to the wider impact of this study, which adds value to the academic and cybersecurity game community. This study affirms games as an effective approach for strengthening cybersecurity decision-making, and helps to address acknowledged issue amongst boards, policymakers, and public.

6   Conclusion and Future Work

The human dimension is of particular interest in cybersecurity games as decision-makers have to make judgements about threats, risks and consequences of their actions. This paper surveys cybersecurity games and compiles a data-set. Through critical review and analysis of the data-set, it presents a criteria to determine how effective cybersecurity games are for assessing decision-making skills. The criteria is composed of game objectives, scenario injects, observation and evaluation methods. This criteria is applied to a sample of games that involve cybersecurity decision-making, to identify state-of-the-art game. Furthermore, the paper reflects on how game format and mechanisms can be improved for developing better decision-making skills.

Future work can include design-led research, where the criteria developed in this paper is used not only assess the effectiveness of cybersecurity games for decision-making skills, but to inform the design of new cybersecurity games. Indeed, design-led research techniques are proved to be clear strengths of HCI research, which have been shown to: *"Improve trust and security online, address issues such as fake news and online bias as well as improve accessibility of technologies and address sustainability of technologies"* [4]. Likewise, the criteria could also be refined through survey of more games. While 46 games informed this study, this could be extended to include a wider sample in which new trends may be incorporated into the criteria. For instance, the results are based on the available information only.

Further research in cybersecurity decision-making can provide significant benefit to the policymaking community. With the average cost of a cyber incident being USD 3.92 million, decision-makers cannot afford to not invest in effective cybersecurity decision-making.

References

1. 2019 Cost of a Data Breach Report. Technical report, Ponemon Institute (2019)
2. Chung, A., Dawda, S., Hussain, A., Shaikh, S.A., Carr, M.: Cybersecurity: policy. In: Shapiro, L., Maras, M.H. (eds.) Encyclopedia of Security and Emergency Management, pp. 1–9. Springer, Cham (2019). https://doi.org/10.1007/978-3-319-69891-5
3. Stern, E.: Designing Crisis Management Training and Exercises for Strategic Leaders (2014). https://www.diva-portal.org/smash/get/diva2:779024/FULLTEXT01.pdf
4. Bonham, J.: Human-computer interaction round table. Technical report, Engineering and Physical Sciences Research Council (2019)
5. Haggman, A.: Cyber wargaming: finding, designing, and playing wargames for cyber security education. Ph.D. thesis, University of London, London, UK (2019)
6. Nagarajan, A., Allbeck, J.M., Sood, A., Janssen, T.L.: Exploring game design for cybersecurity training. In: 2012 IEEE International Conference on Cyber Technology in Automation, Control, and Intelligent Systems (CYBER), pp. 256–262. IEEE (2012)
7. Tioh, J., Mina, M., Jacobson, D.W.: Cyber security training a survey of serious games in cyber security. In: 2017 IEEE Frontiers in Education Conference (FIE), pp. 1–5 (2017)
8. Labuschagne, W.A., Eloff, M.: The effectiveness of online gaming as part of a security awareness program. In: 13th European Conference on Cyber Warfare and Security ECCWS-2014 The University of Piraeus Piraeus, Greece, p. 125 (2014)
9. Rothrock, R.A., Kaplan, J., Van Der Oord, F.: The board's role in managing cybersecurity risks. MIT Sloan Manag. Rev. **59**(2), 12–15 (2018)
10. Hussain, A., Shaikh, S., Chung, A., Dawda, S., Carr, M.: An evidence quality assessment model for cyber security policymaking. In: Staggs, J., Shenoi, s (eds.) ICCIP 2018. IAICT, vol. 542, pp. 23–38. Springer, Cham (2018). https://doi.org/10.1007/978-3-030-04537-1_2
11. de Bruijn, H., Janssen, M.: Building cybersecurity awareness: the need for evidence-based framing strategies. Gov. Inf. Q. **34**(1), 1–7 (2017)
12. On National and International Cyber Security Exercises: Survey, Analysis and Recommendations. Technical report, European Network and Information Security Agency (ENISA) (2012)
13. The 2015 Report on National and International Cyber Security Exercises: Survey, Analysis and Recommendations. Technical report, European Union Agency for Network and Information Security (ENISA) (2015)

14. Ouzounis, E., Trimintzios, P., Saragiotis, P.: National exercise - good practice guide. Technical report, European Network and Information Security Agency (ENISA) (2009)
15. Kick, J.: Cyber exercise playbook. Technical report, The MITRE Corporation (2015)
16. Patriciu, V.-V., Furtuna, A.C.: Guide for designing cyber security exercises. In: Proceedings of the 8th WSEAS International Conference on E-Activities and Information Security and Privacy, E-ACTIVITIES 2009/ISP 2009, pp. 172–177. World Scientific and Engineering Academy and Society (WSEAS) (2009)
17. NVivo Qualitative Data Analysis Software. https://www.qsrinternational.com/nvivo/home
18. NCSC Cyber Attack Categorisation System for UK Incident Response (2017). https://www.ncsc.gov.uk/news/new-cyber-attack-categorisation-system-improve-uk-response-incidents
19. Baltic Cyber Shield (2010). https://ccdcoe.org/uploads/2018/10/BCS2010AAR.pdf
20. Blue Cascades (2018). https://www.regionalresilience.org/blue-cascades--interdependencies.html
21. Cyber 9/12 Strategy Challenge (2018). https://www.atlanticcouncil.org/programs/scowcroft-center-for-strategy-and-security/cyber-statecraft-initiative/cyber-912/
22. Cyber Atlantic (2011). http://www.bic-trust.eu/files/2011/12/slides15.pdf
23. Cyber Storm I, II, III, IV, V, VI (2018). https://www.dhs.gov/cyber-storm
24. GridEx Reports (2018). https://www.nerc.com/pa/CI/CIPOutreach/Pages/GridEX.aspx
25. Jalali, M.S., Siegel, M., Madnick, S.: Decision-making and biases in cybersecurity capability development: evidence from a simulation game experiment. J. Strateg. Inf. Syst. **28**(1), 66–82 (2019)
26. OZON Crisis Exercise (2016). https://www.surf.nl/en/node/566/whitepaper-cyber-crisis-exercise-ozon
27. Deloitte: Quantum Dawn 2 (2013). https://www.sifma.org/wp-content/uploads/2013/07/after-actionreport2013.pdf
28. White Noise - Post Exercise Public Report (2009). https://assets.publishing.service.gov.uk/government/uploads/system/uploads/attachment_data/file/62283/bis-exercise-white-noise.pdf

Mobile Augmented Reality App for Children with Autism Spectrum Disorder (ASD) to Learn Vocabulary (MARVoc): From the Requirement Gathering to Its Initial Evaluation

Kamran Khowaja[1]([✉]) [iD], Dena Al-Thani[1] [iD], Asma Osman Hassan[1] [iD],
Asadullah Shah[2] [iD], and Siti Salwah Salim[3] [iD]

[1] Hamad Bin Khalifa University, Doha, Qatar
kamran.khowaja@gmail.com, {kkhowaja,dalthani}@hbku.edu.qa,
ashassan@mail.hbku.edu.qa
[2] International Islamic University Malaysia, Kuala Lumpur, Malaysia
asadullah@iium.edu.my
[3] University of Malaya, Kuala Lumpur, Malaysia
salwa@um.edu.my

Abstract. The use of different technologies for the intervention of children with autism spectrum disorder (ASD) has increased over the year with the increase in the number of children diagnosed with ASD. In recent years, among the different technologies, the researchers have started to use the augmented reality (AR) to provide the intervention of different skills to children with ASD. The use of AR has many benefits, including ubiquity, minimally work with a camera, among others. Despite several benefits, AR has been underutilized for the vocabulary learning of children with ASD. This paper presents the initial version of the Mobile augmented reality app for children with autism spectrum disorder (ASD) to learn vocabulary (MARVoc). The purpose of developing MARVoc is to support teaching staff at the centers based in Doha, Qatar, to provide an interactive learning environment to children with ASD. The requirements of the MARVoc were gathered from two centers for ASD in Doha; two specific use cases were created from which one use case was finalized for the development of MARVoc. The initial version of the MARVoc was developed; the feedback was taken from the staff working at centers for ASD in Doha, and MARVoc was updated.

Keywords: Autism spectrum disorder (ASD) · Mobile augmented reality (AR) · Language comprehension · Vocabulary · Smartphone · Tablet

1 Introduction

The number of children diagnosed with autism spectrum disorder (ASD) has increased throughout the world in the recent past. ASD is a neurodevelopment disorder, and a child diagnosed with ASD may have an impairment in social communication skills or a repetitive or restricted set of behaviors (*American Psychiatric Association [APA]* 2013).

© Springer Nature Switzerland AG 2020
X. Fang (Ed.): HCII 2020, LNCS 12211, pp. 424–437, 2020.
https://doi.org/10.1007/978-3-030-50164-8_31

According to the research conducted by Alshaban et al. (2019), the prevalence rate of ASD in Qatar among children aged between 5 and 12 years is 1.1%. This is an alarming situation as the earlier the child is diagnosed with ASD; the earlier an intervention can be planned. The research on the use of technology (computer, smartphone, tablet, etc.) based interventions (TBIs) has increased. This can be seen through several review papers that have been written in one decade (Aresti-Bartolome and Garcia-Zapirain 2014; Boucenna et al. 2014; Chen 2012; Diehl et al. 2012; Fletcher-Watson 2014; Ibrahim and Alias 2018; Kagohara et al. 2013; Khowaja et al. 2019; Khowaja et al. 2020; Khowaja and Salim 2013; Khowaja et al. 2019; Knight, McKissick and Saunders 2013; Lorenzo et al. 2019; Marto, Almeida and Gonçalves 2019; Mesa-Gresa et al. 2018; Pennisi et al. 2016; Ramdoss et al. 2012; Ramdoss et al. 2011; Tsikinas and Xinogalos 2019; Zakari, Ma and Simmons 2014). The literature on ASD shows that children diagnosed with ASD face difficulties in interpreting the meaning of the text being read, and vocabulary plays a vital role (Khowaja and Salim 2013). Despite its importance, it is least investigated by the researchers. Among TBIs for children with ASD, serious games have been highly used and provide an active learning environment (Khowaja, Salim, et al. 2019; Noor, Shahbodin and Pee 2012; Tsikinas and Xinogalos 2019; Zakari et al. 2014). Children with ASD learn well visually (Hayes et al. 2010). Serious games provide an education of some content; this makes it different from typical games whose sole purpose is only entertainment. Designing a regular game is hard, so designing a serious game is even harder as the focus must be balanced between educational content and entertainment (Winn 2008). Game designers need to learn frameworks or models to design serious games. Khowaja and Salim (2019) have developed a serious game design framework for the vocabulary learning of children with ASD. Although the framework is specialized, the components used are generic and typically found in most of the serious games. Researchers can use the framework to design, develop, and evaluate serious games for different skills related to children with ASD (Khowaja and Salim 2018).

Each child with ASD is different, Bosseler and Massaro (2003) have suggested that each TBI should be tested with an individual to determine if the solution is feasible for an individual or not. One key issue is the generalization of skills learned through TBI to a natural environment with a different setting, stimuli, etc. Mineo et al. (2009) found that children with ASD prefer to take the lead by assuming the role of someone and perform the given tasks. Taking this into consideration, the use of virtual reality (VR), augmented reality (AR), and mixed reality (MR) where an individual interacts with the technology at their own has increased (Khowaja, Salim et al. 2019). While VR takes the user into the virtual world, AR augments the real world with information from the virtual world. The interaction with the VR world requires at least a specialized VR headset. At the same time, the use of AR applications can minimally work with the smartphone with a camera or any ordinary webcam as well. The use of mobile AR app (MARA) is expected to dominate the market by 2022 in comparison to VR (Merel 2018). From the recent reviews on AR for ASD (Khowaja, Al-Thani et al. 2019; Khowaja et al. 2020; Khowaja, Salim et al. 2019; Marto et al. 2019), it was found that the use AR has increased from the year 2010 onwards. The skills targeted in the studies for ASD include social skills, daily living skills, attention, cognitive skills, communication ability, etc. However, the potential of MARA has been underutilized to provide learning of vocabulary.

To the best of our knowledge, MARA would be first of its kind for the research community as well as the children with ASD in Qatar, their caregivers, and teaching staff working at centers for ASD in Qatar. The use of MARA among locals would allow them to become independent individuals and live a better life.

This research builds on the existing work conducted by the first and last authors. In the existing work, the first author developed a serious game prototype for the desktop application in Kuala Lumpur (KL) Malaysia. The requirements of the prototype were gathered from the center for ASD based in KL. The prototype provided learning of 209 vocabulary items among 11 categories (fruits, animals, birds, etc.) to children with ASD (Khowaja 2017; Khowaja and Salim 2018, 2019). The prototype was improved based on the feedback of the teaching staff and experts (Khowaja, Salim, and Asemi 2015). The prototype was evaluated with five mild children with ASD, recruited from the same center in KL. The results showed improvement in the children from the baseline to the intervention and maintenance.

In this research, the MARA prototype (referred to as MARVoc throughout the manuscript) is used to provide vocabulary learning to children with ASD. The advantage of using MARVoc is its ubiquity, i.e., learning anything supported through an app, anytime, anywhere. The MARVoc can be installed on the tablet PCs, or smartphones that have cameras and support augmented reality application programming interface (API). The MARVoc can be used in different settings, including the classroom, home, or outdoor; the performance of the children can be monitored online by the parents and the caregivers. For any solution to be successful, it is essential to consider the needs of the users, the children with ASD living in Qatar, in the context of this research.

Considering the usefulness of MARVoc and its underutilization for the vocabulary learning among children with ASD, this paper presents a requirement gathering, an initial version of MARVoc prototype, and its evaluation with the teaching staff working at centers for ASD in Qatar.

2   Method

A mixed-methods approach was used with the teaching staff working at centers for ASD in Doha, Qatar, providing to gather the needs of children with ASD. The semi-structured interviews were conducted with the teaching staff first. Then, the use cases were developed based on the requirements gathered from the teaching staff; these use cases were also modified based on the comments of the teaching staff. The concept of use cases was first introduced by the object-oriented community (Jacobson et al. 1992). This concept has been highly used in different fields, including human-computer interaction (HCI). In terms of the HCI, the focus is more on the interaction between the user (also known as an actor) and the system than the user's task only (Rogers, Sharp and Preece 2018). The use cases are easy to develop and modify; the use cases can also be adapted and customized based on the needs of the users. The functionalities of MARVoc were created for the developers to develop an initial version of the prototype. The feedback on the initial version of the prototype was taken from the teaching staff working at two centers for ASD. The feedback from the teaching staff was provided to the developers to update the prototype. The details are described in the following sections.

2.1 Semi-structured Interviews

The purpose of conducting the qualitative study with the teaching staff was to identify: 1) technologies used, 2) instructional content taught, 3) performance assessment, 4) difficulties faced by the children, and 5) instruction methods used. For the study, two centers based in Doha, Qatar, were approached. These centers include Step by Step Center for Special Needs (referred to as CENTER1 in the manuscript) and Shafallah Center for Children with Special Needs (referred to as CENTER2 in the manuscript). The first two authors, the mainly second author, have been working with these two centers in the previous studies. Therefore, the heads of both centers know the researchers. The teaching staff and the students have also interacted with the researchers in earlier studies; thus, they know the researchers and are comfortable working with them. The heads of both centers were communicated to schedule a meeting to brief them at their respective centers about the project, and to take the consent to conduct the qualitative study to gather requirements with the teaching staff. In the meeting, the heads were informed about the purpose of the study. A detailed presentation on the project was also given. The heads, towards the end of the meeting, gave consent to conduct a qualitative study at their centers. A focal person was identified at each center with the help of heads for the main point of communication between researchers and teaching staff.

A total of 27 interviews were conducted at both centers. The interviews at CENTER1 were conducted in English as most of the staff working at the center were foreigners. In contrast, the interviews at CENTER2 were conducted in the Arabic language as the native language of most of the staff working at the center was Arabic. Before the start of the interview, each interviewee was given a consent form to read and sign. At the end of each interview, the staff was given a survey form to gather opinions in terms of difficulties faced, instruction methods, and strategies used based on a 5-points Likert scale (strongly disagree to strongly agree). The interviews conducted in the English language were transcribed, while the interview conducted in the Arabic language were transcribed and then translated into English for the qualitative analysis.

Based on the needs' analysis from the transcription and translation, two cases were developed. The first use case was about the learning of letters and words, while the second use case was about learning of mathematical operations. Both use cases were discussed with the focal persons at both centers, and a mutual decision to choose the first use case was reached.

Based on the needs gathered, a MARA was designed to learn from uppercase and lowercase letters to four-letter consonant, vowel, consonant (CVC) words, and its pronunciation to the construction of short phrases for children with ASD of varying age. For instance, the app can ask a user to form a word based on the picture shown. An uppercase and lowercase alphabet were printed on a card; each card acts as a marker. A marker in an AR is a visual cue that triggers the display of virtual information. When a marker is placed in front of the camera, it will show a 3D object augmented in a natural environment. A user can interact with a 3D object by scaling the size, rotating its shape to see an object from different angles, and hearing its pronunciation multiple times, among others. The app would record all the user's interaction with the app to analyze its performance over the period.

2.2 Use Case: Learning the English Alphabet, Words, and Construction of Short Phrases/Sentences

The details of the chosen use case are as follows:

1. A child picks one card at a time to learn letters from "A" to "Z" or "a" to "z".
2. Scanning a selected card using the camera will augment a 3D uppercase as well as a lowercase letter in real. A child will also get an option to listen to the sound of the letter chosen.
3. A child will learn how to construct three-letter CVC words. To construct a three-letter CVC word, a card corresponding to the letter will be scanned and placed at the actual location that can constitute a word. Scanning each card in front of the Mobile camera will augment the letter in uppercase and lowercase and read aloud the sound. Once all three cards are scanned and placed at their location, if they constitute a word found in the dictionary, an augmented representation of the ob-ject will be shown to the child, and word will be read aloud.
4. A child will learn how to construct four-letter words following the procedure, as mentioned above.
5. To demonstrate the learning of words, a child will learn how to construct phrases/short sentences of four words. While learning the construction of these phrases/short sentences, one or two out words would be randomly placed by the teacher/caregiver. The placement of words would be a guide for the child to think and select the remaining words and place them in the correct sequence. This way, all the words can be scanned from the dictionary to verify if a correct phrase/sentence is constructed. The number of words initially placed by the teacher/caregiver will be based on the need and level of an individual and will slowly fade away based on their progress. For instance, if the phrase/sentence is "A fish can swim," and the word "fish" is scanned and placed on the second position by the teacher/caregiver. The child will see the content augmented as they progress. In the current example, a child will see a fish. Once a child has placed all four words correctly, a child will see an animation of fish swimming in the water. If a child puts an incorrect word, then it will be guided by showing a cross sign at the location where a word is placed and a sound to give them a hint that they need to place another word instead.

2.3 Functionalities

The learning of content incorporated in MARVoc includes:

1. Mixed-mode letters: 26 letter cards that show uppercase and lowercase letters
2. Three-letter and four-letter CVC words that can have a visual representation

   a. CVC words beginning with 'A' or 'a'.
   b. CVC words beginning with 'E' or 'e'.
   c. CVC words beginning with 'I' or 'i'.
   d. CVC words beginning with 'O' or 'o'.
   e. CVC words beginning with 'U' or 'u'.

The MARVoc consists of two phases, namely the learning phase and the activity phase. Each phase is briefly described below:

2.3.1 Learning Phase

In this phase, a child can either select mixed-mode letters or three-letter CVC words to learn. The learning of individual letters and CVC words is explained below:

Mixed-Mode Letters:
A child chooses one card at a time to learn alphabets from 'A' or 'a' to 'Z' or 'z'. Scanning a selected card in front of the camera will augment an alphabet in uppercase as well as lowercase in real. It also shows a 3D pictorial representation of a word starting with the selected alphabet and provides an option to listen to its pronunciation multiple times by clicking on the Speaker button. The child can also perform an interaction with the object using transformation operations like rotating the letter or picture to view either of them from a different angle or scaling their sizes.

CVC Words with Three-Letter:
In this subphase, a child will learn how to construct three-letter words. A card corresponding to an alphabet will be scanned and placed at the actual location that can constitute a word. Scanning each card in front of the camera will augment a letter and its pronunciation will be played. Once all three cards are scanned and placed at their locations; if they constitute a word found in the dictionary, then a child sees an augmented representation of the object and hear the pronunciation of the word, letter-by-letter followed by the complete word. The pronunciation can be played multiple times by clicking on the speaker button.

Note: The child can interact with the visual representation of a letter, or a word like rotating or scaling are the same as explained above.

2.3.2 Activity Phase

In this phase, a child needs to choose one of the following eight activities:

A. Construct three-letter or four-letter words.
B. Construct three-letter or four-letter words starting with a given letter.
C. Construct three-letter or four-letter words ending with a given letter.
D. Construct three-letter or four-letter words that contain a given letter.

Each activity is a timed activity and allows a child to use their imagination to construct as many words as possible. When a child constructs any word, it will:

A. Appreciate if a constructed word is correct and provide an opportunity to interact with the visual representation as mentioned above.
B. Inform the child that word is incorrect and motivate them to construct another word

At the end of the activity:

A. A child will be shown all the words constructed; for each word, a child will also see if a constructed word was correct or incorrect.
B. If all words were correct, then a child will receive a badge as an appreciation. They can collect as many badges as possible.

3 MARVoc Prototype

From the interviews, it was found that iPads are used in the classrooms for teaching and activities. Therefore, it was decided to develop the first version for the iPad only. The initial version of the prototype is developed for an iPad and supports English language only and learning of up to three-letter words. The screenshots of the initial version of MARVoc are shown from Figs. 1, 2, 3, 4, 5, 6. The staff taking part in the usability evaluation was the same who gave interviews. For the evaluation, the staff was briefed about MARVoc, its functionalities, and was allowed to use MARVoc.

Figure 1 shows two options for a child to choose from; the training part is the same as of the learning part, while the activity part is the same as described in subsect. 2.3. If a child selects an option of training, then two options, as shown in Fig. 2, will be

Fig. 1. The first screen to choose an activity or learning

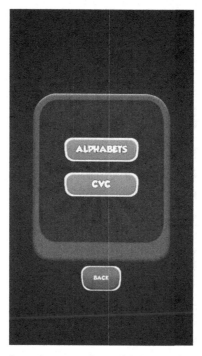

Fig. 2. Second screen to learn alphabets or CVC words

provided to the child. This allows a child to choose either to learn 26 letters from the English alphabet or construction of three-letter CVC words.

Figure 3, Fig. 4, and Fig. 5 are related to the construction of three-letter CVC words. As mentioned in Sect. 2.3, a child will be shown four options to choose from as a part of the activity; these options include the construction of CVC words in random order when a word starts with a specific letter when a word ends with a particular letter or a word which contains a particular letter. The format of learning to construct CVC words of constructing CVC words as a part of an activity is the same. If a child chooses the first option, then a child sees a similar screen, as shown in Fig. 5. However, if a child chooses any other option, then a child sees a screen like Fig. 4; this provides a child an opportunity to choose a letter that will be required in a CVC word to be constructed based on the option chosen, as shown in Fig. 5.

Figure 5 allows a child to construct the CVC words; as per the instructions shown in the dialog box at the center of the screen, a child chose the first option from Fig. 3 and chose the letter "B" from Fig. 4. Once a child knows the instruction, clicking on the close button of the dialog box will make the box disappear from the screen. Based on the option selected, the location to place a letter "B" in the word is randomly chosen by an algorithm. The blue rounded rectangle with a star on the top-left corner and a letter inside indicates that it can be part of the word, while the red rounded rectangle indicates that a child needs to scan a letter for that specific position. The format of a marker for each letter is shown in Fig. 6. The marker shows an uppercase letter in the center, lowercase letter in the lower-right corner, and a pattern in the background. The

Fig. 3. Third screen to choose an option to learn or take part in an activity

background is different for each letter and helps in image detection and recognition when a marker is scanned.

Assume, a child scans a letter "Z" for the second position, since there is no three-letter word which starts with "BZ", a child will see a cross icon in the center of the screen to indicate that they have selected an incorrect letter. Now, assume if a child selected a letter "A"; since there can be a three-letter word which starts with "BA", the current red rounded rectangle will turn into a similar first blue rounded rectangle. Lastly, if a child selects a letter "T" or any other letter to form a three-letter word, present in the dictionary, then the last red rounded rectangle will turn into a blue rounded rectangle like the other rounded rectangles. Then, a child will see a 3D representation of the word and listen to the pronunciation of the word as well. As mentioned earlier, a child can repeatedly listen to the pronunciation of the word and scale and rotate the object.

If at any point a child wants to clear the letters placed so far, then clicking on the "Reset" button will remove the letters placed and allow a child to construct a new word of their choice. If a child wants to select any other letter to be part of the word, then they can click on the "Back" button. Similarly, if a child wants to select any other option as shown in Fig. 3, then clicking on the "Back" button will take them back to Fig. 4, and clicking on the "Back" button again will take them to Fig. 3 to select one of the four options. It is to be noted that the algorithm will still choose the placement of the letter in the word.

Fig. 4. Fourth screen to select a letter to learn or for an activity

3.1 Prototype Feedback

The staff at both centers use several mobile applications as a part of day-to-day teaching or intervention of children with ASD. Therefore, they were used as experts to provide feedback on MARVoc so that usability aspects can be improved before children with ASD start using it for the learning. The feedback provided by the staff are as follows:

- The font face is inconsistent in Fig. 5.
- The background is inconsistent in Fig. 5.
- Animation of rotating lines in the background may be distracting to some children with ASD. There should be an option like a checkbox of "Background animation" to let the user decide if s/he wants an animated background or static.
- Connectivity of the back button on screens is incorrect.
- All the actions performed by the user on the screen needs to be recorded, not just on a specific part like "Training" or "Activity".
- Feedback should be visual (picture and text) and audio.
- Vowel letters (A, E, I, O, U) are missing in the "Select Letters" screen on Fig. 4
- Place "How do you want to create words?" on top of 4 options "Random", "Start with" etc. in Fig. 3.
- The instructions provided in Fig. 5 should be viewable.
- In Fig. 5: When a user clicks on the close button of the dialog box, the instruction/question disappears. It should be placed on the top, followed by the 3 letters.

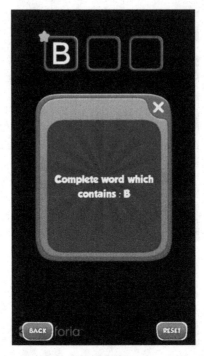

Fig. 5. Fifth screen to construct a three-letter CVC word as a part of the learning or an activity

Fig. 6. An example of a marker used in the MARVoc

- Increase the size of curved rounded rectangles with a letter in Fig. 5.
- A child may not know what does "B" in a curved rounded rectangle in Fig. 5 indicates? They need to start scanning the markers from the "B" so that all three markers are placed next to each other to form a word; otherwise, they may only scan "AT".
- There should be an arrow blink below the first rectangle to indicate waiting for the marker of the first letter to be scanned. This would only be possible when the instruction/question remains on top.

4 Conclusion

This research presents a Mobile augmented reality app for the vocabulary learning of children with ASD (MARVoc). The requirements for the MARVoc were gathered using semi-structured interviews from the teaching staff working at two centers based in Doha, Qatar. These requirements were gathered to ensure that the needs of local children with ASD have been incorporated in MARVoc. Based on the requirements, two detailed use cases were developed and discussed with the focal persons at both centers, and one of the two use cases was finalized for the prototype. The staff working at both centers were given a demonstration of the initial version of the prototype to determine its effectiveness in learning vocabulary for children with ASD. The feedback was taken from the staff, and MARVoc was updated. MARVoc is being deployed at Step by Step Center for Special Needs for use by the staff in the classrooms. MARVoc is also being modified to incorporate four-letter CVC words and construction of short phrases/sentences. The new version of the MARVoc would also include Arabic letters and words so that it can be evaluated with the children with ASD at Shafallah Center for Children with Special Needs. The new version of the MARVoc would support the user to change the user interface from English to Arabic and vice versa.

Acknowledgment. We would like to thank the administration of Step by Step Center for Special Needs, and Shafallah Center for Children with Special Needs in Qatar for allowing their teaching staff to take part in the studies related to our ongoing research.

References

Alshaban, F., et al.: Prevalence and correlates of autism spectrum disorder in Qatar: a national study. J. Child Psychol. Psychiatry **60**(12), 1254–1268 (2019). https://doi.org/10.1111/jcpp.13066

American Psychiatric Association [APA], (2013). Washington, DC

Aresti-Bartolome, N., Garcia-Zapirain, B.: Technologies as Support tools for persons with autistic spectrum disorder: a systematic review. Int. J. Env. Res. Pub. He. **11**(8), 7767–7802 (2014)

Bosseler, A., Massaro, D.W.: Development and evaluation of a computer-animated tutor for vocabulary and language learning in children with autism. J. Autism Dev. Disord. **33**(6), 653–672 (2003)

Boucenna, S., et al.: Interactive technologies for autistic children: a review. Cogn. Comput. **6**(4), 722–740 (2014). https://doi.org/10.1007/s12559-014-9276-x

Chen, W.: Multitouch tabletop technology for people with Autism Spectrum Disorder: a review of the literature. Procedia Comput. Sci. **14**, 198–207 (2012)

Diehl, J.J., Schmitt, L.M., Villano, M., Crowell, C.R.: The clinical use of robots for individuals with Autism Spectrum Disorders: a critical review. Res. Autism Spectrum Disord. **6**(1), 249–262 (2012). https://doi.org/10.1016/j.rasd.2011.05.006

Fletcher-Watson, S.: A targeted review of computer-assisted learning for people with autism spectrum disorder: towards a consistent methodology. J. Autism.Dev. Disord. **1**(2), 87–100 (2014)

Hayes, G.R., Hirano, S., Marcu, G., Monibi, M., Nguyen, D.H., Yeganyan, M.: Interactive visual supports for children with autism. Pers. Ubiquit. Comput. **14**(7), 663–680 (2010)

Ibrahim, Z., Alias, M.: A Review on using assistive technology to enhance social skills competence among children with Autism Spectrum Disorder (ASD). Adv. Sci. Lett. **24**(6), 4250–4254 (2018). https://doi.org/10.1166/asl.2018.11582

Jacobson, I., Christerson, M., Jonsson, P., Overgaard, G.: Object-Oriented Software Engineering: A Use Case Driven Approach. Addison Wesley, Harlow (1992)

Kagohara, D.M., et al.: Using iPods® and iPads® in teaching programs for individuals with developmental disabilities: a systematic review. Res. Dev. Disabil. **34**(1), 147–156 (2013). https://doi.org/10.1016/j.ridd.2012.07.027

Khowaja, K.: A serious game design framework for vocabulary learning of children with autism. (Doctor of Philosophy), University of Malaya (2017)

Khowaja, K., et al.: Use of augmented reality for social communication skills in children and adolescents with autism spectrum disorder (ASD): A systematic review. Paper presented at the 2019 IEEE 6th International Conference on Engineering Technologies and Applied Sciences (ICETAS), Kuala Lumpur, Malaysia, 20–21 December 2019 (2019)

Khowaja, K., et al.: Augmented reality for learning of children and adolescents with autism spectrum disorder (ASD): a systematic review. IEEE Access (2020). https://doi.org/10.1109/ACCESS.2020.2986608

Khowaja, K., Salim, S.S.: A systematic review of strategies and computer-based intervention (CBI) for reading comprehension of children with autism. Res. Autism Spectrum Disord. **7**(9), 1111–1121 (2013)

Khowaja, K., Salim, S.S.: Serious game for children with autism to learn vocabulary: an experimental evaluation. Int. J. Hum-comput. Int. **35**(1), 1–26 (2018). https://doi.org/10.1080/10447318.2017.1420006

Khowaja, K., Salim, S.S.: A framework to design vocabulary-based serious games for children with autism spectrum disorder (ASD). Univ. Access Inf. Soc. (2019). https://doi.org/10.1007/s10209-019-00689-4

Khowaja, K., Salim, S.S., Asemi, A.: Heuristics to evaluate interactive systems for children with Autism Spectrum Disorder (ASD). PLoS ONE **10**(7), e0132187 (2015). https://doi.org/10.1371/journal.pone.0132187

Khowaja, K., Salim, S.S., Asemi, A., Ghulamani, S., Shah, A.: A systematic review of modalities in computer-based interventions (CBIs) for language comprehension and decoding skills of children with autism spectrum disorder (ASD). Univ. Access Inf. Soc. **19**, 213–243 (2020). https://doi.org/10.1007/s10209-019-00646-1

Knight, V., McKissick, B.R., Saunders, A.: A review of technology-based interventions to teach academic skills to students with autism spectrum disorder. J. Autism Dev. Disord. **43**(11), 2628–2648 (2013). https://doi.org/10.1007/s10803-013-1814-y

Lorenzo, G., Lledó, A., Arráez-Vera, G., Lorenzo-Lledó, A.: The application of immersive virtual reality for students with ASD: a review between 1990–2017. Educ. Inform. Tech. **24**(1), 127–151 (2019). https://doi.org/10.1007/s10639-018-9766-7

Marto, A., Almeida, H.A., Gonçalves, A.: Using augmented reality in patients with autism: a systematic review. In: Tavares, J.M.R.S., Natal Jorge, R.M. (eds.) VipIMAGE 2019. LNCVB, vol. 34, pp. 454–463. Springer, Cham (2019). https://doi.org/10.1007/978-3-030-32040-9_46

Merel, T.: Ubiquitous AR to dominate focused VR by 2022 (2018). https://techcrunch.com/2018/01/25/ubiquitous-ar-to-dominate-focused-vr-by-2022/

Mesa-Gresa, P., Gil-Gómez, H., Lozano-Quilis, J.-A., Gil-Gómez, J.-A.: Effectiveness of virtual reality for children and adolescents with Autism Spectrum Disorder: an evidence-based systematic review. Sensors **18**(8), 2486 (2018)

Mineo, B.A., Ziegler, W., Gill, S., Salkin, D.: Engagement with electronic screen media among students with autism spectrum disorders. J. Autism Dev. Disord. **39**(1), 172–187 (2009)

Noor, M., Shahbodin, F., Pee, C.: Serious Game for Autism Children: Review of Literature. Paper presented at the World Academy of Science, Engineering and Technology (2012)

Pennisi, P., et al.: Autism and social robotics: a systematic review. Autism Res. **9**(2), 165–183 (2016). https://doi.org/10.1002/aur.1527

Ramdoss, S., Machalicek, W., Rispoli, M., Mulloy, A., Lang, R., O'Reilly, M.: Computer-based interventions to improve social and emotional skills in individuals with autism spectrum disorders: a systematic review. Dev. Neurorehabil. **15**(2), 119–135 (2012). https://doi.org/10.3109/17518423.2011.651655

Ramdoss, S., et al.: Use of computer-based interventions to improve literacy skills in students with autism spectrum disorders: a systematic review. Res. Autism Spectrum Disord. **5**(4), 1306–1318 (2011)

Rogers, Y., Sharp, H., Preece, J.: Interaction Design: Beyond Human-Computer Interaction, 4th edn. Wiley, Chichester, West Sussex (2018)

Tsikinas, S., Xinogalos, S.: Studying the effects of computer serious games on people with intellectual disabilities or autism spectrum disorder: a systematic literature review. J. Comput. Assist. Learn. **35**(1), 61–73 (2019). https://doi.org/10.1111/jcal.12311

Winn, B.: The design, play, and experience framework. In: Handbook of Research on Effective Electronic Gaming in Education, vol. 3, pp. 1010-1024 (2008)

Zakari, H.M., Ma, M., Simmons, D.: A review of serious games for children with Autism Spectrum Disorders (ASD). In: Ma, M., Oliveira, M.F., Baalsrud Hauge, J. (eds.) SGDA 2014. LNCS, vol. 8778, pp. 93–106. Springer, Cham (2014). https://doi.org/10.1007/978-3-319 11623-5_9

WeRehab: Assisting Cannabis Rehabilitation via Mobile Application

Yuan Long[✉] and Kuang-Yuan Huang

Colorado State University Pueblo, Pueblo, CO 81001, USA
yoanna.long@csupueblo.edu

Abstract. This research aims to develop a mobile application to assist patients undergoing cannabis rehabilitation. The project includes two primary stages. Stage one is an empirical study exploring the impact of different types of social support on rehabbers' behavior in a cannabis rehabilitation discussion group. Stage two oversees the development of a mobile application that addresses the social support research discovered in stage one. The study contributes to both academics and real-world applications.

Keywords: Social support · Cannabis rehabilitation · Informational support · Emotional support · Mobile application

1 Introduction

This research project aims to develop a mobile application for cannabis rehabilitation. The project includes two main stages. Stage one is an empirical study exploring the essential factors constituting social support in a social network community of cannabis rehabilitation. Stage two oversees the development of a mobile application to assist patients of cannabis rehabilitation by addressing the major types of social support discovered in stage one.

The purpose of the first stage is to explore the factors impacting individual's behavior in an online cannabis rehabilitation support group. A discussion forum (cannabisrehab.org) was chosen as the research setting. Six threads with approximately a thousand messages were downloaded as the research database. In each thread, the rehabber who is the initiator starts the thread via posting messages which share experience, express struggles, or ask questions while the rest of the community reply the messages to show their support. Two major types of social support were investigated including both informational support (e.g., suggestions, advices, resources, and referrals, etc.) and emotional support (e.g., sympathy, encouragement, understanding, and relief, etc.). The results indicate that first, the initiators' emotion is greatly impacted by the social support from the community and specifically, informational support which positively affects initiators' emotions.

Based on the results from stage one, stage two aims to develop a mobile application to offer social support by addressing informational support to cannabis rehabbers. The

© Springer Nature Switzerland AG 2020
X. Fang (Ed.): HCII 2020, LNCS 12211, pp. 438–447, 2020.
https://doi.org/10.1007/978-3-030-50164-8_32

major functions of the application include but are not limited to a list of resources, daily digest, self-assessment, a progress monitor, a discussion forum, and messaging.

The rest of the paper is organized as following: we start with a brief literature review and then focus on the two stages of the research including the empirical study and the mobile application development. Finally, we conclude with a discussion on the future research directions derived from the research.

2 Literature Review

Social support is defined as "the exchange of verbal as well as nonverbal messages in order to communicate emotional and informational messages that reduce the retriever's stress" [8]. Individuals join online support groups to seek social support from like-minded people who are experiencing or have experienced similar stressful events. Prior research has suggested that participating in online support groups both increases one's sense of control over the stressful events and brings emotional relief to the participant [1]. Research has also found that participants of online support groups perceive social support that has been received online to be more helpful than support received in face-to-face settings [9].

Two main types of social support have been found to be exchanged online – informational support and emotional support. Different types of social support affect individuals differently. Specifically, informational support affects recipients' evaluation of something external to the subject [4]. For example, learning new skills and strategies via informational support affects individuals' evaluation of the severity and controllability of the stressor. On the other hand, emotional support affects individuals' evaluations and feelings about themselves [4]. For example, emotional support that communicates encouragement, empathy, and compliment can increase one's sense of belonging and self-worth. These affected external (stress) and internal (self) evaluations, through informational and emotional support, should in turn lead to support recipients' emotional restoration [4], both in face-to-face and online [1, 9, 10] settings.

3 Stage 1: Empirical Study

3.1 Research Setting

CannabisRehab (https://www.cannabisrehab.org/), an online discussion forum dedicated to cannabis rehabilitation (recently opened to any drug rehabilitation), was chosen as our research setting. CannabisRehab began online in 2008 (the very first post was published on Nov. 9th, 2008). This website is a free online support group providing *information, support, encouragement and understanding* [2] to assist cannabis rehabilitation. In the past eleven years, the website has hosted more than three thousand threads along with approximately twenty thousand posts and serves close to two thousand registered members [3] with an uncounted number of guests (i.e., the users who visit the website without registering an account).

We chose CannabisRehab as the research site due to three reasons: first, it serves the purpose of our research goal which focuses on the understanding of the use of social networks to support cannabis rehabilitation. Second, it provides a rich source of data by being an active discussion forum spanning over ten years with thousands of posts and users. Third, it is accessible due to its open nature, so we are able to download threads and analyze data.

3.2 Research Questions and Hypotheses

In this research, we aim to investigate: would social network support impact rehabbers emotion? If so, which type of social support, informational or emotional support, plays a more important role?

Specifically, we lay out two hypotheses:

H1. Informational support positively impacts rehabbers' emotion.
H2. Emotional support positively impacts rehabbers' emotion.

3.3 Research Methods

Data Collection. Fifty threads including a total of one thousand and two hundred posts were first downloaded from CannabisRehab. Since the purpose of our research is to investigate the impact of social support on cannabis rehabbers, it requires the thread to have sufficient interaction between the initiator and the respondents, which is indicated by the number of posts included in each thread. After analyzing the fifty threads, we chose the top six that have the largest number of posts as the data source. Table 1 shows the descriptive analysis of these six threads.

Table 1. Descriptive analysis of threads

Thread ID	Total no. of posts	No of posts from rehabber/initiator	No. of replies	% of initiator posts	% of replies	Date of first post	Date of last post	Duration (days)
2	371	262	109	71%	29%	7/7/15	2/6/18	945
8	140	76	64	54%	46%	6/30/16	1/29/18	578
9	140	70	70	50%	50%	5/16/17	1/27/18	256
628	57	30	27	53%	47%	8/6/13	9/2/13	27
768	68	38	30	56%	44%	5/23/13	7/7/13	45
910	41	30	11	73%	37%	1/8/13	2/23/13	46
Total	817	506	311	62%	38%			
Average	136	84	52	62%	38%			

Table 1 depicts a brief picture of the threads (mostly quit journals) on CannabisRehab. There are three details to note here. First, CannabisRehab is not a heavy traffic discussion forum. This may be due to its nature as a focused group on a specific and relatively sensitive topic. Second, the interactions between the rehabber (the person who initiated a thread) and the respondents are diverse. For some threads, the rehabber posts the most. For example, about 70% of the posts were from the rehabber for both thread 2 and thread 910 while the other threads are much more balanced. For example, about half and half is split between the rehabber and the respondents for thread 8, 9, 628, and 768. Third, the majority of the quit journals do not last more than two months. Among the top six quit journals, three lasted more than one year while the rest lasted less than two months.

Data Analysis. Content Analysis has been used as the major analytical method, and a mixed machine vs. human coding procedure has been applied to measure the variables.

The dependent variable in our study is the emotion of the rehabber. Specifically, we used the Linguistic Inquiry and Word Count (LIWC) software package [7] to measure the positive and negative emotions reflected in the word choice of online messages. LIWC is a research tool used to analyze text documents and count the frequencies of the occurrence of words belonging to pre-defined word categories such as pronouns (e.g., I, We, She), biological processes (e.g., abdomen, muscle, sleep), positive emotions (e.g., agree, happy, passion), negative emotions (e.g., anger, anxiety, pathetic), and so on. The LIWC "positive emotions" and "negative emotions" categories were selected to identify words used in a message belonging to either category and count the frequency of occurrence of each of the two word categories.

A Python program was developed to automatically count the number of positive and negative words appearing in each post by the rehabber (the initiator) and then to calculate the percentage of these words to the entire post. The number (0–1) has been used as the indicator of the emotion (positive vs. negative) of the rehabber. For example, a positive or negative number that is close to 1 indicates a high degree of positive or negative emotion while 0 indicates a low degree of positive or negative emotion. The following formula shows the calculation.

Positive (or negative) emotion = No. of positive or negative words/total no. of words in a post by the rehabber.

The two independent variables, including informational support vs. emotional support, have been used to measure different types of social support from the respondents to the rehabber (the initiator). Table 2 shows the definition of the two different types of social support behavior [5, 6]. Note first the recipient in the table refers to the rehabber (the initiator who starts a thread) in our study. And second, Table 2 does not include tangible support and network support in the original behavior codes [5, 6]. These two types of support are mainly applied to physical (face-to-face) instead of virtual (online) support in our study.

To measure informational support vs. emotional support from the respondents, we used sentence as the unit and coded whether this sentence is informational support, emotional support, or neither based on the definition from Table 2. For example, a reply worded as "If you are bored, start playing Baduk (Go, Weiqi)" and "according to this study http://www.researchgate.net/publicat..._imaging_study..." are coded as informational support (suggestion/advice and referral in Table 2, respectively). Additionally, a reply worded as "Hang in there, you can do it!" and "You just slipped" are coded as

Table 2. Definition of social support behavior codes [5, 6]

Support type	Definition
Informational support	
Suggestion/advice	Offers ideas and suggests actions
Referral	Refers the recipient to some other source of help
Situation	Reassesses or redefines the situation
Teaching	Provides detailed information, facts, or news about the situation or about skills needed to deal with the situation
Emotional support	
Relationship	Stresses the importance of closeness and love in relationship with the recipient
Confidentiality	Promises to keep the recipient's problem in confidence
Sympathy	Expresses sorrow or regret for the recipient's situation or distress
Listening	Attentive comments as the recipient's speaks
Understanding/empathy	Expresses understanding of the situation or discloses a personal situation that communicates understanding
Encouragement	Provides the recipient's with hope and confidence
Prayer	Prays with the recipient
Compliment	Says positive things about the recipient or emphasizes recipient's abilities
Validation	Expresses agreement with the recipient's perspective on the situation
Relief of blame	Tries to alleviate the recipient's feelings of guilt about the situation

emotional support (encouragement and relief of blame in Table 2, respectively). Eventually, each reply (a post responded to the rehabber's message) has two separate numbers representing the number of sentences are coded as informational support and emotional support, respectively.

These two variables were manually instead of automatically coded due to three reasons. First, no published word bank (e.g., a word bank similar to LIWC used to code emotion) exists to assist the coding for informational support and emotional support. Second, human raters normally have better comprehension and are more accurate than machines in understanding sentences and their underlying meaning. Third, a little over three hundred replies/messages/posts need to be coded in this study, which is manageable by using the human coders only.

The coding process can be divided into three stages: design, coding, and verification.

The purpose of stage one is to develop the coding rules and the best practices. In this stage, we had two researchers code the same fifty messages.

We decided three outputs: first, a word bank that includes the key words (or the short phrases) indicating either informational support or emotional support. For example, words or phrases such as "hang in", "keep up", "doing well", "strong", "peace", and "love" etc. can be easily found in the sentences showing emotional support. While words or phrases such as "sleep", "beneficial", "brain", "idea", "learning experience", and "resolution" are often found in the sentences showing informational support. Once the word bank is generated, we are able to use it as the reference for the future coding. Additionally, the word bank benefits the follow-up research conducted with Natural Language Processing (a Machine Learning technology) to automatically identify the type of social support.

The second output is a list of quotations including the sentences that are coded as either informational support or emotional support. This list not only helps to verify the coding and solve the discrepancy, it serves as the reference to the future coding as well. Both the first and the second output can be easily achieved by using the software *Atlas.ti*.

The third output is an Excel summary sheet listing the thread number, the post number, the number of sentences that are coded as informational support, and the number of sentences that are coded as emotional support. After back-and-forth discussion, the two researchers achieved 95% agreement on the coding result.

The tasks in stage two are used to train the other researchers. In total, five researchers participated in the coding process. The workload has been divided so that each coder has fifty to sixty messages to code. The coding results were collected two weeks later.

Stage three aims to verify the results. Each coder was assigned ten messages (other than his/her original assignment) and then asked to compare the results. After several rounds of discussion, refining the rules, and even re-coding, the coders achieved 90% agreement.

After a lengthy and comprehensive coding process, we achieved the measurement of the variables including emotional support vs. informational support (from the respondents) and positive vs. negative emotion (of the rehabber/initiator).

Results and Implication. The purpose of the research is to investigate the impact of social support on rehabbers' emotion in the online cannabis rehabilitation community. An assumption has to be made as to what counts as direct impact from the respondent to the rehabber. In a thread, the order of the posts (messages) between the rehabber (i.e., the initiator who starts the thread) and the respondent is random. For example, the following conversation (Fig. 1) illustrates a typical thread in which *I* represents the initiator (the same person throughout a thread) while *R* represents the respondents (who could be different people from the community). Inside of the parentheses shows the date the message has been posted.

It's hard to decide which reply (R) directly impacts the rehabber(I) as there may be a couple of messages in between the rehabber's post which may impact the rehabber's emotion more or less. To be both reasonable and practical, we assume that the single message right before the rehabber's post has a direct impact on the rehabber's emotion in that post.

The following table shows the statistic results using regression analysis.

The results indicate that first, overall social support impacts the rehabber's emotion (statistically significate at 0.002 in Table 3). Second, informational support has a positive impact on rehabbers' emotion so Hypothesis I has been verified (statistically significate

> *Thread: Looking to quit*
> *I(day 1): I really need to quit...*
> *R(day 1): Just know that you can do this...*
> *I(day 1): Hi, thank you!...*
> *I(day 4): Everything stressful in life seems to be happening.*
> *I (day 6): I'm ashamed to say I caved in on 3rd day...*
> *R(day 6): I hope that you will take solace in the fact that you*
> *are actually so much closer to your goal than you think...*
> *I(day 6): Thank you so much for the support...*

Fig. 1. A sample thread

Table 3. Overall fit of the model

ANOVA[a]

Model		Sum of squares	cf	Mean square	F	Sig.
1	Regression	.026	2	.013	6.293	.002[b]
	Residual	.412	199	.002		
	Total	.438	201			

[a]Dependent variable: Pos
[b]Predictors: (Constant). Count_Emo. Count_Info

Table 4. Coefficients of variables

Model		Unstandardized coefficients		Standardized coefficients	t	Sig.
		B	Std. error	Beta		
1	(Constant)	.064	.005		12.942	.000
	Count_Info	.002	.001	.216	3.097	.002
	Count_Emo	.001	.001	.082	1.174	.242

[a]Dependent variable: Pos

at 0.002 in Table 4). Third, the coefficient of emotional support is not significant at 0.05 level therefore Hypothesis II is not supported.

The first hypothesis that proposes informational support has a positive impact on rehabbers' emotion has been supported statistically as expected. Informational support such as suggestions, advices, references, and resources normally answers rehabbers' questions directly and provides objective information to assist in rehabilitation. Rehabbers therefore would receive positive feedback accordingly.

The second hypothesis on the other hand, which proposes emotional support has a positive impact on rehabbers' emotion, is not supported statistically. This could be due to multiple reasons. First, the emotional support, which mostly focuses on sympathy, listening, understanding, empathy, encouragement, and compliment, etc. may not directly answer the rehabbers' questions. This results in the absence of a direct impact on their emotion expressed in the subsequent message. Second, we made an assumption that only a pair of messages right next to each other will have an impact from the respondent to the rehabber (Fig. 1). In reality, a couple of responses may affect a few messages the rehabber posted afterwards. It's hard to tell, but an adjustment of the algorithm to calculate the impact may be possible. Third, we didn't consider the time in between the response and the message posted by the initiator, which may play a role in terms of the impact. For example, the rehabber's emotion may be greatly impacted by whether there is a response and how soon the response appears. In summary, even though in our study, the emotional support does not impact the rehabbers' emotion statistically, it does not mean the former has no contribution to assist in cannabis rehabilitation. Further investigation (possibly a more in-depth qualitative study) is needed to understand the impact of emotional support on the rehabbers' behavior.

4   Stage 2: Practical Application - A Mobile App

Based on the results from stage 1, we developed a mobile application to help assist cannabis rehabilitation. In addition to social network functions such as journaling and messaging, we specifically addressed the informational support by listing the major rehabilitation resources (i.e. online and offline help center), offering rehabilitation knowledge, providing a function for self-assessment on addiction, monitoring the rehabilitation progress, and FAQ. Figure 2 shows the demo of the interface of the application.

This application provides two major modules in addition to the regular functions such as setting and profile. The first module specifically focuses on informational support such as:

- **Resources:** This function provides a list of the major online and offline help centers such as rehab hotlines and local rehab meet groups.
- **Digest:** This function provides constantly updated news/research articles on cannabis rehabilitation. Users can set up a subscription and specify the frequency of articles received through Digest.
- **FAQ:** This function provides commonly asked questions regarding cannabis rehabilitation. The information is from authorized resources with references and links.
- **Self-assessment and progress monitoring:** With this function, users are able to take a self-assessment questionnaire on the addiction symptoms. The score indicates the degree of addiction and the results are visualized via a trendline. The users are able to monitor their own progress as time passes.

The second module provides social network functions such as journals, discussion forums, and in-app messaging. The application was developed via the Apple development platform and is currently in the testing stage.

Fig. 2. The demo of the mobile application

5   Conclusion and Future Research

This paper investigated the impact of two types of social support including informational and emotional support on cannabis rehabbers' behavior. The statistical result shows that informational support affects rehabbers' emotion significantly. Based on the result, we developed a mobile application to assist in cannabis rehabilitation and specifically addresses informational support.

The research is only the beginning in understanding and exploration of what information technology can do to facilitate cannabis rehabilitation. There are quite a few follow-up questions that are worth further investigation. For example, one direction is to include time into the formula and investigate whether the response time impacts rehabbers' emotion. Another interesting direction is to use contemporary machine learning technology, specifically Natural Language Processing (NLP), to identify the questions and subsequent responses. It is similar to Siri in iPhone but in a specific area of cannabis rehabilitation. Ideally, the computer bot can answer the rehabbers' questions by learning from real-life conversations, such as from Cannabisrehab and other similar discussion forums. Those online forums provide a perfect learning environment for the computer bot to identify keywords and classify questions.

References

1. Barak, A., Boniel-Nissim, M., Suler, J.: Fostering empowerment in online support groups. Comput. Hum. Behav. **24**, 1867–1883 (2008)
2. Cannabisrehab online rehab group. https://www.cannabisrehab.org/forums/forumdisplay.php/16-Online-Marijuana-Rehab-Group. Accessed 14 Jan 2020
3. Cannabisrehab forums. https://www.cannabisrehab.org/forums/forum.php. Accessed 14 Jan 2020

4. Cohen, S., McKay, G.: Social support, stress and the buffering hypothesis: a theoretical analysis. In: Baum, A., Singer, J.E., Taylor, S.E. (eds.) Handbook of Psychology and Health, vol. 4, pp. 253–267. Erlbaum, Hillsdale (1984)
5. Cutrona, C.E., Suhr, J.A.: Controllability of stressful events and satisfaction with spouse support behaviors. Commun. Res. **19**(2), 154–174 (1992)
6. Huang, K.Y., Chengalur-Smith, I., Ran, W.: Not just for support: companionship activities in healthcare virtual support communities. Commun. Assoc. Inf. Syst. **34**(1), 29 (2014)
7. Pennebaker, J.W., Boyd, R.L., Jordan, K., et al.: The Development and Psychometric Properties of LIWC2015. University of Texas at Austin, Austin (2015)
8. Pfeil, U.: Online support communities. In: Zaphiris, P., Ang, C.S. (eds.) Social Computing and Virtual Communities, pp. 121–150. Chapman & Hall, London (2009)
9. Wright, B., Bell, S.B.: Health-related support groups on the internet: linking empirical findings to social support and computer-mediated communication theory. J. Health Psychol. **8**(1), 39–54 (2003)
10. Maloney-Krichmar, D., Preece, J.: A multilevel analysis of sociability, usability, and community dynamics in an online health community. ACM Trans. Comput.-Hum. Interact. **8**(2), 201–232 (2005)

Learning Programming in Virtual Reality Environments

Flornaldine Pierre, Fan Zhao[✉], and Anna Koufakou

Florida Gulf Coast University, Fort Myers, FL 33967, USA
fpierre1202@eagle.fgcu.edu, fzhao@fgcu.edu

Abstract. With the increasing popularity of Virtual Reality (VR), more and more studies have been undertaken to identify the applications of VR in different industries, especially in education. There are studies that have developed VR scenarios for training and education. However, few empirical research has been conducted on effects of VR games in higher education. This paper is to study students' acceptance of VR games in higher education and their actual performance through VR learning games. We propose that learning in VR games will positively motivate students' learning attitude in higher education, and learning in VR games will positively improve college students' learning in computer programming.

Keywords: Virtual Reality · Higher education · Programming

1 Introduction

Over the past decade, virtual reality (VR) technology has significantly amplified in prevalence. Whether it is a game or simulation VR is used for a variety of things. VR is typically used with a headset device such as the Oculus Rift™ to immerse the user into computer generated environment. This environment is a computer simulation of real-world scenarios that create a unique engagement improving users' interaction. VR is such an immersive and interactive platform that it could potentially be used to learn new skills and gain valuable knowledge in certain topics. Along with the Internet technologies, computer games and video games are getting popular among all demographical groups. The combination of VR and Games can be very interactive and attractive, especially in learning. However, do users accept this new learning environment, especially on complex topics such as computer programming? Some students may have trouble learning computer science skills in a traditional learning environment. Because of this, the use of a unification of VR and game-based learning methods could potentially be more efficient in gaining computer science skills over a traditional learning environment.

The overall user experience of a student learning through VR is quite an important aspect of the learning process. When a student is fully attentive and comfortable in an environment, it will be much easier for him or her to learn a new concept. If a VR game is adopted to teach a complex computer science subject, it is crucial that the user actually feels comfortable and attentive enough to learn in that particular environment. Surely, a VR environment is immersive and interactive. Are these particular characteristics

X. Fang (Ed.): HCII 2020, LNCS 12211, pp. 448–457, 2020.
https://doi.org/10.1007/978-3-030-50164-8_33

helpful in teaching new skills and subjects? VR technology has unique characteristics and features that may potentially be beneficial for education. This may be beneficial for VR education. This paper explores a study done on STEM and computer programming education through VR and games versus traditional learning environments.

2 Literature Review

Many students have trouble learning from a traditional learning environment. There are also many students who find it much easier to learn using visual methods [1]. A User's Virtual Reality Learning Experience is unique. The user is immersed into an environment usually through a headset and utilizes hand controllers to interact with the environment. A student's experience when using VR-based learning can either positive or negative. Having a positive learning atmosphere will motivate the student to learn as opposed to demotivate. VR is described as Immersion-Interaction-Imagination or I cubed by Burdea and Coiffet [2]. I cubed is an accurate depiction on what a VR experience is. Users are immersed into an imaginative and interactive environment. Both the quality of mental and physical immersion is important in having a successful experience with a VR world [3]. Truchly et al. [4] conducted a study on 52 students in a secondary school to analyze the differences of self-directed learning and VR-based learning. There were two lessons that took place where both groups for each lesson took pre-tests, completed studying, and took post-tests. The experimental groups, however, took part in VR games. The study concluded that learners enjoy the learning process when it is active and visual augmenting. The results of this study shows that the students in the experimental group were a lot more motivated to learn because they were using a new technology like VR (2018). Sutcliffe [5] infers that motivation is an important cognitive aspect when influencing learning and greater motivated students learn more effectively.

Some of the literature reveal reasons, based on their findings, as to why VR may help with learning processes. Most of the literature reveal that VR methods effectively help with the learning processes, based on their studies. Stuchlíková et al. [6] infers that VR education methods help students by using immersive interactive experiences to engage the student with their subject. According to Huang et al. [7], a great sense of presence is created in immersive environments, which strongly motivates the student and allows him or her to cognitively process the learning content efficiently. Learners can gain knowledge by interacting with objects and events from the artificial world. Immersion and simulation properties of VR may provide a great level of realism and interactivity while allowing the user to experience realistic learning situations [7]. VR learning environments offer learners with fast and realistic ways to interact with learning material. By allowing the students to analyze and evaluate their knowledge without the necessity of memorization, the students' creativity, problem solving, and communication skills are improved [6]. It is highly advantageous when students can directly interact with their learning content. Many complex STEM subjects require a high level of creativity and problem-solving skills. Due to its high visualization properties, VR is able to convey complex abstract concepts to users [2].

VR technology have a variety of unique properties that users can utilize. VR uses 3D graphic systems combined with various interface devices to give the effect immersion in an interactive virtual environment [1]. A VR system is capable of detecting user's physical inputs such as gestures and instantaneously respond to the user's activity. Users can simultaneously see the activity changes on screens based on their inputs and movements in the simulation [7]. Hanson and Shelton [8] demonstrate that VR allows students to have control over the 3D objects they see by manipulating, zooming in and out, and touching what they see. In non-immersive environments such as traditional learning environments, learners can hardly manipulate and interact with their learning material immediately [8]. Augmented Reality allows users to view virtual objects in the real world. Augmented reality is closely related to virtual reality as it also allows the manipulation and control over the virtual objects. Siegle's study [9] focuses on augmented reality and mentions apps such as Froggipedia that allows the user to see and interact with a virtual frog and its systems. Siegle [9] infers that 360° video properties allow students to analyze and observe objects and scenes in any direction they choose. Because of this, they can explore the virtual world unlike any way they could in real time.

A study done by Truchly et al. [4] involves two VR applications in subjects of computer networks. The groups in the study completed pre-tests, self-directed studying, and post-tests. The experimental groups, however, used the VR applications. The first lesson was on TCP/IP protocol stacks and the first VR application was a TCP/IP Protocol Stack game. The purpose of this game was to teach protocol stack layers to students with balloons that represent particular protocols [4]. In the TCP/IP experiment, learners were 25% more experienced in the control group as determined by the pretest. Despite this, the experimental group did 10% better than the control group in the post-test and gained 22% of knowledge of the topic whereas the control group lost 13% of knowledge [4]. The second lesson's subject was on firewall systems. The firewall VR game helped students gain an in-depth understanding on how firewall systems and rules functioned. Both groups completed a 39% on average on the pre-test, however the experimental group did 18% better than the control group on the post-test. Huang et al. [7] completed a research study using WVBS-ATS, an interactive web-based 3d VR learning system whose purpose is to teach undergraduate medical students about the structure of the human body. This study was done with 190 university students who were allowed to use the VR system at any time for a month. A survey was given at the conclusion of the study and based on the study, immersion, interaction, and imagination were all considered positive characteristics to improve problem-solving skills. The case study concluded that VR is an effective tool for learners to learn.

Object-Oriented Programming subjects such as encapsulation, abstraction, inheritance, and polymorphism can be complex and strenuous for students to learn. The research study done by Wong et al. [10] involves Odyssey of Phonies, a 2D mobile role-playing game with a purpose of teaching players Object-Oriented Programming. 20 undergraduate students were chosen to participate in the study. The students in the control group took a pre and posttest while the students of the experimental group took both tests and additionally played the game. The case study concluded that the student's understanding of Object-Oriented Programming significantly improved after using the Odyssey of Phonies. Based on their findings they inferred that game-based learning is an effective learning method to learn Object-Oriented Programming.

Gallego-Duran et al. [11] completed a study on game-based learning for logic-thinking and programming. A class on Computational Logics was given to students at the University of Alicante where lessons taught basic Prolog programming. During the years from 2000–2005 for the course, there was an overwhelming lack in student performance. Gallego-Duran et al. [11] inferred that students constantly required a significant amount of assistance, which eventually lead to large amounts of plagiarism and abandonment from students. 1/3rd of students abandoned the course while almost half plagiarized. These harsh statistics proved that most of these students strongly lacked motivation in learning Prolog. Based on their findings, Gallego-Duran et al. [11] inferred that players like to learn and practice by experimenting with environments and receiving feedback. To correct the problem going on in the Computational Logics course, they decided to create PLMan, a Pacman-like game. In PLMan, students control a Pacman-like character using Prolog programs. PLMan instantly gives visual and statistical feedback to the students on their performance. PLMan causes students to use their logic thinking in order to solve the given puzzles. When they receive feedback and results, they utilize those to acquire knowledge and update their code. Two Questionnaires were given to students and teachers to analyze the outcomes of using PLMan. The results showed that in the 2006/2007 term, 71% of students preferred activities from Computational Logics to any other subject activities comparing to fact that majority of the students were uninterested in Computational Logics. A quarter of the students showed enthusiasm for programming activities outside of class. The effects of using PLMan in Computational Logics were overwhelming positive for programming education.

However, few empirical research has been conducted on effects of VR games in higher education. This paper is to study students' acceptance of VR games in higher education and their actual performance through VR learning games.

3 Research Design

We planned three steps in this study. According to a recent survey, we noticed that over 50% of students with business majors in an American university never played VR games. Therefore, our first step is to let students play a VR game.

3.1 Preliminary Usage of VR in Class

In two classes of Introduction of Information Systems (total 72 students), we let students played a simple clue-finding game in a hotel scenario using Oculus Go. We asked students installed the software in their cell phones a day before. In a 75 min class, students were asked to play this game and complete a survey at the end of the class. Figure 1 shows college students playing VR games in a classroom. Figure 2 shows three scenarios in the game.

Fig. 1. Students playing the Oculus VR game

Fig. 2. VR game scenarios

3.2 Students' Acceptance of VR Games in Education

According to the theory of reasoned action (TRA), technology adoption behavior is influenced by belief, attitudes, and intentions. In particular, technology adoption may occur when [12]:

- a new product or service satisfies consumers' existing and unmet need
- a new product or service has a competitive advantage in relation to an existing one
- a painful experience or extreme dissatisfaction of a current product or service
- suppliers have sufficient control over a market to allow them to provide significant incentives to encourage adoption

The most prominent model applied by researchers to explain individual-level technology adoption is Technology Adoption Model (TAM). Based on the belief-attitude-performance chain, TAM is a parsimonious model explaining and predicting user acceptance of an information system (Fig. 3). We adopted TAM in the survey and tested students' attitude toward the VR game, including usefulness, ease of use, satisfaction, and game engagement using VR. Our survey results show that all the factors in the TAM are significantly related. Additionally, in a question asking students' attitude toward VR games in programming learning, 92% of students gave positive answers. Therefore, we believe that teaching programming related knowledge in higher education with VR games will be acceptable by students.

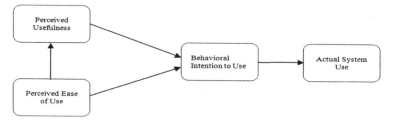

Fig. 3. Technology Adoption Model (TAM)

3.3 Design of a Sorting VR Game

With the confidence of VR game in higher education, we designed a VR game to teach students understanding computer algorithms. We did another survey in the same two classes asking students to list the most difficult algorithms they faced to when they started learning programming. According to the list, the first algorithm we chose is Quick Sort. Quick sort is one of the most useful algorithms in programming. It is a divide-and-conquer algorithm that first choosing a "pivot" element to "partition" the other elements into two sub-arrays, and decide which group is less than or greater than the "pivot". The game was developed in C# with Unity 3D and the VR device we chose is HTC Vive headset.

The followings are the four steps in the game:

Scene 1 (on start of game play):
User interface
- Text directs user to "Choose a pivot"
- Point system is displayed

User interaction
- Select a block

Code
- On select event for when user selects block, it is defined as the pivot for the current iteration of the game
- 2 pointers are automatically defined by game.

Pseudocode:
If pivot is very first or last block:
  Define the 2 blocks on other end as pointers
Else:
  Define left-most and right-most block as 2 pointers

Data
- Pivot
- 2 pointers
- Block items stored in ArrayList to define positions of blocks and calculate pointers
- ArrayList used to define final and correct positions of blocks in arraylist

Scene 2 (sorting process):
User interface
- Text asks user to compare pivot block value and left block value
- Text guides user to swap or move object based on comparison
- Scoring system (shows user current points in game)
- Confirms if user made correct move by X or check

User interaction
- Swaps or moves pointers

Code
- On swap or move of pointer, check if it is correct move.
- If correct move, move on to next step, and increment score
- Else, disregard move and return block to its previous position

Data
- User score
- Pivot
- 2 pointers
- Block items stored in ArrayList to define positions of blocks and calculate pointers
- ArrayList used to define final and correct positions of blocks in arraylist

Scene 3 (partition):
User interface
- Text lets user know partitioning will happen
- Scoring system (shows user current points in game)

User interaction
- User must choose new pivot based on partition

Code
- Game repeats scene 1

Scene 4 (end of game):
User interface
- Text lets user know game is complete
- Displays score

User interaction
- User can play game again

Code
- Checks if current positions correlate to final and correct positions based on ArrayList.

Data
- User score
- Block items stored in ArrayList to define positions of blocks and calculate pointers
- ArrayList used to define final and correct positions of blocks in ArrayList

Figure 4 shows the flow chart of the game and Fig. 5 is an actual game picture.

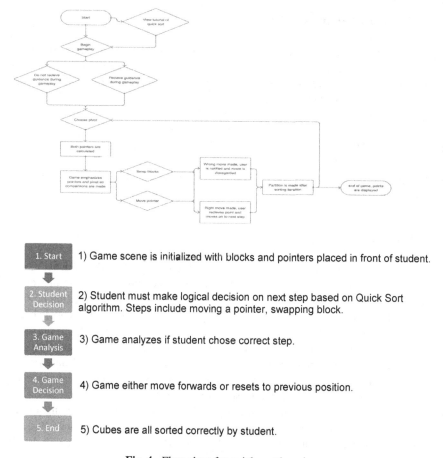

1. Start   1) Game scene is initialized with blocks and pointers placed in front of student.

2. Student Decision   2) Student must make logical decision on next step based on Quick Sort algorithm. Steps include moving a pointer, swapping block.

3. Game Analysis   3) Game analyzes if student chose correct step.

4. Game Decision   4) Game either move forwards or resets to previous position.

5. End   5) Cubes are all sorted correctly by student.

Fig. 4. Flow chart for quick sort learning

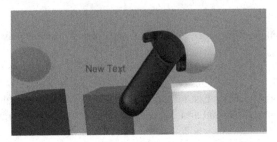

Fig. 5. VR game of quick sort

4   Proposed Research Model

According to the survey using TAM, our students have positive attitude toward learning programming in VR games. Additionally, our literature review shows that students were motivated in learning by VR technology because they will obtain better academic results than they got under the classic learning systems.

Hence, we propose:

H1: Learning in VR games will positively motivate students' learning attitude in higher education.
H2: Learning in VR games will positively improve college students' learning in computer programming.

5   Conclusions

The purpose of this study is to propose a theoretical study regarding the students' acceptance of VR technology and effects of learning in VR games based on a literature review. There are studies that have developed VR scenarios for training and education [1, 6, 7]. Our research highlighted the implications of an application with VR technology in higher education. Since some of the students never played VR games, we let them played an easy game in 75 min. We, then, adopted acceptance research model TAM to assess students' attitude toward learning using VR games. The results is positive. Therefore, we believe VR games can motivate college students in learning with its special characteristics, such as simulation of real-world scenarios, instant interactions, and so on. We proposed that learning in VR games will positively motivate students' learning attitude in higher education, and learning in VR games will positively improve college students' learning in computer programming. Our next step is to test our hypotheses with the VR game we developed.

References

1. Pan, Z., Cheok, A.D., Yang, H., Zhu, J., Shi, J.: Virtual reality and mixed reality for virtual learning environments. Comput. Graph. **30**, 20–28 (2006)
2. Burdea, G., Coiffet, P.: Virtual Reality Technology, 2nd edn. Wiley, New York (1999)

3. Sherman, W.R., Craig, A.B.: Understanding Virtual Reality. Morgan Kaufmann Publishers, New York (2003)
4. Truchly, P., Medvecký, M., Podhradský, P., Vančo, M.: Virtual reality applications in STEM education. In: 16th International Conference on Emerging eLearning Technologies and Applications (ICETA), Starý Smokovec, Slovakia, pp. 597–602 (2018)
5. Sutcliffe, A.: Multimedia and Virtual Reality. Lawrence Erlbaum Associates, New York (2003)
6. Stuchlíková, L., Kósa, A., Benko, P., Juhász, P.: Virtual reality vs. reality in engineering education. In: 15th International Conference on Emerging eLearning Technologies and Applications (ICETA), Stary Smokovec, pp. 1–6 (2017)
7. Huang, H.-M., Rulch, U., Liaw, S.: Investigating learners' attitudes toward virtual reality learning environments: based on a constructivist approach. Comput. Educ. 55(3), 1171–1182 (2011)
8. Hanson, K., Shelton, B.E.: Design and development of virtual reality: analysis of challenges faced by educators. Educ. Technol. Soc. 11(1), 118–131 (2008)
9. Siegle, D.: Seeing is believing: using virtual and augmented reality to enhance student learning. Gifted Child Today 42(1), 46–52 (2019)
10. Wong, Y., Hayati, I., Yatim, M., Hoe, T.: A propriety game based learning mobile game to learn object-oriented programming—Odyssey of Phoenix. In: IEEE 6th International Conference on Teaching, Assessment, and Learning for Engineering (TALE), Teaching, Assessment, and Learning for Engineering (TALE), p. 426 (2017)
11. Gallego-Duran, F.J., Villagra-Arnedo, C., Llorens-Largo, F., Molina-Carmona, R.: PLMan: a game-based learning activity for teaching logic thinking and programming. Int. J. Eng. Educ. 33(2), 807–815 (2017)
12. Fife, E., Pereira, F.: The diffusion of mobile data applications. J. Commun. Netw. 2(3), 5–11 (2003)

Learn to Cook for Yourself: Employing Gamification in a Recipe App Design to Promote a Healthy Living Experience to Young Generation

Pengyu Patrick Ren[✉], Zhenyu Cheryl Qian, and Jung Joo Sohn

Purdue University, West Lafayette, IN, USA
{ren184,qianz,jjsohn}@purdue.edu

Abstract. Nowadays, many young adults are relying on food delivery and unable to cook after they start to live alone. Different kinds of issues exist such as unhealthy diet behavior, environmental pollution, and loss of cooking culture. In this paper, we aim to design a recipe application that can influence young adults and encourage them to cook more and keep a healthier diet. Through a user-centered design approach, we first researched the young adults cooking behavior. After a questionnaire survey and two rounds of interview study, we drew insights from the raw data, which helped determine the design direction and method. In this design, the gamification strategy was selected as the primary feature of design to make the young adults more willing to cook. A recipe app-COOKIT was designed as a game, a repository, and a platform to motivate the cooking experience.

Keywords: Gamification · Cooking motivation · Recipe app design

1 Introduction

When young adults start their higher education or employment, they are also at the stage of forming their health behavioral patterns, which could last a whole lifetime and will influence not only themselves but also their families [1]. One of the most significant parts of their health-related behavioral pattern is their diet, and many problems exist in young people's diets. Breakfast skipping and fast-food consumption are pretty common among young people and could contribute to weight gain then lead to obesity. Young people, especially white-collar workers in China have also become the leading group of consuming delivery food, which is considered as unhealthy as fast-food [2]. Moreover, because of the convenience and the affordable price of fast-food and delivery food, this unhealthy food market is still proliferating, which leads to several issues: Food safety and hygiene are the first significant concerns. Secondly, people who live on fast-food tend to consume unhealthy foods in the long run that contain high sugar and high fat, especially low-price fast-food [3]. The plastic waste generated by the fast-food industry and food delivery is a huge environmental challenge all the countries are facing [4]. Other than that, young people's dependency on food delivery may also endanger the inheritance

© Springer Nature Switzerland AG 2020
X. Fang (Ed.): HCII 2020, LNCS 12211, pp. 458–470, 2020.
https://doi.org/10.1007/978-3-030-50164-8_34

of various traditional cuisine cultures [3]. With fewer and fewer young people cook at home, it is hard to maintain, inherit, and advocate the cooking and dining cultures.

Cooking for oneself is an excellent approach to solve the health issues created by low-quality food, decrease the food-wrapping waste deposit, and protect the cooking culture. Wolfson et al. [5] found that people who cook frequently generally follow a healthier diet than those who seldom cook. One major reason that the young generation is reluctant to cook is that they do not know how to cook. There have already been quite a few recipe applications, such as BigOven, Tasty, and Xiachufang (the most popular recipe app in China). Most of them provide recipe collection and cooking guidance functions. However, there are not many efficient ways to encourage young people to cook. A recipe application might be a useful tool for most people to learn how to cook, but the apps just serve as proper tools, few of them encourage users to cook. Unlike food delivery platforms always offering discounts and coupons to encourage the users to order more [2], the recipe applications have a less positive interaction and encouragements for the users. The motivation for cooking could only originate from the users themselves.

In this research, we utilize the gamification method to design a recipe application. The objectives of this project are to design a new recipe app by employing the gamification method in the app. Compared with the regular recipe apps, this app should build a more engaging environment. The users should be engaged not only in the cooking process but also participate in the whole user experience. In another way, instead of designing a useful tool for cooking guidance, this app should provide a platform or community to help young people learn, enjoy cooking and thus form good cooking and diet habits in the long term.

2   Related Works

2.1   Problems in Young Adults' Diet

During the first screening of literature, we decide to focus on three major problems in the current diet habits of the young generation.

The first issue is the health and safety issue. Because the delivery food and fast food are so convenient and relatively cheap, the quality of the food is relatively low and unhealthy. It tends to use more oil and sugar, thus leads to the over-weight, obesity, and diet-related non-communicable diseases increasing [3]. Besides, about 255 million (234–274) DALYs (Disability Adjusted Life Years) and 11 million deaths were caused by dietary risk factors worldwide in 2017 [6].

The second problem is the environmental issue created by the delivery food waste, which is caused by plastic utensils and packages [3]. Since the restaurants are competing with each other by providing the customers with a better experience, there are more and more disposable utensils and over-designed packages created in the delivery food industry. And it becomes a big challenge for municipal solid waste management [4].

Besides, the food and cooking culture is also endangered because of the delivery of food and fast food. The food preparation time, cooking time, and cooking frequency of Americans have decreased from 1975 to 2006 [7]. Cooking is not only a simple activity for making food, but it is also an important part of a family's own culture and it improves the family bond [3]. If more and more young adults cannot cook in the future, the cooking will be a ritualized symbol but not an everyday activity in future families [3].

2.2 Make Cooking an Engaging Process

How to encourage young adults to cook is the most important research focus of this project. Since most of the young adults have low or no cooking experience, they are not familiar with cooking and not interested in cooking. One of the previous research papers indicates that the facilitators for encouraging cooking are: organizing, planning, and enjoyment of cooking [8]. And these skills or factors enable people to incorporate cooking into their daily life. Organizing and planning the cost and time to find time to cook and cook most efficiently are important skills. And those who can utilize these skills are more willing to cook [8]. Besides, those people who enjoy the cooking process are also highly motivated to cook [8]. Thus, this design also has functions that have been designed to make up for the lack of these skills, and provides the users with a more enjoyable cooking learning guidance.

2.3 Gamification as the Main Method

The gamification method, which refers to "using game-based mechanics, aesthetics and game thinking to engage people, motivate action, promote learning, and solve problems" [9], has been considered as a practical design approach. Because gamification has a positive impact on users' engagement, especially in the short term [10], many mobile applications adopted the gamification method and benefited from it. For example, Walkr, a gamified fitness app launched in 2014, transforms people's walking steps into energy fuel for the spaceship in the app. It encourages people to walk more and is still popular [11]. Another successful example could be the Forest app that helps the users focus on their work and put down their phones. If the user does not play their phone during the preset time, then a tree will be planted in the app [12]. With the points, rewards, and levels in the apps, a gamified app increases the additional value users can get from the app, and it also increases the engagement of the user.

We decided to adopt gamification method into this project and engage the users to learn how to cook, and enjoy the cooking as if they are playing a game. The functions of the app could help the users organize the time, plan, and ingredients to cook more efficiently.

To take full advantage of the gamification method, we chose *Scott Nicholson's 2015 gamification recipe paper* [13] as the major guideline. There are two types of gamification methods: reward-based gamification and meaningful gamification, while the first one is for short-term engagement and the second one is for the long-term value [13]. In our case, the reward mechanism is used to engage the users in the short term. But overall, our meaningful gamification method aims to engage the users in the cooking itself instead of using our app, that is to say, the app is just the tool to help the users get familiar with cooking and interested in it, and they can stop using the app after the cooking habit is formed.

3   User Research and Findings

3.1   User Study

We conducted a questionnaire survey first to understand the young adults' cooking condition. For research convenience, 100 Chinese young adults from 19 to 30 years old have been recruited as the participants through an online survey platform. 96 valid questionnaires were collected eventually from 42 males and 54 females. Through the questionnaire survey, the general cooking condition and recipe app using condition were clear. Also, 60 participants claimed they are willing to accept our further interviews. Then after the questionnaire survey, 12 participants were recruited from the 60 participants for the two rounds of interview, which are for knowing the inconvenience during cooking while using the recipe application and their motivation for cooking.

The interview questions are mixed and listed below:

- How long have you stayed in your city?
- Have you got used to the lifestyle there?
- Are you living alone? Whom do you cook for?
- How often and when do you usually cook? If not very often, why?
- Are you satisfied with your cooking outcomes?
- What kinds of recipes have you used (book, app, video)?
- Do you think the recipes are helpful?
- Do you use a recipe to cook every time?
- Are you satisfied with the recipes you have used? What are the advantages?
- During your recipe using process, what inconvenient experience did you have?
- Why did you start to cook? For what kind of reason?
- If there was any reason, what stops you from cooking sometimes?

After the interviews, we highlighted the keywords in the transcripts of each participant to seek the valuable points and had several discussions about our findings.

3.2   Insights Gained from User Research

The main insights from the research are listed below:

The inconvenience of existing recipe apps. Most of the interviewees and 74% of the questionnaire participants mentioned it was hard to use the touchscreen while their hands are wet, oiled, or occupied. The second frequently-mentioned problem was that when they want to cook a specific dish, they always do not have all the ingredients. Other inconvenient experiences that have been mentioned are: the amounts of the ingredients are unclear in some cases; how long each step should take is unclear, the instruction of one step is too long to memorize, etc.

Different purposes for cooking. When asked about why they start to cook, the general motivation of our interviewees is that most of them start to live alone and try to take care of themselves. Most of them believe home-cooking meals are healthier than the delivery food and the food in the restaurants. More specific reasons that motivate our interviewees to cook are 1. They get interested in a specific dish and want to cook and eat it at home. 2. They miss their hometown cuisine or their parents' dish. 3. They want to save money. 4. They want to cook for their friends or partner. 5. They want to eat healthily or lose weight. Most of our participants have one or two very clear reasons to cook.

Some lack of motivation to cook. Young people may have different reasons to cook. However, they do not cook very frequently. Among our interviewees, only 4 of them cook frequently, at least seven times a week on average. The others mainly cook during the weekend, or at night when they are relatively not busy. The average cooking time is three times per week. Young adults are always busy with their work and life. The first factor that stops many young adults form cooking is the time issue. They think cooking is too time-consuming and they just want to rest after a busy day. The second factor is the delivery food service is too convenient, and many young adults have a strong dependency on it. The third factor is that they think cooking a meal requires a great effort and it is bothering. Many mentioned that it was bothering to go to grocery shopping and prepare all the ingredients, and other than the real cooking process, there are too many preparations like defrosting the meat, washing the ingredients, etc. The fourth factor is that they think cooking is too hard for them after several times of failure. From the interviews, we found out this is mainly because the person is not skilled at cooking, while the dish was not an easy one and requires some cooking experience. Other reasons why they give up cooking are: 1. They do not know what to cook. 2. The dish requires ingredients that they do not have at home. 3. The dish they want to cook is too hard.

4   Design Process

After the user research, we decided on the guidelines of our application design. Increasing people's cooking motivation was defined as our main design goal. Thus, the gamification method was chosen as the main strategy used in the app design. The reasons why people cook were also used to design the features of the app to motivate people in a gamified way. As for the inconveniences during cooking and using an app, we also tried to add functions to improve the user experience of our app. In this design, Chinese dishes and recipes are used as examples.

We first went through several rounds of brainstorming and ideation to come up with some ideas. After the direction has been decided, we confirmed the functional structure of our app. Then we started to design the wireframe and the user interface of the app. In the last step, we made an interactive prototype with animations, which enabled us to test our design (Fig. 1).

4.1   Main Features

There are three main features of this recipe app design to motivate and engage users:

Collectible card game. To adopt the gamification method, the collectible card game has been adapted for the main feature. This type of game encourages players to collect

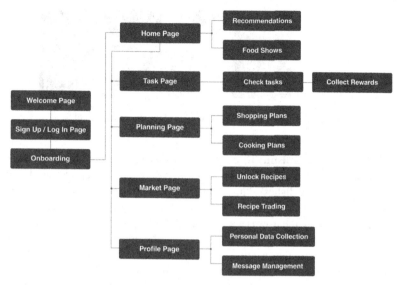

Fig. 1. Information structure of COOKIT

cards, and trade cards with others. In this app, we designed all the recipes into cards. In the beginning, a user could choose ten free recipe cards, and then they can collect more and trade cards with other users. In addition to this, the card system has four features:

1. *Difficulty levels.* All the dishes are categorized into four difficulty levels, from one star to four stars, located at the bottom right corner on the card. The difficulty-level feature makes it more friendly to the new cooks, which guides them to learn to cook from the easiest dishes progressively. This also makes it more challenging for users who have some cooking skills to keep trying more challenging dishes.
2. *Rarity.* The rarity is another feature of this card system, represented by stars in the white, blue, pink, or golden colors. The white star cards are the most common dishes, well-known and cooked by most people no matter at home or in the restaurants. The blue star cards are the regional cuisine. They are based on states or local regions, usually cooked by local people and are unusual and attractive to the people in other regions. The pink star cards are the dishes know by fewer people. They usually require unique ingredients or cooking techniques. The golden dishes are the rarest ones invented by famous cooks and usually only available in some famous restaurants. In summary, the fewer people know the dish, the rarer the dish is in this app. This rarity feature encourages users to seek rarer dishes, thus encourage them to unlock more new dishes and trade with other users. It not only creates more interactions among the users but also keeps this app fresh to them to keep using.
3. *Cuisine cultures.* At the top left corner, it indicates to which cuisine culture the dish belongs. This is a feature that helps the user know more about various cooking cultures and also their diverse tastes.
4. *Like button.* At the top right corner, there is a like button. Once tapped, this dish will enter to the cooking plan, and the app will know more about the user's taste (Fig. 2).

Fig. 2. Difficulty/rarity framework and recipe card examples

Task and Reward mechanism. To engage the users in the short term, the task and reward system has been designed as one of the features. In this app, certain behaviors like "cooking three 1-star dishes", "make cooking plan three times", and "keep cooking for a week" are regarded as tasks. And most tasks encourage the users to cook. After a user cooks a certain dish, the user is encouraged to take a photo of the dish for recording it to the cooking history, the photo-taking also lets the app know this certain dish has been cooked. Once a certain procedure of a task has been implemented successfully, the task will be completed and the reward will be issued to the user. The rewards in this app are coins and EXP (Experience). The coins could be used as money to buy new recipe cards and other services, such as ingredient delivery. The EXP will be used to upgrade a user's level (Fig. 3).

Fig. 3. Task examples

Membership subscription. Users can subscribe to the membership of this app. Membership subscription is not only part of the business model; more importantly, it also encourages the users to use the app more frequently. Additional values will be unlocked with a subscription, such as the ingredients shopping discounts, new recipes unlock every day and a faster EXP growth. Once the users subscribed to the membership, they will try to make the best of the membership benefits, and this also motivates them to keep using the app.

On the other hand, the membership subscription also helps to create a positive word-of-mouth effect if the users value the service [14], which will also benefit the promotion of the app.

4.2 Main Functions

As a recipe app teaching and nurturing the cooking behaviors, there are a group of main functions in the COOKIT:

Smart Recommendations, shopping discounts, and food-related shows. On   the home page, dishes will be recommended based on the time during a day, user's taste, and the ingredients they have. This function makes it easier for the users to decide what dish to cook, and it makes sure they have the ingredients by checking their previous shopping plans. Subscribed users could also get discounts when check-out by showing their QR code in the grocery store that is collaborated with the app. This discount benefit encourages users to buy more ingredients. At the bottom half of the home page, there are food-related shows, which can make the users get interested in a particular dish, and want to cook and eat it. Recommendations will also show up to encourage the users to try to cook it when a particular dish appears (Fig. 4).

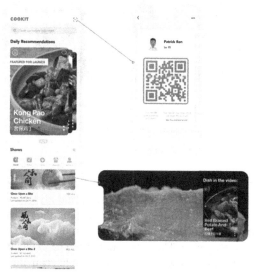

Fig. 4. Smart Recommendations, shopping discounts function, and food-related shows on the home screen

Step by step cooking mode. After a user clicked on a recipe card, it will show the detailed recipe of that dish, which includes the ingredients with amounts, the tips for cooking, and steps with descriptions. Since it is inconvenient to touch the screen during cooking, the app provides a step by step cooking mode. It is another way of showing the recipe with the same content. By tapping the start button, it will go to the step by step cooking mode and play the cooking guidance video of each step. After one step has finished, the next step will play automatically. Each step video will last for the actual cooking time required by that step. It will not only make it easier for the user to follow the steps with voice guidance and videos, but it will also train the users to cook at an appropriate time. Fast forward, rewind, mute, and speed up/down buttons are also provided if a user does not want to follow the auto-play (Fig. 5).

Fig. 5. Recipe screen and step by step cooking mode

Cooking and shopping list planning. Every time a user taps the like icon on the card, the dish will be added to the cooking plan. A user could also make a shopping list in this app. By selecting the date, and then simply dragging the recipe card into the cart, the dish will be added to the cooking plan, and the ingredients for cooking that dish will be generated to the shopping plan. The user could also type in the ingredients manually. After the shopping plan is made, users will receive reminders at the preset time (Fig. 6).

Unlock new recipes like exploring new domains. This app gives new users ten free recipe cards at the beginning, then the users are encouraged to collect more recipes. There are three ways to unlock new recipes in this app: 1. The user could use the coins to purchase recipe bundles to unlock 5 random new recipes. The cards in the bundle will have different rarities, which uses the randomness and the surprise to encourage the users to explore more. The rarer the recipe is, the possibility of getting it is lower. 2. After the users have collected a considerable amount of coins, they can unlock a big number

Fig. 6. Cooking and shopping planning screen

of a certain category of recipes with one purchase, like 500 coins for 50 home-cooking recipe cards. These recipes are relatively cooked more by people and less rare, so it has been made easier for the users to collect them all at once. 3. The user is also encouraged to trade their recipe cards with other users. As it shows in the image, a user can put his or her recipe on the "market" in the app. If other users are interested in that certain recipe, they can buy it with coins. Or they can also message the seller to see what recipe he or she wants, and then trade with their recipe.

The first two ways are designed to create more interactions between the users and the app, by using the randomness to motivate the users to unlock more recipes. The "market" in the app is aimed to create more interactions among the users, build a community in the app, and make the users more engaged (Fig. 7).

Fig. 7. Market screen

Personal data collection. In the profile page, users can edit their personal information like their name and avatar. They can also check their personal data like their level, recipe collection, the dishes they have cooked, the cuisine they have tried, etc.

Messaging center for communication. The last function is the message function. This app allows users to message other users and add friends. It provides a platform for friends to communicate, compete, and trade recipe cards. It also creates opportunities for young adults to make new friends by cooking (Fig. 8).

Fig. 8. Profile and message page

5   Heuristic Evaluation to Assess the Prototype

Heuristic evaluation is a usability testing method where "several expert evaluators are asked to evaluate the user interfaces with sets of principles of an ideal system" [15]. After the design has been finished, we made an interactive prototype of the app to conduct a heuristic evaluation to assess its quality. We recruited five graduate design students as the evaluation experts. Most heuristics are selected which is specialized for gamification design evaluation [16], since gamification is the main method. The other three sets of heuristics that focus on aesthetics, functionality, and usability of the app have also been selected. The 0–4 rating sheet with 14 heuristics and the prototype were provided to each of our evaluators. After the evaluation, evaluators were asked about their overall opinions on the app.

The feedback we received from the participants were generally positive. The evaluation results indicated that the gamification part of our app has no problem. Most of the evaluators think the recipe card design is unique and exciting. They also think the food shows on the home page can really help the users get interested in food and cooking. Overall, their opinion on this app is positive and they are willing to try this app.

There were some valuable negative feedbacks as well. One of the evaluators commented that the information level of this app is not sufficient, if compared with the regular recipe apps. If a user wants to cook a dish which he or she does not own the recipe in this app, there could be some troubles. Take this point into consideration, the number of cards that will be given to the new users worth being considered more. The reward amount, the task difficulty, the cost of unlocking new cards, and the value of each rarity should also be balanced in a better way.

6 Discussion and Conclusion

To encourage young adults to cook more, we designed this recipe app by employing the gamification method. Started with the user research, one round questionnaire survey, and two rounds of interviews have been conducted to understand the current young people's cooking and recipe app using condition. Through the user study, people's cooking motivation and reasons for not cooking were clear, which helped the design process significantly. We designed a collectible recipe app with the inspiration of the collective card game. By encouraging users to collect and trade recipe cards, we promoted the interaction among the users and their engagement in the app. In order to unlock more recipes, a user needs to cook more to earn the coins. Thus, a positive loop of "cooking-being rewarded-unlocking new recipes" was created. Other features of the app such as food shows, shopping discounts, cuisine culture, and personal cooking data collection also give a user more motivation to cook, while the tasks and planning function keeps a user cook regularly.

In this study, the gamification part of the app has no major problem, as the evaluation turned out. However, there are some details and the balance of the system could be polished. Also, the long-term influence on young adults cooking motivation requires the users to use the app in a long time, which is hard to realize with an interactive prototype. Our future work may focus on making a more detailed working prototype and conducting an evaluation of the long-term effect.

References

1. Poobalan, A.S., Aucott, L.S., Clarke, A., Smith, W.C.S.: Diet behaviour among young people in transition to adulthood (18–25 year olds): a mixed method study. Health Psychol. Behav. Med.: Open Access J. 2(1), 909–928 (2014)
2. Daxue Consulting: The food delivery market in Great China in 2019. https://daxueconsult ing.com/o2o-food-delivery-market-in-china/. Accessed 06 Oct 2019
3. Maimaiti, M., Zhao, X., Jia, M., Ru, Y., Zhu, S.: How we eat determines what we become: opportunities and challenges brought by food delivery industry in a changing world in China. Eur. J. Clin. Nutr. 72(9), 1282–1286 (2018)
4. Song, G., Zhang, H., Duan, H., Xu, M.: Packaging waste from food delivery in China's mega cities. Resour. Conserv. Recycl. 130, 226–227 (2018)
5. Wolfson, J.A., Bleich, S.N.: Is cooking at home associated with better diet quality or weight-loss intention? Public Health Nutr. 18(8), 1397–1406 (2015)
6. Afshin, A., et al.: Health effects of dietary risks in 195 countries, 1990–2017: a systematic analysis for the global burden of disease study 2017. The Lancet 393(10184), 1958–1972 (2019)
7. Zick, C.D., Stevens, R.B.: Trends in Americans' food-related time use: 1975–2006. Public Health Nutr. 13(7), 1064–1072 (2010)
8. Wolfson, J.A., Bleich, S.N., Smith, K.C., Frattaroli, S.: What does cooking mean to you? Perceptions of cooking and factors related to cooking behavior. Appetite 97, 146–154 (2016)
9. Kapp, K.M.: The Gamification of Learning and Instruction: Game-Based Methods and Strategies for Training and Education, 1st edn. Wiley, Hoboken (2012). Safari, an O'Reilly Media Company

10. Looyestyn, J., Kernot, J., Boshoff, K., Ryan, J., Edney, S., Maher, C.: Does gamification increase engagement with online programs? A systematic review. PLoS ONE **12**(3), E0173403 (2017)
11. Fourdesire: Make Walking Fun! 5th Anniversary of 'Walkr' Up to 6-million Downloads. https://www.prnewswire.com/news-releases/make-walking-fun-5th-anniversary-of-walkr-up-to-6-million-downloads-300891422.html. Accessed 06 Oct 2019
12. Forest. https://www.forestapp.cc. Accessed 06 Oct 2019
13. Nicholson, S.: A RECIPE for meaningful gamification. In: Reiners, T., Wood, L.C. (eds.) Gamification in Education and Business, pp. 1–20. Springer, Cham (2015). https://doi.org/10.1007/978-3-319-10208-5_1
14. Fu, D., Hong, Y., Wang, K., Fan, W.: Effects of membership tier on user content generation behaviors: evidence from online reviews. Electron. Commer. Res. **18**(3), 457–483 (2018). https://doi.org/10.1007/s10660-017-9266-7
15. Kölling, M., McKay, F.: Heuristic evaluation for novice programming systems. ACM Trans. Comput. Educ. (TOCE) **16**(3), 1–30 (2016)
16. Tondello, G.F., Kappen, D.L., Mekler, E.D., Ganaba, M., Nacke, L.E.: Heuristic evaluation for gameful design. In: Proceedings of the 2016 Annual Symposium on Computer-Human Interaction in Play Companion Extended Abstracts, pp. 315–323 (2016)

Adaptive Puzzle Generation
for Computational Thinking

Marco Scirea[(✉)]

University of Southern Denmark, Odense, Denmark
`msc@mmmi.sdu.dk`
`http://marcoscirea.com`

Abstract. This paper describes a system to generate puzzles with a difficulty degree that adapts to the player. The puzzle is designed with the objective of being used by young pupils, and it is mainly a planning/sequencing task, which is considered one of the aspects of computational thinking. The system is powered by a constrained multi-objective algorithm (NSFI-2Pop) – which evolves the sequences of actions necessary to solve the puzzle – combined with a stochastic algorithm that translates the sequences in playable levels. We also present a pilot evaluation of the system, which seems to indicate that the levels presented to the player are perceived as having an increasing difficulty.

Keywords: Procedural content generation · Evolutionary algorithms · Computational thinking

1 Introduction

Computational thinking (CT) – being able to express problems and solutions in ways that a computer could execute – is becoming increasingly important in young pupils' education, given the increasing digitisation of our world.

Puzzles have been a common method to introduce young pupils to computational thinking [13]. The issue we want to address in this paper is that these puzzles, whether in digital or paper format, only present a static set of challenges and difficulty progression. This approach might work for some pupils, but wouldn't it be better for learning and concept assimilation if we could tailor the puzzles to fit each student's learning? The traditional way to do this, for example in the class, would be for the teacher to create new levels or new puzzles. This is however unpractical and very time consuming, especially if the quality of the new puzzles has to be consistent and high. In the case of digital puzzles it would also require the CT teachers to be programmers, as well as skilled game designers. So our goal here is also to alleviate the workload of teachers, and make it easier for them to assign digital puzzles to their pupils, as part of their augmented classroom [1] or as flipped classroom materials [8].

This paper will focus on logical puzzles in which the solution is unique and represented by a specific sequence of actions. Such puzzles can range from classical problems such as "river crossing puzzles" to puzzles that are closer to

X. Fang (Ed.): HCII 2020, LNCS 12211, pp. 471–485, 2020.
https://doi.org/10.1007/978-3-030-50164-8_35

computer science topics (e.g. *Knight Tour*[1] is a puzzle where the player has to make a knight visit each city in a map/graph once and only once). Examples of such puzzles can be seen in games such as river-crossing puzzles, various puzzles appearing in the *Professor Layton* (Level-5, Matrix Software, 2007–2017) series (e.g. the *Toy Car minigame* in *Professor Layton and the Unwound future* [Level-5, 2008]), *Sokoban* (Thinking Rabbit, 1982), escape-the-room games (e.g. the *Zero Escape* game series [Spike Chunsoft, 2009–2016]), most adventure games (e.g. *The Curse of Monkey Island* [LucasArts, 1997]), and many more. Many puzzles leave more freedom to the player in how to solve them, allowing for more creative problem-solving, but we decided to focus on puzzles with predefined solutions since they are more controllable and allow us to make sure the player has mastered specific concepts when they are able to solve the problem.

In this project we want to generate puzzles (and their solutions) that require the player to reason about sequences of actions, their effect, and how a goal can be achieved in optimal way. Moreover, in order to solve the puzzles, the player has to simulate the effect of a sequence of instructions; when the produced outcome diverges from the player's intuition, the player will be forced to redesign the solution, and improve his or her understanding of the effect of the instructions on the state of the game. These are central aspects of CT: the player has to decompose the problem, formulate an algorithmic sequence of instructions to solve the puzzle, and possibly recognise similar situations from previous puzzles [18]. We decided therefore to evolve puzzle solutions, so our game will always propose the players: i) a solvable puzzle, ii) which include different kinds of challenges, iii) and have an adaptive difficulty level.

Finally, to make the system adapt to the player we introduce a simple player model that keeps track of: what puzzles the player is able to solve as a measure of what concepts have been internalised, and how long does the player take to solve each challenge, giving us a measure of how difficult the puzzle is perceived. This model influences the second and third objective described above, so that the target for the generative system is adjusted as the player is observed playing.

2   Background

2.1   Procedural Content Generation

Procedural content generation is an active field that focuses on generating content for games through AI methods [9]. There has already been some research in generating content for some puzzle games, but without keeping in account the learning aspect [4]. Some examples include: level generation for the *Cut the Rope* (ZeptoLab, 2010) puzzle game [17], generation of *Sokoban* levels [11], and generation of narrative puzzles for adventure games [7]. Moreover, the type of adaptive content generation that this paper describes can be seen as an instance of the experience-driven procedural content generation framework (*EDPCG*) [19], where the game adaptation mechanism generates puzzles with particular elements and challenges in response to the player's actions.

---

[1] https://teachinglondoncomputing.org/puzzles/.

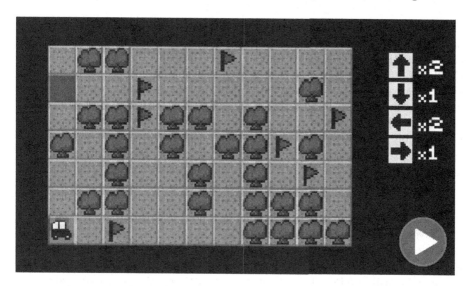

Fig. 1. An example of how the puzzle is presented to the player. See Fig. 2 for the solution to this puzzle. (Color figure online)

2.2 Computational Thinking

Computational thinking has been defined as "a universally applicable attitude and skill set everyone, not just computer scientists, would be eager to learn and use" [18]. That can be seen as a very vague definition, and there is still much debate over a more precise definition of what computational thinking is, and what are its components.

Brennan and Resnick developed a definition of computational thinking that involves three key dimensions: "*computational concepts* (the concepts designers employ as they program), *computational practices* (the practices designers develop as they program), and *computational perspectives* (the perspectives designers form about the world around them and about themselves)" [2]. The computational concepts they identify are: *sequences, loops, parallelism, events, conditionals, operators,* and *data.* Computational practices are defined as *being incremental and iterative, testing and debugging, reusing and remixing,* and *abstracting and modularizing.*

In this paper, our system mostly focuses on *sequences* concepts and on *being incremental and iterative* (since our system generates more and more complex problems), and *testing and debugging* (since the game allows the pupils to plan their solutions and then see how it works, debug it, and improve on it).

2.3 Evolutionary Computation

To generate the puzzles we use an evolutionary algorithm, this is a family of algorithms for global optimisation inspired by biological evolution. These algorithms can create highly optimised solutions for a wide variety of problems and moreover are able to create not just one solution but a wide range of different, but similarly optimised ones. In particular, we use a Multi-Objective Optimisation (MOO) approach: this is defined as the process of simultaneously optimising multiple objective functions. In most multi-objective optimisation problems, there is no single solution that simultaneously optimises every objective. In this case, the objective functions are said to be partially conflicting, and there exists, a number (possibly infinite) of Pareto optimal solutions. To understand what makes a solution better than another the concept of Pareto dominance is introduced: this is a binary relation between two solutions where one solution is Pareto dominant with respect to another solution if, for all objectives, it improves on the other solution.

Many search/optimisation problems have not only one or several numerical objectives, but also a number of constraints - binary conditions that need to be satisfied for a solution to be valid. A number of constraint-handling techniques have been developed to deal with such cases within evolutionary algorithms. The Feasible/Infeasible 2-Population method (FI-2POP) [12] is a constrained evolutionary algorithm that maintains two populations evolving in parallel, where feasible solutions are selected and bred to improve their objective function values, while infeasible solutions are selected and bred to reduce their constraint violations. In each generation, individuals are tested for constraint violations; if they present at least one violation they are moved to the 'Infeasible' population, otherwise they are moved to the 'Feasible' population. An interesting feature of this algorithm is that the infeasible population influences, and sometimes dominates, the genetic material of the optimal solution. Since the infeasible population is not evaluated by the objective function, it does not become fixed in a sub-optimal solution, but rather is free to explore boundary regions, where an optimum solution is most likely to be found.

When dealing with constrained optimisation problems, the approach is usually to introduce penalty functions to act for the constraints. Such an approach favours feasible solutions over the infeasible ones, potentially removing infeasible individuals that may lead to an optimal solution, and finding solutions that can be considered local optimum. There have been many examples of constrained multi-objective optimisation algorithms [3,6,10,14]. In this paper we use an algorithm called Non-dominated Sorting Feasible-Infeasible 2 Populations (NSFI-2POP) [15,16], which combines the benefits of maintaining an infeasible population, free to explore the solution space without being dominated by the objective fitness function(s), and finding the Pareto optimal solution for multiple objectives. This algorithm is essentially a combination of FI-2POP and NSGA-II [5].

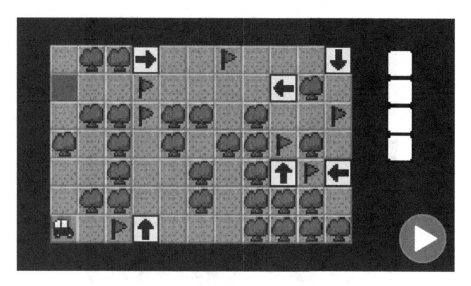

Fig. 2. The solution to the puzzle in Fig. 1.

3   The System

In this section we discuss the details of the implementation of the system, in particular describing how does the game work, how does the puzzle generation work, and how we model the current solving ability of the player.

3.1   The Game

We have chosen to recreate a mini-game from *Professor Layton and the Unwound future* [Level-5, 2008]); the game's goal is for a toy car to reach the goal square, while collecting all the flags on its path (see Fig. 1). Looking at Fig. 1, the car sprite indicates that the starting direction is to the right, the red tile is the goal that the car has to reach, and the flags have to be collected on the way. On the right the direction tiles that the player can drag-and-drop on the game map can be found. Note that direction tiles can only be placed on empty spaces. On the bottom right the play button starts the simulation, so that the player can observe if plan works as expected.

The player interacts with the game by positioning the direction tiles within the game grid, and then by pressing the "play" button the player is able to observe the plan being executed. A small modification to the original game is that, as the car walks over the direction-change tiles, these are picked up, this can create more complex puzzles when the sequence is long enough (see Fig. 12). Note that the player has no way to interact with the game once the simulation has started (apart from aborting it), which means that the player has to create and "test" the plan in its head before being able to see the actual results.

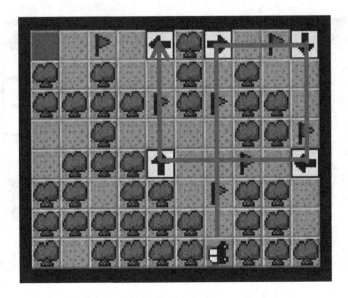

Fig. 3. A visualization of what we consider a *loop* in the context of this game

As discussed in Sect. 2.2, our system mostly focuses on *sequences* concepts, on *being incremental and iterative*, and on *testing and debugging*.

While creating lengthy sequences is the most obvious challenge, puzzles can also include various other features, such as "loops" and recurring paths. By loops we don't mean in the programming sense, but when the player has to make the car follow a path that makes it go through all directions before coming back to the starting one (e.g [left, up, right, down, left], also see Fig. 3).

3.2 Generation of Puzzle from Solution

The evolutionary algorithm generates a set of directions that represent the solution of the puzzle. That is an abstraction, and not a complete level as can be seen in the previous figures. To generate the final level the set is passed to a semi-stochastic algorithm which is described in Fig. 4.

As can be observed in Fig. 4, the algorithm has a stochastic component, meaning that from the same solution different boards can be created (see Fig. 5).

3.3   GA

This section describes details of the evolutionary system where domain-specific choices had to be made that deviate from the more general NSFI-2POP structure defined in Sect. 2.3.

```
L: list of moves
increase: increase in chance of changing direction
P = empty list to hold the path
    carCoordinates = {0,0}
    foreach move m in L:
        changeProbability = 0
        while random number > changeProbability:
            carCoordinate = new position moving by m
            add carCoordinate to P
            changeProbability += increase
        Add an objective in the segment the car has traversed
    spawn car at {0,0}
    spawn goal at last position in P
    foreach tile t not in P:
        if random number > 0.3
            spawn obstacle in t
```

Fig. 4. Level generation algorithm: this transforms the evolved sequence of moves into the actual visual level

Genome Representation. The evolutionary genome consists of a number of values that represent the moves necessary to solve the puzzle. These values are left, right, up, down, and correspond to the tiles that the player has to place on the board (see Fig. 2). The size of the genome is variable, since we want to be able to generate puzzles with different and possibly quite long sequences.

Constraints. We have two constraints in this problem: we do not want to create solutions which contains opposite directions one after the other (e.g [..., left, right, ...]) nor solution that contain the same direction more than once consequently (e.g [..., left, left, ...]). The opposite case is the most crucial, since it would represent an impossible solution (see Fig. 6).

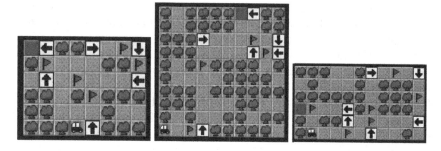

Fig. 5. Three examples of puzzles that are represented by the same solution $\{U, R, D, L, U, L\}$, showing how the system can express the same problem in a number of different ways

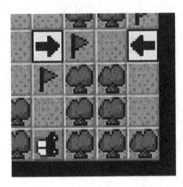

Fig. 6. Example of a situation we would like to avoid and use as a constraint to the evolution

The second case, where we have the same direction more than once consequently, is less critical, but it amounts to the same solution if the two duplicates where one:

$$[up, \textbf{left}, \textbf{left}, up, right] \equiv [up, \textbf{left}, up, right]$$

As such the feasability equation we define is:

$$Feasibility = -\sum_{i=0}^{n-1}(Opposite(i, i+1) + Same(i, i+1))$$

where n is the length of the genome.

The two functions in the above equation are both Boolean ones, returning either 0 or 1 depending if the constraint is satisfied or not. The Feasibility function can return a number between $[0, -2(n-1)]$, where 0 means that the individual satisfies all constraints and can consequently be transferred from the infeasible population to the feasible one.

Fitness Objectives. The objectives used to evolve the individuals in the feasible population are two: the length of the sequence, and the amount of challenges (*loops*, see Sect. 3.1). These objectives do not follow a maximization or minimization problem (e.g. we do not want to evolve towards infinitely large sequences, since it does not make sense to present the player such puzzles). Instead both objectives have a target number, which is variable as time progresses and the player solves puzzles.

These numerical targets are controlled by the player model (see Sect. 3.4), and represent the current difficulty calculated as the one fitting the player's current skill level.

Selection Operator. The feasible population (i.e. that running NSGA-II) utilises a binary tournament selection operator: two random individuals are chosen from the population and compared. The individual that dominates the pair is selected as a parent for a crossover operator, this operator is executed twice to obtain the two parents required by a crossover operator. In the event neither individual dominates the pair, a parent is chosen randomly among the pair. The infeasible population uses a roulette-wheel selection operator: the selection is a stochastic process where individuals have a probability of becoming parents for the next generation proportional to their fitness. In this way individuals with higher fitness are more likely to be selected while individuals with lower fitness have a lesser chance, however they may have genetic material that could prove useful to future generations and are therefore preserved.

Fig. 7. A graphical representation of the crossover process: the two parents are recombined by cutting them at a common index to create two new offspring

Crossover Operator. Both populations adopt a simple single point crossover operator: meaning that a cutting point is chosen, both genomes are split at that index and new individuals are created by recombining the resulting sequences (see Fig. 7).

One adjustment to the canonical single point crossover is necessary, given that in our case the genome length is variable. Quite simply the cutting point is chosen as a number between $[0, smallestN)$, where smallestN is the length of the smallest of the selected genomes. This ensures that the cut always happens at an index that does exist for both genomes. As it can be noticed also in Fig. 8, this operator creates two new individuals that have the same length of the parents. Some more complex crossover operators could create more variation in length sequence; in this first study we decided to use a very commonly used one, since experimentally it doesn't seem to create an issue in how evolution proceeds.

Mutation Operator. The mutation operator gives each gene a probability $1/l$, where l is the genome length, to mutate. This ensures that on average only one gene will mutate but allows for more than one or no mutation to occur. The mutation itself applies one of these operations to the gene g: g changes to represent another direction, g is removed from the genome, a new gene g' (with a randomly chosen direction) is added to the genome after g.

Implementation Details. Other implementation details used to obtain the results discussed later in the paper are here summarised. Our system uses an **elitist strategy**, meaning that a specified number of the best individuals from the current population is allowed to carry on to the next one without being altered.

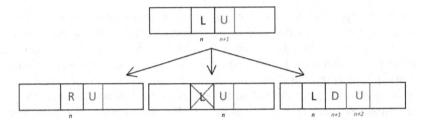

Fig. 8. A representation of the three mutation operators used by our system: the first randomly changes the gene n (in the example from **L**eft to **R**ight), the second removes gene n, and the third inserts a new gene after gene n. Note how the latter two operators change the size of the individual.

The parameters used are:

- Population size: 500
- Generation number: 1000
- Elitist factor: 10%
- Mutation rate: 1/n for each gene, where n is the genome length

We do not present an analysis of the running time of the algorithm but, with these parameters, we obtain a solution in ~10 s.

3.4 Player Model

As mentioned already in Sect. 3.4, player modeling can be split in two large families: model-based (top-down) and model-free (bottom-up) [19]. Our approach uses a model-based approach, meaning that we define a model and use the collected player data to determine the *state* of the player. Since the objective is to control the difficulty of the generated puzzles, the represented state is related to the player's ability to solve the previous puzzles.

For each puzzle we collect some information about the player, these are:

$$Info(p_n) = \{tries, sequenceLength, loops\}$$

where p_n is the n-th puzzle.

Based on the information collected from the gameplay, the target length and target loops of the evolutionary system (as described in Sect. 3.3) are adjusted so that:

- The sequence target length is increased by 2 if the player solved the last puzzle with less than three tries.
- The target loops are increased by 1 if: 1) $targetLength > 5 * targetLoops + 3$ and 2) the player solved the last puzzle with less than three tries. The motivation behind the first part of the if comes from our definition of a loop (see Sect. 3.1) which requires a specific sequence of five directions to be formed.

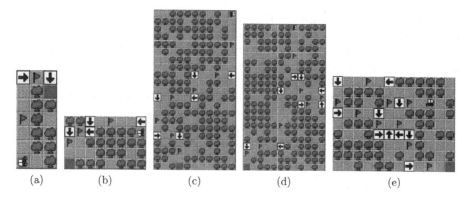

Fig. 9. Example of level progression as can be experienced by the player, starting with a target of $\{3,0\}$ *(a)* and ending at $\{11,2\}$ *(e)*

4   Results and Discussion

This section provides and discusses generated puzzles for various targets, and provides an exploratory evaluation of the dynamic difficulty of the puzzles. This last one is provided by a pilot user study involving three participants.

4.1   Targeted Evolution

Figure 9 shows five generated puzzles of increasing difficulty. As it can be observed, the system is able to produce quite different maps, and as the difficulty increases we see a transition from linear solutions to more complex and sprawling ones that do require deeper thought from the player.

We also would like to discuss Fig. 12, this shows a puzzle evolved to have a quite high complexity. The puzzle appears quite complex even with the solution being displayed, it requires a clever use of the tiles, sometimes in quite unintuitive ways, and requires the player to not only think about where the tiles are placed,

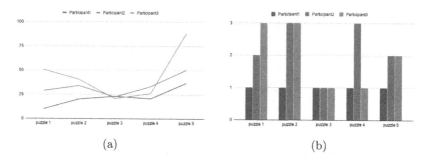

Fig. 10. Visualization of the time the participants took in completing the 5 puzzles (in seconds) (a), and amount of tries needed (b)

but which tiles would disappear once the car travels on them. The participants on the pilot study were asked after the test to try to solve this, and all three had to give up, citing that it was a much more complex task than the ones they tried before. That said, this puzzle is also an example that, while the system creates a solvable puzzle with this type of large solutions, there is room for improvement. In fact, you can observe around the centre of the map that there are two "Down" tiles that appear one after the other in the sequence, which makes one of them superfluous. Possibly a post-processing task could be added to make sure such "extra" tiles would be removed from the final puzzle.

4.2   Pilot User Study

We developed a pilot user study to lightly assess the functioning of the system. The experiment consisted in the participants playing through five puzzles, and of a short survey afterwards. There were 3 participants, with average age 23.6, of which 2 males and 1 female. These were all university students (which can be assumed to have some knowledge of computational thinking), so it's not a sample representative of our target audience, yet they could still give us some initial feedback, especially on playability. During gameplay we collected the time and amount of tries needed to complete the puzzles. The survey consisted in some basic demographic questions, and two specific ones about the experiment itself:

- *Did you feel a sense of progression?*
- *Were you familiar with this type of puzzle?*

Both questions were answerable using a 5-point Likert scale.

As can be observed from Fig. 10a, there seems to be a common pattern with the time to complete the puzzles decreasing after the first puzzle and then increasing towards the fourth and fifth. We hypothesise that the initial decrease in time is due to the participants getting acquainted to the game/interface, and the following increase due to the increasing difficulty. Looking at Fig. 10b we can observe a similar pattern in participants 2 and 3.

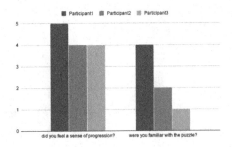

Fig. 11. Participants' answers to the survey

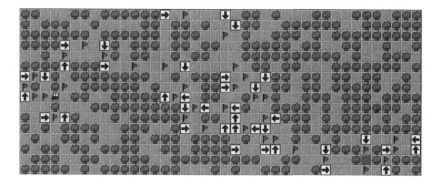

Fig. 12. Example of a generated puzzle with a very large target sequence length (40)

All the participants expressed with a relatively large amount of confidence that they perceived an increase in difficulty Fig. 11. Participant 1 was the only one that was quite familiar with this type of puzzle, which also is reflected into their performance: always solving the puzzle in one try, and very fast solving time also for the first puzzles. That said, we can observe that their solving time also looked like it was increasing towards puzzle 5.

5 Conclusions

This paper presents a novel use of PCG for the generation of puzzles to help pupils learn in a more adaptive ways about some computational thinking concepts, especially sequences. The presented system is able to create a vast variety of puzzles of different difficulties, and can present the player with a progression from simple puzzles to very complex ones.

Of course, this work is still in its infancy, much could be expanded and improved on. In particular the current player modelling is quite simplistic, a more bottom-up approach to creating the model (based on collected player data) would likely lead to more flexible and personalised puzzle generation. We also present a very small user study, which shows some promising results, but that is not nearly enough to reach statistically sound conclusions. Moreover the participants have not been the target audience (young pupils). The next step of this research would be to conduct a more in-depth user-study with our target audience.

That said, we do believe there is a lot of potential in this and similar systems since they would solve one of the main problems educators encounter with using gamification tools for teaching/learning: the content is almost always static and limited! This use of PCG would allow the educator to use the tool for longer and possibly even ask it to generate specific content, without requiring the educator to have either design or programming skills (which is usually the case). Another thing we want to highlight, is that our system can generate a variety of different looking levels, even if they have the same solution, this might be interesting from an educational point of view, to see how groups of students might be able to figure out collectively that they can abstract problems that might look different to the same one.

In conclusion, we presented a system for generating levels of a puzzle game with adaptive difficulty. The difficulty curve is itself controlled by the player performance, and the game was designed with the objective to be able to teach some computational thinking concepts. The system is powered by a constrained multi-objective optimisation evolutionary method.

References

1. Billinghurst, M., Duenser, A.: Augmented reality in the classroom. Computer **45**(7), 56–63 (2012)
2. Brennan, K., Resnick, M.: New frameworks for studying and assessing the development of computational thinking. In: Proceedings of the 2012 Annual Meeting of the American Educational Research Association, Vancouver, Canada, vol. 1, p. 25 (2012)
3. Chafekar, D., Xuan, J., Rasheed, K.: Constrained multi-objective optimization using steady state genetic algorithms. In: Cantú-Paz, E., et al. (eds.) GECCO 2003. LNCS, vol. 2723, pp. 813–824. Springer, Heidelberg (2003). https://doi.org/10.1007/3-540-45105-6_95
4. Colton, S.: Automated puzzle generation. In: Proceedings of the AISB 2002 Symposium on AI and Creativity in the Arts and Science. Citeseer (2002)
5. Deb, K., Pratap, A., Agarwal, S., Meyarivan, T.: A fast and elitist multiobjective genetic algorithm: NSGA-II. IEEE Trans. Evol. Comput. **6**(2), 182–197 (2002)
6. Deb, K., Pratap, A., Meyarivan, T.: Constrained test problems for multi-objective evolutionary optimization. In: Zitzler, E., Thiele, L., Deb, K., Coello Coello, C.A., Corne, D. (eds.) EMO 2001. LNCS, vol. 1993, pp. 284–298. Springer, Heidelberg (2001). https://doi.org/10.1007/3-540-44719-9_20
7. Fernández-Vara, C., Thomson, A.: Procedural generation of narrative puzzles in adventure games: the puzzle-dice system. In: Proceedings of the The Third Workshop on Procedural Content Generation in Games, PCG 2012, Raleigh, NC, USA, pp. 12:1–12:6. ACM, New York (2012). https://doi.org/10.1145/2538528.2538538. http://doi.acm.org/10.1145/2538528.2538538
8. Gilboy, M.B., Heinerichs, S., Pazzaglia, G.: Enhancing student engagement using the flipped classroom. J. Nutr. Educ. Behav. **47**(1), 109–114 (2015)
9. Hendrikx, M., Meijer, S., Van Der Velden, J., Iosup, A.: Procedural content generation for games: a survey. ACM Trans. Multimedia Comput. Commun. Appl. **9**(1), 1:1–1:22 (2013). https://doi.org/10.1145/2422956.2422957. http://doi.acm.org/10.1145/2422956.2422957
10. Isaacs, A., Ray, T., Smith, W.: Blessings of maintaining infeasible solutions for constrained multi-objective optimization problems. In: 2008 IEEE Congress on Evolutionary Computation (IEEE World Congress on Computational Intelligence), pp. 2780–2787. IEEE (2008)
11. Khalifa, A., Perez-Liebana, D., Lucas, S.M., Togelius, J.: General video game level generation. In: Proceedings of the Genetic and Evolutionary Computation Conference 2016, pp. 253–259. ACM (2016)
12. Kimbrough, S.O., Koehler, G.J., Lu, M., Wood, D.H.: On a feasible–infeasible two-population (fi-2pop) genetic algorithm for constrained optimization: distance tracing and no free lunch. Eur. J. Oper. Res. **190**(2), 310–327 (2008)

13. O'Kane, L.: A Computational Thinking Puzzle, July 2016. http://www.icompute-uk.com/news/computational-thinking-puzzle/
14. Ray, T., Kang, T., Chye, S.K.: An evolutionary algorithm for constrained optimization. In: Proceedings of the 2nd Annual Conference on Genetic and Evolutionary Computation, pp. 771–777. Morgan Kaufmann Publishers Inc. (2000)
15. Scirea, M., Togelius, J., Eklund, P., Risi, S.: MetaCompose: a compositional evolutionary music composer. In: Johnson, C., Ciesielski, V., Correia, J., Machado, P. (eds.) EvoMUSART 2016. LNCS, vol. 9596, pp. 202–217. Springer, Cham (2016). https://doi.org/10.1007/978-3-319-31008-4_14
16. Scirea, M., Togelius, J., Eklund, P., Risi, S.: Affective evolutionary music composition with MetaCompose. Genet. Program Evolvable Mach. **18**(4), 433–465 (2017). https://doi.org/10.1007/s10710-017-9307-y
17. Shaker, M., Sarhan, M.H., Naameh, O.A., Shaker, N., Togelius, J.: Automatic generation and analysis of physics-based puzzle games. In: 2013 IEEE Conference on Computational Intelligence in Games (CIG), pp. 1–8, August 2013. https://doi.org/10.1109/CIG.2013.6633633
18. Wing, J.M.: Computational thinking. Commun. ACM **49**(3), 33–35 (2006). https://doi.org/10.1145/1118178.1118215
19. Yannakakis, G.N., Togelius, J.: Experience-driven procedural content generation. IEEE Trans. Affective Comput. **2**(3), 147–161 (2011)

A Systematic Review of Game Learning Research in China

Jingying Wang[1], Qianru Song[2(✉)], Shoubao Gao[2(✉)], and Yuhong Tao[3]

[1] Faculty of Education, Beijing Normal University, Beijing 100875, China
[2] School of Physics and Electronics,
Shandong Normal University, Jinan 250358, Shandong, China
`1452234833@qq.com, gaoshoubao@sdnu.edu.cn`
[3] College of Preparatory Education,
Xinjiang Normal University, Urumqi 833100, Xinjiang, China

Abstract. In recent years, researchers have recognized the educational value of games and gradually introduced them into classroom teaching. With the development of internet technology, the online game industry is also booming and has gradually become mature and increasingly penetrated into people's daily life, which all further stimulate researchers' enthusiasm in game learning research. In order to further understand the evolving path of game-learning research in China and explore the game learning rules, this paper has taken CSSCI in China Knowledge Network Database (CNKI) as the data source, "game" and "learning" as the themes, and has selected 818 articles as the research samples to conduct the research. A bibliometrics software and qualitative text analysis method are employed to analyze the high-frequency keywords and topic changes of the sample literature and to summarize the overall progress of game learning research. The research results show that the research foci in this field are mainly educational games, game based learning, game activities, online games, augmented reality and so on. Research topics mainly include educational games, game based learning, game activities, online games, augmented reality, etc. The application of games in teaching is mainly involved in preschool education and physical education.

Keywords: Gamification · Educational games · Game learning · Educational game design

1 Introduction

In the 1990s, due to the influence of cognitive science, ecological psychology and other disciplines, as well as the fact that the knowledge impartation at that time paid more attention to the integrity of knowledge's internal structure and ignored the practical value, the inert knowledge acquired by students could not effectively provide students with necessary working skills, which caused social dissatisfaction. So scholars in the field of education gradually shifted their research orientation from cognition to situations. The situational learning theory focuses on the interaction between individual students and physical or social contexts. Situational learning theorists believe that situations are important and meaningful part of the whole learning process. Individual's learning activities cannot be separated from specific situations and learning outcomes are affected by situational features and will change accordingly [1]. Since each knowledge points needs to correspond to specific situations and if we consider the individual differences of students, the setting of situation will become more complicated, which has been a problem challenging the situation theory research for long. On the one hand, since the 21st century, the rapid development of internet technology and information technology and their application in the field of education have brought opportunities for scenario setting. On the other hand, researchers have found that games can set immersive situations for learners, effectively enhance learners' learning experience, stimulate their learning interest, tap learning potential and promote learners' development [2].

The concept and application of game have deeply integrated into people's leisure time, work, learning and even into economic activities. Games can not only provide rich and wonderful sensory experience for people, but they can also build another virtual and close to real life space for people to reshape opportunities, improve skills, cultivate abilities and display achievements. Nowadays, children all grow up with the company of games. They get a sense of happiness and achievement in games, so they are eager to engage in a learning process which is as interesting and interactive as games. Professor Edward Castronova, who is engaged in economic and game education research at Indiana University in the United States, points out that the "large-scale migration" of games to human's life has gradually become a new normal in human society, and the investment of a lot of time in games, the integration of game elements and improvement of participatory fun have become the natural choices for future learning [3]. Therefore, game learning has become a research hotspot in the field of education and technology, which has attracted considerable attention worldwide.

Professor Karl M Kapp [4] from the University of Bloomsburg in the U.S. believes that the so-called "Gamification" is to use game mechanisms, game thinking and aesthetic thinking to attract others, encourage behavior, promote learning and solve problems In the field of learning science, game learning refers to integrating game elements into the learning processes, giving full play of games in creating learning situations, stimulating learning interests, maintaining the level of learning motivation and increasing advanced thinking activities. Finally, it points to the optimization of learning processes and the improvement of learning effects.

2 Literature Review

The international research on game based learning can be traced back to the 1980s. At that time, the world's first multiplayer virtual world game - "Underground Castle" came into being. Game developers tried gamification firstly, that is, to turn the non-game things (text system) into games. Since the mid-1980s, researchers have gradually turned the research vision to game learning. In the application of game learning, Ellington, Adinall and Percival [5] proposed that interesting games are of great benefit to develop learners' higher cognitive skills along with higher attention level and longer duration. Dempsey et al. [6] pointed out that game learning can improve learners' self-esteem and change learners' attitudes. Bork and King [7] believed that video games allow learners to conduct real-time brainstorming and arouse inspirations to a large extent. It can be seen that before the 21st century, the focus was on the stimulation of learners' learning interests and the cultivation of metacognitive skills. Researchers believe that games can provide students with more immersive learning opportunities. In these processes, skills will be developed and critical thinking ability can be mastered by solving a series of problems.

In 2003, the term Gamification was formally proposed by the scholar Nick. Since then, Gamification and its derived concept game learning have never faded out of researchers' vision. The research on game learning tends to be diversified, with the main foci are theoretical research, applied technologies and assessment. In the debate on the effectiveness, Lainema and Saarinen [8] introduced two perspectives to study game based learning: experiential learning and constructivism learning theory. They think that experiential learning theory is based on direct experience, while constructivism learning theory is based on the construction of knowledge in the process of problem learning rather than the acquisition of direct experience. Tang and Hanneghan [9] described two ways to design educational games from the perspective of teachers and artists. Zichermann and Cunningham [10] suggested that the elements such as the e-business system that sells cards, player level, badge or trophy, leaderboard, challenge and task, the guidance process and participatory cycle should be added into the design of educational games to improve students' participation and loyalty. Prensky, a well-known scholar, first demonstrated the effectiveness of game learning and analyzed its current application and future prospects. The gamification model has become a new concern in both academia and the game industry. The empirical research was conducted by Michael-D-Hans, who did an effect assessment research by a 16 weeks' comparative experiment between game teaching and non-game teaching [11].

Looking forward, it can be seen that the relationship between game and education is getting closer while there are more and more researches on game based learning. Game based learning and educational games are both important research topics. For example, teachers have used "Civilization" which is developed by "Take 2 Interactive Software" to cultivate students' problem-solving ability in the classroom, and Konami's "Hot Dance Revolution" is also used by consumers to practice dancing. In the game industry, independent industry chains are gradually forming, such as IBM, Cisco, Johnson & Johnson, Alcoa and other enterprises began to use game technology to train employees and contact distant employees, and there are specialized game solution providers, such as Bunchball and Badgeville. It can be seen that with the development of game learning, both educational theories and educational practice and other related industries have made great progresses. These achievements take the advantages of games to facilitate education and create a better future, which are also what researchers expect.

Considering the research in China, most of the research on game learning in China focuses on the setting of game contexts, the design of educational games, the stimulation of learning interests, the students' sense of experience and the empirical research of game effects. However, there is little systematic review on game learning in China. For this reason, this paper intends to use the methods of bibliometrics and knowledge mapping to analyze and summarize the research and application status of game learning in china and offers some prospects to future research foci. Finally, this paper further compares the research themes and methods of game learning between China and western developed countries, which may provide inspirations for the future development of game learning in China.

3 Research Methods and Data Selection

3.1 Research Methods and Tools

In order to exhibit the research context and development of game learning in China since the founding of People's Republic of China, this paper uses Citespace V to visualize the existing research results. With further expectation to make a systematic study on the research track and research status of game learning since the founding of People's Republic of China, qualitative literature analysis has also been employed. Citespace V is a java program developed by Dr. Chen Chaomei of Texas University in the United States to analyze and visualize the co-cited network [12].

3.2 Data Selection

Taking "learning" and "game" as the topic words, limiting the source to CSSCI and the time span from 1949 to now, 818 eligible results have been retrieved as our target data. The Chinese Social Science Citation Index (CSSCI), which is developed by the Chinese Social Science Research and Evaluation Center of Nanjing University, is a key project of both China and its Ministry of Education. Following the law of bibliometrics and adopting the method of combining quantitative and qualitative evaluation, CSSCI selects academic journals with high academic qualities and standard editing from more than 2700 academic journals of Chinese humanities and social sciences as its sources. Therefore, the articles published on CSSCI can represent the highest academic level and latest achievements of Chinese mainland humanities and social sciences research to a large extent. Selecting this database, there are certain guarantees in both academic level and standardization.

4 Research Status of Game Learning in China

We set the time span as 1949–2020 and the length of a single time partition (years per slice) is 1 year; the sources of subject words are title, abstract and keyword; the threshold remains the default state, i.e. the first 50 high frequency or high cited nodes; the node types are author and keyword. Through statistical analysis, this paper thoroughly analyzes the current situations and research trends of game learning since the founding of P.R.C from multiple perspectives.

4.1 Analysis of Highly Influential Research Authors

The research of researchers with high academic influence in a certain field represents the research trends of the whole field and reflects the research practice orientation of certain field. Their research contents are also called the research miniature of a field. Through the analysis of the research author group, we can further grasp the depth and scope of scientific research activities in certain field, which has positive significance for the management, organization, coordination and guidance of scientific research activities [13]. In the 1920s, Lotka [14] considered the uneven distribution between the number of scientists and the number of papers in data research, so he introduced the concept of "scientific productivity", that is, "the number of papers written by individual researchers in a certain time span" and measured the academic writing ability of researchers by this concept. The amount of the author's papers not only represents his activity but also can be used to measure his contribution to social development and human progress. Therefore, with the research on the author's publishing volume and cooperative groups, we can understand the overall situation of the concerning field.

The analysis results of highly influential authors are shown in Table 1. They all have more than 3 posts and they are all productive authors in the field of game learning. Among them, Professor Shang Junjie, who is from the Learning Science Laboratory of Peking University School of Education, has published the most papers on CSSCI. He is interested in learning science and cognitive neuroscience and has made fruitful research results in both disciplines. In the second place, there are four researchers, Pei Lei of the Institute of Basic Education Science of Beijing Institute of Education Sciences, Ma Yingfeng of the Institute of Knowledge Media of Shanxi Normal University, Ma Hongliang of the Department of Education Technology of Shanxi Normal University and Zhuang Shaoyong of the Information Technology Education Promotion Center of the Chinese University of Hong Kong, all of whom have published 6 articles. The above-mentioned authors are highly active in this field and are the core figures in game learning research.

Secondly, the fact that the authors with high contribution rate are mainly from Peking University, Shanxi Normal University and the Chinese University of Hong Kong, further shows that as one of the top institutions in China, Peking University's scientific research strength cannot be underestimated and its scientific research leading ability can easily be seen. Finally, further analysis of the authors shows that a small research team has been formed among Shang Junjie, Peiris, Zhuang Shaoyong, Li Haowen and Li fangle. All the authors are from Beijing and Hong Kong and are in close ties. There is also a partnership between Ma Yingfeng and Ma Hongliang, both of whom are from Shaanxi Normal University. But their research group is small and there is no real research team that has been formed. The results also show that there is close cooperation between and among the researchers within the field but there is less contact with people from other fields, which shows a decentralized state as a whole.

Table 1. List of highly contributing authors.

Rank	Name	Institutions	The amount of articles
1	Shang Junjie	Learning science laboratory, School of education, Peking University	19
2	Pei Leisi	Institute of Basic Education Science, Beijing Academy of Educational Sciences	6
3	Ma Yingfeng	Institute of Knowledge & Media, Shanxi Normal University	6
4	Ma Hongliang	Department of Educational Technology, Shanxi Normal University	6
5	Zhuang Shaoyong	IT Education Promotion Center, Chinese University Hong Kong	6
6	Wu Jianhua	School of Information Management, Central China Normal University	5
7	Li Haowen	IT Education Promotion Center, Chinese University Hong Kong	4
8	Li Fangle	It Education Promotion Center, Chinese University Hong Kong	4
9	Li Yi	Department of Education Technology, School of Education Science, Nanjing Normal University	4
10	Zhang Sujing	School of Education, Hangzhou Normal University	3

4.2 Research Hotspot Analysis

Word frequency analysis is a bibliometrics method that uses the frequency of key words or subject words. It can explain or show the core content of an article and figure out the research hotspot and development trend of certain field. Since key words or subject words of a document are the refinement of the core content of the article; if a key word or topic word repeatedly appears in the literature in its field, this may reflect that the research topic of the key words or subject words is the research hot spot in this field [15]. Through the analysis of the change of key words, we can find the theme change of game learning research [16]. Employing Citespace V word frequency analysis function, which is based on the statistical principles to extract key words from the articles, we can further analyze the frequency of the key words, the relationship between and among the key words in an article and other information like the main year of occurrence, etc. The visualization method can show the frequency and clustering relationship of the key words or of the theme clearly, from which we can analyze game learning research hotspots. Table 2 shows some high-frequency keywords and keywords with high centrality according to Citespace V statistics. Figure 1 shows the research hotspot map generated by Citespace V, that is, high-frequency keyword co-occurrence map.

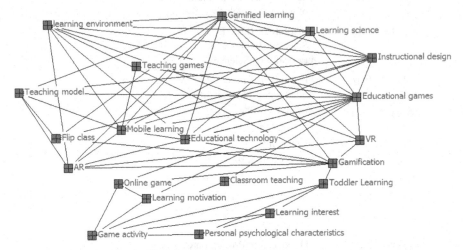

Fig. 1. High frequency keyword co-occurrence map.

The size of the node in Fig. 1 represents the frequency of keywords. The larger the node is, the more frequent the keywords appear. The thickness of the connection represents the frequency of co-occurrence, that is, the closer the connection, the thicker the connection. It can be seen from the figure that "educational games", "game based learning", "online games", "game activities", "augmented reality", "artificial intelligence" and "virtual reality" are the main research contents. The centrality of keywords is a powerful basis for judging the co-occurrence intensity of keywords. The greater the centrality, the stronger the co-occurrence degree of keywords and the greater the influence of the keyword node in all nodes. From the perspective of knowledge theory, the key words with high frequency and centrality are generally the common concerns of many researchers in a period of time, that is, the research hotspot and frontier [17]. In order to further reveal the research hotspots in the field of game learning, Table 2 lists the top 10 keywords in the field of high-frequency keyword centrality, combining with the frequency of keywords to display the research hotspots. It can be seen from the table that the five key words of educational games, game based learning, game activities, online games and augmented reality are all high in centrality and frequency, while the frequency and center of educational games are the highest. So educational games are the most prominent research hotspot and future development trend in this field. Although the frequency of the keywords such as information literacy education games is not high, they are more central, so their co-occurrence with other keywords is strong, which is a potential research hotspot in this field.

Table 2. Ranking of the top 10 high frequency key words in game learning research.

Number	Key words	Coreness	Frequency
1	Education games	0.42	124
2	Game learning	0.27	54
3	Game activities	0.08	27
4	Internet games	0.08	18
5	Strengthen reality	0.06	15
6	Education game design	0.06	3
7	Flipped classes	0.05	6
8	Game design	0.05	6
9	English learning	0.05	4
10	Information literacy education game	0.04	5

4.3 Topic Cluster Analysis

With the present methods, we cannot extract all the keywords contained in an article since generally an article contains more than one topic. If we do not consider all topics to be covered in the extraction, it is likely that all the keywords that are shown on the map will be around one topic and the keywords of other secondary topics might be ignored. So, in order to cover all topics, we can cluster the keywords in the article. Each cluster will be all the key words covered by a topic in an article [18]. Through keyword clustering, we can draw the transition state of each cluster, so as to discover the whole research track and research trends in the field of game teaching research.

As can be seen from Fig. 2, there are 7 keyword clusters in this cluster group, which reflect the research hotspots in the field of learning games since the founding of P.R.C. It can be found from the time axis in this field (Fig. 2), the research time of game activity clustering (#0) and learning interest clustering (#1) is the earliest, and the research mainly focuses on the two levels of children's psychological characteristics and the application of games in classroom teaching, while the other five hot clustering basically began to appear after 2004. Research hotspot clustering (Table 3) lists the top three keywords of LLR tag value of each cluster. The number of nodes is the number of keywords contained in each cluster. The degree of tightness represents the degree of correlation between keywords. The higher the degree of tightness, the better the clustering effect. As for the number of nodes, game activity clustering (#0) contains the most, which shows that in this research hotspot is more common, and the key words such as students' interest, personality and psychological characteristics are the main research issues. From the view of compactness, game activity clustering (#0) and information quality education (#5) are the most closely related, their compactness is above 0.9, followed by artificial intelligence clustering (#2), which shows that game learning research focuses on game activity research and classroom teaching, and psychological research and classroom teaching cases such as interest stimulation and personality psychological

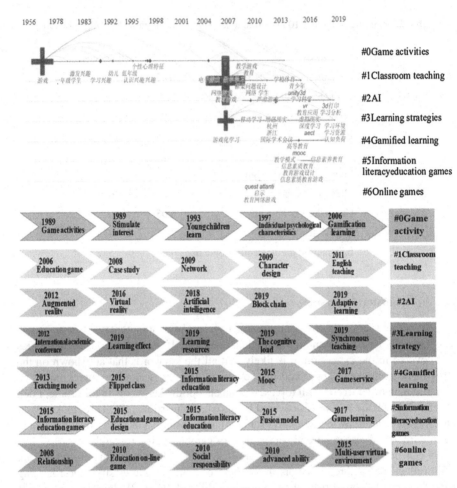

Fig. 2. Game learning research keywords clustering timeline.

characteristics are all among them The implementation of pedagogical research is the main representative.

According to Fig. 2 and Table 3, the research topics of game learning are mainly divided into seven clusters, covering information technology, learning science and psychology. For example, #0 mainly refers to the study of students' psychological characteristics and the stimulation of learning interests, which belongs to the category of psychology. #3 points to learning science, involving the evaluation of learning effect, the development of learning resources and other research directions. According to the induction and analysis of the relevant research hot spots, through the approximate clustering and analysis, the current scholars' research in this field is mainly focused on the following six aspects.

Table 3. Game learning research topic clustering

No.	Nods amount	Closeness	Keywords in the top 3 of LLR tag value	Cluster title
#0	26	0.979	Game activity (16.82); interest (9.47); personality psychological characteristics (9.47)	Game activity
#1	16	0.8	English teaching (7.91); internet (7.91); case study (7.91)	Classroom teaching
#2	16	0.897	Artificial intelligence (10.27); virtual reality (10.27); strengthen reality (10.27)	Artificial intelligence
#3	14	0.889	International academic conference (6.95); learning efficiency (6.95); learning resources (6.95)	Learning strategies
#4	6	0.88	Flipped class (11.92); mooc (7.91); teaching model (7.91)	Gamification
#5	6	0.94	Information literacy education games (23.64); education game design (14.02); information literacy education (9.29)	Information literacy education games
#6	3	0.898	Education online game (8.83); social responsibility (6.22); advanced ability (6.22)	Online games

#1. Game activities. Game activity is the main carrier of game learning. The entertainment elements in games are combined with education and teaching to attract students' attention and stimulate students' interest in learning. Constructivism learning theory, scaffolding theory, situation theory, flow theory and problem-solving learning theory constitute the main body of game learning theory. These theories emphasize the influence of situations on students' participatory interest. Zhong [19] studied the learning interest of learners in game learning with the help of Wiki collaborative lesson preparation platform and action research methodology. The research results showed that the teaching method of game learning has achieved preliminary results and the interest and academic achievements of students have been improved. Augmented reality technology (AR) is a real-time technology to calculate the position and angle of camera images and add corresponding images. The goal of this technology is to integrate the virtual world into the real world on the screen and interact with each other. Compared with traditional video game users, it can obtain a stronger sense of experience and immersion. Hu [20] conducted a research on education games based on AR technology. Guided by the immerse theory and narrative driving theory, the research set challenging learning tasks for learners, in which the influencing factors such as scientific learning interest, game attitude and gender were fully considered. The research results show that learners' scientific learning interest has increased, they are willing to read all kinds of game related information and they are willing to challenge, so as to obtain a strong sense of immersion.

#2.   Classroom teaching. It mainly includes subject teaching, network and case study. As early as 1959, Li [21] published two articles, i.e., "Correctly Arrange the Sports Activities For Preschool Children", and Liang 's [22] "Kindergarten Sports". Games and labor are the main contents of children 's activities. Based on the analysis of the basic task of early childhood education and the characteristics of children in three stages of junior kindergarten class, middle kindergarten class and senior kindergarten class, the paper puts forward the conditions and means of Physical Education in kindergartens, such as reasonable arrangement of children' s sleeping, walking, games, homework and other living systems, and sets games as the main teaching content and teaching methods. Through creative games, activity games and teaching games, we can improve children's health, promote children's physical and mental pleasure, and further develop children's correct ideas and thinking ability. Then, in language learning, such as Chinese Pinyin learning, literacy class, and English teaching, teachers combine games with teaching, which can achieve better results. In recent years, the educational value of video games has been recognized by researchers and has been introduced into classroom teaching. Based on some international application cases of educational games, He [23] analyzed the core elements of integrating educational games into classroom teaching.

#3.   Artificial Intelligence. The rapid development of artificial intelligence technology indicates the arrival of a new era. All countries in the world are trying to seize the opportunity of education development in the era of artificial intelligence. Artificial intelligence has become an important starting point for education reform. The artificial intelligence (Game AI) in games has always been an important factor to attract the young players to get themselves immersed. By using artificial intelligence, virtual reality, augmented reality and other technologies, the scenes in the game can be more lifelike, more intelligent, and even have certain thinking, behavioral judgment abilities, etc. They can bring more thrilling, exciting and diverse experiences and challenges to the players since they are all closer to reality in action, expression, speech or action mode [24]. The adaptive system based on AI is embedded in educational games and thus the internal parameters of education games can be adjusted according to the student variables (such as learning style and cognitive ability, etc.) to adapt the teaching variables required by the students' needs and preferences, such as content sequencing, scaffolding and presentation of learning resources, etc. This may provide students with personalized and appropriate interventions, such as story line, learning pace or difficulty degree [25].

#4.   Learning Strategies. In the whole process of game learning, from the design and development of learning resources to the setting of learning situations, the selection of teaching and learning strategies, as well as the evaluation of students' learning results are all the contents of this research topic. Through literature review, it is found that the relevant research focuses are on the development of learning resources and the evaluation of learning results. For example, Qian [26] and others conducted some research work on the development of learners' attention resources in educational games and proposed that educational games are less attractive than online games. In the design of educational games, we should make clear the audience's positioning, attract learners' attention with practicability, introduce advanced design concepts at home and abroad, mobilize learners' attention with novelty, and enhance the humanized function. All these four development strategies are designed to keep learners' attention with personalized services, to integrate emotional engineering technology, and to use emotional resonance to drive learners' attention. Cao [27] discussed the topic selection of game design. In terms of learning effect evaluation, empirical research is the main method. Li [28] uses meta-analysis method to conduct quantitative analysis on the results of 35 game learning experimental reports at home and abroad from the overall effect, different stages, different knowledge types, different disciplines and other aspects, and objectively examines and evaluates the impact of game learning on students' learning effect.

#5. Game Learning. Under the theme of game learning, we mainly discuss the flipped classroom, MOOC class and other new teaching modes. Zhang [29] discussed some problems about the application of game based learning concept in flipped classroom teaching. They believed that when applying game based learning concept to flipped classroom and to achieve a perfect integration of the two, teachers should master not only the concept of game based learning design, but also the strategies of integrating game based learning design into flipped classroom, such as goal stratification strategy and game level setting strategy, motivation stimulation and reward strategies, communication and feedback, competition, cooperation and reflection strategies and others. Based on the design and implementation of adaptive educational games, Li [30] looked forward to the new ideas brought by flipped classroom, MOOC and big data learning to the application and development of "adaptive" educational games. The combination of MOOC and games not only brings learning pleasure to learners, but also pushes different learning knowledge points for different learners in the game based learning, which can stimulate the enthusiasm of learners to participate in learning and improve the individual's sense of achievement and cognition of knowledge and can provide a strong guarantee for reducing the dropout rate and improving the completion rate.

#6. Information literacy education game. The information literacy education game includes cluster six and cluster seven, which have been the research hotspots since 2013. The basic purpose of information literacy education is to cultivate students' ability to solve problems with information, which is a kind of advanced ability and right the core mechanism of games. Therefore, it has become an important research topic in recent years to carry out information literacy education with the help of games. Relevant researches focus on the research of learning behavior and learning mechanism in the game [31–33], the investigation and research of domestic and international application status [34, 35], and the design and implementation of information literacy education game for a specific purpose, such as Wu [32], following the approach of creating situation-analyzing problems-forming strategies- solving problems-making reflection and summary, taking the methods in book classification and shelving, designed classification problems, password lock solving problems and sorting problems, put them all into a series of game situations, and used flash to edit the little game of *Sailing*. And Wu has also verified the advantages of this kind of games in cultivating students' problem-solving ability.

5 Conclusion and Prospect

This paper selects 818 papers published in the field of game learning since the founding of P.R.C. as research samples and makes a visualized analysis of the research status, hot spots and research topics in the field in the past 70 years with the help of CiteSpace V software. Based on the relevant statistical data and knowledge map, this paper analyzes the high influential authors, research hotspots and research topics respectively and draws the following conclusions:

First of all, we analyzed the highly contributive authors in the field of game learning research in the past 70 years according to the amount of articles published and found several experts and scholars with high reputation in Chinese mainland, such as Shang Junjie, Peiris, Ma Yingfeng, Ma Hongliang and Zhuang Shaoyong. These researchers are very active in the field of game learning research and have achieved considerable research results, which not only promote the development and progress of game learning research to certain extent but also lead the future research direction. After analyzing the top 10 productive authors in the field of game learning in the past 70 years, it is found that Peking University takes the leading role in game learning in China. Through further analysis of the authors, it is found that there is a small research team and close relationship between researchers from Beijing and Hong Kong, including Shang Junjie, Peiris, Zhuang Shaoyong, Li Haowen and Li fangle. The researchers have formed close internal cooperations but there are few external connections and the overall situation is decentralized.

Secondly, through the co-occurrence analysis of high-frequency keywords, education games, game based learning, game activities, online games, augmented reality are the five keywords with high centrality and frequency, while education games takes the highest position in both, so education games is the most prominent research hotspot and future orientation in this field. In addition, the key words in the table, such as education game design, flipped classroom, game design, learning English, information quality education game, are not high in frequency but relatively central, so they share a strong degree with other key words, which are potential research hotspots in this field.

Thirdly, through the clustering analysis of key words, we find that in the past 70 years the present scholars' research in this field mainly focuses on six aspects: game activities, classroom teaching, artificial intelligence, learning strategies, game based learning and information quality education games. In the whole research process, the priority of game design and development is to create high-quality learning experience, simulate the real environment, and guide the design and development of the game with the combination of educational objectives. In the research of experience sense, we should deepen our work in the flow experience, develop more challenging games, and focus on the realization of personalized learning. In the theoretical research, we should focus on the dialectical relationship between "education" and "games"; explore more of the application of interaction theory, hierarchical model and other game design theories in game development; the application of constructivism, behaviorism, situationism and other pedagogical theories in the teaching practice; and the application of psychology theories such as immersion theory, the theory of needs hierarchy and multiple intelligence theory in the process of teacher-student interaction and their application in the theory of students' knowledge growth. All these theoretical applications ultimately point to the cultivation of students' advanced thinking ability, such as growth thinking and innovative thinking. In the application research, the transformation from physical game learning to online game learning has been generally realized, which has formed a network dominated by on-line game learning and supplemented by physical game learning. At the micro level, the new application perspective of turning from the "serious game" to light game has reduced the burden of teachers. In the research of assessment, researchers continue to explore the assessment methods of game learning and diverse evaluation mechanisms have been developed, which mostly cover the evaluation of students' positive learning effect. There is still little assessment and analysis of the negative game learning effect.

Finally, the analysis on the historical development and present status of game learning can provide a driving force for the sustainable development of its research. Summing up the past 70 years' historical experience and reflections, the future research of game learning should also pay attention to the following four aspects.

(1) To employ diversified research methods under an interdisciplinary background. At present, the trend of disciplinary differentiation is increasing, but at the same time, the relationship between disciplines is closer. Interdisciplinary research methods can provide researchers with different perspectives to better solve the problems that cannot be solved by one single discipline. In the application, we should fully consider the adaptability of the problem and the methods, any mechanical borrowing of others' experience will not only fail to solve the problem, but also diminish researchers' interests. Therefore, taking the problem and the essence of the discipline as the starting point and reference, we may choose and use research methods of other disciplines with necessary transformations to obtain new ways or ideas to solve the problems in game learning.

(2) Opportunities and challenges brought by the introduction of business game products in the learning process. With the rapid development of online games, various online games emerge in an endless stream. In order to seize the market, enterprises make full use of virtual reality technology, carefully design game scenes, and constantly optimize the game structure. Compared with educational games, online games developed by enterprises often have better user experience and higher user loyalty. On the one hand, the introduction of business game products into the field of education is an effective way to improve students' participation, stimulate students' interest in learning and enhance their sense of immersion. On the other hand, due to the playful nature of online games is far greater than that of education games, the two are in unbalanced states. Blind introduction of online business games into classroom teaching will lead to challenges such as students' addiction and low fulfillment of educational goals. Therefore, it is necessary for educational researchers to fully understand the advantages and disadvantages of online business games and consider the opportunities and challenges brought by the introduction

of online business games in the field of education and make necessary adaptations in practical uses so that the game is more suitable for classroom teaching.

(3) Improve discipline consciousness and pay attention to system optimization. Although game learning research has a long history and many universities have set up learning science laboratory and basic education science research institutes and other research laboratories, it has not become an independent discipline yet. Therefore, on the one hand, we need to continue to improve the discipline consciousness, optimize the internal system, and gradually establish a mature discipline content system and research framework. On the other hand, on the basis of summing up historical experience, we need to find new research horizons and problem-solving ways through interdisciplinary cooperations, and to break the bottleneck, improve research skills, enrich ideas, and get further development.

(4) Constructing a closed-loop research paradigm guided by a theory-practice-theory model. Practice is the endogenous power of the development of theory. Theory guides practice, and practice promotes theory, thus a closed-loop system can be formed. The combination of theory and practice is the power source of game learning research in this new era, so we should strengthen the theoretical cultivation of researchers and fully integrate the theoretical value into the practice process. On this basis, the practice results will respond to the theoretical development actively, so that the theoretical research can fully absorb the nutrients of the "experimental field", so as to promote the in-depth development of playing in the field of learning, and students can truly experience the fun of the integration of entertainment and teaching.

Acknowledgement. The authors appreciate the support by the National Nature Science Foundation of China (71704116).

References

1. Yao, M.L.: From cognition to situation: the change of learning mode. Educ. Res. **277**, 60–64 (2003)
2. Zhu, Z.T., Deng, P., Sun, L.W.: Entertainment technology: a new territory of educational technology. China Electrification Educ. **220**, 11–14 (2005)
3. Qiu, S.L.: Today, you must know "gamification". http://blog.sina.com.cn/s/blog_5380e3f60102vso1.html. Accessed 31 Jan 2020
4. Kapp, K.M.: The Gamification of Learning and Instruction Fieldbook. Wiley, Hoboken (2013)
5. Ellington, H., Adinall, E., Percival, F.: A Handbook of Game Design. Kogan Page, London (1982)
6. Dempsey, J.V., Lucassen, B.A., Haynes, L.L., Casey, M.S.: Instructional applications of computer games. Cogn. Style, 2–13 (1996)
7. Bonk, C.J., King, K.S.: Computer conferencing and collaborative writing tools: starting a dialogue about student dialogue. In: International Conference on Computer Support for Collaborative Learning L. Erlbaum Associates Inc. (1995)
8. Lainema, T., Saarinen, E.: Explaining the educational power of games. In: Design and Implementation of Educational Games: Theoretical and Practical Perspectives, pp. 17–31. IGI Global (2010)

9. Tang, S., Hanneghan, M.: Designing educational games: a pedagogical approach. In: Gamification for Human Factors Integration: Social, Education, and Psychological Issues, pp. 181–198. IGI Global (2014)

10. Zichermann, G., Cunningham, C.: Gamification by Design: Implementing Game Mechanics in Web and Mobile Apps. O'Reilly Media Inc., Sebastopol (2011)

11. Hanus, M.D., Fox, J.: Assessing the effects of gamification in the classroom: a longitudinal study on intrinsic motivation, social comparison, satisfaction, effort, and academic performance. Comput. Educ. **80**, 152–161 (2015)

12. Chen, C.M.: Searching for intellectual turning points: progressive knowledge domain visualization. Proc. Natl. Acad. Sci. **101**, 5303–5310 (2004)

13. Qiu, J.P., Ma, R.M.: A CSSCI-based bibliometric study of library, information and archive management. J. Chin. Libr. **161**, 24–29 (2006)

14. Lotka, A.J.: The frequency distribution of scientific productivity. J. Wash. Acad. Sci. **16**(12), 317–323 (1926)

15. Qiu, J.P., Wen, F.F.: Visualization analysis of the research front and hot domains of library and information science in the past five years: studies based on the quantitative analysis of 13 high-impact international journals. J. Chin. Libr. **192**, 51–60 (2011)

16. Bao, X.Y., Zhao, Y.X.: Research progress and prospect of gamified learning. e-Educ. Res. **268**, 45–52 (2015)

17. Hou, J.H.: Visualizing the institution cooperation of international energy technology. J. Intell. **5**, 422–430 (2009)

18. Xie, Q.Z., Tan, Q.P., Yan, Y.: An approach of automatic key phrase extraction based on graph and clustering. J. Zhengzhou Univ. (Nat. Sci. Ed.) **2**, 81–85 (2018)

19. Zhong, H.R., Zhou, Z.H.: Impacts of game-based learning on learning motivation: an action research. Mod. Educ. Technol. **3**, 91–94 (2012)

20. Yang, W.Y., Hu, W.P.: The characteristics and influential factors of immersion in mobile game of science with AR. Mod. Distance Educ. Res. **147**, 105–112 (2017)

21. Lin, J.S.: Properly organizing physical activities for preschool children. Qian Xian **10**, 24–25 (1959)

22. Liang, G.G.: Kindergarten sports. J. Shanghai Univ. Sport. **3**, 27–31 (1959)

23. He, B.X., Zhuang, K.J., Ma, Y.F.: Game learning analytics: a core factor for integrating educational games into classroom. e-Educ. Res. **305**, 96–101 (2018)

24. Tao, K.: From trigger to association: a new probe into the path of gamification learning: taking artificial intelligence and cognitive skill trees in games as examples. Mod. Distance Educ. **147**, 72–77 (2013)

25. Wang, G.X., Wang, Y.: Development of contextualized narrative games supporting smart learning and verification of learning effects. Distance Educ. China **410**, 20–28 + 92–93 (2019)

26. Qian, L., Jin, K., Zhang, S.J.: Strategies about exploiting the attention resource of learners in educational games. J. Distance Educ. **6**, 93–97 (2010)

27. Cao, P.G., Zhang, H.: Talking about the subject selection of educational learning games digital learning resources. Chin. Ed. J. **6**, 59–62 (2015)

28. Li, Y.B., Song, J.Y., Yao, Q.H.: Research on influence of gamification learning method on students' learning effect: meta-analysis based on 35 experiments and quasi-experimental studies. e-Edu. Res. **319**, 56–62 (2019)

29. Zhang, J.L., Zhang, B.H.: Application of game based learning in flipped classroom. J. Distance Educ. **112**, 73–78 (2013)

30. Li, X.: A structure design model of adaptive educational games and its experiment. J. Distance Educ. **126**, 97–103 (2015)

31. Wu, J.H., Ban, L.N., Li, X.: A preliminary study on transfer of learning in information literacy educational game. Doc. Inf. Knowl. **174**, 88–94 (2016)

32. Wu, J.H., Chen, Y.N., Harrison, H.Y., Zhang, S.T.: Design of problem solving oriented information literacy educational game. Libr. Inf. Serv. **424**, 6–12 (2015)
33. Zhang, L.: Research on educational mechanisms of information literacy embedded in games. Res. Libr. Sci. **19**, 10–13 (2015)
34. Hong, Y.: Survey of and reflection on Chinese and American university library information literacy education game. Libr. Inf. **5**, 70–77 (2015)
35. Zhao, Y.L., He, Y.: Application of video games in overseas classroom teaching and its revelation. Prim. Second. Sch. Abroad **1**, 23–30 (2015)

Conceptual Change in Preschool Science Education: Evaluating a Serious Game Designed with Image Schemas for Teaching Sound Concept

Yiqi Xiao[1]([⊠]) [iD] and Chenhan Jiang[2] [iD]

[1] University of Shanghai for Science and Technology, Shanghai 200093, China
yiqi.xiao@usst.edu.cn
[2] Tongji University, Shanghai 200092, China
chenhan0713@126.com

Abstract. Restructuring and developing child's conceptions and explanatory models about the nature science is a key issue for elementary education. This study evaluates an interactive game that makes use of specific instructional strategy to facilitate children's learning of sound concept. By extracting image schemas which exist in children's mental models of understanding sound concept and its scientific explanations, a tablet-based serious game was designed through expressing the analogies where these image schemas were used. The degree of children's conceptual change was compared by implementing pre-, post- and delayed posttest. The results showed that children who had experienced the serious game more accurately answered relevant questions and explained sound concepts. Since conceptual change requires a long-term learning process, the main purpose of study is to help children quickly acquire a basic understanding of the science concept and enhance their learning motivation in kindergarten class.

Keywords: Conceptual change · Preschool children · Science education · Serious game · Image schemas · Design method

1 Introduction

Conceptual change is a learning process in which students' pre-instructional conceptions are restructured to facilitate the acquisition of science concepts (Duit 2003). The students, especially the preschool children, tend to interpret natural phenomena with pre-existing knowledge that is contradictory to the scientific view (Vosniadou 1994). As a result of daily interaction with the environment, children acquire knowledge about the real world mainly from direct experience and observation. Therefore, many of children's conceptions are ego-centric (Piaget 1929) and perception-oriented, and characterized by the animism (Piaget 1972) and pre-casual reasoning. In fact, children's early understanding of science is usually built on intuitive knowledge in the form of naive theories (Pine et al. 2001). In order to make children's conceptions conform to the accepted scientific

© Springer Nature Switzerland AG 2020
X. Fang (Ed.): HCII 2020, LNCS 12211, pp. 503–520, 2020.
https://doi.org/10.1007/978-3-030-50164-8_37

ideas and correct the misconceptions (a frequently used term is *alternative conceptions*), instructional strategies are required for educators. In previous studies researchers have explored the game-based learning (GBL) for science education, however, many studies more focus on what roles the educational games play in promoting knowledge construction of middle school or undergraduate students (Gauthier and Jenkinson 2017; Cheng et al. 2015), instead of their effects on restructuring children's existing beliefs.

The goal of the paper is designing an educative and amusing tablet-based serious game that provide children with visual representations of scientific concepts, and thus laying a foundation for them to understand abstract scientific knowledge. According to the analogical reasoning theory, the present exploratory case intended to bridge the gap between familiar knowledge of children and scientific explanations through the visual representations in interactive games and the game activities. To this end, the authors tries to visualize the *image schemas* on which children's and scientific conceptions are based in the game interface.

This paper begins with an overview of the related works about instructional strategies and image schema theory. On this basis, a table-based game prototype for teaching sound concept is designed as a case study. After that, the results of pre-, post- and delayed post-test are compared to examine the extent of conceptual change.

2 Background

2.1 Instructional Strategies for Conceptual Change

The game design for science learning needs to accord with the teaching process of constructing new concepts. Regarding the teaching method, two basic strategies, *assimilation* and *accommodation*, are initially proposed by Posner et al. (1982). Many instructional strategies have developed from this guideline. Assimilation refers to the integration of new concepts with children's original idea. The instructor has to guide the students to accept new concepts with their existing concepts or to link the abstract concepts with common experiences (Hewson and Hewson 1983) by using particular strategies, for example, the analogical reasoning (Brown and Clement 1989; Chiu and Lin 2005). Based on the structure mapping theory (Gentner 1983), this kind of reasoning uses the analogical connection between prior knowledge and the target knowledge in learning domain to easily explain science concepts. Using this strategy, children are likely to easier understand the electric current, for example, when it is compared to water flow, and many similar examples are discussed in previous studies. As the way of radically reconstructing concepts, accommodation is a process in which children's conceptions are challenged, abandoned or reformed, finally resulting in the acceptance of scientific conceptions. To achieve the effective conceptual change, a large number of pedagogical researches have attempted to create conflicts between children's early beliefs and the reality. These cognitive conflicts are commonly produced by the experiences that provide learners with the evidence to contradict their existing conceptions (Kang et al. 2004), thus learners will be confused and dissatisfied with their own conceptions. The strategies for resolving cognitive conflicts include using laboratory activities, showing students the computer simulations of natural phenomena (Bell and Trundle 2008) or experimental results, and group discussion (Coştu et al 2007).

The present work mainly focuses on assimilation strategy to promote conceptual change, because the lack of relevant knowledge might limit the young learners, especially the preschoolers, to update their explanations for the cognitive conflict. We make use of image schema as the structure of analogy that can relate children's ideas to scientific ideas when playing the interactive game.

2.2 Image Schemas

Image schema is a concept originated from the domain of Cognitive Linguistics, which is initially used to expound the mapping structure between source domain and target domain of a metaphor. Johnson (1987) defined image schemas as "recurring dynamic patterns of our perceptual interaction and daily activities" that relate and organize human experience. According to Mandler's work (2005), the motion of an object along paths and its locations in space is more attractive to infants than its visual characteristics such as the color and shape. According to Mandler (2014), in infancy and early childhood, humans repeatedly experience the simple events occurred in the movement of objects and the spatial relations of objects, then begin to realize some concepts like *path, target, border* and *blockage*. As a result, these pre-conceptual structures are represented in languages, and become the building blocks for people to understand abstract concept and reason about the world. People will use image schemas subconsciously as the cognitive *structure* when it is required to learn new knowledge through the old.

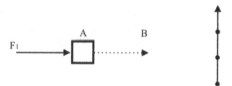

Fig. 1. The diagrams of COMPULSION and SCALE image schema.

As Hurtienne (2017) noted, there are two ways that humans use image schemas to understand new concepts. One is to understand the target knowledge with image schemas of the current knowledge. For example, some children believe that the wind causes the moving of clouds (Piaget 1930), just like the fallen leaves float as wind blows. The movement of leaves is indeed due to the force exerted by airflow of wind, so the COMPULSION image schema can be identified. However, children can borrow this idea to explain how the clouds move. The other is to relate image schema(s) to a concept (Hurtienne 2017). For example, if children only view the boiling process as a phenomenon when the temperature continues to rise (SCALE image schema), they might think that the temperature of a boiling liquid keeps rising upon continued heating (Coştu et al. 2007). The SCALE schema, for this case, exists in the scientific explanation of boiling. However, it is not enough for children to learn the boiling concept only by using SCALE schema: they requires clear and understandable ways of showing them other knowledge about boiling, just as they can look the rising temperature as SCALE.

In this paper the authors hypothesize that visualizing the image schemas is helpful for children to figuratively understand the science concepts.

The image schemas are not only useful in structuring the meaning of language, they can be also identified from drawings and activities. For the language material, it is recommended to extract image schemas by literally explaining the words and sentences (Hurtienne et al. 2015; Winkler et al. 2016) with the help of an interpreter who well knows all the image schemas. Except identifying image schemas from utterance, experts can explain the meaning of sign languages, hand gestures and simple drawings with the diagrams of image schemas (Fig. 1). For example, "pressing a button" instantiates the PATH, COMPULSION, and CONTAINER image schema, which represents the movement trajectory, the acting force, and the new state the system enters in, respectively (Asikhia et al. 2015).

3   Design Process

3.1   Objective

Sound is one of the most directly perceived and frequently occurred physical phenomena in our daily life. The investigation in previous study (Mazens and Lautrey 2003) suggests a hierarchy of children's understanding of the sound, showing that very small proportion of preschoolers believe that the sound is the effect of vibration rather than a kind of substance. The majority of young children are able to notice the basic sound phenomena, but it is difficult for them to fully accept their scientific explanations. In this study the authors explored children's understanding of sound (i.e., the big concept) in two aspects, namely the production of sound and sound propagation (Hrepic 2010), by asking children 16 questions (Table 1). Seven of the questions are concerned with the two topics (loudness and pitch) regarding the production of sound. The rest of the questions involves how the sound transmits in space and through the mediums.

3.2   Method

A predict-observe-explain (POE) task (White and Gunstone 1992) was prepared for children to answer each question. The POE task requires children to make a prediction about the consequence of a question, then explain the prediction and finally reconcile the paradox between their explanation and an experimental result. Children were asked to fulfill the task for each question in the order as depicted in Table 1. First, children were asked to judge whether a statement is correct. Next, they had to give reasons or examples to support a prediction after they had made it. If a child did not immediately response to a question or make an explanation, the interviewer should encourage him or her to articulate what he or she knows about that. Thereafter, the consequence of each question were tested by a little experiment with simple devices. This method has been widely adopted by researchers for the investigation of existing conceptions, and it is also the standard procedure that previous researches followed in the pre-, post-, and delayed post-test.

In the pre-test before our design process, 20 preschoolers (11 boys and 9 girls whose average age is 5 years and 11 months) and five teachers participated in this research in

Table 1. The questionnaire for pre-test.

Topic 1: The amplitude of vibration

1. Striking an object with greater force causes louder sound

2. When you hammer a clenched fist on a table, other objects on the table will be shaken

3. Big sound in the air can shake an erected pencil on the table

4. Big sound in the air can cause ripples

Topic 2: The pitch depends on the frequency of vibration

5. Striking a longer tuning fork causes higher pitch

6. Knocking a glass full of water causes higher pitch than knocking an empty glass

7. Two metal blocks, a pyramid and a cylinder. Striking the pyramid causes higher pitch

Topic 3: The sound propagation in the space

8. The person who stands closer to a sound source can hear louder sound

9. The person who stands 1 m before a sound source can hear louder sound than the one stands 1 m behind it

10. Sound only goes to the listener from the mouth of speaker along a sequential trajectory

11. Shouting in this classroom produces echoes

Topic 4: The sound propagation through transmission mediums

12. We can hear the sound of bell outside this closed classroom

13. When a lid covers the device which is playing music, we cannot hear the sound

14. When the device which is playing music is put in a balloon, we cannot hear the sound

15. We cannot hear the sound made by a device in water

16. When you cover ears and make a sound by yourself, you can still hear that sound clearly

a privately-owned kindergarten. Pair of children were interviewed together in a quiet classroom in order that two children will compete to respond and debate each other. If, however, one of the children always echoed the other's views, the teacher must take measures to arouse the child to give individual opinions. All the dialogues in interview were recorded.

In addition to verbal description, experimenter asked the children to draw the explanatory models as pictorial representations (Rice et al. 1998; Edens and Potter 2003). A camera recorded how children portrayed the reason why they thought a question was true or false with diagrams and simple drawings. For example, they needed to draw the process how the sound transmits between two spaces and transmits 'from here to there'. The duration of pre-test was limited to one hour and, after that, the experimenter gave every children candies as the reward for participation.

3.3 Data Collection

The languages children participants used and the pictures they drew revealed their explanatory models of the questions. In most of the cases children are unable to logically describe what causes the sound and the factors that make a different sound. Twelve children correctly answered the relevance of loudness of sound and the magnitude of external force exerted on the object, while only five thought that the pitch is related to the mass of objects which determined the frequency of its vibration. There were two children who mentioned a concept 'vibration', however, they failed to elaborate on the concept as it was merely a term they learned from children's books. The children participants were inclined to use the modes of moving material objects to explain how sound is transmitted, even though most of them recognized that the sound is 'different' from visible objects.

A number of image schemas identified from the conceptions were chosen to construct analogical elements in the game. We merely cited the analysis of question 13 (Q13) as typical of the identification process. When children participants found they can hear the music emitted from a mobile phone that was covered by the lid of a tin box, one of them, P7, said the sound 'came to my ear because it was big enough to break through that lid'. He further explained his theory and noted the center of the lid was easier for the sound to penetrate. Table 2 presented the four image schemas identified from his response and the drawing. On the other hand, some image schemas were extracted from the scientific conception of sound propagation, i.e., a mechanical (longitudinal) wave is transmitted through mediums and will attenuate due to various resistance factors (Table 3).

Table 2. An example of identifying image schemas from a child's explanation for Q13.

PATH	Extracted from the phrase 'came to my ear' and the line that links the space inside the lid and the exterior space on children's drawings
COMPULSION	Extracted from the sentence 'big enough to break through the lid'. It has the sense of exerting force on the lid
BLOCKAGE	Extracted from the phrase 'break through', as it suggests that the lid is a barrier the sound can break through
CENTER-PERIPHERY	Extracted from the word 'center'. In children's eyes the center of lid might be easier to be penetrated

To explain what was observed in the experiment for Q13, many children participants argued that (i) the lid was too *thin* to be completely soundproofed (BLOCKAGE image schema), or (ii) the sound *'leaked out'* of the confined space *through* the small gap between edge of the lid and tabletop (PATH image schema), or (iii) the longer the distance between sound source and listener is, the smaller the sound the listener can hear (SCALE image schema). In addition, P8 and P20 believed that the sound was *blocked* by the lid, so it *rebounded* and went out through gaps or small holes (BLOCKAGE image schema). In our design process the transcribed text of children's answers to all the questions of topic 4 was analyzed. The image schemas which most frequently appeared in children's conceptions of this topic included PATH, BLOCK-AGE, and SCALE. Researchers designed game contents which expressed these image schemas, making analogies between scientific interpretations and children's familiar knowledge.

Table 3. The image schemas identified from scientific explanation of sound propagation, the underlined schemas are those which also exist in children's mental models.

Image schemas	Annotations	Interaction design
PATH	The abstract *trajectory* along which the sound transmits	Dragging an icon which represents 'a sound' and moving it to other places on the screen
CENTER-PERIPHERY	Sound spreads *in all directions*	The loudness of sound reduces as the distance between the icon and sound source increases
BLOCKAGE	The transmission medium which can *reflect* a sound	When the icon is dragged to an area which represent solid or liquid medium, the sound will decay significantly
IN-OUT	A sound 'enters *into*' a different medium and transmit through it	When the icon is dragged within an area which represent solid or liquid medium, the loudness of sound will slowly change
SCALE	A sound is *gradually* decaying in the course of passing through mediums	The sound gradually becomes weaker when the icon passes through more than one areas which represent solid or liquid mediums

3.4 Game Design

The game system consists of two components: the scenes and the sound sources. The two types of scenes are (i) desktop scene and (ii) space scene (Fig. 2). The first version of prototype comprises two different pages for each type. Each page can simulate a particular situation in real world and the multiple interactive pages prolong the playing time, thereby deepening children's understanding of the analogies with repeated practices. The interactions in desktop scenes are set for learning the topic 1 and topic 2, while those in space scenes are aimed at facilitating children to rethink their understandings of topic 3 and topic 4.

As the upgraded version of desktop scenes, space scenes contain more interactions and more functions. Children players were allowed to add any of the sound sources to a scene or to interact with the virtual objects in that scene to receive audio feedbacks.

They can freely choose the sound sources (including three types of animals and one sound-producing apparatus) from the graphical menu below the main interface where sound sources can be placed. Using the sounds from nature and everyday environment such as twittering, chirping and ringing was an approach to motivate children to explore the game.

The desktop scene does not support adding sound sources; a player can only select the tools in the menu to interact with the elements and areas of interface to get audio feedbacks. When tapping one of the graphical areas as depicted in Fig. 3, system will respond with corresponding sound, i.e., the sound of tapping the glass or porcelain, and more taps bring bigger sound. If the player stops tapping for a while, then that sound will gradually fade and finally cease. When tapping the background area of game interface the player can hear a sound of knocking on the door. Tapping on a different graphical area in a desktop scene results in a different pitch. In line with the actual situations, a larger area which represents a bigger object always responds with lower pitch when it is tapped. This design is a reflection of the metaphor 'LESS IS UP' where the UP-DOWN image schema is used. If the children players interact with different two areas with the same number of taps, they can compare the two sounds in terms of pitch at the same level of loudness.

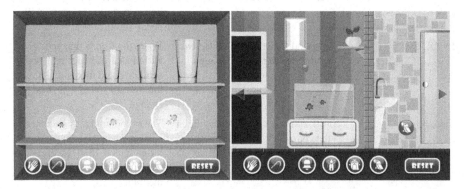

Fig. 2. The samples of game interface: desktop scene (left) and space scene (right).

The interactions in space scenes are used to simulate the propagation and attenuation of sound. To add a sound source, the player has to first tap on an icon in the menu and then tap any place of the game space; then a new icon will appear in that place. The player can also tap that icon and then taps the game space to move the sound source. In this way, if the icon in menu is tapped in the second time, the sound source is cancelled. Moreover, a long press on the sound source can create a colored circle which can be dragged within the area of game space. The longer the linear distance between a circle and its sound source is, the weaker the sound can be heard, as the circle denotes the point to which a sound is transmitted.

In the space scenes, players are provided with many possibilities of interaction that bring varying feedback. For example, the player can add a sound source in the area which represents room space; the loudness of sound greatly reduce when the circle is moved into areas which represent solid or liquid medium. If the circle is dragged within such an area, the loudness will not dramatically change. However, the loudness of sound will further reduce to a very low level when the circle passes through a wall or an obstacle and enters into another space. The significant decrease in loudness suggests that the sound is partly reflected and partly absorbed as it passes to a new medium. When the circle returns to the area where its sound source is, the linear distance shall, as mentioned above, decide the loudness of that sound. Children can also add a sound source to the area of 'table' or 'fish tank' to experience what happens when a sound is emitted from the sound source in a confined space or in water. The system enables children to create and adjust a couple of ambient sounds for the purpose of comparing the effect of sound propagation through the air and other mediums.

4   Evaluation

4.1 Participants

All the children and teachers who had participated in the pre-test were invited again to take part in two tests of summative evaluation (a post-test and a delayed post-test). The time span between pre-test and the evaluation tests is three weeks. Through compari three tests, researchers can judge how much the conceptual change of children is facilitated by the game, and can assess the effect of game training for children on retaining the scientific ideas.

4.2 Procedure

The evaluation work started with playing game in an one-week science course, and the post-tests were conducted thereafter. Twenty children were divided into five groups, each was accompanied and managed by one teacher. The kindergarten staffs arranged a quiet classroom which was suitable for solitary play, in doing so no child was disturbed by other's activities. The playing time for each child lasted usually no more than 1 h. In this period, children were not limited to playing, also they could communicate to the teacher or even do some non-game activities. Nevertheless, the teachers monitored children's behaviors and guided them to experience all the interactions of the game. When a different interaction was triggered, the teacher usually gave a hint to children about the reason why there was a different sound, and directly instructed them to interpret the system feedback. A camera mounted on tripod captured the behavior data in game session for subsequent analysis.

The next phase of evaluation was the post- and delayed post-test. Children participants engaged in post-test in their first science class next week (the time span between last-time game-playing and the post-test varied from one to three days), and two weeks later the delayed post-test was conducted. Researchers specifically developed other two questionnaires for these two tests where the content of questions, as well as the experiment material, was distinct from each other, but the questions for each topic were based on the same science concept. For comparison purposes, the numbers of questions in each of the two tests are the same as those in the pre-test, and so is the total number of questions for each topic. Data collection through implementing the POE tasks focused on the following aspects: children's predictions, explaining the predictions, and explanations for experimental results. Researchers then interviewed the five teacher participants after all tests were finished in order to know the benefits and shortcomings of our design from the educators' view.

Table 4. The measurement categories.

Measurements	Descriptions
True responses/reasons	The number of correct prediction of questions and the number of questions that were correctly explained
Number of correct answers	The number of both correctly predicting a question and correctly explaining either the prediction or the experimental result. 'Correctly' means no obvious misconceptions
Response time	The time children spent in responding to a question and finding the explanation for the prediction and the experimental result
Understanding level	The degree of conceptual change that resulted in higher level of understanding sound concepts
Game playing time	The total time children spent in playing the time until they decided to stop
Frequency of distraction	The frequency that children were distracted from the game at playtime
Teachers' comments	Teachers' opinions on the game design and game-based learning

4.3 Measurements

The measurements used for evaluating the game-based learning process included three categories as listed in Table 4.

The degree of conceptual change was measured based on the dialogues with children using four subcategories: number of *true responses* to the questions and *true reasons*, number of *correct answers*, *response time*, and *understanding level*. When a child felt unable to predict a question or to explain the reason for a prediction or an experimental result, these 'no responses' equated to false responses, but in these situations the time children spend in responding to questions would be still considered in statistical analysis.

Understanding level is measured by the similarity between children's conception and scientific explanation to indicate the stages of the development of children's mental models towards scientific models. Researchers formulated a scoring rubric (Table 5) specially to measure children's understanding level of the sound concept. Table 5 specified the three dimensions of this rubric. Each dimension contained a rating scale of achievement and the quality definitions of the levels, referring to previous studies (Mazens and Lautrey 2003; Hrepic 2010). Dimension 1 served as a tool for overall rating of children's view on the nature of sound. The descriptions of levels in dimension 2 expressed the assessor's rating of children's mental models of sound production (children's responses to topic 1 and 2), and dimension 3 presented different understanding levels of sound

Table 5. The scoring rubric for evaluating understanding levels.

Dimension 1 The nature of sound
1 Sound is a thing or an entity
2 Sound is a kind of 'substance' that is too small to be seen
3 Sound is a transparent and invisible substance like the smell or ghost
4 Sound is immaterial, and it is an effect of the impact or other activities
5 Sound is a wave phenomenon that can be perceived by auditory organs of humans and animals
Dimension 2 Sound production
1 The sound is produced by the objects, creatures and the environment
2 Sound comes from the air, or the movement of air
3 Sound is a non-solid substance like the air, and it emerges because the 'particles' of sound are disturbed
4 Sound is the result of disturbance created by the motion of particles. There will be no sound without any external forces exerted on the objects
5 Sound is the vibration of the particles that propagate as an audible wave
Dimension 3 Sound propagation
1 Sound only exists in the air. It moves away from the source and moves toward the listener along a trajectory
2 Sound can find its way to transmit, propagate and spread in the space
3 Sound can penetrate some kinds of substance, and it is continuously passed to the other mediums
4 Sound propagates through the connection of objects. The poor contact or long distance between objects results in the incomplete sound transmission
5 Sound is the traveling disturbance of particles of the transmission mediums

propagation (children's responses to topic 3 and 4). Ratings were based on the best reason children gave us to explain their predictions and the consequences of experiments, so the score of a 'no response' is zero.

The playability of game was measured by two subcategories: *playing time* and *frequency of distraction*. Video recordings documented various actions the children took to explore the game or to discuss with teacher or ask for guidance. All the time spent in taking such actions were regarded as playing time, see Fig. 3. The evaluation focused on the playability issue as the study has to explore:

- If there was a positive effect on the conceptual change when children had more intently engaged in the game with longer time.
- If the game appealed to both boys and girls so that the learning effect was not influenced by gender.

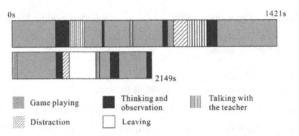

Fig. 3. The game timeline of participant No.14.

4.4 Data Analysis

Conceptual Change

In the post- and delayed post-test, children significantly more correctly predicted ($\chi^2 = 23.46$, df = 2, $p < 0.001$) and explained the questions ($\chi^2 = 31.01$, df = 2, $p < 0.001$), and finally explained more experimental results ($\chi^2 = 21.43$, df = 2, $p < 0.001$) compared to the pre-test, as-shown in Fig. 4a. The increment rate of true responses in two evaluation tests (Pre-/Post-test: 31.6%; Pre-/Delayed test: 35.5%) is not so great in comparison with the increase in explaining predictions (Pre-/Post-test: 175.7%; Pre-/Delayed test: 140.5%) and experimental results (Pre-/Post-test: 82.4%; Pre-/Delayed test: 68.9%). This may be because children can guess the right answer from two options, i.e., yes or no, can or cannot. In this way children more often made the right predictions in pre-test, but they usually had a confused look on their faces when the results of experimental verification were shown to them. Actually, children found true reasons for explaining only about 11.6% of all the questions and about 23.1% of the experiments on average.

Figure 4b shows the number of correct answers in the three tests where each children correctly answered only 2.5 among 16 questions on average before the game-based

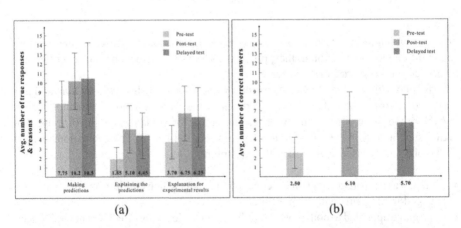

(a)   (b)

Fig. 4. The mean number of true responses and true answers to the reasons in the POE tasks (a); the mean number of correct answers (b).

learning. In many times children did not find the true reasons without the experimental results. Statistics showed that the number of correct answers in either post-test ($z = -3.85$, $p < 0.001$) or delayed post-test ($z = -3.84$, $p < 0.001$) is significantly larger than that in pre-test, Comparing with the post-test, a slightly smaller number of correct answers in the delayed post-test ($z = -1.14$, $p = 0.25$) was detected. This result indicates a positive effect of the game training and the gamification of learning process on fostering a relatively scientific understanding of the sound concept. A relatively scientific understanding meant the children had discarded initial ideas and turned to use incomplete scientific ideas to superficially explain the phenomena. It was almost impossible for preschoolers to describe a precise and complete scientific model in theory, even though they were allowed to learn with more time.

Children's understanding level in the post-test is also significantly higher than the pre-test, in terms of The Nature of Sound ($t(19) = -10.23$, $p < 0.001$), Sound Production ($t(19) = -8.02$, $p < 0.001$) and Sound Propagation ($t(19) = -10.91$, $p < 0.001$). In delayed post-test there is a slight decrease in understanding level, in comparison with the post-test (The Nature of Sound: $t(19) = 1.41$, $p = 0.173$; Sound Production: $t(19) = 1.47$, $p = 0.158$; Sound Propagation: $t(19) = 0.73$, $p = 0.735$), see Fig. 5a.

According to the qualitative analysis of children's utterances, a considerable number of the preschoolers aged 5–6 years compared the sound to wind or water in pre-test because they were cognizant of the difference between sound and many kinds of solid substance. After the game session, children participants more or less changed their conceptions that sound was the 'special' substance, even 65% (13/20) participants used words like 'pervasive' or 'unseen' to define sound. Despite a number of children did not try to explain the nature of sound with fluid or smoke anymore in evaluation test, only a few of them (3/20) began to realize that sound wave is related to the vibration. After game-based learning, children were more active to recall many different kinds of sounds, but also most of them (18/20) were unable to clearly explain how the sounds are produced. By contrast, the improvement of children's understanding of sound propagation is more significant. In the pre-test children used to view space as the only channel of sound transmission. In the post-test and the delayed post-test, there were 12 and 10 kids believed that sound could affect many objects and the surroundings respectively. This indicated a notable change of the way they understood sound propagation.

The evaluation involves analyzing children's response time for asking a question, which is considered to be an indicator of whether they have clear ideas about sound. Except for explaining the prediction ($\chi^2 = 6.30$, df = 2, $p < 0.05$), either the response time of making prediction ($\chi^2 = 3.90$, df = 2, $p = 0.142$) or explaining experimental result ($\chi^2 = 4.90$, df = 2, $p = 0.086$) in evaluation test is not significantly less than pre-test. In the tests children did not tend to easily predict a question unless they already had an explanation. So if they could find the theory to support a prediction, they appeared more confident and responded more quickly. In the pre- and post-test, children took less time in explaining the predictions, and in comparison, they took more time to ponder on the reason for experimental results (Fig. 5b). However, in the delayed post-test a decrease of time in responding to the experimental results was detected. Children participants were more quickly to find a reason or recall what they had learned when experimenter showed them the answer of question with an experiment in this final test. This indicates

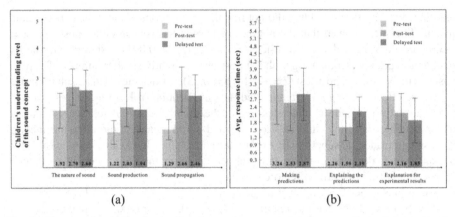

Fig. 5. The mean level of understanding the sound concepts (a); the mean time of responding to the POE tasks (b).

that children have been impressed with the game mechanics and what they observed in previous experiments. As a result, the experiments in delayed test evoked their memories to some degree.

In addition, statistical results showed that the standard deviations of some measurements about conceptual change were a bit high. In the post-test some children successfully changed their explanatory models for some questions, in contrast to others who still adhered to their own conceptions or failed to learn new knowledge. This was probably because the children participants differed greatly in the learning skill and the interest in this educational game, and also in the prior knowledge they had acquired in childhood.

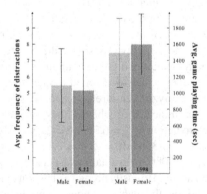

Fig. 6. The mean frequency of distractions (left) and the mean time of playing game (right).

Playability

In the game session, there is no significant difference in both the game playing time ($F_{(1,18)} = 0.554$, $p = 0.55$) and frequency of distraction ($F_{(1,18)} = 0.048$, $p = 0.83$) between boys and girls (Fig. 6). As observed from video recordings, children participants displayed a strong interest in the game interface and the interactions at the beginning of test. They normally became less focused and tired of playing again what they had experienced over time. The game playing time of all participants varied from 12 m 38 s to 37 m 3 s. Although the performances of two girls were distinctly better (see the behavior pattern of P14 in Fig. 3), but as a whole, children's engagement in playing game was not evidently influenced by gender.

During the playing time, children frequently talked with teacher as well as the experimenter about their daily life, prior experiences, and everything they suddenly thought of. Some children did not have a feeling of being tested and many of their activities were not relevant to our test. These were evidences that children were not always immersed in game in the course of testing, rather, they disengaged from the game activity at times in free-play.

Table 6. The correlations between two indicators of playability and the level of children's understanding of sound.

	Game playing time	Frequency of distraction
The nature of sound (post-test)	0.674**	−0.505*
(delayed post-test)	0.745**	−0.656**
Sound production (post-test)	0.787**	0.787**
(delayed post-test)	0.878**	0.878**
Sound propagation (post-test)	0.635**	−0.241
(delayed post-test)	0.568**	−0.362

** Correlation is significant at the 0.01 level (2-tailed)
* Correlation is significant at the 0.05 level (2-tailed)

Statistical results show a correlation between the indicators of playability and the number of correct answers. There is a significant positive correlation (post-test: $r = 0.721$, $p < 0.001$; delayed post-test: $r = 0.815$, $p < 0.001$) of the game playing time and the number of correct answers, which is negatively correlated with the frequency of distraction (post-test: $r = -0.492$, $p < 0.05$; delayed post-test: $r = -0.457$, $p < 0.05$). The correlation of children's understanding level and their involvement in game session is also demonstrated (Table 6). This study proved a positive effect on conceptual change through the learning by game-playing—finally children participants could accept and have a rough idea of the reason for some sound phenomena. It is worth noting that the game, as an instructional tool, may give rise to new alternative conceptions once the dynamic effects, animations or the artistic expression of game elements are misunderstood by kids. Fortunately, such cases were rare in the two evaluation tests. It is concluded that this game provides an impetus to children's conceptual change in the early stage of science education since it promotes their understanding to a certain level. The game experience is also vital in children's learning of very abstract science concept in school education.

Teachers' Comments

Researchers discussed with the teachers about the practical effect of this work. Teachers' comments can be summarized as follow:

- Designing a tablet-based interactive game in the way of stressing the analogies of science concepts (bridging with image schemas) helped the young children a lot in learning basic science knowledge. Children were likely to use intuitive thinking to explain the sound, and they often seemed incapable of explaining why a prediction they made was wrong when showing them an unexpected experimental result. The characteristics of children's thinking model limited them to learn the abstract knowledge and physical laws in the young age. The design idea of explaining the profound concepts with simple game tasks led children to use the imagery thinking to understand them. The game-based intervention stimulated children's interest in primary science as well.
- The game was designed for changing children's wrong conceptions for science learning, in fact, some of children had no ideas and they did not know how to respond to some questions in the first place. This meant the improvement of children's performance was not fully the result of conceptual change. Moreover, the game performed an outstanding effect on knowledge construction, in part due to children are good at memorizing new knowledge. The learning method through game should be extended to primary schools and integrated with other teaching strategies to further explain to children the scientific ideas and solidify their knowledge about science.

5   Discussions and Conclusions

The present work places emphasis on designing a game prototype which is installed on tablet computer for children to understand some basic laws about sound through the game interactions (inputs) and multi-modal feedback (outputs). In order to express the scientific ideas in a persuasive and readily understandable manner, researchers adopted a classical strategy—analogical reasoning—to construct the similarities between children's conception and the widely-accepted science knowledge. The similarities can be found by revealing the image schemas exist in both the anchor concept and target concept. Therefore, designing with image schemas is an attempt to combine the instructional strategy with games. By this means children will begin to know the general explanations of scientific phenomena in the right age (5 years to 7 years old), and this may be beneficial for them to gain deeper insight into scientific models in the future.

Based on this theoretical basis, a learning-specific serious game was designed and evaluated in authentic teaching environment. Results suggest that the game-playing may have a positive effect on the conceptual change in the following three aspects.

First, when children interact with the game system, the interactions convey the stimuli and cues which repeatedly remind them of the knowledge about sound. This is helpful for children to insist on their existing scientific concepts not only, but also to associate the realistic situations with game situation so as to explain what they have experienced in real world. As shown in the results, children participants correctly answered more questions in the post-test. The misconceptions of some children were resistant indeed, but they learned to reason sound phenomena in consistence with the scientific view to some extent in post- and delayed post-test.

Second, as an example that children reached a higher level of understanding the sound, they more frequently abandoned the idea of comparing the sound to visible and touchable things, e.g., P13 said the sound can pass through a wall but raindrops cannot. However, the children did use words and sentences to describe the vibration or disturbance very few times, and obviously these concepts are constituted by a group of basic concepts such as energy and particles which are beyond the scope of young kids' knowledge. In consideration of that, researchers do not expect that the game contributes to a full conceptual change, instead they hope it just allows children to doubt about the misconceptions by sparking their interest in thinking and learning. For the older children who can understand more abstract concepts, it is also valuable to impart science knowledge to them with analogical, interactive and interesting games which may be the powerful aid in curricular teaching.

Third, the new conceptions about sound children had formed through the game playing experience were stored in their long-term memory. Comparative analysis showed there is no statistically significant difference between post-test and delayed post-test scores in most of the measurements (an exception is the understanding level of sound propagation in post- and delayed post test: $t(19) - 2.34, p < 0.05$), indicating that children participants basically retained the conceptions in memory. However, standard deviation of the results of delayed post-test is larger compared to the post-test, suggesting that the game-based learning was not so effective in knowledge retention for some children.

Some future works remain to be done to enrich the current practice. To further assess the design method used in this study, it should be applied to designing serious games for other physical concepts such as force, light, thermo, and dissolution, and even more concepts about nature science. As a pilot study focused on the children from the top class of a kindergarten, the research have not been continued in a follow-up study in primary schools. Thus far, the differences in the degree of conceptual change between preschool children and the pupils are unknown. In addition, this study was conducted in class time when the children were accompanied by their teachers. As the parents play a different role in the growth and education of children, future researches should consider the extension of game-playing to family hour, and explore the potential of collaborative mode of game-based learning. Currently, the findings in this research may provide new insights into the methodology of designing serious games for the learning-through-play in early education.

References

Asikhia, O.K., Setchi, R., Hicks, Y., Walters, A.: Conceptual framework for evaluating intuitive interaction based on image schemas. Interact. Comput. **27**(3), 287–310 (2015)

Bell, R.L., Trundle, K.C.: The use of a computer simulation to promote scientific conceptions of moon phases. J. Res. Sci. Teach. **45**(3), 346–372 (2008)

Brown, D.E., Clement, J.: Overcoming misconceptions via analogical reasoning: abstract transfer versus explanatory model construction. Instr. Sci. **18**, 237–261 (1989)

Cheng, M.T., Chen, J.H., Chu, S., et al.: The use of serious games in science education: a review of selected empirical research from 2002 to 2013. J. Comput. Educ. **2**(3), 353–375 (2015)

Chiu, M.H., Lin, J.W.: Promoting fourth graders' conceptual change of their understanding of electric current via multiple analogies. J. Res. Sci. Teach. **42**(4), 429–464 (2005)

Coştu, B., Ayas, A., Niaz, M., Ünal, S., Çalik, M.: Facilitating conceptual change in student understanding of boiling concept. J. Sci. Educ. Technol. **16**(6), 524–536 (2007)

Duit, A.: Conceptual change: a powerful framework for improving science teaching and learning. Int. J. Sci. Educ. **25**(6), 671–688 (2003)

Edens, K.M., Potter, E.: Using descriptive drawings as a conceptual change strategy in elementary science. School Sci. Math. **103**(3), 135–144 (2003)

Gauthier, A., Jenkinson, J.: Serious game leverages productive negativity to facilitate conceptual change in undergraduate molecular biology: a mixed-methods randomized trial. Int. J. Game. Base. Learn. **7**(2), 20–34 (2017)

Gentner, D.: Structure mapping: a theoretical framework for analogy. Cogn. Sci. **7**, 155–170 (1983)

Hewson, M.G., Hewson, P.W.: Effect of instruction using students' prior knowledge and conceptual change strategies on science learning. J. Res. Sci. Teach. **20**(8), 731–743 (1983)

Hrepic, Z.: Identifying students' mental models of sound propagation: The role of conceptual blending in understanding conceptual change. Phys. Rev. Special Top. Phys. Educ. Res. **6**(2), 020114 (2010)

Hurtienne, J., Klöckner, K., Diefenbach, S., et al.: Designing with image schemas: Resolving the tension between innovation, inclusion and intuitive use. Interact. Comput. **27**(3), 235–255 (2015)

Hurtienne, J.: How cognitive linguistics inspires HCI: Image schemas and image-schematic metaphors. Int. J. Hum-Comput. Int. **33**(1), 1–20 (2017)

Johnson, M.: The Body in the Mind: The Bodily Basis of Meaning, Imagination, and Reason. The University of Chicago Press, Chicago and London (1987)

Kang, S., Scharmann, L.C., Noh, T.: Reexamining the role of cognitive conflict in science concept learning. Res. Stud. Sci. Educ. **34**, 71–96 (2004)

Mandler, J. M.: How to build a baby: III. Image schemas and the transition to verbal thought. In: Hampe, B., Grady, J.E. (eds.) From Perception to Meaning: Image Schemas In Cognitive Linguistics, pp. 137–163, Berlin, Germany: Mouton de Gruyter (2005)

Mandler, J.M., Cánovas, C.P.: On defining image schemas. Lang. Cogn. Neurosci. **6**(4), 510–532 (2014)

Mazens, K., Lautrey, J.: Conceptual change in physics: children's naive representations of sound. Cogn. Develop. **115**, 1–18 (2003)

Piaget, J.: The Child Conception of the World. Harcourt Brace, New York (1929)

Piaget, J.: The Child's Conception of Physical Causality. Harcourt Brace, New York (1930)

Piaget, J.: The Principles of Genetic Epistemology. Basic Books, New York (1972)

Pine, K., Messer, D., John, K.: Children's misconceptions in primary science: a survey of teacher's views. Res. Sci. Technol. Educ. **19**(1), 79–96 (2001)

Posner, G.J., Strike, K.A., Hewson, P., et al.: Accommodation of a scientific conception: toward a theory of conceptual change. Sci. Educ. **66**(2), 211–227 (1982)

Rice, D.C., Ryan, J.M., Samson, S.M.: Using concept maps to assess student learning in the science classroom: must different methods compete? J. Res. Sci. Teach. **35**(10), 1103–1127 (1998)

Vosniadou, S.: Capturing and modeling the process of conceptual change. Learn. Instr. **4**, 45–69 (1994)

White, R.T., Gunstone, R.F.: Probing Understanding. Falmer, London (1992)

Winkler, A., Baumann, K., Huber, S. et al.: Evaluation of an application based on conceptual metaphors for social interaction between vehicles. Paper presented at the meeting of DIS 2016, Brisbane, Australia (2016)

A Mixed Method Approach to Evaluate Web 2.0 Applications in Business Games

Susann Zeiner-Fink[(⊠)], Anne Goy, and Angelika C. Bullinger

Chemnitz University of Technology, 09111 Chemnitz, Germany
{susann.zeiner-fink,anne.goy,
angelika.bullinger-hoffmann}@mb.tu-chemnitz.de

Abstract. Business games are useful tools for analyzing communication, processes and correlations in business contexts. They help to reduce the complexity of the problems faced by real companies to substantial parts. In addition to informal learning, they also help to stimulate explicit and implicit knowledge. Thus, business games increase the motivation to learn and improve knowledge acquisition. There are only a few findings linking general conditions to high-quality results of business games. Based on a business game, this paper presents an approach that uses a mixed method evaluation design to examine a Web 2.0 application in a production setting; psychological elements in the game; and the competence development of the participants. Overall, 194 participants responded to questionnaires and 60 interviews that measured the participants' learning effects and game experiences. The most important results which need to be referred for implementation in business games are identified as flow, motivation, realism and learning.

Keywords: Business games · Mixed methods · Web 2.0 application · Storytelling

1 Introduction

As a result of industrial digitization, new human-machine interfaces are being implemented in production environments. Employees therefore need to implement new technological developments to their daily work. Innovative learning approaches, such as business games, provide the opportunity to facilitate an appropriate close to reality learning environment, simulating dynamic and complex systems and close to practice problems. The participants are confronted with a specific task or problem in an artificial environment with the possibility to give different actions a trial. From this they gain knowledge and skills that enable them to act in future real-life situations [1]. Furthermore, business games are characterized by creativity, flexibility, uncertainty, and openness and give participants enough space and scope to act [2]. In contrast to real problems, wrong decisions in a simulated environment have no serious effects. Thus, errors provide useful guidance for learning from mistakes by experiencing near realistic consequences [2, 3]. Participants get the opportunity to take part in the game actively and

© Springer Nature Switzerland AG 2020
X. Fang (Ed.): HCII 2020, LNCS 12211, pp. 521–531, 2020.
https://doi.org/10.1007/978-3-030-50164-8_38

directly by taking over different roles and have an impact on the simulation results. Business games deal with specialized and factual communication and interaction decisions. These are predetermined and regulated by the events, as well as the goals of the game, in combination with the pre-defined rules and game environments [4]. Due to the high complexity of the business game method, a competent implementation and coordination of the interests of all participants is required [5].

Additionally, learning effects, game experience and behavioral changes of the participants in the game are difficult to measure and there are only a few studies examining the topic of 'learning by games' or influencing factors which support learning [6–8]. Nevertheless, the expansion and development of innovative simulation game-oriented methods that are specifically designed to address critical situations and challenges in companies, seems indispensable given the wide range of capabilities and the effectiveness of business games [2, 5, 8].

Only a few reports in literature refer to a mixed methods approach in business games evaluation [9]. Based on a business game, this paper presents an approach that uses a mixed method evaluation design, examining three factors being: Web 2.0 application in a production setting; psychological elements in the game; and the competence development of the participants. This paper attempts to investigate an evaluation design which includes a questionnaire and storytelling.

Hence, after a short overview of the main elements in business games, this paper will introduce a newly-developed business game. Two methods of evaluation are employed and results of the business game evaluation are introduced. Finally, starting points for further research in this field are shown.

2   Elements of Business Games and How to Evaluate Them

According to findings in literature, Trautwein [8] examines key factors that influence the success of business games. These include the demographics of participants who directly take part in the game (gender, age, educational background, technical background), group-specific aspects (cooperation during the game, atmosphere, task allocation), and framework conditions of the game (realism, traceability). In business games, an indirect and creative learn-through-experimentation reality is set. Participants gain knowledge in a game-based environment via incidental learning while focusing on problem solving tasks [2]. Therefore, learning components need to be implemented in a business game. In this survey learning base on Kolb's experiential learning [10] and the action-orientated learning base on Ameln and Kramer [1]. Additionally, the flow component (absent-mindedness, concentration and control) based on Csikszentmihalyi [11] needs to be focused on in business games as well. Flow can improve learning outcomes and is positively linked to motivation and task requirements [11]. To create problem-solving tasks with realistic context in games, it is useful to implement challenges which closely relate to reality. Thus, in the investigated business game, a human-machine interaction is implemented. To test the whether this close to reality challenge suits the recruitment of the participants well, we evaluate two versions of the business game: with and without microblogging. To summarize what we want to investigate in this paper:

- What is the main criteria that influences the success of the game?
- How do the participants assess the two versions of the business game concerning motivation, learning, flow, game design and success of the game?

To answer these questions, a combination of qualitative and quantitative methods seems to be suitable. A mixed method evaluation design could increase the significance of the test results [12]. Thus, the evaluation is based on the logical evaluation model of Kriz und Hense [4]. Implemented methods include a standardized questionnaire from Trautwein [8] and a storytelling interview according to Thier [13].

3 Evaluation Design

The business game was developed to explore how technical changes influence routine tasks, in this case, within a production environment. Thus, a Web 2.0 microblogging application was implemented into a tangible experience. The main part of the game is a LEGO® vehicle production line, where computer-based technology is used as a communication tool between the implemented assembly lines (see Fig. 1).

Fig. 1. Overview of the business game

To get quick familiarity with the game process, the assembly line was kept simple. It consists of three different production processes and one management department. Various common business problems may occur during three business years. Thus, the participants need to clarify typical organizational and production challenges. The game operates with a minimum of eleven participants and a duration of approximately four hours [14]. To test the interaction and gameplay with Web 2.0 technologies, the game was tested *with* ($n = 158$), and *without* ($n = 37$) *the microblogging tool*.

To evaluate the business game, an explanatory sequential mixed method design was used [15]. The first part of the survey contained a questionnaire ($N = 195$) which was handed out after the game. The participants got numbers to keep track during the evaluation process. The implemented questionnaire consisted of 64 semi-structured and structured questions. Measured categories included previous experience, realism, satisfaction, motivation, learning, flow, success of the business game, skills acquisition and game design (based on i.e. [8]). The categories were measured with a 6-point Likert scale from "*1 = strongly agree*" to "*6 = strongly disagree*".

After a period of either four weeks or a year, the participants attended a story telling interview ($N = 60$). The participants should respond to the question which was their main experience during the game.

The game has been played in 34 test runs between 2012 and 2018. 195 participants (response rate 88.07%) with an average age of 26.16 ($SD = 7.08$) answered the questionnaire. 103 participants were male, 92 were female. The sample was subdivided into 134 students and 65 employees. 40 participants attended the interview after four weeks, 20 participants attended the interview after a year.

Statistic Software SPSS (IBM SPSS Statistics 26) was used for quantitative data analysis. Due to large group sample sizes and the data structure, parametric data analysis was applied. If not otherwise specified, t-test and a univariate ANOVA was used. The parametric effect size d, was calculated according to Cohen [16]. The interviews were analyzed by the structured quality content analysis of Kuckartz [17]. To compare the results of the quantitative and qualitative data, the same categories were used.

4   Results

As a result of the reliability analysis, the items of the total scale, whose values for $\alpha <$ 0.6 are different, were considered individually in the survey [18].

The reliability analysis was followed by a one-factorial ANOVA with a post-hoc Scheffé test. Significant differences emerged from the respective professions for the categories prior experience, realism, success of the game, satisfaction, competence acquisition, engagement, flow and motivation, as well as for the individual items regarding the material usage of the LEGO® bricks, event cards and the Web 2.0 application, the traceability of the game results, structure, fun and the rewarding participation in the business game. The Scheffé test also shows that there is a significant difference between the different groups of students, employees and others with regard to the implemented categories (see Table 1).

Afterwards, a multiple linear regression was calculated for the success of the game as dependent variable: $R^2 = .773$, $F(16,101) = 21.52$, $p = .000$. A quality of .773 was gained. The categories realism ($p = .007$), motivation ($p = .007$) and flow ($p = .022$) unravel the variance with a significant positive effect. Thus, the regression shows that these three categories have the greatest impact on the success of the game. Therefore, a t-test for a group comparison regarding these three categories followed. To explain the most relevant results, we focused on the following most distinctive findings.

4.1   Microblogging

The results show (see Table 2) that the participants who attended the game with microblogging assess the usage of microblogging as moderate. They also stated that

Table 1. Significant results of ANOVA and Scheffé

category	ANOVA			profession	Scheffé	
	F	*p*	η^2		*p 1*	*p 2*
microblogging	$F(2,121) = 6.17$	.003*	.09	--	--	--
realism	$F(2,121) = 10.97$	<.001*	.15	st < e, o	>.001	.011
motivation	$F(2,121) = 4.67$	.011*	.07	e > st, o	.028	0.23
flow	$F(2,121) = 4.64$	.011*	.08	--	--	--
learning	$F(2,121) = 1.40$	.250	.02	--	--	--
succes of the game	$F(2,121) = 7.48$	.001*	.11	e > st, o	.001	.037

*$p < .001$
st = students
e = employees
o = others

they gained a high level of learning of microblogging. They rather less agreed, that microblogging was intuitive. Furthermore, they indicated that they had experiences with microblogging before the game.

Table 2. Descriptive results of participants who attended the game with microblogging

Items	*M*	*SD*
usages of microblogging	2.91	1.40
learning trough microblogging	2.71	1.45
microblogging is intuitive	3.35	1.43
experience of microblogging before the game	4.75	1.46

According to inferential statistical analysis, the t-test showed a significance difference for the variables' success of the game ($t(193) = -2.228, p = .027, d = -0.407$) and realism ($t(191) = -2.013, p = .045, d = -0.372$). Both variables were rated slightly better *without* than *with microblogging* (see Table 3).

The effect sizes according to Cohen [16] can be classified as small. There was no difference in mean values for the interesting variables of motivation, success of learning and flow. The variant of the game *without microblogging* was assessed slightly better than *with microblogging*, descriptively. The storytelling interviews confirm these statements:

"(…) communication, so the two managing directors, my colleague and I, we often have to fly to Russia because we need to clarify problems and explain new tasks. In the beginning everything went more or less well, over the IT systems and with the time and with the time pressure it turned out that it is better to have a meet in person to explain that employees should be more aware of things than simply tell them via chat, for example." (I_044; 5-5).

Table 3. Descriptive results of the category microblogging

Items	M	SD	n
with microblogging			
success	2.45	1.03	158
realism	2.53	1.09	158
without microblogging			
success	2.45	.78	37
realism	2.53	.74	37

Previously analysis showed differences between participants attending the game. Thus, the following section shows the results of students and employees.

4.2 Success of the Game

The overall model was significant ($F(3,191) = 2.86$, $p = .038$, adjusted $R^2 = .028$, $n = 195$). It was shown that both professions, employee or student ($F(1,191) = 1.256$, $p = .264$, $d = 0.168$), as well as the simulation game variation (whether the game was played *with* or *without microblogging* ($F(1,191) = 3.78$, $p = .053$, $d = 0.278$)) had no significant connection to the simulation's success. In addition, there was an insignificant interaction between profession and microblogging on the simulation success ($F(1,191) = .236$, $p = .627$, $d = 0.063$). The effect size for the overall model ($d = 0.424$) according to Cohen [16] can be classified as small. The univariate ANOVA of the categories of realism, motivation, flow and learning was not significant.

Descriptively, it was shown that both groups rated the simulation success for the variation *without microblogging* slightly better as *with microblogging* (see Table 4). It was also shown that the employees generally rate the success of the game for both variants better compared to the students.

Table 4. Descriptive results of the category success of the game

Item	M	SD	n
with microblogging			
employee	2.24	.82	53
student	2.55	1.11	105
without microblogging			
employee	1.97	.88	12
student	2.09	.74	25

Additionally, the interviews show no difference between the two groups when assessing the success of the game: "*In any case, it was a meaningful experience that might help you later in your professional life and where you might remember, you could do that at the time or the solution I tried at that time was crap. After all, you can exclude them.* " (I_017; 34-35).

4.3 Realism

Descriptively, the data shows that both groups rated the realism in the variation *without microblogging* slightly higher than *with microblogging* (see Table 5). It was also shown that the employees generally rate the realism in both conditions higher in comparison to the students.

Table 5. Descriptive results of the category realism

Item	M	SD	n
with microblogging			
employee	2.32	.90	53
student	2.63	1.17	104
without microblogging			
employee	1.96	.78	12
student	2.23	.72	24

These results are confirmed in the storytelling Interviews: After four weeks, the most of the students and employees mentioned that the game *without microblogging* was more realistic than with the IT tool. Surprisingly, after a year, the participants tend to assess the game more realistic, regardless if the microblogging tool was added or not. *"I was positively surprised how one is influenced by external influences or influences in a completely different direction, as you actually think, at the beginning. Well, very interesting and good." (I_018; 17-17). They connected the experience to their daily work: "This is actually a reliving of things that you also know from your normal job. And as soon as the communication channels get longer, the communication gets worse."* (I_008; 46-46).

4.4 Motivation

The descriptive data of motivation shows that both groups rated the variation *without microblogging* slightly higher than *with* (see Table 6). Also, the data shows that the employees were slightly more motivated in both variants than the students.

After four weeks the students and employees stated that they were highly motivated during the game both *with* and *without microblogging: "Good, we felt good. So my group felt good because everyone worked together well." (I_45; 27-28).* Regarding the fun category during the game *with microblogging*, higher frequencies can be found in the interviews of the employees after one year than after four weeks. The opposite was found in the student interviews. In comparison, lower frequencies can be found in the interviews of the employees after four weeks of the fun category *without microblogging* than after a year. All students stated that they had fun during the game.

Table 6. Descriptive results of the category motivation

Item	M	SD	n
with microblogging			
employee	1.84	.69	53
student	2.07	1.04	105
without microblogging			
employee	1.79	1.00	12
student	1.81	.82	25

4.5 Flow

Descriptively, the data shows that the students had a higher experience of flow *without microblogging*. Regarding the employees, the results are different: They gained a higher experience of flow *with the microblogging tool* (see Table 7).

Table 7. Descriptive results of the category flow

Item	M	SD	n
with microblogging			
employee	1.96	.50	38
student	2.17	.73	91
without microblogging			
employee	2.03	.62	12
student	1.97	.63	23

During the game the participants were focused on their task: *"It was fun. I was totally in the game. And I felt comfortable, in the pre-assembly."* (I_041; 2-2). *With microblogging*, the students stated that time went by very quickly. Only one third of the employees mentioned this after four weeks and half of them after a year. *Without microblogging*, the participants did not mention any time component during the interviews.

4.6 Learning

The data shows descriptively that both groups rate the learning success in the variation *without microblogging* slightly higher than *with microblogging* (see Table 8). In addition, the employees rate the success of learning higher than the students in the variant *with microblogging*. The data of the version *without microblogging* shows no difference between employees and students.

During the storytelling interviews all participants stated that they gained knowledge during the game - whether it was *with* or *without microblogging*: *"They all understood what it was about, in the sense of 'If it is further away, you have more coordination effort*

Table 8. Descriptive results of the category learning

Item	M	SD	n
with microblogging			
employee	2.89	1.20	53
student	2.87	1.29	105
without microblogging			
employee	2.38	1.42	12
student	2.77	1.40	24

and more racing'." (I_004; 9-9). Three quarter of the employees and only few of the students attending the game *without microblogging* mentioned that after four weeks, they could transfer the knowledge into their own field. All employees stated after one year that they draw from previously gained knowledge. Only one third of the students mentioned this during the interviews. In the game *with microblogging* half of the employees made this reference. Surprisingly almost all of the students mentioned after four weeks they could draw from previously gained knowledge during the game: *"In any case, I found the most important thing was the PC. At the beginning, I could not cope with it, it was the hardest thing. Although it worked then. I think you can handle it then and that was actually quite good."* (I_012; 2-2). Only one third mentioned this after one year.

5 Discussion

In general, the results show high values, descriptively. There are only marginal differences without practical significance. Regarding this, the results suggest that the game tends to be rated better *without the microblogging component*. One explanation could be that the human-machine interface was found to be disruptive during the routine tasks in the game process. Evidence could be found during the storytelling interviews showing a strong correlation between the microblogging variable and the category of lurking factors. Accordingly, employees rated the business game with higher values than the students for the categories: success of the business game, realism, motivation, and learning (descriptive differences with higher effects). This could be due to the fact that they had already gained more active work experience, having previously dealt with more flow. Supporting this, employees experienced higher levels of flow when microblogging was included in the game. This was also confirmed during the employee interviews. Comparatively, students tended to experience higher levels of flow *without microblogging*, this was not confirmed during their interviews, however. During the interviews, all participants stated that they were focused on their tasks and that time flew by. The high game involvement which was directly connected with the game elements, put the participants in the position of a game setting where they did not realize that learning took place by playing. Only when the participants were asked directly about their learning of subtopics, they confirm any sense of new knowledge gain. It should be noted that the learning was measured only via self-evaluation, so the findings of learning naturally correlated with in-game success and motivation. With regard to the participants' previous experiences on their learning effects, the data shows that learning increased when participants had previously gained multiple experiences. It was found that participants with fewer prior experiences rejected the notion that they were able to improve their learning. According to the high similarity between the mean values of the implemented items, it could be assumed that the research design is suitable for these categories.

6 Conclusion

The results confirm theoretical findings found in literature. The high accordance of the items regarding the implemented categories of realism, motivation, flow, learning, and success of business games, indicates that the game met the expectations of the participants. This confirmation proves objective number one. The results also indicated that the business game with the microblogging tool implemented challenged the participants more than the game without this component. This proves objective two.

Furthermore, it could be assumed that flow, motivation and a human-machine-interaction have an impact on learning effects. The data showed that learning was clearly not taken into account.

Regarding the sample size, the results are supposed to be generalizable and provide some evidence about the evaluation of business games and game-based learning. Additionally, the findings show only the effects and no causality of the categories evaluated.

The research objectives of implementing a mixed method approach in business games were achieved due to the fact that the results show that the used methods consider a high degree of the participants' individual background. Nevertheless, additional evaluation methods in the field of qualitative and quantitative research could lead to more meaningful results. In addition, the presented methods show only one of the possible combinations of different method variants, which can be further supplemented. Moreover, this mixed method approach has not yet been used in the business game context. Further research in this field would be needed. Thus, this paper contributes to the mixed method approach by showing that these evaluation methods can generate insights that could otherwise be lost in surveys.

References

1. von Ameln, F., Kramer, J.: Organisationen in Bewegung bringen. Springer, Heidelberg (2016). https://doi.org/10.1007/978-3-662-48197-4
2. Klippert, H.: Planspiele. 10 Spielvorlagen zum sozialen, politischen und methodischen Lernen in Gruppen. 5th edn. Beltz, Weinheim, Germany (2008)
3. Rohn, W.E.: Ursprung und Entwicklung des Planspiels. In: Geilhardt, T., Mühlbradt, T. (eds.) Planspiele im Personal- und Organisationsmanagement (Schriftenreihe Psychologie und innovatives Management), pp. 57–69. Verlag für Angewandte Psychologie, Göttingen, Germany (1995)
4. Kriz, W.C., Hense, J.U.: Theory-oriented evaluation for the design of and research in gaming and simulation. Simul. Gaming 37(2), 268–283 (2006)

5. Wein, B., Willems, R., Quanjel, M.: Planspielsimulationen. In: Herz, D., Blätte, A. (eds.) Simulation und Planspiel in den Sozialwissenschaften. Eine Bestandsaufnahme der internationalen Diskussion, pp. 15–63. LIT Verlag, Münster, Germany (2000)

6. Kriz, W.C., Auchter, E.: 10 years of evaluation research into gaming simulation for german entrepreneurship and a new study an its long-term effects. Simul. Gaming **47**(2), 179–205 (2016)

7. Schwägele, S.: Planspiel - Lernen - Lerntransfer. Eine subjektorientierte Analyse von Einflussfaktoren. Ph. D Dissertation. University of Bamberg. Bamberg, Germany (2015)

8. Trautwein, C.: Unternehmensplanspiele im industriebetrieblichen Hochschulstudium. Analyse von Kompetenzerwerb, Motivation und Zufriedenheit am Beispiel des Unternehmensplanspiels TOPSIM - General Management II. 1st edn. Ph. D Dissertation. University of Hohenheim. Gabler Verlag | Springer Fachmedien Wiesbaden GmbH, Wiesbaden, Germany (2011)

9. Lohmann, J. R.: Simulations Matter. Wirkungsweisen und Mehrwert von Politiksimulationen. Ph. D Dissertation. University of Passau, Passau, Germany (2019)

10. Kolb, A.Y., Kolb, D.A., Passarelli, A., Sharma, G.: On becoming an experiential educator :the educator role profile. Simul. Gaming **45**(2), 204–234 (2014)

11. Shernoff, D.J., Csikszentmihalyi, M., Shneider, B., Shernoff, E.S.: Student engagement in high school classrooms from the perspective of flow theory. Sch. Psychol. Quarterly **18**(2), 158–176 (2003)

12. Mayring, P.: Einführung in die qualitative Sozialforschung. Eine Anleitung zu qualitativem Denken. 5th edn. Beltz, Weinheim, Germany (2002)

13. Thier, K.: Storytelling. Eine Methode für das Change-, Marken-, Projekt- und Wissensmanagement. 3rd edn. Springer, Berlin, Germany (2017). http://dx.doi.org/10.1007/978-3-662-49206-2

14. Fink, S., Bullinger, A. C., Kiili, K.: Measuring game experience and learning effects of business games. In: Proceedings of the 45th Conference of the International Simulation and Gaming Association, pp. 140–153. (2014)

15. Creswell, J.W.: A Concise Introduction to Mixed Methods Research. Sage, Los Angeles (2015)

16. Cohen, J.: Statistical Power Analysis for the Behavioral Sciences, 2nd edn. Lawrence Erlbaum Associates, Hillsdale (1988)

17. Kuckartz, U.: Qualitative Inhaltsanalyse. Methoden, Praxis, Computerunterstützung (Grundlagentexte Methoden). 4th edn. Beltz Juventa, Weinheim, Germany (2018). http://ebooks.ciando.com/book/index.cfm?bok_id/2513416

18. Brosius, F.: SPSS 21. Fundierte Einführung in SPSS und in die Statistik; alle statistischen Verfahren mit praxisnahen Beispielen; inklusive CD-ROM. 1st edn. Mitp Verl.-Gruppe Hüthig Jehle Rehm, Heidelberg, Germany (2013)

Correction to: Guidance Is Good or Avoid Too Much Hand-Holding? Proposing a Controlled Experiment on the Impact of Clear Proximal Goals on Digital Game Enjoyment

Owen Schaffer

Correction to:
Chapter "Guidance Is Good or Avoid Too Much
Hand-Holding? Proposing a Controlled Experiment
on the Impact of Clear Proximal Goals on Digital Game
Enjoyment" in: X. Fang (Ed.): *HCI in Games*, LNCS 12211,
https://doi.org/10.1007/978-3-030-50164-8_12

The original version of this chapter was revised. The number of versions of the game has been corrected to four.

The updated version of this chapter can be found at
https://doi.org/10.1007/978-3-030-50164-8_12

Author Index

Printed in the United States
By Bookmasters